# DEAD SEA SCROLLS, REVISE AND REPEAT

# EARLY JUDAISM AND ITS LITERATURE

Rodney A. Werline, General Editor

*Editorial Board:*
Randall D. Chesnutt
Kelley N. Coblentz Bautch
Maxine L. Grossman
Carol Newsom

Number 52

# DEAD SEA SCROLLS, REVISE AND REPEAT

## New Methods and Perspectives

*Edited by*

Carmen Palmer, Andrew R. Krause,
Eileen Schuller, and John Screnock

Atlanta

Copyright © 2020 by Society of Biblical Literature

All rights reserved. No part of this work may be reproduced or transmitted in any form or by any means, electronic or mechanical, including photocopying and recording, or by means of any information storage or retrieval system, except as may be expressly permitted by the 1976 Copyright Act or in writing from the publisher. Requests for permission should be addressed in writing to the Rights and Permissions Office, SBL Press, 825 Houston Mill Road, Atlanta, GA 30329 USA.

Library of Congress Cataloging-in-Publication Data

Names: Palmer, Carmen, editor. | Krause, Andrew R., editor. | Schuller, Eileen M., 1946– editor. | Screnock, John, editor.
Title: Dead Sea Scrolls, revise and repeat : new methods and perspectives / edited by Carmen Palmer, Andrew R. Krause, Eileen Schuller, and John Screnock.
Description: Atlanta : SBL Press, [2020] | Series: Early Judaism and its literature; 52 | Includes bibliographical references and index.
Identifiers: LCCN 2019059604 (print) | LCCN 2019059605 (ebook) | ISBN 9781628372731 (paperback) | ISBN 9780884144359 (hardback) | ISBN 9780884144366 (ebook)
Subjects: LCSH: Dead Sea scrolls. | Qumran community.
Classification: LCC BM487 .D44977 2020  (print) | LCC BM487  (ebook) | DDC 296.1/55—dc23
LC record available at https://lccn.loc.gov/2019059604
LC ebook record available at https://lccn.loc.gov/2019059605

# Contents

Acknowledgments ..................................................................................vii
Abbreviations ........................................................................................ix

Introduction: New Approaches to Old Questions
    Andrew R. Krause, Carmen Palmer, and John Screnock......................1

### Part 1. Law, Language, and Literary Formation

Rule Texts from Qumran on the Spectrum of Jewish
    Legal Development
    Sarianna Metso ..................................................................................23

A Legal Approach to Textual Authority at Qumran:
    The Penal Codes as a Test Case
    Jonathan Vroom ................................................................................35

Assessing the Character of Hebrew in the Dead Sea Scrolls:
    Historical Linguistics, Numerical Syntax, and the
    Notion of a Distinct Dead Sea Scrolls Hebrew
    John Screnock ..................................................................................59

Variant Readings in the Aramaic Dead Sea Scrolls: A Tool for
    Ongoing Research on the Textual Status and Linguistic Settings
    of Ancient Jewish Aramaic Literature
    Andrew B. Perrin and Brandon Diggens ...........................................93

Isaiah at Qumran and in the Gospel of Matthew
    Kyung S. Baek ................................................................................119

### Part 2. Space and Time

The Threat of the Monstrous in the Scrolls
    Heather Macumber ........................................................................145

Sectarian Identity and Angels Associated with Israel:
   A Comparison of Daniel 7–12 with 1QS,
   11QMelchizedek, and 1QM
   Matthew L. Walsh ........................................................................169

Function and Creativity in the Hebrew, Aramaic,
   and Cryptic Calendars from Qumran
   Helen R. Jacobus .........................................................................199

Spirits of Controversy in My Bodily Structures:
   Spatiality of Body and Community in Qumran
   Apotropaic Prayers
   Andrew R. Krause .......................................................................251

Part 3. The Body

Sexuality and Self-Deprecation in the Thanksgiving Psalms:
   Questions of Celibacy and the Presence of Women in the Yaḥad
   Nicholas Meyer ............................................................................279

Masculinities and the Men of the Qumran Communities:
   Reevaluating the Ideals of Purification, Power, and
   Performance in the Dead Sea Scrolls
   Jessica M. Keady .........................................................................305

Circumcision of the Heart in the Dead Sea Scrolls
   and in the Second Temple Period: Spiritual,
   Moral, and Ethnic
   Carmen Palmer ...........................................................................327

Experiencing the Solidity of Spaces in the Qumran Hodayot
   Angela Kim Harkins ...................................................................353

Contributors .............................................................................................373
Ancient Sources Index ...........................................................................379
Author Index ...........................................................................................397

# Acknowledgments

Many of the chapters in this volume began as papers at two special sessions held at the Canadian Society of Biblical Studies in May 2016 and 2017. We would like to extend thanks to the Canadian Society of Biblical Studies for including these sessions and to all our colleagues who attended and provided insightful feedback. This volume was inspired, in part, by the desire to foster further conversation and collegiality among the scholars working with the Dead Sea Scrolls and beyond. We would also like to thank all our colleagues who contributed chapters to this volume, the contents of which explore new methods, reassess former conclusions with creativity and insight, and offer a multitude of ideas to spark further thought and consideration. We are grateful to Eileen Schuller for her guidance, mentorship, and insight shared throughout the compilation of the volume. We are also grateful to Nicole L. Tilford, of SBL Press, and Rodney Werline, editor of the series Early Judaism and Its Literature, for all their assistance in improving and bringing this volume to completion. May the conversations begun in this volume continue to *be revised and rewritten in the days and years ahead.*

# Abbreviations

## Dead Sea Scrolls

| | |
|---|---|
| 1Q8 | Isaiah[b] |
| 1Q19 | Noah |
| 1Q20 | Genesis Apocryphon |
| 1Q21 | Testament of Levi *or* Aramaic Levi Document |
| 1Q23 | Enoch, Giants[a] |
| 1Q24 | Enoch, Giants[b]? |
| 1Q26 | Instruction |
| 1Q27 | Mysteries |
| 1Q32 | New Jerusalem |
| 1Q71 | Daniel[a] |
| 1Q72 | Daniel[b] |
| 1QapGen | Genesis Apocryphon |
| 1QH[a] | Hodayot[a] *or* Thanksgiving Hymns[a] |
| 1QM | Milḥamah *or* War Scroll |
| 1QpHab | Pesher Habakkuk |
| 1QS | Serekh ha-Yaḥad *or* Rule of the Community |
| 2Q24 | New Jerusalem |
| 2Q26 | Enoch, Giants |
| 364-DCT | 364-Day Calendar Traditions |
| 3Q4 | Pesher Isaiah |
| 3Q14 | Unclassified fragments |
| 3Q15 | Copper Scroll |
| 4Q2 | Genesis[b] |
| 4Q7 | Genesis[g] |
| 4Q10 | Genesis[k] |
| 4Q55 | Isaiah[a] |
| 4Q56 | Isaiah[b] |

| | |
|---|---|
| 4Q57 | Isaiah$^c$ |
| 4Q58 | Isaiah$^d$ |
| 4Q59 | Isaiah$^e$ |
| 4Q60 | Isaiah$^f$ |
| 4Q61 | Isaiah$^g$ |
| 4Q62 | Isaiah$^h$ |
| 4Q63 | Isaiah$^j$ |
| 4Q64 | Isaiah$^k$ |
| 4Q65 | Isaiah$^l$ |
| 4Q66 | Isaiah$^m$ |
| 4Q67 | Isaiah$^n$ |
| 4Q68 | Isaiah$^o$ |
| 4Q69 | Isaiah$^p$ |
| 4Q69a | Isaiah$^q$ |
| 4Q69b | Isaiah$^r$ |
| 4Q159 | Ordinances$^a$ |
| 4Q161 | Pesher Isaiah$^a$ |
| 4Q162 | Pesher Isaiah$^b$ |
| 4Q163 | Pesher Isaiah$^c$ |
| 4Q164 | Pesher Isaiah$^d$ |
| 4Q165 | Pesher Isaiah$^e$ |
| 4Q169 | Pesher Nahum |
| 4Q174 | Florilegium, also Midrash on Eschatology$^a$ |
| 4Q176 | Tanḥumim |
| 4Q177 | Catena A, also Midrash on Eschatology$^b$ |
| 4Q184 | Wiles of the Wicked Woman |
| 4Q186 | Horoscope |
| 4Q196 | Tobit$^a$ |
| 4Q197 | Tobit$^b$ |
| 4Q198 | Tobit$^c$ |
| 4Q199 | Tobit$^d$ |
| 4Q201 | Enoch$^a$ |
| 4Q202 | Enoch$^b$ |
| 4Q203 | Enoch, Giants$^a$ |
| 4Q204 | Enoch$^c$ |
| 4Q205 | Enoch$^d$ |
| 4Q206 | Enoch$^e$ |
| 4Q207 | Enoch$^f$ |
| 4Q208 | Enoch, astronomical books$^a$ |

| | |
|---|---|
| 4Q209 | Enoch, astronomical books$^b$ |
| 4Q210 | Enoch, astronomical books$^c$ |
| 4Q211 | Enoch, astronomical books$^d$ |
| 4Q212 | Enoch$^g$ |
| 4Q213 | Levi$^a$ |
| 4Q213a | Levi$^b$ |
| 4Q213b | Levi$^c$ |
| 4Q214 | Levi$^d$ |
| 4Q214a | Levi$^e$ |
| 4Q214b | Levi$^f$ |
| 4Q216 | Jubilees$^a$ |
| 4Q217 | Jubilees$^b$? |
| 4Q218 | Jubilees$^c$ |
| 4Q219 | Jubilees$^d$ |
| 4Q220 | Jubilees$^e$ |
| 4Q221 | Jubilees$^f$ |
| 4Q222 | Jubilees$^g$ |
| 4Q223 | Jubilees$^h$ |
| 4Q246 | Apocryphon of Daniel |
| 4Q251 | Halakha A |
| 4Q252 | Commentary on Genesis A |
| 4Q256 | Serekh ha-Yaḥad$^b$ *or* Rule of the Community$^b$ |
| 4Q258 | Serekh ha-Yaḥad$^d$ *or* Rule of the Community$^d$ |
| 4Q259 | Serekh ha-Yaḥad$^e$ *or* Rule of the Community$^e$ |
| 4Q261 | Serekh ha-Yaḥad$^g$ *or* Rule of the Community$^g$ |
| 4Q265 | Miscellaneous Rules |
| 4Q266 | Damascus Document$^a$ |
| 4Q267 | Damascus Document$^b$ |
| 4Q269 | Damascus Document$^d$ |
| 4Q270 | Damascus Document$^e$ |
| 4Q274 | Toḥorot A |
| 4Q285 | Sefer ha-Milḥamah |
| 4Q286 | Berakhot$^a$ |
| 4Q287 | Berakhot$^b$ |
| 4Q288 | Berakhot$^c$ |
| 4Q289 | Berakhot$^d$ |
| 4Q290 | Berakhot$^e$ |
| 4Q299 | Mysteries$^a$ |
| 4Q300 | Mysteries$^b$ |

| | |
|---|---|
| 4Q301 | Mysteries[c]? |
| 4Q317 | Cryptic A Phases of the Moon |
| 4Q318 | Zodiology and Brontology |
| 4Q319 | Otot |
| 4Q320 | Calendrical Document Mishmarot A |
| 4Q321 | Calendrical Document Mishmarot B |
| 4Q321a | Calendrical Document Mishmarot C |
| 4Q322 | Mishmarot A |
| 4Q324 | Mishmarot C |
| 4Q325 | Calendrical Document Mishmarot D |
| 4Q332 | Historical Text D |
| 4Q334 | Ordo |
| 4Q364 | Reworked Pentateuch[b] *or* 4QPentateuch[b] |
| 4Q365 | Reworked Pentateuch[c] *or* 4QPentateuch[c] |
| 4Q385 | Pseudo-Ezekiel[a] |
| 4Q394 | Miqṣat Maʿaśê ha-Torah[a] |
| 4Q400 | Shirot ʿOlat Hashabbat[a] *or* Songs of the Sabbath Sacrifice[a] |
| 4Q401 | Shirot ʿOlat Hashabbat[b] *or* Songs of the Sabbath Sacrifice[b] |
| 4Q403 | Shirot ʿOlat Hashabbat[d] *or* Songs of the Sabbath Sacrifice[d] |
| 4Q405 | Shirot ʿOlat Hashabbat[f] *or* Songs of the Sabbath Sacrifice[f] |
| 4Q415 | Instruction[a] |
| 4Q416 | Instruction[b] |
| 4Q417 | Instruction[c] |
| 4Q418 | Instruction[d] |
| 4Q418a | Instruction[e] |
| 4Q434 | Barkhi Nafshi[a] |
| 4Q435 | Barkhi Nafshi[b] |
| 4Q436 | Barkhi Nafshi[c] |
| 4Q437 | Barkhi Nafshi[d] |
| 4Q438 | Barkhi Nafshi[e] |
| 4Q444 | Incantation |
| 4Q471 | War Scroll-like Text B |
| 4Q482 | Jubilees[i]? |
| 4Q491 | Milḥamah[a] |
| 4Q492 | Milḥamah[b] |
| 4Q493 | Milḥamah[c] |
| 4Q494 | Milḥamah[d] |
| 4Q495 | Milḥamah[e] |
| 4Q496 | Milḥamah[f] |

| | |
|---|---|
| 4Q497 | War Scroll-like Text A |
| 4Q502 | Rituel de mariage *or* Ritual of Marriage |
| 4Q503 | Prières quotidiennes *or* Daily Prayers |
| 4Q504 | Dibre Hame'orot$^a$ *or* Words of the Luminaries$^a$ |
| 4Q509 | Prières pour les fêtes$^c$ |
| 4Q510 | Shirot$^a$, Songs of the Sage$^a$, *or* Songs of the Maskil$^a$ |
| 4Q511 | Shirot$^b$, Songs of the Sage$^b$, *or* Songs of the Maskil$^b$ |
| 4Q512 | Ritual Purity B |
| 4Q514 | Ordinances$^c$ |
| 4Q530 | Enoch, Giants$^b$ |
| 4Q531 | Enoch, Giants$^c$ |
| 4Q532 | Enoch, Giants$^d$ |
| 4Q534 | Noah$^a$ |
| 4Q541 | Apocryphon of Levi$^b$? |
| 4Q542 | Testament of Qahat |
| 4Q543 | Visions of Amram$^a$ |
| 4Q544 | Visions of Amram$^b$ |
| 4Q545 | Visions of Amram$^c$ |
| 4Q546 | Visions of Amram$^d$ |
| 4Q547 | Visions of Amram$^e$ |
| 4Q548 | Visions of Amram$^f$ |
| 4Q549 | Visions of Amram$^g$? |
| 4Q552 | Four Kingdoms$^a$ |
| 4Q553 | Four Kingdoms$^b$ |
| 4Q554 | New Jerusalem$^a$ |
| 4Q555 | New Jerusalem$^b$ |
| 4Q556 | Vision$^a$ |
| 4Q558 | Vision$^b$ |
| 4Q560 | Exorcism |
| 4Q561 | Physiognomy/Horoscope |
| 4Q564 | Aramaic F |
| 5Q3 | Isaiah |
| 5Q15 | Unclassified fragments |
| 6Q8 | Enoch, Giants |
| 6Q17 | Calendrical Document |
| 11Q5 | Psalms Scroll$^a$ |
| 11Q10 | Targum of Job |
| 11Q11 | Apocryphal Psalms$^a$ |
| 11Q13 | Melchizedek |

| | |
|---|---|
| 11Q14 | Sefer ha-Milḥamah |
| 11Q18 | New Jerusalem |
| 11Q19 | Temple Scroll |
| 11Q29 | Fragment related to Serekh ha-Yaḥad |
| ALD | Aramaic Levi Document |
| CD | Cairo Genizah copy of the Damascus Document |
| D | Damascus Document |
| M | Milḥamah |
| Mur 3 | Isaiah |
| S | Serekh ha-Yaḥad (Manual of Discipline) |
| SM | Sefer ha-Milḥamah |
| TTS | Treatise on the Two Spirits |

Abbreviations

| | |
|---|---|
| AB | Anchor Bible |
| *ABD* | Freedman, David Noel, ed. *Anchor Bible Dictionary*. 6 vols. New York: Doubleday, 1992. |
| AcBib | Academia Biblica |
| *AfO* | *Archiv für Orientforschung* |
| AfOB | Archiv für Orientforschung: Beiheft |
| AGJU | Arbeiten zur Geschichte des antiken Judentums und des Urchristentums |
| *AHES* | *Archive for History of Exact Sciences* |
| A.J. | Josephus, *Antiquitates judaicae* |
| ANEM | Ancient Near East Monographs |
| ANES | Ancient Near Eastern Studies |
| ANYAS | Annals of the New York Academy of Sciences |
| AOAT | Alter Orient und Altes Testament |
| *Astr.* | Manilius, *Astronomica* |
| b. Shabb. | Babylonian Talmud Shabbat |
| BC | Bloomsbury Companions |
| BETL | Bibliotheca Ephemeridum Theologicarum Lovaniensium |
| BI | Biblical Intersections |
| *Bib* | *Biblica* |
| *Bib. hist.* | Diodorus Siculus, *Bibliotheca historica* |
| *BibInt* | *Biblical Interpretation* |
| BibInt | Biblical Interpretation Series |
| BibOr | Biblica et Orientalia |

| | |
|---|---|
| *BIOSCS* | *Bulletin of the International Organization for Septuagint and Cognate Studies* |
| *B.J.* | Josephus, *Bellum judaicum* |
| BJS | Brown Judaic Studies |
| *BN* | *Biblische Notizen* |
| *BW* | Bible and Women |
| BZAW | Beihefte zur Zeitschrift für die alttestamentliche Wissenschaft |
| *C&D* | *Crime and Delinquency* |
| ca. | circa |
| CBET | Contributions to Biblical Exegesis and Theology |
| *CBQ* | *Catholic Biblical Quarterly* |
| CEJL | Commentaries on Early Jewish Literature |
| CJA | Christianity and Judaism in Antiquity |
| CM | Cuneiform Monographs |
| CNIP | CNI Publications |
| col(s). | column(s) |
| CQS | Companion to the Qumran Scrolls |
| *CS* | *Cognitive Science* |
| CSCA | Cambridge Studies in Cultural Anthropology |
| CSCO | Corpus Scriptorum Christianorum Orientalium |
| CSHJ | Chicago Studies in the History of Judaism |
| *CSR* | *Cognitive Systems Research* |
| *CT* | *Communications Theory* |
| *CurBR* | *Currents in Biblical Research* |
| DCLS | Deuterocanonical and Cognate Literature Series |
| *DDD* | Toorn, Karel van der, Bob Becking, and Pieter W. van der Horst, eds. *Dictionary of Deities and Demons in the Bible*. Leiden: Brill, 1995. |
| *De Lys.* | Dionysius of Halicarnassus, *Commentaries on the Attic Orators: Lysias* |
| DHR | Dynamics in the History of Religions |
| DJD | Discoveries in the Judaean Desert |
| *DSD* | *Dead Sea Discoveries* |
| DSS | Dead Sea Scrolls |
| *DSSR* | Parry, Donald W., and Emanuel Tov, eds. *Dead Sea Scrolls Reader*. 2nd ed. 2 vols. Leiden: Brill, 2013. |
| *EA* | *English in Australia* |

| | |
|---|---|
| *EDEJ* | Collins, John J., and Daniel C. Harlow, eds. *Eerdmans Dictionary of Early Judaism*. Grand Rapids: Eerdmans, 2010. |
| *EDSS* | Schiffman, Lawrence H., and James C. VanderKam, eds. *Encyclopedia of the Dead Sea Scrolls*. 2 vols. New York: Oxford University Press, 2000. |
| EJL | Early Judaism and Its Literature |
| ELT | *English Language Teaching* |
| 1 En. | 1 Enoch |
| 2 En. | 2 Enoch |
| *ErIsr* | *Eretz-Israel* |
| Exod. Rab. | Exodus Rabbah |
| FAT | Forschungen zum Alten Testament |
| frag. | fragment(s) |
| Gen. Rab. | Genesis Rabbah |
| *Geog.* | Strabo, *Geographica* |
| GKC | Kautzsch, Emil, ed. *Gesenius' Hebrew Grammar*. Translated by Arthur E. Cowley. 2nd ed. Oxford: Clarendon, 1910. |
| GS | *Gender Society* |
| HB | Hebrew Bible |
| HBAI | *Hebrew Bible and Ancient Israel* |
| Hen | *Henoch* |
| HOS | Handbook of Oriental Studies |
| HS | Homage Series |
| HSM | Harvard Semitic Monographs |
| HSS | Harvard Semitic Studies |
| HTR | *Harvard Theological Review* |
| HUCA | *Hebrew Union College Annual* |
| HUCM | Monographs of the Hebrew Union College |
| *Hypoth.* | Philo, *Hypothetica* |
| IBHS | Waltke, Bruce K., and Michael O'Connor. *An Introduction to Biblical Hebrew Syntax*. Winona Lake, IN: Eisenbrauns, 1990. |
| IEJ | *Israel Exploration Journal* |
| IELOA | Instruments pour l'étude des langues de l'Orient ancien 5 |
| IJS | IJS Studies in Judaica |
| IOS | *Israel Oriental Studies* |
| JAJ | *Journal of Ancient Judaism* |
| JAJSup | Journal of Ancient Judaism Supplements |
| JANES | *Journal of the Ancient Near Eastern Society* |

| | |
|---|---|
| JAOS | *Journal of the American Oriental Society* |
| JBL | *Journal of Biblical Literature* |
| JCS | *Journal of Cuneiform Studies* |
| JESHO | *Journal of the Economic and Social History of the Orient* |
| JJI | *Journal of Jewish Identities* |
| JJS | *Journal of Jewish Studies* |
| JJTP | *Journal of Jewish Thought and Philosophy* |
| JNES | *Journal of Near Eastern Studies* |
| Joüon | Joüon, Paul. *A Grammar of Biblical Hebrew*. Translated and revised by T. Muraoka. 2 vols. Rome: Pontifical Biblical Institute, 1991. |
| JQR | *Jewish Quarterly Review* |
| JSem | *Journal of Semitics* |
| JSHJ | *Journal for the Study of the Historical Jesus* |
| JSJ | *Journal for the Study of Judaism in the Persian, Hellenistic, and Roman Periods* |
| JSJSup | Supplements to the Journal for the Study of Judaism |
| JSNT | *Journal for the Study of the New Testament* |
| JSNTSup | Journal for the Study of the New Testament Supplement Series |
| JSOT | *Journal for the Study of the Old Testament* |
| JSOTSup | Journal for the Study of the Old Testament Supplement Series |
| JSPSup | Journal for the Study of the Pseudepigrapha Supplement Series |
| JSQ | *Jewish Studies Quarterly* |
| JSS | *Journal of Semitic Studies* |
| Jub. | Jubilees |
| JVI | *Journal of Value Inquiry* |
| KUSATU | *Kleine Untersuchungen zur Sprache des Alten Testaments und seiner Umwelt* |
| l(l). | line(s) |
| LHBOTS | The Library of Hebrew Bible/Old Testament Studies |
| LSTS | The Library of Second Temple Studies |
| LXX | Septuagint |
| m. | Mishnah |
| MB | *Mitteilungen und Beiträge der Forschungsstelle Judentum der Theologischen Fakultät Leipzig* |
| Mek. Shir. | Mekilta Shirata |

| | |
|---|---|
| *MG* | *Materia Giudaica* |
| *Migr.* | Philo, *De migratione Abrahami* |
| *Mos.* | Philo, *De vita Mosis* |
| MT | Masoretic Text |
| *MTSR* | *Method & Theory in the Study of Religion* |
| NA$^{27}$ | *Novum Testamentum Graece*, Nestle-Aland, 27h ed. |
| NA$^{28}$ | *Novum Testamentum Graece*, Nestle-Aland, 28th ed. |
| *NABU* | *Nouvelles assyriologiques brèves et utilitaires* |
| *Nat.* | Pliny, *Naturalis historia* |
| *NLH* | *New Literary History* |
| *NovT* | *Novum Testamentum* |
| NovTSup | Supplements to Novum Testamentum |
| *NRN* | *Nature Reviews Neuroscience* |
| NRSV | New Revised Standard Version |
| n.s. | new series |
| NTOA | Novum Testamentum et Orbus Antiquus |
| NTS | *New Testament Studies* |
| NTSI | New Testament and the Scriptures of Israel |
| OAWPHK | Österreichische Akademie der Wissenschaften. Philosophisch-Historische Klasse |
| OBO | Orbis Biblicus et Orientalis |
| OLC | hexaplaric recension of Origen; Lucianic text; catena group |
| *Opif.* | Philo, *De opificio mundi* |
| OTE | *Old Testament Essays* |
| OTL | Old Testament Library |
| OTP | Charlesworth, James H., ed. *Old Testament Pseudepigrapha*. 2 vols. New York: Doubleday, 1983, 1985. |
| *OtSt* | *Oudtestamentische Studiën* |
| PAM | Palestine Archaeological Museum |
| PFES | Publications of the Finnish Exegetical Society |
| *Phaen.* | Aratus, *Phaenomena* |
| PI | Philosophers' Imprint |
| PJEGLMBS | *Proceedings, Journal of the Eastern Great Lakes and Midwest Biblical Societies* |
| pl(s). | plate(s) |
| PS | *Psychological Science* |
| PT | *Poetics Today* |
| PTRS | *Philosophical Transactions of the Royal Society B* |
| PTSDSSP | Princeton Theological Seminary Dead Sea Scrolls Project |

| | |
|---|---|
| QG | Philo, *Quaestiones et solutiones in Genesin* |
| QE | Philo, *Quaestiones et solutions in Exodum* |
| RB | *Revue biblique* |
| RBS | Resources for Biblical Study |
| RCPP | Routledge Contemporary Political Philosophy |
| REL | *Revue des Etudes Latines* |
| Rel | *Religion* |
| RevOrChr | *Revue de l'Orient Chretien* |
| RevQ | *Revue de Qumran* |
| RGRW | Religions in the Graeco-Roman World |
| RSL | *Reti, Saperi, Linguaggi* |
| SALALS | *Southern African Linguistics and Applied Languages Studies* |
| SBLDS | Society of Biblical Literature Dissertation Series |
| SBT | Studies in Biblical Theology |
| SciCon | *Science in Context* |
| SDSSRL | Studies in the Dead Sea Scrolls and Related Literature |
| Sem | *Semiotica* |
| Shabb. | Shabbat |
| SJLA | Studies in Judaism in Late Antiquity |
| SJOT | *Scandinavian Journal of the Old Testament* |
| SJSHR | Studien zu den Jüdischen Schriften aus hellenistisch-römanischer |
| SJT | *Scottish Journal of Theology* |
| SP | Samaritan Pentateuch |
| Spec. | Philo, *De specialibus legibus* |
| SPhA | Studies in Philo of Alexandria |
| SSECJ | Studies in Scripture in Early Judaism and Christianity |
| SSLL | Studies in Semitic Languages and Linguistics |
| SSN | Studia Semitica Neerlandica |
| ST | *Studia Theologica* |
| STAC | Studies and Texts in Antiquity and Christianity |
| StBibLit | Studies in Biblical Literature |
| STDJ | Studies on the Texts of the Desert of Judah |
| SUNT | Studien zur Umwelt des Neuen Testaments |
| s.v. | *sub verbo*, under the word |
| SVTP | Studia in Veteris Testamenti Pseudepigraphica |
| SWAMW | Scientific Writings from the Ancient and Medieval World |
| TAC | Time, Astronomy, and Calendars |
| TAPS | Transactions of the American Philosophical Society |

| | |
|---|---|
| TBN | Themes in the Biblical Narrative |
| *TCS* | *Trends in Cognitive Sciences* |
| TSAJ | Texte und Studien zum antiken Judentum |
| *TWQ* | *Theologisches Wörterbuch zu den Qumrantexten* |
| UCOP | University of Cambridge Oriental Publications |
| *UTLJ* | *University of Toronto Law Journal* |
| VAR | variant reading |
| *Virt.* | Philo, *De virtutibus* |
| *Vita* | Josephus, *Vita* |
| *VT* | *Vetus Testamentum* |
| VTSup | Supplements to Vetus Testamentum |
| WAC | Wise, Michael, Martin Abegg Jr., and Edward Cook. *The Dead Sea Scrolls: A New Translation*. HarperSanFrancisco, 1996. |
| WBC | Word Biblical Commentary |
| WMANT | Wissenschaftliche Monographien zum Alten und Neuen Testament |
| WUNT | Wissenschaftliche Untersuchungen Neuen Testament |
| *ZA* | *Zeitschrift für Assyriologie* |
| *ZAW* | *Zeitschrift für die alttestamentliche Wissenschaft* |

# Introduction: New Approaches to Old Questions

Andrew R. Krause, Carmen Palmer, and John Screnock

*Dead Sea Scrolls, Revise and Repeat* has two primary aims: to bring new methodologies to the study of the Dead Sea Scrolls (DSS) and to reassess earlier conclusions about the DSS—specifically, those dealing with the identity of the movement(s) associated with Qumran and the DSS. Many of the chapters in this volume began in the context of a two-year special session offered at the Canadian Society of Biblical Studies. Those revised studies, along with additional studies that serve to broaden the scope, address these aims in different ways. Over the past decade, scholars have increasingly acknowledged variegation and development in the Yaḥad movement.[1] Scholars are reconsidering past hypotheses and reconstructions that limited the Yaḥad to the site of Qumran, as well as the traditional set of so-called sectarian features used to identify texts belonging to the movement.

Because texts must be understood in light of the people and communities who produced and received them, the identity of the movement continues to attract scholarly attention. This volume is meant to help us rethink the identity of the group, without treating the movement as a static, homogenous whole. Using the DSS themselves as the primary investigative tool, we aim to further our understanding of the people and the movement (or movements) associated with Qumran, their outlook on the world, and what binds them together. Many of the studies in this volume address identity questions directly, reassessing established conclusions regarding such issues as the categorization of rule texts, reuse of scripture, significance of angelic fellowship, varieties of calendrical use, and celibacy within the Qumran movement.

---

1. See John J. Collins, *Beyond the Qumran Community: The Sectarian Movement of the Dead Sea Scrolls* (Grand Rapids: Eerdmans, 2010).

Often, the best way to reassess the conclusions of past scholarship is to apply new methods. Of the essays that take this kind of methodological focus, some are less direct in addressing identity questions; however, all come to conclusions that challenge past views. These studies draw on a variety of interdisciplinary methods and theories that are relatively new to DSS scholarship: spatial theory, legal theory, historical linguistics, ethnicity theory, cognitive literary theory, monster theory, and masculinity theory. While recent methodologically focused volumes on the DSS have addressed some of these areas, this volume brings refinement and clarification in terms of both the theoretical framework and the application of many of these methods.

## Methodology, Reassessment, and Interdisciplinarity in Dead Sea Scrolls Studies

Our focus on interdisciplinary approaches, as well as the notion of DSS studies as a distinct field,[2] can be situated within the history of scholarship by means of an analogy to other fields. The disciplinary setting and methodological development of Ugaritic studies, for example, helps to clarify the position of DSS studies. When clay tablets were discovered at Ras Shamra in the late 1920s, modern humans knew the city and people of Ugarit only indirectly[3] and had never encountered the Ugaritic language. There were, therefore, no Ugariticists, so scholars from other fields worked together to make sense of the evidence they were finding. They applied existing methods from archaeology, paleography, history, Semitics, and ancient Near Eastern studies. Still today, the study of Ugarit and Ugaritic is best situated in the larger contexts provided by these and other fields; literary studies, sociology, anthropology, linguistics, and history are applicable wherever human society is present. However, Ugarit's subject matter is unique and therefore requires specifically crafted methods of analysis.[4] More importantly, its subject matter deserves study in its own right. Though Ugarit provides important contextualization for biblical texts, for example, the

---

2. We are using the term *DSS studies* to include both studies pertaining to the DSS and studies pertaining to the history and archaeology of the site of Qumran.

3. For example, in the Amarna Letters.

4. The writing system, for example, is one of the only alphabetic systems that uses cuneiform (Old Persian is another); its decipherment could not be accomplished by simply applying methods from another field.

material from this field has significance beyond its utilization in the study of the Bible. The history, language, archaeology, and literature of Ugarit are worthy of study in their own right, without any subsequent goals to serve in other fields. It is therefore right that we approach the material from Ugarit as a sort of area study in miniature, so that the particular contours of this place-time-people cluster are appreciated and understood, and its study safeguarded.

When a new field such as Ugaritic studies is born,[5] it is initially interdisciplinary out of necessity, because it has no methods of its own. It then develops methods specifically designed for its unique needs and subject material. When it has its own methodological basis and has applied it extensively to the evidence, a field often enters a third phase, during which it returns to interdisciplinarity. Throughout these three phases, the reassessment of past models is vital to the growth of any field. As with Ugaritic, DSS scholarship began as an interdisciplinary endeavor; the field has long since passed into the second phase of methodological uniformity, and in recent years has (re)turned to interdisciplinary methods. Throughout its existence, DSS studies has undergone a continual process of reevaluation and scrutiny.

Discovered two decades after the Ugaritic material, the DSS similarly created their own small field of study, initially requiring the importation of methods from other fields (e.g., archaeology, Hebrew Bible, paleography). The DSS and the cluster of issues related to them (e.g., the identity of the Yaḥad and the significance of the geographical site of Qumran) rightly constitute an area with its own field of study—though these topics also ought to be studied in connection to, and in the context of, larger disciplines. Fortunately, scholars did not have to decipher the script and language of the DSS; that knowledge was already available from Jewish Studies and the Hebrew Bible. This fact, together with the longer timeline of Ugarit (many layers of the site are yet to be excavated, and texts continue to be found), means that DSS studies has progressed through the initial stage of methodological development more quickly than Ugaritic studies, which is still deciphering texts and developing its own methods.[6]

---

5. Here we refer to new fields born from new evidence (e.g., Akkadian material in the nineteenth century), rather than from new methods (e.g., generative linguistics) or from attention to a previously unstudied subject (e.g., translation studies).

6. We continue to find textual and other material evidence at Ugarit and locations

Though much of the initial work happened behind closed doors, since the earliest study of the DSS scholars have debated and reassessed the reconstruction, meaning, and sociohistorical context of these important finds from Caves 1 to 11. Since Emanuel Tov became the editor in chief of the Discoveries in the Judaean Desert (DJD) series, leading to the rapid publication of the remaining texts, scholars have brought an ever-widening set of skills and techniques to this endeavor. As a result, monographs and edited volumes reassessing past readings and historical reconstructions have proliferated. In the later 1990s, several scholars began to reassess the findings of the past generation. Scholars such as Elisha Qimron, Lawrence Schiffman, and Hartmut Stegemann revolutionized the study of the DSS by directly questioning past studies. Stegemann greatly advanced the manuscript reconstruction of badly damaged scrolls and rejected the traditional Qumran-Essene hypothesis in favor of a more nuanced reconstruction based on careful analysis of the texts themselves.[7] Stegemann was followed by other scholars who contextualized the group or groups responsible for the so-called sectarian literature from Qumran, including Gabriele Boccaccini and the Groningen School.[8] The new series from Brill, Studies on the Texts of the Desert of Judah (STDJ), became a venue for full monograph-length studies; in the early 1990s this series also published the proceedings from key conferences such as the Madrid Congress, the first meeting of the International Organization for Qumran Studies, and a landmark volume reviewing the first four decades of DSS research.[9] All of these provided

---

nearby, and though several reference grammars have been published, there remain substantial disagreements about fundamental aspects of Ugaritic language.

7. Hartmut Stegemann, *Die Essener, Qumran, Johannes der Täufer und Jesus* (Freiburg: Verlag Herder, 1993); Elisha Qimron, *The Temple Scroll: A Critical Edition with Extensive Reconstructions* (Jerusalem: Israel Exploration Society, 1996); Lawrence H. Schiffman, *Reclaiming the Dead Sea Scrolls: The History of Judaism, the Background of Christianity, the Lost Library of Qumran* (New York: Doubleday, 1994).

8. Gabriele Boccaccini, *Beyond the Essene Hypothesis* (Grand Rapids: Eerdmans, 1998); Florentino García Martínez and Julio Trebolle Barrera, *The People of the Dead Sea Scrolls: Their Writings, Beliefs, and Practices*, trans. Wilfred G. E. Watson (Leiden: Brill, 1995).

9. Julio Trebolle Barrera and Luis Vegas Montaner, eds., *The Madrid Qumran Congress: Proceedings of the International Congress on the Dead Sea Scrolls, Madrid, 18–21 March, 1991*, 2 vols., STDJ 11 (Leiden: Brill, 1992); George J. Brooke, ed., *New Qumran Texts and Studies: Proceedings from the First Meeting of the International Organization for Qumran Studies, Paris 1992*, STDJ 15 (Leiden: Brill, 1994); Devorah

the second generation of DSS scholars a chance to offer more precision to the philological and historical study of the DSS. The series has continued to publish edited volumes with perspectives on specific issues and genres of the DSS, originating in various conferences of the Orion Center at the Hebrew University of Jerusalem or the International Organization for Qumran Studies; many of these were dedicated to scholars from the first generation of DSS studies.[10] Indeed, the international conferences held at regular—and frequent—intervals in these years played a very significant role in establishing DSS studies as a subdiscipline in its own right. Especially important were a series of volumes that sought to reassess DSS studies around the fiftieth anniversary of the discovery of the Cave 1 scrolls.[11] As the DJD volumes continued to appear, so too did volumes of ever-expanding interdisciplinary critiques of past readings.

In 2006, around the sixtieth anniversary of the discovery of the DSS, Eileen Schuller proposed that

> after a half-decade where textual, philological, and historical scholars carried most of the burden, it is now the time for drawing other scholars and resources into the study of the scrolls. On the one hand, there is still much that the "hard scientists," working in specialties as diverse and complex as AMS (accelerator mass spectography), archeobotany, DNA analysis, and INAA (instrumental neutron activation analysis) can contribute.... But equally exciting is what scholars who are trained in the

---

Dimant and Uriel Rappaport, *The Dead Sea Scrolls: Forty Years of Research*, STDJ 10 (Leiden: Brill, 1992).

10. E.g., Moshe Bernstein, Florentino García Martínez, and John Kampen, eds., *Legal Texts and Legal Issues*, STDJ 23 (Leiden: Brill, 1997); David Goodblatt, Avital Pinnick, and Daniel R. Schwartz, eds., *Historical Perspectives: From the Hasmoneans to Bar Kokhba in Light of the Dead Sea Scrolls*, STDJ 37 (Leiden: Brill, 2001); Daniel K. Falk, Florentino García Martínez, and Eileen M. Schuller, eds., *Sapiential, Liturgical, and Poetic Texts from Qumran*, STDJ 35 (Leiden: Brill, 2001); Esther G. Chazon, *Liturgical Perspectives: Prayer and Poetry in Light of the Dead Sea Scrolls*, STDJ 48 (Leiden: Brill, 2003).

11. Robert A. Kugler and Eileen M. Schuller, eds., *The Dead Sea Scrolls at Fifty*, EJL 15 (Atlanta: Scholars Press, 1997); Stanley E. Porter and Craig A. Evans, eds., *The Scrolls and the Scriptures: Qumran Fifty Years After*, JSPSup 26 (Sheffield: Sheffield Academic, 1997); Peter W. Flint and James C. VanderKam, eds., *The Dead Sea Scrolls after Fifty Years: A Comprehensive Reassessment*, 2 vols. (Leiden: Brill, 1998–1999); Lawrence H. Schiffman, Emanuel Tov, and James C. VanderKam, eds., *The Dead Sea Scrolls Fifty Years after Their Discovery* (Jerusalem: Israel Exploration Society, 2000).

various humanistic and social scientific methodologies and disciplines might contribute.... Drawing upon a wider variety of specialties with a more interdisciplinary perspective will cause the scrolls to be read in new ways that will generate new questions and, almost certainly, new issues and problems to be considered.[12]

For Schuller, this profusion of new studies—which had already begun to some extent—would not take the place of the past historical, manuscript, and philological studies, which themselves still needed reevaluation. Rather, they would supplement the work already done and lead to better readings and deeper historical insight. For example, Hannah Harrington brought social-scientific interests in purity and taboo, informed by the work of Mary Douglas and Jacob Milgrom.[13] Judith Newman and Daniel Falk applied the ritual theories of Victor Turner and Catherine Bell to the liturgical scrolls and other Second Temple prayer texts.[14] Spurred by the work of Schuller herself, several scholars utilized gender and other embodiment theories.[15] Russell Arnold, Angela Kim Harkins, and Newman have combined philosophical and sociological theories together in their work on DSS ritual texts, while Carol Newsom, Jutta Jokiranta, Alex Jassen, and Alison Schofield have consistently used sophisticated social-scientific theories in their studies of Yaḥad social organization.[16]

---

12. Eileen M. Schuller, *The Dead Sea Scrolls: What Have We Learned?* (Louisville: Westminster John Knox, 2006), 107–8.

13. Hannah K. Harrington, *The Impurity Systems of Qumran and the Rabbis: Biblical Foundations* (Atlanta: Scholars Press, 1993); Harrington, *The Purity Texts*, CQS 5 (London: T&T Clark, 2004).

14. Daniel K. Falk, *Daily, Sabbath, and Festival Prayers in the Dead Sea Scrolls*, STDJ 27 (Leiden: Brill, 1998); Judith H. Newman, *Praying by the Book: The Scripturalization of Prayer in Second Temple Judaism*, EJL 14 (Atlanta: Society of Biblical Literature, 1999). See also Mark J. Boda, Daniel K. Falk, and Rodney A. Werline, eds., *Seeking the Favor of God*, 3 vols., EJL 21–23 (Atlanta: Society of Biblical Literature, 2006–2008).

15. Cecilia Wassen, *Women in the Damascus Document*, AcBib 21 (Atlanta: Society of Biblical Literature, 2005); Hanna Tervanotko, *Denying Her Voice: The Figure of Miriam in Ancient Jewish Literature*, JAJSup 23 (Göttingen: Vandenhoek & Ruprecht, 2016); Jessica M. Keady, *Vulnerability and Valour: A Gendered Analysis of Everyday Life in the Dead Sea Scrolls Communities*, LSTS 91 (London: Bloomsbury, 2017).

16. Russell C. D. Arnold, *Social Role of Liturgy in the Religion of the Qumran Community*, STDJ 60 (Leiden: Brill, 2006); Angela Kim Harkins, *Reading with an "I" to the Heavens: Looking at the Qumran Hodayot through the Lens of Visionary Tradition*,

Hebraists have included (and sometimes focused on) the evidence from the DSS in their assessment of ancient Hebrew.¹⁷ Further, the DSS have been analyzed by methods from the digital humanities.¹⁸ Many of these studies have been grouped with other theoretical studies in various volumes or series, rather than with DSS-specific studies. However, the tradition continues of collected volumes that are devoted to exploring new approaches and questions.¹⁹

---

Ekstasis 3 (Berlin: de Gruyter, 2011); Judith H. Newman, *Before the Bible: Liturgical Body and the Formation of Scriptures in Early Judaism* (Oxford: Oxford University Press, 2018); Carol A. Newsom, *The Self as Symbolic Space: Constructing Identity and Community at Qumran*, STDJ 52 (Leiden: Brill, 2004); Alex P. Jassen, *Mediating the Divine: Prophecy and Revelation in the Dead Sea Scrolls and Second Temple Judaism*, STDJ 68 (Leiden: Brill, 2007); Alison Schofield, *From Qumran to the Yaḥad: A New Paradigm of Textual Development for the Community Rule*, STDJ 77 (Leiden: Brill 2009); Jutta Jokiranta, *Social Identity and Sectarianism in the Qumran Movement*, STDJ 105 (Leiden: Brill, 2013).

17. Most notably, in STDJ's collection of volumes on the Hebrew of the Dead Sea Scrolls and Ben Sira (vols. 26, 33, 36, 73, 108, 114, 124); and in studies by Elisha Qimron, *A Grammar of the Hebrew of the Dead Sea Scrolls* (Jerusalem: Yad Izhak Ben-Zvi, 2018); and Eric Reymond, *Qumran Hebrew: An Overview of Orthography, Phonology, and Morphology*, RBS 76 (Atlanta: SBL Press, 2014). Studies that draw explicitly on new methods from linguistics include Jacobus A. Naudé, "Diachronic Syntax and Language Change: The Case of Qumran Hebrew," *SALALS* 18 (2000): 1–14; Ken M. Penner, *The Verbal System of the Dead Sea Scrolls: Tense, Aspect, and Modality in Qumran Hebrew Texts*, SSN 64 (Leiden: Brill, 2014); Robert D. Holmstedt and John Screnock, "Writing a Descriptive Grammar of the Syntax and Semantics of the War Scroll (1QM): The Noun Phrase as Proof of Concept," in *The War Scroll, Violence, War and Peace in the Dead Sea Scrolls and Related Literature: Essays in Honour of Martin G. Abegg on the Occasion of His Sixty-Fifth Birthday*, ed. Kipp Davis et al., STDJ 115 (Leiden: Brill, 2015), 67–106.

18. E.g., Maruf A. Dhali et al., "A Digital Palaeographic Approach towards Writer Identification in the Dead Sea Scrolls," in *Proceedings of the Sixth International Conference on Pattern Recognition Applications and Methods, ICPRAM 2017, Porto, Portugal, February 24–26, 2017* (Setúbal, Portugal: SciTePress, 2017), 693–702.

19. The following volumes, for example, focus on reassessment of past conclusions, application of new methods, or both: Jonathan G. Campbell, William John Lyons, and Lloyd K. Pietersen, *New Directions in Qumran Studies: Proceedings of the Bristol Colloquium on the Dead Sea Scrolls*, LSTS 52 (London: T&T Clark, 2005); Michael Thomas Davis and Brent A. Strawn, eds., *Qumran Studies: New Approaches, New Questions* (Grand Rapids: Eerdmans, 2007); Florentino García Martínez and Mladen Popović, eds., *Defining Identities: We, You, and the Other in the Dead Sea Scrolls; Proceedings of the Fifth Meeting of the IOQS in Gröningen*, STDJ 70 (Leiden: Brill, 2008); Daniel K.

The refined and concentrated use of social theory has led scholars such as John Collins, Joan Taylor, and Schofield to articulate increasing problems with the traditional Qumran-Essene hypothesis.[20] Much recent discussion has tended to present the Yaḥad movement as a more complex and diffuse group of communities spread throughout Judea, though as yet no full and comprehensive consensus has emerged to explain exactly how such communities related and interacted with one another, whether geographically or conceptually. That scholarship is now in a state of flux, and that this is a time of experimentation with different models and social theories is reflected in the different terminologies found in the essays of this volume and even in different uses and presuppositions for the same terms: *movement, community, group, sectarian.*

In summary, the first waves of DSS scholarship accomplished the important task of deciphering the material evidence and uncovering the sociohistorical milieu of the DSS. This methodological focus on fundamental issues was attended by the temptation to leverage the DSS for impact (e.g., theories about nascent Christianity). Scholars quickly moved on to the development of field-specific methods, and the more the evidence has been accurately quantified the less attention has been allocated to some of the earlier questions. Although some scholars had moved beyond foundational methods such as material reconstruction and paleography within a few decades of the DSS's discovery, even these more traditional approaches are being reapplied and renewed, especially with advances from the digital humanities.

---

Falk et al., *Qumran Cave 1 Revisited: Texts from Cave 1 Sixty Years after Their Discovery; Proceedings of the Sixth Meeting of the IOQS in Ljubljana*, STDJ 91 (Leiden: Brill, 2010); Maxine L. Grossman, ed., *Rediscovering the Dead Sea Scrolls: An Assessment of Old and New Approaches and Methods* (Grand Rapids: Eerdmans, 2010); Sarianna Metso, Hindy Najman, and Eileen M. Schuller, eds., *The Dead Sea Scrolls: Transmission of Traditions and the Production of Texts*, STDJ 92 (Leiden: Brill, 2010); Charlotte Hempel, ed., *The Dead Sea Scrolls: Texts and Contexts*, STDJ 90 (Leiden: Brill, 2010); Shani Tzoref and Lawrence H. Schiffman, eds., *The Dead Sea Scrolls at Sixty*, STDJ 89 (Leiden: Brill, 2010); Devorah Dimant, ed., *The Dead Sea Scrolls in Scholarly Perspective: A History of Research*, STDJ 99 (Leiden: Brill, 2012). For a recent, interdisciplinary collection from a single author, see George J. Brooke, *Reading the Dead Sea Scrolls: Essays in Method*, EJL 39 (Atlanta: Society of Biblical Literature, 2013).

20. Collins, *Beyond the Qumran Community*; Joan E. Taylor, *The Essenes, the Scrolls, and the Dead Sea* (Oxford: Oxford University Press, 2012); Schofield, *From Qumran to the Yaḥad*.

The progress made in the last thirty years has spurred scholars from around the world to offer fresh insight into the publication of these texts, rereading of the data, and entirely new hypotheses regarding the community or movement that produced them. Works meant to challenge past hypotheses and conclusions have nearly become a subgenre of DSS studies. While some of these studies are monographs, they are most often edited volumes that bring a variety of new approaches to bear on the task of understanding Qumran, the Yaḥad movement, and the DSS. The present volume purposefully and unapologetically situates itself in this tradition of reassessment and exploration of interdisciplinarity. Of course, all studies on the DSS aim to add new knowledge, though not all seek to reassess the field and its methodologies. This volume is not presented for the sake of proffering new fads or doing away with the work of the past. It comes with full acknowledgment that we are standing on the shoulders of giants as we bring forward new methods and theories in a spirit of self-renewing discourse.

## Chapter Outlines

Each section and chapter contributes in some fashion to the overarching matter of identity.

The first section addresses matters of law, language, and literary formation. Sarianna Metso and Jonathan Vroom both reassess perceptions of law in the DSS and within the broader context of Jewish legal development. Metso reassesses the so-called rule texts from Qumran by taking a sweeping view of the Damascus Document (D) and Serekh ha-Yaḥad (S, Rule of the Community) alongside other legal texts that originated within Second Temple Jewish communities. In drawing on this new and broader framework instead of the usual scholarly categories of halakic or rule texts, Metso discovers the role that revelatory authority plays in "the level of scribal manipulations permitted." Metso forwards her argument by examining examples from across the spectrum of editorial approaches that were employed by Second Temple era scribes in regard to the laws of Leviticus, in the Samaritan Pentateuch, 4QPentateuch (4Q364–367), 11QTemple (11Q19), and D and S. On one end of the spectrum, the book of Leviticus in the Samaritan Pentateuch does not show editorial intervention typical of the Samaritan Pentateuch. On the other end of the spectrum are the communities responsible for D and S, which undertook a highly creative approach to scriptural traditions. Metso highlights examples where passages from Leviticus are used to address entirely different topics, such as the use of Lev 10:10 in the Cairo Genizah copy of the Damascus Document (CD) VI, 14–21 to distinguish between insiders and outsiders in the community, instead of Levitical injunctions regarding clean and unclean. Metso uses these examples to observe sociological differences regarding dissimilar leadership roles in the communities behind these texts. In the Essene community, the Teacher and the scribes who came after him viewed themselves as recipients of revelation, permitting revelatory modifications to legal material. In contrast, Moses was considered the final legal prophet in the Samaritan community, and thus further legal innovations were not possible.

Vroom draws on legal theory to reassess the genre and function of the rule texts pertaining to the DSS and their underlying communities, including S, D, and Miscellaneous Rules (4Q265). Instead of taking the view that these texts should be understood as binding law, Vroom finds agreement with those who conclude that the rule texts should be viewed as didactic texts, "meant to instill community values." Vroom's methodological innovation is in how he addresses the question of the authority of the texts. First, Vroom explains the two types of authority that legal theorists distinguish, namely, practical authority and epistemic authority, and the types of interpretive practices they engender. In the case of practical authority, the addressee will be concerned with compliance with a command, whereas with epistemic authority the addressee will be interested in engaging reason. After laying out the groundwork to legal theory, Vroom applies it to the Qumran penal codes by working through a series of examples. These examples highlight that while the laws were viewed with authority, the various reinterpretations of each suggest a lack of interest in how to comply and a much stronger interest in epistemic authority. Vroom concludes the chapter by discussing the value in thinking through the lens of epistemic authority: this method permits scholars to see the texts as authoritative but not representative of binding law.

Two chapters address matters of language. First, John Screnock's chapter reassesses the notion that Qumran Hebrew was a distinct dialect closely associated with the "sectarians who supposedly lived at Qumran." Drawing on historical linguistics, Screnock analyzes the syntax of cardinal numbers to conclude that the Hebrew of the DSS prefers the order number-noun, just as do Biblical and Mishnaic Hebrew. This conclusion differs from Qimron's argument that noun-number ordering distinguished the Hebrew of the DSS. Screnock advances his study in the following steps: First, he introduces the field of historical linguistics, which explains language variations vis-à-vis both controlled features of stylistics and uncontrollable features including dialect, register, and diachrony (constrainment by temporal location). Second, Screnock defines his parameters and assembles the data in the DSS, including DSS witnesses with ten or more "tokens" (instances where the order of a number phrase can be discerned). Third, Screnock's interpretation of the data establishes that number-noun order is preferred and that those cases of noun-number ordering can be explained according to stylistics, especially list style. Screnock concludes the study by observing that there is more continuity than differentiation between Hebrew in the DSS and earlier Hebrew and by discussing classicizing and a specific case in the War Scroll.

The second chapter that addresses the matter of language is that of Andrew B. Perrin and Brandon Diggens, who present the first complete and consolidated list of textual variants from Aramaic DSS that are attested in multiple manuscripts. The transcriptions of the texts they assess (1 Enoch, Aramaic Levi Document, Astronomical Enoch, Tobit, Four Kingdoms, New Jerusalem, and Visions of Amram) are taken from the DJD editions (or from other editions if not included in DJD). Perrin and Diggens limit the study to variants that yield a change in a text's semantics as well as to variants relevant to the development of Aramaic language. An example highlighting semantic variants includes pluses or minuses of content, such as the presence or absence of secondary discourse markers in Four Kingdoms. Examples related to development in the Aramaic language include differences in scribal preference for plene or defective spelling and interchanged gutturals or sibilants (Enochic Book of Watchers and Book of Dreams) and the interchange of *he* and *aleph* (Tobit). Perrin and Diggens conclude the study with an appendix of instances within Edward Cook's *Dictionary of Qumran Aramaic* where Cook provides alternate readings to those given in DJD or aligns with a reading from another scholarly edition. This study presents known textual information in a new manner so as to facilitate further study and questions.

Kyung S. Baek's chapter rounds out the section, reconsidering questions about the formation of biblical texts and the reuse of scripture within various traditions. Baek pays tribute to the late Professor Peter Flint, who was an active member of the Canadian Society of Biblical Studies and a participant in the sessions where many of the chapters in this book first took form. Baek extends Flint's findings regarding the extensive use of Isaiah in the DSS in order to shed light on the Gospel of

Matthew's use of Isaiah. He first offers an overview on the use of Isaiah in the DSS as a comparative tool. The textual variants evident in the text, notes Baek, "suggest a fluidity of the text of Isaiah during the time of its composition." Baek then moves to his study of Matthew's use of Isaiah. While not implying a direct influence, Baek is interested in the findings that might arise from noting a common scribal practice such as the fluidity found in Matthew. Baek charts three primary ways that Matthew reworks Isaiah: Matthew's use of fulfillment quotations, whose purpose is to contemporize prophetic texts; Matthew's use of citations, those with an introductory formula serving to authenticate the person of Jesus and those without serving to incorporate the original historical context of the text into the present; and Matthew's use of allusions to Isaiah that offer themes to unite the Matthean community.

The second section focuses on matters of space and time. In the first chapter in this section, Heather Macumber assesses space through monster theory and perceived demonic threats on the cosmic world of the communities of the DSS. Macumber draws on monster theory in an assessment of Songs of the Sage (4Q510–511) to demonstrate how a retreat to the wilderness, both real and metaphorical, leaves members of the movement susceptible to demonic attack. Monster theory, Macumber explains, is a methodological tool to understand a culture through the study of the monsters it creates and vilifies, as they indicate any given community's concerns. Because members of the Qumran movement removed themselves physically and geographically to achieve spiritual purification and revelation, they also made themselves susceptible to demonic attack, as the wilderness was a place of chaos. In her assessment of Songs of the Sage, Macumber argues that the Maskil wards off attack as a sort of gatekeeper through the establishment of cosmic boundaries, which include protection against the fragile physical and spiritual selves of community members. Furthermore, community members themselves become hybrid beings like monsters, as their identity becomes ambiguously located between human and angelic beings. With the use of monster theory, the study highlights the physical and ontological liminal status of community members.

Matthew L. Walsh takes up the discussion of angelology to conclude that sectarian boasting of relationship with angels associated with Israel served to promote a particular identity. Walsh compares DSS deemed sectarian (S, 11QMelchizedek [11Q13], and the War Scroll [1QM]) with a nonsectarian Second Temple–period text (Dan 7–12). Walsh begins with a study of Dan 7–12, emphasizing that in these chapters victory is decreed for the heavenly Israel, paralleling victory for the deliverance of the earthly Israel as well. Heavenly and earthly realms are connected, and all Israel is included. Walsh then moves on to the comparisons among sectarian texts discussing angelic communities. The Treatise on the Two Spirits (1QS III, 13–IV, 26) in the Rule of the Community (1QS) instructs that angelic assistance is "an integral component of what it means to be the true Israel." In 11QMelchizedek, to be a member of the sect and the true Israel, one must be in "the lot of the angel to whom the God of Israel has delegated great power and authority." Finally, Walsh turns to the War Scroll, where he observes a dependence on and yet a reenvisioning of Daniel, whereby the heavenly Israel and earthly Israel together form God's lot. Thus the claim of angelic fellowship and the precise nature and extent of this claim played a key role in shaping the identity of this movement.

The third chapter in this section deals more specifically with time: Helen R. Jacobus offers a fresh perspective on Qumran calendar scholarship. The study contradicts the standard view that the Qumran community only used a solar calendar (364-Day Calendar Traditions), a calendar that was not used among the rest of Jewish society. Jacobus observes that there were a variety of calendars in use for different occasions within late Second Temple Judaism. Jacobus lays out her careful argument in the following manner: First, Jacobus demonstrates that the 364-Day Calendar Traditions are not unique to Qumran. For example, Calendrical Document Mishmarot A (4Q320) exhibits the 364-Day Calendar Traditions, yet predates the existence of the sectarian movement at the site of Qumran; Commentary on Genesis A (4Q252), which contains the only unbroken reference to the 364-day year, "has no identifiable sectarian morphology or contextual features." Next, Jacobus questions the commonly held argument that the 364-day calendar was not intercalated at Qumran (the process of adding days or months to keep the calendar in line with the seasons), and therefore deemed fictional and ideal. She argues that some form of intercalation seems likely to have been developed and applied. Jacobus uses Astronomical Enoch[a–b] (4Q208–209) as a case study for this perspective, arguing that 4Q208–209 draws on a synchronistic solar calendar of 360 days (integrating the zodiac) and the 354-day lunar calendar. She advances this study by reconstructing the year, supported in fragments in 4Q208–209, by using the template of Zodiac Calendar (4Q318); the zodiac signs correspond to the gate numbers shown in 4Q208–209, the efficacy of which can be tested against various astronomical online tools. For Jacobus, the evidence suggests "a culture of knowledge and educational transmission within the region" of calendrical systems combined in creative ways.

The final chapter in this section may serve as a segue between the focus on space and time and the next section's focus on the body. Andrew R. Krause works with critical spatial theory to assess the manner in which the Yaḥad movement communicated impurity, sin, and atonement in a bodily fashion, both individual and community. Krause uses spatial theory to describe how the notion of physical enclosures, serving as protective spaces, may also apply to the physical body as a protective space. Krause demonstrates that spirits (whether good or evil) and the sectarian body are connected and do not form a body/soul antithesis. Krause draws on a selection of Qumran apotropaic prayers, including those found within the Aramaic Levi Document, 4QIncantation (4Q444), 4QShirot (4Q400–407), the Treatise of the Two Spirits (esp. 1QS IV, 15–26), the Hymn of the Maskil (1QS IX, 25–XI, 15), and the Hodayot (1QH[a]). These apotropaic prayers are spatial not only in their performance but also in their desired effect of keeping evil spirits out of specific spaces. The body becomes the primary protective space, serving as the location for positive spirits to ward off evil ones. In particular, the heart is the primary locus for the God-granted positive spirits of knowledge, truth, and righteousness; conversely, the heart is where these positive spirits may be forced out by evil spirits, such as Belial himself. That the spirits of knowledge and truth are granted by God alone safeguards the Yaḥad's claims to special revelation but also explains their experiences of spiritual failure.

The studies in the third section relate to the theme of the body. In the first essay in this section, Nicholas Meyer reexamines DSS perceptions toward celibacy and sexuality. Meyer reassesses the scholarly conclusion that a positive view toward sexuality was the norm within the sectarian movement, arguing instead that celibacy was required for an elite component of Yaḥad members who strove for perfect holiness with a priesthood among angels. Meyer advances this argument by means of a textual study of the Hodayot. He uncovers the Hodayot's negative view of sexuality first through charting comparative passages in S, D, and the Temple Scroll (11Q19) that suggest a practice of celibacy within the sectarian movement as a means to commune with a priestly, heavenly world. Next, Meyer distills four features within the Hodayot: a focus on the earthly nature of humanity (contrasted with the heavenly realm), the prevalence of terms reflecting humanity's sexuality, the rapport between this sexuality and ritual impurity, and finally a negative estimation of this impurity in light of heavenly communion. Meyer's study calls attention to a stream within the sectarian movement for which the earthly body, that of both male and female, was seen to be impure as a "symptom of priestly concerns for ritual purity and heavenly worship." The way in which Meyer frames this study invites us to rethink questions about the presence and status of women within different parts of this movement.

In the next chapter on the body, Jessica M. Keady draws on masculinity studies to assess the day-to-day construction of the ideal male within the Qumran communities. Using the hegemonic position of the ideal male, Keady assesses the War Scroll as a case study to discover the fashion in which readers viewed everyday life in this document as a way to prepare for eschatological battle. The idealized male was pure and ready to provoke violence, and any man who was ritually impure and could not partake in battle was thus lacking in masculinity. Thus masculinity was related to purity, and masculinity was fluid, just as were purity and impurity. Priests and Levites played an important role during war to further buttress the goal of masculine perfection and readiness for violence. This ideal provided a model to which to aspire on a daily basis; to be less than pure would leave these men vulnerable in relation to power and performance. The use of masculinity studies permits readers to see that men, and not only women, display fluctuating levels of impurity within the Qumran communities.

The third chapter in this section on the body is that of Carmen Palmer, who draws on ethnicity theory to reassess the motif of circumcision of the heart found within the DSS and other late Second Temple literature. Within ethnicity theory, features of kinship and culture, including religious practice, together constitute a full, ethnic identity. Palmer proposes that the motif of heart circumcision, as a type of spiritualizing or religious practice, does not supersede matters of kinship and descent, evidenced through physical circumcision. This conclusion goes against scholarship that argues that spiritualization within the sectarian movement affiliated with the DSS suggests that kinship is no longer of importance. Palmer undertakes a reassessment of the circumcision motifs, both physical and of the heart, found in selected texts. The conclusions demonstrate that matters of kinship and culture are always interconnected between the two types of circumcision, although each text differs with respect to the permeability of heart circumcision. Where the Scrolls are concerned, the theme of circumcision of the heart is particular to the Yaḥad (Serekh) tradition and represents a type of secondary conversion, following physical circumcision, that is exclusive to group members. For Jubilees, exclusive eighth-day physical circumcision is necessary for heart circumcision, demonstrating a full ethnic integration. In the writings of Philo, physical circumcision eradicates the pleasures that delude the mind and elucidates heart circumcision, which is spiritual and of the mind. Finally, in Romans, heart circumcision enables a dual ethnicity, whether Jew and Christ follower or gentile and Christ follower.

Finally, Angela Kim Harkins draws on cognitive literary theory "to consider how spaces are described in the Qumran *hodayot* in such a way as to allow for the phenomenon of immersive reading," where immersive reading is the achievement of "an experience of presence in a narrative world." Cognitive literary theory, as applied to narrative spaces, "considers how the embodied experience of reading could engage immersive cognitive processes of mental imaging" through certain practices. The chapter proceeds with the examination of two elements that encourage an immersive experience. The first element is the use of counterintuitive landscape features that destabilize and cause the reader to slow down the pace of reading, allowing for deeper emotional engagement with the text. Using 1QH$^a$ XVI, 5–XVII, 36 as an example, Harkins notes how counterintuitive landscape features are integrated into the passage's description of a wetland garden, such as the trees of life serving as exotic cultivar and the presence of otherworldly angelic beings, from the garden of Eden (Gen 3:24) in 1QH$^a$ XVI, 6–7. Counterintuitive also is the "unexpected change in tone" seen in the shift in the text's focus to the speaker's "affliction and misery." The second element that encourages an immersive experience is the use of enactive reading combined with first-person narration. These enactive, embodied experiences are described as either interoceptive, which include "bodily experiences associated with the viscera," or proprioceptive, which entail "embodied sensations of moving through space." Harkins offers the example of 1QH$^a$ XVI, 26–XVII, 16 with regard to interoception, experienced through the hymnist's emotional distress connected to visceral sensations, such as a burning fire in the bones (XVI, 31). Proprioception experiences are described in XVI, 5–XVII, 36 in terms of how the hymnist's body "interacts with the wetland garden." Harkins concludes the chapter with the observation that through such processes, the ancient reader may have been able to access "experiences of presence" extending to the body and not only the mind.

We are only beginning to uncover the richness of what the DSS have to offer. The need continues for further reevaluation of earlier conclusions along with the application of new methodologies if we are to discover fully what the DSS can reveal about Judaism, Hebrew language, scripture in the Second Temple period, Hellenistic Judaism, early Christ followers, and other ancient Mediterranean groups. Besides the great potential for DSS studies themselves to advance, there is also potential for DSS studies to lead the way for other fields by modeling methodological advancement and pioneering interdisciplinary approaches.

## Bibliography

Arnold, Russell C. D. *Social Role of Liturgy in the Religion of the Qumran Community*. STDJ 60. Leiden: Brill, 2006.
Bernstein, Moshe, Florentino García Martínez, and John Kampen, eds. *Legal Texts and Legal Issues*. STDJ 23. Leiden: Brill 1997.
Boccaccini, Gabriele. *Beyond the Essene Hypothesis*. Grand Rapids: Eerdmans, 1998.
Boda, Mark J., Daniel K. Falk, and Rodney A. Werline, eds. *Seeking the Favor of God*. 3 vols. EJL 21–23. Atlanta: Society of Biblical Literature, 2006–2008.
Brooke, George J., ed. *New Qumran Texts and Studies: Proceedings from the First Meeting of the International Organization for Qumran Studies, Paris 1992*. STDJ 15. Leiden: Brill, 1994.
———. *Reading the Dead Sea Scrolls: Essays in Method*. EJL 39. Atlanta: Society of Biblical Literature, 2013.
Campbell, Jonathan G., William John Lyons, and Lloyd K. Pietersen. *New Directions in Qumran Studies: Proceedings of the Bristol Colloquium on the Dead Sea Scrolls*. LSTS 52. London: T&T Clark, 2005.
Chazon, Esther G. *Liturgical Perspectives: Prayer and Poetry in Light of the Dead Sea Scrolls*. STDJ 48. Leiden: Brill, 2003.
Collins, John J. *Beyond the Qumran Community: The Sectarian Movement of the Dead Sea Scrolls*. Grand Rapids: Eerdmans, 2010.
Davis, Michael Thomas, and Brent A. Strawn, eds. *Qumran Studies: New Approaches, New Questions*. Grand Rapids: Eerdmans, 2007.
Dhali, Maruf A., Sheng He, Mladen Popović, Eibert Tigchelaar, and Lambert Schomaker. "A Digital Palaeographic Approach towards Writer Identification in the Dead Sea Scrolls." Pages 693–702 in *Proceedings of the Sixth International Conference on Pattern Recognition Applications and Methods, ICPRAM 2017, Porto, Portugal, February 24–26, 2017*. Setúbal, Portugal: SciTePress, 2017.

Dimant, Devorah, ed. *The Dead Sea Scrolls in Scholarly Perspective: A History of Research.* STDJ 99. Leiden: Brill, 2012.
Dimant, Devorah, and Uriel Rappaport. *The Dead Sea Scrolls: Forty Years of Research.* STDJ 10. Leiden: Brill, 1992.
Falk, Daniel K. *Daily, Sabbath, and Festival Prayers in the Dead Sea Scrolls.* STDJ 27. Leiden: Brill, 1998.
Falk, Daniel K., Florentino García Martínez, and Eileen M. Schuller, eds. *Sapiential, Liturgical, and Poetic Texts from Qumran.* STDJ 35. Leiden: Brill, 2001.
Falk, Daniel K., Sarianna Metso, Donald W. Parry, and Eibert J. C. Tigchelaar, eds. *Qumran Cave 1 Revisited: Texts from Cave 1 Sixty Years after Their Discovery; Proceedings of the Sixth Meeting of the IOQS in Ljubljana.* STDJ 91. Leiden: Brill, 2010.
Flint, Peter W., and James C. VanderKam, eds. *The Dead Sea Scrolls after Fifty Years: A Comprehensive Reassessment.* 2 vols. Leiden: Brill, 1998–1999.
García Martínez, Florentino, and Mladen Popović, eds. *Defining Identities: We, You, and the Other in the Dead Sea Scrolls; Proceedings of the Fifth Meeting of the IOQS in Gröningen.* STDJ 70. Leiden: Brill, 2008.
García Martínez, Florentino, and Julio Trebolle Barrera. *The People of the Dead Sea Scrolls: Their Writings, Beliefs, and Practices.* Translated by Wilfred G. E. Watson. Leiden: Brill, 1995.
Goodblatt, David, Avital Pinnick, and Daniel R. Schwartz, eds. *Historical Perspectives: From the Hasmoneans to Bar Kokhba in Light of the Dead Sea Scrolls.* STDJ 37. Leiden: Brill, 2001.
Grossman, Maxine L., ed. *Rediscovering the Dead Sea Scrolls: An Assessment of Old and New Approaches and Methods.* Grand Rapids: Eerdmans, 2010.
Harkins, Angela Kim. *Reading with an "I" to the Heavens: Looking at the Qumran Hodayot through the Lens of Visionary Tradition.* Ekstasis 3. Berlin: de Gruyter, 2011.
Harrington, Hannah K. *The Impurity Systems of Qumran and the Rabbis: Biblical Foundations.* Atlanta: Scholars Press, 1993.
———. *The Purity Texts.* CQS 5. London: T&T Clark, 2004.
Hempel, Charlotte, ed. *The Dead Sea Scrolls: Texts and Contexts.* STDJ 90. Leiden: Brill, 2010.
Holmstedt, Robert D., and John Screnock. "Writing a Descriptive Grammar of the Syntax and Semantics of the War Scroll (1QM): The Noun Phrase as Proof of Concept." Pages 67–106 in *The War Scroll, Violence,*

*War and Peace in the Dead Sea Scrolls and Related Literature: Essays in Honour of Martin G. Abegg on the Occasion of His Sixty-Fifth Birthday*. Edited by Kipp Davis, Dorothy M. Peters, Kyung S. Baek, and Peter W. Flint. STDJ 115. Leiden: Brill, 2015.

Jassen, Alex P. *Mediating the Divine: Prophecy and Revelation in the Dead Sea Scrolls and Second Temple Judaism*. STDJ 68. Leiden: Brill, 2007.

Jokiranta, Jutta. *Social Identity and Sectarianism in the Qumran Movement*. STDJ 105. Leiden: Brill, 2013.

Keady, Jessica M. *Vulnerability and Valour: A Gendered Analysis of Everyday Life in the Dead Sea Scrolls Communities*. LSTS 91. London: Bloomsbury, 2017.

Kugler, Robert A., and Eileen M. Schuller, eds. *The Dead Sea Scrolls at Fifty*. EJL 15. Atlanta: Scholars Press, 1997.

Metso, Sarianna, Hindy Najman, and Eileen M. Schuller, eds. *The Dead Sea Scrolls: Transmission of Traditions and the Production of Texts*. STDJ 92. Leiden: Brill, 2010.

Naudé, Jacobus A. "Diachronic Syntax and Language Change: The Case of Qumran Hebrew." *SALALS* 18 (2000): 1–14.

Newman, Judith H. *Before the Bible: Liturgical Body and the Formation of Scriptures in Early Judaism*. Oxford: Oxford University Press, 2018.

———. *Praying by the Book: The Scripturalization of Prayer in Second Temple Judaism*. EJL 14. Atlanta: Society of Biblical Literature, 1999.

Newsom, Carol A. *The Self as Symbolic Space: Constructing Identity and Community at Qumran*. STDJ 52. Leiden: Brill, 2004.

Penner, Ken M. *The Verbal System of the Dead Sea Scrolls: Tense, Aspect, and Modality in Qumran Hebrew Texts*. SSN 64. Leiden: Brill, 2014.

Porter, Stanley E., and Craig A. Evans, eds. *The Scrolls and the Scriptures: Qumran Fifty Years After*. JSPSup 26. Sheffield: Sheffield Academic, 1997.

Qimron, Elisha. *A Grammar of the Hebrew of the Dead Sea Scrolls*. Jerusalem: Yad Izhak Ben-Zvi, 2018.

———. *The Temple Scroll: A Critical Edition with Extensive Reconstructions*. Jerusalem: Israel Exploration Society, 1996.

Reymond, Eric. *Qumran Hebrew: An Overview of Orthography, Phonology, and Morphology*. RBS 76. Atlanta: SBL Press, 2014.

Schiffman, Lawrence H. *Reclaiming the Dead Sea Scrolls: The History of Judaism, the Background of Christianity, the Lost Library of Qumran*. New York: Doubleday, 1994.

Schiffman, Lawrence H., Emanuel Tov, and James C. VanderKam, eds.

*The Dead Sea Scrolls Fifty Years after Their Discovery*. Jerusalem: Israel Exploration Society, 2000.

Schofield, Alison. *From Qumran to the Yaḥad: A New Paradigm of Textual Development for the Community Rule*. STDJ 77. Leiden: Brill 2009.

Schuller, Eileen M. *The Dead Sea Scrolls: What Have We Learned?* Louisville: Westminster John Knox, 2006.

Stegemann, Hartmut. *Die Essener, Qumran, Johannes der Täufer und Jesus*. Freiburg: Verlag Herder, 1993.

Taylor, Joan E. *The Essenes, the Scrolls, and the Dead Sea*. Oxford: Oxford University Press, 2012.

Tervanotko, Hanna. *Denying Her Voice: The Figure of Miriam in Ancient Jewish Literature*. JAJSup 23. Göttingen: Vandenhoek & Ruprecht, 2016.

Trebolle Barrera, Julio, and Luis Vegas Montaner, eds. *The Madrid Qumran Congress: Proceedings of the International Congress on the Dead Sea Scrolls, Madrid, 18–21 March, 1991*. 2 vols. STDJ 11. Leiden: Brill, 1992.

Tzoref, Shani, and Lawrence H. Schiffman, eds. *The Dead Sea Scrolls at Sixty*. STDJ 89. Leiden: Brill, 2010.

Wassen, Cecilia. *Women in the Damascus Document*. AcBib 21. Atlanta: Society of Biblical Literature, 2005.

# Part 1
## Law, Language, and Literary Formation

# Rule Texts from Qumran on the Spectrum of Jewish Legal Development

Sarianna Metso

Scholarly discussions pertaining to the Dead Sea Scrolls tend to treat the so-called rule texts from Qumran, such as the Damascus Document and the Community Rule, in a category of their own. In this chapter I will aim at a more sweeping view and will examine these texts in the broader frame of postexilic Jewish legal development. The focus here will be on the impulses that drove legal activity in various Second Temple Jewish communities and how those impulses translated into different attitudes toward the Mosaic Torah. Comparisons will be made with the attitudes of communities as different as those behind the Samaritan Pentateuch, 4QPentateuch (formerly known as 4QReworked Pentateuch), and the Temple Scroll (11Q19). I argue that what distinguishes the various legal works is how revelatory authority was viewed in the communities that produced them and that sociological factors quite likely played a significant role in shaping scribes' exegetical techniques.

There are two interrelated points I would like to submit for discussion: first, modern concepts used to categorize legal material were likely not known to the scribes who created this material; second, what distinguishes legal works is the view of revelatory authority held by the communities that produced them. On the first point, although the scribes of the Second Temple period seem to have employed a variety of approaches in generating, interpreting, and transmitting legal material, there is little evidence that the kind of categories that we as scholars have commonly assigned to this material to mark distinctions—such as halakic rules versus rules related to community organization—would have been operational in the minds of the scribes of the Second Temple period. The evidence rather suggests that in the minds of the scribes, all legal activity formed an extension of the Torah of Moses, irrespective of whether the law was derived exegetically, whether it arose from the everyday needs of communal life, or whether it received scriptural justification only secondarily or perhaps none at all.¹

So, it is important to recognize that the categories we commonly use are not native or emic but etic and largely anachronistic.² Just as important as it has been in some other areas of Qumran studies to free our minds

---

1. For example, Aharon Shemesh writes, "Any attempt to differentiate between injunctions grounded in the Pentateuch and anonymous sectarian legislation is an external distinction imposed by contemporary scholars, which had no reality for the sectarians for whom both were the living word of God." See Shemesh, "The Scriptural Background of the Penal Code in the *Rule of the Community* and *Damascus Document*," *DSD* 15 (2008): 217-18. In the context of Qumran material, the question of legal derivation has been widely discussed, and not all scholars agree. For a summary of varying views see Sarianna Metso, "When the Evidence Does Not Fit: Method, Theory, and the Dead Sea Scrolls," in *Rediscovering the Dead Sea Scrolls: An Assessment of Old and New Approaches and Methods*, ed. Maxine L. Grossman (Grand Rapids: Eerdmans, 2010), 14-21. The point on legal activity forming an extension of the Torah of Moses has been made already by, e.g., Mayer I. Gruber in reference to the traditions underlying the Mishnah. See Gruber, "The Mishnah as Oral Torah: A Reconsideration," *JSJ* 15 (1984): 112-22. He concludes that while "some of the laws contained in the Mishnah purport to be of divine origin, and they have a clear basis in Scripture," others "have little or no Scriptural basis," although they claim to have one (121). Yet some of the laws "purport to be the legislation of named or unnamed mortal authorities including the pre-exilic prophets" (121). The laws of the Mishnah ought to be viewed as stemming "from *numerous* corpora" (122). Lutz Doering has similarly argued that "while scriptural predisposition and support should thus be taken seriously, the establishment of halakah should not be considered a predominantly exegetical enterprise." See Doering, "Parallels without 'Parallelomania': Methodological Reflections on Comparative Analysis of Halakhah in the Dead Sea Scrolls," in *Rabbinic Perspectives: Rabbinic Literature and the Dead Sea Scrolls*, ed. Stephen D. Fraade, Aharon Shemesh, and Ruth A. Clements, STDJ 62 (Leiden: Brill, 2006), 17.

2. This is true of not only the terms and categories *biblical* and *rewritten Bible* but of the category of *halakic* as well. While the term *halakah* is commonly applied to certain texts found at Qumran, as a technical term it became introduced only in rabbinic literature. While some have seen the pejorative expression דורשי החלקות ("Seekers of Smooth Things"), used in 4QpNah (4Q169) as a pun on the Pharisees, reflecting the later usage of the term, the word *halakah* as a legal term is not found in the Scrolls. See John P. Meier, "Is There *Halaka* (the Noun) at Qumran?," *JBL* 122 (2003): 15-56; Dennis Green, "Halakhah at Qumran? The Use of √הלך in the Dead Sea Scrolls," *RevQ* 22 (2005): 235-51.

from categories taken for granted,³ it is necessary for us to recognize the fluid character of the legal material. Although categories such as *halakic texts* and *rule texts* may perhaps serve as convenient shorthands in certain modern contexts, on closer inspection these distinctions seem not to be entirely justified, whether we examine these texts from the perspective of the derivation of laws, level of authority, or the intended audience. Since I have made this argument more extensively elsewhere,⁴ it will suffice to briefly summarize it here.

Regarding the perspective of legal derivation, no clear differences emerge, for a single document can combine material from a variety of legal enterprises: some arose from scriptural exegesis, others sprung from the practical demands of community life or organization, and yet others represent cases where a simple practical rule was secondarily furnished with a scriptural hook or prooftext. Regarding the perspective of the level of authority, it is equally difficult to draw clear-cut distinctions between the laws of the Torah, halakic rules, and rules pertaining to community life, since the penal codes preserved at Qumran in particular display a mindset that appears to treat the rules generated by the community life and organization as equally authoritative as the rules of the Torah. Regarding the perspective of the intended audience, there is similarly little distinction discernible between halakah and community legislation, for both—although always created within a specific group—aim at positing an ideal of proper behavior for true Israel.

If the scholarly categories commonly used do not serve well to accurately reflect the character of the legal material of the Second Temple period, might it make sense to look for additional and perhaps alternative avenues to explain the evidence? This question brings me to my second point, which concerns the factors that could explain the variety of approaches that Second Temple scribes employed in generating, interpreting, and transmitting legal material. Understandably, the main focus of scholarly analysis so far has been on the exegetical techniques used in various Second Temple legal texts, but as we try to characterize the legal

---

3. Eugene Ulrich, *The Dead Sea Scrolls and the Developmental Composition of the Bible*, VTSup 169 (Leiden: Brill, 2015), 15–27.

4. See Sarianna Metso, "Challenging the Dichotomy between Halakhah and Community Legislation," in *Crossing Imaginary Boundaries: The Dead Sea Scrolls in the Context of Second Temple Judaism*, ed. Mika S. Pajunen and Hanna Tervanotko, PFES 108 (Helsinki: Finnish Exegetical Society, 2015), 61–70.

traditions in texts as varied as the Samaritan Pentateuch, the Temple Scroll, or the Rule Texts from Qumran, the question arises: why was it permissible in certain Jewish communities for scribes to exhibit a very high level of editorial freedom, while in other, roughly contemporary, Jewish communities it was not? I would like to posit that what distinguishes the various legal works is how revelatory authority was viewed in the communities that produced them and that sociological factors quite likely played a significant role in shaping scribes' exegetical techniques.

To illuminate this point, I would like to consider the polarities of editorial approach that scribes in various Second Temple communities took in regard to the laws of Leviticus. As we examine the Samaritan legal approach in the context of a larger corpus of ancient Jewish literature, it appears to stand at one end of a continuum, the other end of which is demonstrable in many of the so-called community compositions found at Qumran, such as the Community Rule and the Damascus Document.

As is already well known, the text of the Samaritan Pentateuch was almost totally a nonsectarian version circulating in Judah and the wider circles of Palestine during the late Second Temple period. This version is often called pre-Samaritan or Proto-Samaritan, and its principal characteristic—as already seen in the Qumran (that is, Judean) scrolls of Exodus and Numbers—is the insertion of large additions into the earlier text as seen in the MT tradition.[5] Although several books of the joint Judean-Samaritan Pentateuch, Exodus and Deuteronomy in particular, underwent editing of this type before the few distinctly Samaritan features were added to the text, the book of Leviticus seems to have escaped this type of editorial intervention.[6] This is highly surprising, for the legal sections of the Pentateuch are demonstrably repetitious and occasionally conflicting, and one would expect them to have triggered large-scale harmonization.[7]

---

5. For discussion, see, e.g., Sidnie White Crawford, "Pentateuch as Found in the Pre-Samaritan Texts and 4QReworked Pentateuch," in *Changes in Scripture: Rewriting and Interpreting Authoritative Traditions in the Second Temple Period*, ed. Hanne von Weissenberg (Berlin: de Gruyter, 2011), 123–36; Ulrich, *Dead Sea Scrolls*, 215–27.

6. For a more detailed discussion of the text-critical character of SP-Leviticus than the one presented here, see Sarianna Metso, "SP and Ancient Texts Close to SP: Leviticus," in *The Textual History of the Bible*, ed. Armin Lange and Emanuel Tov (Leiden: Brill, 2017), 1B:93–98.

7. Although the large-scale changes in the narrative sections of the pre-Samaritan version are often described as editorial or harmonizing, it should be kept in mind that

Several explanations have been offered. Moshe Bernstein has suggested that it was the sanctity of the legal material that prevented major editorial changes.[8] In contrast, Molly Zahn has proposed that the narrative frames of the pentateuchal legal codes were dissimilar enough that the scribes would consider their individual laws as not directly equivalent or conflicting and thus not requiring harmonization.[9] Michael Segal rejects the view that the editorial goal in the heavily edited narrative sections of the Pentateuch would have been harmonization in the first place. He argues that the scribes' goal was rather in a mechanical fashion to provide the source in each instance of quotation. Legal sections seldom contain "internal references to earlier source material that should have been known to the reader from any other section of the Pentateuch. Without any such references, there is no reason for the scribe to copy material into the legal corpora."[10]

Any of these explanations seems plausible to me, but I would like to raise yet another possibility for consideration. Magnar Kartveit points out that the editorial reworking in Exodus and Deuteronomy aims at

---

harmonizing features were common in the texts stemming from this period and were not exclusively a pre-Samaritan phenomenon. For discussion, see Emanuel Tov, "The Nature and Background of Harmonizations in Biblical Manuscripts," *JSOT* 31 (1985): 7; Esther Eshel and Hanan Eshel, "Dating the Samaritan Pentateuch Compilation in Light of the Qumran Biblical Scrolls," in *Emanuel: Studies in Hebrew Bible, Septuagint, and Dead Sea Scrolls in Honor of Emanuel Tov*, ed. Shalom M. Paul et al., VTSup 94 (Leiden: Brill, 2003), 217–21; Robert T. Anderson and Terry Giles, *The Samaritan Pentateuch: An Introduction to Its Origin, History, and Significance for Biblical Studies*, RBS 72 (Atlanta: Society of Biblical Literature, 2012), 60–69. For Emanuel Tov's more recent view on the use of the term *harmonizing*, see his *Textual Criticism of the Hebrew Bible*, 3rd ed. (Minneapolis: Fortress, 2012), 80, 82–83.

8. Moshe J. Bernstein, "What Has Happened to the Laws? The Treatment of Legal Material in 4QReworked Pentateuch," *DSD* 15 (2008): 47.

9. Molly Zahn writes: "The priestly legislation in Leviticus and Numbers has as its narrative setting God's speech to Moses from the tent of meeting (Lev 1:1; Num 1:1). The Covenant Code (Exodus 21–23), on the other hand, is situated at Mount Sinai, while Deuteronomy's law code is spoken by Moses on the plains of Moab. Though it is explicitly noted that Moses decrees the laws in accordance with God's instructions (Deut 1:3; 6:1), there is no identification of the law code itself with God's earlier revelation on Sinai." See Zahn, *Rethinking Rewritten Scripture: Composition and Exegesis in the 4QReworked Pentateuch Manuscripts*, STDJ 95 (Leiden: Brill, 2011), 175 n. 74.

10. Michael Segal, "The Text of the Hebrew Bible in Light of the Dead Sea Scrolls," *MG* 12 (2007): 17.

highlighting the "prophetic primacy" of Moses.[11] In addition, he offers the insight that "the prophets to succeed [Moses] will be preachers of the law. Thus a double defense against intruders is built up: Moses is the reference point of prophecy, and his successors are preachers of the law revealed to him."[12] Although the focus of Kartveit's book is not on Leviticus or the legal sections of the Pentateuch to any noticeable extent, this observation, I think, has relevance for our discussion of the legal sections as well: if law received and preached by Moses had revelatory character, it had to be perfect. It could only be interpreted, not modified. In this light, the editorial restraint evident in the Samaritan Pentateuch of Leviticus makes complete sense.

Let us now consider the very different way Leviticus traditions are treated in manuscripts commonly labeled as community compositions. As is well known, the scribes responsible for creating documents such as the Damascus Document and the Community Rule were highly creative in their approach to scriptural traditions. To describe one example: in the Cairo Genizah copy of the Damascus Document (CD) VI, 14–21 quoting Lev 10:10, the text of Leviticus is used to bolster community discipline and cohesion, although the original context of the Leviticus quote addresses an entirely different topic.

Leviticus 10:10 says: "You are to distinguish [ולהבדיל] between the holy and the common, and between the unclean and the clean" (NRSV). In the book of Leviticus, this injunction anticipates the individual laws of Lev 11–15 concerning clean and unclean animals, purification of a woman after childbirth, diagnosis and cleansing of leprosy and bodily discharges, and rules for offerings that atone for uncleanness. In CD (VI, 14–21), however, this injunction quoted from Lev 10:10 is used for a quite different purpose. The spotlight is not on cultic or ritual purity, but the distinction concerns the separation between the community members and outsiders. Thus, in the text of CD, the scribe brings the concepts of clean and unclean, sacred and profane into an entirely new perspective.[13]

---

11. Magnar Kartveit, *The Origin of the Samaritans*, VTSup 128 (Leiden: Brill, 2009), 281.

12. Kartveit, *Origin of the Samaritans*, 284.

13. For a fuller discussion, see Sarianna Metso, "The Character of Leviticus Traditions at Qumran," in *In the Footsteps of Sherlock Holmes: Studies in the Biblical Text in Honour of Anneli Aejmelaeus*, ed. Kristin De Troyer, T. Michael Law, and Marketta Liljeström, CBET 72 (Leuven: Peeters, 2014), 651–55.

Other examples could be mentioned as well. Particularly revealing are cases such as the one in 1QS V, 13–20, where an earlier version of 4QS$^{b, d}$ (4Q256, 4Q258) lacks the scriptural proof texts, but the longer version of 1QS adds them.[14] When using the phrase "lest he burden him with iniquity and guilt" (פן ישיאנו עוון אשמה), drawn from Lev 22:16, the text of 1QS agrees with the original scriptural context of the quote: both texts involve concern for the cultic purity of the community when holy food is consumed. In 1QS, however, the notion of impurity that can make the entire community bear the guilt is expanded to embrace not only cultic matters but also matters of work and property. These latter areas of concern render community members more likely to have contact with outsiders and thus more susceptible to teachings not sanctioned by the leaders of the Yaḥad. The editorial work evident in 1QS seems to have served the goal of providing scriptural justification (not yet in 4QS$^{b, d}$) for the rule of separating from outsiders.[15]

When we seek to find reasons for the differing attitudes toward legal material that the scribes in Samaritan and Essene communities exhibited, it is enlightening to consider the possibility of dissimilar leadership roles in the two communities.[16] Pesher Habakkuk ascribes to the Teacher of Righteousness prophetic interpretive authority (1QpHab VII, 4–5). In the Essene community, the Teacher was more than an interpreter of legal traditions. He was a recipient of revelation. Therefore, all scripture, including legal material, was open to revelatory modification. Even after the Teacher's death, in communities such as the one at Qumran, revelation was considered as ongoing, and new regulations emerging from legal innovation were ascribed revelatory character, even when their connection with

---

14. The redactional development of the Community Rule has been widely debated. For a summary of the discussion, see, e.g., Sarianna Metso, *The Serekh Texts*, LSTS 62 (London: T&T Clark, 2007), 15–20.

15. I have discussed 1QS V, 13–20 more extensively in "When the Evidence Does Not Fit," 14–21.

16. For further discussion on the topic of leadership and social structures in Second Temple Jewish communities, see, e.g., Lawrence H. Schiffman, "Utopia and Reality: Political Leadership and Organization in the Dead Sea Scrolls Community," in Paul et al., *Emanuel: Studies in Hebrew Bible*, 413–27; Diana V. Edelman and Ehud Ben Zvi, eds., *Leadership, Social Memory, and Judean Discourse in the Fifth–Second Centuries BCE* (Sheffield: Equinox, 2016); Jutta Jokiranta, "Sociological Approaches to Qumran Sectarianism," in *The Oxford Handbook of the Dead Sea Scrolls*, ed. Timothy H. Lim and John J. Collins (Oxford: Oxford University Press, 2010), 200–231.

the Torah was only superficial. In contrast, in the Samaritan community—as convincingly argued by Kartveit—Moses was considered as having been the final legal prophet and the community leaders mere preachers of the law. In that community, no further legal innovation could be ascribed the aegis of revelation.

Two distinct works found at Qumran, 4QPentateuch (4Q364–367, *olim* 4QRP) and the Temple Scroll, can be viewed on the spectrum between the Samaritan Pentateuch and the Essene rule texts. Although both 4QPentateuch and the Temple Scroll are presumably non-Essene works, in the communities behind these works there may have been leaders claiming revelatory authority similar to the Teacher of Righteousness. Thus, to understand the textual character of the Samaritan Pentateuch as compared with other Second Temple Jewish material, it is necessary to pay attention to possible sociological factors alongside possible scribal and interpretive practices.

Typologically, the Samaritan Pentateuch belongs between the pre-Samaritan and 4QPentateuch traditions. Bernstein and Zahn have noted that while in minor variants 4QPentateuch is very similar to the Samaritan Pentateuch, the type of the topical rearrangements that occur in 4QPentateuch do not appear in the Samaritan Pentateuch.[17] This indicates that the editorial reworking in the Samaritan Pentateuch is more conservative than that of 4QPentateuch.

A continuation of this line of development can be seen in the Temple Scroll. The author of the work did not hesitate to imply revelatory authority; the work is written in the first-person from the mouth of God. The purpose and literary genre of the Temple Scroll are debated among scholars. Was the work meant as the final, sixth book to complete the existing pentateuchal Torah, as a replacement of the entire existing Torah, or perhaps as scriptural interpretation?[18] Sidnie White Crawford concludes that all these characterizations—"a pseudepigraph, a *sefer torah* (Book of the

---

17. See Bernstein, "What Has Happened," 32–33; Zahn, *Rethinking Rewritten Scripture*, 173–75.

18. On the first option, see Hartmut Stegemann, "The Origins of the Temple Scroll," in *Congress Volume Jerusalem 1986*, ed. John A. Emerton, VTSup 40 (Leiden: Brill, 1998), 235–56. On the second option, see Ben-Zion Wacholder, *The Dawn of Qumran: The Sectarian Torah and the Teacher of Righteousness*, HUCM 8 (Cincinnati: Hebrew Union College Press, 1983). On the third option, see Dwight D. Swanson, *The Temple Scroll and the Bible: The Methodology of 11QT*, STDJ 14 (Leiden: Brill, 1995).

Law), and a 'Rewritten Bible'"—are "in one sense or another, correct, but all of them are necessary to capture the full flavor of the scroll."[19]

The community compositions found at Qumran, such as the Damascus Document (D) and the Community Rule (S), can be considered as yet another step in the line of Jewish legal development. The feature that places the legal works on the spectrum (SP-Leviticus, 4QPentateuch, 11QTemple, D, and S) is how revelatory authority was understood in the communities behind these works and what kind of textual manipulation was permitted. The scribes of the Essene community, who thought they were imbued with the same revelatory authority as their Teacher, were immersed in scriptural material when composing new regulations for community life and saw their new regulations as prophetically sanctioned extensions of the laws of the Torah. In fact, unlike the Samaritan community, the community of Essenes appears to have made little distinction between the laws of the Torah and their community regulations. While study of the exegetical character of pre-Samaritan and Essene writings is necessary for describing the differences, a consideration of sociological factors turns out to be profitable in explaining the differences. As the examples from the Second Temple compositions I have discussed above demonstrate, the degree of revelatory interpretation changes the intent and therefore the meaning of the text of the Torah.

In summary, if Moses was considered the final legal prophet in the Samaritan communities, as Kartveit has argued, then no further legal innovation could happen under the umbrella of revelation. In contrast, at Qumran revelation was considered by the leaders as ongoing; therefore, new regulations resulting from legal innovation had revelatory character, whether or not stemming from the Torah. The varying views of revelation in Second Temple communities determined the level of scribal manipulation permitted. While the study of exegetical techniques used in the Second Temple legal writings is interesting and often illuminating, the scholarly categories commonly used do not always serve well to describe the scribal mindsets that lay behind the texts. A consideration of sociological factors and leadership structures in Second Temple communities may open a new and more emic avenue in explaining the differences in various communities.

---

19. Sidnie White Crawford, *The Temple Scroll and Related Texts*, CQS 2 (Sheffield: Sheffield Academic, 2000), 17.

## Bibliography

Anderson, Robert T., and Terry Giles. *The Samaritan Pentateuch: An Introduction to Its Origin, History, and Significance for Biblical Studies.* RBS 72. Atlanta: Society of Biblical Literature, 2012.

Bernstein, Moshe J. "What Has Happened to the Laws? The Treatment of Legal Material in 4QReworked Pentateuch." *DSD* 15 (2008): 24–49.

Crawford, Sidnie White. "Pentateuch as Found in the Pre-Samaritan Texts and 4QReworked Pentateuch." Pages 123–36 in *Changes in Scripture: Rewriting and Interpreting Authoritative Traditions in the Second Temple Period.* Edited by Hanne von Weissenberg. Berlin: de Gruyter, 2011.

———. *The Temple Scroll and Related Texts.* CQS 2. Sheffield: Sheffield Academic, 2000.

Doering, Lutz. "Parallels without 'Parallelomania': Methodological Reflections on Comparative Analysis of Halakhah in the Dead Sea Scrolls." Pages 13–42 in *Rabbinic Perspectives: Rabbinic Literature and the Dead Sea Scrolls.* Edited by Stephen D. Fraade, Aharon Shemesh, and Ruth A. Clements. STDJ 62. Leiden: Brill, 2006.

Edelman, Diana V., and Ehud Ben Zvi, eds. *Leadership, Social Memory, and Judean Discourse in the Fifth–Second Centuries BCE.* Sheffield: Equinox, 2016.

Eshel, Esther, and Hanan Eshel. "Dating the Samaritan Pentateuch Compilation in Light of the Qumran Biblical Scrolls." Pages 215–40 in *Emanuel: Studies in Hebrew Bible, Septuagint, and Dead Sea Scrolls in Honor of Emanuel Tov.* Edited by Shalom M. Paul, Robert A. Kraft, Lawrence H. Schiffman, and Weston W. Fields. VTSup 94. Leiden: Brill, 2003.

Green, Dennis. "Halakhah at Qumran? The Use of √הלך in the Dead Sea Scrolls." *RevQ* 22 (2005): 235–51.

Gruber, Mayer I. "The Mishnah as Oral Torah: A Reconsideration." *JSJ* 15 (1984): 112–22.

Jokiranta, Jutta. "Sociological Approaches to Qumran Sectarianism." Pages 200–231 in *The Oxford Handbook of the Dead Sea Scrolls.* Edited by Timothy H. Lim and John J. Collins. Oxford: Oxford University Press, 2010.

Kartveit, Magnar. *The Origin of the Samaritans.* VTSup 128. Leiden: Brill, 2009.

Meier, John P. "Is There *Halaka* (the Noun) at Qumran?" *JBL* 122 (2003): 15–56.

Metso, Sarianna. "Challenging the Dichotomy between Halakhah and Community Legislation." Pages 61–70 in *Crossing Imaginary Boundaries: The Dead Sea Scrolls in the Context of Second Temple Judaism*. Edited by Mika S. Pajunen and Hanna Tervanotko. PFES 108. Helsinki: Finnish Exegetical Society, 2015.

———. "The Character of Leviticus Traditions at Qumran." Pages 645–58 in *In the Footsteps of Sherlock Holmes: Studies in the Biblical Text in Honour of Anneli Aejmelaeus*. Edited by Kristin De Troyer, T. Michael Law, and Marketta Liljeström. CBET 72. Leuven: Peeters, 2014.

———. *The Serekh Texts*. LSTS 62. London: T&T Clark, 2007.

———. "SP and Ancient Texts Close to SP: Leviticus." Pages 93–98 in *The Textual History of the Bible*. Vol. 1B. Edited by Armin Lange and Emanuel Tov. Leiden: Brill, 2017.

———. "When the Evidence Does Not Fit: Method, Theory, and the Dead Sea Scrolls." Pages 14–21 in *Rediscovering the Dead Sea Scrolls: An Assessment of Old and New Approaches and Methods*. Edited by Maxine L. Grossman. Grand Rapids: Eerdmans, 2010.

Schiffman, Lawrence H. "Utopia and Reality: Political Leadership and Organization in the Dead Sea Scrolls Community." Pages 413–27 in *Emanuel: Studies in Hebrew Bible, Septuagint, and Dead Sea Scrolls in Honor of Emanuel Tov*. Edited by Shalom M. Paul, Robert A. Kraft, Lawrence H. Schiffman, and Weston W. Fields. VTSup 94. Leiden: Brill, 2003.

Segal, Michael. "The Text of the Hebrew Bible in Light of the Dead Sea Scrolls." *MG* 12 (2007): 5–20.

Shemesh, Aharon. "The Scriptural Background of the Penal Code in the *Rule of the Community* and *Damascus Document*." *DSD* 15 (2008): 191–224.

Stegemann, Hartmut. "The Origins of the Temple Scroll." Pages 235–56 in *Congress Volume Jerusalem 1986*. Edited by John A. Emerton. VTSup 40. Leiden: Brill, 1998.

Swanson, Dwight D. *The Temple Scroll and the Bible: The Methodology of 11QT*. STDJ 14. Leiden: Brill, 1995.

Tov, Emanuel. "The Nature and Background of Harmonizations in Biblical Manuscripts." *JSOT* 31 (1985): 3–29.

———. *Textual Criticism of the Hebrew Bible*. 3rd ed. Minneapolis: Fortress, 2012.

Ulrich, Eugene. *The Dead Sea Scrolls and the Developmental Composition of the Bible*. VTSup 169. Leiden: Brill, 2015.

Wacholder, Ben-Zion. *The Dawn of Qumran: The Sectarian Torah and the Teacher of Righteousness*. HUCM 8. Cincinnati: Hebrew Union College Press, 1983.

Zahn, Molly. *Rethinking Rewritten Scripture: Composition and Exegesis in the 4QReworked Pentateuch Manuscripts*. STDJ 95. Leiden: Brill, 2011.

# A Legal Approach to Textual Authority at Qumran: The Penal Codes as a Test Case

Jonathan Vroom

One of the key questions in the study of the Dead Sea Scrolls (DSS) and their underlying communities is the question of the genre of the rule texts: the Serekh texts (S), the Damascus texts (D), and 4Q265.[1] On the one hand, numerous scholars assume that the rule texts functioned as law. According to these scholars, the rule texts functioned as a sort of legal constitution for the community; members were bound by its stipulations, and adjudicators applied its laws in community discipline proceedings.[2] This approach has implications for how one reconstructs

---

1. The S tradition is represented by the well-preserved 1QS scroll, along with twelve fragmentary texts from Caves 4, 5, and 11. For an overview of the manuscripts see Sarianna Metso, *The Serekh Texts*, LSTS 62 (New York: T&T Clark, 2007), 1–6. The D tradition is represented by the well-preserved Damascus Document manuscripts from Cairo Genizah (CD A and CD B), along with ten fragmentary texts from Caves 4, 5, and 6. For an overview of the manuscripts see Charlotte Hempel, *The Damascus Texts* (Sheffield: Sheffield Academic, 2000), 19–24. 4Q265, a fragmentary scroll, attests to both S-like and D-like features. It is important for the present discussion because it preserves a penal code that is related to that of S and D. For an overview see Hempel, *Damascus Texts*, 93–101.

2. For example, Hanne von Weissenberg states: "Qumranic legal texts such as the Community Rule would have been authoritative in as much as they were normative laws, constituting legally binding norms for their community. Their authority would have functioned on the level of practical, daily life." See von Weissenberg, "Defining Authority," in *In the Footsteps of Sherlock Holmes: Studies in the Biblical Text in Honour of Anneli Aejmelaeus*, ed. Kristin De Troyer, T. Michael Law, and Marketta Liljeström, CBET 72 (Leuven: Peeters, 2014), 690. See also Eyal Regev, "Between Two Sects: Differentiating the Yaḥad and the Damascus Covenant," in *The Dead Sea Scrolls: Texts and Contexts*, ed. Charlotte Hempel, STDJ 90 (Leiden: Brill, 2010), 439–42; James Nati, "The Community Rule or Rules for the Communities? Contextualizing the Qumran

the communities that underlie the DSS. Specifically, it is assumed that each version of a rule text reflects a particular community. Thus, 1QS was the rule text of one particular community—perhaps the one that resided at Qumran—while 4QS$^e$ (4Q259), with its alternative rules (particularly its penal code), reflects another community.[3] While these reconstructed communities are related—either reflecting one community that has evolved and developed over time or different branches of a broad sectarian movement—they are distinct.[4]

On the other hand, some scholars argue that the rule texts should not be understood as legal texts at all.[5] They instead were didactic texts that instilled community values. Rather than functioning as a list of rules and laws dictating what members could or could not do, they were, in some way, didactic and ideological.[6] According to this approach, although the rule texts are certainly a valuable source for historical reconstructions of sectarian communities, it should not be assumed that each version of a text—each version of S and D in particular—reflects a distinct community.

In this essay, I will draw from legal theory to provide a new means of addressing this question of the rule texts' genre and function. More specifically, I will reframe this issue as a question of the type of authority these texts held. I will focus on the penal codes in particular: Did the various

---

Serekhim," in *Sibyls, Scriptures, and Scrolls: John Collins at Seventy*, ed. Joel Baden, Hindy Najman, and Eibert J. C. Tigchelaar, JSJSup 175 (Leiden: Brill, 2017), 925–27; and E. P. Sanders, *Paul and Palestinian Judaism: A Comparison of Patterns of Religion* (Philadelphia: Fortress, 1977), 325.

3. Yonder Moynihan Gillihan, for example, states: "I will take 1QS as the normative rule for the *Yaḥad*, even if some of the *Yaḥad's* cells were governed by other recensions such as 4QS$^{b,\,d}$ and 4QS$^e$." See Gillihan, *Civic Ideology, Organization, and Law in the Rule Scrolls: A Comparative Study of the Covenanters' Sect and Contemporary Voluntary Associations in Political Context*, STDJ 97 (Leiden: Brill, 2012), 9.

4. For a discussion of these explanations for the legal differences between the rule texts see my discussion in Jonathan Vroom, *The Authority of Law in the Hebrew Bible and Early Judaism: Tracing the Origins of Legal Obligation from Ezra to Qumran*, JSJSup 187 (Leiden: Brill, 2018), 54–55.

5. See, e.g., Philip R. Davies, "Redaction and Sectarianism in the Qumran Scrolls," in *The Scriptures and the Scrolls: Studies in Honour of A. S. van der Woude on the Occasion of His Sixty-Fifth Birthday*, ed. Casper J. Labuschagne, Antonius Hilhorst, and Florentino García Martínez (Leiden: Brill, 1992), 152–63; Sarianna Metso, "Problems in Reconstructing the Organizational Chart of the Essenes," *DSD* 16 (2009): 391–93.

6. See my overview, in section 3, of the various didactic and ideological explanations that have been argued for the rule texts.

penal codes possess legal authority, as the Torah may have for the sectarian communities? Or did they hold some other form of nonlegal authority? Put differently, did the rule texts produce the same normative impact that statutes and constitutions do today, which entail binding obligations, or did they produce a different type of normative impact? In the end, my legal-theoretical analysis will support the second position concerning the nature and function of the rule texts—that they were didactic and ideological, rather than strictly legal.

The essay will be divided into three main sections. First, I will draw from legal theory to provide a framework for distinguishing between two types of authority: (1) practical authority, which is akin to law, producing binding obligations, and (2) epistemic authority, which is akin to wisdom instruction, producing nonbinding norms. Furthermore, I will argue that it is possible to determine which type of authority a text held by analyzing the manner in which it was interpreted/interpretively rewritten. Texts that possess practical/legal authority are interpreted in a certain way, while texts that possess epistemic authority are interpreted differently. Second, I will apply this theoretical framework to a selection of laws from the various penal codes that have been preserved. Here I will argue that the Qumran penal codes were not treated as binding law. Third, I will suggest that the rule texts are best understood as epistemic authorities. This theory corresponds with a number of previous analyses of the rule texts.

## 1. Two Types of Textual Authority

Legal theorists make a distinction between two types of authority. The first is known as *practical authority*, which is primarily concerned with its addressees' actions. Practical authorities tell their subjects what to do and what not to do; they make commands and impose binding obligations. Law is the obvious example of a practical authority, but it also applies to a general's orders to his troops, company policies, or a parent's house rules for their children. Examples in the ancient world would be a king's edict or a judge's verdict. The second type of authority is *epistemic authority*. This concerns authority over one's beliefs. An example of an epistemic authority would be a doctor's recommendation for an influenza vaccination or an expert witness's testimony in court. Examples in the ancient world would be a sage's instructions to his students or a prophetic warning to turn away from idols. In each case, the one in possession of epistemic authority has more (or special access to) knowledge than his addressees on a particular matter. While an epistemic authority often gives directives with normative content, in the sense that they seek to influence their addressees' practical reasoning and decision making, epistemic authorities do not and cannot impose binding norms on their addressees. In short, practical authorities command, while epistemic authorities persuade.[7]

## 1.1. The Normative Impact of Practical and Epistemic Authorities

The chief difference between practical and epistemic authority lies in the way that each affects its addressees' practical reasoning. For this I turn to Joseph Raz's well-known theory on the authority of law: the preemption thesis. This an essential element of his account of the law's authority.[8] The preemption thesis is the best means of explaining the impact that a practical authority's directives have on its addressees. According to the preemption thesis, law's authority operates by providing reasons for action that preempt its subjects' other reasoning, such that they feel obligated to comply simply based on its say-so. He explains as follows:

> A simplified picture captures the gist of the matter: laws are normally made to settle actual or possible disagreements about which standards those subject to them should follow.... So the law sets things straight: telling people "this is what you should do and whether you agree that this is so or not, now that it is the law that you should you have the law as a new, special kind of reason to do so." The law is a special kind of reason for it displaces the reasons which it is meant to reflect. It functions as court decisions do: the litigants disagree about what they have reason to do. The court determines matters. Of course they may still disagree [... but it] does not matter. The court's decision settles matters. It displaces the original reasons (the cause of action) and now the parties are bound by the decision instead. Similarly, a law, when it is binding, pre-empts the reasons which it should have reflected, and

---

7. For further introductory comments on these two types of authority see Dudley Knowles, *Political Obligation: A Critical Introduction*, RCPP (London: Routledge, 2010), 34–35.

8. Joseph Raz's full theory on the authority of law is known as the service conception of law's authority. It is composed of three theses: (1) the content-independent thesis, (2) the normal justification thesis, and (3) the preemption thesis. See Raz, *The Morality of Freedom* (Oxford: Clarendon, 1986), 38–69. I will focus solely on the preemption thesis.

whether it successfully reflects them or not it displaces them, and is now a new source of duties.[9]

Although Raz's full theory on the law's authority is debated, it is widely agreed that the preemption thesis explains how legal authority operates: it operates by providing preemptive reasons for action.[10]

One of the clearest examples of a law's preemptive reason-giving power from early Jewish sources is the scene in 1 Macc 2:29–38, where a group was butchered because they refused to defend themselves from attack on the Sabbath. For them, the Torah's Sabbath prohibition was nonnegotiable binding law. It provided a reason for action (or in this case nonaction) that preempted all other practical reasoning, even the strongest of reasons for action: self-defense. They felt obligated to comply with the Torah's demand even when it resulted in death. Similarly, in the episode of Daniel and the lions' den from Dan 6, King Darius was bound by his decree to throw Daniel in the den despite the fact that he did not want to (v. 14). For Darius, the decree was a reason for action that displaced his other reasons for action, such that he was obligated to comply based on its mere say-so. As Frederick Schauer states: "Law makes us do things we do not want to do."[11] This is how practical authorities affect their subjects' practical reasoning.

By contrast, epistemic authorities have a much different normative effect on their subjects' practical reasoning. Epistemic authorities only have the power to displace one's reasons for belief; they do not displace reasons for action. In other words, epistemic authorities work by persuasion. For

---

9. Joseph Raz, introduction to *Between Authority and Interpretation: On the Theory of Law and Practical Reason*, ed. Joseph Raz (Oxford: Oxford University Press, 2009), 7.

10. For example, while critiquing Raz's theory of law's authority, Scott Hershovitz acknowledges that "the preemption thesis tells us what an authoritative order does." See Hershovitz, "The Role of Authority," *PI* 11 (2011): 2. Similarly, Frederick Schauer states that "rules function as rules by excluding or pre-empting what would otherwise be good reasons for doing one thing or another." See Schauer, *Thinking Like a Lawyer: A New Introduction to Legal Reasoning* (Cambridge: Harvard University Press, 2009), 61. For the most significant critique of Raz see Stephen L. Darwall, *Morality, Authority, and Law: Essays in Second-Personal Ethics* (Oxford: Oxford University Press, 2013), 135–78.

11. This is the first line of his most recent book. See Frederick F. Schauer, *The Force of Law* (Cambridge: Harvard University Press, 2015), 1.

example, we treat a doctor's recommendation for an influenza vaccination much differently than we treat a legally mandated vaccination, even though they both come from authoritative sources. If we follow the doctor's directive, we do so because we *believe* something to be true about what she says, because the doctor's knowledge on vaccinations is superior to ours. What the doctor tells us about the benefits of a given vaccination displaces our own beliefs about it. But the newly adopted beliefs about vaccinations are only *added* to our reasons for action. They do not displace our other reasons for action.

Arie Rosen, for example, describes the normative impact of epistemic authority as follows:

> Although both types of authority [practical and epistemic] are practical, in the sense that they ultimately guide our actions and behavior, they have a different impact on what we believe to be the right course of action. In order to affect our practical reasoning, epistemic authority has to influence our personal beliefs regarding what is right and wrong, proper and improper.... It tells us not only what to do but what to believe.[12]

By contrast, practical authorities tell their subjects what to do and what not to do regardless of what they believe. Rosen writes: "What we are urged to respect in decisionist [practical authority's] directives is not ... the impact it should have on our beliefs and convictions but the directive's particular content, the arbitrary element that is left to the discretion of the person in authority."[13] Thus, while practical authority preempts one's reasons for action—such that we feel obligated to comply regardless of what we believe—epistemic authority only adds to one's reasons for action, by displacing one's reasons for belief. This explains why one type of authority commands, while the other persuades.

## 1.2. Interpretive Reasoning with Practical and Epistemic Authorities

One of the unique features of practical authority, which is important for the question of identifying textual authority in ancient Jewish sources, is that practical authorities are interpreted in a unique and identifiable

---

12. Arie Rosen, "Two Logics of Authority in Modern Law," *UTLJ* 64 (2014): 675–76.
13. Rosen, "Two Logics of Authority," 680.

way. Specifically, the primary questions that underlie the interpretation of a practical authority are the following: *What does it mean to follow this directive?* and *What does and does not count as compliance?* Because of the reason-preempting nature of practical authority's directives, its addressees do not and cannot ask the question of why act or do one thing or another; the only question they are left with is how to comply with the demand. This unique mode of interpretive reasoning underlies the military adage "When I say jump, you say: How high?" With the directives of an epistemic authority, their addressees must still consider reasons as to whether to follow the directive; they are allowed to say: "Why should I jump? Give me a good reason." With practical authorities, the only questions the subjects are allowed to ask is: "How high? What height of jump counts as compliance with the command?" Thus, the interpretive engagement with the directives of an epistemic authority is of a different kind from that of practical authority.

This difference in interpretive reasoning can be demonstrated with the famous contradictory aphorisms of Prov 26:4–5:

> Do not answer fools according to their folly,
>   or you will be a fool yourself.
> Answer fools according to their folly,
>   or they will be wise in their own eyes. (NRSV)

The direct contradiction between these directives prevents any reader from following them based on their mere say-so. In other words, they cannot be treated as law, as preemptive reasons for action. As an epistemic authority, the proverb provides a good (as opposed to a preemptive) reason to answer a fool and a good (as opposed to a preemptive) reason to refrain from answering a fool. Epistemic authorities, therefore, call their addressees to engage reason, rather than preempt it. In other words, they must decide for themselves which course of action is best, in their particular situation, taking both directives into consideration. By contrast, if one of these directives were treated as law—both cannot be treated as such—then it would produce an entirely different type of interpretive reasoning. The addressee would ask questions such as: *What counts as folly? What does it mean to answer according to folly? And what qualifies as a fool?* Once the deliberations as to whether to follow the directive are eliminated, however—that is, once such reasoning is preempted—then the only questions left are *What does it mean to follow this directive? And what does and does not count as compliance? What do the words of the command mean?* This produces a unique mode of interpretation, which focuses on the meaning of the specific wording of the directive, as opposed to its underlying rationale.

## 2. Interpretive Engagement in the Transmission of the Qumran Penal Codes

The fact that binding norms produce a unique and identifiable mode of interpretation makes it possible to determine whether ancient interpreters viewed their received traditions as practical authorities or epistemic authorities. For example, the Cairo Genizah copy of the Damascus Document's (CD) interpretation of the Torah's Sabbath law (X, 14–XI, 18) demonstrates an intense concern with the question of what does and does not count as compliance; the scribe spent the better part of two columns delineating the boundaries of the word *work*. This suggests that that scribe viewed the Torah's law as a practical authority. While it is true that the scribe responsible for CD's Sabbath interpretation was likely drawing from contemporary interpretive traditions, this does not negate the fact that the text's intense concern with the meaning of the law's specific words reflects a legal understanding of the law.[14] The question, therefore, for the rule texts is: do we find a similar type of interpretive reasoning underlying the interpretive rewriting among the S, D, and 4Q265 traditions? There is no question that there is intentional interpretive creativity in their reformulation among the various traditions.[15] What I seek to determine here is the mode of interpretive reasoning that underlies that reformulation.

The penal codes found in S, D, and 4Q265 provide a particularly fruitful avenue of inquiry.[16] Not only do they contain the clearest law-like language among the rule texts, particularly the if-then casuistic style, but

---

14. For a more complete discussion see Vroom, *Authority of Law*, 39–47.

15. For a comparison of the rule texts' rewriting with that of so-called biblical texts from the same period, see Charlotte Hempel, "Pluralism and Authoritativeness: The Case of the S Tradition," in *Authoritative Scriptures in Ancient Judaism*, ed. Mladen Popović, JSJSup 141 (Leiden: Brill, 2010), 193–208; Annette Steudel, "The Damascus Document (D) as a Rewriting of the Community Rule," *RevQ* 25 (2012): 605–20.

16. They are found primarily in 1QS VI, 24–XII, 25; 4QS$^e$ I, 4–15; II, 3–9; 4QS$^g$ (4Q261) 3, 2–4; 4a–b, 1–7; 5a–c, 1–9; 6a–e, 1–5; CD XIV, 18–22; 4QD$^a$ (4Q266) 10 I–II; 4QD$^e$ (4Q270) 7 I; and 4Q265 4 I, 2–II, 2. Small bits and pieces of penal codes are also found in 4QS$^d$ (4Q258), 4QD$^b$ (4Q267), 4QD$^d$ (4Q269), and 11Q29.

they also reflect an obvious literary connection,[17] though the direction of dependence is debated. I will assume that D generally precedes S, though both were being transmitted throughout the late Second Temple period, which means the direction of dependence for any interpretive change should be taken on a case-by-case basis.

## 2.1. The Omission of Laws Concerning Women in S

I begin with the well-known departure of the S tradition from the D tradition in laws that deal with women. While the D tradition's penal code (found in 4QD$^e$ [4Q270]) prohibits members from grumbling against fathers and mothers, S appears to switch this to grumbling against the foundation of the community and against peers.

1QS VII, 17–18

והאיש אשר ילון על יסוד היחד ישלחהו ולוא ישוב ואם על רעהו ילון אשר לוא
במשפט ונענש ששה חודשים

4QD$^e$ 7 I, 13–14

[ואשר ילו]ן֯ על האבות [ישלח] מן העדה ולא ישׁ֯וֹב [ואם] על האמות ונעֹנַש
עֲשֹׂר[ת] יׂמים[18]

---

17. Both Hempel and Metso frequently refer to the penal codes as hard evidence for a literary relationship between the S and D communities in particular. See, for example, Charlotte Hempel, *The Qumran Rule Texts in Context: Collected Studies*, TSAJ 154 (Tübingen: Mohr Siebeck, 2013), 44. She writes: "The presence of the penal code material in 4QD that parallels 1QS VI, 24–VII, 25 is of paramount importance for the question of the relationship between both documents." See also Sarianna Metso, "The Relationship between the Damascus Document and the Community Rule," in *The Damascus Document: A Centennial of Discovery; Proceedings of the Third International Symposium of the Orion Center for the Study of the Dead Sea Scrolls and Associated Literature*, ed. Joseph M. Baumgarten, Esther G. Chazon, and Avital Pinnick (Leiden: Brill, 2000), 87–90. The penal code in 1QS in particular bares similarity to the casuistic section of the covenant code (Exod 21:1–22:16). For further comment see Marcus K. M. Tso, *Ethics in the Qumran Community: An Interdisciplinary Investigation*, WUNT 2/292 (Tübingen: Mohr Siebeck, 2010), 174–75.

18. For this reconstruction see Joseph M. Baumgarten, James H. Charlesworth et al., "The Damascus Document," in *Damascus Document II, Some Works of the Torah, and Related Documents*, vol. 3 of *The Dead Sea Scrolls: Hebrew, Aramaic, and Greek Texts with English Translations*, ed. James H. Charlesworth (Tübingen: Mohr Siebeck, 1994), 154 n. 251. For an alternative reconstruction see Elisha Qimron, *The Dead Sea*

1QS VII, 17–18
And a man who grumbles against the foundation of the community shall be sent away and shall not return. But if he grumbles against his peer which is not by law, he shall be fined six months.[19]

4QD<sup>e</sup> 7 I, 13–14
[And whoever grum]bles against the fathers [shall be sent away] from the congregation and shall not return. [But if he grumbles] against the mothers then he shall be fined ten days.

The most natural explanation for this difference is that the S scribes sought to eliminate any mention of women and family life because they were part of an all-male celibate community.[20] As a consequence, they altered the formulation of the law, swapping offenses against mothers and fathers for offenses against peers and the foundation of the community.

What is notable about this reformulation of the earlier law is that the earlier version must have been considered authoritative for the S community. It would have been much easier to dispense with those laws altogether. That the S scribes sought to retain as much of the rules as they could suggests that they were important—even authoritative. Instead of simply eliminating the family laws, the scribes interpretively reformulated them such that they would fit within their all-male community.

The authority that the D penal code held for the S scribes, however, does not appear to have been practical/legal authority. In their reformulation of the law, it is clear that the S scribes are not concerned with the typical questions that occupy the subjects of a practical authority. If they understood D's laws as a practical authority, their interpretive efforts would have been spent addressing the question of what it means to grumble: what does and does not qualify as grumbling? That is the type of interpretive reasoning that is applied to practical authorities. That the S scribes

---

*Scrolls: The Hebrew Writings* (Jerusalem: Yad Ben-Zvi, 2010), 1:56. He suggests the verb ירשע was used instead of ילון. This would make the parallel with 1QS less clear.

19. Unless otherwise indicated, translations are mine.

20. This conclusion is bolstered by the immediately preceding law in D, which prohibits fornication (זנה) with one's wife, which is absent in S. For further discussion see Sidnie White Crawford, "Not according to Rule: Women, the Dead Sea Scrolls and Qumran," in *Emanuel: Studies in Hebrew Bible, Septuagint, and Dead Sea Scrolls in Honor of Emanuel Tov*, ed. Shalom M. Paul et al., VTSup 94 (Boston: Brill, 2003), 148–50.

chose to reinterpret the law so as to eliminate references to women and family life, while ignoring the question of what does and does not count as compliance, suggests that D was not considered as a legally binding text. Rather, it was likely an epistemic authority.

## 2.2. Serekh Editing of D: The Case of the *Rabbîm*

A second interpretive change in the penal codes can be found in D's version of the law against leaving community meetings. As argued by Charlotte Hempel, the D version reflects editing by a Serekh community, particularly the addition of the word *rabbîm* (הרבים).[21]

1QS VII, 10–11

וכן לאיש הנפסׄר במושב הרבים אשר לוא בעצה וחנם

And likewise for the man who leaves the meeting of the *rabbîm* without permission or reason

4QD[a] 10 II, 6–8

[וכן לאיש הנפ]טר [אשר] לוׄ בעצת הרׄ[בׄ]יׄ[ם וׄ]חׄ[נם]

[And likewise for the man who lea]ves [with]out the permission of the *ra[bb]î[m* or reason

According to Hempel, the reference to the *rabbîm* in D was added by an S redactor. The most common self-designation in D is עדה, while the most common term in S is הרבים.[22] This leads Hempel to believe that 1QS VII, 10–11 preserves the earlier form of this law and 4QD[a] reflects a later ideological change in the direction of S.[23]

If this explanation is correct, then it is another example of an interpretive change made within the transmission of the rule-text penal codes that

---

21. See Charlotte Hempel, "The Penal Code Reconsidered," in *Legal Texts and Legal Issues: Proceedings of the Second Meeting of the International Organization for Qumran Studies, Cambridge 1995; Published in Honour of Joseph M. Baumgarten*, ed. Moshe J. Bernstein, Florentino García Martínez, and John I. Kampen (Boston: Brill, 1997), 342–43; Hempel, *The Laws of the Damascus Document: Sources, Tradition, and Redaction*, STDJ 29 (Leiden: Brill, 1998), 146–48.

22. According to Hempel, הרבים occurs in 1QS thirty-four times, while only nine times in D texts ("Penal Code Reconsidered," 342–43).

23. For an alternative argument see Reinhard G. Kratz, "Der 'Penal Code' und das Verhältnis von Serekh-Yachad (S) und Damascusschrift (D)," *RevQ* 25 (2011): 205–6.

pays no attention to the questions of what does and does not count as compliance. For example, if this law were to be treated as a preemptive reason for action, then it would have to specify what אשר לוא בעצה וחנם (without permission or reason) means: *Is there a means of obtaining permission? What qualifies as permission? Who gives this permission?* Their interpretive efforts were not expended on these practical issues; instead, their interpretative change was motivated by purely ideological considerations, meant to reinforce the identity of the S community.[24]

## 2.3. Adding Levels of Exclusion to S

A third interpretive change among the penal codes can be found in 1QS's rendering of D's law concerning one who betrays the community. In 4QD$^e$, there is a law that specifies two years of separation for betraying the community and walking in the stubbornness of one's heart. The 1QS scribe, or perhaps the scribe responsible for his *Vorlage*, added levels of exclusion to this punishment:

4QD$^e$ 7 I, 8–10
והאי[ש אשר תזוע [רוחו מיסוד היחד לבגוד באמת וללכת בשרירות לבו]
[ו][הֹֽו][בדל שתי שנ]ים וֹנֶעֱנָש ששים [יום ובמלאות לו שתי שנים ישאלו הרבים]
על דֹּבָ[רו ואם יקרב] וֹיֹכֹתֹוֹ[בוהו בתכונו ואחר ישאל אל המשפט][25]

1QS VII, 18–21
והאיש אשר תזוע רוחו מיסוד היחד לבגוד באמת וללכת בשרירות לבו אם ישוב
ונענש שתי שנים ברשונה[26] לוא יגע בטהרת הרבים[27] ובשנית לוא יגע משקה[28]
הרבים ואחר כול אנשי היחד ישב ובמלואת לו שנתים ימים ישאלו הרבים על
דבריו ואם יקרבהו ונכתב בתכונו ואחר ישאל אל המשפט

---

24. This is very similar to Metso's explanation for the development of S, in which 1QS represents a later edition of S with a more advanced self-understanding of the community's identity. See Sarianna Metso, *The Textual Development of the Qumran Community Rule*, STDJ 21 (Boston: Brill, 1997), 143–50.

25. My reconstruction here follows Qimron, *Dead Sea Scrolls*, 1:56.

26. There is an erasure at this point in the text.

27. At the beginning of the next line רבים has been erased.

28. At this point בטהרת was erased, and משקה is written above in the interlinear space.

4QD$^e$ 7 I, 8–10
[A ma]n whose [spirit] trembles [before the foundation of the community, betraying the truth and he has walked in the stubbornness of his heart, then] he shall be se[parated two years and f]ined 60 [days. And when the two years are completed, the many shall consider] his ca[se, and if he is admitted] he shall be inscr[ibed in his rank and may then deliberate concerning the law.]

1QS VII, 18–21
A man whose spirit trembles before the foundation of the community, betraying the truth and he has walked in the stubbornness of his heart, then he shall be fined two years. <u>During the first year he shall not touch the pure meal of the many, and during the second year he shall not touch the drink of the many. And he shall sit below all the men of the Community.</u> And when the two years are completed, the many shall consider his case, and if he is admitted he shall be inscribed in his rank and may then deliberate concerning the law.

When the 1QS scribe composed his version of D's law, he added levels of exclusion to the two-year punishment. In the first year the offender is excluded from the pure meal of the community, and in the second year the offender is excluded from the pure drink. The laws in 1QS and D are otherwise basically the same.[29]

Whatever his reason for this change, what I want to highlight is that, once again, his activity did not address questions of the meaning of the law's requirement. *What does it mean to walk in the stubbornness of one's heart and betray the truth? What qualifies as a violation of that rule?* If the scribe had been bothered by these questions, it stands to reason that he would have somehow addressed them. Instead, he expended his interpretive efforts adding a detail to the law that fails to bring any clarity whatsoever to the question of what it means to follow this law and what does or does not constitute a violation of the law. While it is possible to interpret binding law for other purposes, when written norms hold practical authority, interpreters will primarily be concerned with the question of what qualifies as compliance.[30] Thus, the lack of attention to such questions suggests that

---

29. See Alex P. Jassen, "The Rule of the Community," in *Outside the Bible: Ancient Jewish Writings Related to Scripture*, ed. Louis H. Feldman, James L. Kugel, and Lawrence H. Schiffman (Philadelphia: Jewish Publication Soceity of America, 2013), 2952.

30. Both Schauer and Rosen note that one of the key features of practical

this scribe responsible for this plus did not consider his version of the penal code to be a practical authority for his community.

## 2.4. Correcting Punishment Durations in S Manuscripts

The fourth difference among the Qumran penal codes, which has received much attention in recent years, is the changes to the punishment lengths within S manuscripts.[31] Two have been preserved:

| Offense | 1QS penalty | 4QS$^e$ penalty |
| --- | --- | --- |
| Bearing a grudge | Fined one year (corrected from six months) | Fined six months |
| Exposing oneself | Fined thirty days | Fined sixty days |

While 1QS VII, 13-14 prescribes a thirty-day fine for exposing oneself, 4QS$^e$ I, 11-13 requires a sixty-day fine.[32] Similarly, while 1QS VII, 7-8

---

authorities is that their interpreters are primarily concerned with their specific verbal formulation. Schauer, for example, states: "One of the principal features of rules—and the feature that makes them rules—is that what the rule says really matters.... A big part of a rule's 'ruleness' is tied up with the language in which a rule is written. Central to what rules are and how they function is that what the rule says is the crucial factor, even if what the rule says seems wrong or inconsistent with the background justifications lying behind the rule, and even if following what the rule says produces a bad result on some particular occasion" (*Legal Reasoning*, 17-18). Similarly, Rosen states: "While the exercise of one type of authority [epistemic authority] invites us to focus on the directive's epistemic significance, which transcends the particularity of the instructor's intentions or specific way of saying things, the exercise of the other type [decisionist authority] invites us to focus on the particular content of a directive" ("Two Logics of Authority," 685).

31. These changes are important for Alison Schofield, *From Qumran to the Yaḥad: A New Paradigm of Textual Development for the Community Rule*, STDJ 77 (Boston: Brill, 2009), 115-16. She is followed by other others (see discussion below).

32. Because only the ים is clearly preserved, it is possible to reconstruct a thirty-day punishment (שלשים), rather than sixty days (ששים), though according to Schofield, who places much weight on this variant, sixty seems most likely given the spacing (*From Qumran to the Yaḥad*, 110 n. 119). For reading ששים see Elisha Qimron and James H. Charlesworth, "4QS MSS A-J," in *Rule of the Community and Related Documents*, vol. 1 of *The Dead Sea Scrolls: Hebrew, Aramaic, and Greek Texts with English Translations*, ed. James H. Charlesworth, PTSDSSP 1 (Tübingen: Mohr Siebeck, 1994), 84. Obviously if "thirty" is the correct reading, then this discussion becomes moot.

prescribes a one-year punishment for bearing a grudge, 4QS$^e$ I, 4 only requires a six-month penalty.³³ What is more, the one-year penalty from 1QS was written in the interlinear space by a second hand, corrected from six months.

These changes, particularly the interlinear corrections, lead some scholars to conclude that the rule texts were actively used to govern community life; the change to the punishment duration indicates that the texts were updated to reflect changes to the community's legal practices. Alison Schofield, for example, writes:

> The emendation in 1QS attests to the scribes' dynamic engagement with the text, where a second scribe updated the legal code to reflect what must have been an actual change in punishment length. Such scribal activity would have been unnecessary if this was a mere literary record, and this is the strongest evidence that this text reflects the praxis of a living community.³⁴

This is essential to her theory that each version of S governed a geographically distinct cell of the broad Yaḥad movement; several other scholars follow Schofield on this point.³⁵

While it is not impossible to explain these changes to the punishment lengths as the result of changes to a community's legal practices, I would suggest that such a conclusion is unlikely. As discussed above, when a rule is treated as law, it preempts all other reasons for action, such that the interpreter is only left with the question of what does and does not count as compliance. If the laws were treated this way, then it stands to reason that interpreters would expend their interpretive efforts addressing questions concerning the offenses: *What does it mean to bear a grudge? What qualifies as exposing oneself? What does and does not count as compliance?* There are a host of questions that the scribe left unaddressed.

---

33. It must be noted that this a reconstruction. Only the יום is clearly preserved from the supposed ששה חודשים reconstruction. See Philip Alexander and Geza Vermes, *Qumran Cave 4.XIX: Serekh Ha-Yaḥad*, DJD XXVI (Oxford: Clarendon, 1998), 135–36.

34. Schofield, *From Qumran to the Yaḥad*, 118.

35. Schofield, *From Qumran to the Yaḥad*, 115–18. See also John J. Collins, *Beyond the Qumran Community: The Sectarian Movement of the Dead Sea Scrolls* (Grand Rapids: Eerdmans, 2010), 3; Gillihan, *Civic Ideology, Organization, and Law*, 14–18; Nati, "Community Rule," 925–27.

Grudge bearing, for example, deals with one's emotional state, which makes the statement seem more like a moral imperative rather than a legal prohibition. It is true that, in the sect's judicial context, grudges refer to one's failure to immediately report an offense, which is an element of the community's law of reproof, discussed in 1QS V, 24–VI, 1 and CD IX, 2–8. According to this law, an offender cannot be punished unless an accuser brings reproof (הוכח) to the overseer. This reproof must be reported immediately. Anyone who waits "day to day" (מיום ליום; CD IX, 6) will be guilty of bearing a grudge. The offense of grudge bearing, however, is not framed as a crime of omission, whereby one neglects to fulfill his legal obligation to report an offense. Rather, the offense is presented as the harboring of ill feelings toward a peer. According to the interpretation of Lev 19:17–18 in CD IX, 2–8, bearing such a grudge is tantamount to hating one's neighbor. As Lawrence Schiffman states: "If one fails to reprove his fellow, he may come to hate him."[36] Thus the offense that the penal code addresses is the harboring of ill feelings toward a peer. If this is the case, then why would a scribe who makes the effort to update the duration of the punishment for this offense not also take the time to add some specificity to the offense itself—to shed some light on the vexing question of what does and does not count as compliance with such a rule? Grudge bearing is virtually unintelligible as law. Because law provides reasons for action—as opposed to beliefs or emotions—it simply cannot prohibit grudge bearing.

Furthermore, if we assume for a moment that this change to the punishment length was made by a scribe who sought to revise the existing penalty for grudge bearing, then we also have to assume that the community's judges were bound to the specific wording of the text and could not exercise discretion. In other words, we would have to assume that the punishment for any given offense was standardized across each community and that its adjudicators could not issue a more lenient punishment until

---

36. See Lawrence H. Schiffman, "Reproof as a Requisite for Punishment in the Law of the Dead Sea Scrolls," in *Jewish Law Studies II: The Jerusalem Conference Volume*, ed. Bernard S. Jackson (Atlanta: Scholars Press, 1986), 68. More recently, while discussing the rebuke passage in CD VI, 20–VII, 3, Matthew Goldstone argues that by framing the legal obligation of rebuke as an admonition against grudge-bearing, the CD scribe "highlights the moral dimension of the commandment." See Goldstone, *The Dangerous Duty of Rebuke: Leviticus 19:17 in Early Jewish and Christian Interpretation*, JSJSup 185 (Leiden: Brill, 2018), 31. Similarly, in the penal code, the prohibition against grudge bearing (as opposed to a command to immediately report an offense, which is an action that the law can govern) reflects the law's nonlegal character.

the written laws were changed. After all, when a norm is treated as a preemptive reason for action—as law—it means that judges are handcuffed by its specific wording; they are obligated to render verdicts that they may not even agree with.[37] This seems unlikely. Even in modern law, it is recognized that sentencing should be left up to the discretion of judges, though they typically must work within a sentencing range (e.g., ten to twenty-five years for second-degree murder).[38] Every case has mitigating factors or extenuating circumstances that must be taken into account when assigning specific penalties. This may well have been the case for the sect's judges as well. They would be presented with the facts of each case, render a verdict, and issue a penalty—whether separation from the community or from the meal and whether for a few days or years—while taking all circumstances into account. If the community judges had this type of discretion, which seems intuitive, then there would be no need to correct the law in the first place, in which case the change to the penalty says nothing about the nature and function of the penal codes.

This discretion with punishments was likely also the case with the other offense where the penalty may have been changed within S manuscripts: the offense of exposing oneself. It seems unlikely that adjudicators would assign the same penalty for the one who briefly exposed his buttocks because he neglected to tie his robe properly as the one who brazenly flaunted his genitals. Yet if we assume that the penalty was changed to correct the law according to contemporary practice, then we would also have to assume that the penal codes dictated one standard punishment for each offense and that adjudicators were bound to apply that one punishment for every occurrence of that offense. If, however, judges were free to exercise their discretion when rendering a punishment, as was almost certainly the case, then there would be no need to update the older penalty length, since their decision was not based on applying a fixed, prescribed punishment in the first place. Therefore, not only does the scribe responsible for these

---

37. According to Schauer, this is the best evidence for law's authority—when a judge acts against reason to follow the law (*Force of Law*, 67–75).

38. This is standard practice in most legal systems, though there has been a shift toward more determinate sentencing (which still retains a degree of discretion). For a discussion of the debate between determinate and indeterminate sentencing, and how each approach has been used in the past, see Yan Zhang, Lening Zhang, and Michael S. Vaughn, "Indeterminate and Determinate Sentencing Models: A State-Specific Analysis of Their Effects on Recidivism," *C&D* 60 (2014): 694–98.

changes ignore the question of what counts as compliance with the law—the main indication that a norm is being treated as binding law—but also it is unlikely that penalty lengths had any bearing on judicial decisions beyond mere example.

While the question remains as to why a scribe would have changed a penalty—whether scribal error or for some unknown interpretive reason—these changes should not be taken as evidence for the legal/practical nature of the rule texts. These changes should also not be taken as evidence for distinct sectarian communities. If the penal codes' main function was not practical/legal, then a single community could very well tolerate seemingly contradictory laws. For example, the rule against public nudity would serve the same didactic/ideological function whether the penalty was six months or one year. While the penal codes certainly reflect the kinds of behaviors that were punished in community meetings and are therefore a valuable source for our understanding community life, we cannot assume that they were treated as rules—as preemptive reasons for action.

### 3. Reading the Penal Codes as Epistemic Authorities

If I am correct that the penal codes, and rule texts more broadly, did not possess practical (legal) authority, then the question must be asked: why were they written? If they were not law, then what were they? While space does not permit a full discussion,[39] I would suggest that it is best to think of the (so-called) rule texts as epistemic authorities. It is counterintuitive to think that they possessed no authority. It is unhelpful to say that they were descriptive, rather than prescriptive, since that implies that they had no normative impact whatsoever on community life; a dichotomy between descriptive and prescriptive is misleading, since it implies that a text is either legally binding or has no normative value.[40] The concept of epistemic authority is helpful because it allows us to view the rule texts as authoritative, having an impact on community life, while not restricting us to view them as binding law, simply listing the actions that members could and could not do, along with their corresponding penalties.

---

39. See further discussion see Vroom, *Authority of Law*, 168–71.

40. This descriptive-prescriptive dichotomy has become a popular way of discussing biblical law. See, for example, Michael Lefebvre, *Collections, Codes, and Torah: The Re-characterization of Israel's Written Law*, LHBOTS 451 (New York: T&T Clark, 2006), 23–30.

As for the question of how this epistemic authority was brought to bear on community life, impacting beliefs and ultimately decision making, a number of compatible suggestions have already been given. For example, Sarianna Metso argues that they were didactic, rather than legal; they were "records of community traditions—post-scriptive rather than prescriptive—important for members, particularly for new members, to study."[41] Alternatively, speaking of the Damascus tradition, Steven Fraade uses the concept of performativity, which refers to "how texts actively and transformatively engage their audiences in the process of conveying meaning and cultivating identity."[42] He argues that the laws of D "functioned not just juridically, but also (if not mainly) pedagogically and liturgically, that is rhetorically and performatively, in a particular social setting." He goes on to suggest that the ceremonial reading of the text "would have functioned as a reminder, even a reenactment, for its audience of their original entry and annual reconfirmation into the covenant."[43] In this way, the rule texts would have affected members' beliefs and values in a way that would have solidified their allegiance to the community, ultimately influencing their decision making.

Another account of the rule texts that is compatible with my epistemic-authority theory is given by Carol Newsom and further expanded by Jutta Jokiranta. They focus on the texts' role in identity formation. Newsom argues that the form of 1QS functions to create a symbolic world that cultivates sectarian identity. She writes:

> The Serekh ha-Yahad is thus roughly shaped as a virtual experience of the discourse and praxis that members would experience as they entered the community and became increasingly proficient in its figured world. This is so ... whether or not the descriptions in the Serekh

---

41. Metso argues this based on the fact that the rule texts contain a variety of genres, not just laws; that they contain conflicting laws; and that there is no reference to written texts in the passages that describe adjudication. See Metso, "Problems in Reconstructing," 390–93. For a similar explanation see Lawrence H. Schiffman, *Sectarian Law in the Dead Sea Scrolls: Courts, Testimony, and the Penal Code*, BJS 33 (Chico, CA: Scholars Press, 1983), 157–59.

42. Steven D. Fraade, "Ancient Jewish Law and Narrative in Comparative Perspective: The *Damascus Document* and the Mishnah," in *Legal Fictions: Studies of Law and Narrative in the Discursive Worlds of Ancient Jewish Sectarians and Sages*, ed. Stephen D. Fraade, JSJSup 147 (Leiden: Brill, 2011), 230 n. 5.

43. Fraade, "Ancient Jewish Law," 239–40.

ha-Yahad reflect the precise practices of the community at any given time. What we have here is how the community represents itself to itself, not so much in terms of precise information as in ethos, values, and sensibilities.[44]

According to this explanation, the reading/reciting of the rule texts—or portions thereof—would create/reinforce community identity and values. Jokiranta pushes Newsom's identity-formation approach further, drawing from social-identity theory. She states: "The penal code is one part of the construction of the community of counsel. It promotes the continuance of the shared social identity: *the awareness of being part of the righteous counseling, and emotional reliance on the trustworthiness of the group.*"[45] In this way, the penal codes would strengthen members' commitment to the community and its practices, which would, in turn, affect their practical decision making.

## 4. Conclusion

While much more could be said about how the penal codes, and rule texts more broadly, functioned as epistemic authorities, my goal in this essay was to argue that they should not be viewed as binding law. Among the sampling of interpretive rewriting that was examined here, there is no evidence that the sectarian scribes viewed the laws as practical authorities. Unlike contemporary Torah-interpretive texts, such as the Sabbath passage of CD X, 14–XI, 18 (see section 2), the interpretive reasoning reflected in the Qumran rule texts shows no concern with the question of what does and does not qualify as compliance. Rather, the manner in which they were interpretively rewritten suggests that they possessed epistemic authority, rather than practical/legal authority.

---

44. Carol A. Newsom, *The Self as Symbolic Space: Constructing Identity and Community at Qumran*, STDJ 52 (Leiden: Brill, 2004), 148.

45. Jutta Jokiranta, "Social Identity in the Qumran Movement: The Case of the Penal Code," in *Explaining Christian Origins and Early Judaism: Contributions from Cognitive and Social Science*, ed. Petri Luomanen, Ilkka Pyysiäinen, and Risto Uro, BibInt 89 (Leiden: Brill, 2007), 295, emphasis original.

## Bibliography

Alexander, Philip, and Geza Vermes. *Qumran Cave 4.XIX: Serekh Ha-Yaḥad*. DJD XXVI. Oxford: Clarendon, 1998.

Baumgarten, Joseph M., James H. Charlesworth, Lidija Novakovic, and Henry W. M. Rietz. "The Damascus Document." Pages 1–185 in *Damascus Document II, Some Works of the Torah, and Related Documents*. Vol. 3 of *The Dead Sea Scrolls: Hebrew, Aramaic, and Greek Texts with English Translations*. Edited by James H. Charlesworth. Tübingen: Mohr Siebeck, 1994.

Collins, John J. *Beyond the Qumran Community: The Sectarian Movement of the Dead Sea Scrolls*. Grand Rapids: Eerdmans, 2010.

Crawford, Sidnie White. "Not according to Rule: Women, the Dead Sea Scrolls and Qumran." Pages 127–50 in *Emanuel: Studies in Hebrew Bible, Septuagint, and Dead Sea Scrolls in Honor of Emanuel Tov*. Edited by Shalom M. Paul, Robert A. Kraft, Lawrence H. Schiffman, and Weston W. Fields. VTSup 94. Boston: Brill, 2003.

Darwall, Stephen L. *Morality, Authority, and Law: Essays in Second-Personal Ethics*. Oxford: Oxford University Press, 2013.

Davies, Philip R. "Redaction and Sectarianism in the Qumran Scrolls." Pages 152–63 in *The Scriptures and the Scrolls: Studies in Honour of A. S. van der Woude on the Occasion of His Sixty-Fifth Birthday*. Edited by Casper J. Labuschagne, Antonius Hilhorst, and Florentino García Martínez. Leiden: Brill, 1992.

Fraade, Steven D. "Ancient Jewish Law and Narrative in Comparative Perspective: The *Damascus Document* and the Mishnah." Pages 227–54 in *Legal Fictions: Studies of Law and Narrative in the Discursive Worlds of Ancient Jewish Sectarians and Sages*. Edited by Steven D. Fraade. JSJSup 147. Leiden: Brill, 2011.

Gillihan, Yonder Moynihan. *Civic Ideology, Organization, and Law in the Rule Scrolls: A Comparative Study of the Covenanters' Sect and Contemporary Voluntary Associations in Political Context*. STDJ 97. Leiden: Brill, 2012.

Goldstone, Matthew S. *The Dangerous Duty of Rebuke: Leviticus 19:17 in Early Jewish and Christian Interpretation*. JSJSup 185. Leiden: Brill, 2018.

Hempel, Charlotte. *The Damascus Texts*. Sheffield: Sheffield Academic, 2000.

———. *The Laws of the Damascus Document: Sources, Tradition, and Redaction*. STDJ 29. Leiden: Brill, 1998.

———. "The Penal Code Reconsidered." Pages 337–48 in *Legal Texts and Legal Issues: Proceedings of the Second Meeting of the International Organization for Qumran Studies, Cambridge 1995; Published in Honour of Joseph M. Baumgarten*. Edited by Moshe J. Bernstein, Florentino García Martínez, and John I. Kampen. Boston: Brill, 1997.

———. "Pluralism and Authoritativeness: The Case of the S Tradition." Pages 193–208 in *Authoritative Scriptures in Ancient Judaism*. Edited by Mladen Popović. JSJSup 141. Leiden: Brill, 2010.

———. *The Qumran Rule Texts in Context: Collected Studies*. TSAJ 154. Tübingen: Mohr Siebeck, 2013.

Hershovitz, Scott. "The Role of Authority." *PI* 11 (2011): 1–19.

Jassen, Alex P. "The Rule of the Community." Pages 2923–74 in *Outside the Bible: Ancient Jewish Writings Related to Scripture*. Edited by Louis H. Feldman, James L. Kugel, and Lawrence H. Schiffman. Philadelphia: Jewish Publication Society of America, 2013.

Jokiranta, Jutta. "Social Identity in the Qumran Movement: The Case of the Penal Code." Pages 277–98 in *Explaining Christian Origins and Early Judaism: Contributions from Cognitive and Social Science*. Edited by Petri Luomanen, Ilkka Pyysiäinen, and Risto Uro. BibInt 89. Leiden: Brill, 2007.

Knowles, Dudley. *Political Obligation: A Critical Introduction*. RCPP. London: Routledge, 2010.

Kratz, Reinhard G. "Der 'Penal Code' und das Verhältnis von Serekh-Yachad (S) und Damascusschrift (D)." *RevQ* 25 (2011): 199–227.

Lefebvre, Michael. *Collections, Codes, and Torah: The Re-characterization of Israel's Written Law*. LHBOTS 451. New York: T&T Clark, 2006.

Metso, Sarianna. "Problems in Reconstructing the Organizational Chart of the Essenes." *DSD* 16 (2009): 388–415.

———. "The Relationship between the Damascus Document and the Community Rule." Pages 85–93 in *The Damascus Document: A Centennial of Discovery; Proceedings of the Third International Symposium of the Orion Center for the Study of the Dead Sea Scrolls and Associated Literature*. Edited by Joseph M. Baumgarten, Esther G. Chazon, and Avital Pinnick. Leiden: Brill, 2000.

———. *The Serekh Texts*. LSTS 62. New York: T&T Clark, 2007.

———. *The Textual Development of the Qumran Community Rule*. STDJ 21. Boston: Brill, 1997.

Nati, James. "The Community Rule or Rules for the Communities?: Contextualizing the Qumran *Serekhim*." Pages 916–39 in *Sibyls, Scriptures, and Scrolls: John Collins at Seventy*. Edited by Joel Baden, Hindy Najman, and Eibert J. C. Tigchelaar. JSJSup 175. Leiden: Brill, 2017.

Newsom, Carol A. *The Self as Symbolic Space: Constructing Identity and Community at Qumran*. STDJ 52. Leiden: Brill, 2004.

Qimron, Elisha. *The Dead Sea Scrolls: The Hebrew Writings*. Vol. 1. Jerusalem: Yad Ben-Zvi, 2010.

Qimron, Elisha, and James H. Charlesworth. "4QS MSS A–J." Pages 53–103 in *Rule of the Community and Related Documents*. Vol. 1 of *The Dead Sea Scrolls: Hebrew, Aramaic, and Greek Texts with English Translations*. Edited by James H. Charlesworth, Jacob Milgrom, Elisha Qimrom, Lawrence H. Schiffman, Loren T. Stuckenbruck, and Rozann E. Whitaker. Tübingen: Mohr Siebeck, 1994.

Raz, Joseph. Introduction to *Between Authority and Interpretation: On the Theory of Law and Practical Reason*. Edited by Joseph Raz. Oxford: Oxford University Press, 2009.

———. *The Morality of Freedom*. Oxford: Clarendon, 1986.

Regev, Eyal. "Between Two Sects: Differentiating the *Yaḥad* and the Damascus Covenant." Pages 431–49 in *The Dead Sea Scrolls: Texts and Contexts*. Edited by Charlotte Hempel. STDJ 90. Leiden: Brill, 2010.

Rosen, Arie. "Two Logics of Authority in Modern Law." *UTLJ* 64 (2014): 669–702.

Sanders, E. P. *Paul and Palestinian Judaism: A Comparison of Patterns of Religion*. Philadelphia: Fortress, 1977.

Schauer, Frederick F. *The Force of Law*. Cambridge: Harvard University Press, 2015.

———. *Thinking Like a Lawyer: A New Introduction to Legal Reasoning*. Cambridge: Harvard University Press, 2009.

Schiffman, Lawrence H. "Reproof as a Requisite for Punishment in the Law of the Dead Sea Scrolls." Pages 59–74 in *Jewish Law Studies II: The Jerusalem Conference Volume*. Edited by Bernard S. Jackson. Atlanta: Scholars Press, 1986.

———. *Sectarian Law in the Dead Sea Scrolls: Courts, Testimony, and the Penal Code*. BJS 33. Chico, CA: Scholars Press, 1983.

Schofield, Alison. *From Qumran to the Yaḥad: A New Paradigm of Textual Development for the Community Rule*. STDJ 77. Boston: Brill, 2009.

Steudel, Annette. "The Damascus Document (D) as a Rewriting of the Community Rule." *RevQ* 25 (2012): 605–20.

Tso, Marcus K. M. *Ethics in the Qumran Community: An Interdisciplinary Investigation.* WUNT 2/292. Tübingen: Mohr Siebeck, 2010.

Vroom, Jonathan. *The Authority of Law in the Hebrew Bible and Early Judaism: Tracing the Origins of Legal Obligation from Ezra to Qumran.* JSJSup 187. Leiden: Brill, 2018.

Weissenberg, Hanne von. "Defining Authority." Pages 679–96 in *In the Footsteps of Sherlock Holmes: Studies in the Biblical Text in Honour of Anneli Aejmelaeus.* Edited by Kristin De Troyer, T. Michael Law, and Marketta Liljeström. CBET 72. Leuven: Peeters, 2014.

Zhang, Yan, Lening Zhang, and Michael S. Vaughn. "Indeterminate and Determinate Sentencing Models: A State-Specific Analysis of Their Effects on Recidivism." *C&D* 60 (2014): 693–715.

# Assessing the Character of Hebrew in the Dead Sea Scrolls: Historical Linguistics, Numeral Syntax, and the Notion of a Distinct Dead Sea Scrolls Hebrew

John Screnock

In past scholarship on the Hebrew found in the Dead Sea Scrolls (DSS), there seems to have been an impulse to look for and highlight anything *different*—as has been true in many areas of study aimed at the DSS. This impulse was reflected early on in the concept of Qumran Hebrew, a distinct dialect or phase of ancient Hebrew closely associated with the sectarians who supposedly lived at Qumran.[1] When we consider the Hebrew of the DSS in the context of historical linguistics, however, it appears in a somewhat different light. Such contextualization mitigates the impression of otherness for the Hebrew in the DSS, instead painting a picture of continuity with Hebrew used in other corpora. I will illustrate the point by looking at the syntax of cardinal numerals in particular. Scholars of the DSS were eager to define Dead Sea Scrolls Hebrew[2] as different in the area

---

1. Qumran Hebrew's distinctiveness and its link to the sectarian group come to the fore most clearly in William Schniedewind's work, e.g., "Qumran Hebrew as an Antilanguage," *JBL* 118 (1999): 235–52; see also Eric Reymond, *Qumran Hebrew: An Overview of Orthography, Phonology, and Morphology*, RBS 76 (Atlanta: SBL Press, 2014), 13–14, on others with a similar approach. Even the more typical approaches to the Hebrew of the DSS, however, contain similar emphases on distinctiveness and connection to the Yaḥad. See, e.g., Takamitsu Muraoka, "An Approach to the Morphosyntax and Syntax of Qumran Hebrew," in *Diggers at the Well*, ed. Takamitsu Muraoka and John F. Elwolde (Leiden: Brill, 2000), 193–214; and Elisha Qimron, *A Grammar of the Hebrew of the Dead Sea Scrolls* (Jerusalem: Yad Izhak Ben-Zvi, 2018), one of whose aims is to "demonstrate essential differences and establish the uniqueness of the DSS language" (2).

2. I hesitate even to use such a term, because I do not think the Hebrew found in the DSS is fundamentally different from Hebrew in other earlier and contemporane-

of numeral syntax, maintaining that the usual order of number phrases in the DSS was *noun-number* (the noun precedes the cardinal numeral that quantifies it). Whereas the Hebrew found in most of the Hebrew Bible has the order *number-noun* (as in example 1), so-called Late Biblical Hebrew supposedly began to use the variant order *noun-number* (as in example 2), a trend supposedly continued in DSS Hebrew.

1. CD 10:4, עשרה אנשים, "ten men"[3]
2. 1QM 2:1, ראשים שנים עשר, "twelve chiefs"

By *number phrase*, I do not mean a phrase headed by a numeral (as in *verb phrase*, which is headed by a verb), but any noun phrase containing a cardinal numeral. Because ordinal numerals take adjectival syntax, I do not include them in my discussion here.[4]

In fact, when we bring a methodology that draws on historical linguistics, the uses of noun-number order in the DSS should *not* lead to this conclusion, for two reasons. First, in the Hebrew used in texts before and after the DSS the order noun-number is abnormal, entailing that no historical development ever took place; the Hebrew of the Mishnah clearly prefers number-noun order, and the argument that Late Biblical Hebrew moved toward noun-number order is flawed. Second, when all of the data are taken into account—*all* of the number phrases where the order can be discerned, in any text containing a statistically significant number of tokens—the Hebrew of the DSS itself shows a clear preference for number-noun order, as in Late Biblical Hebrew and the Mishnah. In light of this evidence, the notion that noun-number order somehow increased or even prevailed in the DSS should be abandoned. Moreover, other areas where the DSS are said to differ from the Hebrew in preceding texts should be reconsidered using a historical-linguistic framework.

---

ous texts. However, it is a concept maintained by other scholars—as such, when I use the term *Dead Sea Scrolls Hebrew*, I always mean it in scare quotes, as so-called Dead Sea Scrolls Hebrew.

3. All translations are mine unless noted otherwise.

4. See John Screnock, "The Syntax of Cardinal Numerals in Judges, Amos, Esther, and 1QM," *JSS* 63 (2018): 128. Alexandra Borg's discussion of the יום הששי construction in the DSS involves ordinals, but only insofar as they are adjectives. See "Some Observations on the יום הששי Syndrome in the Hebrew of the Dead Sea Scrolls," in Muraoka and Elwolde, *Diggers at the Well*, 26–39.

My study proceeds in three parts. First, I summarize the work of previous scholars on the syntax of cardinal numerals in the DSS, with particular focus on the order of noun and number. Because few have attended to numeral syntax in ancient Hebrew generally, my main interlocutor is Elisha Qimron, whose reference grammar is the authoritative voice on the Hebrew of the DSS.[5] Second, I summarize a historical-linguistic approach to the study of ancient Hebrew. Third, I present the evidence from the DSS and discuss its interpretation in historical-linguistic context.

## 1. Elisha Qimron on the Syntax of Numerals

Elisha Qimron's *Hebrew of the Dead Sea Scrolls* (1986) was for a long time the most comprehensive treatment of Hebrew in the DSS, paralleling reference grammars for Biblical Hebrew in its coverage—orthography, phonology, morphology, syntax, and vocabulary.[6] Martin Abegg's important overview of Hebrew in the DSS (1998) has similar coverage and is substantial and useful—but out of necessity it is quite brief, at just over thirty pages.[7] Recently, Eric Reymond published an extensive study of orthography, phonology, and morphology in the DSS, extending and revising the work of earlier scholars, especially Qimron's *Hebrew of the Dead Sea Scrolls*.[8] This work does not, however, consider syntax, including the syntax of numerals. Qimron's *Grammar of the Hebrew of the Dead Sea Scrolls* (2018) updates his earlier work; the amount of revision to the 1986 grammar varies depending on the particular area of language under consideration.

---

5. Elisha Qimron, *The Hebrew of the Dead Sea Scrolls*, HSS 29 (Atlanta: Scholars Press, 1986). Qimron recently published a revised version of the work: *A Grammar of the Hebrew of the Dead Sea Scrolls* (Jerusalem: Yad Izhak Ben-Zvi, 2018). Both the 1986 version (itself a condensed revision of his dissertation) and the 2018 version are important for my discussion, since the former is indicative of the approach and conclusions typical of DSS scholarship, while the latter is more authoritative; moreover, taken in tandem these hint at ways in which Qimron's thinking may have developed.

6. E.g., *IBHS*, Joüon, GKC.

7. Martin G. Abegg, "The Hebrew of the Dead Sea Scrolls," in *The Dead Sea Scrolls after Fifty Years: A Comprehensive Assessment*, ed. Peter W. Flint and James C. VanderKam (Leiden: Brill, 1998), 1:325–58.

8. Reymond, *Qumran Hebrew*. As Jared Jacobs notes, "In order to understand fully Reymond's arguments, the reader needs to be familiar with Kutscher, Qimron, and others." See Jacobs, review of Eric Reymond, *Qumran Hebrew*, *JSS* 62 (2017): 262.

In his 1986 grammar, Qimron addresses the syntax of cardinal numerals over two pages.[9] He begins with a distinction made by some scholars for Hebrew in the Hebrew Bible: "Classical" Biblical Hebrew takes number-noun order, while noun-number order sometimes occurs in "late biblical books."[10] Though brief, this statement signals to the reader a robust approach to the historical development of Hebrew: the traditional division between Classical Biblical Hebrew and Late Biblical Hebrew, and the practice of identifying features (e.g., Aramaisms) that betray Late Biblical Hebrew.[11] Though Qimron later gives further nuance to the discussion, noting objections to the idea that noun-number order increased in Late

---

9. Qimron, *Hebrew of the Dead Sea Scrolls*, 85–86. Though just two pages, this is one of the most extensive discussions of numeral syntax in the DSS. For an earlier, critical engagement of Qimron's 1986 grammar, which I draw on in sections below, see Screnock, "Syntax of Cardinal Numerals," 133–34. Qimron focuses on two particular areas of numeral syntax: the order of numeral and noun, and the order of measuring expressions; this focus appears to reflect the focus of earlier scholarship on the Hebrew found in the Bible, in particular Robert Polzin, *Late Biblical Hebrew: Toward an Historical Typology of Biblical Hebrew Prose*, HSM 12 (Missoula, MT: Scholars Press, 1976), 58–64. Qimron's discussion of "phrases of measures, weight, time, etc.," may, depending on how "etc." is understood, indicate a focus on measures and related expressions (e.g., frequency and duration) but not all numerals (Qimron, *Hebrew of the Dead Sea Scrolls*, 85; Qimron, *Grammar of the Hebrew*, 440). See also Adina Moshavi and Susan Rothstein, "Indefinite Numerical Construct Phrases in Biblical Hebrew," *JSS* 63 (2018): 108–14. Qimron's examples, however, include phrases that are not measures or related: e.g., 1QM 9:14, מגנים שלוש מאות ("three hundred shields") and שערים שנים ("two gates"). Given how he contextualizes this section in the discussion of numerals generally in ancient Hebrew (see below), it is clear that Qimron's comments are meant to apply to all number phrases.

10. Qimron, *Hebrew of the Dead Sea Scrolls*, 85.

11. Later, Qimron signals again that he is plugged into this framework, using the terminology *postexilic Hebrew* for Late Biblical Hebrew and alluding to the potential influence of Aramaic (Qimron, *Grammar of the Hebrew*, 441, 442; Qimron, *Hebrew of the Dead Sea Scrolls*, 86). See Qimron, *Grammar of the Hebrew*, 33, where Qimron specifies his method as "comparison [of DSS Hebrew] with other types of early Hebrew [= Classical Biblical Hebrew and Late Biblical Hebrew] and Aramaic"; see also Qimron, *Hebrew of the Dead Sea Scrolls*, 15. Although Qimron does not privilege Tiberian Biblical Hebrew as equivalent to Biblical Hebrew—seeking to draw on Babylonian Hebrew, Samaritan Hebrew, and Greek and Latin transliterations as equal witnesses to ancient Hebrew—this principle seems to apply to phonology and morphology, not syntax (see Qimron, *Grammar of the Hebrew*, 51–52). In his analysis of numeral syntax, anyway, Qimron's main points of reference are Classical Biblical Hebrew and Late Biblical Hebrew as understood via the MT.

Biblical Hebrew,[12] at this point in his presentation the reader understands that noun-number order is indicative of later texts. Qimron then cites four cases of noun-number order in the Cairo Genizah copy of the Damascus Document (CD)—in context, the reader is likely to infer that *this* is the payoff we have been looking for, a significant linguistic difference in the DSS. After making the caveat that "in the other DSS [number-noun] order dominates," Qimron confirms the reader's inference: "CD reflects a real Qumranic feature."[13] How can CD contain the real feature of the language when the other feature dominates in other DSS? Alongside the chronological element—DSS Hebrew continues a trend observed in Late Biblical Hebrew[14]—Qimron's argument involves a stylistic element: DSS Hebrew is distinct from literary Hebrew, found in the Bible, the Mishnah,[15] and some DSS. In the case of numerals, it seems that Qimron (in 1986) is suggesting that the presence of noun-number order in CD gives us a glimpse of the actual spoken language,[16] which is suppressed in other DSS.

The brevity of Qimron's statement so far—consisting of just one paragraph—should not cause us to underestimate its impact.[17] Qimron's 1986 grammar remains the first port of call for many students and scholars who

---

12. Qimron, *Hebrew of the Dead Sea Scrolls*, 86.

13. Qimron, *Hebrew of the Dead Sea Scrolls*, 85. Qimron cites two counterexamples against CD from 1QM and 1QS.

14. Notably, at the end of the section on numerals, Qimron again ties into the chronological argument: cases of noun-number order "are almost exclusive to post-exilic Hebrew," suggesting "their lateness" (*Grammar of the Hebrew*, 442; *Hebrew of the Dead Sea Scrolls*, 86).

15. He refers to "literary [Mishnaic Hebrew]" (Qimron, *Hebrew of the Dead Sea Scrolls*, 85). For an overview of scholarly views on literary versus spoken language in the DSS, see Reymond, *Qumran Hebrew*, 14–18.

16. For Qimron, the language used in the DSS reflects the Hebrew spoken in Jerusalem at the time: "Most of the [DSS] were copied in the Herodian era when Hebrew was still spoken. [They reflect] the language of the Capital in the late Second Temple period. ... The Hebrew of the DSS is a Hebrew idiom of the Second Temple period from Jerusalem or its vicinity. It records the spoken language of that time" (Qimron, *Grammar of the Hebrew*, 33).

17. Other scholars follow Qimron's assessment; see, e.g., Steven E. Fassberg, "Dead Sea Scrolls: Linguistic Features," in *Encyclopedia of Hebrew Language and Linguistics*, ed. Geoffrey Khan et al., vol. 1 (Leiden: Brill, 2013), 667. Elsewhere, however, Fassberg is more nuanced: "In the Dead Sea Scrolls, [numeral-noun] order is dominant, though there are exceptions." See Fassberg, "Shifts in Word Order in the Hebrew of the Second Temple Period," in *Hebrew in the Second Temple Period: The Hebrew of*

are curious about a point of grammar in the DSS. Reference grammars often do not have space for more than a few sentences on specific issues, and as such this paragraph is easily read as a strong statement that DSS Hebrew uses noun-number order.

In his 1998 overview of Hebrew in the DSS, Abegg writes, "By far the most common use of the numbers 3–10 is in apposition before the substantives they modify."[18] Because Abegg follows an organizational scheme for numerals common to reference grammars,[19] however, readers are liable to miss the importance of the five words "before the substantives they modify," given that the section on numerals 3–10 is but one of seven sections on numerals. Several of these sections do not comment on order, and others state that either number-noun or noun-number order is possible. Abegg's portrayal is accurate but does not mitigate the impact and influence of Qimron's voice on the particular issue of order in number phrases.

There are important changes to Qimron's first paragraph in his 2018 grammar. Qimron no longer refers to noun-number order as "a real Qumranic feature," instead saying that this order is "occasionally attested" in the DSS.[20] The removal of this phrase and its juxtaposition with number-noun order in other DSS also mitigates the insinuation that noun-number order belongs to a nonliterary style of Hebrew associated with the DSS. Together with the more cautious phrase "occasionally attested," the following descriptive statement can be interpreted as softening the claim for distinct numeral syntax in the DSS: "Note that in literary Mishnaic Hebrew and thereafter the classical order predominates."[21] Nevertheless, the 2018 grammar retains the notion that noun-number order distinguishes DSS Hebrew: "The word order *noun-numeral* ... characterizes late Hebrew."[22]

---

the Dead Sea Scrolls and of Other Contemporary Sources, ed. Steven E. Fassberg, Moshe Bar-Asher, and Ruth A. Clements, STDJ 108 (Leiden: Brill, 2013), 63.

18. Abegg, "Hebrew of the Dead Sea Scrolls," 354.

19. See Screnock, "Syntax of Cardinal Numerals," 128 n. 9.

20. Qimron, *Grammar of the Hebrew*, 440; compare Qimron, *Hebrew of the Dead Sea Scrolls*, 85.

21. Qimron, *Grammar of the Hebrew*, 440; compare Qimron, *Hebrew of the Dead Sea Scrolls*, 85.

22. Qimron, *Grammar of the Hebrew*, 441; Qimron, *Hebrew of the Dead Sea Scrolls*, 86. By *late Hebrew*, Qimron does not mean Late Biblical Hebrew, given that

After his discussion of order in number phrases generally, Qimron moves to phrases involving "the kind of measure e.g. אורך ['length']."[23] From this point onward, the 1986 and 2018 versions do not differ in substance. Qimron again situates DSS Hebrew in the context of classical and postexilic Hebrew in the Hebrew Bible: classical texts have the "kind of measure" word after the number, while postexilic texts introduce a "late construction," with the word preceding the number.[24] Three examples and two further references from the DSS follow. Qimron groups the order of this type of phrase with noun-number order in number phrases and calls this order "character[istic of] late Hebrew."[25]

The section on numerals concludes by mentioning the debate over Qimron's initial premise—that Classical Biblical Hebrew uses number-noun order, but Late Biblical Hebrew shifts to noun-number order. "Scholars are divided as to whether this phenomenon is late, since it is frequent in lists and administrative documents."[26] This caveat does not, however, apply to the DSS and specifically the examples he has mustered, since they "are not restricted to lists or administrative documents"[27]— an important point I will challenge below. Because noun-number order occurs "almost exclusive[ly in] post-exilic Hebrew and Aramaic," for Qimron this feature of DSS Hebrew is clearly a late feature.[28]

---

he goes on to cite the Copper Scroll (3Q15) and Bar Kokhba with the logical connector "thus."

23. Qimron, *Grammar of the Hebrew*, 440; Qimron, *Hebrew of the Dead Sea Scrolls*, 85.

24. Qimron, *Grammar of the Hebrew*, 440–41; Qimron, *Hebrew of the Dead Sea Scrolls*, 85.

25. See above. In contrast, Fassberg distinguishes between the word order of number phrases and the order of these other phrases ("Shifts in Word Order," 63–65).

26. Qimron, *Grammar of the Hebrew*, 441; Qimron, *Hebrew of the Dead Sea Scrolls*, 86. Indeed, it seems to me that in 2018 there is no longer a debate: scholars agree that the order *noun-number*, though abnormal, is used in many texts both early and late, *within lists*. See Steven Weitzman, "The Shifting Syntax of Numerals in Biblical Hebrew: A Reassessment," *JNES* 55 (1996): 177–85, esp. 179–81. However, Fassberg states, "Most scholars believe that this shift in [the order of number phrases] reflects a diachronic development," citing studies from 1909, 1971, and 1976 ("Shifts in Word Order," 64).

27. Qimron, *Grammar of the Hebrew*, 442; Qimron, *Hebrew of the Dead Sea Scrolls*, 86.

28. Qimron, *Grammar of the Hebrew*, 442; Qimron, *Hebrew of the Dead Sea Scrolls*, 86.

## 2. Historical Linguistics

When we follow principles established in historical linguistics, a different interpretation of the data in the DSS emerges.[29] In this section, I briefly outline the principles that are relevant to the issue of numeral syntax in the DSS.[30]

A variety of factors can result in linguistic variation, only one of which is diachronic development. When I teach, I often have students from various parts of the United States, the United Kingdom, and British Commonwealth countries—all native English speakers. Though we clearly exist in the same location at the same time, there is language variation between us. So linguistic variation is not always diachronic in nature. On the other hand, if an English speaker were to travel back in time one hundred years, there would be differences between their English and the English used by people in the same region. So diachronic development is an excellent candidate for explaining language variation. David Crystal divides potential causes for variation into two types: those the speaker can control and those she cannot control.[31] Controllable features are what are referred to as stylistics, the features that a speaker/writer uses to serve the particular purposes of language use—for example, specialist language (e.g., scientific or medical), formal versus informal language, and written versus spoken language.[32] Uncontrollable features are not

---

29. Many Hebraists draw explicitly on historical linguistics. See, e.g., Jacobus A. Naudé, "The Transitions of Biblical Hebrew in the Perspective of Language Change and Diffusion," in *Biblical Hebrew: Studies in Chronology and Typology*, ed. Ian Young (London: T&T Clark, 2003), 189–214; John A. Cook, "Detecting Development in Biblical Hebrew Using Diachronic Typology," in *Diachrony in Biblical Hebrew*, ed. Cynthia L. Miller-Naudé and Ziony Zevit (Winona Lake, IN: Eisenbrauns, 2012), 83–95; B. Elan Dresher, "Methodological Issues in the Dating of Linguistic Forms: Considerations from the Perspective of Contemporary Linguistic Theory," in Miller-Naudé and Zevit, *Diachrony in Biblical Hebrew*, 19–38; Robert D. Holmstedt, "Investigating the Possible Verb-Subject to Subject-Verb Shift in Ancient Hebrew: Methodological First Steps," *KUSATU* 15 (2013): 3–31; John Screnock and Robert D. Holmstedt, *Esther* (Waco, TX: Baylor University Press, 2015), 17–32; Screnock, "Complex Adding Numerals and Hebrew Diachrony," *JBL* 137 (2018): 789–819.

30. See Screnock, "Complex Adding Numerals," 792–93.

31. David Crystal, "New Perspectives for Language Study. 1: Stylistics," *ELT* 24 (1970): 103.

32. Crystal, "New Perspectives," 99; for his full typology see 103–5. See also David

truly uncontrollable to the language user—insofar as one can always imitate another manner of speaking—but have to do with how one normally would speak or one's native way of speaking.[33] These belong to three categories, each constrained by a different type of boundary within which the speaker is located: dialect (constrained by geographic location), register (constrained by social class), and diachrony (constrained by temporal location).[34]

Controllable and uncontrollable features intersect at many points; for example, lower-class dialects are often associated with informal language, and dialect and diachrony can be used as stylistic features (e.g., in style switching and classicism, respectively). Diachronic development is often involved when we find two or more forms of a single language coexisting synchronically.[35] Explaining language variation by appealing to stylistics, dialect, or register, then, must take into account the relationship of these three to diachrony and situate the use of stylistics, and so on, vis-à-vis diachrony.[36]

In order to chart diachronic change with any degree of certainty, the amount of data in use must be statistically significant.[37] A handful of cases in a given text is not enough evidence from which to draw conclusions; the issue here is not the total number of occurrences of a given feature but the total number of occurrences in individual texts. If a text contains only a few instances of a feature, we unfortunately cannot use that text for diachronic analysis of the feature.

Diachronic change occurs in a more-or-less predictable way, with individual aspects of a language changing gradually over time. The

---

Crystal, "Style: The Varieties of English," in *The English Language*, ed. Whitney F. Bolton and David Crystal (London: Sphere Books, 1988), 207–9.

33. As Crystal notes, "Most people normally do not talk as if they were from a different area, class or time from the one to which they actually belong" ("Style," 206).

34. See Crystal, "New Perspectives," 103; Crystal, "Style," 203–6.

35. See Aaron Hornkohl, *Ancient Hebrew Periodization and the Language of the Book of Jeremiah: The Case for a Sixth-Century Date of Composition*, SSLL 74 (Leiden: Brill, 2014), 22. I argue, for example, that an appeal to dialect or register (specifically, language of the P source) to explain variation in the order of adding numerals must necessarily involve diachrony (Screnock, "Complex Adding Numerals," 815).

36. See Crystal on situating stylistic analysis in the context of normal language use ("New Perspectives," 99–100).

37. Screnock and Holmstedt, *Esther*, 23; Screnock, "Complex Adding Numerals," 792–93.

change from מַמְלָכָה to מַלְכוּת,³⁸ for example, did not happen immediately, with one generation suddenly preferring the latter. Rather, historical linguists argue for a process of change and gradual diffusion. Initially, the old feature is the only option; if a language user innovates a new feature and other people start to use the new feature, it may then increasingly gain in popularity; eventually, the new feature all but replaces the old feature, though the old feature often continues to be used sparsely.³⁹ The existence of an early feature does not make a text early, since early features often hang around at the end of this process of change; similarly, a late feature does not make a text late, since the use of a new feature starts relatively early in the process of diffusion. There are three distinct phases in the process: old-feature dominance, mixed use, and new-feature dominance.⁴⁰ Since languages are made up of individual features, which change gradually, it follows that languages change gradually over time as well. The way in which this happens, however, does not mirror the way in which individual features develop; a language as it exists on the ground, among everyday people, does not shift from old-temporal dialect to new-temporal dialect with a transition stage in between. Languages

---

38. Dresher, "Methodological Issues," 33–35.

39. Walt Wolfram and Natalie Schilling-Estes, "Dialectology and Linguistic Diffusion," in *The Handbook of Historical Linguistics*, ed. Brian D. Joseph and Richard D. Janda (London: Blackwell, 2003), 713–35; Mark Hale, *Historical Linguistics: Theory and Method* (Malden, MA: Blackwell, 2007), 27–47; Naudé, "Transitions of Biblical Hebrew," esp. 199–200; Jacobus A. Naudé, "Diachrony in Biblical Hebrew and a Theory of Language Change and Diffusion," in Miller-Naudé and Zevit, *Diachrony in Biblical Hebrew*, 61–81; Screnock and Holmstedt, *Esther*, 21.

40. Some historical linguists note that the process of diffusion, when plotted as a $y$ value along an $x$-axis of time, can be approximated by a Sigmoid curve. See Charles Bailey, *Variation and Linguistic Theory* (Arlington, VA: Center for Applied Linguistics, 1973), 77; see also Naudé, "Transitions of Biblical Hebrew," 200; Robert D. Holmstedt, "Historical Linguistics and Biblical Hebrew," in Miller-Naudé and Zevit, *Diachrony in Biblical Hebrew*, 102–3; Holmstedt, "Investigating the Possible Verb-Subject to Subject-Verb Shift," 12–13; Robert Rezetko and Ian Young, *Historical Linguistics and Biblical Hebrew: Steps toward an Integrated Approach*, ANEM 9 (Atlanta: SBL Press, 2014), 223–25. Sometimes, features enter a language for a time only to fall out of favor, never replacing the old feature—i.e., the process resembles a bell curve instead of an S-curve. See Dean Forbes, "Two Candidate Approaches to Text Sequencing: An Addendum to 'The Diachrony Debate: A Tutorial on Methods,'" *JSem* 26 (2017): 710–16. Texts with a clear *terminus ad quem* and/or *terminus post quem* are thus important for suggesting or eliminating the possibility of a bell curve.

are made up of hundreds of changing features, none of which develop at exactly the same rate.⁴¹

Three points from the preceding summary are particularly salient for our analysis of the order of number phrases. First, if a language has acquired a new feature, the new feature remains; it does not disappear suddenly and the language revert to the old feature. Second, explanations of linguistic variation that appeal to style, dialect, and register must take diachronic change into account. Third, as most Hebraists now recognize, a few occurrences of a unique feature do not constitute language change or entail that the unique feature is characteristic of the text or corpus in which it is found.

## 3. The Order of Number Phrases in the Dead Sea Scrolls

Qimron's discussion of order in number phrases includes references to fewer than twenty cases. What does the situation look like when we cast our net more broadly and consider all the evidence in the DSS? In this section, I present the data more fully and interpret it according to the principles of historical linguistics.

The definition of our corpus is crucial. For this study, I began by including every DSS witness with ten or more tokens. A token is an instance where the order of a number phrase can be discerned. Some scrolls with more than ten tokens, however, are unfortunately unusable for one reason or another. I do not include the Temple Scroll (11Q19), 4Q252, and 4Q365, which make significant use of earlier texts, weaving them together in a way that makes it difficult to discern where the language of the earlier text ends and the language of the scroll begins.⁴² A number of texts contain numerals without overt nouns—for example, 4Q317 fragment 1+1a ii:12, בעשרה בו ("on the tenth [day] in it [= the month]"), or 4Q365 fragment 2 ii:2, ששים באמה ("sixty in cubits")—in which case it is impossible to determine the order of the number phrase.⁴³ In the former example, if the

---

41. Holmstedt, "Historical Linguistics and Biblical Hebrew," 101–4.
42. See Screnock, "Complex Adding Numerals," 794; and see Qimron's remarks on biblical manuscripts in the DSS (*Grammar of the Hebrew*, 50–51). On the character of the Temple Scroll, for example, see Dwight D. Swanson, *The Temple Scroll and the Bible: The Methodology of 11QT*, STDJ 14 (Leiden: Brill, 1995).
43. Texts that do not have enough tokens after cases with covert nouns are eliminated include 4Q317, 4Q321, 4Q321a, 4Q325, 4Q365a, and 4Q394. Regarding the example from 4Q317, the dating formula with בו is diachronically significant but falls

noun were overt—ביום עשרה בו or יוֹם בו or בעשרת יוֹם—the example would fall into the unique category where a cardinal is used as an ordinal. In such cases, the order noun-number is not at all unusual, reflecting the adjectival syntax of ordinal numbers, which follow the noun they modify.[44] I therefore do not include 4Q321, which contains ten cases of cardinals used as ordinals[45]—for example, 4Q321 1:4, בעשתי עשר החודש ("on the eleventh month")—but which otherwise contains very few number phrases with overt nouns. Similarly, I do not include cases of אחד, which takes adjectival syntax.[46] Finally, several texts with high amounts of numerals cannot be included because they are too fragmentary; after eliminating cases where lacunae prohibit the determination of order, these texts contain very few or no tokens.[47]

Given the general lack of usable evidence, I have included all texts with *close to* ten tokens: CD, 1QS, 1QS[a], 1QM, 3Q15, 4Q265, 4Q266, 4Q403, 4Q405, and the account of David's compositions in 11Q5 27.[48] In

---

outside the scope of this study. See Ronald Bergey, "Late Linguistic Features in Esther," *JQR* 75 (1984): 72; Screnock and Holmstedt, *Esther*, 130–31. Regarding the example from 4Q365, while semantically equivalent to ששים אמה ("sixty cubits"), syntactically the two phrases are not equivalent; the syntax of ששים באמה is reflected in the fuller translation "[the value] sixty in [terms of the measure of the] cubit."

44. Joüon, §142o.

45. All of 4Q321's ordinal-use cardinals use the number-noun order characteristic of cardinals, rather than the noun-number order characteristic of ordinals; they would not, therefore, complicate my analysis if included.

46. See Screnock, "Syntax of Cardinal Numerals," 128–29; Moshavi and Rothstein, "Indefinite Numerical Construct Phrases," 104 n. 15.

47. After eliminating evidence because of these factors, the texts with ten or more numerals that I do not include are as follows: Temple Scroll, 4Q159, 4Q252, 4Q270, 4Q317, 4Q320, 4Q321, 4Q321a, 4Q324d, 4Q325, 4Q334, 4Q364, 4Q365, 4Q365a, 4Q385, 4Q394, 4Q491, 4Q496, and 4Q503.

48. Within these texts, I of course exclude individual points of evidence for the same reasons as above: quotes of earlier texts (e.g., CD 19:2 quotes Deut 7:9), cases where the noun is not overt, or places that are too fragmentary. 4Q265 has nine tokens, 1QS[a] has six, and 11Q5 has five. I include 11Q5 in particular because it has evidence that complicates my analysis. According to the reconstruction of 4Q334 frag. 2–4, there are several places with noun-number, but the text is far too fragmentary to know whether these reconstructions are correct; notably, the reconstructed text is clearly a list, explaining the use of noun-number order if the reconstruction is correct. For the reconstruction, see Shemaryahu Talmon, Jonathan Ben-Dov, and Uwe Glessmer, *Qumran Cave 4.XVI: Calendrical Texts*, DJD XXI (Oxford: Clarendon, 2001), 175.

the evidence from the Songs of the Sabbath Sacrifice (4Q403 and 4Q405), the phrases "seven words of wonder" and similar phrases are used repeatedly. This does not, however, entail that each token should not be given full weight as evidence. To the contrary, each time such a phrase is used there is the potential for alteration of syntax. There is considerable variability, in fact, in the structure and even gender agreement of these phrases. Each case, therefore, counts as one token of evidence, even if it is identical to other cases.

My use of CD deserves additional discussion, given Qimron's comments about the evidence in medieval CD manuscripts. Qimron suggests that the Cairo Genizah manuscripts were "distorted by the copyists of the Medieval age and thus [do] not reflect the DSS language, especially in its phonology and morphology."[49] As such, Qimron states explicitly, in the introductions to his 1986 and 2018 grammars, that he has not included evidence from Cairo Genizah CD in his study.[50] Yet, in his analysis of numeral syntax, he clearly *has* included this evidence. The four cases he cites in 1986 are noted only as CD, giving column and line numbers from Cairo Genizah manuscripts A and B.[51] In 2018, he notes that two of the four cases are supported by extant evidence in the DSS.[52] Though the medieval scribes may have rendered the earlier language of CD inaccessible in terms of phonology and morphology, it seems that Qimron tacitly endorses the use of manuscripts A and B as evidence for the syntax of the DSS. In my analysis of CD, I began by analyzing Cairo Genizah manuscripts A and B, which contain a sufficient number of tokens for evaluation. I cross-checked all of these tokens against the manuscripts of CD in the DSS. Because the DSS manuscripts are quite fragmentary, working backward from the medieval material in this manner makes sense. 4Q266 (4QD^a) is listed as a separate entry in my data because it contains ten usable tokens of evidence that are not extant in Cairo Genizah manuscripts A and B.

---

49. Qimron, *Grammar of the Hebrew*, 50; see also Qimron, *Hebrew of the Dead Sea Scrolls*, 15.

50. Qimron, *Grammar of the Hebrew*, 50; see also Qimron, *Hebrew of the Dead Sea Scrolls*, 15.

51. Qimron, *Hebrew of the Dead Sea Scrolls*, 85.

52. Qimron, *Grammar of the Hebrew*, 440.

## 3.1. The Data

In light of Qimron's portrayal of numeral syntax, the data from my corpus are surprising.

> Number-noun order: **CD** 4:15, 16–17, 21; 7:6, 12; 9:22–23^; 10:4^, 6^, 6–7^, 7^, 8^; 12:5; 13:1; 14:7^, 9^twice, 13; 19:1, 2; 20:22; **1QS** 3:18; 7:3, 4, 5, 6, 8twice, 9, 10, 11, 12twice, 13, 14, 14–15, 18, 19, 22; 8:1; **1QS**a 1:8twice, 10, 12, 13, 26; **1QM** 1:13; 2:4, 6, 9twice, 13, 14; 3:14twice; 4:5, 15twice, 16twice, 17; 5:1, 2, 3twice, 7twice, 12, 13thrice, 14, 16; 6:1twice, 2, 4thrice, 8, 8–9, 9twice, 10, 14twice; 7:1twice, 2, 3, 9–10, 14thrice, 15twice, 16, 18; 8:1–2, 4, 6, 8–9, 13, 14; 9:4twice, 4–5, 11, 12twice, 13twice; 11:8–9; 16:7; **3Q15** 4:8*; 7:5*; **4Q265** frag. 4 i:4, 6, 9, 11, 12; ii:2; frag. 7 ln. 5, 6, 15; **4Q266** frag. 6 ii:3; frag. 10 ii:1, 3, 3–4, 4, 6twice, 7, 8, 13; **4Q403** frag. 1 i:1, 2, 3, 4, 5, 11, 12, 13, 16, 19, 20, 21–22, 22, 23, 24, 25; ii:11, 21, 22, 27; **4Q405** frag. 3 ii:2, 4, 5, 8, 13, 16; frag. 8–9 ln. 5; frag. 13 ln. 3, 4twice, 5; frag 15ii–16 ln. 5; frag. 20ii–22 ln. 6; frag. 64–67 ln. 2, 3; **11Q5** 27:7*, 8*
>
> Noun-number order: **CD** 1:5–6^, 10^; 14:21!; 20:15; **1QS** 8:1; **1QM** 2:1, 2; **3Q15** throughout*; **11Q5** 27:4–5*, 5–7*; 9–10*

References followed by an asterisk (*) indicate number phrases that are used in lists. CD references followed by a caret (^) indicate where DSS fragments clearly support the evidence in Cairo Genizah manuscripts A and B; CD 14:21 is marked by ! because its parallel in 4Q266 contains opposing evidence (see section 3.2.4).[53] There are five further cases that I have not included but that possibly contain number-noun order: in CD 14:4, 6; and 19:1, the interpretation is unclear; in 4Q403 fragment 1 i:20, 26, slight lacunae prevent certainty. An additional case in 1QM 2:1 (אבות העדה שנים וחמשים, "fifty-two [?] fathers of the congregation"?) likely reflects noun-

---

53. The parallels are as follows: CD 1:4–5 (4Q266 frag. 2 i:10 and 4Q268 frag. 1 l. 13), 10 (4Q266 frag. 2 i:13); 9:22–23 (4Q270 frag. 6 iv:12); 10:4 (4Q270 frag 6 iv:16), 6 (4Q266 frag. 8 iii:6), 6–7 (4Q266 frag. 8 iii:6 and 4Q270 frag. 6 iv:17), 7 (4Q270 frag. 6 iv:17), 8 (4Q270 frag. 6 iv:18); 14:7 (4Q267 frag. 9 v:11), 9 (4Q266 frag. 10 i:2 and 4Q267 frag. 9 v:13–14), 21 (4Q266 frag. 10 ii:1). Of the twenty cases of number-noun order in CD, nine are present in Cave 4 fragments; of the four cases of noun-number order, two are present in Cave 4 fragments, while another is present but takes number-noun order.

number order; given the lack of context (the last line of col. I is not extant) we cannot be certain, but it is reasonable to think it patterns with the following two number phrases in 2:1–2, taking noun-number order. Finally, two number phrases with noun-number order that I include from 11Q5 27:5–7 and 9–10 are debatable (see section 3.2.1).

When we set the tallies for each text side by side, a fairly clear picture of the situation in the DSS comes into view.[54]

|  | Normal/unmarked order: number—noun | Abnormal/marked order: noun—number |
| --- | --- | --- |
| CD | 20–23 | 4 |
| 1QS | 19 | 1 |
| 1QSª | 6 | 0 |
| 1QM | 68 | 2–3 |
| 3Q15 | 2 | approx. 70+ |
| 4Q265 | 9 | 0 |
| 4Q266 | 10[52] | 0 |
| 4Q403 | 20–22 | 0 |
| 4Q405 | 15 | 0 |
| 11Q5 27 | 2 | 1–3 |

Of all of the texts for which we have enough data to determine a preferred order for number phrases, only the Copper Scroll (3Q15) contains a significant amount of noun-number tokens. Eight other texts with adequate data exhibit a preference for number-noun order, while the five tokens from 11Q5 27 are split.

3.2. Interpreting the Data

The Copper Scroll, our one text that overwhelmingly prefers noun-number order, is anomalous linguistically in the context of the rest of the DSS.[55]

---

54. These two figures include only the number phrases in 4Q266 that are not found in Cairo Genizah manuscripts A and B.
55. See Qimron, *Grammar of the Hebrew*, 50 n. 25: "The language of this scroll differs so markedly from the language of the other scrolls that it should be treated

More importantly, like the cases of noun-number order in 11Q5, the Copper Scroll's number phrases all occur within a list. As Qimron notes, the order noun-number is often used in lists.[56] Indeed, the earlier argument for an increased use of noun-number order in Late Biblical Hebrew is faulty because it *excluded* data from lists in the classical corpus but *included* data from lists in the late corpus.[57] Texts from various times—early and late—used noun-number order in lists; in other words, this is a *synchronic* language variation, not diachronic development. There are many examples of noun-number order from lists in classical texts:

3. Josh 15:41, עָרִים שֵׁשׁ־עֶשְׂרֵה, "sixteen cities"
4. Num 7:84, מִזְרְקֵי־כֶסֶף שְׁנֵים עָשָׂר, "twelve bowls of silver"

This synchronic variation is about stylistics. The order noun-number appears to be used in particular contexts as part of a set of genre features associated with lists. As such, the evidence from the Copper Scroll—which is essentially a long list of treasures and their locations—does not indicate any historical development to the language. Rather, it participates in a well-known, *marked* use of noun-number order. Similarly, the passage in 11Q5 27 is a list at the point where up to three cases of noun-number order occur. Leaving aside the data from the Copper Scroll and 11Q5 27, we find that the texts that are stylistically neutral contain few cases of noun-number order.

Having accounted for data in the Copper Scroll's and 11Q5 27, interpreting the remainder of the data is relatively straightforward. Here I set aside the few remaining cases of noun-number order—but I will return to them below (sections 3.2.1–3.2.4), after sketching a general interpretation of the data. The argument for increased use of noun-number order in Late Biblical Hebrew fails, and there is no trajectory of change based on the data from the Hebrew Bible. In ancient Hebrew before the DSS, the normal/

---

separately." To give just two examples, masculine plurals end in ־ין, and complex teen numerals often exhibit phonetic elision—e.g., 3Q15 1:4, שבעשרה ("seventeen," i.e., שבע עשרה; see also 2:8; 11:10; and compare 8:5–6, where the two *ayin*s remain distinct because of a line break), and 9:2, שלושרא ("thirteen," i.e., שלוש עשרה).

56. Qimron, *Grammar of the Hebrew*, 441–42; Qimron, *Hebrew of the Dead Sea Scrolls*, 86.

57. See Gary Rendsburg, "Late Biblical Hebrew and the Date of P," *JANES* 12 (1980): 71; Weitzman, "Shifting Syntax of Numerals," 179.

unmarked order of number phrases is number-noun.[58] Significantly, the Hebrew used in the Mishnah overwhelmingly favors the same order, number-noun.[59] Recalling the principles of historical linguistics outlined in section 2, when diachronic change occurs the new feature that has replaced the old continues to be used. That the Hebrew in the Mishnah does not use noun-number order suggests very strongly that no diachronic development ever took place. When we add to this contextual evidence from before and after the DSS, the limited distribution of noun-number order in the DSS makes sense. The simplest way to reconstruct the historical development of number phrase order from the classical texts to the Mishnah is that *there was no development*. An argument in favor of dialect or idiolect causing variation here[60] would be similarly unnecessary: given the paucity of noun-number order in the DSS, the simplest explanation of our data is that ancient Hebrew at all times used number-noun order, with marked noun-number order reserved for stylistic variation.

A full consideration of the data within a historical linguistic framework shows that Qimron's account of numeral syntax is inadequate. His argument that the DSS show a growing trend of noun-number order in later Hebrew lacks in two ways. First, it does not fit the expected pattern of diachronic language development: number-noun order is normal and unmarked in the language of texts earlier and later than the DSS (esp. the Hebrew Bible and the Mishnah), making it highly unlikely that noun-number order was normal and unmarked in the intervening period. If one were to argue that a specific idiolect, style, or dialect is in play,[61] I

---

58. Screnock, "Syntax of Cardinal Numerals," 132–33.

59. Moses H. Segal, *A Grammar of Mishnaic Hebrew* (Oxford: Clarendon, 1927), §394; so Qimron, *Grammar of the Hebrew*, 440; Qimron, *Hebrew of the Dead Sea Scrolls*, 85; Fassberg, "Shifts in Word Order," 64.

60. As is perhaps suggested in Qimron, *Hebrew of the Dead Sea Scrolls*, 85; see in section 1 above. One might respond that most of the DSS and the Mishnah reflect a literary register of Hebrew, which retained earlier features of the language in spite of diachronic change in the spoken language. For the particular linguistic element in question, however, we cannot posit a classicism without first establishing a diachronic development (see section 2 above)! Moreover, texts of the Hebrew Bible are just as likely to be using (a) literary register(s), and given other linguistic changes evidenced in the Mishnah we *would* expect its language to reflect vernacular features in use in the preceding period (i.e., the time of the DSS).

61. As is perhaps hinted at in Qimron, *Hebrew of the Dead Sea Scrolls*, 85; see section 1 above.

would counter that arguing for such synchronic variety requires contextualization in normal language use, including the relationship of idiolect, and so on, to Hebrew's diachronic progression (see section 2). Given the shape of the actual data (see the next point), there is no need to appeal to style, dialect, or idiolect to explain the language of the DSS; it simply uses normal language in this particular area (numeral syntax), language we would expect. Second, it does not fit the actual data when considered fully. Overwhelmingly, the DSS themselves prefer number-noun order. Granted, Qimron notes that most DSS prefer number-noun order. However, in the case of his star witness[62]—CD, where Qimron finds the most examples (four) of noun-number order—missing in Qimron's discussion is the fact that CD itself prefers number-noun order and that one of the four noun-number cases is problematic (see section 3.2.4). Especially in the 1986 version of the grammar, but remaining to an extent in 2018, Qimron contravenes his principle of "[ignoring] isolated features in favor of systematic phenomena."[63]

In no way do I mean to devalue Qimron's work as a whole. Given the scope of his task—tracking hundreds of linguistic features in the DSS—no one can reasonably expect his grammar to be perfect in every way. Instead, my point is to caution us in how we use past scholarship, especially authoritative works such as Qimron's grammar. His work is (rightly) foundational to most linguistic study of the DSS. Yet, like all past scholarship, it must be continually questioned and reworked.

### 3.2.1. Alternative Interpretations of Aberrant Cases

Returning now to the seven cases of noun-number in the DSS outside lists, it is important to note that cases of (what appears to be) noun-number order are found outside lists in older texts as well, as in the following examples from the classical corpus.

5. 1 Kgs 7:3, עַל־הָעַמּוּדִים אַרְבָּעִים וַחֲמִשָּׁה, "upon forty-five columns"
6. Gen 49:28, שִׁבְטֵי יִשְׂרָאֵל שְׁנֵים עָשָׂר, "the twelve tribes of Israel"

---

62. Note that according to Qimron in *Hebrew of the Dead Sea Scrolls*, CD preserves the "real Qumran feature" in contrast to other DSS (85).

63. Qimron, *Hebrew of the Dead Sea Scrolls*, 15.

To begin with, we may be wrong to interpret many of these cases as single number phrases. In all the cases of noun-number order, it is not difficult to take an alternative interpretation, understanding two appositional phrases instead of a single number phrase, and resulting in a more stuttering or punctual style, as in these representative examples:

7. 1QM 2:2, ראשי המשמרות ששה ועשרים במשמרותם ישרתו, "The chiefs of the courses, twenty-six, shall serve in their courses" (WAC)
8. 1QS 8:1, בעצת היחד שנים עשר איש וכוהנים שלושה תמימים בכול הנגלה, "In the council of the Yaḥad [there should be] twelve men, and [there should be] priests, three [of them], blameless in all that is revealed"

Even in CD's four cases, all of which are temporal adjuncts to the verb, we could understand two individual phrases. Consider a contrasting example from Gen 7:4.

9. Gen 7:4, לְיָמִים עוֹד שִׁבְעָה, "for days, still/more, seven"
10. CD 20:15, בשנים ארבעים, "according to years, forty" (?)

In Gen 7:4, the translation "for seven more days" is better English, but does not reflect the Hebrew syntax, where the adverb עוֹד ("yet, still, more") splits the noun and numeral.

Though such interpretations are possible, they are not always convincing, and to dismiss all of the noun-number cases through this possibility might amount to special pleading. I therefore suggest below other possible synchronic explanations for the abnormal data.

3.2.2. List Style

Given a number of examples from the DSS and Hebrew Bible, I wonder whether the noun-number order often used in lists derives from the general staccato syntax of lists, where apposition is used generously. In other words, the basis of single number phrases with noun-number order is something more complex, consisting of at least two phrases. In examples 11 and 12, it is clear that we do not have a single number phrase; example 13 is therefore best read in a similar way, but in another context could be taken as a single number phrase.

11. Ezra 2:58, כָּל־הַנְּתִינִים וּבְנֵי עַבְדֵי שְׁלֹמֹה שְׁלֹשׁ מֵאוֹת תִּשְׁעִים וּשְׁנָיִם, "all the temple servants and sons of the servants of Solomon: three hundred and ninety-two"
12. Ezra 2:6, בְּנֵי־פַחַת מוֹאָב לִבְנֵי יֵשׁוּעַ יוֹאָב אַלְפַּיִם שְׁמֹנֶה מֵאוֹת וּשְׁנֵים עָשָׂר, "the sons of Paḥat-Moab, that is, the sons of Yeshua and Yoab: two thousand, eight hundred and twelve"
13. Ezra 2:5, בְּנֵי אָרַח שְׁבַע מֵאוֹת חֲמִשָּׁה וְשִׁבְעִים, "seven hundred and seventy-five sons of Araḥ" or "the sons of Araḥ: seven hundred and seventy-five"

Phrases such as ככרין שבעין ("seventy talents") in example 14 are single number phrases, but they developed from the staccato appositional syntax "talents, seventy."

14. 3Q15 2:6, בור ב]ו [כלין וכסף ככרין שבעין, "[in] a pit in it: vessels and silver, seventy talents"

The point is that list stylistics involve two features that affect our interpretation of the data. In addition to noun-number order being used frequently in lists (discussed above), the underlying appositional syntax of lists can result in placement of numerals alongside nouns that is liable to misinterpretation as a single number phrase.

The numerals in 11Q5 27 present an excellent example. There, the best interpretation of the text is one in which list style is used, resulting in numerals and nouns in apposition, *not* as single number phrases. This interpretation is not necessarily prompted by the abnormality of noun-number order, but by the general difficulty of understanding single number phrases here—in other words, this is not special pleading. If these are truly number phrases, the numeral and the preceding noun quantified by it are separated by noun-phrase internal prepositional phrases:

15. 11Q5 5–7, שיר לשורר לפני המזבח על עולת התמיד לכול יום ויום לכול ימי השנה ארבעה וששים ושלוש מאות, "three hundred and sixty-four songs to sing before the altar accompanying the daily perpetual burnt offering for all the days of the year" (translation based on WAC)
16. 11Q5 27:9–10, שיר לנגן על הפגועים ארבעה, "four songs for charming the demon-possessed with music" (WAC)

In the first case, 11Q5 27:5–7, the internal prepositional phrase is very long—twelve words. Is it reasonable to interpret each of these excerpts as a single noun phrases? Consider the English translations approximating this syntax: "four for-charming-the-possessed songs" (27:9–10), and "364 to-sing-before-the-altar-accompanying-the-perpetual-offering-for-every-day-for-all-the-days-of-the-year songs" (5–7). The first is awkward but processable; the second is not, and therefore should not be interpreted as a single noun phrase.

These difficulties, together with contextual sensitivity to the entire passage, suggest an interpretation of the passage with staccato list stylistics. The translation by Michael Wise, Martin Abegg, and Edward Cook (WAC) is instructive.

17. 11Q5 27:4–10, ויכתוב תהלים שלושת אלפים ושש מאות ושיר לשורר לפני
המזבח על עולת התמיד לכול יום ויום לכול ימי השנה ארבעה וששים ושלוש
מאות ולקורבן השבתות שנים וחמשים שיר ולקורבן ראשי החודשים ולכול ימי
המועדות ולים הכפורים שלושים שיר ויהי כול השיר אשר דבר ששה ואבעים
וארבע מאות ושיר לנגן על הפגועים ארבעה ויהי הכול ארבעת אלפים וחמשים

> He wrote: psalms, three thousand six hundred; songs to sing before the altar accompanying the daily perpetual burnt offering for all the days of the year, three hundred and sixty-four; for the Sabbath offerings, fifty-two songs; and for the new moon offerings, all the festival days, and the Day of Atonement, thirty songs. The total of all the songs that he composed was four hundred and forty-six, not including four songs for charming the demon-possessed with music. The sum total of everything, psalms and songs, was four thousand and fifty. (WAC)

The WAC translation of the passage itself anticipates some of the difficulties, as well as contextual sensitivity to the punctual style of a list. WAC renders the first and second potential number phrases as two noun phrases in apposition ("psalms, three thousand six hundred" and "songs ... for all the days of the year, three hundred and sixty-four"), the third and fourth potential number phrases (with number-noun order!) as number phrases ("fifty-two songs"), and the sixth potential number phrase (the fifth and seventh number phrases are predicate complements and thus do not belong syntactically with an overt noun) as a number phrase ("four songs"). Of the three potential cases with noun-number order, WAC only takes the last as a number phrase. I suggest that it, too, should be interpreted with punctual, list syntax: שיר לנגן על הפגועים ארבעה, "as for the שיר whose purpose is to play music for those who encountered evil: [there are] four."

We could understand the two cases of noun-number order in 1QM similarly. Both fall within the second column, where full predications are used but the text is easily interpreted as having list syntax at points—like 11Q5 27. Here, however, I suggest that the numerals and nouns in question are indeed single number phrases and that they take noun-number order in accordance with list stylistics.

18. 1QM 2:1–3, ואת ראשי הכוהנים יסרוכו אחר כוהן הראש ומשנהו <u>ראשים</u> <u>שנים עשר</u> להיות משרתים בתמיד לפני אל <u>וראשי המשמרות ששה ועשרים</u> במשמרותם ישרתו ואחריהם ראשי הלויים לשרת תמיד שנים עשר אחד לשבט They should order the chiefs of the priests after the chief priest and his deputy: <u>twelve chiefs</u> to be serving in the continual offering before God. <u>The twenty-six chiefs of the courses</u>: they shall serve in their courses. After them the chiefs of the Levites serve continually, twelve in all, one to a tribe. (based on WAC)

This interpretation of the text fits well with other linguistic features: the use of the infinitive להיות in line 1 instead of a finite verb suggests a list without full predication, while the double fronting of ראשי המשמרות ששה ועשרים ("the twenty-six chiefs of the courses") and במשמרותם ("in their courses") before the verb ישרתו ("they will serve") in line 2 suggests punctual, list style. If the text preceding אבות העדה שנים וחמשים ("fifty-two [?] fathers of the congregation"?) were extant, I suspect it would fit the same style. The cases of noun-number order in 11Q5 and 1QM, then, can justifiably be understood as participating in the stylistics of lists.

3.2.3. Phrase-Internal Fronting

Another potential synchronic explanation for noun-number order is phrase-internal fronting. Although the internal word order of noun phrases in Hebrew is relatively inflexible, the alteration between unmarked number-noun order and marked noun-number order in number phrases is a potential exception. Given the examples of noun-number word order in the DSS, I wonder whether the variations in order might be tied—like variations in word order at the clause level—to focus. Specifically, noun-number order might mark the noun within the number phrase for in situ focus (focusing without movement to the front of the clause).

19. 1QS 8:1, בעצת היחד שנים עשר איש וכוהנים שלושה, "In the council of the Yaḥad [there should be] twelve men, and three priests"

The phrase "three priests" might stress priests: in contrast to the Yaḥad members without special status ("twelve men"), it is important that these three are priests. The cases of noun-number order in 1QM also lend themselves to contrast and in situ focus.

20. 1QM 2:1–2, ואת ראשי הכוהנים יסרוכו ... ראשים שנים עשר להיות משרתים בתמיד לפני אל וראשי המשמרות ששה ועשרים במשמרותם ישרתו
    "They should order the chiefs of the priests [...]. Twelve chiefs ought to be serving in the continual offering before God, and the twenty-six chiefs of the courses should serve in their courses."

In contrast to other individuals discussed in the passage, especially the immediately preceding "fathers of the congregation" (אבות העדה), the ones responsible for the continual offering need to be *chief priests*; the fronting of ראשים ("chiefs") in ראשים שנים עשר ("twelve chief [priests]") might help to communicate this emphasis. Similarly, the twenty-six "chiefs of the courses"—who are known in context and thus articulated (ראשי המשמרות, "the chiefs of the courses")—are to serve in those very courses, and no one else; thus, ראשי המשמרות ששה ועשרים ("twenty-six chiefs of the courses") instead of ששה ועשרים ראשי המשמרות ("twenty-six chiefs of the courses" without focus).

The cases in 11Q5, though easily explicable as partaking in the typical style of a list, might also work with this analysis.

21. 11Q5 27:4–10, ויכתוב תהלים שלושת אלפים ושש מאות ושיר לשורר לפני המזבח ... ארבעה וששים ושלוש מאות ולקורבן השבתות שנים וחמשים שיר ולקורבן ראשי החודשים ולכול ימי המועדות ולים הכפורים שלושים שיר
    He wrote three thousand six hundred *psalms*, three hundred and sixty-four *songs* to sing before the altar..., for the Sabbath offerings, fifty-two songs, and for the new moon offerings [etc.], thirty songs.

The fronting of תהלים ("psalms") and שיר ("song") may contrast the two types of literature ("3,600 *psalms* and 364 *songs*"), with the contrast no longer necessarily in the following two number phrases "fifty-two songs" and "thirty songs" (since "song" has already been introduced).[64]

Though contextual factors do not suggest a contrastive reading as strongly, similar interpretations are possible for the four noun-number cases in CD. For example, CD 1:5–6, בקץ חרון שנים שלוש מאות ותשעים לתיתו אותם ביד נבוכדנאצר, "in the time of wrath, three hundred and ninety *years* from his giving them over to Nebuchadnezzar." In other words, the "time of wrath" was very long, measured in years rather than months or days.

Without cross-linguistic evidence supporting my suggestion here—I am not aware of other languages where noun-phrase internal fronting marks focus—it is difficult to corroborate. This is just one way to interpret some of the aberrant evidence, most of which can also be explained as partaking in list stylistics.

3.2.4. Corrupted Data

One of the four cases of noun-number order in CD may not reflect the premedieval form of the text. Manuscript A's text of 14:21 has large lacunas on either side, leaving little context for reconstruction. Moreover, what seems to be a clear parallel (the basis of manuscript A's reconstruction) in 4Q266 fragment 10 ii:1 contains a different number with different order.

22. CD 14:21, ונ]ענש ימים ששה ואשר ידב]ר, "and h]e should be punished for six days. And as for the one who speaks ..."

23. 4Q266 frag 10 ii:1, ונענש מאה יום ואם בדבר, "and he should be punished for a hundred days. And if in a matter of ..."

Whether or not the two texts are in fact parallel, it is clear from other number phrases in 4Q266 in similar contexts that 4Q266 prefers number-noun order.[65] This suggests that manuscript A's number phrase in CD 14:21 does not accurately reflect the Hebrew of the Second Temple period.

---

64. Interpreting the number phrase in ll. 9–10 as further contrast might be possible, though not likely.

65. 4Q266 frag. 10 ii:6, 8; 4Q270 frag. 7 i:9, 14, all contain the same expression ("he should be punished for *x* years") with number-noun order. None have corresponding text extant in the Cairo Genizah manuscripts.

## 3.2.5. Summary of Synchronic Explanations

The aberrant number phrases with noun-number order can be explained in a variety of ways. It is widely recognized that number phrases with this order occur in lists. Above I suggest that such order may also occur because of internal fronting, though the idea is tenuous; and that reinterpretation of these aberrant number phrases as two distinct phrases (a noun and a numeral) in apposition is preferable in many cases, especially within lists.

## 3.3. Measurement Expressions

None of the data I present and analyze in sections 3.1–2 directly address Qimron's second phenomenon, discussed briefly in section 1. As I noted there, Qimron posits a diachronic development in phrases that use a word denoting the "kind of measure," a development supposedly exhibited in the DSS. This second phenomenon is not about the order of numeral and noun in a number phrase but the order of a measurement expression and the noun it describes. Consider Qimron's first example:

24. 1QM 4:15, אות כול העדה אורך ארבע עשרה אמה, "The banner of the whole congregation shall be fourteen cubits long" (WAC)

אורך, "length," is neither a measure nor a numeral; אמה, "cubit," is the measure that specifies the length (אורך) of the banner and is itself quantified by the numeral ארבע עשרה ("fourteen"). In this and Qimron's other two examples, the measure אמה ("cubit") follows the numeral that quantifies it—in other words, the order is number-noun.[66] Furthermore, the numeral ארבע עשרה ("fourteen") does not interact syntactically with אורך ("length"); rather, it is embedded within the measurement phrase. Qimron's cases, then, do not exhibit the order measure–number or even kind of measure–number, but rather kind of measure–measure.

In my view, the words אורך ארבע עשרה אמה do not constitute a single phrase (unlike English "fourteen cubits long"). אורך does not take different syntax by virtue of being a "kind of measure"; instead, it is the subject of a null copula, with the predicate compliment "fourteen cubits."

---

66. Qimron's example from Late Biblical Hebrew, on the other hand, has the measure אמות ("cubits") before the numeral: 2 Chr 3:3, רֹחַב אַמּוֹת עֶשְׂרִים, "the width was twenty cubits."

I translate, "As for the banner of the whole congregation, [its] length is fourteen cubits." In this understanding, each constituent is in its right place: in null copula (verbless) clauses, the subject (אורך) ought to precede the predicate (ארבע עשרה אמה), with topicalization occurring at the front (אות כול העדה).⁶⁷ Though measure words in measurement phrases do bear many similarities to numerals in number phrases, and we could understand a single phrase "fourteen cubits of length," Qimron does not sufficiently demonstrate that the syntax of measurement phrases and number phrases are likely to be identical.⁶⁸ If we were to track the order of measurement phrases—which I have not done for this study—I wonder whether the same problems would arise for an analysis positing diachronic development.⁶⁹

## 4. Conclusion

When the language of the DSS is considered in a historical-linguistic framework, we find that the syntax of number phrases—specifically, their order—agrees with periods of Hebrew that preceded and followed. There was no diachronic change to the order of number phrases, from number-noun in Classical Biblical Hebrew to noun-number in DSS Hebrew. Rather, the order of number phrases in all of ancient Hebrew was number-noun, with a few synchronic reasons for marked variation.

Of the ten texts for which we have enough data to determine a preferred order for number phrases, only the Copper Scroll contains a significant amount of noun-number tokens. Besides being a linguistic

---

67. Randall Buth, "Word Order in the Verbless Clause: A Generative-Functional Approach," in *The Verbless Clause in Biblical Hebrew: Linguistic Approaches*, ed. Cynthia Miller (Winona Lake, IN: Eisenbrauns, 1999), 79–108.

68. Note that Qimron does connect the two: he refers to "the same practice" of inverting order for both of these kinds of phrase and labels the order of these "two word categories" as "*noun-numeral*" (Qimron, *Grammar of the Hebrew*, 440–41; Qimron, *Hebrew of the Dead Sea Scrolls*, 85–86). On measure words in measurement phrases bearing many similarities to numerals in number phrases, see Moshavi and Rothstein, "Indefinite Numerical Construct Phrases," 109–11.

69. Fassberg notes a few further examples but does not treat the evidence exhaustively ("Shifts in Word Order," 65). It is possible that the order of these phrases is typically measure-noun throughout ancient Hebrew (including Late Biblical Hebrew and the DSS), with aberrant noun-measure order (e.g., 1 Kgs 9:28; Num 18:16) occurring throughout ancient Hebrew.

anomaly, this text is essentially a list, explaining the high use of abnormal noun-number order. Number-noun order is the normal, unmarked order of number phrases in the DSS. When we look back to the Hebrew Bible and forward to the Mishnah, we find that the same is true of the language found there. No solid evidence exists for a development in the order of number phrases at any point in ancient Hebrew. The abnormal, marked occurrences of noun-number order—occurring in the DSS and in other corpora—can be explained in a variety of ways. Chiefly, the stylistics of lists are to blame: staccato, appositional syntax characterizes lists, leading both to cases where two separate phrases are liable to be confused for a number phrase and to the use of noun-number order for number phrases in lists. Outside lists, some of the cases of number phrases with noun-number order outside may in fact be two distinct phrases, or may result from a phrase internal strategy for marking focus. We also saw one example where the language of the DSS may have been altered during the medieval period.

The method we bring to the task is essential. If we come to the DSS looking for abnormalities in language, we are sure to find them. It is incorrect, however, to conclude that such abnormalities characterize the Hebrew of the DSS, and moreover that the language of the DSS is unique as a result. Instead of this haphazard approach, we ought to collect all of the data and place it in its historical-linguistic context. When we do this, we discover that the abnormalities are not characteristic of the DSS, that the same abnormalities can be found in the language of other texts, and that the language of the DSS fits right in with the language of earlier and later corpora.

***

Unlike the order of number phrases, an aspect of numeral syntax that did develop over time is the order of numerals within complex adding numerals.[70] By contrasting an old feature (increasing order, e.g., 1s–10s–100s) and a new feature (decreasing order, e.g., 100s–10s–1s), we can track a progression from old-feature dominance to mixed use to new-feature dominance, with the new feature persisting at the end of the process. Within the DSS, the Copper Scroll uses only decreasing order, while the

---

70. See Screnock, "Complex Adding Numerals," 801–13.

War Scroll classicizes, using increasing order in nine out of ten instances. Though the War Scroll does not classicize in many other areas of language, the use of increasing order would have helped to give the text an air of antiquity.[71] I disagree with Qimron, who states, "The claim that the scribes at Qumran sometimes used deliberate classicism [should be rejected]. How can these scribes be both modernizers and archaisers?"[72] Qimron's argument seems to reflect a view that the people writing the scrolls were using the "new" language features for the first time (thus the term *modernizers*), but those features may already have been a part of the language known by those writing the scrolls. Though some features in the DSS may be new from our perspective (in contrast to our earlier evidence for ancient Hebrew), these features may nevertheless have been in use for some time (and we simply have no extant evidence of them).[73] To answer Qimron's question, these scribes were not necessarily modernizers—they used the language as they inherited it, quite possibly without introducing new features; and their archaizing was not total or complete—for some features they used classicisms, but not all.[74] It is even possible, though not probable, that the scribes *were* language innovators for some features, while classicizing with others—though they would have done these two things for different reasons.

Interestingly, the material evidence for 1QM lends weight to my analysis—that the language is classicizing in the order of complex adding numerals.[75] 1QM 2:10 reads, ומלחמת המחלקות בעתש ועשרים הנותרות, "and the war of divisions during the remaining twenty-nine [years]." The *ayin* following *bet* in בעתש was half-written—only the right stroke[76]—and

---

71. The book of Exodus, on which the War Scroll is based to an extent, prefers increasing order, and its language is at the beginning of the transition stage from old feature to new feature (Screnock, "Complex Adding Numerals," 807–13).

72. Qimron, *Grammar of the Hebrew*, 51 n. 27.

73. Notably, Qimron thinks that the DSS reflect the language as spoken in Jerusalem (*Grammar of the Hebrew*, 33).

74. It would be much more difficult to mimic an older stage in language *completely* than to mimic select aspects of it.

75. See my brief comment in Screnock, "Complex Adding Numerals," 803 n. 44.

76. Sukenik suggests that this is the "initial stroke of a ש," which indeed it could be on purely graphic reasoning, since the initial strokes of *ayin* and *shin* are identical. I am not aware of an explanation, however, for why the scribe would have started to write *shin*. See Eleazar Sukenik, *The Dead Sea Scrolls of the Hebrew University* (Jerusalem: Magnes Press, 1955).

then *tav* and *shin* are written immediately after, with space for another letter following *shin*.

Did the scribe begin to write the *ayin* in תשע ("nine") at the start of the word instead of the end? This is highly unlikely. Rather, the scribe—knowing the text had the number twenty-nine at this point—began to write the number according to the Hebrew he spoke, using decreasing order (עשרים ותשע). The initial *ayin*—only half written—is the *ayin* from the start of עשרים ("twenty"). The scribe caught his mistake—either by looking at his *Vorlage* or recalling the correct wording[77]—and began to write תשע instead. I am uncertain why he did not erase the first stroke of *ayin* and why he did not write *ayin* at the end of תשע,[78] but the cause of the error in the first place is the discord between the scribe's vernacular and the classicizing language of the War Scroll.

\*\*\*

I have argued that authoritative resources on the DSS, such as Qimron's grammar, should be used with caution and constantly questioned and revised. In this study I have focused on the order of number phrases; I suspect that other—though not all—areas of syntax in Qimron's grammar might be open to similar critique based on historical-linguistic method. Though the labors of Qimron and other past scholars—all impressive linguists and masters of the material in the DSS—are monumental, we nevertheless must continue to rethink their work, particularly in the area of syntax.

As a concluding thought, it is worth considering the role that supposed Qumran Hebrew or Dead Sea Scrolls Hebrew has played in our conception of the DSS and the group(s) responsible for them. Whether implicitly, or explicitly—as in William Schniedewind's idea of Qumran Hebrew as "antilanguage"[79]—viewing the Hebrew of the DSS as de facto

---

77. On the interplay of long-term memory, short-term memory, reading, and language, see Jonathan Vroom, "The Role of Memory in *Vorlage*-Based Transmission: Evidence from Erasures and Corrections," *Textus* 27 (2018): 258–73.

78. Perhaps he left the details of the correction to a supervising scribe who never ended up checking the first scribe's work.

79. Schniedewind, "Qumran Hebrew as an Antilanguage." By citing Schniedewind, I do not mean to criticize his work or imply that it is incorrect. A community only needs to focus on a few features of language to create an antilanguage, and the

a unique variety of Hebrew has reinforced the notion of the DSS and the community/ies behind them as distinct, unique, and sectarian. But does the language used in the DSS suggest a community isolated and distinct from the rest of the Jewish world? Probably not. In my impression, though differences with the Hebrew of the Hebrew Bible are emphasized, in the end the Hebrew of the DSS is not all that different. In the case of numeral syntax, in particular, the evidence points to continuity with ancient Hebrew as used outside the DSS.

## Bibliography

Abegg, Martin G. "The Hebrew of the Dead Sea Scrolls." Pages 325–58 in *The Dead Sea Scrolls after Fifty Years: A Comprehensive Assessment*. Vol. 1. Edited by Peter W. Flint and James C. VanderKam. Leiden: Brill, 1998.

Bailey, Charles. *Variation and Linguistic Theory*. Arlington, VA: Center for Applied Linguistics, 1973.

Bergey, Ronald. "Late Linguistic Features in Esther." *JQR* 75 (1984): 66–78.

Borg, Alexandra. "Some Observations on the יום חשישי Syndrome in the Hebrew of the Dead Sea Scrolls." Pages 26–39 in *Diggers at the Well*. Edited by Takamitsu Muraoka and John F. Elwolde. Leiden: Brill, 2000.

Buth, Randall. "Word Order in the Verbless Clause: A Generative-Functional Approach." Pages 79–108 in *The Verbless Clause in Biblical Hebrew: Linguistic Approaches*. Edited by Cynthia Miller. Winona Lake, IN: Eisenbrauns, 1999.

Cook, John A. "Detecting Development in Biblical Hebrew Using Diachronic Typology." Pages 83–95 in *Diachrony in Biblical Hebrew*. Edited by Cynthia L. Miller-Naudé and Ziony Zevit. Winona Lake, IN: Eisenbrauns, 2012.

Crystal, David. "New Perspectives for Language Study. 1: Stylistics." *ELT* 24 (1970): 99–106.

———. "Style: The Varieties of English." Pages 199–222 in *The English Language*. Edited by Whitney F. Bolton and David Crystal. London: Sphere Books, 1988.

---

idea is possible for some texts. It is important, however, that we not jump in the direction of antilanguage with everything we see in the DSS—as I have demonstrated in the case of numeral syntax, where the language of the DSS is not unique.

Dresher, B. Elan. "Methodological Issues in the Dating of Linguistic Forms: Considerations from the Perspective of Contemporary Linguistic Theory." Pages 19–38 in *Diachrony in Biblical Hebrew*. Edited by Cynthia L. Miller-Naudé and Ziony Zevit. Winona Lake, IN: Eisenbrauns, 2012.

Fassberg, Steven E. "Dead Sea Scrolls: Linguistic Features." Pages 663–69 in *Encyclopedia of Hebrew Language and Linguistics*. Vol. 1. Edited by Geoffrey Khan, Shmuel Bolozky, Steven E. Fassberg, Gary A. Rendsburg, Aaron D. Rubin, Ora R. Schwarzwald, and Tamar Zevi. Leiden: Brill, 2013.

———. "Shifts in Word Order in the Hebrew of the Second Temple Period." Pages 57–71 in *Hebrew in the Second Temple Period: The Hebrew of the Dead Sea Scrolls and of Other Contemporary Sources*. Edited by Steven E. Fassberg, Moshe Bar-Asher, and Ruth A. Clements. STDJ 108. Leiden: Brill, 2013.

Forbes, Dean. "Two Candidate Approaches to Text Sequencing: An Addendum to 'The Diachrony Debate: A Tutorial on Methods.'" *JSem* 26 (2017): 710–16.

Hale, Mark. *Historical Linguistics: Theory and Method*. Malden, MA: Blackwell, 2007.

Holmstedt, Robert D. "Historical Linguistics and Biblical Hebrew." Pages 97–124 in *Diachrony in Biblical Hebrew*. Edited by Cynthia L. Miller-Naudé and Ziony Zevit. Winona Lake, IN: Eisenbrauns, 2012.

———. "Investigating the Possible Verb-Subject to Subject-Verb Shift in Ancient Hebrew: Methodological First Steps." *KUSATU* 15 (2013): 3–31.

Hornkohl, Aaron. *Ancient Hebrew Periodization and the Language of the Book of Jeremiah: The Case for a Sixth-Century Date of Composition*. SSLL 74. Leiden: Brill, 2014.

Jacobs, Jared. Review of Eric Reymond, *Qumran Hebrew*. *JSS* 62 (2017): 261–63.

Moshavi, Adina, and Susan Rothstein. "Indefinite Numerical Construct Phrases in Biblical Hebrew." *JSS* 63 (2018): 99–123.

Muraoka, Takamitsu. "An Approach to the Morphosyntax and Syntax of Qumran Hebrew." Pages 193–214 in *Diggers at the Well*. Edited by Takamitsu Muraoka and John F. Elwolde. Leiden: Brill, 2000.

Naudé, Jacobus A. "Diachrony in Biblical Hebrew and a Theory of Language Change and Diffusion." Pages 61–81 in *Diachrony in Biblical*

*Hebrew*. Edited by Cynthia L. Miller-Naudé and Ziony Zevit. Winona Lake, IN: Eisenbrauns, 2012.

———. "The Transitions of Biblical Hebrew in the Perspective of Language Change and Diffusion." Pages 189–214 in *Biblical Hebrew: Studies in Chronology and Typology*. Edited by Ian Young. London: T&T Clark, 2003.

Polzin, Robert. *Late Biblical Hebrew: Toward an Historical Typology of Biblical Hebrew Prose*. HSM 12. Missoula, MT: Scholars Press, 1976.

Qimron, Elisha. *A Grammar of the Hebrew of the Dead Sea Scrolls*. Jerusalem: Yad Izhak Ben-Zvi, 2018.

———. *The Hebrew of the Dead Sea Scrolls*. HSS 29. Atlanta: Scholars Press, 1986.

Rendsburg, Gary. "Late Biblical Hebrew and the Date of P." *JANES* 12 (1980): 71.

Reymond, Eric. *Qumran Hebrew: An Overview of Orthography, Phonology, and Morphology*. RBS 76. Atlanta: SBL Press, 2014.

Rezetko, Robert, and Ian Young. *Historical Linguistics and Biblical Hebrew: Steps toward an Integrated Approach*. ANEM 9. Atlanta: SBL Press, 2014.

Schniedewind, William. "Qumran Hebrew as an Antilanguage." *JBL* 118 (1999): 235–52.

Screnock, John. "Complex Adding Numerals and Hebrew Diachrony." *JBL* 137 (2018): 789–819.

———. "The Syntax of Cardinal Numerals in Judges, Amos, Esther, and 1QM." *JSS* 63 (2018): 125–54.

Screnock, John, and Robert D. Holmstedt. *Esther*. Waco, TX: Baylor University Press, 2015.

Segal, Moses H. *A Grammar of Mishnaic Hebrew*. Oxford: Clarendon, 1927.

Sukenik, Eleazar. *The Dead Sea Scrolls of the Hebrew University*. Jerusalem: Magnes, 1955.

Swanson, Dwight D. *The Temple Scroll and the Bible: The Methodology of 11QT*. STDJ 14. Leiden: Brill, 1995.

Talmon, Shemaryahu, Jonathan Ben-Dov, and Uwe Glessmer. *Qumran Cave 4.XVI: Calendrical Texts*. DJD XXI. Oxford: Clarendon, 2001.

Vroom, Jonathan. "The Role of Memory in *Vorlage*-Based Transmission: Evidence from Erasures and Corrections." *Textus* 27 (2018): 258–73.

Weitzman, Steven. "The Shifting Syntax of Numerals in Biblical Hebrew: A Reassessment." *JNES* 55 (1996): 177–85.

Wolfram, Walt, and Natalie Schilling-Estes. "Dialectology and Linguistic Diffusion." Pages 713–35 in *The Handbook of Historical Linguistics*. Edited by Brian D. Joseph and Richard D. Janda. London: Blackwell, 2003.

# Variant Readings in the Aramaic Dead Sea Scrolls: A Tool for Ongoing Research on the Textual Status and Linguistic Setting of Ancient Jewish Aramaic Literature

Andrew B. Perrin and Brandon Diggens

Varied Editorial Approaches to Presenting Variant Readings

The Aramaic Dead Sea Scrolls (DSS) are among the first and last fragmentary finds from the Judaean wilderness to make their way out of the Qumran caves and into modern published editions. While discovery, acquisition, and sifting of the DSS fragments continued in the early 1950s, by mid-decade some first-generation Scrolls scholars promptly provided their impressions of these ancient finds. In 1953, the first volume of the Discoveries in the Judaean Desert of Jordan included a number of fragments from Aramaic texts.[1] By 1956, Nahman Avigad and Yigael Yadin presented a volume on the then-known material of the Genesis Apocryphon.[2] In that same year, Józef Milik published fragments of the Prayer of

---

This research was undertaken thanks to funding from a Social Sciences and Humanities Research Council of Canada Insight Grant and the Canada Research Chair in Religious Identities of Ancient Judaism.

1. Józef T. Milik and Dominique Barthélemy, *Qumran Cave 1*, DJD I (Oxford: Clarendon, 1955). The volume included fragments of the Birth of Noah (1Q19), a brief section of Genesis Apocryphon (1Q20), materials of Aramaic Levi Document (1Q21), and fragments of two manuscripts later identified as coming from the Book of Giants (1Q23–24), as well as an appendix including transcription and notes of the Cave 1 Daniel fragments (1Q71–72). In this first installment of the series, editors noted textual differences between the Qumran Daniel fragments and the MT. For the Aramaic Levi Document they presented one apparent variant with the Genizah text but consistently noted the location of corresponding text in the Aramaic Levi Bodleian materials and parallels in Greek Testament of Levi for all fragments in question.

2. Nahman Avigad and Yigael Yadin, *A Genesis Apocryphon: A Scroll from the Wil-*

Nabonidus and Pseudo-Daniel in an article that remains essential reading on those Aramaic compositions.³ While there were other studies, partial editions, and transcriptions of the Aramaic texts in the initial decades of Qumran research, the full picture of these materials remained unknown until the early 1990s, when, as the familiar story goes, the entire library was reverse-engineered and suddenly available for scholars and the public.

Critical editions of many Aramaic texts, however, were spread over several Discoveries in the Judaean Desert (DJD) volumes in the 1990s and 2000s. Eventually, Émile Puech published the bulk of the Aramaic finds in some of the last volumes of the DJD project, providing a sort of inclusio to the long process of publishing the Aramaic DSS fragments that started decades prior.⁴

Users of the DJD series will know that there is both uniformity and diversity in the structure and layout of individual volumes. As the series grew, changed, and evolved, so did its approach, method, and scope. With a project of this size and duration, there are understandably degrees of differences as editors were given latitude to present the materials in a way they felt fit with the material evidence and met the aims of a critical edition as they understood it. One area where there is discontinuity across the series, however, is the manner of the presentation or depth of discussion given to textual variations evident in overlaps between manuscripts of the same composition.

In most cases, the collation and presentation of textual variants was a treatment given to those scrolls containing writings eventually canonized in the Hebrew Bible and Old Testament. This is not without good reason. From an early time, scholars recognized (and popularized) the significance of the biblical scrolls for rethinking, reevaluating, or even revising the texts of the Hebrew Scriptures. Scanning the footnotes of most modern Bible translations or apparatuses of critical editions shows that

---

derness of Judea; Description and Contents of the Scroll, Facsimiles, Transcription, and Translation of Columns II, XIX–XXII (Jerusalem: Magnes and Heikhal Ha-Sefer, 1956).

3. Józef T. Milik, "'Prière de Nabonide' et autres écrits d'un cycle de Daniel," *RB* 63 (1956): 407–15.

4. Émile Puech, *Qumrân Grotte 4.XXII: Textes araméens, première partie; 4Q529–549*, DJD XXXI (Oxford: Clarendon, 2001); Puech, *Qumrân Grotte 4.XXVII: Textes araméens, deuxième partie; 4Q550–4Q575a, 4Q580–4Q587*, DJD XXXVII (Oxford: Clarendon, 2009). See introductory paragraphs below for primary source bibliography of individual Aramaic works among the DSS.

the Qumran discoveries are continually evolving the content and shape of Scripture as we learn more of the early textual development, transmission, and reception of the books received as authoritative in Judaism and Christianity. To do this sort of work, variant lists and apparatuses are essential.[5]

Yet, as Charlotte Hempel recently reminded our guild, we need to treat would-be biblical books and so-called nonbiblical texts among the Qumran collection with the same methodological rigor when exploring the development of complex literary traditions in ancient Judaism.[6] In light of this call to action, we might consider why few editions of the Aramaic texts included a formal list of textual variants and what that might tell us about our cultural, theological, or academic biases that prioritize canonical writings.

Compare, for example, the varied approaches and data for the following works comprising or including Aramaic content. Perhaps not surprising given their eventual canonical status, the fragmentary content of Daniel and Ezra's Aramaic sections came with full lists of textual variants between the Qumran materials and later witnesses.[7] Beyond these, the Aramaic Levi Document and Astronomical Enoch are the only Aramaic texts among the

---

5. See now especially Eugene Ulrich, *The Qumran Biblical Scrolls: Transcriptions and Textual Variants*, VTSup 134 (Leiden: Brill, 2010), which distills the textual data from the larger publication project of the biblical scrolls. For readers with little or no knowledge of ancient languages, the inclusion and explanation of variant readings was also a major feature of Martin Abegg Jr., Peter Flint, and Eugene Ulrich, *The Dead Sea Scrolls Bible: The Oldest Known Bible Translated for the First Time into English* (New York: HarperOne, 1999). How to navigate and integrate such data into new translations or critical editions is very much an open question. For the differing approaches and aims of recent or ongoing projects on the Hebrew Bible, see the collection of essays by project leaders or contributors of *Biblia Hebraica Quinta*, *Biblia Qumranica*, *Hebrew University Bible Project*, and *Oxford Hebrew Bible* (now *The Hebrew Bible: A Critical Edition*) in the thematic issue of *HBAI* 2 (2013). For a broader context of current questions and methodological approaches, see now John S. Kloppenborg and Judith H. Newman, eds., *Editing the Bible: Assessing the Task Past and Present* (Atlanta: Society of Biblical Literature, 2012).

6. Charlotte Hempel, "From A–Z: The Relegation of the A-List of Biblical History in the Dead Sea Scrolls" (paper presented at the International Meeting of the Society of Biblical Literature, Helsinki, 2 August 2018).

7. The Cave 4 items relevant to these works were published by Eugene Ulrich, "Daniel," in *Qumran Cave 4.XI: Psalms to Chronicles*, by Eugene Ulrich et al., DJD XVI (Oxford: Clarendon, 2000), 239–89; Ulrich, "Ezra," in Ulrich et al., *Qumran Cave 4.XI*, 291–93.

DSS that were published with a variant list in their DJD editions.[8] Others, such as Joseph Fitzmyer's erudite treatments of the Aramaic and Hebrew fragments of Tobit, included selective discussions of variations between the Qumran fragments and subsequent witnesses in a brief comments section.[9] Writings that were lost until their modern discovery present their own set of challenges: their unknown or lack of reception means we do not have external witnesses for comparisons of highly fragmentary texts. For example, Visions of Amram is a formidable text, and Puech's edition

---

8. Much in the style and form of the comparisons of the biblical Scrolls, Stone and Greenfield highlighted differences among the Qumran Cave 4 texts and with the Cairo Genizah materials. See Michael E. Stone and Jonas C. Greenfield, "Aramaic Levi Document," in *Qumran Cave 4.XVII: Parabiblical Texts, Part 3*, by George J. Brooke et al., DJD XXII (Oxford: Clarendon, 1996), 1–72. The integration of data from the Mount Athos Greek materials, however, were not included in the apparatuses until the subsequent publication by Jonas C. Greenfield, Michael E. Stone, and Esther Eshel, *The Aramaic Levi Document: Edition, Translation, Commentary*, SVTP 19 (Leiden: Brill, 2004). See also the important treatment by Drawnel, which includes incisive comments and detailed notes on transcription or textual differences yet also does not consolidate this data in a single place. See Henryk Drawnel, *An Aramaic Wisdom Text from Qumran: A New Interpretation of the Levi Document*, JSJSup 86 (Leiden: Brill, 2004). Norin preliminarily explored the issue of early and late readings or forms revealed by the variant readings across all ALD witnesses. See Stig Norin, "The Aramaic Levi—Comparing the Qumran Fragments with the Genizah Text," *SJOT* 27 (2013): 118–30. Perrin studied the potential of variant editions, or more likely only variant passages, of the Aramaic Levi Document in light of the Qumran fragments. See Andrew B. Perrin, "The Textual Forms of Aramaic Levi Document at Qumran," in *Reading the Bible in Ancient Traditions and Modern Editions: Studies in Memory of Peter W. Flint*, ed. Andrew B. Perrin, Kyung S. Baek, and Daniel K. Falk, EJL 47 (Atlanta: SBL Press, 2017), 431–52. Such studies indicate how some of the questions and insights pioneered largely in the domain of the biblical scrolls are only recently coming to the fore for research on the Aramaic DSS. For overlaps and variants among the Astronomical Book fragments, see Eibert J. C. Tigchelaar and Florentino García Martínez, "4QAstronomical Enoch[a–b] (4Q208–209)," in *Qumran Cave 4.XXVI: Cryptic Texts*, by Stephen J. Pfann; *Miscellanea, Part 1*, by Philip S. Alexander et al., DJD XXXVI (Oxford: Clarendon, 2000), 95–172.

9. See Joseph Fitzmyer, "Tobit," in *Qumran Cave 4.XIV: Parabiblical Texts, Part 2*, by Magen Broshi et al., DJD XIX (Oxford: Clarendon, 1995), 1–76. In most cases, the complete discussion of textual variety between all the Tobit witnesses came in Fitzmyer's later commentary. See Joseph A. Fitzmyer, *Tobit*, CEJL (Berlin: de Gruyter, 2003). Hallermayer took a similar approach in her edition, as textual variants are reserved for commentary or footnotes not presented in an apparatus. See Michaela Hallermayer, *Text und Überlieferung des Buches Tobit*, DCLS 3 (Berlin: de Gruyter, 2008).

is foundational for the access and study of these fragmentary materials.[10] However, while overlaps are clearly marked for each fragment, transcriptions are unaccompanied by variant lists.

One of the main outcomes and oft-repeated insights of Qumran scholarship is that the canon of Scripture did not yet exist in the mid–Second Temple period, and the shape and content of many writings were still developing and/or circulating in more than one form or edition.[11] Agreed. Yet, while scholarship has generally recognized this need for nuance and emphasized the importance of avoiding canonical anachronism, in many ways noncanonical literature has been treated differently, or, at least, the questions asked of it are not the same as those pressed to materials carrying content of eventual biblical writings.[12] The unique opportunity of the Aramaic DSS, then, is to study how traditions developed as scribes plied their craft in a set of writings that includes items across all subsequently developed canonical or cultural categories (such as, Bible, Apocrypha, Pseudepigrapha) yet from a time *before* all of these boundaries were set in place.[13]

---

10. See Émile Puech, "Visions de 'Amram," in Puech, *Qumrân Grotte 4.XXII*, 283–405. Duke's proposed critical text and arrangement does note variants between the fragments as well as alternate transcription proposals following his synthesized sections. See Robert R. Duke, *The Social Location of the Visions of Amram (4Q543–547)*, StBibLit 135 (New York: Lang, 2010).

11. The most perspective insight on this topic is by Mika Pajunen, "Bible," in *The T&T Clark Companion to the Dead Sea Scrolls*, ed. George J. Brooke and Charlotte Hempel, BC (London: Bloomsbury, 2018), 367–75.

12. Mroczek's study underscored that the canonical and conceptual image of the Bible has still served as a guide for how many scholars frame questions and engage ancient source materials. See Eva Mroczek, *The Literary Imagination in Jewish Antiquity* (Oxford: Oxford University Press, 2016).

13. All of these terms, and the modern conceptions or collections they bring to mind, must be used with great caution. For calls to nuance, see Loren T. Stuckenbruck, "Apocrypha and Pseudepigrapha," *EDEJ* 143–62; Hindy Najman, review of *Old Testament Pseudepigrapha: More Noncanonical Scriptures*, ed. Richard J. Bauckham, James R. Davila, and Alexander Panayotov, *DSD* 22 (2015): 211–14. We deploy them here for heuristic purposes to illustrate the reach and representation of the Aramaic texts in subsequent bodies of literature. Additionally, we need to bear in mind that, in the same way that our manuscript evidence for the Aramaic texts is fragmentary, so too is our knowledge of their reception. Just because an ancient text was brought to our modern attention through a new discovery does not mean that it did not serve the ideological interests or practical needs of communities in antiquity in some unknown

## Developing a Tool for Studying the Textual Status of the Aramaic Texts

The foregoing observations are less a critique on the content or quality of scholarly editions—in most instances, the textual information is there—than on the manner of presentation. Having a variant list ready at hand will benefit a number of areas of current study and enable new questions for the future. These include but are not limited to articulating the early textual status of Aramaic writings, exploring evidence of secondary contributions or interpretations of transmitted content, revealing perspectives on scribal innovations reflected in material philology, and uncovering ancient understandings of language at the levels of corpus and cognitive linguistics. In many cases, we are only beginning to explore these topics for the fragmentary Aramaic DSS and the cultures that penned or preserved them.

To enable ongoing inquiry in these and other areas, what follows are lists of all the variant readings that exist among those Aramaic manuscripts at Qumran that exhibit certain overlaps. To facilitate easy access, our data are separated into lists for each work in question. Brief paragraphs introduce each composition and include a selective commentary on items within the list. We developed these lists using the following principles:

- DJD served as our base transcription. In cases where Aramaic materials were not included in the DJD series, we note what editions served as our departure point.[14]
- All items in the variant readings were checked against both PAM (Palestine Archaeological Museum) image plates and more recently available digital images on the Leon Levy Digital Dead Sea Scrolls Library.
- Our collations include variant readings based on extant text. When pertinent, we include minor reconstructions made in light of extant overlaps with another Qumran fragment.
- The lists present differences only between the Qumran materials, not variants with later witnesses when available.

---

way. Lack of reception in a canon does not necessarily imply lack of reception in other ways that are lost on us centuries later.

14. For preliminary editions or textual studies relevant to each work, see also the bibliographies included at the outset of the relevant DJD volume.

- Our primary interest is in true variants (i.e., differences that result in a change in the semantics of the text). However, we also include variations that are relevant to studying the state or development of Aramaic language (orthography and morphology) and scribal approaches (use of abbreviations or symbols).
- Apart from those items included in the appendix, our present data set does not include transcription differences that result from the comparison of editions outside DJD.

Deviations from these parameters relevant to a specific manuscript or series of variant readings are discussed in the header paragraphs below.

### Enochic Book of Watchers and Book of Dreams

The discovery of Aramaic originals of many writings known subsequently in the Ethiopic book of 1 Enoch both provided fresh materials for study and opened up new questions regarding the early configuration of separate Enochic writings.[15] In the case of 4Q206, content from the Book of Watchers (1 En. 1–36), Book of Dreams (1 En. 83–90), and Book of Giants were included on the same scroll. This presents a host of yet-unanswered codicological and traditional questions. For the present purposes, we include the relevant materials for these traditions in the same list. Since the materials related to the Astronomical Book (1 En. 72–82) were found independently in the manuscript evidence at Qumran, these are introduced and presented separately.

The variants of these Enochic manuscripts illustrate the general range of differences characteristic of the Aramaic texts. It seems some scribes preferred defective over plene spellings (compare וֹכֹל in 4Q201 1 II, 2 with כֹול[ו in 4Q204 1 I, 21). There is also ample evidence for interchanged gut-

---

15. The primary Aramaic texts relevant here include 4Q201–202, 4Q204–207, and 4Q212. Aspects of these were published in Józef T. Milik, *The Books of Enoch: Aramaic Fragments of Qumrân Cave 4* (Oxford: Clarendon, 1976), with additional materials found in the following: Loren T. Stuckenbruck, "4QEnoch<sup>a</sup> (4Q201 2–8)," in Pfann, *Qumran Cave 4.XXVI*, 3–7; Stuckenbruck "4QEnoch<sup>f</sup> ar (4Q206 2–3)," in Pfann, *Qumran Cave 4.XXVI*, 42–48. To date, the leading integration of the Aramaic readings from the Qumran Cave 4 materials into a text-critically informed translation is that in George W. E. Nickelsburg, *1 Enoch 1: A Commentary on the Book of 1 Enoch, Chapters 1–36, 81–108*, Hermeneia (Minneapolis: Augsburg Fortress, 2001).

turals or sibilants. Note, for example, the different spellings of the name Aseael in 4Q201 1 III, 9 (עסאל) and 4Q204 1 II, 26 (עשׂא[ל]). We also see the change from use of *zayin* to *dalet* with the formation of the relative particle in one area of overlap (זי in 4Q206 4 II, 13 and די in 4Q205 2 I, 26), which seems to be a feature of middle Aramaic.[16] Relevant here are the set of variants involving the use or nonuse of the relative particle in overlapping texts (4Q201 1 II, 5–6 and 4Q 204 1 I, 24–25). The manuscripts also include a few genuine semantic variants. See, for example where 4Q201 1 II, 1 reads חֹ [זו] לֹאֹרְעֹהֹ ("see the earth") against 4Q204 1 I, 20, which includes חזוא לכון ל[א]רעא ("see for yourself the earth"). Elsewhere, 4Q204 1 XII, 29 includes the reading קליפיא ("the bark") where the overlap in 4Q206 1 XXVI, 16 reads קלפוהי ("its bark").

Finally, there do not appear to be any variant readings among those materials assigned to the Book of Giants. Besides the five manuscripts whose identification with Enoch's Book of Giants is "virtually certain" (1Q23, 4Q203, 4Q530, 4Q531, and 6Q8), Loren Stuckenbruck determined five more are either probable or merely plausible (1Q24, 2Q26, 4Q532, 4Q556, and 4Q206 2–3) copies.[17] Due to their fragmentary nature and modest overlap, there are no certain variants among these. Milik, however, proposed an overlap between 4Q206 and 4Q556, so long as one of the two words therein was a variant. While Stuckenbruck is correct that neither

---

16. For discussions on the diachronic development of this form, see Ursula Schattner-Rieser, *L'araméen des manuscrits de la mer Morte, I: Grammaire*, IELOA 5 (Prahins: Éditions du Zèbre, 2004), 35–36; Takamitsu Muraoka, *A Grammar of Qumran Aramaic*, ANES 38 (Leuven: Peeters, 2011), 4.

17. Loren T. Stuckenbruck, *The Book of Giants from Qumran*, TSAJ 63 (Tübingen: Mohr Siebeck, 1997), 41. While Milik's earlier study is not without its problems, it remains essential for the study of many of these materials (*Books of Enoch*, 298–339). For the official publication and, in some cases, reeditions of the Book of Giants fragments or related texts, see: Józef T. Milik, "Deux apocryphes en Araméen (1Q23, 1Q24)," in Milik and Barthélemy, *Qumran Cave 1*, 97–99; Maurice Baillet, "Un apocryphe de la Genese (6Q8)," in *Les "Petites Grottes" de Qumrân*, by Maurice Baillet, Józef T. Milik, and Roland de Vaux, DJD III (Oxford: Clarendon, 1962), 116–19; Loren T. Stuckenbruck, "6QpapGiants ar (Re-edition)," in Pfann, *Qumran Cave 4.XXVI*, 73–94; Émile Puech, "Livre des Geants (530–533, 203 1)," in Puech, *Qumran Grotte 4.XXII*, 9–94; Stuckenbruck, "4QEnoch[a] (4Q201 2–8)"; Puech, "4QGéants[a] ar (4Q203)," in Puech, *Qumran Cave 4.XXVII*, 507–8. For the uncertain texts, see: Milik, "Deux apocryphes en Araméen," 99; Puech, "Livre des Géants (530–533, 203 1)," 95–104; Puech, "4QProphétie[a] ar (4Q556)," in Puech, *Qumran Cave 4.XXVII*, 155–58; Stuckenbruck, "4QEnoch[f] ar (4Q206 2–3)."

Variant Readings in the Aramaic Dead Sea Scrolls 101

the variant nor the overlap are conclusive, we include it here as a point of interest: compare הוה שפיך in 4Q206 2, 2 with הוה משתפך 4Q556 6, 2.[18]

Variants

לְאַרְעָֿה [חֹ[זו] 4Q201 1 II, 1 ] חזוא לכון ל[א]רעא 4Q204 1 I, 20 (1 En. 2.2)
וֹאֹ[תבו]ננו 4Q201 1 II, 1 ] ואתבוננא 4Q204 1 I, 20 (1 En. 2.2)
בעבד֯ה 4Q201 1 II, 1 ] בעובד]ה 4Q204 1 I, 20 (1 En. 2.2)
וֹכֹל 4Q201 1 II, 2 ] וֹ[כֹ]ל 4Q204 1 I, 21 (1 En. 2.2)
דֹּעֲלֵיהן 4Q201 1 II, 5 ] די עליהון 4Q204 1 I, 24 (1 En. 3.1)
ותלת 4Q201 1 II, 6 ] ודתלת 4Q204 1 I, 25 (1 En. 3.1)
א[ילניה 4Q201 1 II, 9 ] אילניא 4Q204 1 I, 28 (1 En. 5.1)
כלהן 4Q201 1 II, 9 ] כולהון 4Q204 1 I, 28 (1 En. 5.1)
בהן 4Q201 1 II, 9 ] וב[הֹון 4Q204 1 I, 28 (1 En. 5.1)
הוֹא לעלם 4Q201 1 II, 11 ] חי[א די לכול עלם 4Q204 1 I, 30 (1 En. 5.1)
מלכה֯ 4Q201 1 III, 2 ] מ[לכא 4Q202 1 II, 7 (1 En. 6.4)
ואלין 4Q201 1 III, 5 ] [וֹ]אֹלן 4Q204 1 II, 24 (1 En. 6.7)
עסאל 4Q201 1 III, 9 ] עשאֹ[ל 4Q204 1 II, 26 (1 En. 6.8)
עסר 4Q201 1 III, 10 ] עשר]יֹ 4Q202 1 II, 15 (1 En. 6.8)
עסר 4Q201 1 III, 11 ] עשֹ[ר 4Q204 1 II, 28 (1 En. 6.8)
תשעת לה 4Q201 1 III, 12 ] תשעת עשר[י לה 4Q202 1 II, 17 (1 En. 6.8)
עס[ר]תֹאֹ רבני רב[נ]יֹ 4Q201 1 III, 13 ] רֹבני עשֹ[רתא 4Q202 1 II, 17 (1 En. 6.8)
עסר]תֹאֹ 4Q201 1 III, 13 ] עשֹ[רתא] 4Q202 1 II, 17 (1 En. 6.8)
כל 4Q201 1 III, 14 ] כו]ל 4Q202 1 II, 18 (1 En. 7.1)
חרשה 4Q201 1 III, 15 ] לחר[שֹׁתֹא 4Q202 1 II, 19 (1 En. 7.1)
מדֹקִן 4Q204 1 XII, 29 ] מדקק 4Q206 1 XXVI, 16 (1 En. 31.3)
קליפיא 4Q204 1 XII, 29 ] קלפוהי 4Q206 1 XXVI, 16 (1 En. 31.3)
אחזיאת 4Q204 1 XII, 30 ] [אֹחזֹ]יֹת 4Q206 1 XXVI, 17 (1 En. 32.1)
ורעדין 4Q204 4, 1 ] דֹּ[חֹ]לֹ[יֹ]ן 4Q205 2 II, 30 (1 En. 89.29) רע[דֹּין וֹדֹּחֹלֹ]יֹן
די 4Q205 2 I, 26 ] זי 4Q206 4 II, 13 (1 En. 89.12)
ראם 4Q205 2 II, 27 ] רם 4Q206 4 III, 19 (1 En. 89.29)
ענא 4Q205 2 II, 29 ] ענֹ[הֹ 4Q206 4 III, 21 (1 En. 89.30)

### Aramaic Levi Document

Six manuscripts of the Aramaic Levi Document were found in Qumran Cave 4 (4Q213, 4Q213a, 4Q213b, 4Q214, 4Q214a, and 4Q214b). The previously

---

18. Stuckenbruck, *Book of Giants*, 189.

published materials from Cave 1 (1Q21) were reclassified as an additional copy in view of the later finds.[19] These benefit from the later known witnesses to the work in multiple collections and languages.[20]

Internally, the Qumran texts reveal only a handful of variants between the seven texts. Many are orthographical (כֹ[ל] [4Q213 1 II, 4] or בֹּוֹלֹ [4Q214b 8, 1]). One variant reading is syntactical, involving the appositional order of words: יעקוב אבי (4Q213b 1, 4) with אבי יע[קב (1Q21 4, 1). While it goes beyond the bounds of our current data, the Qumran texts did confirm a new Aramaic background for a reading only previously known in the Greek Mount Athos text. Where the Cairo Genizah text reads ואשא, the Qumran materials read ראשא (1Q21 45, 1; 4Q214 2, 3; 4Q214b 2–3, 8), which shows the reading τὴν κεφαλήν is likely derived from a lost *Vorlage* that paralleled the Cave 4 witnesses in this instance.

Variants

אבי יע[קב מעשר] 1Q21 4, 1 (ALD 8)[21] ] יעקוב אבי מעשר 4Q213b 1, 4
כֹ[ל] 4Q213 1 II, 4 ] בֹּוֹלֹ 4Q214b 8, 1 (ALD 96)
מ[טמריא 4Q214b 8, 2 (ALD 97)[22] ] מטמרה 4Q213 1 II, 6

---

19. For the published editions, see Józef T. Milik, "Testament de Lévi (1Q21)," in Milik and Barthélemy, *Qumran Cave 1*, 87–90; Stone and Greenfield, "Aramaic Levi Document," 1–72. For synopses of all manuscripts including their proposed paleographical dates, see Greenfield, Stone, and Eshel, *Aramaic Levi Document*, 4.

20. For transcriptions of all Aramaic, Greek, and Syriac materials see, Drawnel, *Aramaic Wisdom Text*.

21. 4Q213b agrees with the Cairo Genizah text (Greenfield, Stone and Eshel, *Aramaic Levi Document*, 70). For another potential variant between the Qumran fragments, and certainly with the Cairo Genizah fragments, see 4Q214 2, 3 // 1Q21 45, 1 // 4Q214b 2–6 I, 9. Since these three places are highly fragmentary in the Qumran texts and debated among scholars, we do not include the material in our list. See the transcriptions and comments of Greenfield, Stone, and Eshel, *Aramaic Levi Document*, 84; Drawnel, *Aramaic Wisdom Text*, 185.

22. Greenfield, Stone, and Eshel are inconsistent on this point: under their variant section of the text they read מטמרא but מטמריא in their commentary (*Aramaic Levi Document*, 106, 213). Drawnel, however, is correct that the *yod* is "absent in the manuscript" (*Aramaic Wisdom Text*, 201).

## Astronomical Enoch

Fragments of at least four Aramaic manuscripts have a plausible relationship to the Astronomical Book of Enoch (4Q208–211).[23] These exhibit minor overlap and variation between select fragments (4Q208 23, 4Q210 1 II), which may have extended further than we can know given the fragmentary nature of the texts.

There is, for example, what appears to be a difference in the length of text as revealed by an apparent minus in 4Q209. Where 4Q209 23, 7–8 includes room for approximately three words, the corresponding content line in 4Q210 1 II, 18–19 has additional space and includes limited content regarding the rising of the moon. These fragments also include a number of prepositional and conjunctive differences. In one instance, this involves different compound preposition clusters: where 4Q209 23, 5 reads ובדכן (i.e., ו + ב + די + כן), the overlapping text in 4Q210 1 II, 16 has בדיל כן.[24]

One of the most consistent threads of variation involves the (non) use of a medial *nun* on some forms in 4Q210, many of which were corrected via supralinear insertions in combination with scratched out characters. For example, the initial form מאיאן becomes מנאין at 4Q210 1 II, 16, where the corresponding text of 4Q209 23, 5 reads מאין. Given the cluster of corrections involving the words involving *nun* in 4Q209 23, it is likely these additions to the text were undertaken at the same time. The motivation for these corrections—whether textual, scribal, or linguistic—is open to debate.[25]

---

23. For 4Q208–209, see Tigchelaar and García Martínez, "4QAstronomical Enoch[a–b]." For 4Q208–209 as well as 210–211, see also Milik's *Books of Enoch*, 273–97. These materials now benefit from a fresh treatment by Henryk Drawnel, *The Astronomical Book (4Q208–211) from Qumran: Text, Translation, and Commentary* (Oxford: Oxford University Press, 2011).

24. For discussion on compound prepositions, see Muraoka, *Grammar of Qumran Aramaic*, 83–84; see also Schattner-Rieser, *L'araméen des manuscrits*, 96.

25. Milik suggests that the updated form מנאין was intended to bring the text into alignment with contemporary spelling for the relative "whence" (*Books of Enoch*, 291). Tigchelaar and García Martínez argue, however, that Milik's transcription is fine but his resulting translation ("there") "is not an exact rendering of the Aramaic" ("4QAstronomical Enoch[a–b] ar," 161). They suggest the form here and elsewhere in the fragment should be read as the noun "vessels." Beyer proposed that the form is a plural of מאה, that is, "hundreds." See Klaus Beyer, *Die aramäischen Texte vom Toten Meer samt den Inschriften aus Palästina, dem Testament Levis aus der Kairoer Genisa,*

Variants

קׅדמיה 4Q209 23, 3 ] קדמיא 4Q210 1 II, 15 (1 En. 77.1)
מאץ 4Q209 23, 5 ] מא{י׳}אׄ 26 4Q210 1 II, 16 (1 En. 77.2)
ומאץ 4Q209 23, 5 ] ומ{י׳}אן 27 4Q210 1 II, 16 (1 En. 77.2)
כוכבין 4Q209 23, 5 ] כֿוכביא 4Q210 1 II, 16 (1 En. 77.2)
ובדכן 4Q209 23, 5 ] בדיל כ]ן 4Q210 1 II, 16 (1 En. 77.2)
ומתכנסין 4Q209 23, 6 ] ומתכ<נ>סין 4Q210 1 II, 17 (1 En. 77.3)
כל 4Q209 23, 6 ] {ו}כֿל 4Q210 1 II, 17 (1 En. 77.3)
למדנחי 4Q209 23, 6 ] למדנח 4Q210 1 II, 17 (1 En. 77.3)
דרחיץ ירחין בהשתֿלֿ] מותהון 4Q209 23, 7–8 ] זרחיןׄ [וחזית תלת תֿ ארעא
בכל יום וי[וֿםֿ לאתחזיא עָ]ל ארעא וחזית תלת ... ת ארעא] 4Q210 1 II,
18–19 (1 En. 77.3)
בדי 4Q209 23, 8 ] די 4Q210 1 II, 18 (1 En. 77.3)
מאׅ[י׳]ןׄ 4Q209 23, 8] 4Q210 1 II, 18 28מׄיאץ (1 En. 77.3)
זרחיןׄ 4Q209 23, 8 ] {ש}דׄרחיץ 4Q210 1 II, 18 (1 En. 77.3)
מנהון 4Q209 23, 8 ] מנהׄוןׄ 4Q210 1 II, 19 (1 En. 77.3)

## Tobit

Cave 4 held four fragmentary Aramaic copies of the book of Tobit (4Q196–199) and a single Hebrew translation (4Q200).[29] As Fitzmyer demonstrated, in structure and detail these materials provide early Semitic language witnesses to the text from the so-called long version found in the Old Latin and Sinaiticus, with only occasional minor agreements in words or phrasing to the short version.

---

*der Fastenrolle und den alten talmudischen Zitaten: Ergänzungsband* (Göttingen: Vandenhoeck & Ruprecht, 1994), 255.

26. The textual variant is complicated by an apparent series of interventions. See Milik, *Books of Enoch*, 288; Tigchelaar and García Martínez, "4QAstronomical Enoch[a–b] ar," 159–60.

27. Here too, the text and interventions are difficult to decipher. See Milik, *Books of Enoch*, 288; Tigchelaar and García Martínez, "4QAstronomical Enoch[a–b] ar," 159–60.

28. For discussion of the correction and resulting variant, see Milik, *Books of Enoch*, 288; Tigchelaar and García Martínez, "4QAstronomical Enoch[b] ar," 159–60.

29. For complete publication, see Fitzmyer, "Tobit." It is possible that the fragment 3Q14 4 includes content from Tob 7:1–2. Baillet only briefly hints at this possibility, which seems more likely in view of the now-known texts of 4Q196 14 II, 6–8 and 4Q197 4 III, 2–5. See Maurice Baillet, "Fragments isolés," in Baillet, Milik, and de Vaux, *Les "Petites Grottes" de Qumran*, 103.

The textual variants between the Qumran Aramaic texts are few but of various types. These include morphological or phonological interchanges of final *he* and *aleph* (במה, 4Q196 14 II, 8; כמא, 4Q197 4 III, 4). Similarly, earlier in the same fragments we see the *haphel* and *aphel* used interchangeably (וה[ש]כֹּחו, 4Q196 14 II, 6; ואשכחֹו, 4Q197 4 III, 3).[30] Another sort of verbal-syntactical variant is found in the use of *lamed* as a direct-object marker in 4Q197 4 II, 10 on the form ולאמי, where the overlapping text of 4Q196 14 I, 6 reads ואמי. One known variant reveals an early scribal blunder. Where 4Q196 18, 16 reads the confusing form ובקדה, the overlapping material in 4Q198 1, 2 reads ופקדה. As Fitzmyer and Edward Cook note, the *bet* in 4Q196 is likely a scribal error for the intended verb פקד found in 4Q198.[31]

Finally, as was the case with Aramaic Levi Document above, in a very few instances the Qumran Tobit materials provide entirely new readings unknown from later traditions. Note, for example, Azariah's appeal to Tobias as אחי ("*my* brother") in 4Q196 14 I, 9, where most later witnesses here read only "brother" (ἀδελφός in all Greek versions).

Variants
    4Q196 13, 2–3 [עזריה] אֹחי אמֹ[ר לי][ ...מה סם ב[לֹבֹב
    4Q197 4 I, 12 (Tob 6:7) [וא]מר לה עזריה אחי מה סם בלבב]
    4Q197 4 I, 12 (Tob 6:7) וֹבכֹ]בדה [ 4Q196 13, 3 וכבֹדֹה
    4Q197 4 II, 10 (Tob 6:15) ולאמי [ 4Q196 14 I, 6 ואמי
    4Q197 4 III, 3 (Tob 7:1) ואשכחֹו] [ 4Q196 14 II, 6 וה[ש]כֹּחו
    4Q197 4 III, 4 (Tob 7:2) כמא [ 4Q196 14 II, 8 כמה
    4Q198 1, 2 (Tob 14:3) ופקדה [ 4Q196 18, 16 ובקדה

---

30. Variation in these forms is well-noted in the corpus as a whole and, as Muraoka underscores, there is "no functional difference" between them (*Grammar of Qumran Aramaic*, 109). The linguistic variation opens the question of whether such shifts in language are not only diachronic but also relevant to studies in cognitive linguistics and scribal understandings or preferences. Cook comments that certain linguistic preferences, such as these verbal stems, seem "to have depended on the whim of the scribe." See Edward M. Cook, "The Aramaic of the Dead Sea Scrolls," in *The Dead Sea Scrolls after Fifty Years: A Comprehensive Assessment*, ed. Peter W. Flint and James C. VanderKam (Leiden: Brill, 1998), 1:373.

31. See Edward M. Cook, *Dictionary of Qumran Aramaic* (Winona Lake, IN: Eisenbrauns, 2015), 193.

## Four Kingdoms

The Aramaic Four Kingdoms is represented by four fragmentary manuscripts at Qumran (4Q552, 4Q553, 4Q553a).[32] While the modest overlap between these reveals but four textual variants, some are of semantic significance. Note, for example, the following variant involving either a plus or minus of content. When dialoguing with the tree in the symbolic dream-vision account, 4Q553 3+2 II+4, 5 relates the seer's words as ושאלתה ואמרת לה מן שמך ("and I inquired of it and said to it, 'What is your name?'"). Alternatively, 4Q552 1 II, 8 does not include the second introductory discourse marker and reads ושאלתה מן שׁמ[ך] ("and I asked it, 'What is [your] name?'"). This variant could be explained in one of two ways. On the one hand, if 4Q553 is the older reading, then we might presume that parablepsis by homoioteleuton occurred when the scribe's eye skipped from the final *he* of ושאלתה to the final *he* of לה. On the other hand, if 4Q552 is the older reading, then ואמרת לה may have been added to clarify an implied level of discourse. Either way, this reading illustrates again that these early Aramaic manuscripts from Qumran *do* reveal variation and, at times, it is indeterminate which reading is earlier.

Variants

    4Q553 3+2 II+4, 2 וקמו אלניא ] 4Q552 1 II, 2 וקאם אילנא

    4Q553 3 + 2 II+4, 3 אחזה ] 4Q552 1 II, 3 אחזא

    4Q552 1 II, 6–8 אחרנא[ די נ[חית למערבא ל[משלט וקאם](?)[ למשנק ושאלתה ] 4Q553 3+2 II+4, 5 אחרנא ושאלתה

    4Q553 3+2 II+4, 5–6 ושאלתה ואמרת לה מן שמד ] 4Q552 1 II, 8 ושאלתה מן שׁמ[ך

## New Jerusalem

Second only to the Enochic works, the Aramaic New Jerusalem is represented by more copies across more caves than any other writing among the Aramaic DSS. A total of seven copies have been identified (1Q32, 2Q24, 4Q554, 4Q554a, 4Q555, 5Q15, 11Q18).[33] Given this representation, it is

---

32. For publication, see Émile Puech, "Les Quatre Royaumes," in Puech, *Qumran Grotte 4.XXVII*, 57–90.

33. The New Jerusalem texts are published in several DJD(J) volumes: Józef T. Milik, "Description de la Jérusalem Nouvelle (1Q32)," in Milik and Barthélemy,

perhaps not surprising that the New Jerusalem fragments also reveal the most variant readings in overlapping texts. These too fall on a spectrum.

There are a large number of differences related to the preference for either *he* or *aleph* in final positions. Intriguingly, there is some vacillation between these even within the same manuscripts. For example, 4Q554 1 III, 15 reads גויא, and 5Q15 1 I, 18 has גויה. Then shortly after, we find the reverse: 4Q554 1 III, 21 reads גֹוֹהֹ where 5Q15 1 II, 4 has גוא.[34] There are some pluses or minuses of both conjunctions (ולכל at 4Q554 1 II, 13 compared with לכל at 5Q15 1 I, 1) and prepositions (לאמי[ן] at 4Q554 1 II, 20 compared with אמי[ן] at 5Q15 1 I, 5).

Finally, some of the New Jerusalem fragments feature ciphered numbers (4Q554, 4Q554a) where the other manuscripts used written cardinal numbers in square script. This is an important scribal feature, yet in no places do we find a variant in the traditional sense involving different figures.[35] Along with this, where 5Q15 and 11Q18 write out complete measurement (אמין, "cubits") there are at least two instances where אמין has been abbreviated to simply *aleph* (4Q554 1 III, 14; 4Q554 1 III, 18). Here, too, while these dif-

---

Qumran Cave 1, 134; Maurice Baillet, "Description de la Jérusalem Nouvelle (2Q24)," in Baillet, Milik, and de Vaux, *Les "Petites Grottes" de Qumrân*, 84–89; Milik, "Description de la Jérusalem Nouvelle (5Q15)," in Baillet, Milik, and de Vaux, *Les "Petites Grottes" de Qumrân*, 184–92; Florentino García Martínez and Eibert J. C. Tigchelaar, "11QNew Jerusalem ar (11Q18)," in *Manuscripts from Qumran Cave 11 (11Q2–18, 11Q20–31)*, by Florentino García Martínez, Eibert J. C. Tigchelaar, and Adam S. van der Woude, DJD XXIII (Oxford: Clarendon, 1998), 305–56; Émile Puech, "Jérusalem Nouvelle (4Q554–555)," in Puech, *Qumran Grotte 4.XXVII*, 91–152. See also the important independent edition by Lorenzo DiTommaso, *The Dead Sea New Jerusalem Text: Contents and Contexts*, TSAJ 110 (Tübingen: Mohr Siebeck, 2005).

34. Compare also the series of nearly all configurations of possible spellings for the following: סחר סחר (4Q554 1 II, 13), סוחר סחור (5Q15 1 I, 1), and סחור סח[ור] (2Q24 1 2). Milik proposed that the formation of the forms in 5Q15 may be a Hebraism (Milik, "Description de la Jérusalem Nouvelle [5Q15]," 184).

35. The following references are for all overlaps where either 4Q544 or 4Q554a has a ciphered number and another New Jerusalem fragment has a written cardinal number: 4Q554 1 II, 12 // 2Q24 1, 1; 4Q554 1 II, 12–13 // 5Q15 1 I, 1; 4Q554 1 II, 14 // 5Q15 1 I, 1–2; 4Q554 1 II, 14 // 2Q24 1, 3 // 5Q15 1 I, 1–2; 4Q554 1 II, 15 // 5Q15 1 I, 2; 4Q554 1 II, 17 // 5Q15 1 I, 3; 4Q554 1 II, 18 // 5Q15 1 I, 4; 4Q554 1 II, 18 // 5Q15 1 I, 4; 4Q554 1 II, 19 // 5Q15 1 I, 5; 4Q554 1 II, 20 // 5Q15 1 I, 5; 4Q554 1 II, 21 // 5Q15 1 I, 6; 4Q554 1 III, 13 // 5Q15 1 I, 16; 4Q554 1 III, 14 // 5Q15 1 I, 17; 4Q554 1 III, 16 // 5Q15 1 I, 19; 4Q554 1 III, 18 // 5Q15 1 II, 1; 4Q554 1 III, 18 // 5Q15 1 II, 1; 4Q554a 1, 5 // 5Q15 1 II, 8; 4Q554a 1, 7 // 5Q15 1 II, 11.

ferences are significant for studies in scribal culture and material philology, they fall beyond the bounds of the present data set.

Variants
    5Q15 1 I, 1 לכל [ 4Q554 1 II, 13 ולכל
    2Q24 1, 2 סחור סח[ור]; 5Q15 1 I, 1 סוחר סחור [ 4Q554 1 II, 13 סֹחרֹ סחרֹ
    5Q15 1 I, 1 לפרזֹתא [ 4Q554 1 II, 13 לפרזיתא
    תלתה א[מ]ין עשרין [וחדה] .vac [ וכדן 4Q554 1 II, 14 תלתה אמין ריٜ וכֹדֹן 5Q15 1 I, 1–2
    2Q24 1, 3 אח[זי]נֹ[י ] כול משחת [ 4Q554 1 II, 14 [א]חֹזיני מש[ח]תֹ
    5Q15 1 I, 3 פֹותֹ[י ] 4Q554 1 II, 16 פתי
    5Q15 1 I, 4 פותי [ 4Q554 1 II, 18 פתיה
    5Q15 1 I, 4 אֹפֹוֹ]תי [ 4Q554 1 II, 18 ופתי
    5Q15 1 I, 5 אמי[ן] [ 4Q554 1 II, 20 לאמי[ן
    5Q15 1 I, 17 ית [ 4Q554 1 III, 14 ותֹ]רין [
    5Q15 1 I, 17 אורכה [ 4Q554 1 III, 14 ארכה
    5Q15 1 I, 18 אסף [ 4Q554 1 III, 15 אסוף
    5Q15 1 I, 18 אוחרן [ 4Q554 1 III, 15 אחרן
    5Q15 1 I, 18 ותרעא [ 4Q554 1 III, 15 ותרעה
    5Q15 1 I, 18 כותלא [ 4Q554 1 III, 15 כתלא
    5Q15 1 I, 18 גויֹה [ 4Q554 1 III, 15 גויא
    5Q15 1 I, 19 רֹוֹמֹ]ה [ 4Q554 1 III, 16 ורומה
    5Q15 1 II, 2 תרֹעֹ [ 4Q554 1 III, 18 תרעא
    5Q15 1 II, 2 אחזיא]ני [ 4Q554 1 III, 19 אחזיני
    5Q15 1 II, 3 ואורכה [ 4Q554 1 III, 20 וארכה
    5Q15 1 II, 4 גוא [ 4Q554 1 III, 21 גֹוֹהֹ
    5Q15 1 II, 7 פותאהון [ 4Q554a 1, 4 פת]ֹיהון
    5Q15 1 II, 7 ארוך [ 4Q554a 1, 4 ארך
    5Q15 1 II, 13 עשרה [ 4Q554a 1, 10 עש[רֹ]א
    5Q15 1 II, 13 ופותֹ]יהון [ 4Q554a 1, 10 ופתיהון
    11Q18 20, 5 ] הֹיֹ[ 2Q24 4, 14 הות

## Visions of Amram

At least five manuscripts of Visions of Amram were discovered in Qumran Cave 4 (4Q543–547).[36] An additional two manuscripts (4Q548 and

---

36. For 4Q543–547, see Puech, "Visions de 'Amram."

4Q549) are often clustered with these more certain manuscripts, yet these do not exhibit overlaps or feature topics and discourse that cohere with the content of 4Q543–547.

The majority of variants among the fragments of 4Q543–547 are orthographic in nature (4Q543 4, 2 // 4Q547 1–2 III, 6; 4Q544 1, 2 // 4Q545 1a–b II, 15), involve shifts in guttural uses (exchange between *aleph* and *he* in 4Q544 1, 1 // 4Q545 1a–b II, 13; or once between *het* and *he* at 4Q543 5–9, 7 // 4Q544 1, 14), morphological differences regarding pronominal suffixes (4Q543 5–9, 7 // 4Q544 1, 14 and 4Q543 2a–b, 1 // 4Q545 1a I, 14), or verbal sufformatives and syntax (4Q543 5–9, 7 // 4Q544 1, 14; 4Q544 1, 1 // 4Q545 1a–b II, 13).

At least two semantic variants warrant comment, not least to reiterate the often-indeterminate nature of their origins or hints toward scribal interactions with the developing tradition. Compare the phrase בחזוי ("in my vision") in 4Q544 1, 10 with בחזות ("in visions of") in 4Q547 1–2 III, 9. The latter occurs on the edge of a narrow fragment, making it difficult to discern what the original phrase of the dream-vision formula may have read.[37] The penultimate entry in this list is, in the end, no variant at all. It began as a textual difference, which was obviated via an erasure demonstrating ongoing editorial activity. The stylistic idiom of "taking a wife for oneself" appears in many places in the Aramaic corpus to emphasize the importance of marriage within a kinship group.[38]

Variants

מִמַּרְכֹה 4Q543 2a–b, 1 ] ממרך 4Q545 1a I, 14
וּ[בְּבוֹל 4Q547 1–2 III, 6 ] ובכל 4Q543 4, 2
וְאַנְפּיוה 4Q544 1, 14 ] וא[נְ]פּיהי 4Q543 5–9, 7
הָעְבְן 4Q544 1, 14 ] חעבון 4Q543 5–9, 7
וּלְעַמְרה 4Q545 1a–b II, 13 ] ולמעמרא 4Q544 1, 1
עֲבִידְתֵּנְא 4Q545 1a–b II, 15 ] עבדתנא 4Q544 1, 2

---

37. Puech reconstructed the suffixed noun ראשי ("my head"), as in Dan 2:28; 4:2 (5), 7 (10), 10 (13); and 7:1 ("Visions de 'Amram," 379). Duke accepted that Puech's reconstruction "seems reasonable" (*Social Location*, 20). In Daniel, however, the phrase "visions of my/your head" (חזוי ראשי/ך) is predominantly coupled with "while upon my/your bed" (על משכבי/ך). The latter element is not found in the partially overlapping text of 4Q544 1, 10. It is possible, then, that in this manuscript Amram referred to "visions of the night."

38. See 1Q20 20, 9, 34; 4Q197 4 I, 19; 4 II, 3; and 11Q19 56, 18.

שׂגיּ 4Q544 1, 2 ] שׂ[גיאין ] 4Q545 1a–b II, 15
ולה 4Q544 1, 3 ] ולא 4Q545 1a–b II, 17
אנחנא 4Q544 1, 4 ] אנחנה 4Q545 1a–b II, 19
אנתה אחֹ]רי 4Q544 1, 8 ] אֹחרי {לי} אֹ[נֹתהֹ 4Q547 1–2 III, 7
בחזוֹי 4Q544 1, 10 ] בחזות 4Q547 1–2 III, 9

## Appendix: New or Confirmed Readings from Cook's *Dictionary of Qumran Aramaic*

Until relatively recently, the lack of a specialized lexical resource on the Qumran Aramaic texts meant scholars were forced to cull information from a handful of grammars, concordances, databases, and dictionaries, none of which were tailored to the texts at hand or fully and consistently integrated their lexical data.[39] Cook's *Dictionary of Qumran Aramaic* rectified this situation.

One of the added benefits of the volume is the impressive number of places where Cook proposes improvements on the transcription of words or phrases in the Qumran Aramaic texts. In the spirit of consolidating and presenting data relevant to the continued linguistic and textual study of the Qumran Aramaic texts, the following lists all instances where Cook critiques a reading found in the editions that served as his base text and provides an alternate reading or aligns with a reading found in another scholarly edition. Note, however, that we collate neither when a reading is stated as uncertain nor when an array of possible alternatives is presented without a determination of the best reading. Proposed reconstructions are generally not included, save for when a partially extant word is in question. For the sake of brevity, variations in diacritics between one transcription or another are generally not included. The list is ordered according the Qumran composition, fragment, and line number, with page numbers included for individual lexical entries. The data here is based on information presented solely in the dictionary itself. For full bibliographic information on all editions and studies referenced in the notations below, see Cook's full works cited list.[40]

---

39. Specialized grammars of the Qumran Aramaic finds now include those by Schattner-Rieser, *L'araméen des manuscrits*; Muraoka, *Grammar of Qumran Aramaic*.
40. Cook, *Dictionary of Qumran Aramaic*, 261–65.

# Variant Readings in the Aramaic Dead Sea Scrolls 111

- 1Q20 0, 8 אֲנִיתִי (Milik). With Machiela, Cook reads אנחנא (*Dictionary of Qumran Aramaic*, 16).
- 1Q20 0, 13. With Fitzmyer, Cook reads בעד מל[וה]י (*Dictionary of Qumran Aramaic*, 36).
- 1Q20 2, 22. With Machiela (see also Greenfield and Sokoloff), Cook reads רֹט עַל חנוך (*Dictionary of Qumran Aramaic*, 220).
- 1Q20 2, 23 לארקבת (Abegg and Wise), לְאַרְךְ מַת (Fitzmyer). With Dupont-Sommer, Cook reads לה קדמת (*Dictionary of Qumran Aramaic*, 206).
- 1Q20 6, 3 אֹוחת (Abegg and Wise). With Beyer (see also Machiela), Cook reads ארחת (*Dictionary of Qumran Aramaic*, 102).
- 1Q20 7, 19 להעדותני (Fitzmyer), לסעדותי (Machiela). With Beyer, Cook reads לסֹעדותני (*Dictionary of Qumran Aramaic*, 167).
- 1Q20 20, 26. With Fitzmyer and Machiela, Cook reads יתוך (*Dictionary of Qumran Aramaic*, 252).
- 1Q20 20, 29. Cook reads חי instead of הו (see Machiela; Cook, *Dictionary of Qumran Aramaic*, 62, 82).
- 1Q20 21, 32–33 וֹשׂגיאין (Machiela). Cook reads בֹּעגיאין (*Dictionary of Qumran Aramaic*, 172).
- 4Q197 4 III, 11 טב (Beyer). With Fitzmyer, and in light of LXX, Cook reads טֹבֹ[ח] (*Dictionary of Qumran Aramaic*, 94).
- 4Q201 1 II, 1 בֹּסֹרכן (Milik), [ה]לכן (Langlois). Cook reads לכן (*Dictionary of Qumran Aramaic*, 64).
- 4Q201 1 II, 4 מיבישן (Milik). With Langlois, Cook reads כִּיבישין (*Dictionary of Qumran Aramaic*, 98).
- 4Q201 1 II, 13. With Langlois, Cook reads בפם (*Dictionary of Qumran Aramaic*, 192).
- 4Q201 1 III, 19 וֹקשרין (Milik). With Sokoloff and Langlois, Cook reads ושריו (*Dictionary of Qumran Aramaic*, 215).
- 4Q201 1 III, 20 בֹּנֹף (Milik). With Langlois, Cook reads either בזה or בנה (*Dictionary of Qumran Aramaic*, 116).
- 4Q201 1 IV, 1 חבר[וֹ] (Milik). With Beyer and Langlois, Cook reads חבר[ין] (*Dictionary of Qumran Aramaic*, 75).
- 4Q202 1 II, 27 מֹבֹונא (Milik). With Beyer and Stadel, Cook reads תכונא (*Dictionary of Qumran Aramaic*, 253).
- 4Q204 1 VI, 13 [את]חזֹית (Milik). Cook reconstructs חזֹית[א] (*Dictionary of Qumran Aramaic*, 81).
- 4Q204 1 VI, 14. With Beyer, Cook reads בגזירוֹ גזֹ[ר עליכ]ון (*Dictionary of Qumran Aramaic*, 44).

- 4Q205 5 II, 17. Milik's reading: [בֹּל יֹהֹ]דת מריא, "very precarious." Cook proposes מֹל ○[ (*Dictionary of Qumran Aramaic*, 35).
- 4Q206 4 I, 21 [ז]ירו מֹ[ן] (Milik). Informed in part by Beyer, Cook reads [ורימנ]יא (*Dictionary of Qumran Aramaic*, 216).
- 4Q206 4 II, 20 נת[ר] (Milik). Cook reads נֹת[ת] (*Dictionary of Qumran Aramaic*, 162).
- 4Q211 1 I, 3 ועא (Drawnel). Cook reads יעא (*Dictionary of Qumran Aramaic*, 105).
- 4Q213a 3–4, 2 אשֹבען (Stone and Greenfield). With Drawnel, Cook reads ובען (*Dictionary of Qumran Aramaic*, 229).
- 4Q213a 3–4, 6 חסיה (Stone and Greenfield). With Puech and Drawnel, Cook reads חסדה (*Dictionary of Qumran Aramaic*, 88).
- 4Q214b 2–6 I, 4. With Beyer, Cook reads וסוגדֹהֹ (*Dictionary of Qumran Aramaic*, 164).
- 4Q246 1 I, 5. Cook reads נחשירוֹן (*Dictionary of Qumran Aramaic*, 155).
- 4Q461 1 I, 2. With Popović, Cook reads אֹרין (*Dictionary of Qumran Aramaic*, 24).
- 4Q530 1 I, 7 [ה]וֹקֹרת (Stuckenbruck, Beyer), אֹחרת (Puech). Cook reads [א]חֹדת (*Dictionary of Qumran Aramaic*, 106).
- 4Q530 2 II+6–12, 16 גברוֹא (Puech). Cook reads גבריא (*Dictionary of Qumran Aramaic*, 43).
- 4Q530 2 II+6–12, 24 כֹפנוהֹי (Puech). With Machiela and Perrin, Cook reads תֹּנֹדֹע (*Dictionary of Qumran Aramaic*, 118).
- 4Q530 2 II+6–12, 24 איתיו (Puech). With Stuckenbruck, Beyer, and Machiela and Perrin, Cook reads איתֹי (*Dictionary of Qumran Aramaic*, 8–9).
- 4Q530 2 II+6–12, 24. With Machiela and Perrin, Cook reads ארבא (*Dictionary of Qumran Aramaic*, 21–22).
- 4Q531 15, 3 אֹחרת (Puech). Cook reads אֹחדת (*Dictionary of Qumran Aramaic*, 6).
- 4Q531 22, 8 אוש (Milik), איליֹ (Stuckenbruck, Beyer). With Puech, Cook reads איש (*Dictionary of Qumran Aramaic*, 8).
- 4Q534 1 I, 4 לטיש (Starky), מלוהי (Beyer), כלהון (Fitzmyer), כלייש (Carmignac), כלטיש (Puech). Cook reads כלטוש (*Dictionary of Qumran Aramaic*, 128).
- 4Q534 7 I, 1 א{{מ}}ז (Puech). Cook reads ומא (*Dictionary of Qumran Aramaic*, 49).
- 4Q541 9 I, 6 באיש יאפיך (Puech). Cook reads באיש ואפיד (*Dictionary of Qumran Aramaic*, 21).

- 4Q542 1 II, 7 לבלמֹ] (Puech), לבלב̇]לה[ (Beyer). Cook proposes perhaps reading [לבלח̇]ודיהון (*Dictionary of Qumran Aramaic*, 35).
- 4Q544 1, 13 כפ[תן (Puech). Cook reads ואימ[תן (*Dictionary of Qumran Aramaic*, 8, 52, 197).[41]
- 4Q544 1, 13 ח̇שֹל (Puech). Cook reads דֹחִיל (*Dictionary of Qumran Aramaic*, 52).
- 4Q544 2, 16 [מ]צליא (Puech). Cook reads עֹליא (*Dictionary of Qumran Aramaic*, 160).
- 4Q548 1 II+2, 7 חרֹא (Puech, Beyer). Cook reads חדֹא (*Dictionary of Qumran Aramaic*, 91).
- 4Q556 1, 6. Cook reads חדתא, which supersedes חרתא of the *Dead Sea Scrolls Concordance* (*Dictionary of Qumran Aramaic*, 77).
- 4Q556a 5 I, 7. With Puech, Cook reads פתגמא, which supersedes בתגמא of the *Dead Sea Scrolls Concordance* (*Dictionary of Qumran Aramaic*, 196).
- 4Q558 29, 4 יתיתר (Beyer), א]יתותר[ (Puech). Cook reads יתותר (*Dictionary of Qumran Aramaic*, 108).
- 4Q558 33 I, 8. With Puech, Cook reads וֹחהֹא[ר], which supersedes חוֹא at 4Q558 37 I, 7 of the *Dead Sea Scrolls Concordance* (*Dictionary of Qumran Aramaic*, 220).
- 4Q558 33 II, 5. With Puech, Cook reads בלאו, which supersedes מלאו of the *Dead Sea Scrolls Concordance* (*Dictionary of Qumran Aramaic*, 35).
- 4Q558 51 II, 4. Cook reads קש̇]יטא. See also Stökl Ben Ezra (Cook, *Dictionary of Qumran Aramaic*, 215).
- 4Q558 57, 4 תוֹת[ (Puech). Cook reads תזף (*Dictionary of Qumran Aramaic*, 101).
- 4Q560 1 I, 5. With Puech, Cook reads מחתא די, which supersedes מחתורי of the *Dead Sea Scrolls Concordance* (*Dictionary of Qumran Aramaic*, 136).
- 4Q561 1 I, 5 מג[דמין (Puech). Cook reads מה[דמ̇ין, noting also a possible scribal error for [מ]גרמין (*Dictionary of Qumran Aramaic*, 61).
- 4Q564 1 II, 2 ש̇ידין (Puech). Cook reads עוֹיֹדין (*Dictionary of Qumran Aramaic*, 175).

---

41. For a supporting analysis of Cook's reading here and the next lemma, see now also Andrew B. Perrin, "Another Look at Dualism in 4QVisions of Amram," *Hen* 36 (2014): 106–17.

- 4Q565 1, 3 אלה (Puech). Cook reads אשה (*Dictionary of Qumran Aramaic*, 26).
- 4Q586 b, 2 יתעבוהן (Puech). Cook suggests ית עביהן (*Dictionary of Qumran Aramaic*, 257).
- 11Q10 11, 8 ה[צו]מ[ו] (Sokoloff), ט[ב]ה (Beyer). With García Martínez et al., Cook reads מ[מ]ו[ון]ה (*Dictionary of Qumran Aramaic*, 141).
- 11Q10 28, 5–6. Cook reads ט[פי] (*Dictionary of Qumran Aramaic*, 97).
- 11Q10 32, 9 יס[דד] (Sokoloff). Cook reads ילג[ז] (*Dictionary of Qumran Aramaic*, 26).

## Bibliography

Abegg, Martin, Jr., Peter Flint, and Eugene Ulrich. *The Dead Sea Scrolls Bible: The Oldest Known Bible Translated for the First Time into English*. New York: HarperOne, 1999.

Avigad, Nahman, and Yigael Yadin. *A Genesis Apocryphon: A Scroll from the Wilderness of Judea; Description and Contents of the Scroll, Facsimiles, Transcription, and Translation of Columns II, XIX–XXII*. Jerusalem: Magnes & Heikhal Ha-Sefer, 1956.

Baillet, Maurice. "Description de la Jérusalem Nouvelle (2Q24)." Pages 84–89 in *Les "Petites Grottes" de Qumrân*. By Maurice Baillet, Józef T. Milik, and Roland de Vaux. DJD III. Oxford: Clarendon, 1962.

———. "Fragments isolés." Pages 102–4 in *Les "Petites Grottes" de Qumrân*. By Maurice Baillet, Józef T. Milik, and Roland de Vaux. DJD III. Oxford: Clarendon, 1962.

———. "Un apocryphe de la Genese (6Q8)." Pages 116–19 in *Les "Petites Grottes" de Qumrân*. By Maurice Baillet, Józef T. Milik, and Roland de Vaux. DJD III. Oxford: Clarendon, 1962.

Beyer, Klaus. *Die aramäischen Texte vom Toten Meer samt den Inschriften aus Palästina, dem Testament Levis aus der Kairoer Genisa, der Fastenrolle und den alten talmudischen Zitaten: Ergänzungsband*. Göttingen: Vandenhoeck & Ruprecht, 1994.

Cook, Edward M. "The Aramaic of the Dead Sea Scrolls." Pages 359–78 in *The Dead Sea Scrolls after Fifty Years: A Comprehensive Assessment*. Vol. 1. Edited by Peter W. Flint and James C. VanderKam. Leiden: Brill, 1998.

———. *Dictionary of Qumran Aramaic*. Winona Lake, IN: Eisenbrauns, 2015.

DiTommaso, Lorenzo. *The Dead Sea New Jerusalem Text: Contents and Contexts*. TSAJ 110. Tübingen: Mohr Siebeck, 2005.

Drawnel, Henryk. *An Aramaic Wisdom Text from Qumran: A New Interpretation of the Levi Document*. JSJSup 86. Leiden: Brill, 2004.

———. *The Astronomical Book (4Q208–211) from Qumran: Text, Translation, and Commentary*. Oxford: Oxford University Press, 2011.

Duke, Robert R. *The Social Location of the Visions of Amram (4Q543–547)*. StBibLit 135. New York: Lang, 2010.

Fitzmyer, Joseph. "Tobit." Pages 1–76 in *Qumran Cave 4.XIV: Parabiblical Texts, Part 2*. By Magen Broshi et al. DJD XIX. Oxford: Clarendon, 1995.

———. *Tobit*. CEJL. Berlin: de Gruyter, 2008.

García Martínez, Florentino, and Eibert J. C. Tigchelaar. "11QNew Jerusalem ar (11Q18)." Pages 305–56 in *Manuscripts from Qumran Cave 11 (11Q2–18, 11Q20–31)*. By Florentino García Martínez, Eibert J. C. Tigchelaar, and Adam S. van der Woude. DJD XXIII. Oxford: Clarendon, 1998.

Greenfield, Jonas C., Michael E. Stone, and Esther Eshel. *The Aramaic Levi Document: Edition, Translation, Commentary*. SVTP 19. Leiden: Brill, 2004.

Hallermayer, Michaela. *Text und Überlieferung des Buches Tobit*. DCLS 3. Berlin: de Gruyter, 2008.

Hempel, Charlotte. "From A–Z: The Relegation of the A-List of Biblical History in the Dead Sea Scrolls." Paper presented at the International Meeting of the Society of Biblical Literature. Helsinki, 2 August 2018.

Kloppenborg, John S., and Judith H. Newman, eds. *Editing the Bible: Assessing the Task Past and Present*. Atlanta: Society of Biblical Literature, 2012.

Milik, Józef T. *The Books of Enoch: Aramaic Fragments of Qumrân Cave 4*. Oxford: Clarendon, 1976.

———. "Description de la Jérusalem Nouvelle (1Q32)." Page 134 in *Qumran Cave 1*. By Józef T. Milik and Dominique Barthélemy. DJD I. Oxford: Clarendon, 1955.

———. "Description de la Jérusalem Nouvelle (5Q15)." Pages 184–92 in *Les "Petites Grottes" de Qumrân*. By Maurice Baillet, Józef T. Milik, and Roland de Vaux. DJD III. Oxford: Clarendon, 1962.

———. "Deux apocryphes en Araméen (1Q23, 1Q24)." Pages 97–99 in *Qumran Cave 1*. By Józef T. Milik and Dominique Barthélemy. DJD I. Oxford: Clarendon, 1955.

———. "'Prière de Nabonide' et autres écrits d'un cycle de Daniel." *RB* 63 (1956): 407–15.

———. "Testament de Lévi (1Q21)." Pages 87–90 in *Qumran Cave 1*. By Józef T. Milik and Dominique Barthélemy. DJD I. Oxford: Clarendon, 1955.

Milik, Józef T., and Dominique Barthélemy. *Qumran Cave 1*. DJD I. Oxford: Clarendon, 1955.

Mroczek, Eva. *The Literary Imagination in Jewish Antiquity*. Oxford: Oxford University Press, 2016.

Muraoka, Takamitsu. *A Grammar of Qumran Aramaic*. ANES 38. Leuven: Peeters, 2011.

Najman, Hindy. Review of *Old Testament Pseudepigrapha: More Noncanonical Scriptures*. Edited by Richard J. Bauckham, James R. Davila, and Alexander Panayotov. *DSD* 22 (2015): 211–14.

Nickelsburg, George W. E. *1 Enoch 1: A Commentary on the Book of 1 Enoch, Chapters 1–36, 81–108*. Hermeneia. Minneapolis: Augsburg Fortress, 2001.

Norin, Stig. "The Aramaic Levi—Comparing the Qumran Fragments with the Genizah Text." *SJOT* 27 (2013): 118–30.

Pajunen, Mika. "Bible." Pages 367–75 in *The T&T Clark Companion to the Dead Sea Scrolls*. Edited by George J. Brooke and Charlotte Hempel. BC. London: Bloomsbury, 2018.

Perrin, Andrew B. "Another Look at Dualism in *4QVisions of Amram*." *Hen* 36 (2014): 106–17.

———. "The Textual Forms of Aramaic Levi Document at Qumran." Pages 431–52 in *Reading the Bible in Ancient Traditions and Modern Editions: Studies in Memory of Peter W. Flint*. Edited by Andrew B. Perrin, Kyung S. Baek, and Daniel K. Falk. EJL 47. Atlanta: SBL Press, 2017.

Puech, Émile. "4QGéants[a] ar (4Q203)." Pages 507–8 in *Qumran Cave 4.XXVII: Textes araméens, deuxième partie; 4Q550–4Q575a, 4Q580–4Q587*. By Émile Puech. DJD XXXVII. Oxford: Clarendon, 2009.

———. "4QProphétie[a] ar (4Q556)." Pages 155–58 in *Qumrân Grotte 4.XXVII: Textes araméens, deuxième partie; 4Q550–4Q575a, 4Q580–4Q587*. By Émile Puech. DJD XXXVII. Oxford: Clarendon, 2009.

———. "Jérusalem Nouvelle (4Q554–555)." Pages 91–152 in *Qumrân Grotte 4.XXVII: Textes araméens deuxième partie; 4Q550–4Q575a,*

4Q580–4Q587. By Émile Puech. DJD XXXVII. Oxford: Clarendon, 2009.

———. "Les Quatres Royaumes." Pages 57–90 in *Qumran Grotte 4.XXVII: Textes araméens, deuxième partie; 4Q550–4Q575a, 4Q580–4Q587.* By Émile Puech. DJD XXXVII. Oxford: Clarendon, 2009.

———. "Livre des Géants (530–533, 203 1)." Pages 9–104 in *Qumrân Grotte 4.XXII: Textes araméens, première partie; 4Q529–549.* By Émile Puech. DJD XXXI. Oxford: Clarendon, 2001.

———. *Qumrân Grotte 4.XXII: Textes araméens, première partie; 4Q529–549.* By Émile Puech. DJD XXXI. Oxford: Clarendon, 2001.

———. *Qumrân Grotte 4.XXVII: Textes araméens, deuxième partie; 4Q550–4Q575a, 4Q580–4Q587.* By Émile Puech. DJD XXXVII. Oxford: Clarendon, 2009.

———. "Visions de 'Amram." Pages 283–405 in *Qumrân Grotte 4.XXII: Textes araméens, première partie; 4Q529–549.* By Émile Puech. DJD XXXI. Oxford: Clarendon, 2001.

Schattner-Rieser, Ursula. *L'araméen des manuscrits de la mer Morte, I: Grammaire.* IELOA 5. Prahins: Éditions du Zèbre, 2004.

Stone, Michael E., and Jonas C. Greenfield. "Aramaic Levi Document." Pages 1–72 in *Qumran Cave 4.XVII: Parabiblical Texts, Part 3.* By George J. Brooke et al. DJD XXII. Oxford: Clarendon, 1996.

Stuckenbruck, Loren T. "4QEnoch$^a$ (4Q201 2–8)." Pages 3–7 in *Qumran Cave 4.XXVI: Cryptic Texts.* By Stephen J. Pfann et al. *Miscellanea, Part 1.* By Philip S. Alexander et al. DJD XXXVI. Oxford: Clarendon, 2000.

———. "4QEnoch$^f$ ar (4Q206 2–3)." Pages 42–48 in *Qumran Cave 4.XXVI: Cryptic Texts.* By Stephen J. Pfann et al. *Miscellanea, Part 1.* By Philip S. Alexander et al. DJD XXXVI. Oxford: Clarendon, 2000.

———. "6QpapGiants ar (Re-edition)." Pages 73–94 in *Qumran Cave 4.XXVI: Cryptic Texts.* By Stephen J. Pfann et al. *Miscellanea, Part 1.* By Philip S. Alexander et al. DJD XXXVI. Oxford: Clarendon, 2000.

———. "Apocrypha and Pseudepigrapha." *EDEJ* 143–62.

———. *The Book of Giants from Qumran.* TSAJ 63. Tübingen: Mohr Siebeck, 1997.

Tigchelaar, Eibert J. C., and Florentino García Martínez. "4QAstronomical Enoch$^{a-b}$ (4Q208–209)." Pages 95–172 in *Qumran Cave 4.XXVI: Cryptic Texts.* By Stephen J. Pfann et al. *Miscellanea, Part 1.* By Philip S. Alexander et al. DJD XXXVI. Oxford: Clarendon, 2000.

Ulrich, Eugene. "Daniel." Pages 239–89 in *Qumran Cave 4.XI: Psalms to Chronicles.* By Eugene Ulrich et al. DJD XVI. Oxford: Clarendon, 2000.

———. "Ezra." Pages 291–93 in *Qumran Cave 4.XI: Psalms to Chronicles*. By Eugene Ulrich et al. DJD XVI. Oxford: Clarendon, 2000.
———. *The Qumran Biblical Scrolls: Transcriptions and Textual Variants*. VTSup 134. Leiden: Brill, 2010.

# Isaiah at Qumran and in the Gospel of Matthew

Kyung S. Baek

## 1. Introduction

Eugene Ulrich and Peter Flint have made a substantial contribution to scholarship on Isaiah at Qumran. Over a period of roughly thirty years, not only did they write extensively on Isaiah, but their research informed some of their widely held conclusions regarding the biblical Dead Sea Scrolls (DSS). Discoveries in the Judaean Desert (DJD) XXXII, based on the Isaiah scrolls of Cave 1 (1QIsa$^a$ and 1QIsa$^b$ [1Q8]), was the culmination of their work.[1] Building on their research, this article is a tribute to Flint in which I attempt to extend some of their findings into Matthew's use of Isaiah.

In both the DSS and the Gospel of Matthew, Isaiah is important and used in a variety of ways. Arguably, Isaiah is the best-known prophetic book for early Jewish and Christian interpretation, being frequently cited in Second Temple Jewish literature as well as in the New Testament. In the DSS, its significance is evidenced not only by its many manuscripts but also by its use in commentaries (pesharim) and its numerous occurrences in quotations, citations, and allusions. Similarly, in the New Testament, Isaiah is one of the most-quoted books in the Hebrew Bible.[2]

---

Peter W. Flint passed away suddenly on November 3, 2016. It was an honor to be invited to present a memorial paper on May 27, 2017, at the Annual Meeting of the Canadian Society of Biblical Studies. This article was developed from that invitation, and I want to thank the editors for its inclusion in this volume.

1. Peter W. Flint and Eugene Ulrich, *Qumran Cave 1.I–II: The Isaiah Scrolls*, 2 vols., DJD XXXII (Oxford: Clarendon, 2010).

2. See Craig A. Evans, "From Gospel to Gospel: The Function of Isaiah in the New Testament," in *Writing and Reading the Scroll of Isaiah: Studies of an Interpretive Tradition*, ed. Craig C. Broyles and Craig A. Evans (Leiden: Brill, 1997), 2:651.

These similarities suggest that Isaiah at Qumran could shed some light on Matthew's use of Isaiah in its explicit and implicit references—that is, in fulfillment quotations, citations, and allusions.

Furthermore, this multiplicity of uses of Isaiah at Qumran and in Matthew seems to illustrate Matthew's repertoire of hermeneutical strategies in its presentation of Jesus's identity and authority as the Messiah (1:1). Matthew uses fulfillment quotations to reveal divine activity as actualized prophecy—revealing Jesus's identity and divine protection. Matthew uses citations with an introductory formula to support Jesus's authority in continuity with the Hebrew scriptures (i.e., placing them in the mouth of Jesus). Matthew uses nonintroductory citations as idiomatic expressions for Jesus's teaching and actions. Matthew uses allusions of Isaiah thematically to persuade its readers regarding the person and purpose of Jesus as the servant of the Lord, call to true worship, and God's deliverance and restoration of Israel.

## 2. Isaiah at Qumran

### 2.1. Peter Flint and DJD XXXII

Appropriately, this article begins with a short tribute to Flint and his work on Isaiah.[3] As an enthusiastic spokesperson for the DSS, his passion and commitment were exemplary and infectious when he presented his research, published his findings, and trained the next generation of DSS scholars.[4] Often collaborating with his students and colleagues, he edited and wrote more than eleven books and eighty-five articles and presented over one hundred conference papers.[5]

In working on Isaiah, Peter, a careful text critic and technician, researched the minutia of the DSS: meticulously examining and transcribing texts, compiling lists of variant readings, and examining their

---

3. To many who knew Peter, he was not just a scholar but a trusted colleague and friend. He tirelessly advocated for his graduate students and paved opportunities for junior scholars.

4. From 2000 to 2016, Peter held a Tier 1 Canada Research Chair in Dead Sea Scrolls Studies that supported his research program.

5. See Andrew B. Perrin, Kyung S. Baek, and Daniel K. Falk, *Reading the Bible in Ancient Traditions and Modern Editions: Studies in Memory of Peter W. Flint*, EJL 47 (Atlanta: SBL Press, 2017), 679–90.

features and characteristics.[6] The pinnacle of his research was the publication of the two-volume set of DJD XXXII (*Qumran Cave 1.I–II: The Isaiah Scrolls*): volume 1 contains the photographic plates and transcriptions of 1QIsa[a] and 1QIsa[b], and volume 2 includes an introduction to 1QIsa[a] and 1QIsa[b] (covering their discovery, photography, and linguistic profile,[7] commentary on their physical descriptions and contents, paleography and dating, scribal practices and scribal marks, orthography, sense divisions, and textual character) as well as a list of textual variants. However, Peter's research on Isaiah did not end with DJD XXXII. Having established the text and variants of Isaiah, he began investigating Isaiah's influence and use not only at Qumran but also in broader Second Temple literature. Peter's research vision was especially evident in his final two articles: "Interpreting the Poetry of Isaiah at Qumran: Theme and Function in the Sectarian Scrolls" and "The Interpretation of Scriptural Isaiah in the Qumran Scrolls: Quotations, Citations, Allusions, and the Form of the Scriptural Source Text."[8]

## 2.2. Isaiah at Qumran

DJD XXXII lays a foundation for understanding the book of Isaiah as well as some aspects of the DSS and Second Temple Judaism. Isaiah is among the most popular books at Qumran, with twenty-two copies found among the DSS: two copies in Cave 1 (1QIsa[a], 1QIsa[b]); eighteen copies in Cave 4 (4QIsa[a–o] [4Q55–68], 4QpapIsa[p] [4Q69], 4QIsa[q–r] [4Q69a, 4Q69b]); one copy in Cave 5 (5QIsa [5Q3]); and one copy at Murabba'at (MurIsa [Mur

---

6. Peter's earliest publications of Isaiah were in 1988: "From Tarshish to Carthage: The Septuagint Translation of 'Tarshish' in Isaiah 23," *PJEGLMBS* 8 (1988): 127–33; "The Septuagint Version of Isaiah 23:1–14 and the Massoretic Text," *BIOSCS* 21 (1988): 35–54.

7. Martin Abegg Jr. wrote this section.

8. Peter W. Flint, "Interpreting the Poetry of Isaiah at Qumran: Theme and Function in the Sectarian Scrolls," in *Prayer and Poetry in the Dead Sea Scrolls and Related Literature: Essays in Honor of Eileen Schuller on the Occasion of Her Sixty-Fifth Birthday*, ed. Jeremy Penner, Ken M. Penner, and Cecilia Wassen, STDJ 98 (Leiden: Brill, 2012), 151–84; Flint, "The Interpretation of Scriptural Isaiah in the Qumran Scrolls: Quotations, Allusions, and the Form of the Biblical Text," in *A Teacher for all Generations: Essays in Honor of James C. VanderKam*, ed. Eric F. Mason et al., JSJSup 153 (Leiden: Brill, 2012), 398–406.

3]).⁹ Although many are fragmentary, with varying degrees of completeness, these manuscript copies of Isaiah range over nearly two centuries, from about 125 BCE (i.e., 1QIsa<sup>a</sup>) to about 60 CE (i.e., 4QIsa<sup>c</sup>).[10] In addition to these twenty-two copies, six pesharim on Isaiah were also found at Qumran (3Q4, 4Q161, 4Q162, 4Q163, 4Q164, 4Q165). Furthermore, Isaiah is one of the most quoted books among the DSS, being cited at least twenty-three times in the sectarian writings.[11] Further accentuating its significance, 1QS VIII, 14 quotes Isaiah as a means of expressing the community's self-identity (see Isa 40:3).[12] Therefore, we can reasonably conclude that Isaiah was important and viewed as authoritative scripture for the Qumran movement. In sum, Isaiah's influence at Qumran should not be underestimated, with its high number of manuscripts, pesharim,[13] and frequent use in quotations, citations, and allusions.[14]

---

9. Only Psalms, with thirty-seven, and Deuteronomy, with thirty, have more manuscripts.

10. Eugene Ulrich, "An Index of the Passages in the Biblical Manuscripts from the Judean Desert (Part 2: Isaiah–Chronicles)," *DSD* 2 (1995): 88–92; Peter W. Flint, "The Book of Isaiah in the Dead Sea Scrolls," in *The Bible as Book: The Hebrew Bible and the Judaean Desert Discoveries*, ed. Edward D. Herbert and Emanuel Tov (London: British Library and Oak Knoll, 2002), 229–51.

11. See Francis J. Morrow Jr., "The Text of Isaiah at Qumran" (PhD diss., Catholic University of America, 1973), 205–13, where he has a nine-page list of occurrences of Isaiah in the DSS. Furthermore, many citations of Isaiah often focus on the text and interpretation of Isaiah's message: CD IV, 12–14 (Isa 24:17); VII, 11–12 (Isa 7:17); VIII, 1–2 (Isa 7:17); 1QS V, 17 (Isa 2:22); VIII, 13–14 (Isa 40:3); 1QM XI, 11–12 (Isa 31:8); 4Q162 (Isa 5:11–14); 4Q163 (Isa 30:15–18); 4Q174 1–2 I, 15–16 (Isa 8:11); 4Q176 1–2 I, 4 (Isa 40:1–5); 4Q265 2, 3–5 (Isa 54:1–2); 4Q266 3 I, 7 (Isa 24:17); 11Q13 II, 23 (Isa 52:7); XI, 11–12 (Isa 31:8).

12. Isaiah 40:3 is quoted at Qumran and in all four gospels for the purpose of self-identification (1QS VIII, 13–14; Matt 3:3; Mark 1:3; Luke 3:4; John 1:23). As a fulfillment of Isaiah's prophecy, the sectarian community seems to have separated themselves from others by going out into the wilderness to prepare the way of the Lord.

13. Like the twelve Minor Prophets (but unlike Jeremiah and Ezekiel), there are Isaiah pesharim that contain important themes such as the shoot of David (4Q161) and the Chosen One (4Q164).

14. See George J. Brooke, "Isaiah in the Pesharim and Other Qumran Texts," in Broyles and Evans, *Writing and Reading the Scroll of Isaiah*, 2:609–12, where he lists four uses of Isaiah: (1) legal, (2) eschatological, (3) poetic, and (4) exhortatory.

## 2.3. The Great Isaiah Scroll (1QIsa<sup>a</sup>)

The Great Isaiah Scroll (1QIsa<sup>a</sup>), also named the Isaiah Scroll of Saint Mark's Monastery, deserves special attention from among the Isaiah scrolls. Possibly the best-known DSS today, 1QIsa<sup>a</sup> is a magnificent manuscript housed at the Shrine of the Book and recognized as a national treasure of Israel. Well-preserved and in excellent condition, it contains all sixty-six chapters of Isaiah in fifty-four columns with only the occasional lacuna due to leather damage or minor deteriorations in the parchment.[15] In most instances, only a few words and phrases have been lost, while the vast majority is clear enough to be read with the naked eye.[16] 1QIsa<sup>a</sup> is among the first group of manuscripts discovered in Cave 1 at Qumran, in late 1946 or early 1947.[17] Dating from the Hasmonean period, 1QIsa<sup>a</sup> is the oldest manuscript copy of Isaiah found at Qumran (ca. 150–125 BCE).[18]

For examining the use of Isaiah in Matthew, four considerations should focus our attention. (1) The study of 1QIsa<sup>a</sup> has provided significant insights into the development of Hebrew Bible texts.[19] (2) Although many variant readings of Isaiah are minor and inconsequential, there are

---

15. Written on seventeen sheets of velum, 1QIsa<sup>a</sup> is 7.34 meters long with an average height of 26.2 centimeters. Thus, it is the longest scroll among the biblical scrolls and second longest among all the Scrolls, with only 11QT<sup>a</sup> (11Q19) being longer (8.148 meters). 1QIsa<sup>a</sup> accounts for about 24–25 percent of the biblical corpus of the HB found at Qumran.

16. For examples of manuscript damage in 1QIsa<sup>a</sup>, see Isa 1:21, 23–26; 2:15, 17, 19–21; 5:10–14; 7:9–12, 14–15; 8:7; 10:13–14; 14:27, 29; 45:10–14.

17. See Weston W. Fields, *The Dead Sea Scrolls: A Full History* (Leiden: Brill, 2009), 13, 24; John C. Trever, *The Untold Story of the Dead Sea Scrolls* (Westwood, NJ: Revell, 1965); Trever, *The Dead Sea Scrolls: A Personal Account*, rev. ed. (Piscataway, NJ: Gorgias, 2005), 98.

18. 1QIsa<sup>a</sup> provides an important glimpse into the textual history of the book of Isaiah. Dated to about 125 BCE, the scroll succeeds the date of the LXX translation of Isaiah (ca. 140 BCE or late second century) and precedes the dates of the MT-aligned manuscripts (e.g., 1QIsa<sup>b</sup>, ca. 50 BCE). See Abi T. Ngunga and Joachim Schaper, "Isaiah," in *The T&T Clark Companion to the Septuagint*, ed. James K. Aitken (London: Bloomsbury T&T Clark, 2015), 458.

19. As Eugene Ulrich aptly states, "The very first scriptural manuscript [i.e., 1QIsa<sup>a</sup>] discovered at Qumran and published already by 1950 is, in a condensed form, a compendium of most of the learnings to be gained about the Scriptures in the Second Temple period" (Ulrich and Flint, *Qumran Cave 1.I–II*, 2:128).

hundreds of real variants.[20] This presence of many variations and corrections and a divergent textual character from that of the MT suggest scribal innovation and error. (3) These types of variants suggest a fluidity of the text of Isaiah during the time of its composition.[21] (4) The study of 1QIsa[a] and its variants has given a greater prominence to the LXX, which has often been characterized as a somewhat careless representation of the Hebrew and imaginative in its exegesis.[22]

### 3. Matthew's Use of Isaiah

How does research on Isaiah at Qumran clarify aspects of its use in the Gospel of Matthew? Without forcing a direct connection or influence between the DSS and the New Testament, similarities suggest at least a shared social milieu with common authoritative traditions and scribal practices.[23] Both the DSS and Matthew highly value the Hebrew scriptures, as they persistently quote, cite, and allude to them. As Richard Hays states:

> Even if the Gospel writers were questioning and reorganizing their inherited "religious categories," there is nonetheless a certain obvious sense in which the Gospels arose out of the religious and cultural matrix of the Old Testament. Jesus and his first followers were Jews whose symbolic world was shaped by Israel's Scripture: their ways of interpreting the

---

20. The vast majority of variations are relatively minor and are simply due to differences in spelling (orthography), suffixes and endings (morphology), and pronunciation (phonology).

21. See Eugene Ulrich, *The Dead Sea Scrolls and the Developmental Composition of the Bible*, VTSup 169 (Leiden: Brill, 2015), 115–16. For example, Isa 2:9b–10 is not present in 1QIsa[a], but these verses (with slightly varying forms) are found in 4QIsa[a], 4QIsa[b], the MT, and the LXX (see Isa 40:6–8). This minus suggests that these verses were secondary to 1QIsa[a]'s earlier text form and therefore an instability of the text of Isaiah.

22. This characterization has been based on the false assumption that the Greek translator(s) was translating from a Hebrew text very similar to the MT. However, because of the Hebrew text of 1QIsa[a], the value of the LXX has been elevated, as it represents another Hebrew text.

23. See George J. Brooke, *The Dead Sea Scrolls and the New Testament* (Minneapolis: Fortress, 2005), 1–26.

world and their hopes for God's saving action were fundamentally conditioned by the biblical stories of God's dealings with the people Israel.[24]

Matthew, like the DSS, develops a complex intertextual web of Hebrew Bible quotations, citations, and allusions. Although this web is difficult to grasp, Matthew deliberately and explicitly aids his audience at times by identifying some of his textual sources (e.g., 24:15; see Mark 13:14).

Concerning Matthew's use of Isaiah, "Isaiah plays a profound role in the message of the gospel of Matthew."[25] Various forms suggest an inventory of functions in Matthew's use of the Hebrew Bible. However, before delving into the evidence, two considerations, although obvious, should be stated: (1) finding explicit citations is rather easy, while identifying implicit citations and allusions is notoriously difficult—such identifications are subjective and nearly impossible to distinguish from idiom; and (2) citations with and without introductions operate differently. In sum, Matthew's different uses of Isaiah correspond to different purposes, such that we can see Matthew's hermeneutical repertoire with regards to his use of the Hebrew Bible.

### 3.1. Matthew's Fulfillment Quotations

Eleven of Matthew's explicit citations of the Hebrew Bible occur in fulfillment quotations. Unique to Matthew,[26] these quotations have two features that distinguish them from other quotations in the New Testament: (1) they occur as narrative comments outside Jesus's story and (2) they contain an introductory statement using the lexemes "fulfill" (πληρόω) and "prophet" (προφήτης).[27] Out of eleven fulfillment quotations, five (or possibly six) quote Isaiah.

---

24. Richard B. Hays, *Echoes of Scripture in the Gospels* (Waco, TX: Baylor University Press, 2016), 5.

25. Richard Beaton, "Isaiah in Matthew's Gospel," in *Isaiah in the New Testament*, ed. Steve Moyise and Maarten J. J. Menken, NTSI (London: T&T Clark, 2005), 63.

26. Matthew 3:3 is not unique to Matthew (see Mark 1:3; Luke 3:4; John 1:23).

27. For example, Matt 1:23, Τοῦτο δὲ ὅλον γέγονεν ἵνα πληρωθῇ τὸ ῥηθὲν ὑπὸ κυρίου διὰ τοῦ προφήτου λέγοντος (All this took place to fulfill what had been spoken by the Lord through the prophet), and 4:14, ἵνα πληρωθῇ τὸ ῥηθὲν διὰ Ἡσαΐου τοῦ προφήτου λέγοντος (so that what had been spoken through the prophet Isaiah might be fulfilled) are typical for fulfillment quotations, with minor changes. All English translations of the New Testament are according to the NRSV.

1. **Matt 1:22-23 quotes Isa 7:14**
2. Matt 2:15b quotes Hos 11:1
3. Matt 2:17-18 quotes Jer 31:15 (identifies the prophet Jeremiah)
4. Matt 2:23 quotes Judg 13:5 or **Isa 11:1**
5. **Matt 3:3 quotes Isa 40:3 (identifies the prophet Isaiah)**
6. **Matt 4:15-16 quotes Isa 8:23-9:1 (identifies the prophet Isaiah)**
7. **Matt 8:17 quotes Isa 53:4 (identifies the prophet Isaiah)**
8. **Matt 12:17-21 quotes Isa 42:1-4 (identifies the prophet Isaiah)**
9. Matt 13:35 quotes Ps 78:2
10. Matt 21:4-5 quotes Zech 9:9 (see **Isa 62:11**)
11. Matt 27:9-10 quotes Zech 11:12-13 (see Jer 18:1-2; 32:6-9; identifies the prophet Jeremiah; see Matt 26:15)

This high percentage of occurrences as well as four direct references to the prophet Isaiah seems to indicate Isaiah as a preferred text of Matthew.

A couple of points regarding fulfillment quotations should be noted before considering Matthew's fulfillment quotations in light of Isaiah at Qumran. First, Matt 3:3 is included in this list, although it lacks πληρόω and is not unique to Matthew (see Mark 1:3; Luke 3:4; John 1:23).[28] Matthew seems to adopt Mark 1:3 along with its use of Malachi and Isaiah and then adapts it for his own purposes as a fulfillment quotation. Second, it is difficult to identify Matt 2:23's Hebrew Bible referent. The altered introductory formula—a change of "prophet" from the singular to the plural—has produced two alternative proposals for this quotation: (1) Maarten Menken suggests that Matt 2:23 refers to Judg 13:5, due to Matthew's literary context and for linguistic reasons;[29] and (2) Joseph Fitzmyer, taking the quotation at face value, suggests that there is no known referent.[30] Whatever the case may be, and even if Matt 2:23 does not quote Isa 11:1, at least half of Matthew's fulfillment quotations still cite Isaiah, emphasizing its importance.

---

28. It sits outside the narrative and identifies the prophet Isaiah.

29. Maarten J. J. Menken, *Matthew's Bible: The Old Testament Text of the Evangelist* (Leuven: Peeters, 2004), 162.

30. Joseph A. Fitzmyer, "The Use of Explicit Old Testament Quotations in Qumran Literature and the New Testament," in *The Semitic Background of the New Testament: Combined Edition of "Essays on the Semitic Background of the New Testament" and "A Wandering Aramean"; Collected Aramaic Essays* (Grand Rapids: Eerdmans, 1997), 14-15. See also CD IX, 8-9; XVI, 10.

In *Matthew's Bible*, Menken examines Matthew's quotations of the Hebrew Bible in an attempt to uncover the text-type behind each quotation.[31] From these fulfillment quotations that do not quite match the MT or LXX, Menken states that there is no indication that Matthew translated a Hebrew text or revised the LXX himself. However, he suggests Matthew used a revised LXX that was in closer agreement with the Hebrew.[32] This is debatable or at the very least uncertain for a number of reasons. (1) Whenever Matthew quotes from the Hebrew Bible in parallel with Mark, it is identical with the LXX text (Matt 3:3; Mark 1:3). If Matthew has a revised LXX text of Isaiah, why would he consistently choose to follow Mark's LXX, especially when Matthew revises and corrects the text of Mark in other instances? (2) Although Matthew's quotation of Isa 11:1 is questionable in 2:23, it does raise the possibility of translating from Hebrew to Greek. (3) Also, in Matt 27:9–10, not only does Matthew misidentify Jeremiah the prophet as his reference, but there seems to be a cluster of themes from Zech 11:12–13; Jer 18:1–2; 32:6–9, suggesting variation and complexity in his use of the Hebrew Bible. All this to say, as one examines Matthew's quotations, rather than suggesting a strict copying of a revised LXX, it seems from the variety of changes that a more fluid transmission, or possibly translation, is at work in these texts, originating from the author.

Interestingly, this raises a question: What scrolls did the author of Matthew have at hand in producing his text? The Gospel of Mark? The book of Isaiah? Something like 1QIsa$^a$ is probably the best example of what Matthew may have had when composing his text. Therefore, as Ulrich Luz suggests after investigating Matthew's quotations:

> Obviously, the synagogue library was no longer accessible to the evangelist. This has several results: for one, it is confirmed that the Matthean

---

31. Menken, *Matthew's Bible*. See also Krister Stendahl, *The School of St. Matthew and Its Use of the Old Testament*, 2nd ed. (Philadelphia: Fortress, 1968); Robert H. Gundry, *The Use of the Old Testament in St. Matthew's Gospel with Special Reference to the Messianic Hope* (Leiden: Brill, 1967).

32. Menken indicates that revising the LXX was a widespread phenomenon with multiple centers during this period (*Matthew's Bible*, 180–82). Although debatable, this does account for the minor differences between Matthean Sondergut and those taken from Mark (which is virtually identical to the LXX). For example, Matt 1:23 quotes Isa 7:14b primarily from the LXX, with two minor changes—λήμψεται (she will receive) to ἕξει (she will have), and καλέσεις (you will call) to καλέσουσιν (they will call)—while Matt 3:3, quoting Isa 40:3 (see Mark 1:3), is identical to the LXX.

community no longer lived within the synagogue union. In its library, there was a scroll of Isaiah; Isaiah plays the most important role of all prophets—in Matthew, as elsewhere in early Christianity. Of the Isaiah quotations the evangelist has compared at least some with the text of his Bible, the Septuagint. No other prophetic scroll can be assumed to have been in the Matthean community library, not even a Jeremiah scroll.[33]

Although the exact number of scrolls that were at hand is indeterminable, Luz's suggestion gives a practical picture of what may have been accessible to the author by limiting the number of scrolls from the Hebrew scriptures.[34]

Therefore, in attempting to identify the text-type(s) of the version(s) of Isaiah used by Matthew, I applied some of Flint and Ulrich's work on the text and variant readings of Isaiah at Qumran (DJD XXXII), but it produced very few results.[35] Although variant readings are valuable in observing scribal innovations as well as textual emendation and manuscript development, the added layer of translation makes the task of identification too complex and subjective.

However, one aspect of Isaiah at Qumran that pertains to Matthew's fulfillment quotations is its use in Qumran pesharim.[36] Although Matthew's quotations are not pesher-like and should be classified differently due to their form, they do function similarly, as they both contemporize the prophetic texts. In addition, Matthew seems to have some knowledge of ancient Near Eastern divination, with his use of magi (2:1–2), blessings and curses (5:1–12; 23:13–36), divine messengers (1:20, 24), signs (12:39; 16:4), and dream-visions (1:20; 2:13–15; 17:9).[37] Given this awareness of

---

33. Ulrich Luz, *Matthew 21–28*, Hermeneia (Minneapolis: Fortress, 2005), 157–58.

34. Luz suggests this due to Matthew's misidentification of Matt 27:9–10. Matthew quotes Zech 11:12–13 but incorrectly identifies the prophet Jeremiah.

35. See appendix.

36. Pesher can be understood as divine revelation that contemporizes an authoritative text for its intended audience (1QpHab VIII, 8–11; see Hab 2:5–6). See Daniel A. Machiela, "The Qumran Pesharim as Biblical Commentaries: Historical Context and Lines of Development," *DSD* 19 (2012): 313–62; Alex P. Jassen, "The Pesharim and the Rise of Commentary in Early Jewish Scriptural Interpretation," *DSD* 19 (2012): 363–98.

37. See Martti Nissinen, "How Prophecy Became Literature," *SJOT* 19 (2005): 154–55; Nissinen, "Prophecy and Omen Divination," in *Divination and Interpretation of Signs in the Ancient World*, ed. Amar Annus (Chicago: Oriental Institute, 2010), 225–66; Scott B. Noegel, "'Sign, Sign, Everywhere a Sign': Script, Power, and Interpretation in the Ancient Near East," in Annus, *Divination and Interpretation of Signs*,

divination, it seems that Matthew connects fulfillment quotations from the Hebrew prophets with dream-visions.

- Joseph's dream-vision (1:20) with quotation from Isa 7:14 (1:23)
- Magi's dream-vision (2:12) with quotation from Mic 5:2, 4 (2:6)
- Joseph's dream-vision (2:13) with quotations from Hos 11:1 (2:15) and Jer 31:15 (2:18)
- Joseph's dream-vision (2:19, 22) with quotation from Isa 11:1 or Judg 13:5 (2:23)
- Pilate's wife's dream-vision (27:19) with quotation from Zech 11:12–13; see Jer 18:1–2, 19:1–13, 32:6–9 (27:9–10)

Together with dream-visions, Matthew's fulfillment quotations are revelatory—divine disclosure—acting as a running commentary whose aim is to authenticate Jesus's identity as the Messiah (1:22–23; see Isa 7:14).[38] This pairing of quotations outside the narrative and dream-visions within the story emphasizes divine revelation and intervention. Like dream-visions that are of divine origin, Jesus's identity and story are viewed as enigmatic revelation that needs to be interpreted through the Hebrew Bible (i.e., Matthew's fulfillment quotations). In addition, they are authenticated as God grants divine insight.[39] Thus, sharing the same conceptual world as ancient Near Eastern divination and framed by the fulfillment of the prophet's words, Matthew's quotations of Isaiah are used to reveal the divine will and bring these passages to his present time.[40]

---

146–62. On dream-visions, specifically, in Jesus's transfiguration (Matt 17:9; see Mark 9:9; Luke 9:36), only Matthew contains the word ὄναρ (dream-vision) rather than ἐνύπιον (dream; Acts 2:17).

38. See George J. Brooke, "Aspects of Matthew's Use of Scripture," in Mason et al., *Teacher for All Generations*, 821–38; Brooke, "Prophets and Prophecy in the Qumran Scrolls and the New Testament," in *Text, Thought, and Practice in Qumran and Early Christianity: Proceedings of the Ninth International Symposium of the Orion Center for the Study of the Dead Sea Scrolls and Associated Literature, Jointly Sponsored by the Hebrew University Center for the Study of Christianity, 11–13 January, 2004*, ed. Ruth A. Clements and Daniel R. Schwartz, STDJ 84 (Leiden: Brill, 2009), 47; Kyung S. Baek, "Prophecy and Divination in the Gospel of Matthew: The Use of Dream-Visions and Fulfillment Quotations," in Perrin, Baek, and Falk, *Reading the Bible*, 653–78.

39. See Baek, "Prophecy and Divination in the Gospel of Matthew," 672–74.

40. DSS research is moving from focusing exclusively on texts and textuality (i.e., transmitting records, literature, and ideas) to viewing manuscripts as material phe-

Finally, the author uses fulfillment quotations in service of his purpose to motivate the audience to believe his narrative presentation.[41] As Christopher Stanley states, "To quote from an outside text in order to lend support to an argument is a rhetorical act.... Quotations are meant to affect an audience; otherwise, there is no reason to include them in a literary work."[42] Therefore, the quotations, as prooftexts, are meant to fulfill prophecy retrospectively—that is, they are read backward in light of new revelatory events. According to Matthew, the Torah and the Prophets are fulfilled in Jesus (5:17).[43]

## 3.2. Matthew's Citations

Unlike fulfillment quotations, Matthew's Hebrew Bible citations are located within the story rather than within comments on the story. With roughly thirty-one citations in total, twenty have an introductory formula, and eleven do not. All these citations are found in direct speech and put in the mouths of various characters—primarily Jesus. Matthew cites Isaiah seven times and places the citations in Jesus's mouth, three times with an introductory formula and four without.

- Jesus to the disciples (13:13–15 cites Isa 6:9–10 LXX; see Ezek 12:2) with introduction (see Mark 4:12; Luke 8:10; Acts 28:26–27; Rom 11:8)
- Jesus to Pharisees (15:8–9 cites Isa 29:13 LXX; see Ezek 33:31) with introduction (see Mark 7:6–7; Col 2:22)
- Jesus in the temple (21:13 cites Isa 56:7; see Jer 7:11) with introduction (see Mark 11:17; Luke 19:46; Phil 4:18)
- Jesus to the crowd (8:11 cites Isa 43:5; 49:12) without introduction (see Luke 13:29; Acts 18:9–10)

---

nomena concerned more toward use and media (i.e., amulets, inscriptions, and texts as media).

41. Steve Moyise, *Evoking Scripture: Seeing the Old Testament in the New* (London: T&T Clark, 2008), 128.

42. Christopher D. Stanley, *Arguing with Scripture: The Rhetoric of Quotations in the Letters of Paul* (London: T&T Clark, 2004), 9. See also William Harris, *Ancient Literacy* (Cambridge: Harvard University Press, 1989); Harry Gamble, *Books and Readers in the Early Church: A History of Early Christian Texts* (New Haven: Yale University Press, 1995).

43. Hays, *Echoes of Scripture in the Gospels*, 4–5.

- Jesus to John the Baptist (11:5 cites Isa 61:1; 35:4–6) without introduction
- Jesus to John the Baptist (11:23 cites Isa 14:11, 13–15) without introduction
- Jesus to his disciples (24:7 cites Isa 19:2) without introduction
- Jesus to his disciples (24:29 cites Isa 13:10; 24:23; see Ezek 32:7; Joel 2:10, 31; 3:15) without introduction

We can tentatively draw two conclusions from these citations. Matthew seems to use introductory formula citations differently from his nonintroductory citations. (1) Two formula citations include Isaianic texts as fulfilled prophecy (13:14–15; 15:8–9).[44] These two, plus the third formula citation with introduction (21:13), have the function of validating and authenticating Jesus and his use of the Hebrew scriptures.[45] Their purpose is to emphasize Matthew's continuity with the Hebrew scriptures and Jesus's authority from the Hebrew scriptures. Although the citation is important, the prophet Isaiah as an authoritative tradition from the past as a bridge to Matthew's present is the focal point. This emphasis and explicit reference to the prophet Isaiah seems to dislodge the citation from its original context and transport its content into Matthew's narrative. Moreover, in its goal of establishing continuity between the scriptures and Jesus's words, the citation is adopted and adapted as a way to confirm Jesus's authority and reinforce his teachings and actions (see 5:17; 13:52).[46]

(2) Alternatively, citations without an introduction operate idiomatically and thematically, incorporating the original historical context into the present.[47] Idioms are difficult to identify, since multiple scriptural

---

44. Matthew 13:14–15 cites Isa 6:9–10 LXX (see Mark 4:12; Luke 8:10) with an introductory formula, καὶ ἀναπληροῦται αὐτοῖς ἡ προφητεία Ἡσαΐου ἡ λέγουσα ("with them indeed is fulfilled the prophecy of Isaiah that says"). Again, Isaiah and prophecy are mentioned in Matt 15:7–9, as it cites Isa 29:13 LXX (see Mark 7:6–7), ἐπροφήτευσεν περὶ ὑμῶν Ἡσαΐας λέγων ("Isaiah prophesied rightly about you when he said").

45. Matthew 21:13 cites Isa 56:7 LXX with the introductory formula γέγραπται ("it is written"). In the temple, Jesus combines Isa 56:7 LXX and Jer 7:11 as the reason for his actions of driving out those who were selling and buying and overturning the tables of money changers and sellers.

46. Moyise, *Evoking Scripture*, 128.

47. Fitzmyer examines Hebrew Bible quotations at Qumran and the New Testament and separates them by three introductory statements (to write, to say, and others) and categorizes them into four classes: (1) literal or historical class, where the

passages usually contain similar language.⁴⁸ Similarly, Matthew contains language from more than one scriptural passage and sometimes has multiple uses of a phrase. For example, Matt 8:11 cites Isa 43:5, "from east and west" (ἀπὸ ἀνατολῶν καὶ δυσμῶν; see Isa 49:12; 59:19), which often refers to the ingathering of the dispersed nation of Israel at the eschatological banquet; however, Jesus transforms the idiom to include gentiles in the banquet. In addition, Matt 11:5 cites Isa 61:1 (see Isa 26:19; 29:18; 35:5–6; 42:18; Ps 146:7–8) as an answer to John the Baptist's question, "Are you the one who is to come, or are we to wait for another?" This list of miraculous activity alludes to God's deliverance (see Luke 4:18–19). Finally, Matt 24:29 cites Isa 13:10 and 24:23 (see Isa 34:4), with their proclamations concerning the day of the Lord. Although one cannot be certain from where they developed or whether they arose from one or more traditions, idiomatic expressions based in common knowledge become the basis and catalyst in Matthew for Jesus's teaching and actions as he changes their common understanding.⁴⁹ In sum, citations with introductions are prophetic utterances by Matthew's Jesus, stressing the position of his authority, while citations without introductions are idiomatic expressions that are spoken and altered by Jesus to emphasize the content of his teaching.

### 3.3. Matthew's Allusions

Matthew frequently alludes to Isaiah, but allusions are difficult to identify.⁵⁰ Allusions are by definition elusive, since some information is being with-

---

Hebrew Bible is quoted in the same sense as the original writers; (2) modernization class, where the Hebrew Bible is applied to the new event of the reader; (3) accommodation class, where the Hebrew Bible is taken from its original context and deliberately modified and adapted into a new situation; and (4) eschatological class, where the Hebrew Bible is expressed as a promise or threat for the eschaton ("Use of Explicit Old Testament Quotations," 16–17).

48. Julie A. Hughes, *Scriptural Allusions and Exegesis in the Hodayot*, STDJ 59 (Leiden: Brill, 2006), 46–47.

49. Gillian Lane-Mercier's parodic approach recasts ideas and language by using quotations to mix voices or as a springboard for further ideas. See Lane-Mercier, "Quotation as Discursive Strategy," *Kodikas* 14 (1991): 199–214.

50. See NA²⁷ and NA²⁸ for a list of allusions of Isaiah in Matthew. One interesting note when comparing the two editions is the omission or addition of some Isaiah allusions (e.g., Matt 2:10 [Isa 39:2] in NA²⁷ and not in NA²⁸; and Matt 5:5 [Isa 60:21;

held.[51] Often, identifying allusions in the New Testament is accomplished by designating a minimum number of words, or forms of words, that must agree between an allusion and its source in order to establish a definite relationship.[52] However, this is essentially impossible for Matthew's allusions, because they may rely on the Hebrew text of Isaiah (either the MT or some other version at variance with the MT), the Greek text of Isaiah (again, either the LXX or its many known or unknown versions at variance with the LXX), or perhaps even scribal innovation or modification of a passage or another version.[53] Furthermore, allusions do not always need a minimum number of words. For example, Craig Evans examines the use of Isaiah in Matthew through the theme and occurrences of the word "gospel" (בשר).[54]

---

65:9] in NA[28] and not in NA[27]). Also see Richard B. Hays, who sets out seven criteria to provide a measure of control in verifying the presence of scriptural allusions: (1) availability, (2) volume, (3) recurrence, (4) thematic coherence, (5) historical plausibility, (6) history of interpretation, and (7) satisfaction. See Hays, *Echoes of Scripture in the Letters of Paul* (New Haven: Yale University Press, 1989).

51. Usually an allusive reference works depending on the skills and background of the reader; however, Julie Hughes proposes that allusions work even when the reader does not recognize the source (*Scriptural Allusions and Exegesis*, 49).

52. Hughes develops a method for identifying and categorizing quotations, citations, and allusions (*Scriptural Allusions and Exegesis*, 50–54). Quotations are subdivided into Q1 (50 percent or more correspondence in lexemes with citation formulae without clear delimitation) and Q2 (50 percent or more correspondence in lexemes and identified with a specific figure or previously known writing). Citations are classified as C (50 percent or more correspondence in lexemes without citation formulae), and allusions are divided into A1a (less than 50 percent correspondence in lexemes with a *hapax legomenon*), A1b (less than 50 percent correspondence in lexemes, group of words with similar syntactical relationship), A1c (less than 50 percent correspondence in lexemes with common occurring phrase), and A1d (less than 50 percent correspondence in lexemes).

53. See Michael Knowles, *Jeremiah in Matthew's Gospel: The Rejected Prophet Motif in Matthean Redaction*, JSNTSup 68 (Sheffield: Sheffield Academic, 1993), 162.

54. Evans, "From Gospel to Gospel," 651–91. Evans identifies more allusions of Isaiah in Matthew: 5:34–35 (Isa 66:1); 11:4–5 // Luke 17:18–23 (Isa 35:5–6; 61:1–2; see 42:18); 11:23 // Luke 10:15 (Isa 14:13–15); 13:13 // Mark 4:12 // Luke 8:10 (Isa 6:10 Targum); 15:8–9 // Mark 7:6–7 (Isa 29:13); 16:19 (Isa 22:22 LXX and Targum); 21:13 // Mark 11:17 // Luke 19:46 (Isa 53:11–12); 21:33 // Mark 12:1 // Luke 20:9 (Isa 5:1–7); 24:29 // Mark 13:24–25 // Luke 21:25 (Isa 13:10; 24:19; 34:4); 24:31 (Isa 27:13); and 26:52 (Isa 50:11 Targum).

Allusions of Isaiah are scattered throughout Matthew.[55] The presence of authorial intention regarding allusions is debatable and virtually impossible to prove for each specific instance; however, generally there does seem to be authorial intention. When all possible allusions to Isaiah are examined, it is surprising to find only three major themes that Matthew incorporates from Isaiah: (1) the servant of the Lord, (2) true worship, and (3) God's deliverance and restoration. Even more astonishing is the coordination between these Isaianic allusions and Matthew's other uses of the Hebrew Bible. First, Matthew alludes to the servant of the Lord about nine times: 3:16–17 (see Isa 42:1; 11:2); 5:39 (see Isa 50:6); 13:16 (see Isa 52:15); 20:28 (see Isa 53:10–12); 26:28 (see 53:12); 26:67 (see Isa 50:6; 53:3); 27:12 (see Isa 53:7); 27:30 (see Isa 50:6); and 27:38 (see Isa 53:12).[56] Furthermore, this theme prominently appears in Matthew's fulfillment quotations (4:15–16; 8:17; 12:17–21). Second, true worship echoes throughout Matthew four times: 5:34–35 (see Isa 66:1); 6:16 (see Isa 58:5–14); 25:35 (see 58:7).[57] True worship is also the subject of citations with introductions (13:13–15; 15:8–9; 21:13). Third, the Isaianic theme of God's deliverance and restoration is found in Matthew six times: 2:11 (see Isa 60:6); 5:4 (see Isa 61:2); 6:19 (see Isa 51:8); 24:35 (see Isa 40:8); 24:37 (see Isa 54:9); and 26:39 (see Isa 51:17–22).[58] God's deliverance and restoration is also found in Matthew's citations without introductions (8:11; 11:5; 24:7, 29).[59]

---

55. Matthew 4:5 (see Isa 48:2; 52:1); Matt 4:7 (see Isa 7:12); Matt 5:14 (see Isa 2:2); Matt 6:6 (see Isa 26:20); Matt 6:7 (see Isa 1:15); Matt 6:9 (see Isa 63:16; 64:7–8; 29:23); Matt 8:28 (see Isa 65:4); Matt 11:21 (see Isa 23); Matt 11:29 (see Isa 28:12); Matt 11:22 (see Isa 34:8); Matt 11:23 (see Isa 14:11–15); Matt 11:25 (see Isa 29:14); Matt 12:43 (see Isa 34:14); Matt 16:19 (see Isa 22:22); Matt 16:23 (see Isa 8:14); Matt 21:33 (see Isa 5:1–7); Matt 21:42 (see Isa 28:16; 8:14); Matt 23:13 (see Isa 5:8–20); Matt 23:23 (see Isa 1:17); Matt 24:7 (see Isa 19:2); Matt 26:75 (see Isa 22:4); and Matt 27:43 (see Isa 36:7, 20).

56. Some allusions are disputable: 13:16 (see Isa 52:15); 20:28 (see Isa 53:10–12); 26:28 (see Isa 53:12).

57. Matthew 9:14 (see Isa 58:3) is questionable. True worship goes along with Matthew's emphasis on righteousness. See Benno Przybylski, *Righteousness in Matthew and His World of Thought* (Cambridge: Cambridge University Press, 1980).

58. One could also include these allusions, but they are questionable: 5:3 (see Isa 57:15; 61:1); 5:11 (see Isa 51:7); 12:29 (see Isa 49:24–25; 53:12); 24:31 (see Isa 27:13); and 14:25 (see 43:16).

59. For example, the centurion's inclusion in the eschatological banquet, Jesus's performance of signs as the coming one, and the signs of end of the age seem to echo God's deliverance and restoration from Isaiah.

Although this connection between Isaianic allusions and Matthew's uses of the Hebrew Bible could be purely coincidental, it is a surprising pattern.

Nonetheless, the function of allusions is to have an effect on the readers to elicit from them a response, conviction, and action (i.e., a performative function).[60] Allusions have a double referent—a meaning that is found in the immediate situation within the gospel and a meaning created by the allusion. Therefore, allusions simultaneously activate two texts.[61] As a literary device signaled by a verbal parallel, they impart meaning to a text. Brian Nolan writes:

> A scriptural allusion may be defined as a conscious evocation of an OT personage, event, institution, passage, or literary technique, made by the writer in order to communicate through the medium of received religious tradition. No clearly defined set of rules can be given for gauging the precise influence of an OT theme, passage, or reality, or an apparent parallel in Matthew. But two criteria are certainly valid. For that influence to be highly significant, there must be both a series of verbal similarities between the texts, and a theological motive giving them some coherence and direction.[62]

Similarities or contrasts between texts may encourage readers to interpret them in light of one another. Moreover, Christopher Stanley suggests that the use of allusions gives a sense of solidarity or reinforces belonging to a particular community.[63] Matthew's allusions to these Isaianic themes—servant of the Lord, true worship, and God's deliverance and restoration of Israel—may therefore function in part as an attempt to unite the Matthean community together around the teachings and actions of Jesus.

---

60. See Richard S. Briggs, *Words in Action: Speech Act Theory and Biblical Interpretation* (Edinburgh: T&T Clark, 2001), 3–27.

61. Moyise, *Evoking Scripture*, 130.

62. Brian M. Nolan, *The Royal Son of God: The Christology of Matthew 1–2 in the Setting of the Gospel*, OBO 23 (Göttingen: Vandenhoeck & Ruprecht, 1979), 23.

63. Christopher D. Stanley, "The Rhetoric of Quotations: An Essay on Method," in *Early Christian Interpretation of the Scriptures of Israel: Investigations and Proposals*, ed. Craig A. Evans and James A. Sanders, JSNTSup 148, SSEJC 5 (Sheffield: Sheffield Academic, 1997), 44–58.

## 4. Conclusion

This article began as a memorial tribute to Peter Flint, highlighting his work on Isaiah at Qumran and culminating in the publication of DJD XXXII. Isaiah's importance among the DSS is echoed in the Gospel of Matthew. Matthew's purpose in using Isaiah is to undergird Jesus's identity and authority. Matthew's quotations, citations, and allusions to the book of Isaiah suggest an inventory of hermeneutical strategies: (1) fulfillment quotations as divine revelation and realized prophecy revealing Jesus's identity, (2) citations with introductory formula to support Jesus's authority in continuity with the Hebrew scriptures, (3) nonintroductory citations as idiomatic expressions of Jesus's words and actions; and (4) allusions that coordinate Isaianic themes with Jesus in an attempt to bring Matthew's readers to solidarity (i.e., the Gospel of Jesus the Messiah as the servant of the Lord bringing about God's restoration of Israel and calling his followers to true worship). This variety illustrates his repertoire of hermeneutical strategies in presenting Jesus as the Messiah.

## Appendix

| Matt 1:23 | Isa 7:14 LXX |
|---|---|
| ἰδοὺ ἡ παρθένος ἐν γαστρὶ ἕξει καὶ τέξεται υἱόν, καὶ καλέσουσιν τὸ ὄνομα αὐτοῦ Ἐμμανουήλ | ἰδοὺ ἡ παρθένος ἐν γαστρὶ λήμψεται καὶ τέξεται υἱόν, καὶ καλέσεις τὸ ὄνομα αὐτοῦ Ἐμμανουήλ |

1QIsa<sup>a</sup>

ה[נ]ה העלמה הרה וילדת בן וקרא שמו עמנואל

7:14  (29)  וקרא 1QIsa<sup>a</sup> LXX<sup>S</sup> ] את- MT LXX
7:14  (29)  עמנואל 1QIsa<sup>a</sup> "LXX (Ἐμμανουήλ) α' σ' ] עמנו אל MT (see 8:8, 10)

---

Matt 3:3
(Mark 1:3; Luke 3:4; John 1:23)

Isa 40:3 LXX

φωνὴ βοῶντος ἐν τῇ ἐρήμῳ· ἑτοιμάσατε τὴν ὁδὸν κυρίου, εὐθείας ποιεῖτε τὰς τρίβους αὐτοῦ.

Φωνὴ βοῶντος ἐν τῇ ἐρήμῳ Ἑτοιμάσατε τὴν ὁδὸν Κυρίου, εὐθείας ποιεῖτε τὰς τρίβους τοῦ θεοῦ ἡμῶν.

1QIsa<sup>a</sup>

קול קורא במדבר פנו דרך יהוה וישרו בערבה מסלה לאלוהינו

40:3   (2)   וישרו 1QIsa<sup>a</sup> ] ישרו 1QIsa<sup>b</sup> MT LXX; ישרו׳[ 4QIsa<sup>b</sup>

40:3   (2)   בערבה 1QIsa<sup>a</sup> 4QIsa<sup>b</sup> MT ] > LXX

---

Matt 4:15–16                                    Isa 8:23–9:1 LXX

γῆ Ζαβουλὼν <u>καὶ</u> γῆ Νεφθαλίμ, <u>ὁδὸν</u>         χώρα Ζαβουλών, ἡ γῆ Νεφθαλείμ, καὶ
<u>θαλάσσης</u>, πέραν τοῦ Ἰορδάνου, Γαλιλαία      οἱ λοιποὶ οἱ τὴν παραλίαν καὶ πέραν τοῦ
τῶν ἐθνῶν, ὁ λαὸς ὁ <u>καθήμενος</u> ἐν σκότει      Ἰορδάνου, Γαλειλαία τῶν ἐθνῶν. ὁ λαὸς ὁ
φῶς <u>εἶδεν</u> μέγα, <u>καὶ τοῖς καθημένοις</u> ἐν      πορευόμενος ἐν σκότει, ἴδετε φῶς μέγα·
χώρᾳ <u>καὶ</u> σκιᾷ θανάτου φῶς <u>ἀνέτειλεν</u>       οἱ κατοικοῦντες ἐν χώρᾳ σκιᾷ θανάτου,
<u>αὐτοῖς</u>.                                           φῶς λάμψει ἐφ᾽ ὑμᾶς.

1QIsa<sup>a</sup>

ארץ זבולון והארץ נפתלי והאחרון הכביד דרך הים עבר הירדן גליל הגואים
העם ההולכים בחושך ראו אור גדול יושבי בארץ צלמות אור נגה עליהם

8:22–23  (16–17)   כעת הרישון<sup>23</sup> ... כ׳לו 1QIsa<sup>a</sup> (see 3:11 VAR) ] ... כי לא<sup>23</sup> 
              כעת הראשון MT; καὶ οὐκ ... ἕως καιροῦ.<sup>23[9:1]</sup>Τοῦτο πρῶτον ποίει LXX

8:23   (16)   מעופף 1QIsa<sup>a</sup> ] מועף MT

8:23   (17)   והארץ ... ארץ 1QIsa<sup>a</sup> LXX ] וארצה ... ארצה MT

8:23[9:1]  (17–18)   והאחרון הכביד 1QIsa<sup>a</sup> MT ] καὶ οἱ λοιποὶ οἱ τὴν παραλίαν
              κατοικοῦντες LXX

8:23[9:1]  (18)   דרך הים 1QIsa<sup>a</sup> MT σ′ ] tr post Νεφθαλίμ LXX; > LXX<sup>S*OLC</sup>

8:23[9:1]  (18)   הגואים 1QIsa<sup>a</sup> MT (הגוים) LXX<sup>S*OLC</sup> ] + τὰ μέρη τῆς Ιουδαίας
              LXX

9:1[2]   (19)   בארץ צלמות 1QIsa<sup>a</sup> MT ] ἐν χώρᾳ καὶ σκιᾷ θανάτου LXX

---

Matt 8:17                                       Isa 53:4 LXX

<u>αὐτὸς τὰς ἀσθενείας</u> ἡμῶν <u>ἔλαβεν</u> καὶ <u>τὰς</u>    ὗτος τὰς ἁμαρτίας ἡμῶν φέρει καὶ περὶ
<u>νόσους ἐβάστασεν</u>.                            ἡμῶν ὀδυνᾶται,

1QIsa<sup>a</sup>

אכן חולייניו הואה נשא ומכאובינו סבלם

53:4  (9)  חשבנוהי 1QIsaᵃ ] נהו- 1QIsaᵇ MT
53:4  (9)  ומוכה 1QIsaᵃ LXX (vid) ] מכה 1QIsaᵇ MT

| Matt 12:18–21 | Isa 42:1–4 LXX |
|---|---|
| ἰδοὺ ὁ παῖς μου <u>ὃν ᾑρέτισα</u>, ὁ <u>ἀγαπητός</u> <u>μου εἰς ὃν εὐδόκησεν</u> ἡ ψυχή μου· <u>θήσω</u> τὸ πνεῦμά μου ἐπ' αὐτόν, <u>καὶ</u> κρίσιν τοῖς ἔθνεσιν <u>ἀπαγγελεῖ. οὐκ ἐρίσει οὐδὲ</u> <u>κραυγάσει, οὐδὲ ἀκούσει τις ἐν ταῖς</u> <u>πλατείαις τὴν φωνὴν</u> αὐτοῦ. κάλαμον <u>συντετριμμένον οὐ κατεάξει καὶ λίνον</u> <u>τυφόμενον οὐ σβέσει, ἕως ἂν ἐκβάλῃ εἰς</u> <u>νῖκος</u> τὴν κρίσιν. καὶ τῷ ὀνόματι αὐτοῦ ἔθνη ἐλπιοῦσιν. | Ἰακὼβ ὁ παῖς μου, ἀντιλήμψομαι αὐτοῦ· Ἰσραὴλ ὁ ἐκλεκτός μου, προσεδέξατο αὐτὸν ἡ ψυχή μου· ἔδωκα τὸ πνεῦμά μου ἐπ' αὐτόν, κρίσιν τοῖς ἔθνεσιν ἐξοίσει· οὐ κεκράξεται οὐδὲ ἀνήσει, οὐδὲ ἀκουσθήσεται ἔξω ἡ φωνὴ αὐτοῦ. κάλαμον τεθλασμένον οὐ συντρίψει, καὶ λίνον καπνιζόμενον οὐ σβέσει, ἀλλὰ εἰς ἀλήθειαν ἐξοίσει κρίσιν· ἀναλάμψει καὶ οὐ θραυσθήσεται, ἕως ἂν θῇ ἐπὶ τῆς γῆς κρίσιν· καὶ ἐπὶ τῷ ὀνόματι αὐτοῦ ἔθνη ἐλπιοῦσιν. |

1QIsaᵃ

הנה עבדי אתמוכה בו בחירי רצתה נפשי נתתי רוחי עליו ומשפטו לגואים יוציא.
לוא יזעק ולוא ישא ולוא ישמיע בחוץ קולו.
קנה רצוץ לוא ישבור ופשתה כהה לוא יכבה לאמת יוציא משפט.
ולוא יכהה ולוא ירוץ עד ישים בארץ משפט ולתורתיו איים ינחילו. [[ ]]

42:1  (10)  הנה 1QIsaᵃ MT (הן) Matt 12:18 ] Ἰακώβ LXX (see 41:8)
42:1  (10)  אתמוכה 1QIsaᵃ ] אתמך MT
42:1  (10)  בחירי 1QIsaᵃ MT Matt ] pr Ἰσραήλ LXX (see 41:8)
42:1  (10)  ומשפטו 1QIsaᵃ ] משפט MT LXX
42:2  (11)  יזעק 1QIsaᵃ ] יצעק MT
42:3  (12)  יכבה 1QIsaᵃ LXX (vid) ] יכבנה MT
42:4  (12)  ולוא יכהה 1QIsaᵃ ] לא יכהה 4QIsaʰ MT; ἀναλάμψει LXX
42:4  (13)  ולתורתיו 1QIsaᵃ ] ולתרתו 4QIsaʰ; וּלְתוֹרָתוֹ MTᴸ LXX
42:4  (13)  ינחילו 1QIsaᵃ ] יחילו 4QIsaʰ; יְיַחֵילוּ MTᴸ LXX (ἐλπιοῦσιν)

## Bibliography

Baek, Kyung S. "Prophecy and Divination in the Gospel of Matthew: The Use of Dream-Visions and Fulfillment Quotations." Pages 653–78 in *Reading the Bible in Ancient Traditions and Modern Editions*. Edited by Andrew B. Perrin, Kyung S. Baek, and Daniel K. Falk. EJL 47. Atlanta: SBL Press, 2017.

Beaton, Richard. "Isaiah in Matthew's Gospel." Pages 63–78 in *Isaiah in the New Testament*. Edited by Steve Moyise and Maarten J. J. Menken. NTSI. London: T&T Clark, 2005.

Briggs, Richard S. *Words in Action: Speech Act Theory and Biblical Interpretation*. Edinburgh: T&T Clark, 2001.

Brooke, George J. "Aspects of Matthew's Use of Scripture." Pages 821–38 in *A Teacher for All Generations: Essays in Honor of James C. VanderKam*. Edited by Eric F. Mason, Samuel I. Thomas, Kelley Coblentz Bautch, Alison Schofield, Eugene Charles, Angela Kim Harkins, and Daniel A. Machiela. JSJSup 153. Leiden: Brill, 2012.

———. *The Dead Sea Scrolls and the New Testament*. Minneapolis: Fortress, 2005.

———. "Isaiah in the Pesharim and Other Qumran Texts." Pages 609–32 in *Writing and Reading the Scroll of Isaiah: Studies of an Interpretive Tradition*. Vol. 2. Edited by Craig C. Broyles and Craig A. Evans. VTSup 70. Leiden: Brill, 1997.

———. "Prophets and Prophecy in the Qumran Scrolls and the New Testament." Pages 31–48 in *Text, Thought, and Practice in Qumran and Early Christianity: Proceedings of the Ninth International Symposium of the Orion Center for the Study of the Dead Sea Scrolls and Associated Literature, Jointly Sponsored by the Hebrew University Center for the Study of Christianity, 11–13 January, 2004*. Edited by Ruth A. Clements and Daniel R. Schwartz. STDJ 84. Leiden: Brill, 2009.

Evans, Craig A. "From Gospel to Gospel: The Function of Isaiah in the New Testament." Pages 651–91 in *Writing and Reading the Scroll of Isaiah: Studies of an Interpretative Tradition*. Vol. 2. Edited by Craig C. Broyles and Craig A. Evans. VTSup 70. Leiden: Brill, 1997.

Fields, Weston W. *The Dead Sea Scrolls: A Full History*. Leiden: Brill, 2009.

Fitzmyer, Joseph A. "The Use of Explicit Old Testament Quotations in Qumran Literature and the New Testament." Pages 3–58 in *The Semitic Background of the New Testament: Combined Edition of "Essays on the Semitic Background of the New Testament" and "A Wandering Aramean"; Collected Aramaic Essays.* Grand Rapids: Eerdmans, 1997.

Flint, Peter W. "The Book of Isaiah in the Dead Sea Scrolls." Pages 229–51 in *The Bible as Book: The Hebrew Bible and the Judaean Desert Discoveries.* Edited by Edward D. Herbert and Emanuel Tov. London: British Library & Oak Knoll, 2002.

———. "From Tarshish to Carthage: The Septuagint Translation of 'Tarshish' in Isaiah 23." *PJEGLMBS* 8 (1988): 127–33.

———. "The Interpretation of Scriptural Isaiah in the Qumran Scrolls: Quotations, Allusions, and the Form of the Biblical Text." Pages 398–406 in *A Teacher for All Generations: Essays in Honor of James C. VanderKam.* Edited by Eric F. Mason, Samuel I. Thomas, Kelley Coblentz Bautch, Alison Schofield, Eugene Charles, Angela Kim Harkins, and Daniel A. Machiela. JSJSup 153. Leiden: Brill, 2012.

———. "Interpreting the Poetry of Isaiah at Qumran: Theme and Function in the Sectarian Scrolls." Pages 161–95 in *Prayer and Poetry in the Dead Sea Scrolls and Related Literature: Essays in Honor of Eileen Schuller on the Occasion of Her Sixty-Fifth Birthday.* Edited by Jeremy Penner, Ken M. Penner, and Cecilia Wassen. STDJ 98. Leiden: Brill, 2012.

———. "The Septuagint Version of Isaiah 23:1–14 and the Masoretic Text." *BIOSCS* 21 (1988): 35–54.

Flint, Peter W., and Eugene Ulrich. *Qumran Cave 1.* Vol 1, *The Isaiah Scrolls.* Part 1, *Plates and Transcriptions.* DJD XXXII. Oxford: Clarendon, 2010.

———. *Qumran Cave 1.* Vol. 2, *The Isaiah Scrolls.* Part 2, *Introductions, Commentary, and Textual Variants.* DJD XXXII. Oxford: Clarendon, 2010.

Gamble, Harry. *Books and Readers in the Early Church: A History of Early Christian Texts.* New Haven: Yale University Press, 1995.

Gundry, Robert H. *The Use of the Old Testament in St. Matthew's Gospel with Special Reference to the Messianic Hope.* Leiden: Brill, 1967.

Harris, William. *Ancient Literacy.* Cambridge: Harvard University Press, 1989.

Hays, Richard B. *Echoes of Scripture in the Gospels.* Waco, TX: Baylor University Press, 2016.

———. *Echoes of Scripture in the Letters of Paul.* New Haven: Yale University Press, 1989.

Hughes, Julie A. *Scriptural Allusions and Exegesis in the Hodayot*. STDJ 59. Leiden: Brill, 2006.

Jassen, Alex P. "The Pesharim and the Rise of Commentary in Early Jewish Scriptural Interpretation." *DSD* 19 (2012): 363–98.

Knowles, Michael. *Jeremiah in Matthew's Gospel: The Rejected Prophet Motif in Matthean Redaction*. SNTSup 68. Sheffield: Sheffield Academic, 1993.

Lane-Mercier, Gillian. "Quotation as Discursive Strategy." *Kodikas* 14 (1991): 199–214.

Luz, Ulrich. *Matthew 21–28*. Hermeneia. Minneapolis: Fortress, 2005.

Machiela, Daniel A. "The Qumran Pesharim as Biblical Commentaries: Historical Context and Lines of Development." *DSD* 19 (2012): 313–62.

Menken, Maarten J. J. *Matthew's Bible: The Old Testament Text of the Evangelist*. Leuven: Peeters, 2004.

Morrow, Francis J., Jr. "The Text of Isaiah at Qumran." PhD diss., Catholic University of America, 1973.

Moyise, Steve. *Evoking Scripture: Seeing the Old Testament in the New*. London: T&T Clark, 2008.

Nissinen, Martti. "How Prophecy Became Literature." *SJOT* 19 (2005): 154–55.

———. "Prophecy and Omen Divination." Pages 225–66 in *Divination and Interpretation of Signs in the Ancient World*. Edited by Amar Annus. Chicago: Oriental Institute, 2010.

Ngunga, Abi T., and Joachim Schaper. "Isaiah." Pages 456–68 in *The T&T Clark Companion to the Septuagint*. Edited by James K. Aitken. London: Bloomsbury T&T Clark, 2015.

Noegel, Scott B. "'Sign, Sign, Everywhere a Sign': Script, Power, and Interpretation in the Ancient Near East." Pages 146–62 in *Divination and Interpretation of Signs in the Ancient World*. Edited by Amar Annus. Chicago: Oriental Institute, 2010.

Nolan, Brian M. *The Royal Son of God: The Christology of Matthew 1–2 in the Setting of the Gospel*. OBO 23. Göttingen: Vandenhoeck & Ruprecht, 1979.

Perrin, Andrew B., Kyung S. Baek, and Daniel K. Falk. *Reading the Bible in Ancient Traditions and Modern Editions: Studies in Memory of Peter W. Flint*. EJL 47. Atlanta: SBL Press, 2017.

Przybylski, Benno. *Righteousness in Matthew and His World of Thought*. Cambridge: Cambridge University Press, 1980.

Stanley, Christopher D. *Arguing with Scripture: The Rhetoric of Quotations in the Letters of Paul*. London: T&T Clark, 2004.

———. "The Rhetoric of Quotations: An Essay on Method." Pages 44–58 in *Early Christian Interpretation of the Scriptures of Israel: Investigations and Proposals*. Edited by Craig A. Evans and James A. Sanders. JSNTSup 148. SSEJC 5. Sheffield: Sheffield Academic, 1997.

Stendahl, Krister. *The School of St. Matthew and Its Use of the Old Testament*. 2nd ed. Philadelphia: Fortress, 1968.

Trever, John C. *The Dead Sea Scrolls: A Personal Account*. Rev. ed. Piscataway, NJ: Gorgias, 2005.

———. *The Untold Story of the Dead Sea Scrolls*. Westwood, NJ: Revell, 1965.

Ulrich, Eugene. *The Dead Sea Scrolls and the Developmental Composition of the Bible*. VTSup 169. Leiden: Brill, 2015.

———. "An Index of the Passages in the Biblical Manuscripts from the Judean Desert (Part 2: Isaiah–Chronicles)." *DSD* 2 (1995): 88–92.

# Part 2
# Space and Time

# The Threat of the Monstrous in the Scrolls

Heather Macumber

The desire for communion with angels and the divine world is found throughout the Dead Sea Scrolls (DSS). In the Songs of the Sabbath Sacrifice, the community pictures its members as priests who are able to join in the praises of the angels in the heavenly temple (4Q400 2, 5–7). In the Hodayot we hear that the worshiper is purified "and so that he may take (his) place before you with the everlasting host and the [eternal] spirit[s]" (1QH$^a$ XIX, 16).[1] Yet there is an undercurrent of unease that flows throughout some of these texts where one detects the danger of associating with the divine. A binary understanding of the world is established in the Treatise on the Two Spirits, where "in the hand of the Prince of Lights is dominion over all the sons of justice; they walk on paths of light. And in the hand of the Angel of Darkness is total dominion over the sons of deceit; they walk on paths of darkness" (1QS III, 20–21). There is a real threat residing in all community members regarding their spiritual and physical state. This aspiration to achieve communion with the angelic hosts makes the community members vulnerable to demonic attack and shows the fault lines in their own world. I will focus primarily on the Songs of the Sage (4Q510–4Q511) that are typically identified as antidemonic songs to demonstrate how demons threaten the community's boundaries both spatially and ontologically. My main methodology is that of monster theory, a way of understanding a culture by examining the monsters it produces. As demonstrated in texts such as Songs of the Sage, the effect

---

1. All citations of the Hodayot follow Hartmut Stegemann, Eileen Schuller, and Carol A. Newsom, *Qumran Cave 1.III: 1QHodayot$^a$, with Incorporation of 1QHodayot$^b$ and 4QHodayot$^{a-f}$*, DJD XL (Oxford: Clarendon, 2009). All other citations from the DSS follow Florentino García Martínez and Eibert J. C. Tigchelaar, *The Dead Sea Scrolls Study Edition*, 2 vols. (Leiden: Brill, 1997–1998).

is a community that guards against demonic attack by policing both the physical bodies and the spiritual selves of its members. By distancing its members from other Jewish traditions and aligning closely with the divine world, the community creates a new identity that threatens normative boundaries between the earthly and heavenly realms.

## 1. Monster Theory

Monsters are boundary creatures that escape easy classification. They are familiar specters that reappear through time and cultures, and yet they remain deeply unsettling. Monster theory as a discipline seeks to read cultures through the monsters that it creates and even vilifies.[2] Modern monsters are generally understood as evil beings that bring harm to humanity. However, ancient understandings of monsters differ significantly from modern views, as these creatures were recognized as warnings or extraordinary signs from the divine.[3] Their strangeness or otherness challenges the status quo of a society, often uncovering fears and taboos deeply rooted in cultures.[4] This is especially true of monsters that are hybrid beings whose mixing of categories threatens the boundaries of what societies consider normative.[5] These monstrous creations are the symbolic Other that allows the dominant culture to outline who is considered an insider or an outsider.[6] Timothy Beal speaks of the monster as "a horrific figure of otherness within sameness."[7] Monsters are figures

---

2. Jeffrey J. Cohen, "Monster Culture (Seven Theses)," in *Monster Theory: Reading Culture*, ed. Jeffrey J. Cohen (Minneapolis: University of Minnesota Press, 1996), 3–25.

3. The term *monster* is derived from both the Latin *monstrare*, "to show/demonstrate," and *monere*, "warning." See Émile Benveniste, *Pouvoir, droit, religion*, vol. 2 of *Le vocabulaire des institutions indo-européennes* (Paris: Les éditions de minuit, 1969), 255.

4. Beal uses the term *unheimlich* to capture the disturbance monsters impose on a society's sense of order and identity. See Timothy K. Beal, *Religion and Its Monsters* (New York: Routledge, 2002), 5.

5. Claude Moussy, "Esquisse de l'histoire de monstrum," *REL* 55 (1977): 351.

6. Many marginalized groups historically were depicted using monstrous language and imagery. As Gilmore states, "The impulse to create monsters stems from the need of the majority to denigrate those who are different, be they the lower classes, foreigners, or marginalized deviant groups." See David Gilmore, *Monsters: Evil Beings, Mythical Beasts, and All Manner of Imaginary Terrors* (Philadelphia: University of Pennsylvania Press, 2003), 14.

7. Beal, *Religion and Its Monsters*, 4.

that both disturb the normal order of society and simultaneously reveal the deepest insecurities of a culture.[8] The strength of monster theory is that it does not primarily concern itself with the origins of these monsters but with how they function in society as indicators of a community's fears and prejudices.[9]

## 2. Monsters at Qumran

There is no specific word for monster in the DSS, and it is easy to begin corralling all the references to evil spirits and beings under the label of monster. However, monster theory appropriately resists such easy classification and insists on a deeper understanding that monsters' roles are ambiguous. A monster is not primarily identified as an evil being but one that is different, caught between categories and threatening.[10] All these descriptors would apply equally to those beings called angels as much as those known as demons. Angels are liminal beings that operate in the boundaries between heaven and earth and defy human categories of classification. They, like many monsters, are typically hybrid creatures that combine human and animal characteristics. Examples include the cherubim as winged sphinxes (1 Kgs 6:27; Ezek 10:2–20) and the seraphim pictured as winged serpent creatures with the human characteristic of speech (Num 21:6; Deut 8:15; Isa 6:2; 30:6), as well as the ophanim, who mix both human and nonanimate elements (1 En. 61.10; 71.7; 2 En. 20.1; 4Q403 1 II, 15–16). The term *monstrous* is not relegated to beings considered evil but more accurately describes beings that cross boundaries both physically and ontologically.

Similarly, the English term *demon* is less than helpful for describing the range of harmful spirits that threaten and afflict the community. The Greek word *daimon* does not necessarily imply an evil spirit but more accurately is used to denote a lesser god who could act either positively or

---

8. Beal, *Religion and Its Monsters*, 4–5.

9. Important studies on monster theory or monster studies include Noel Carroll, *The Philosophy of Horror: Or, Paradoxes of the Heart* (New York: Routledge, 1990); Marie Hélène Huet, *Monstrous Imagination* (Cambridge: Harvard University Press, 1993); Cohen, "Monster Culture"; Beal, *Religion and Its Monsters*; Gilmore, *Monsters*; Niall Scott, *Monsters and the Monstrous: Myths and Metaphors of Enduring Evil* (Amsterdam: Rodopi, 2007); Stephen T. Asma, *On Monsters: An Unnatural History of Our Worst Fears* (Oxford: Oxford University Press, 2009).

10. Cohen, "Monster Culture," 6.

negatively.[11] In the DSS, a variety of terms are used to label these beings that pose a threat to the community. Specifically, in 4Q510 and 4Q511 one finds the following types of malevolent beings: spirits of angels of destruction, spirits of the bastards, demons, Lilith, the destroyer, and evil spirits. As noted above, a key identifier of monsters is that they challenge boundaries and potentially act as forces of chaos and disorder.[12] This is especially true of demons or spirits found in Second Temple Judaism that are pictured as a composite of both human and angelic natures.[13] This hybrid understanding of the nature of demonic beings can be traced back to the Book of Watchers and its etiology of evil spirits. The improper mixing of categories begins with the illicit union of the angels and human women, resulting in a race of giants, hybrid beings who are both angelic and human. The angel Gabriel is sent to destroy these creatures (1 En. 10.9), but like so many monsters, they cannot be completely destroyed.[14] Instead evil spirits emanate from their bodies (1 En. 15.11–16.1), who have harmful intentions toward humanity.[15] These spirits are known as demons, and it is their hybrid identity as both angelic and human that makes them so dangerous. As Philip Alexander notes, they not only harass humans but can "invade the human body" because they seek to regain an earthly and physical form.[16] The influence of the Book of Watchers on the Qumran community is consistently noted, and even the terminology in the DSS reflects this origin. For instance, in the Songs of the Sage, the

---

11. Manfred Hutter, "Demons and Benevolent Spirits in the Ancient Near East: A Phenomenological Overview," in *Angels: The Concept of Celestial Beings; Origins, Development and Reception*, ed. Friedrich V. Reiterer, Tobias Nicklas, and Karin Schöpflin, DCLS (Berlin: de Gruyter, 2007), 21.

12. Cohen, "Monster Culture," 6.

13. Demons "belong to an intermediate category of being that is part angelic and part human." See Philip Alexander, "The Demonology of the Dead Sea Scrolls," in *The Dead Sea Scrolls after Fifty Years: A Comprehensive Assessment*, ed. Peter W. Flint and James C. VanderKam (Leiden: Brill, 1999), 2:339.

14. A common thesis of monster theory is that the monster never truly dies but escapes only to reappear again. Cohen states, "No monster tastes of death but once" ("Monster Culture," 5).

15. The destructive nature of these spirits is aptly described in 1 En. 15.11–12, which highlights the multiple ways that they inflict harm and turn against humanity.

16. Alexander, "Demonology," 339. See also Loren Stuckenbruck, "Satan and Demons," in *Jesus among Friends and Enemies*, ed. Chris Keith and Larry Hurtado (Grand Rapids: Baker Academic, 2011), 173–97.

term "spirits of the bastards" is listed among other demonic forces, likely referring back to the illicit union between the Watchers and the human women of 1 Enoch that produced the evil spirits.[17] Similarly, 11Q11 V, 6 relates, "Who are you, [oh offspring of] man and of the seed of the ho[ly] ones?" The hybrid nature of these beings would be particularly disturbing for the Qumran community, who maintained strict purity rules.[18]

### 3. The Threat of Monsters

Monsters, whether beneficial or harmful, live and operate in liminal locations often at the borders of the human world. Noel Carroll describes these locations as "environs outside of and unknown to ordinary social discourse."[19] These cosmic locations, found in peripheral or marginal locations, take many forms in Jewish literature, including mountains, the wilderness, and the sea, among others. In particular, the wilderness or desert is known in the ancient world as the abode of demons and spirits.[20] The Hebrew term *midbār*, translated as "wilderness" rather than "desert," gives a better sense that this is a location that is uninhabited and not domesticated by civilizations.[21] In biblical texts, the wilderness is the home of wild creatures and demons (Job 24:5; Ps 74:14; Isa 34:12–15). It also becomes symbolic for the fate of cities that receive divine judgment and are reduced to rubble (Isa 5:6; Zeph 2:9).[22] The wilderness becomes

---

17. Ida Frölich, "From Pseudepigraphic to Sectarian," *RevQ* 21 (2004): 405.

18. Frölich notes, "The author of the *Songs to the Sage* makes the unclean demons counterparts of his own group, the righteous elect loving purity" ("From Pseudepigraphic to Sectarian," 405).

19. Carroll, *Philosophy of Horror*, 35.

20. Mark S. Smith, *The Origins of Biblical Monotheism: Israel's Polytheistic Background and the Ugaritic Texts* (Oxford: Oxford University Press, 2001), 28–30.

21. Talmon reiterates that the Hebrew term *midbār* is more appropriate than the English word *desert*. See Shemaryahu Talmon, "The 'Desert Motif' in the Bible and Qumran Literature," in *Biblical Motifs: Origins and Transformations*, ed. Alexander Altmann (Cambridge: Harvard University Press, 1966), 39. For a discussion of the real/metaphorical experience of wilderness, see George J. Brooke, "Isa 40:3 and the Wilderness Community," in *New Qumran Texts and Studies*, ed. George J. Brooke with Florentino García Martínez (Leiden: Brill, 1994), 124.

22. Alison Schofield, "The Em-bodied Desert and Other Sectarian Spaces in the Dead Sea Scrolls," in *Constructions of Space IV: Further Developments in Examining Ancient Israel's Social Space*, ed. Mark K. George (New York: Bloomsbury, 2013), 163.

synonymous with a place of chaos that has escaped the order and stability of settled areas. In Isa 34, an oracle against Edom, the prophet proclaims that it will revert to a wilderness as "Thorns shall come up over its palaces, nettles and thistles in its fortresses" (Isa 34:13).[23] Moreover, it will become the home of jackals, ostriches, wild animals, and also demons, including Lilith (Isa 34:13–14). This association of the wilderness with demonic spirits is further illustrated in 2 Bar 10.6–8: "I call the sirens from the sea, and you, liliths, from the desert and demons and jackals from the forest."[24] In this instance, these monstrous creatures are called out from the uninhabited regions to lament over a destroyed Jerusalem that has itself become a wilderness.[25]

While the wilderness is a place of chaos, it is also a place of revelation in the biblical texts, where one encounters the divine. Hagar, expecting death in her exile to the wilderness, finds not only physical sustenance but a divine encounter (Gen 16:7–14; 21:15–19). Moreover, Moses and later Elijah escape to the wilderness only to experience the divine at remote mountains (Exod 3; 1 Kgs 19). This is echoed in the wilderness traditions of early Israel, who receive the law and divine provision; however, their desert experience is also marked by disobedience. Thus, the wilderness becomes a place for spiritual purification as well as a place of revelation.[26] Into this matrix, the sectarian community that produced the DSS fashioned the identity of its members as a people distinct from the Jerusalem cult.[27] This was done mainly for community members to dis-

---

23. Unless otherwise indicated, all translations are mine.

24. Translation from Liv Ingebord Lied, *The Other Lands of Israel: Imaginations of the Land in 2 Baruch*, JSJSup 129 (Leiden: Brill, 2008), 113.

25. Lied, *The Other Lands of Israel*, 113.

26. Hindy Najman, "Towards a Study of the Uses of the Concept of Wilderness in Ancient Judaism," *DSD* 13 (2006): 99–113, esp. 109; see also Alison Schofield, "The Wilderness as Literary Motif in the Dead Sea Scrolls," in *Israel in the Wilderness*, ed. Kenneth E. Pomykala (Leiden: Brill, 2008), 38.

27. It is difficult to determine the exact nature of the Qumran community and to postulate its composition. Collins has argued against the idea of identifying the Yaḥad as exclusively the Qumran community but instead seeing it as an umbrella term for the diversity of groups that adhered to a similar viewpoint. See John J. Collins, "Forms of Community in the Dead Sea Scrolls," in *Emanuel: Studies in the Hebrew Bible, Septuagint, and Dead Sea Scrolls in Honor of Emanuel Tov*, ed. Shalom M. Paul et al., VTSup 94 (Leiden: Brill, 2003), 97–111. I use the terms *Qumran community* and *Yaḥad movement* interchangeably to indicate that there is not one monolithic com-

connect from what they saw as the corrupt priesthood and pollution of the temple.[28] However, in the process the community also drew a strong boundary between its members and what they came to see as the Other. This boundary was both geographical and metaphorical. In their removal to the desert, the sectarians envisioned themselves as creating an alternate temple mirroring the heavenly one.[29] The community reenacts Isa 40:3 and literally moves into the desert in an attempt to distance its members from the influence of the Jerusalem temple and to draw closer to God and the angelic host.[30]

The wilderness in these texts becomes a third space—a liminal location—where human and divine beings interact.[31] This is highlighted especially in works such as Songs of the Sabbath Sacrifice (4Q400 2, 5-7) and the Hodayot (e.g., 1QH<sup>a</sup> XI, 22-24; XII, 25-26; XIX, 13-17), where

---

munity but that there are diverse groups spread out geographically that would find common ground with one another. See also Alison Schofield, "Between Center and Periphery: The Yaḥad in Context," *DSD* 16 (2009): 330-50.

28. They saw themselves as "a holy house for Israel and the foundation of the holy of holies for Aaron.... and it will be a house of perfection and truth and truth in Israel" (1QS VIII, 5-9). See John J. Collins, "Powers in Heaven: God, Gods, and the Angels in the Dead Sea Scrolls," in *Religion in the Dead Sea Scrolls*, ed. John J. Collins and Robert A. Kugler (Grand Rapids: Eerdmans, 2003), 13.

29. Collins, "Powers in Heaven," 13. This is especially pronounced in the Songs of the Sabbath Sacrifice. Newsom argues that the language of the songs was designed to "create a sense of the presence of the heavenly temple." See Carol Newsom, *Songs of the Sabbath Sacrifice: A Critical Edition* (Atlanta: Scholars Press, 1985), 59, 72.

30. Najman, "Towards a Study," 100. See also Esther G. Chazon, "Human and Angelic Prayer in Light of the Dead Sea Scrolls," in *Liturgical Perspectives: Prayer and Poetry in Light of the Dead Sea Scrolls*, ed. Esther G. Chazon, STDJ 48 (Leiden: Brill, 2003), 35-47; Chazon, "Liturgical Communion with Angels at Qumran," in *Sapiential, Liturgical and Poetical Texts from Qumran*, ed. Daniel K. Falk, Florentino García Martínez, and Eileen M. Schuller, STDJ 35 (Leiden: Brill, 2000), 95-105. By using the term *desert* or *wilderness* I am not assuming that everyone would need to literally move to the wilderness to identify with these texts and the symbolic concept of the wilderness.

31. I am using Soja's understanding of third space here as lived experience combining both the real and the imagined. See Edward W. Soja, *Thirdspace: Journeys to Los Angeles and Other Real-and-Imagined Places* (Oxford: Blackwell, 1996), 5-6. For discussions of the wilderness as third space, see Lied, *Other Lands of Israel*, 13-15; Laura Feldt, "Wilderness and Hebrew Bible Religion—Fertility, Apostasy and Religious Transformation in the Pentateuch," in *Wilderness in Mythology and Religion: Approaching Religious Spatialities, Cosmologies, and Ideas of Wild Nature*, ed. Laura Feldt (Berlin: de Gruyter, 2012), 59-61.

the community and the Maskil join the worship of angels.[32] However, in their effort to distance themselves from the polluting effects of the Jerusalem temple and to commune with God, the community members make themselves vulnerable to the monstrous inhabitants of the wilderness that surrounds them. Thus, the more they seek divine contact, the more susceptible they become to demonic attack. In the Songs of the Sage, the desire of the community to attain the status of the angels is clear. In 4Q511 35, 3–4, the Maskil states, "God makes (some) ho[ly] for himself like an everlasting sanctuary, and there will be purity amongst those purified. And they shall be priests, his just people, his army and servants, the angels of his glory." The liminal setting of the wilderness allows the community to interact with the angels, but the forces of the demonic world are also a continuing reality. As Laura Feldt notes, the wilderness acts as an ambiguous space as it "oscillates between benign and malign."[33]

## 4. Songs of the Sage

As the community strived to identify and worship with the divine, it is not surprising to find protections against the demonic forces also at work in this wilderness location.[34] The Songs of the Sage (4Q510 and 4Q511)

---

32. See Judith H. Newman, "The Thanksgiving Hymns of 1QH$^a$ and the Construction of the Ideal Sage through Liturgical Performance," in *Sibyls, Scriptures and Scrolls: John Collins at Seventy*, ed. Joel Baden, Hindy Najman, and Eibert J. C. Tigchelaar, JSJSup 175 (Leiden: Brill, 2017), 953; John J. Collins, "The Angelic Life," in *Metamorphoses: Resurrection, Body and Transformative Practices in Early Christianity*, ed. Turid Karlsen Seim and Jorunn Økland, Ekstasis 1 (Berlin: de Gruyter, 2009), 302.

33. Feldt, "Wilderness and Hebrew Bible Religion," 82.

34. In addition to the Songs of the Sage (4Q510–511) other examples of defenses against demons include 11Q11 (11QApocryphal Psalms$^a$) and 4Q560 (4QExorcism). For discussions of demonology at Qumran see the following: Douglas L. Penny and Michael O. Wise, "By the Power of Beelzebub: An Aramaic Incantation Formula from Qumran (4Q560)," *JBL* 113 (1994): 627–50; Philip S. Alexander, "'Wrestling against Wickedness in High Places': Magic in the Worldview of the Qumran Community," in *The Scrolls and the Scriptures: Qumran Fifty Years After*, ed. Stanley E. Porter and Craig A. Evans, LSTS 26 (Sheffield: Sheffield Academic, 1997), 318–37; Esther Eshel, "Demonology in Palestine in the Second Temple Period" (PhD diss., Hebrew University, 1999); Alexander, "Demonology of the Dead Sea Scrolls," 331–53; Eshel, "Apotropaic Prayers in the Second Temple Period," in Chazon, *Liturgical Perspectives*, 69–88; Archie T. Wright, *The Origin of Evil Spirits: The Reception of Genesis 6:1–4 in Early Jewish Literature*, WUNT 2/198 (Tübingen: Mohr Siebeck, 2005); Loren

are chief examples of apotropaic prayers with the aim of reestablishing the cosmic boundaries around the community.[35] Alexander argues that these prayers were preventative in nature and meant to stave off attack to members both individually and communally.[36] In 4Q510, the purpose of the Maskil's prayer is to "declare the splendour of his radiance in order to frighten and terri[fy]" (4Q510 1, 4), while in 4Q511 the same idea of terrifying is present but expressed as "to startle those who terrify" (4Q511 8, 4). In each case, it is the Maskil and by extension members of the community who are verbally interacting with the spirits to subdue them and keep their attacks at bay. Their weapon is their praise of God's splendor and specifically "the splendour of his radiance" (4Q510 1, 4).[37] These texts differ from other magical incantation texts in that they do not summon the name of YHWH to frighten away the demons.[38] As Bilhah Nitzan has noted, "Accordingly, the songs are not merely ceremonial accompaniment to acts of war, but themselves constitute the instruments of war."[39] The following section examines three components of the Songs of the Sage as

---

Stuckenbruck, "Prayers of Deliverance from the Demonic in the Dead Sea Scrolls and Related Early Jewish Literature," in *The Changing Face of Judaism, Christianity and Other Greco-Roman Religions in Antiquity; Presented to James H. Charlesworth on the Occasion of His Sixty-Fifth Birthday*, ed. Ian H. Henderson and Gerbern S. Oegema, SJSHR 2 (Gütersloh: Gütersloher Verlagshaus, 2006), 146–65; Ida Frölich, " 'Invoke at Any Time': Apotropaic Texts and Belief in Demons in the Literature of the Qumran Community," *BN* 137 (2008): 41–74; Hermann Lichtenberger, "Spirits and Demons in the Dead Sea Scrolls," in *Text, Thought, and Practice in Qumran and Early Christianity: Proceedings of the Ninth International Symposium of the Orion Center for the Study of the Dead Sea Scrolls and Associated Literature, Jointly Sponsored by the Hebrew University Center for the Study of Christianity, 11–13 January, 2004*, ed. Ruth A. Clements and Daniel R. Schwartz, STDJ 84 (Leiden: Brill, 2009), 267–80; Frölich, "Theology and Demonology in Qumran Texts," *Hen* 32 (2010): 101–29.

35. The Songs of the Sage (4Q510–511) date to the end of the first century BCE and are quite damaged in sections. See Maurice Baillet, ed., *Qumran grotte 4.III (4Q482–4Q520)*, DJD VII (Oxford: Clarendon, 1982), 215, 219.

36. Alexander, "Demonology of the Dead Sea Scrolls," 345.

37. Bilhah Nitzan, *Qumran Prayer and Religious Poetry*, STDJ 12 (Leiden: Brill, 1994), 237.

38. Bilhah Nitzan, "Hymns from Qumran—4Q510–4Q511," in *The Dead Sea Scrolls: Forty Years of Research*, ed. Devorah Dimant and Uriel Rappaport, STDJ 10 (Leiden: Brill, 1992), 54. This is in contrast to 11Q11, often compared to the Songs of the Sage, which does call on the name of God to protect the community.

39. Nitzan, *Qumran Prayer*, 237.

they relate to their function as defensive prayers: (1) the establishment of cosmic boundaries, (2) the vulnerability of the body and spirit, and (3) the formation of a hybrid identity. In their desire to commune with the divine, the community members move physically further into the wilderness, resulting in a community caught between the divine and earthly worlds.

## 4.1. Establishment of Cosmic Boundaries

As noted above, in ancient and modern traditions, monsters inhabit peripheral locations that assume liminal connotations. One finds numerous references to such cosmic geographical boundaries throughout the Songs of the Sage. In 4Q511, the Maskil makes reference to the boundaries of the earthly and cosmic world:

> In their eras may the seas bl[ess] him, and may all their living things declare […] beauty, may all of them exult before the God of justice in jubi[lations of] salvation. For there is n[o] destroyer in their regions, and evil spirits do not walk in them. For the glory of the God of knowledge shines out through his words, and none of the sons of wickedness is able to resist. (4Q511 1, 3–8)

This passage points to the coming judgment of God on the demonic creatures that awaits them in the eschaton. Specific reference is made to "seas" and "all their living things" that will bless and praise God. The reference to the seas that "bless him" is noteworthy, as typically the seas are pictured in conflict with God. In the Psalms, God tames the "voice" of the sea by rebuking and silencing it.[40] That the sea here is pictured as blessing God is a radical portrait of God's kingship over this cosmic space that is normally at odds with God. Elsewhere in the Hebrew Bible, the "living things" are also found with reference to the cosmic sea that houses both sea creatures and more fearsome monsters (Gen 1:20–21; Ps 104:25–26).[41] The passage is damaged, so it is not clear whether other regions of the world were also included, but the sea is typically a prime locale for monstrous creatures

---

40. The following psalms describe God's kingship over the seas: Pss 29:3–4; 65:7; 93:3–4. Specifically, Ps 93:3 makes reference to the "voice" of the floods and the "thunders of mighty waters." For a helpful discussion of these passages see Debra Scoggins Ballentine, *The Conflict Myth and the Biblical Tradition* (Oxford: Oxford University Press, 2015), 81–82.

41. Ballentine, *Conflict Myth*, 87.

(Pss 74:13–14; 89:9–10; Isa 27:1; 51:9–10).[42] There is a strong tradition of God as the divine warrior that battles against the sea by setting boundaries for it and by subduing the monsters within it. Finally, the phrase "there is no destroyer in their regions, and evil spirits do not walk in them" points to a future time when the evil spirits will be eradicated from creation. Joseph Angel draws attention to the theme of light and its relation to the knowledge of God throughout 4Q510–511.[43] It is "the glory of the God of knowledge" that "shines out" through the words of the Maskil that is responsible for the annihilation of the evil spirits.[44]

Moreover, the Maskil in fragment 30 again makes reference to God's control over the cosmos:

> you have sealed [... ea]rth ... [...] and deep are [... the] heavens and the abysses and [...] You, my God have sealed them all up, and nobody opens them. And to whom [...] Can perhaps the waters of the deep be gauged in the hollow of a man's hand? And [the span of the heavens] be calculated in palms? (4Q511 30, 1–4)

Here we have reference to the deep and the abyss—all liminal locations that are typical haunts of demons. This passage likely reflects the belief that in the final days these deep cosmic locales will be sealed up again and that the demonic forces will be unable to escape.[45] This future judgment on evil spirits is also found in 1 En. 16.1-2 and the Hodayot.[46] Elsewhere the Songs of the Sage accept the fact for the present time that they will continue to experience attack from demonic spirits, as found in 4Q510 1, 7–8, which states, "Not for an everlasting destruction [but ra]ther for the era of the humiliation of sin." As Nitzan notes, the Songs of the Sage differ in that "the Sage from Qumran only scares the evil spirits away, in a somewhat

---

42. For the sea as a cosmic site, see John Day, *God's Conflict with the Dragon and the Sea: Echoes of a Canaanite-Myth in the Old Testament*, UCOP 35 (Cambridge: Cambridge University Press, 1985).

43. Joseph L. Angel, "Maskil, Community, and Religious Experience in the Songs of the Sage (4Q510-511)," *DSD* 19 (2012): 11.

44. Angel, "Maskil, Community and Religious Experience," 11.

45. Nitzan, "Hymns from Qumran," 60.

46. Nitzan notes similar themes found in 1QH$^a$ XI, 17–19 concerning Sheol and the Pit that seal up the unjust ("Hymns from Qumran," 60).

temporary fashion."⁴⁷ In the related 11QApocryphal Psalms,⁴⁸ the attack of "the offspring of man and the seed of the holy ones" must be continually repelled with the use of this incantation, though in this instance with the name of YHWH:

> An incanta]tion in the name of YHW[H. Invoke at an]y time. the heave[ns. When] he comes upon you in the nig[ht,] you shall [s]ay to him: Who are you, [oh offspring of] man and of the seed of the ho[ly] ones? Your face is a face of [delus]ion, and your horns are horns of illu[si]on. You are darkness and not light, [injus]tice and not justice. [...] the chief of the army. YHWH [will bring] you [down] [to the] deepest [Sheo]l, [he will shut] the two bronze [ga]tes through [which n]o light [penetrates.] [On you shall] not [shine the] sun, whi[ch rises] [upon the] just man to ... (11Q11 V, 4–11)

The demonic forces that threaten the present community are on borrowed time. They will soon be relegated back to their border lands, but only through the actions of God as mediated through the Maskil and the community. Monster theory assumes that the monster never dies but always is resurrected to attack again.⁴⁹ This aligns with the Songs of the Sage, which conceives of a continuous battle between the community and the demonic until the final judgment. The Maskil's identity as gatekeeper is fashioned in opposition to the Other, envisioned not only by the evil spirits but those that do not follow the path of the community.⁵⁰

## 4.2. The Vulnerability of the Body and Spirit

The context and frequency of these prayers is not clear from the text.⁵¹ Though the songs are addressed with *lmśkyl*, they do not necessarily imply

---

47. Nitzan, "Hymns from Qumran," 55.
48. 11Q11 is often considered part of a larger group of incantation prayers for protection against evil spirits. The group also includes 4Q510, 4Q511, 4Q444, 4Q560, and 11Q5. See Wright, *Origin of Evil Spirits*, 183.
49. Cohen, "Monster Culture," 5.
50. Newsom describes the Maskil's role in the following way: "He lets in, and he keeps out. No one comes into the community except through his judgment. As a boundary marking figure he must face both to the outside and to the inside." See Carol A. Newsom, *The Self as Symbolic Space: Constructing Identity and Community at Qumran*, STDJ 52 (Leiden: Brill, 2004), 170.
51. Numerous contexts are proposed by scholars, including at the end of the year

authorship but likely their function as a song for the Maskil to sing.[52] Furthermore, it is not only the body of the Maskil that is under attack but that of the community as a whole. The Maskil makes references to the larger community and the community's acts of worship: "[May] all those of perfect behaviour praise him. With the lyre of salvation [may] they [op]en their mouth for God's kindnesses. May they search for his manna" (4Q511 10, 8–9). The references to plurality in "all those of perfect behaviour" as well as "their mouth" demonstrate that this is a communal exercise.[53] Alexander notes that the use of "Amen, amen" in the benediction of 4Q511 also implies a shared experience.[54] This communal identity is manifested not only in praising God but in the combined struggles of the community members against demonic attack. The Songs of the Sage follow other familiar doctrines, such as that of the Treatise on the Two Spirits, which states, "and all the spirits of his lot cause the sons of light to fall" (1QS III, 24). There is a very real sense that demons or evil spirits pose a risk for the community (4Q510 1, 6). That these attacks are not isolated is made clear as the Maskil reports he is only able to repel the spirits rather than eradicate them (4Q511 35, 6–8).

The Maskil receives special attention in the Songs of the Sage as the chief figure to ward off the demonic forces and to draw firmer boundaries around the community.[55] In the same way the physical space, the wilderness, was vulnerable to demonic attack, in the Songs of the Sage it is clear that the individual and corporate body are also susceptible. In 4Q510 and 4Q511 the Maskil recounts the purpose of demonic attack: "And I, a Sage declare the splendour of his radiance in order to frighten and terr[ify] all the spirits of the ravaging angels and the bastard spirits, demons, Lilith, owls and [jackals ...] and those who strike unexpectedly to lead astray the spirit of knowledge, to make their hearts forlorn" (4Q510 1, 4–6). The

---

(Nitzan, *Qumran Prayer*, 238) and during an annual covenant ceremony (Eshel, "Apotropaic Prayers," 83–84).

52. Alexander, "Wrestling against Wickedness," 319.

53. Angel notes the communal nature of the songs, implied by the plural references to "mouths" and "lips," among others ("Maskil, Community, and Religious Experience," 2–3).

54. Alexander, "Wrestling against Wickedness," 321.

55. On the role of the Maskil, see Carol Newsom, "The Sage in the Literature of Qumran: The Functions of the Maskil," in *The Sage in Israel and the Ancient Near East*, ed. John G. Gammie and Leo G. Perdue (Winona Lake, IN: Eisenbrauns, 1990), 373–82.

Maskil is pictured as one who is at work keeping the demonic forces at bay, especially those that "strike unexpectedly," with the result of making "their hearts forlorn." This is done through the use of liturgy in singing these songs that focus on the "splendour of his radiance" (4Q510 1, 4). This fits well with Carol Newsom's description of the Maskil as "a gateway or boundary marking figure" who has the main responsibility of accepting or denying entry into the community.[56] He is a liminal figure who stands between the community and its opponents.

There is no doubt that the DSS speak of the spiritual and psychological danger posed by spirits and demons.[57] However, the effect on the physical body is also an important consideration, especially since the Songs of the Sage incorporate references to the body in the defense against the demons. The body itself is a site of vulnerability with relation to the demons who attack it. This is not isolated to the Songs of the Sage but is found in other texts such as 11Q5, containing a prayer of deliverance against demons. It states, "Let not Satan rule over me, nor an evil spirit; let neither pain nor evil purpose take possession of my bones" (11Q5 XIX, 15–16). Prior to this plea for deliverance, the writer of 11Q5 asks for forgiveness from sin and to be cleansed from iniquity as well as a request for a spirit of faith and knowledge (ll. 13–15). The physical body and the spiritual self cannot be separated here, as the writer is aware of their close interrelations. In the Songs of the Sage, the use of body language both as a weapon and a site of vulnerability with relation to the demonic is found in 4Q511:

> in God's council. Because He has placed [the wisdom] of his intelligence [in my] hea[rt, and on my tongue] the praises of his justice and […] …
> And through my mouth he startles [all the spirits of] the bastards, to subjugate [all] impure [sin]ners. For in the innards of my flesh is the foundation of [… and in] my body wars. (4Q511 48, 49+51, 1–4)

---

56. Newsom, *Self as Symbolic Space*, 170.

57. Alexander argues that the demonic attacks were primarily psychological rather than involving physical symptoms or even bodily possession ("Wrestling against Wickedness," 324). This might be too sharp a dichotomy, as elsewhere in the Scrolls there is evidence that demonic attack was thought to result in sickness, such as in the Genesis Apocryphon (1QapGen [1Q20] XX, 16–29), and even death, as found in Tobit (Tob 3:8; 6:8, 14–15; 8:2). See also Jub. 10.7–14. Moreover, Stuckenbruck distinguishes between the terminology of demonic attack and possession. See Loren Stuckenbruck, *The Myth of Rebellious Angels*, WUNT 335 (Tübingen: Mohr Siebeck, 2014), 176.

The text is fragmentary, but one can see that divine knowledge and insight are internalized by the Maskil as they are placed in his heart and on his tongue. It is specifically through the mouth of the Maskil that words of praise come forth to terrify the demons that threaten him and the community. It is through song and worship that the Maskil is able to protect the community, using his body as a weapon armed with divine wisdom.[58] Yet the Maskil also reveals the fragility of the body as a site of internal battle. Though the line is fragmentary, the use of *bāśār*, "flesh," points to the corruptive human nature that lies within each individual's body.[59]

Moreover, throughout the Songs of the Sage there is reference to the purity of the Maskil as a prerequisite for his election (4Q511 18). Yet it is evident that that the Maskil's body is also a point of vulnerability, described as a fragile vessel. An attitude of humility concerning his origins is displayed: "And I, [I will praise yo]u, for on account of your glory you have [pla]ced knowledge in my foundation of dust, to [...], even though I am a formation from spat saliva, I am moulded [from clay], and of darkness is [my] mixtu[re ...] ... and iniquity in the innards of my flesh" (4Q511 28+29, 2-4). This attitude of abasement but sharp expectation of divine favor is similar to what we find in the Hodayot and what Newsom calls "part of the practice of the construction of the self."[60] Similarly, the speaker makes reference to himself as "a creature of clay" and states, "for I have stationed myself in the wicked realm and with the vile by lot" (1QH$^a$ XI, 24–26). As noted above, this feeling of worthlessness is tied to the body as the location of sin, especially when using the term *bāśār*, "flesh."[61] Newsom further notes the connection between *bāśār* and the image of body as derived from dust and clay.[62] A similar idea is found in 4Q511, as

---

58. Newman has noted the use of the Maskil's body in the Hodayot as part of his role "to provide a continuous intercessory link to the divine" ("Thanksgiving Hymns of 1QH$^a$," 957).

59. The term *bāśār* is used twenty-nine times in the Hodayot to indicate the sinful inclinations of humanity. It is not disconnected from the body but rather is an integral part of the body along with the spirit. See Alexandria Frisch and Lawrence H. Schiffman, "The Body in Qumran Literature: Flesh and Spirit, Purity and Impurity in the Dead Sea Scrolls," *DSD* 23 (2016): 163.

60. See Newsom, *Self as Symbolic Space*, 173; Newman, "Thanksgiving Hymns of 1QH$^a$," 947.

61. Frisch and Schiffman, "Body in Qumran Literature," 159.

62. Carol Newsom, "Flesh, Spirit, and the Indigenous Psychology of the Hodayot," in *Prayer and Poetry in the Dead Sea Scrolls and Related Literature: Essays in Honor of*

the speaker understands that iniquity is found in the "innards of my flesh" and in a body molded from dust and clay. Although the Maskil and by extension the community strived for identification with the divine, they were constantly aware of their own fragile physical and spiritual selves. Thus, the Songs of the Sage are an important part of the community's liturgy to secure protection from the outside threat of demons but also to guard against the inner danger of each community member's own corruptible nature.

### 4.3. Hybrid Identity

The line between the individual and the community is not perfectly clear, as the Maskil serves both as a teacher and exemplar to the rest of the community.[63] Angel notes, "the Maskil's self-description is not so much the personalized expression of an individual, as it is a formulaic expression of communal ideals."[64] A large part of the identity and purpose of the community was to seek communion with God and angelic beings. In 4Q511, after the Maskil startles those who terrify, he states that God "will hide me ... among his holy ones" (4Q511 8, 7–8). In fragment 35 there is an ambiguous identification of the human community with the angelic one: "Among the holy ones, God makes (some) ho[ly] for himself like an everlasting sanctuary, and there will be purity among those purified. And they shall be priests, his just people, his army and servants, the angels of his glory" (4Q511 35, 2–4). Although these texts are antidemonic, they also represent the desire for a communion with the angelic host and the negation of normative boundaries separating the divine and human. This desire to be hidden among the angels and to identify so strongly with the divine beings is an example of boundary crossing by the Maskil and larger community. Although the community members are characterized by multiple dualisms—insider versus outsider, sons of light versus sons of darkness, and pure versus impure—their identity is not fixed but marked by hybridity. As Newsom has noted, the construction of the self is not done in a vacuum but in a deliberate manner by "contesting

---

*Eileen Schuller on the Occasion of Her Sixty-Fifth Birthday*, ed. Jeremy Penner, Ken M. Penner, and Cecilia Wassen, STDJ 90 (Leiden: Brill, 2012), 343–45.

63. Newsom, "Sage in the Literature," 382.

64. Angel, "Maskil, Community, and Religious Experience," 13. See also Newsom, *Self as Symbolic Space*, 189.

other constructions of meaning in the discursive community of Second Temple Judaism."[65] In order to construct their own identity, the sectarians required an Other against which they were set apart. While that Other is their human counterpart in Jewish communities from which they have separated, it is imperative to remember their self-construction is also vis-à-vis the divine realm.

In the sectarians' dualistic view, their opponents in other Jewish communities were the "sons of darkness" aligned with the demonic world.[66] Their physical removal to the wilderness not only brought them into a liminal location but also results in a hybrid state. They do not fit normative categories, as they participate simultaneously in the divine and earthly worlds, as demonstrated in the following text:

> He placed [I]srael [in t]welve camps … […] the lot of God with the ange[ls of] his glorious luminaries. On his name he instituted the pr[ai]se of their […] according to the feasts of the year, [and] the communal [do]minion, so that they would walk [in] the lot of [God] according to [his] glory, [and] serve him in the lot of the people of his throne. For the God of … (4Q511 2 I, 7–10)

Therefore, community members became caught between the earthly and divine worlds, suspended between these categories.[67] In effect, their own self-understanding led them to embody an identity of otherness and hybridity. The members identified with the angelic host but continued to acknowledge their own human limitations as they experienced constant attack from malevolent spirits. Thus, the community members constructed their own identity in such a way that they, like monsters, were hybrid beings who refused easy classification.[68] In their attempts to bridge the gap between the earthly and divine worlds, they called into question the boundaries between human and divine beings.

Monster theory approaches the study of monsters as a method of reading cultures that produce and interact with them. However, it not only

---

65. Newsom, *Self as Symbolic Space*, 193.

66. For a discussion of the multiple dualisms operating in the Scrolls, see Wright, *Origin of Evil Spirits*, 170–71.

67. Collins has called this a "two-sided existence" in which the hymnist is "set apart from all that and can join with the angels in praising God" ("Angelic Life," 304).

68. This is a central tenant of Monster theory as outlined by Cohen ("Monster Culture," 6–7).

studies the monsters but, more importantly, understands that "the monster notoriously appears at times of crisis as a kind of third term that problematizes the clash of extremes."[69] In the case of the Qumran community, the presence of demons as exemplified in the Yaḥad's apotropaic prayers demonstrates each member's liminal status both physically and ontologically. The withdrawal of the community members to the desert prompted a reappraisal of how they related to the divine world and perhaps even changed their own self-understanding of their status in the human realm. They were surrounded by monstrous beings, both angelic and demonic, caught between both extremes that vied for their allegiance. From the perspective of the Maskil and the community, the Other consisted of those outside their community who had effectively aligned themselves with the forces of darkness and impurity.[70] However, by studying the Yaḥad's relationship with the monsters that surrounded its members, it is clear that the community members had more in common with these monsters than with their human counterparts elsewhere. In fact, the Maskil and his followers had become "other," and like the monsters they both admired and reviled, they force us to reconsider "new and interconnected methods of perceiving the world."[71]

## 5. Conclusion

The wilderness locale for the Yaḥad movement was not a static entity but one that was imbued with symbolic significance.[72] It was also a lived-out space in which the community members carefully regulated their behaviors and solidified their identities against others. The texts I have considered, particularly the Songs of the Sage, are often called antidemonic or magical texts. While this is true, it does not capture completely the larger signifi-

---

69. Cohen, "Monster Culture," 6.
70. George W. E. Nickelsburg, "The We and the Other in the Worldview of 1 Enoch, the Dead Sea Scrolls, and Other Early Jewish Texts," in *The "Other" in Second Temple Judaism: Essays in Honor of John J. Collins*, ed. Daniel C. Harlow et al. (Grand Rapids: Eerdmans, 2011), 273.
71. Cohen, "Monster Culture," 7.
72. See Lied: "The Land is always localised and is always presented by familiar terms and imageries, but it is also always more than a location, or a territory, and more than the allusions and connotations associated with the Land-theme. The land is the spatial outcome of the creative recombination of location and conventional concepts through Israel's collective religious practices" (*Other Lands of Israel*, 17).

cance of these texts, as we see the community and especially the Maskil, who interacts with the cosmic world. One of the primary purposes for the identification and move to the wilderness was to seek communion with angelic beings. As I argued, the desire to cross from the earthly to the divine realm put the community at risk. The more community members attempted to identify with the angelic host, the more they needed to guard against demonic attack. The construction of the world into the insiders and outsiders is called into question when the Yaḥad's relationship to the divine world is integrated into this matrix. Yaḥad members constructed their identity in contrast to the Other, those they considered impure and wicked, who were excluded from the community, but by striving for divine communion they also effectively became Other. Yaḥad members were a hybrid community caught between their fragile human states and their desire to join the angelic community while constantly guarding against the attack of malevolent spirits who attempted to breach their spiritual and physical defenses.

## Bibliography

Alexander, Philip S. "The Demonology of the Dead Sea Scrolls." Pages 331–53 in *The Dead Sea Scrolls after Fifty Years: A Comprehensive Assessment*. Vol. 2. Edited by Peter W. Flint and James C. VanderKam. Leiden: Brill, 1999.

———. "'Wrestling against Wickedness in High Places': Magic in the Worldview of the Qumran Community." Pages 318–37 in *The Scrolls and the Scriptures: Qumran Fifty Years After*. Edited by Stanley E. Porter and Craig A. Evans. LSTS 26. Sheffield: Sheffield Academic, 1997.

Angel, Joseph L. "Maskil, Community, and Religious Experience in the Songs of the Sage (4Q510–511)." *DSD* 19 (2012): 1–27.

Asma, Stephen T. *On Monsters: An Unnatural History of Our Worst Fears*. Oxford: Oxford University Press, 2009.

Baillet, Maurice, ed. *Qumran grotte 4.III (4Q482–4Q520)*. DJD VII. Oxford: Clarendon, 1982.

Ballentine, Debra Scoggins. *The Conflict Myth and the Biblical Tradition*. Oxford: Oxford University Press, 2015.

Beal, Timothy K. *Religion and Its Monsters*. New York: Routledge, 2002.

Benveniste, Émile. *Pouvoir, droit, religion*. Vol. 2 of *Le vocabulaire des institutions indo-européennes*. Paris: Les éditions de minuit, 1969.

Brooke, George J. "Isa 40:3 and the Wilderness Community." Pages 117–32 in *New Qumran Texts and Studies*. Edited by George J. Brooke with Florentino García Martínez. Leiden: Brill, 1994.

Carroll, Noel. *The Philosophy of Horror: Or, Paradoxes of the Heart*. New York: Routledge, 1990.

Chazon, Esther G. "Human and Angelic Prayer in Light of the Dead Sea Scrolls." Pages 35–47 in *Liturgical Perspectives: Prayer and Poetry in Light of the Dead Sea Scrolls*. Edited by Esther G. Chazon. STDJ 48. Leiden: Brill, 2003.

———. "Liturgical Communion with Angels at Qumran." Pages 95–105 in *Sapiential, Liturgical and Poetical Texts from Qumran*. Edited by Daniel K. Falk, Florentino García Martínez, and Eileen M. Schuller. STDJ 35. Leiden: Brill, 2000.

Cohen, Jeffrey J. "Monster Culture (Seven Theses)." Pages 3–25 in *Monster Theory: Reading Culture*. Edited by Jeffrey J. Cohen. Minneapolis: University of Minnesota Press, 1996.

Collins, John J. "The Angelic Life." Pages 291–310 in *Metamorphoses: Resurrection, Body and Transformative Practices in Early Christianity*. Edited by Turid Karlsen Seim and Jorunn Økland. Ekstasis 1. Berlin: de Gruyter, 2009.

———. "Forms of Community in the Dead Sea Scrolls." Pages 97–111 in *Emanuel: Studies in the Hebrew Bible, Septuagint, and Dead Sea Scrolls in Honor of Emanuel Tov*. Edited by Shalom M. Paul, Robert A. Kraft, Lawrence H. Schiffman, and Weston W. Fields. VTSup 94. Leiden: Brill, 2003.

———. "Powers in Heaven: God, Gods, and the Angels in the Dead Sea Scrolls." Pages 9–28 in *Religion in the Dead Sea Scrolls*. Edited by John J. Collins and Robert A. Kugler. Grand Rapids: Eerdmans, 2003.

Day, John. *God's Conflict with the Dragon and the Sea: Echoes of a Canaanite-Myth in the Old Testament*. UCOP 35. Cambridge: Cambridge University Press, 1985.

Eshel, Esther. "Apotropaic Prayers in the Second Temple Period." Pages 69–88 in *Liturgical Perspectives: Prayer and Poetry in Light of the Dead Sea Scrolls*. Edited by Esther G. Chazon. STDJ 48. Leiden: Brill, 2003.

———. "Demonology in Palestine in the Second Temple Period." PhD diss., Hebrew University, 1999.

Feldt, Laura. "Wilderness and Hebrew Bible Religion—Fertility, Apostasy and Religious Transformation in the Pentateuch." Pages 55–94 in *Wilderness in Mythology and Religion: Approaching Religious Spatialities,*

*Cosmologies, and Ideas of Wild Nature*. Edited by Laura Feldt. Berlin: de Gruyter, 2012.

Frisch, Alexandria, and Lawrence H. Schiffman. "The Body in Qumran Literature: Flesh and Spirit, Purity and Impurity in the Dead Sea Scrolls." *DSD* 23 (2016): 155–82.

Frölich, Ida. "From Pseudepigraphic to Sectarian." *RevQ* 21 (2004): 395–406.

———. "'Invoke at Any Time': Apotropaic Texts and Belief in Demons in the Literature of the Qumran Community." *BN* 137 (2008): 41–74.

———. "Theology and Demonology in Qumran Texts." *Hen* 32 (2010): 101–29.

García Martínez, Florentino, and Eibert J. C. Tigchelaar. *The Dead Sea Scrolls Study Edition*. 2 vols. Leiden: Brill, 1997–1998.

Gilmore, David. *Monsters: Evil Beings, Mythical Beasts, and All Manner of Imaginary Terrors*. Philadelphia: University of Pennsylvania Press, 2003.

Huet, Marie Hélène. *Monstrous Imagination*. Cambridge: Harvard University Press, 1993.

Hutter, Manfred. "Demons and Benevolent Spirits in the Ancient Near East: A Phenomenological Overview." Pages 21–34 in *Angels: The Concept of Celestial Beings; Origins, Development and Reception*. Edited by Friedrich V. Reiterer, Tobias Nicklas, and Karin Schöpflin. DCLS. Berlin: de Gruyter, 2007.

Lichtenberger, Hermann. "Spirits and Demons in the Dead Sea Scrolls." Pages 267–80 in *Text, Thought, and Practice in Qumran and Early Christianity: Proceedings of the Ninth International Symposium of the Orion Center for the Study of the Dead Sea Scrolls and Associated Literature, Jointly Sponsored by the Hebrew University Center for the Study of Christianity, 11–13 January, 2004*. Edited by Ruth A. Clements and Daniel R. Schwartz. STDJ 84. Leiden: Brill, 2009.

Lied, Liv Ingeborg. *The Other Lands of Israel: Imaginations of the Land in 2 Baruch*. JSJSup 129. Leiden: Brill, 2008.

Moussy, Claude. "Esquisse de l'histoire de monstrum." *REL* 55 (1977): 345–69.

Najman, Hindy. "Towards a Study of the Uses of the Concept of Wilderness in Ancient Judaism." *DSD* 13 (2006): 99–113.

Newman, Judith H. "The Thanksgiving Hymns of 1QH$^a$ and the Construction of the Ideal Sage through Liturgical Performance." Pages 940–57 in *Sibyls, Scriptures and Scrolls: John Collins at Seventy*. Edited by Joel

Baden, Hindy Najman, and Eibert J. C. Tigchelaar. JSJSup 175 Leiden: Brill, 2017.

Newsom, Carol. "Flesh, Spirit, and the Indigenous Psychology of the Hodayot." Pages 339–54 in *Prayer and Poetry in the Dead Sea Scrolls and Related Literature: Essays in Honor of Eileen Schuller on the Occasion of Her Sixty-Fifth Birthday*. Edited by Jeremy Penner, Ken M. Penner, and Cecilia Wassen. STDJ 90. Leiden: Brill, 2012.

———. "The Sage in the Literature of Qumran: The Functions of the Maskil." Pages 373–82 in *The Sage in Israel and the Ancient Near East*. Edited by John G. Gammie and Leo G. Perdue. Winona Lake, IN: Eisenbrauns, 1990.

———. *The Self as Symbolic Space: Constructing Identity and Community at Qumran*. STDJ 52. Leiden: Brill, 2004.

———. *Songs of the Sabbath Sacrifice: A Critical Edition*. Atlanta: Scholars Press, 1985.

Nickelsburg, George W. E. "The We and the Other in the Worldview of 1 Enoch, the Dead Sea Scrolls, and Other Early Jewish Texts." Pages 262–78 in *The "Other" in Second Temple Judaism: Essays in Honor of John J. Collins*. Edited by Daniel C. Harlow, Matthew Goff, Karina Martin Hogan, and Joel S. Kaminsky. Grand Rapids: Eerdmans, 2011.

Nitzan, Bilhah. "Hymns from Qumran—4Q510–4Q511." Pages 53–63 in *The Dead Sea Scrolls: Forty Years of Research*. Edited by Devorah Dimant and Uriel Rappaport. STDJ 10. Leiden: Brill, 1992.

———. *Qumran Prayer and Religious Poetry*. STDJ 12. Leiden: Brill, 1994.

Penny, Douglas L., and Michael O. Wise. "By the Power of Beelzebub: An Aramaic Incantation Formula from Qumran (4Q560)." *JBL* 113 (1994): 627–50.

Schofield, Alison. "Between Center and Periphery: The *Yaḥad* in Context." *DSD* 16 (2009): 330–50.

———. "The Em-bodied Desert and Other Sectarian Spaces in the Dead Sea Scrolls." Pages 155–74 in *Constructions of Space IV: Further Developments in Examining Ancient Israel's Social Space*. Edited by Mark K. George. New York: Bloomsbury, 2013.

———. "The Wilderness as Literary Motif in the Dead Sea Scrolls." Pages 37–53 in *Israel in the Wilderness*. Edited by Kenneth E. Pomykala. Leiden: Brill, 2008.

Scott, Niall. *Monsters and the Monstrous: Myths and Metaphors of Enduring Evil*. Amsterdam: Rodopi, 2007.

Smith, Mark S. *The Origins of Biblical Monotheism: Israel's Polytheistic Background and the Ugaritic Texts.* Oxford: Oxford University Press, 2001.

Soja, Edward W. *Thirdspace: Journeys to Los Angeles and Other Real-and-Imagined Places.* Oxford: Blackwell, 1996.

Stegemann, Hartmut, Eileen Schuller, and Carol A. Newsom. *Qumran Cave 1.III: 1QHodayot$^a$, with Incorporation of 1QHodayot$^b$ and 4QHodayot$^{a-f}$.* DJD XL. Oxford: Clarendon, 2009.

Stuckenbruck, Loren. *The Myth of Rebellious Angels.* WUNT 335. Tübingen: Mohr Siebeck, 2014.

———. "Prayers of Deliverance from the Demonic in the Dead Sea Scrolls and Related Early Jewish Literature." Pages 146–65 in *The Changing Face of Judaism, Christianity and Other Greco-Roman Religions in Antiquity: Presented to James H. Charlesworth on the Occasion of His Sixty-Fifth Birthday.* Edited by Ian H. Henderson and Gerbern S. Oegema. SJSHR 2. Gütersloh: Gütersloher Verlagshaus, 2006.

———. "Satan and Demons." Pages 173–97 in *Jesus among Friends and Enemies.* Edited by Chris Keith and Larry Hurtado. Grand Rapids: Baker Academic, 2011.

Talmon, Shemaryahu. "The 'Desert Motif' in the Bible and Qumran Literature." Pages 31–63 in *Biblical Motifs: Origins and Transformations.* Edited by Alexander Altmann. Cambridge: Harvard University Press, 1966.

Wright, Archie T. *The Origin of Evil Spirits: The Reception of Genesis 6:1–4 in Early Jewish Literature.* WUNT 2/198. Tübingen: Mohr Siebeck, 2005.

# Sectarian Identity and Angels Associated with Israel: A Comparison of Daniel 7–12 with 1QS, 11QMelchizedek, and 1QM

Matthew L. Walsh

## Introduction

One of the many intriguing developments of Second Temple Judaism was its detailed speculation regarding the angelic realm, and it is the early Jewish fascination with angels[1] that will be the focus of this essay. More specifically, I will utilize the belief that certain angels were thought to be closely associated with Israel and, in turn, employ this conviction to shed light on sectarian identity in the Dead Sea Scrolls (DSS). Two hallmarks of the association between the angels and Israel will serve as points of departure. First, angels associated with Israel were cast as having different vocations, but my main interest here is in angelic warrior-guardians, who strove against the angels associated with Israel's enemies in the celestial realm and/or were granted a prominent role in the eschatological deliverance of God's people.[2] Second, a crucial component of the presentation

---

This study adapts and condenses aspects of Matthew L. Walsh, *Angels Associated with Israel in the Dead Sea Scrolls: Angelology and Sectarian Identity at Qumran*, WUNT 2/509 (Tübingen: Mohr Siebeck, 2019), especially 56–83, 149–201.

1. The broadest treatment of the subject is Michael Mach, *Entwicklungsstadien des jüdischen Engelglaubens in vorrabbinischer Zeit*, TSAJ 34 (Tübingen: Mohr Siebeck, 1992). For a concise introduction, see Larry W. Hurtado, "Monotheism, Principal Angels, and the Background of Christology," in *The Oxford Handbook of the Dead Sea Scrolls*, ed. Timothy H. Lim and John J. Collins (Oxford: Oxford University Press, 2010), 546–56.

2. For a recent treatment of this angelic vocation, see Aleksander R. Michalak, *Angels as Warriors in Late Second Temple Jewish Literature*, WUNT 2/330 (Tübingen:

of these angels was that they were envisioned within apocalyptic worldviews that assumed, as Darrell Hannah puts it, that "earthly realities reflect and mirror heavenly ones."[3] There was thus thought to be a connection or correspondence between the realms. This is relevant, of course, because, from the early days of the investigation of the DSS, scholars have been intrigued by the claims of the sect to have a unique relationship with the angels. Compositions such as the Hodayot (1QH$^a$) and the War Scroll (1QM) have been understood as containing boasts of fellowship with the angels prior to the postmortem experiences anticipated in Dan 12:2–3, 1 En. 104.2–6, and Wis 5:5.

But, as Eileen Schuller has recently highlighted, there is a lack of consensus as to what exactly is being claimed in sectarian angelic fellowship passages,[4] and it is with this observation that I hint at the direction of my study. First, I assume that the sect's well-known devotion to halakic matters and their negative view of outsiders meant that they viewed themselves as the true Israel; indeed, I propose that boasts of angelic fellowship only bolstered the sect's assertions to be the legitimate people of God. Second, to understand sectarian angelic fellowship claims and differentiate them from the relatively widespread early Jewish assumption of a correspondence between heaven and earth, it is necessary to compare sectarian texts with late Second Temple texts found at Qumran adduced as having a nonsectarian provenance.

Since Dan 7–12 is arguably the paradigmatic nonsectarian exemplar of Israel having angelic guardians whose struggles in heaven were intimately related to those of the nation on earth, I will begin by looking at these chapters of the book of Daniel. In addition to examining how angelic

---

Mohr Siebeck, 2012). Another important role in which angels were cast is that of priests who were envisioned as ministering in the heavenly temple. For discussion of these angels, see Joseph L. Angel, *Otherworldly and Eschatological Priesthood in the Dead Sea Scrolls*, STDJ 86 (Leiden: Brill, 2010).

3. Darrell D. Hannah, "Guardian Angels and Angelic National Patrons in Second Temple Judaism and Early Christianity," in *Angels: The Concept of Celestial Beings; Origins, Development and Reception*, ed. Friedrich V. Reiterer, Tobias Nicklas, and Karen Schöpflin, DCLS (Berlin: de Gruyter, 2007), 420. Contra Crispin H. T. Fletcher-Louis, *All the Glory of Adam: Liturgical Anthropology in the Dead Sea Scrolls*, STDJ 42 (Leiden: Brill, 2001), who largely denies the notion of a correspondence between heaven and earth and instead has proposed that many references to angels are, in actuality, humans in their redeemed state.

4. Eileen M. Schuller, "Recent Scholarship on the Hodayot," *CurBR* 10 (2011): 151.

guardians associated with Israel contribute to Dan 7–12, I will note the relationship between these angels and Daniel's understanding of Israel, thereby setting the stage for a comparison with sections of three compositions of sectarian provenance: 1QS, 11QMelchizedek (11Q13), and 1QM.

## Nonsectarian Texts: Daniel 7–12

Angels associated with Israel are central to the worldview of Dan 7–12, as these chapters reveal that the persecutions of the Jews at the hands of Antiochus Epiphanes are only part of a larger reality: the evil that is transpiring on earth is parallel to a battle in heaven, with the outcome of the earthly conflict determined by events in the heavenly realm. The severity of the situation is highlighted by descriptions of the oppression of the angelic host, who are defended by their leader, Michael. Indeed, chapters 7–12 as a unit reveal the centrality of angels associated with Israel in the mind of its composer(s) and/or compiler(s).[5] In the words of John Collins,

> What we find in the visions [of Dan 7–12] is not just a reaction to the events of the Maccabean period but a way of perceiving those events that is quite different from what we find in the books of Maccabees.... Behind the wars of the Hellenistic princes lies the heavenly combat between the angelic princes.... The first objective of the book is to persuade its readers of the reality of this supernatural dimension. The struggle is not ultimately between human powers or within human control.... The beast from the sea will be destroyed, and Michael will prevail in the heavenly combat. The very fact that the situation is beyond human control is, in the end, reassuring, for it is in the hand of God, the holy ones, and the angelic prince, Michael.[6]

---

5. Source-critical discussions of Dan 7–12 are complex, not least because ch. 7 is written in Aramaic, whereas chs. 8–12 are composed in Hebrew. For a discussion of the source-critical issues of Dan 7–12 vis-à-vis its angelology, see Michael Segal, who argues that ch. 7 provided the "theological underpinnings of the national [angelic] princes" found in chs. 10 and 12. See Segal, "Monotheism and Angelology in Daniel," in *One God, One Cult, One Nation: Archaeology and Biblical Perspectives*, ed. Reinhard G. Kratz and Hermann Spieckmann, BZAW 405 (Berlin: de Gruyter, 2010), 419. This is an important observation, as it suggests that Dan 7 anticipates the more explicit descriptions of Israel's angelic guardians later in the book. See further below.

6. John J. Collins, *Daniel: A Commentary on the Book of Daniel*, Hermeneia (Minneapolis: Fortress, 1993), 61.

In this section, I will mainly address aspects of chapters 7, 8, 10, and 12 of Daniel.

## Daniel 7

After the description of four violent and terrifying beasts, including the exceedingly arrogant horn of the fourth beast, Daniel recounts the climax of the first part of his vision, where we encounter the enigmatic "one like a son of man":

חזה הוית בחזוי ליליא וארו עם־ענני שמיא כבר אנש אתה הוה ועד־עתיק יומיא
מטה וקדמוהי הקרבוהי
ולה יהיב שלטן ויקר ומלכו וכל עממיא אמיא ולשניא לה יפלחון שלטנה שלטן
עלם די־לא יעדה ומלכותה די־לא תתחבל

> As I watched in the night visions, I saw one like a human being coming with the clouds of heaven. And he came to the Ancient One and was presented before him. To him was given dominion and glory and kingship that all peoples, nations, and languages should serve him. His dominion is an everlasting dominion that shall not pass away, and his kingship is one that shall never be destroyed. (7:13–14)[7]

The identity of the "one like a son of man" is the subject of prolonged debate, but the interpretation accepted here is that this figure is a highly exalted heavenly being, the chief angelic guardian of God's people, perhaps Michael.[8] This reading makes good sense in light of the remainder

---

7. English translations of the Hebrew Bible are from the NRSV.

8. For a history of interpretation, see Collins, *Daniel*, 304–11, 318–19. Collins has championed the interpretation of the "one like a son of man" as Michael. See John J. Collins, "The Son of Man and the Saints of the Most High in the Book of Daniel," *JBL* 93 (1974): 50–68; Collins, *Daniel*, 310–11, 318–19. As noted above, Segal has argued that that final form of Dan 10–12 is the product of different authors, and while he considers the references to Michael in chs. 10 and 12 to be secondary, he argues that these additions were influenced by Dan 7:13–14 ("Monotheism and Angelology," 405–20). Alternatively, the "one like a son of man" has been identified as an unnamed angelic leader (e.g., Ferch), Gabriel (e.g., Zevit), or perhaps a celestial being who outranks Michael but should be identified with other elite principal angel figures of the Second Temple period (e.g., Bampfylde, Heiser). See Arthur J. Ferch, "The Apocalyptic 'Son of Man' in Daniel 7" (PhD diss., Andrews University, 1979), 105; Ziony Zevit, "The Structure and Individual Elements of Daniel 7," *ZAW* 80 (1960): 394–96; Gillian

of chapter 7, which continues by revealing that the same fortunes of the "one like a son of man" will be those of the "holy ones of the Most High," which is likely a reference to the collective angelic host,[9] who are said to possess the kingdom forever (v. 18). But chapter 7 also notes the hardships of the "holy ones," as verse 21 reads: "[the] horn made war with the holy ones and was prevailing over them." Elaborating on this statement, verse 25 discloses that the horn is a king who, among other blasphemous acts, "shall speak words against the Most High, [and] attempt to wear out the holy ones of the Most High." According to verse 22, this affliction is reversed by the judgment of the "Ancient One," a point that serves to reinforce both the interconnected fates of the "holy ones of the Most High" and the "one like a son of man"[10] and that they are ultimately dependent on divine judgment.

The persecuted Jews themselves are almost certainly the referent of verse 27, where it is said that the "people of the holy ones of the Most High" will be given "the kingship and dominion and the greatness of the kingdom under the whole heaven." Here, two observations are key. First, chapter 7 seemingly differentiates between the "holy ones of the Most High" and the "people of the holy ones of the Most High."[11] Second, "people of the holy ones of the Most High" is a designation that suggests a close association between the Jewish people and their angelic guardians, and the genitive is best taken as indicating that the people belong to the angels in a tutelary sense.[12] Moreover, as with the "one like a son of man" and the "holy ones of the Most High," verses 26–27 announce that the

---

Bampfylde, "The Prince of the Host in the Book of Daniel and the Dead Sea Scrolls," *JSJ* 14 (1983): 129–34; Michael J. Heiser, "The Divine Council in the Late Canonical and Non-canonical Second Temple Jewish Literature" (PhD diss., University of Wisconsin–Madison, 2004), §§6.2–3, 7.4.

9. For the angelic interpretation of the "holy ones," see the helpful excursus of Collins, *Daniel*, 313–19.

10. The coming of the "one like a son of man" in the visionary sequence (7:13–14) directly follows the judgment scene of the fourth beast and its horn (7:11–12), at which the "Ancient One" (7:9–10) presumably presides.

11. Contra Vern S. Poythress, "The Holy Ones of the Most High in Daniel VII," *VT* 26 (1976): 208–13, who describes the designation "holy ones" and "people of the holy ones" as synonymously referring to Israel, but this reading too readily discounts the correspondence between heaven and earth that undergirds Dan 7–12.

12. So Luc Dequeker, "The Saints of the Most High in Qumran and Daniel," *OtSt* 18 (1973): 155–56, 179–87; see also Collins, *Daniel*, 315, 322.

fortunes of the "people of the holy ones" are ultimately dependent on the judgment of the heavenly court.

Returning briefly to the subject of the beasts, the interpretation provided by the angelic attendant in verses 17–18 is brief: the four beasts represent four kings/kingdoms. But in light of the aspects of chapter 7 just discussed (not to mention chs. 8–12), viewing the beasts as symbols for earthly kings and kingdoms likely does not exhaust their meaning. If, as some have argued, the symbolism of the beasts includes the heavenly or angelic powers that lie behind the respective earthly kings/kingdoms,[13] then the interpretation of the "one like a son of man" as an angel constitutes a powerful announcement: the dominion granted to the leader of the righteous angelic host means that, in the end, the celestial forces behind Antiochus will be defeated. As Collins notes, "To the pious Jews of the Maccabean era, who had a lively belief in supernatural beings, nothing could be more relevant"[14] than the belief that the leader of the angelic host, the host itself, and the people of God, would together receive dominion, glory, and kingship.

---

13. On the beasts as representing more than earthly kings/kingdoms and the relationship of ch. 7 to what follows, see the comments of Chrys C. Caragounis, who writes: "The oscillation between king and kingdom observable in the text, obtains also between the king on the one hand and the entity that is conceived of as being the core in the concept of 'Beast' on the other. The recognition of the dynamic nature of the text is of crucial importance for understanding the nature of the concept of 'Beast.'... Our author is grappling with his problem on a two-dimensional basis. While cogitating on human affairs the author goes beyond what is observable in the empirical realm. He introduces his readers to another plane, the plane of vision, where earthly phenomena are seen to have their invisible counterparts to 'events' beyond the world of sense. More than this, there is a causal connection between the invisible and the visible worlds. Earthly events are not simply the result of the whim of earthly potentates; they are to be explained by reference to realties in the invisible world. It is this double dimension in the author's perspective which renders the concept of 'Beast' a complex concept of ambivalent nature.... What is perhaps only implicit as yet in chapter 7 become quite explicit in [ch. 10]. Here, two of the beasts/kingdoms, Persia and Greece, are described as having a 'prince,' ... who tries to thwart God's purpose by opposing the angelic emissary. That these 'princes' cannot possibly refer to ... human kings is placed beyond reasonable doubt in verse 21 which in identical terms speaks of the angel Michael as the 'prince' of the Jews." See Caragounis, *The Son of Man: Vision and Interpretation*, WUNT 38 (Tübingen: Mohr Siebeck, 1986), 69–70. For similar comments, see Collins, *Daniel*, 312 n. 306, 320.

14. Collins, *Daniel*, 318.

## Daniel 8

Daniel 8 addresses the same historical concerns as chapter 7, and it has been suggested that the former, which marks the book's transition to Hebrew, is dependent on the latter.[15] The earthly and cosmic impact associated with the persecutions of Antiochus, who is again symbolized by a little horn, are the focus, and the chapter ends with a brief yet hopeful polemic indicating that the oppressor will meet his demise through divine intervention.[16]

Chapter 8 utilizes the widespread ancient Near Eastern motif that the stars are gods or angelic beings, and while the astral host can be cast as either for or against the God of Israel (e.g., Isa 24:21-23; Job 38:7), it is obvious in 8:10-12 that the stars are the victims of the horn's aggression and therefore represent righteous angels:[17]

ותגדל עד־צבא השמים ותפל ארצה מן־הצבא ומן־הכוכבים ותרמסם
ועד שר־הצבא הגדיל וממנו הורם התמיד והשלך מכון מקדשו
וצבא תנתן על־התמיד בפשע ותשלך אמת ארצה ועשתה והצליחה

> [The horn] grew as high as the host of heaven. It threw down to earth some of the host and some of the stars, and trampled on them. Even against the prince of the host it acted arrogantly; it took the regular burnt offering away from him and overthrew the place of his sanctuary. Because of wickedness, the host was given over to it together with the regular burnt offering; it cast truth to the ground, and kept prospering in what it did.

---

15. On the complementary relationship between the two chapters, see John E. Goldingay, *Daniel*, WBC 30 (Dallas: Word, 1989), 201; Collins, *Daniel*, 342.

16. As Goldingay implies, the absence of any mention of divine intervention until the very end of the chapter highlights the severity of persecutions of Antiochus (*Daniel*, 204). But note the insightful observation of Carol A. Newsom with Brennan W. Breed, who, in reference to the fact that Antiochus's demise is communicated by only three Hebrew words (ובאפס יד ישבר), "But he shall be broken, and not by human hands," point out: "The rhetorical economy of the text deflates Antiochus's massive pretentions." See Newsom and Breed, *Daniel: A Commentary*, OTL (Louisville: Westminster John Knox, 2014), 272.

17. See Collins, *Daniel*, 332, who describes the angels as "good." Alternatively, the stars were considered to be manifestations of divine beings, though the distinction is sometimes unclear. See Collins, *Daniel*, 331; see also Goldingay, *Daniel*, 209-10; E. Theodore Mullen Jr., *The Assembly of the Gods: The Divine Council in Canaanite and Early Hebrew Literature*, HSM 24 (Chico, CA: Scholars Press, 1980), 194-96.

The angelic stars and the trampling they endure from the horn are reminiscent of the war the horn waged against the worn-out holy ones of Dan 7 and highlights the similarities between the two chapters. Chapter 8 also emphasizes a cosmic dimension associated with the assaults of Antiochus. Indeed, the direness of the situation is underscored in that even the "prince of the host"—possibly a reference to the chief of the righteous angelic forces[18]—bears the brunt of the horn's arrogance. That verse 11 states that the host is "given over" to the horn continues the bleak description of righteous angels under attack.

One of the ways Dan 8 emphasizes the correspondence between heaven and earth is by alternating references to each realm. This oscillation can occur abruptly: after a rather lengthy description of the power of the goat and its horns (vv. 5–9), which symbolize events on earth, attention is suddenly given to the cosmic disturbances associated with the horn (vv. 10–11).[19] But chapter 8 can also exhibit this oscillation within one line, as verse 12 mentions both the afflictions of the angelic host and the disruption of temple sacrifices. Thus, in the same breath, the impact of the horn is said to touch heaven and earth, and "here again, the empirical

---

18. Given that 8:11 continues by mentioning that the horn "took the regular burnt offering away from *him* and overthrew the place of *his* sanctuary"—with the antecedent of the pronouns almost certainly referring to the "prince of the host"—the epithet is often understood as a description of the God of Israel; that the interpretation section of the passage apparently refers to the "prince of the host" as the שר־שרים, "prince of princes" (8:25), is said to strengthen the identification. The translators of the NRSV apparently concur with this evaluation, as is evidenced by the capitalization of the epithet (i.e., "Prince of princes"), both here and in the parallel to Dan 8:11 at 11:36: "The king shall act as he pleases. He shall exalt himself and consider himself greater than any god, and shall speak horrendous things against the God of gods." See John J. Collins, "Prince שר," *DDD*, 662–64; see also Louis F. Hartman and Alexander A. DiLella, *The Book of Daniel*, AB 23 (Garden City, NY: Doubleday, 1978), 236; Newsom, *Daniel*, 264. If this interpretation is correct, Dan 8 is a rare instance of the use of שר as an epithet for the God of Israel (see 1QH$^a$ XVIII, 10; 4Q417 2 I, 5; 4Q418 140, 4). However, following medieval commentator Ibn Ezra, some scholars have allowed for the possibility that this figure is Michael. See Andre Lacocque, *The Book of Daniel*, trans. David Pellauer (Atlanta: John Knox, 1979), 162; Goldingay, *Daniel*, 210. Additionally, it has been proposed that the "prince of the host" and the "one like a son of man" are the same figure, who should be differentiated from the lower-ranking Michael (see Bampfylde, "Prince of the Host," 129–34; Hesier, "Divine Council," §§6.2–6.3).

19. Goldingay, *Daniel*, 205.

tribulation of the Jewish people is understood to have its counterpart in the heavenly battle."[20]

Daniel 10–12

The final section of the book of Daniel is composed of an initial vision (10:1–11:1), which serves as an introduction for an angel-mediated discourse containing the *ex eventu* prophecy of the history of the fourth–second centuries BCE (11:2–12:4); an epilogue (12:5–13) follows this discourse. But chapter 10 is far from superfluous introductory material: the vision is vital for understanding chapter 11 in that the former elucidates the latter by providing a glimpse of "what is really going on."[21] In other words, the cryptic imagery of chapters 7–8 is made explicit in chapter 10: the struggle of God's people on earth corresponds to the battles of their angelic counterparts in heaven. Chapters 10–12 are clear, however, that this struggle will end in Michael's victory, which means victory for Israel.[22]

In Dan 10–12, Michael is three times referred to as a שר, "prince" (see 10:13, 21; 12:1), a designation indicating that his role corresponds to that

---

20. Collins, *Daniel*, 333–35. See Lacocque, who not only supports the interpretation that the "prince of the host" is Michael but also sees the epithet as simultaneously referring to the high priest (*Book of Daniel*, 162). While this view is quite speculative, it is likely an attempt to underscore the relationship between the realms.

21. Collins, *Daniel*, 61. On the priority of the heavenly world at Qumran, see Philip Alexander, *The Mystical Texts: Songs of the Sabbath Sacrifice and Related Manuscripts*, LSTS 61, CQS 7 (London: T&T Clark, 2006), especially 42, 47, 61.

22. As previously mentioned, Segal has argued that the passages referring to angelic princes in Dan 10 and 12 (10:13, 20–21; 12:1) are secondary, deliberately added to complement the picture of Dan 7–8, namely, that "the Lord renders judgment on the nations of the world, including Israel. Each of these nations is depicted by a supernatural being, and in the case of Israel, by a divine entity second in rank only to God himself" (Segal, "Monotheism and Angelology," 419). Segal suggests that his analysis helps to make sense of awkward "seams" in the text, e.g., the tribulation and arrival of Michael at 12:1 (cited below) *after* the demise of Antiochus at the end of ch. 11. But whether original or added later—though it could not have been much later—the result is the same: the author(s) was/were attempting to convey a worldview that presupposed a correspondence between heaven and earth. See Collins, who does not consider these passages secondary and notes that the "at that time" of 12:1 refers to "the time of the king's invasion of Israel and his death, which is in 'the time of the end' (11:40) and is the time of the decisive heavenly intervention" (*Daniel*, 390).

of the שר פרס, "the prince of Persia" (10:13, 20) and the שר־יון, "the prince of Greece" (10:20). The term *prince* likely stems, in part, from reflection on the שר־צבא־יהוה of Josh 5:13–14, and in the context of chapter 10 is meant to convey that, in Michael, Israel has a devoted angelic guardian par excellence.[23]

Due to chapter 10's description of Michael as only אחד השרים הראשנים, "one of the chief princes" (v. 13), some commentators, as noted above, have rejected the idea that Michael is the ranking angel in the minds of Daniel's author(s).[24] But this reading should not be too hastily accepted, as there are hints that Michael is exemplary or even extraordinary among the angels. First, 10:21 is clear that the unnamed angel who requires assistance in the struggle against the angelic princes of Persia and Greece has only Michael to rely on:

ואין אחד מתחזק עמי על־אלה כי אם־מיכאל שרכם

There is no one with me who contends against these princes except Michael, your prince.

The implication is that the other angels are either unwilling to help or, more likely, outmatched.[25] As we have seen, chapters 7 and 8 describe the collective angelic host as being oppressed by the little horn, and so it is plausible that chapter 10 underscores the severity of the persecution by reiterating that even God's angels—with the exception of the unnamed angel and Michael—are too weak (on their own) to contend successfully against their celestial enemies.[26]

Second, Michael's role is affirmed as central to the triumph of Israel in the eschatological scenario of chapter 12:

---

23. Hartman and DiLella, *Daniel*, 282–83; see also Michalak, *Angels as Warriors*, 104–5.

24. I.e., Michael is viewed as inferior to the more elite "one the like a son of man" (7:13–14) and "prince of the host" (8:11) (see Bampfylde, "Prince of the Host," 129–34; Hesier, "Divine Council," §§6.2–6.3).

25. See Todd R. Hanneken, who argues that Dan 10 is an example of angelic "inefficiency" or "inefficacy" in apocalypses. See Hanneken, *The Subversion of the Apocalypses in the Book of Jubilees*, EJL 34 (Atlanta: Society of Biblical Literature, 2012), 68–69.

26. See Lacocque: "Only 'Michael, your prince' is faithful, but he will suffice" (*Book of Daniel*, 213).

ובעת ההיא יעמד מיכאל השר הגדול העמד על־בני עמך והיתה עת צרה אשר
לא־נהיתה מהיות גוי עד העת ההיא ובעת ההיא ימלט עמך כל־הנמצא כתוב בספר

> At that time Michael, the great prince, the protector of your people, shall arise. There shall be a time of anguish, such as has never occurred since nations first came into existence. But at that time your people shall be delivered, everyone who is found written in the book. (12:1)

The opening statement of this verse is difficult to reconcile with interpretations of the book of Daniel that view Michael as inferior to other angels. However, even if, in theory, Michael was thought to have superiors in the angelic hierarchy, it makes little difference insofar as it is Michael's role as the guardian of Israel that is clearly celebrated in the closing lines of the book.

Finally, chapter 12 makes important claims regarding the people of God. After announcing Michael's role, verse 1 not surprisingly refers to the cessation of Israel's hardships. In other words, while the imagery of hostile beasts and animals and the behind-the-scenes glimpses into the heavenly world that dominate Dan 7–12 work together to reveal that history is progressing according to a divinely ordained plan, verse 1 is clear that the telos of this plan is the eschatological deliverance of God's people. Also, Dan 12:3 is important for what it says regarding the resurrected state of at least some of those who rise to eternal life:[27]

והמשכלים יזהרו כזהר הרקיע ומצדיקי הרבים ככוכבים לעולם ועד:

> Those who are wise shall shine like the brightness of the sky, and those who lead many to righteousness, like the stars forever and ever. (12:3)

Again, the notion of the astral host is in view, with verse 3 asserting that the wise will receive an angel-like exaltation in heaven at the resurrection.[28] Significantly, Goldingay suggests that this distinction is related to

---

27. Hartman and DiLella, *Daniel*, 310, stress that not everyone who is resurrected shines like the stars, as this is reserved for the wise; see also Collins: "Only in the case of the wise *Maskilim* are we given any information about the resurrected state" (*Daniel*, 392).

28. As is frequently highlighted, the picture here resembles 1 En. 104.2–6, and thus an association or fellowship with the angels is likely in view. See Collins, *Daniel*, 393. Contra Goldingay, *Daniel*, 308.

the connection between heaven and earth presupposed throughout Dan 7–12: "those who are wise"—literally, the *maskilim*—who demonstrate their faithfulness through wise teaching and suffering (see 11:33), will be honored by being granted the prestige and privileges of heaven and its inhabitants, the angels to whom the *maskilim* correspond.[29] Yet despite this apparent privilege and distinct status, it has been rightly observed that the orientation of the *maskilim*—those ostensibly responsible for the book of Daniel—is "outward" insofar as they continue to function "within the larger community"[30] and are not antagonistic toward broader Judaism. Such statements are supported by the solidarity Daniel shows with his fellow Jews when he says that he was "confessing my sin and the sin of my people Israel" (9:20).[31]

Summary of Daniel 7–12

In short, Dan 7–12 reveals the conviction that the happenings of the heavenly realm were part of a fuller reality that had profound relevance for the Jews who composed and first heard the book of Daniel. Despite the chaotic persecutions that overwhelmed even the angelic host, God had decreed victory for his angels and their leader—who effectively constitute heavenly Israel—and this verdict is paralleled by the decree given for the deliverance of Israel on earth from Antiochus and his forces. While Daniel appears to set the *maskilim* apart for a privileged, angel-like afterlife, the work as whole is not exclusivist: solidarity with wider Israel is emphasized,

---

29. Goldingay, *Daniel*, 308–9.

30. John J. Collins also notes that even if "the commitment of the masses appears uncertain, ... there is no evidence of separate organization, such as we find at Qumran. The temple and central institutions of the religion are evidently not rejected [by the *maskilim*], although for the present they are defiled." See Collins, *The Apocalyptic Imagination: An Introduction to Jewish Apocalyptic Literature*, 2nd ed. (Grand Rapids: Eerdmans, 1998), 112. On those responsible for the book of Daniel, see Collins: "There can be little doubt that the author of Daniel belonged to this circle and that the instruction they impart corresponds to the apocalyptic wisdom of the book" (*Daniel*, 385). See also George W. E. Nickelsburg, who notes that the character Daniel is "a stand-in for the real authors (the *maskilim*)." See Nickelsburg, *1 Enoch 1: A Commentary on the Book of 1 Enoch, Chapters 1–36; 81–108*, Hermeneia (Minneapolis: Fortress, 2001), 68.

31. See Newsom, who observes that ch. 9 "focuses extensively on the relationship between YHWH and Israel—a topic absent from the other chapters" (*Daniel*, 287).

and thus there is nothing to suggest that the anticipated angelic succor would be limited to a select few.

Sectarian Texts: 1QS, 11QMelchizedek, and 1QM

The picture of the sectarian texts is simultaneously familiar and distinct. Before looking at the War Scroll, which is obviously dependent on the book of Daniel, I will briefly examine a section of 1QS known as the Treatise on the Two Spirits and 11QMelchizedek, as these texts not only share affinities with Daniel but also reveal convictions that may have served as the conceptual foundations for the lofty boasts of 1QM.

The Treatise on the Two Spirits (1QS III, 13–IV, 26)

While there is debate regarding the provenance of the dualistic Treatise on the Two Spirits, especially the history of its relationship to the Serekh tradition,[32] it is evident that, at minimum, Treatise on the Two Spirits has been adopted and granted a prominent position in 1QS, a quintessential sectarian document. More to the point, Treatise on the Two Spirits immediately follows 1QS's covenant renewal ceremony (I, 13–III, 12), which Shemaryahu Talmon has described as "confirmation of [the sectarian]

---

32. Since 1QS was among the first texts discovered and because the manuscripts found in Cave 1 included several documents universally considered to be of sectarian provenance, scholars have often concluded that the dualistic outlook of Treatise on the Two Spirits (TTS) was a foundational component of the Qumran movement's theology. As Charlotte Hempel highlights, the dualistic designation "Sons of Light" has been frequently employed in the early secondary literature as a designation for those responsible for the Scrolls with little or no qualification (e.g., Wernberg-Møller). See Hempel, "The Treatise on the Two Spirits and the Literary History of the Rule of the Community," in *Dualism in Qumran*, ed. Geza G. Xeravits, LSTS 76 (London: Continuum, 2010), 102; Preben Wernberg-Møller, *The Manual of Discipline: Translated and Annotated with an Introduction*, STDJ 1 (Leiden: Brill, 1957), 47. But the discovery of shorter recensions of the Community Rule from Cave 4—texts that lack TTS as well as other material—has problematized the understanding that TTS and its dualistic outlook were integral parts of the Serekh tradition from its inception. On 1QS as a developmental expansion of the tradition, see Sarianna Metso, *The Textual Development of the Qumran Community Rule*, STDJ 21 (Leiden: Brill, 1997). On the Cave 4 fragments as an abbreviation of the tradition reflected in 1QS, see Philip S. Alexander, "The Redaction History of the Serekh Ha-Yahad: A Proposal," *RevQ* 17 (1996): 437–56.

community's claim to be the only legitimate heir to biblical Israel," that is, the true people of God.³³ The contribution the dualism of Treatise on the Two Spirits makes to such claims is that it "absolutizes" them.³⁴

With this in mind, it is intriguing what Treatise on the Two Spirits says about the assistance the righteous have in their struggle against the forces of darkness. After outlining that the wicked "Angel of Darkness" and his retinue not only lead the nonsectarian "Sons of Deceit" but also have a hand in causing the sectarian "Sons of Light" to stumble (III, 21–22), the column continues with the brief yet powerful affirmation that

ואל ישראל ומלאך אמתו עזר לכול בני אור

The God of Israel and his Angel of Truth help all the Sons of Light. (24–25)³⁵

---

33. Shemaryahu Talmon, "The Community of the Renewed Covenant: Between Judaism and Christianity," in *The Community of the Renewed Covenant*, ed. Eugene Ulrich and James C. VanderKam, CJA 10 (Notre Dame: University of Notre Dame Press, 1994), 13–14. On the sect as the true Israel, specifically as it relates to 1QS, see Lawrence H. Schiffman: "All in all, the authors of the various sectarian texts found at Qumran saw both the people and the Land of Israel in ideal terms. They expected that as the true Israel, separated from both errant Jews and from the non-Jewish world, they could live a life of perfect holiness and sanctity." See Schiffman, "Israel," *EDSS* 1:390. John S. Bergsma stresses that "the identification of the *Yahad* with 'Israel' in 1QS … is very strong," even if the Qumran movement hoped that wider Israel would recognize the error of their ways and acknowledge the sectarian covenant as the only legitimate religious foundation for the nation. See Bergsma, "Qumran Self-Identity: 'Israel' or 'Judah'?," *DSD* 15 (2008): 178. For similar comments, see Sarrianna Metso, *The Serekh Texts*, LSTS 62 (London: T&T Clark, 2007), 24; Richard J. Bautch, *Glory and Power, Ritual and Relationship: The Sinai Covenant in the Post-exilic Period*, LHBOTS (London: T&T Clark, 2009), 139–40; John J. Collins, *The Scriptures and Sectarianism: Essays on the Dead Sea Scrolls*, WUNT 332 (Tübingen: Mohr Siebeck, 2014), 181–82.

34. As George W. E. Nickelsburg explains, TTS "encompasses all of humanity in its scope," and from the perspective of the Qumran movement, "the rest of Israel—to say nothing of humanity—constitutes the Other, as darkness is other than light." See Nickelsburg, "The We and the Other in the Worldview of 1 Enoch, the Dead Sea Scrolls, and Other Early Jewish Texts," in *The "Other" in Second Temple Judaism: Essays in Honor of John J. Collins*, ed. Daniel C. Harlow et al. (Grand Rapids: Eerdmans, 2011), 262–78.

35. Text and translations are based on Elisha Qimron, "The Rule of the Community (1QS)," in *Rule of the Community and Related Documents*, vol. 1 of *The Dead*

The placement of this announcement means that at the heart of Treatise on the Two Spirits is the declaration that to be counted among the Sons of Light—that is, to be a sect member or part of the true Israel—is not simply to be on the righteous or victorious side of a dualistic divide, as important as that was; it means that one's help in the midst of the cosmic struggle between good and evil is the God of Israel and his Angel of Truth.[36] That the sect claimed the God of Israel's Angel of Truth as *their* help is no small contention, because it is effectively an usurpation of the angelic assistance that in texts such as Daniel is the hope of the nation more broadly defined.[37] In the context of the Community Rule, this angelic assistance also seems to be considered an integral component of what it means to be the true Israel.

11QMelchizedek (11Q13)

The fragmentary pesher 11QMelchizedek outlines the career of its namesake, a figure of extraordinarily high rank and privilege, and here I accept the common identification of Melchizedek as an angelic benefactor of God's people.[38] Particularly noteworthy is how the text assigns God's pre-

---

*Sea Scrolls: Hebrew, Aramaic, and Greek Texts with English Translations*, ed. James H. Charlesworth, PTSDSSP 1 (Tübingen: Mohr Siebeck, 1994), 5–51.

36. This epithet is likely another designation for the "Prince of Light" (see 1QS III, 20); on the identity of this figure vis-à-vis other Second Temple–period principal angels, see below. On the importance of angel-led dualism to sectarian self-conception, see Cecilia Wassen, "Good and Bad Angels in the Construction of Identity in the Qumran Movement," in *Gottesdienst und Engel im antiken Judentum und frühen Christentum*, ed. Jörg Frey and Michael R. Jost, WUNT 2/446 (Tübingen: Mohr Siebeck, 2017), 73–75, 89. On the importance of being on the righteous or victorious side, see the comments of Ruth M. M. Tuschling, *Angels and Orthodoxy: A Study of the Development in Syria and Palestine from the Qumran Texts to Ephrem the Syrian*, STAC 40 (Tübingen: Mohr Siebeck, 2007), 115, 136.

37. Darrell D. Hannah rightly observes that the sect claimed Israel's angel succor as their own. See Hannah, *Michael and Christ: Michael Traditions and Angel Christology in Early Christianity*, WUNT 2/109 (Tübingen: Mohr Siebeck, 1999), 75.

38. Dated on the basis of paleography to the first century BCE, fourteen fragments and two columns of text (with vestiges of a third) were discovered. Hebrew text, sigla, and translations cited here are from Florentino García Martínez, Eibert J. C. Tigchelaar, and Adam S. van der Woude, *Manuscripts from Qumran Cave 11 (11Q2-18, 11Q20-31)*, DJD XXIII (Oxford: Clarendon, 1998), 221–41. For a helpful overview of the issues and support for the angelic interpretation of Melchizedek, see Eric F. Mason, *"You Are a Priest Forever": Second Temple Jewish Messianism and the Priestly*

rogatives to Melchizedek. The best-known example of this is the text's quotation of Psalm 82:1, where it is Melchizedek who now "takes his place in the divine council" in order to judge (II, 10). But, most significantly, II, 8 states that atonement in the eschatological jubilee will be for

כול בני [אור ו]א[נש]י [גורל מל]כי [צדק

all the sons of [light and for] the men of the lot of Mel[chi]zedek.

The line is frequently restored with the word אור,[39] thus resulting in the "Sons of Light," the (perhaps adopted) dualistic designation for members of the Qumran movement, which is also used in 1QS and 1QM.

Furthermore, that the "men of the lot of Melchizedek" is parallel to the "Sons of Light" suggests that to be a sect member is, by definition, to be able to claim Melchizedek as one's angelic redeemer. If the restoration at II, 9 is correct,[40] an intimate connection with the angels is further emphasized when the beneficiaries of Melchizedek's assistance are referred to as ע[ם קדושי אל, "the people of the holy ones of God." Like the phrase found in Dan 7:27, this language is best understood as positing a tutelary relationship between heaven and earth,[41] as this aptly characterizes Melchizedek's role in 11QMelchizedek. Thus, like 1QS, a key aspect of what it means to be a sect member—and therefore a member of the true Israel—is to be in the lot of the angel to whom the God of Israel has delegated great power and authority.

---

*Christology of the Epistle to the Hebrews*, STDJ 74 (Leiden: Brill, 2008), 168–90. More specifically, Annette Steudel summarizes a common observation when she states that this figure seems to be "almost identical" with the Prince of Light(s) and God's Angel of Truth from 1QS III, as well as Michael as portrayed in Dan 7–12 and 1QM XVII, 5–9 (see below). See Steudel, "Melchizedek," *EDSS* 1:536. Contra Heiser, who contends, once again, that while an identification should be made between Melchizedek, the Prince of Light(s), and God's Angel of Truth, as well as the Danielic "one like a son of man" and the "Prince of the Host," this lofty figure should be differentiated from Michael, who occupies a lower rank ("Divine Council," §7.4); see Bampfylde, "Prince of the Host," 129–34.

39. See García Martínez, Tigchelaar, and van der Woude, *Manuscripts from Qumran Cave 11*, 227.

40. See García Martínez, Tigchelaar, and van der Woude, *Manuscripts from Qumran Cave 11*, 227, 229, 231.

41. As noted above, Dequeker views the people as those who "belong or pertain to the angels" ("Saints of the Most High," 155–56); see also Collins, *Daniel*, 315–16.

## The War Scroll

It is clear that the War Scroll is indebted to the book of Daniel,[42] evident not least by its expectation of eschatological angelic assistance for God's people. But here this hope is combined with the sectarian claims of a uniquely close relationship with their angelic guardians that surpasses even that claimed by Treatise on the Two Spirits and 11QMelchizedek. The resulting fusion of these convictions amounts to a grandiose statement on the self-identity of the sectarians, who were convinced that they would fight in conjunction with the angels at the eschatological war.[43]

It was noted above how tutelary readings of "people of the holy ones" in Dan 7:27 and 11Q13 II, 9, fit very well with the correspondences between heaven and earth that are assumed in those texts. While the syntax is open to interpretation, 1QM has two occurrences of a similar phrase. The first is found at X, 9–10, which is a prayer that begins with the rhetorical question:

ומיא --------[44] כעמכה ישראל אשר בחרתה לכה מכול עמי הארצות
עם קדושי ברית

---

42. On the influence of the book of Daniel on the War Scroll, see, e.g., Jean Duhaime, *The War Texts: 1QM and Related Manuscripts*, CQS 6 (London: T&T Clark, 2006), 65–71; Collins, *Scriptures and Sectarianism*, 102–16.

43. As with 1QS, the presence of dualistic terminology (e.g., "Sons of Light") has traditionally led to the conclusion that the "Israel" of 1QM is the sect. However, source-critical scholarship on 1QM has prompted the realization that this identification requires nuance, since even before the M-tradition manuscripts and related materials from Cave 4 were published, scholars recognized that different traditions had been brought together in 1QM. In short, the view espoused here is that, even if sources were used that originally referred to Israel in a broad(er) sense, the Israel of 1QM is sectarian-defined. This is not to deny that the Qumran movement may have hoped that other Jews would join their ranks. However, such a scenario would only be possible upon acceptance of the sectarian covenant. See, e.g., E. P. Sanders, *Paul and Palestinian Judaism: A Comparison of Patterns of Religion* (Philadelphia: Fortress, 1977), 254. For a recent and detailed treatment of the subject, see Brian Schultz, *Conquering the World: The War Scroll (1QM) Reconsidered*, STDJ 76 (Leiden: Brill, 2009).

44. There is a horizontal scribal notation in this line. See Jean Duhaime, "War Scroll," in *Damascus Document, War Scroll and Related Documents*, vol. 2 of *The Dead Sea Scrolls: Hebrew, Aramaic, and Greek Texts with English Translations*, ed. James H Charlesworth, PTSDSSP 2 (Tübingen: Mohr Siebeck, 1995), 116 n. 122.

who -------- is like your people Israel whom you have chosen for yourself among all the peoples of the lands,
the holy people of the covenant[45]

Duhaime's translation reveals that he understands קדושי as an attributive adjective.[46] But many have read קדושי as a substantive, resulting in the translation "the people of the holy ones of the covenant."[47] Given the widespread recognition of the influence of Dan 7–8 on this line,[48] that X, 10 envisions a tutelary correspondence between heaven and earth makes good sense.

Similar language is found in another prayer, this time in XII, 8: כיא קדוש אדוני ומלך הכבוד אתנו עם קדושים. The translation of the first part of the line, "for holy is the Lord and the king of glory is with us," is relatively clear, but the next phrase, עם קדושים, has been variously interpreted. Jean Duhaime translates it as "together *with* the holy ones," thus taking עם as the preposition עִם.[49] However, for two reasons it is better to read עם

---

45. Hebrew text, sigla, and translations are from Duhaime, "War Scroll," 80–141.

46. Duhaime, "War Scroll," 117. See also Jean Carmignac, *La Règle de la guerre: Des Fils de lumière contre les Fils de ténèbres; Texte restauré, traduit, commenté par Jean Carmignac* (Paris: Letouzey et Ané, 1958), 145, who seemingly understands the word as an attributive as well.

47. For discussion, see Dequeker, "Saints of the Most High," 155; Collins, *Daniel*, 315. More recently, see Robert D. Holmstedt and John Screnock, "Writing a Descriptive Grammar of the Syntax and Semantics of the War Scroll (1QM): The Noun Phrase as Proof of Concept," in *The War Scroll, Violence, War and Peace in the Dead Sea Scrolls and Related Literature: Essays in Honour of Martin G. Abegg on the Occasion of His Sixty-Fifth Birthday*, ed. Kipp Davis et al., STDJ 115 (Leiden: Brill, 2015), 82, who place the occurrence of קדושי in X, 10 in their list of 1QM's substantival adjectives. On the association of angels with the Sinai covenant, see Jub. 1.27–29, 2.1; Josephus, *A.J.* 15.136; Acts 7:53; Gal 3:19; Heb 2:2. Moreover, the manner by which 1QM X elaborates on עם קדושי ברית has a covenantal flavor: the passage continues by stating that the people of Israel were the privileged recipients of the law and angelic revelation (see Dequeker, "Saints of the Most High," 157).

48. Even among those who translate עם קדושי ברית as "holy people of the covenant"; see, e.g., the comment of Carmignac, "Daniel (7, 27 et 8, 24) a créé l'expression 'le peuple des saints' et elle est passée dans le 'style' de Qumrân," who also notes that there is similar language elsewhere in 1QM (see XII, 8; VI, 6; XVI, 1) (*La Règle de la guerre*, 145).

49. Duhaime, "War Scroll," 121. See, e.g., Jan van der Ploeg, *Le Rouleau de la guerre: Traduit et annoté, avec une introduction*, STDJ 2 (Leiden: Brill, 1959), 47; Hol-

as עַם, "people," and in apposition to אתנו, "with us."⁵⁰ The first reason "people of the holy ones" should be the preferred over "together with the holy ones" is that it avoids the grammatically awkward construction of having two prepositions, אֶת and עִם, side by side.⁵¹ Second and more significantly, עם קדושים is immediately followed by three parallel statements that give practical, wartime expression to the presupposition that the people have an intimate connection with the angels (see XII, 8–9).⁵² Thus, reading "people of the holy ones" at XII, 8 as a tutelary genitive is also apropos.

That both 1QM X, 10 and XII, 8 should be understood as referring to the "people of the holy ones" is arguably reinforced by two occurrences of what Collins dubs the "reverse" of the phrase.⁵³ The first of these is found at VI, 6 and comes at the end of a rule for battalion formation and the descriptions of the inspirational words to be written on the javelins of those assembled for battle. After stating that the warriors will use their weapons to enact the judgment of God on their enemies, the section concludes with this triumphant exclamation:

והיתה לאל ישראל המלוכה ובקדושי עמו יעשה חיל

And the kingship shall belong to the God of Israel and among the holy ones of his people he shall do worthily.

The second occurrence of the phrase is like the first and is found at XVI, 1, functioning as the climax of a hortatory address the high priest is to recite to the warriors:

אל ישראל קרא חרב על כול הגואים ובקדושי עמו יעשה גבורה

---

mstedt and Screnock, "Writing a Descriptive Grammar," 83. Also see 1QH<sup>a</sup> XI, 22–23; XIX, 14–15, where עַם is virtually certain.

50. I.e., "For the Lord is holy, the king of glory is with us, the people of the holy ones." See, e.g., the translations of Carmignac, *La Règle de la guerre*, 178; Yigael Yadin, *The Scroll of the War of the Sons of Light against the Sons of Darkness*, trans. Batya Rabin and Chaim Rabin (Oxford: Oxford University Press, 1962), 316; Dequeker, "Saints of the Most High," 159.

51. So Dequeker, "Saints of the Most High," 159.

52. I will address the content of the statements in XII, 8–9 below.

53. Collins, *Daniel*, 315.

> The God of Israel has summoned a sword against all the nations, and among the holy ones of his people he will do mightily.

While Luc Dequeker contends that "people of the holy ones" and "holy ones of his people," are two sayings that "must have the same meaning,"[54] I would propose there is an important nuance: that is, "holy ones of his people" may suggest that the holy ones belong to the people or that the people can lay claim to these angelic holy ones in some way. Given the grand and cosmic scale on which the war is envisioned in 1QM,[55] it is conceivable that this phrase contributed to the rallying cry of the document and to the formation of the War Scroll's readers, the prospective human combatants. As Carol Newsom has argued, even nonpolemical sectarian texts that share affinities with other late Second Temple texts were intended to be formative and can be polemical, for the simple reason that "every act of formation is also an act of estrangement. Every act of discourse is also an act of counter-discourse.... [Other language] can appear faulty and defective or shallow and superficial."[56] How much more, then, would the formational import be, when language from the influential book of Daniel is reversed and employed in an overtly polemical text such as 1QM?

The bold assertion that the angels in some way belong to the people functions well as a rationale for the text's best-known claim: that the human warriors expected the angels to be their wartime comrades. For example, 1QM VII, 6 states that

מלאכי קודש עם צבאותם יחד

the holy angels are together with their armies

This is echoed by the parallel statements of XII, 8–9, which read:

---

54. Dequeker, "Saints of the Most High," 155; see also Collins, *Daniel*, 315–16, who seems to follow Dequeker's assumption that the phrases have the same meaning, yet, as already noted, he simultaneously refers to "holy ones of the people" as the *reverse* of the Danielic phrase "people of the holy ones."

55. On the sectarians as viewing themselves as God's decisive counterstrike against wickedness; see Carmignac, *La Règle de la guerre*, 92.

56. Admittedly, Newsom's words are in reference to the Hodayot's function in shaping sectarian identity, but the principle is relevant here. See Carol A. Newsom, *The Self as Symbolic Space: Constructing Identity and Community at Qumran*, STDJ 52 (Leiden: Brill, 2004), 269.

גבוֹ֯ [...] צִּבא מלאכים בפקודינו
וגבור המלחֹ[מה] בעדתנו וצבא רוחיו עם צעדינו

gbw [...]⁵⁷ the host of angels (is) among our numbered men,
and the mighty one of wa[r] (is) in our congregation, and the host of his spirits (is) with our foot-soldiers

In light of these statements, angelic "assistance," though not incorrect, is descriptively deficient, as it goes beyond what we see in Daniel and other texts, with scholars rightly citing 1QM as an eschatological and martial example of the sectarian concept of angelic fellowship.[58]

A final set of observations will illustrate not only 1QM's dependence on Daniel but also how the sectarians have reenvisioned it. Near the end of the extant document, column XVII, 5–8 speaks of the final victory:

היום מועדו להכניע ולהשפיל שר ממשלת
רשעה וישלח עזר עֹוֹלָֹמִֹיֹם לגֹוֹרֹל [פ]ֹדֹותו בגבורת מלאך האדיר למשרת מיכאל
באור עולמים
להאיר בשמחה בֹרית ישראל⁵⁹ שלום וברכה לגורל אל להרים באלים משרת
מיכאל וממשלת
ישראל בכול בשר ישמח צדק בֹמרומים וכול בני אמתו יגילו בדעת עולמים

Today is His appointed time to subdue and to humble the Prince of the dominion of wickedness. He will send eternal assistance to the lot to

---

57. Duhaime does not attempt to restore the small tear between גבוֹ and צּבא, but see Carmignac, who proposes גבורות, which both carries the appropriate sense and adequately fills the space; i.e., "the mighty deeds of the host of angels are among our numbered men" (Duhaime, "War Scroll," 121; Carmignac, *La Règle de la guerre*, 179).

58. On the interaction of angels and humans in 1QM, see Schäfer, who uses "fellowship" with the angels; Tuschling, who refers to "communion" with the angels; and Hannah, who speaks of the soldiers' "companionship" with the angels. See Peter Schäfer, *The Origins of Jewish Mysticism* (Tübingen: Mohr Siebeck, 2009), 151–52; Tuschling, *Angels and Orthodoxy*, 119; Hannah, *Michael and Christ*, 59. Michalak dubs the humans and angels as "brothers in arms"; Sullivan contends that "the term 'utopian' might be appropriate…, insomuch as the War Scroll seems to describe a synergy between humans and angels as the 'Sons of Light.'" See Michalak, *Angels as Warriors*, 152; Kevin P. Sullivan, *Wrestling with Angels: A Study of the Relationship between Angels and Humans in Ancient Jewish Literature and the New Testament*, AGJU 55 (Leiden: Brill, 2004), 156 n. 44.

59. On the restoration of ברית ישראל from fragments, see Duhaime, "War Scroll," 132.

> be redeemed by Him through the might of an angel: He has magnified the authority of Michael in eternal light, to light up in joy the covenant of Israel, peace and blessing to the lot of God, so as to raise among the gods the authority of Michael and the dominion of Israel over all flesh. Righteousness shall rejoice up on high, and all sons of His truth shall be glad in eternal knowledge.

It is helpful to view the beginning of this passage as answering a series of implied questions: How will God win the war and defeat the angelic leader of wickedness and his forces? By sending help to his redeemed lot. What is the means by which God will help? Via the "might of an angel," who is frequently identified as Michael, though some have suggested that this is an even higher-ranking angel, whose lofty stature ensures the eminence of Michael and the forces he commands.[60] While both interpretations have merit, this angel's identity is not a primary concern here. More significant for the purposes of this study is that the answer to the third implied question—What are the results of this angelic help?—includes two references to "the authority of Michael." Thus, even if the מלאך of line 6 is not Michael, 1QM is seemingly at pains to underscore Michael's exaltation.

---

60. The reading adopted here is that of Yadin, who understands האדיר to be a verb (see Isa 42:21; Yadin, *Scroll of the War*, 340). However, this word is frequently taken to be an adjective modifying מלאך, resulting in the translation "majestic angel." While there are admittedly various valid translations of ll. 6–7, reading האדיר as an adjective may not be the preferable option because it means that the clause following it is without a verb. See, e.g., Duhaime, who is forced to supply a verb (in parentheses): "He has sent an everlasting help to the lot whom he has redeemed through the might of the *majestic* angel. (He will set) the authority of Michael in everlasting light" ("War Scroll," 133). Heiser argues that this angel should be identified with others from the Qumran texts and the Hebrew Bible, including the Prince of Light(s), God's Angel of Truth, Melchizedek, the "one like a son of man," and the Prince of the Host ("Divine Council," §7.4). But, to reiterate, Heiser excludes Michael from this list. As it pertains to 1QM XVII, though he follows Yadin in reading האדיר of l. 6 as a verb, Heiser interprets the phrase בגבורת מלאך as adverbially related to האדיר and thus deems the sense to be as follows: "by the might of an angel (i.e., Michael's superior) God has magnified the authority of Michael." While this reading makes it easier to posit a distinction between Michael and his angelic superior, I am not convinced that it necessitates a subordinate Michael. Instead, it may be that Michael himself is the מלאך through whom God magnifies "Michael's authority," a designation that should be understood in a collective sense (see further below). That the exaltation of "Michael's authority" is said to be "among the gods" (באלים) is an additional challenge to viewing Michael as holding a subordinate rank.

Moreover, the full answer to the third implied question, which is showcased in lines 6–8, complements the close relationship between angels and humans discussed thus far:

### Parallelism of 1QM XVII, 6–8

| | |
|---|---|
| להאיר בשמחה ברית ישראל | האדיר למשרת מיכאל באור עולמים |
| to light up in joy the covenant of Israel | He has magnified *the authority of Michael* in eternal light |
| שלום וברכה לגורל אל | |
| Peace and blessing to the *lot of God* | |
| וממשלת ישראל בכול בשר | להרים באלים משרת מיכאל |
| and *the dominion of Israel* over all flesh | so as to raise among the gods *the authority of Michael* |

A number of items require comment. First, that there is an intimate connection between heaven and earth is indicated by two statements that parallel Michael and Israel, the first of which uses light/illumination (אור) imagery. Second, ברית ישראל is a clear reference to God's people,[61] but more curious is משרת מיכאל, which is obviously angelic, but in what sense? While it may be that משרה refers to the archangel's literal "authority,"[62] it

---

61. Specifically, those who accept the sectarian reconstitution of Israel; see above. See also, e.g., Davidson, who in reference to 1QM XVII, 7–8 states that "Israel (the sect) will gain dominance over all flesh"; Davies also specifies the sect as the "true Israel." See Maxwell J. Davidson, *Angels at Qumran: A Comparative Study of 1 Enoch 1–36, 72–108 and Sectarian Writings from Qumran*, JSPSup 11 (Sheffield: JSOT Press, 1992), 226; Philip R. Davies, *1QM, the War Scroll from Qumran: Its Structure and History*, BibOr 32 (Rome: Biblical Institute Press, 1977), 81. This identification is confirmed by the use of "absolutizing" dualistic terminology similar to that of 1QS: e.g., גורל (see 1QM I, 5–14; 1QS III, 24; 11Q13 II, 8), ממשלה (see 1QM I, 6; 1QS III, 20–26; 11Q13 II, 9), and בני אמת (e.g., 1QS IV, 5–6; see Davies, *1QM, the War Scroll*, 80–81).

62. I concur with the readings of משרת that understand it to be the construct form of the noun מִשְׂרָה (see Isa 9:5–6) rather than a participle of שרת. For discussion, see Carmignac, *La Règle de la guerre*, 239.

more likely includes a collective character: that is, משרת מיכאל is a reference to the righteous angels Michael assists and those through and over whom he has sway.⁶³ The advantage of the latter understanding is that it better complements the collectivity of both ברית ישראל in the first parallel and ממשלת ישראל⁶⁴ in the second. Thus, we have in this passage the leader of the angelic host (= the angel of line 6, who may be Michael [or Michael's superior]), the collective angelic host (= the authority of Michael, who are the forces under Michael's command [which undoubtedly includes their leader/namesake]), and the people (= the covenant/dominion of Israel [namely, the sectarian-defined people of God]).⁶⁵ Moreover, the connection between the Michael-led angelic forces and Israel on earth suggests that the former effectively constitute the guardians of heavenly Israel in a manner reminiscent of Dan 7–12; and that the amalgam of the heavenly Israel and earthly Israel into one eschatological army is a sectarian usurpation and widening of the apocalyptic notion that "earthly realities reflect and mirror heavenly ones."⁶⁶ With these things in mind, the mention of Michael, Israel's angelic prince and guardian par excellence (see Dan 10:21, 23; 12:1), is no accident. Third, in the midst of the two lines that mention Michael and Israel, a blessing is pronounced on the גורל אל. While this phrase may initially seem awkward or extraneous, its placement underscores 1QM's focus on the human-angel composition of the Sons of Light. In short, heavenly Israel and the true earthly Israel, *as a unit*, constitute

---

63. Davidson, *Angels at Qumran*, 227; see also Carmignac, *La Règle de la guerre*, 238.

64. The collective sense of ממשלה is clearly present in 1QS III, 20–26, where the "dominion" of the Prince of Light includes the "Sons of Righteousness"; see 2 Chr 32:9, where ממשלה refers to Sennacherib's "military forces." Davies suggests that the ממשלה of XVII, 8 is that of the "true Israel," a statement followed by parenthetical references to Dan 7:22, 27 (*1QM, the War Scroll*, 81). Davies offers no commentary, but these verses pertain to the possession of the kingdom by the "holy ones" (7:22) and "the people of the holy ones" (7:27), thus suggesting that he reads ממשלה collectively.

65. As noted above, Collins observes the same threefold distinction in Dan 7 (i.e., "one like a son of man," holy ones, and people of the holy ones; see *Daniel*, 318).

66. Hannah "Guardian Angels," 420. On column XVII as similar to Dan 7, see Duhaime, who observes that "the victory in col. 17 is that of [God's] appointed angel. [A result] of this victory is the exaltation of Michael over all gods, perhaps in the manner of the exaltation of the 'one like a son of man' in Daniel 7." See Jean Duhaime, "Dualistic Reworking in the Scrolls from Qumran," *CBQ* 49 (1987): 51. On the Michael-led angels as heavenly Israel, see Collins, who speaks of the "synergism between the faithful Israelites on earth and their angelic counterparts in heaven" (*Daniel*, 318).

"God's lot"[67]—a fact immediately reinforced by the second Michael-Israel parallel. Fourth, sectarian usurpation of the authority of Michael—that is, Israel's angelic succor—for themselves performs an "apologetic function, justifying the secession from mainstream Judaism"[68] insofar as "those who do not stand with the right leaders and the cosmic powers behind them will suffer destruction by the wrath of God."[69]

## Conclusions

As the "people of the holy ones" (see 11Q13 II, 9; 1QM X, 10; XII, 8), the sectarians of the Qumran movement were convinced that they had a special connection to Israel's angelic succor, which in Dan 7–12 is ostensibly available to the nation more generously defined. Indeed, the Treatise on the Two Spirits, 11QMelchizedek, and the War Scroll each suggest that the sectarians' close relationship to their celestial guardians was an integral component of what it meant to be the true Israel. To be sure, the book of Daniel also dubs faithful Jews as "people of the holy ones." But the Qumran movement's bold references to the angels as the "holy ones of his people" (see 1QM VI, 6; XVI, 1), point to the belief that they somehow laid claim to their angelic succor. If correct, this idea may have contributed to the even loftier conviction that, as "God's lot," the angels of heavenly Israel would fight as comrades with the warriors of the true earthly Israel, namely, the sectarian soldiers. For a group that considered itself alone to be the inheritors of biblical Israel, there arguably would have been no better claim than to boast that fidelity to the sectarian covenant included martial fellowship with the army of heavenly Israel. Finally, the War Scroll, like the book of Daniel, casts Michael as Israel's angelic guardian par excellence, who, if not foremost among his fellows, seems to have been envisioned as exalted by his angelic superiors for the well-being and glory of those he represents.

---

67. Technically, Davidson is correct that 1QM has the sectarians as belonging to the "lot of God" rather than to the lot of an angel (see 11QMelch, where sect members are part of "Melchizedek's lot"; see Davidson, *Angels at Qumran*, 224–27). But the significance of this observation could easily be overstated since here the chosen leader of God's lot is an angel.

68. So Tuschling, though if it is correct that the initial reasons for secession were halakic, then the angelological claims were likely used to bolster the primary halakic concerns (see Tuschling, *Angels and Orthodoxy*, 117; Collins, *Scriptures and Sectarianism*, 194).

69. Duhaime, "Dualistic Reworking," 55.

In the War Scroll, however, it is sectarian-defined Israel who is exalted with the "authority of Michael." Thus, while scholars have sometimes disagreed as to the precise meaning of angelic fellowship claims at Qumran, this study has demonstrated that at least part of the meaning is to be found in the contribution these boasts make to the identity of the sect as the true people of God.

## Bibliography

Alexander, Philip. *The Mystical Texts: Songs of the Sabbath Sacrifice and Related Manuscripts*. LSTS 61. CQS 7. London: T&T Clark, 2006.

———. "The Redaction History of the Serekh Ha-Yahad: A Proposal." *RevQ* 17 (1996): 437–56.

Angel, Joseph L. *Otherworldly and Eschatological Priesthood in the Dead Sea Scrolls*. STDJ 86. Leiden: Brill, 2010.

Bampfylde, Gillian. "The Prince of the Host in the Book of Daniel and the Dead Sea Scrolls." *JSJ* 14 (1983): 129–34.

Bautch, Richard J. *Glory and Power, Ritual and Relationship: The Sinai Covenant in the Post-exilic Period*. LHBOTS 471. London: T&T Clark, 2009.

Bergsma, John S. "Qumran Self-Identity: 'Israel' or 'Judah'?" *DSD* 15 (2008): 172–89.

Caragounis, Chrys C. *The Son of Man: Vision and Interpretation*. WUNT 38. Tübingen: Mohr Siebeck, 1986.

Carmignac, Jean. *La Règle de la guerre: Des Fils de lumière contre les Fils de ténèbres; Texte restauré, traduit, commenté par Jean Carmignac*. Paris: Letouzey et Ané, 1958.

Collins, John J. *The Apocalyptic Imagination: An Introduction to Jewish Apocalyptic Literature*. 2nd ed. Grand Rapids: Eerdmans, 1998.

———. *Daniel: A Commentary on the Book of Daniel*. Hermeneia. Minneapolis: Fortress, 1993.

———. "Prince שר." *DDD* 662–64.

———. *The Scriptures and Sectarianism: Essays on the Dead Sea Scrolls*. WUNT 332. Tübingen: Mohr Siebeck, 2014.

———. "The Son of Man and the Saints of the Most High in the Book of Daniel." *JBL* 93 (1974): 50–66.

Davidson, Maxwell J. *Angels at Qumran: A Comparative Study of 1 Enoch 1–36, 72–108 and Sectarian Writings from Qumran*. JSPSup 11. Sheffield: JSOT Press, 1992.

Davies, Philip R. *1QM, the War Scroll from Qumran: Its Structure and History*. BibOr 32. Rome: Biblical Institute Press, 1977.

Dequeker, Luc. "The Saints of the Most High." *OtSt* 18 (1973): 108–87.

Duhaime, Jean. "Dualistic Reworking in the Scrolls from Qumran." *CBQ* 49 (1987): 32–56.

———. "War Scroll." Pages 80–141 in *Damascus Document, War Scroll and Related Documents*. Vol. 2 of *The Dead Sea Scrolls: Hebrew, Aramaic, and Greek Texts with English Translations*. Edited by James H. Charlesworth. PTSDSSP 2. Tübingen: Mohr Siebeck, 1995.

———. *The War Texts: 1QM and Related Manuscripts*. CQS 6. London: T&T Clark, 2006.

Ferch, Arthur J. "The Apocalyptic 'Son of Man' in Daniel 7." PhD diss., Andrews University, 1979.

Fletcher-Louis, Crispin H. T. *All the Glory of Adam: Liturgical Anthropology in the Dead Sea Scrolls*. STDJ 42. Leiden: Brill, 2001.

García Martínez, Florentino, Eibert J. C. Tigchelaar, and Adam S. van der Woude. *Manuscripts from Qumran Cave 11 (11Q2–18, 11Q20–31)*. DJD XXIII. Oxford: Clarendon, 1998.

Goldingay, John E. *Daniel*. WBC 30. Dallas: Word, 1989.

Hannah, Darrell D. "Guardian Angels and Angelic National Patrons in Second Temple Judaism and Early Christianity." Pages 413–35 in *Angels: The Concept of Celestial Beings; Origins, Development and Reception*. Edited by Friedrich V. Reiterer, Tobias Nicklas, and Karen Schöpflin. DCLS. Berlin: de Gruyter, 2007.

———. *Michael and Christ: Michael Traditions and Angel Christology in Early Christianity*. WUNT 2/109. Tübingen: Mohr Siebeck, 1999.

Hanneken, Todd R. *The Subversion of the Apocalypses in the Book of Jubilees*. EJL 34. Atlanta: Society of Biblical Literature, 2012.

Hartman, Louis F., and Alexander A. DiLella. *The Book of Daniel*. AB 23. Garden City, NY: Doubleday, 1978.

Heiser, Michael. "The Divine Council in the Late Canonical and Noncanonical Second Temple Jewish Literature." PhD diss., University of Wisconsin-Madison, 2004.

Hempel, Charlotte. "The Treatise on the Two Spirits and the Literary History of the Rule of the Community." Pages 102–20 in *Dualism in Qumran*. Edited by Geza G. Xeravits. LSTS 76. London: Continuum, 2010.

Holmstedt, Robert D., and John Screnock. "Writing a Descriptive Grammar of the Syntax and Semantics of the War Scroll (1QM): The Noun

Phrase as Proof of Concept." Pages 67–106 in *The War Scroll, Violence, War and Peace in the Dead Sea Scrolls and Related Literature: Essays in Honour of Martin G. Abegg on the Occasion of His Sixty-Fifth Birthday*. Edited by Kipp Davis, Dorothy M. Peters, Kyung S. Baek, and Peter W. Flint. STDJ 115. Leiden: Brill, 2015.

Hurtado, Larry W. "Monotheism, Principal Angels, and the Background of Christology." Pages 546–54 in *The Oxford Handbook of the Dead Sea Scrolls*. Edited by Timothy H. Lim and John J. Collins. Oxford: Oxford University Press, 2010.

Lacocque, Andre. *The Book of Daniel*. Translated by David Pellauer. Atlanta: John Knox, 1979.

Mach, Michael. *Entwicklungsstadien des jüdischen Engelglaubens in vor-rabbinischer Zeit*. TSAJ 34. Tübingen: Mohr Siebeck, 1992.

Mason, Eric F. *"You Are a Priest Forever": Second Temple Jewish Messianism and the Priestly Christology of the Epistle to the Hebrews*. STDJ 74. Leiden: Brill, 2008.

Metso, Sarianna. *The Serekh Texts*. LSTS 62. London: T&T Clark, 2007.

———. *The Textual Development of the Qumran Community Rule*. STDJ 21. Leiden: Brill, 1997.

Michalak, Aleksander R. *Angels as Warriors in Late Second Temple Period Literature*. WUNT 2/330. Tübingen: Mohr Siebeck, 2012.

Mullen, E. Theodore, Jr. *The Assembly of the Gods: The Divine Council in Canaanite and Early Hebrew Literature*. HSM 24. Chico, CA: Scholars Press, 1980.

Newsom, Carol A. *The Self as Symbolic Space: Constructing Identity and Community at Qumran*. STDJ 52. Leiden: Brill, 2004.

Newsom, Carol A., with Brennan W. Breed. *Daniel: A Commentary*. OTL. Louisville: Westminster John Knox, 2014.

Nickelsburg, George W. E. *1 Enoch 1: A Commentary on the Book of 1 Enoch, Chapters 1–36, 81–108*. Hermeneia. Minneapolis: Fortress, 2001.

———. "The We and the Other in the Worldview of 1 Enoch, the Dead Sea Scrolls, and Other Early Jewish Texts." Pages 262–78 in *The "Other" in Second Temple Judaism: Essays in Honor of John J. Collins*. Edited by Daniel C. Harlow, Matthew Goff, Karina Martin Hogan, and Joel S. Kaminsky. Grand Rapids: Eerdmans, 2011.

Ploeg, Jan van der. *Le Rouleau de la guerre: Traduit et annoté, avec une introduction*. STDJ 2. Leiden: Brill, 1959.

Poythress, Vern S. "The Holy Ones of the Most High in Daniel VII." *VT* 26 (1976): 208–13.
Qimron, Elisha. "The Rule of the Community (1QS)." Pages 5–51 in *Rule of the Community and Related Documents*. Vol. 1 of *The Dead Sea Scrolls: Hebrew, Aramaic, and Greek Texts with English Translations*. Edited by James H. Charlesworth. PTSDSSP 1. Tübingen: Mohr Siebeck, 1994.
Sanders, E. P. *Paul and Palestinian Judaism: A Comparison of Patterns of Religion*. Philadelphia: Fortress, 1977.
Schäfer, Peter. *The Origins of Jewish Mysticism*. Tübingen: Mohr Siebeck, 2009.
Schiffman, Lawrence H. "Israel." *EDSS* 1:388–91.
Schuller, Eileen M. "Recent Scholarship on the Hodayot." *CurBR* 10 (2011): 119–62.
Schultz, Brian. *Conquering the World: The War Scroll (1QM) Reconsidered*. STDJ 76. Leiden: Brill, 2009.
Segal, Michael. "Monotheism and Angelology in Daniel." Pages 405–20 in *One God, One Cult, One Nation: Archaeology and Biblical Perspectives*. Edited by Reinhard G. Kratz and Hermann Spieckmann. BZAW 405. Berlin: de Gruyter, 2010.
Steudel, Annette. "Melchizedek." *EDSS* 1:535–37.
Sullivan, Kevin P. *Wrestling with Angels: A Study of the Relationship between Angels and Humans in Ancient Jewish Literature and the New Testament*. AGJU 55. Leiden: Brill, 2004.
Talmon, Shemaryahu. "The Community of the Renewed Covenant: Between Judaism and Christianity." Pages 3–24 in *The Community of the Renewed Covenant*. Edited by Eugene Ulrich and James C. VanderKam. CJA 10. Notre Dame: University of Notre Dame Press, 1994.
Tuschling, Ruth M. M. *Angels and Orthodoxy: A Study of the Development in Syria and Palestine from the Qumran Texts to Ephrem the Syrian*. STAC 40. Tübingen: Mohr Siebeck, 2007.
Walsh, Matthew L. *Angels Associated with Israel in the Dead Sea Scrolls: Angelology and Sectarian Identity at Qumran*. WUNT 2/509. Tübingen: Mohr Siebeck, 2019.
Wassen, Cecilia. "Good and Bad Angels in the Construction of Identity in the Qumran Movement." Pages 71–97 in *Gottesdienst und Engel im antiken Judentum und frühen Christentum*. Edited by Jörg Frey and Michael R. Jost. WUNT 2/446. Tübingen: Mohr Siebeck, 2017.

Wernberg-Møller, Preben. *The Manual of Discipline: Translated and Annotated with an Introduction*. STDJ 1. Leiden: Brill, 1957.

Yadin, Yigael. *The Scroll of the War of the Sons of Light against the Sons of Darkness*. Translated by Batya Rabin and Chaim Rabin. Oxford: Oxford University Press, 1962.

Zevit, Ziony. "The Structure and Individual Elements of Daniel 7." *ZAW* 80 (1960): 394–96.

# Function and Creativity in the Hebrew, Aramaic, and Cryptic Calendars from Qumran

Helen R. Jacobus

The Qumran calendars are part of ancient Near Eastern and Greek and Mesopotamian Hellenistic cultures, where calendrical plurality was the norm during this period. The full extent of the nature of the diversity of the Qumran calendrical fragments in Hebrew and Aramaic and in cryptic scripts is still unknown. Here, the term *calendrical texts* refers to those texts that contain tabular, technical, and calendrical data as part of a fixed cycle for the purpose of liturgical practices or for astronomical purposes, which in antiquity included the astral sciences. The standard hypothesis is that the community responsible for compiling and preserving the Dead Sea Scrolls (DSS) followed a different calendar from that of the rest of Jewish society.[1] The nature of what was, precisely, the assumed, singular normative Jewish calendar, which Shemaryahu Talmon describes as "lunar," is in the main not precisely defined but presumed to be related to the current Jewish calendar.[2] The traditional status quo holds that the purported calendrical differences constituted a religious and political controversy; however, as this contribution demonstrates, the calendars at Qumran do not support the theory of a calendar controversy among homogenous

---

1. James C. VanderKam, "Calendrical Texts and the Origins of the Dead Sea Scrolls Community," in *Methods of Investigation of the Dead Sea Scrolls and the Khirbet Qumran Site: Present Realities and Future Prospects*, ed. Michael O. Wise et al., ANYAS 722 (New York: New York Academy of Sciences, 1994), 371–88; VanderKam, *Calendars in the Dead Sea Scrolls: Measuring Time* (London: Routledge, 1998), 113–16.

2. Shemaryahu Talmon, "Calendars and Mishmarot," *EDSS* 1:108–17; Talmon, "The Calendar of the Covenanters of the Judean Desert," in *The World of Qumran from Within: Collected Studies* (Jerusalem: Magnes, 1989), 147–99.

Jewish communities.[3] The nature and content of early Jewish calendars—solar, luni-solar, and luni-solar-zodiacal—that existed and that were used for different purposes in late Second Temple Judaism remains the subject of investigation.

Background to Different Concepts of Calendrical Time in Early Judaism

The concept of calendrical time in these manuscripts is multilayered. One could use the fourth day of creation, Gen 1:14–19 (4QGen$^b$ [4Q2] 1 I, 16–22; 4QGen$^g$ [4Q7] 2, 2–8; Gen 1:14–16, 4QGen$^k$ [4Q10] 1–4), as a rough point of departure in that the luminaries and the stars are used to demark units of festivals (מועדים), days, and years. In some Hebrew texts weeks are included within calendrical cycles, reflecting the seven-day week, culminating with the Sabbath. In Jubilees the moon is included in the fourth day of creation (Jub. 2.5 // 4Q216 VI, 5) but removed from the rewritten version of Gen 1:14 for calendrical time reckoning (Jub. 2.9 // 4Q216 IV, 7b–9). This is in contrast to its reception in Ps 104:19 (not extant in the DSS) and Ben Sira: Sir 43:6–8 (extant in manuscript B from the Genizah and part-extant in manuscript M from Masada) and Sir 50:6 (preserved in manuscript B).

The calendrical rendering in Jub. 6.23–38 (not found in Hebrew at Qumran) includes weeks and is divided into a fifty-two-week year: thirteen weeks comprising 91 days in each quarter of the year, consisting of one 31-day month and two 30-day months, equating to the 364-day-year, Sabbath-structured schematic calendar. The 31-day months that commence each quarter (the days of remembrance, Jub. 6.23) are the first, fourth, seventh, and tenth months. Jubilees does not have the days of the week, but in the Hebrew calendars from Qumran the year begins on the fourth day of the week, coinciding with the day of the creation of luminaries in Gen 1:14–19.[4]

---

3. So also Sacha Stern, "The Sectarian Calendar of Qumran," in *Sects and Sectarianism in Jewish History*, ed. Sacha Stern, IJS 12 (Leiden: Brill, 2011), 52–74. On the status quo, see Shemaryahu Talmon, "Yom Hakippurim in the Habakkuk Scroll," *Bib* 32 (1951): 549–63; Talmon, "The Calendar Controversy in Ancient Judaism: The Case of the Community of the Renewed Covenant," in *Technological Innovations, New Texts, and Reformulated Issues: The Provo International Conference on the Dead Sea Scrolls*, ed. Donald W. Parry and Eugene Ulrich, STDJ 30 (Leiden: Brill, 1999), 379–95.

4. The critical editions of most of the Hebrew calendrical texts are contained in Shemaryahu Talmon, Jonathan Ben-Dov, and Uwe Glessmer, *Qumran Cave 4.XVI: Calendrical Texts*, DJD XXI (Oxford: Clarendon, 2001). The preambles to 4Q320

Another difference is that in the Hebrew Qumran calendrical texts, the first, fourth, seventh, and tenth months are 30-day months; the 31-day months are the third, sixth, ninth, and twelfth months, completing, not beginning, each quarter of the year. Hence, the dates of the calendar and the festivals fall on the same day of the week in each year.

These differences led Annie Jaubert to refer to the Hebrew Qumran calendrical texts as the "Jubilees-Qumran" calendar; in developing the observations of Dominique Barthélemy, she posited that the Qumran model was an ancient Jewish calendar that was evidenced in the Hexateuch, not the later books and those with foreign calendars, and that the Jubilees narrative preserved a biblical 364-day year calendar.[5] Furthermore, despite assertions by several scholars to the contrary, Jaubert's findings with regard to Sabbath avoidance in the Hexateuch and the book of Jubilees (arguing that the patriarchs journeyed on Sunday, Wednesday,

---

and 4Q319 describe the creation of the luminaries with reference to the first of the twenty-four priestly courses in the *mishmarot* texts (Gamul), which differs from the biblical ritual (Jehoiarib in 1 Chr 24). In the War Scroll (1QM) II, 1–6, twenty-six priestly divisions are described but not listed by name. A small fragment from the calendar on papyrus (the only known such instance) was found in Cave 6, 6Qpap-Calendrical Doc (6Q17). See Maurice Baillet, "17. Fragment de Calendrier," in *Les "Petites Grottes" de Qumrân*, by Maurice Baillet, Józef T. Milik, and Roland de Vaux, DJD III (Oxford: Clarendon, 1962), 132–33. Discussions in Martin G. Abegg Jr., "The Calendar at Qumran," in *Theory of Israel*, vol. 1 of *Judaism in Late Antiquity, Part 5: The Judaism of Qumran; A Systemic Reading of the Dead Sea Scrolls*, ed. Alan J. Avery-Peck, Jacob Neusner, and Bruce Chilton, HOS 1/56 (Leiden: Brill, 2001), 145–72; Jonathan Ben-Dov, *Head of All Years: Astronomy and Calendars in Their Ancient Context*, STDJ 78 (Leiden: Brill, 2008); Michael Wise, Martin Abegg Jr., and Edward Cook, eds., *The Dead Sea Scrolls: A New Translation* (New York: HarperCollins, 1996), 380–86, 389–408.

5. Annie Jaubert, *The Date of the Last Supper*, trans. Isaac Rafferty (Staten Island, NY: Alba House, 1965), 15–52; Annie Jaubert, "Le calendrier des Jubilés et de la secte de Qumrân. Ses origines bibliques," *VT* 3 (1953): 250–64; Jaubert, "Le calendrier des Jubilés et les jours liturgiques de la semaine," *VT* 7 (1957), 35–61; Stéphane Saulnier, *Calendrical Variations in Second Temple Judaism: New Perspectives on the "Date of the Last Supper" Debate*, JSJSup 159 (Leiden: Brill, 2012), 19–50; Helen R. Jacobus, *Zodiac Calendars in the Dead Sea Scrolls and Their Reception: Ancient Astronomy and Astrology in Early Judaism*, IJS 14 (Leiden: Brill, 2014), 24–29; Dominique Barthélemy, "Notes en marge de publications récentes sur les manuscrits de Qumrân," *RB* 59 (1952): 199–203. "Jubilees-Qumran" calendar is the terminology used by Jaubert in accordance with her hypothesis that this calendar was ancient (*Date of the Last Supper*, 38, 52).

and Friday only, not on the Sabbath) have not been shown to be incorrect, and, in fact, the opposite situation is the case.[6]

## The 364-Day Calendar

Following Philip Callaway, Uwe Glessmer promoted the term "364-Day Calendar Traditions," removing the solar element from the schematic nature of the calendar.[7] However, it cannot be ruled out that its basic form was regarded as an ideal solar calendar. The 364-day year is the foundation of the *mishmarot*, the calendars of the priestly courses, based on a rotating six-year (sexennial) cycle, consisting of a three-year (triennial) cycle, repeated. It is also the basis of 4QOtot (4Q319), whereby the *mishmarot* are divided into six periods of forty-nine years (a jubilee cycle). This is the longest metacycle in the calendrical texts: 294 years (6 × 49).

The Jubilees-Qumran calendar is found in a late second-century *mishmarot* text, 4Q320, predating the accepted earliest period of habitation of the sectarian community at Qumran, in the early first century.[8] Either its users were not confined to the site, or it was used by different groups, as suggested by the Masada fragment of Shirot ʿOlat Hashabbat (Mas1K).[9]

---

6. Despite the title of Wacholder and Wacholder's article, its data do not disprove Jaubert's hypothesis that in Jubilees the patriarchs favored traveling on Monday, Wednesday, and Friday, and avoided the Sabbath. See Ben-Zion Wacholder and Sholom Wacholder, "Patterns of Biblical Dates and Qumran's Calendar: The Fallacy of Jaubert's Hypothesis," *HUCA* 66 (1995): 1–40. See also Abegg, "Calendar at Qumran," 147 n. 7; Roger T. Beckwith, *Calendar, Chronology and Worship*, AGJU 61 (Leiden: Brill, 2005), 54–66.

7. Uwe Glessmer, "Calendars in the Qumran Scrolls," in *The Dead Sea Scrolls after Fifty Years: A Comprehensive Assessment*, ed. Peter W. Flint and James C. VanderKam (Leiden: Brill, 1999), 2:231; Philip Callaway, "The 364-Day Calendar Traditions at Qumran," in *Mogliany 1989: Papers on the Dead Sea Scrolls Offered in Memory of Jean Carmignac; Part I: General Research on the Dead Sea Scrolls, Qumran, and the New Testament; the Present State of Qumranology*, ed. Zdzislaw Jan Kapera (Krakow: Enigma, 1993), 19–29.

8. Jodi Magness, *The Archaeology of Qumran and the Dead Sea Scrolls*, SDSSRL (Grand Rapids: Eerdmans, 2002), 47–72; Eric M. Meyers, "Khirbet Qumran and Its Environs," in *The Oxford Handbook of the Dead Sea Scrolls*, ed. Timothy H. Lim and John J. Collins (Oxford: Oxford University Press, 2010), 21–45. 4QCalendrical Document/Mishmarot A (4Q320) is dated by paleography to 125–100 BCE (see Talmon, Ben-Dov, and Glessmer, *Qumran Cave 4.XVI*, 41).

9. See also Carol A. Newsom, "Sectually Explicit: Literature from Qumran," in

The months have ordinal numbers in the *mishmarot* texts, with the year beginning in the spring. Double-dating with an ordinal month and the equivalent Aramaic translation of the Babylonian month name exists in so-called historical texts from Qumran (4Q322a 2, 4Q332 2).[10] The Aramaic month names were in use in the late biblical books Esther, Zechariah, and Nehemiah, in 1–2 Maccabees (which mainly uses Macedonian month names), in dated legal documents in the Elephantine papyri, and in the Aramaic zodiac calendar text in 4Q318 (see below).

4QOtot is part of the same scroll as the Cave 4 copy of the Community Rule, 4QS$^e$ (Serekh ha-Yaḥad) = 4Q259 IV, 9–VII, 1–8 and unplaced fragments, which does not have the Maskil's hymn. Conversely 1QS (100–75 BCE), which is earlier than 4Q259 (50–25 BCE), does not have 4QOtot, but the Maskil's hymn and its prologue (1QS IX, 26 // 4Q259 IV, 8) in the columns where the extended *mishmarot* cycle of 4QOtot is placed in the text of 4Q259.[11] In addition to the *mishmarot*, the 364-day-year forms the basis of other calendrical texts that do not include the priestly courses, and

---

*The Hebrew Bible and Its Interpreter*, ed. William H. Propp, Baruch Halpern, and David Noel Freedman (Winona Lake, IN: Eisenbrauns, 1990), 167–87.

10. The critical editions are Eibert J. C. Tigchelaar, "322a. 4QHistorical Text H?," in *Qumran Cave 4.XXVIII: Wadi Daliyeh II: The Samaria Papyri for Wadi Daliyeh*, by Douglas M. Gropp; *Miscellanea, Part 2*, DJD XXVIII (Oxford: Clarendon, 2001), 125–28; Joseph A. Fitzmyer, "332. 4QHistorical Text D," in *Qumran Cave 4.XXVI: Cryptic Texts*, by Stephen J. Pfann; *Miscellanea, Part 1*, by Philip S. Alexander et al., DJD XXXVI (Oxford: Clarendon, 2000), 281–86.

11. Metso argues that 4QS$^e$ is a later copy of an earlier recension of the Rule, contrary to the view of the editors of the Cave 4 versions of the text, Alexander and Vermes, who state that 4QOtot is a later addition. See Sarianna Metso, *The Textual Development of the Qumran Community Rule*, STDJ 21 (Leiden: Brill, 1997), 48–51, 69–74; Philip Alexander and Geza Vermes, *Qumran Cave 4.XIX: Serekh Ha-Yaḥad*, DJD XXVI (Oxford: Clarendon, 1998), 9–15, 59–60, 114–24, 150–52, 158–62; Talmon, Ben-Dov, and Glessmer, *Qumran Cave 4.XVI*, 195–244; Florentino García Martínez and Eibert J. C. Tigchelaar, *The Dead Sea Scrolls Study Edition* (Leiden: Brill, 1997–1998), 1:92–95, 532–37. For further references, see Helen R. Jacobus, "Calendars in the Qumran Collection," in *The Dead Sea Scrolls at Qumran and the Concept of a Library*, ed. Sidnie White Crawford and Cecilia Wassen, STDJ 116 (Leiden: Brill, 2015), 233–34; Jacobus, "Calendars," in *The T&T Clark Companion to the Dead Sea Scrolls*, ed. George J. Brooke and Charlotte Hempel, BC (London: Bloomsbury, 2018), 243.

other texts concerned with festivals, such as those with the Temple Scroll festivals, and liturgical texts with calendrical structures.[12]

---

12. Such as Songs of the Sabbath Sacrifice [ShirShabb$^{a-h}$] (4Q400–407), [11QShirShabb] (11Q17), [MasShirShabb] Mas1k. See Carol Newsom, *Songs of the Sabbath Sacrifice: A Critical Edition* (Atlanta: Scholars Press, 1985); Newsom, "4Q400–4Q407, Mas1K, *4QShirot 'Olat ha-Shabbat$^{a-h}$*," in *Qumran Cave 4.VI: Poetical and Liturgical Texts, Part 1*, by Esther Eshel et al., DJD XXI (Oxford: Clarendon, 1998), 173–401; Newsom, "1K. *MasShirot 'Olat ha-Shabbat*," in Eshel et al., *Qumran Cave 4.VI*, 239–52; Newsom, *Angelic Liturgy: Songs of the Sabbath Sacrifice*, vol. 4 B of *The Dead Sea Scrolls: Hebrew, Aramaic and Greek Texts with English Translations*, ed. James H. Charlesworth and Carol A. Newsom (Tübingen: Mohr Siebeck, 1999). Possibly 4QDaily Prayers (4Q503), which comprises one month in the 364-day calendar, harmonized with the phases of the moon. See Maurice Baillet, "503. Prières quotidiennes," in *Qumrân Grotte 4.III: 4Q482–4Q520*, ed. Maurice Baillet, DJD VII (Oxford: Clarendon, 1982), 105–36; Joseph M. Baumgarten, "4Q503 (Daily Prayers) and the Lunar Calendar," *RevQ* 12 (1986): 399–407; Francis Schmidt, "Le Calendrier Liturgique des Prières Quotidiennes (4Q503)," in *Le Temps et les Temps: Dans les littératures juives et chrétiennes au tourant de notre ère*, ed. Christian Grappe and Jean-Claude Ingelaere, JSJSup 112 (Leiden: Brill, 2006), 55–88; Michael O. Wise, "Second Thoughts on *dwq* and the Synchronistic Calendar," in *Pursuing the Text: Studies in Honour of Ben Zion Wacholder on the Occasion of His Seventieth Birthday*, ed. John C. Reeves and John Kampen, JSOTSup 184 (Sheffield: Sheffield Academic, 1994), 98–120; Martin G. Abegg Jr., "Does Anyone Really Know What Time It Is? A Re-examination of 4Q503 in Light of 4Q317," in Parry and Ulrich, *Technological Innovations, New Texts*, 396–406; Helen R. Jacobus, "Qumran Calendars and the Creation: A Study of 4QcryptA Lunisolar Calendar (4Q317)," *JAJ* 4 (2013): 72–74. For different types of calendrical texts, see Armin Lange and Ulrike Mittmann-Richert, "Annotated List of the Texts of the Judaean Desert Classified by Content and Genre," in *The Texts in the Judaean Desert: Indices and an Introduction to the Discoveries in the Judean Desert Series*, by Emanuel Tov, DJD XXXIX (Oxford: Clarendon, 2002), 133–36. Texts concerned with the Temple Scroll festivals include 11QTemple$^{a-b}$ (11Q19–20), 4Q364a, 4Q325, 4Q324d, 4Q326, 4Q327. There is a scholarly discussion as to whether the dates of the Temple Scroll festivals were calibrated according to the 364-day calendar, since there is a record of different dates for these feasts, according to a tradition in later sources. For full summaries of these arguments and references, see Michael A. Daise, "The *Temple Scroll* Calendar: Revisiting the Feast of Oil in the Calendrical Documents/ *Mišmarot*," in *With Wisdom as a Robe: Qumran and Other Jewish Studies in Honour of Ida Fröhlich*, ed. Károly Dániel Dobos and Miklós Kőszeghy (Sheffield: Sheffield Academic, 2009), 329–38; James C. VanderKam, "The Temple Scroll and the Book of Jubilees," in *Temple Scroll Studies*, ed. George J. Brooke, JSPSup 7 (Sheffield: Sheffield Academic, 1989), 214–18.

The exegetical text, 4QCommentary on Genesis A (4Q252), which contains the only unbroken reference to the 364-day year (4Q252 II, 2–3: "Noah went forth from the ark at the end of a complete תמימה year of three hundred and sixty-four days") in the DSS, does not exhibit the standard, polemical, or linguistic characteristics of the sectarian texts.[13] Furthermore, David's Compositions, 11Q5 (11QPsa) XXVII, 5–9 in the Psalms Scroll, which, in enumerating David's songs and psalms includes a reference to 364 days of the year, also has no identifiable sectarian morphological or contextual features.[14]

## Intercalation

Notably, since the 364-day year is about one-and-a-quarter days shorter than the actual solar year, this schematic year would gradually slip out of alignment with the seasons. This would affect the festival calendars of the *mishmarot*, Temple Scroll, and the biblical and Second Temple precepts for observing seasonally related rituals for the festivals: after seventy years, the date of Passover would be in the winter. Therefore, if the 364-Day Calendar Traditions were to be used in practice, intercalation according to some method would be essential (that is, by the addition of a certain number of

---

13. Timothy H. Lim, "The Chronology of the Flood Story in a Qumran Text (4Q252)," *JJS* 43 (1992): 288–98; George J. Brooke, "The Genre of 4Q252: From Poetry to Pesher," *DSD* 1 (1994): 161, 165–67; Brooke, "The Thematic Content of 4Q252," *JQR* 85 (1994): 38–41; Brooke, "252. 4QCommentary on Genesis A," in *Qumran Cave 4.XVII: Parabiblical Texts, Part 3*, by George J. Brooke et al., DJD XXII (Oxford: Clarendon, 1996), 185–207; Brooke, "254a. 4QCommentary on Genesis D," in Brooke et al., *Qumran Cave 4.XVII*, 233–36; Moshe J. Bernstein, "4Q252: From Re-written Bible to Biblical Commentary," *JJS* 45 (1994): 4–9.

14. James A. Sanders, *The Psalms Scroll of Qumrân Cave 11 (11QPsa)*, DJD IV (Oxford: Clarendon, 1965), 9, 91–93. 11QPsa XXVII, 5–7: "3,600 psalms; and songs to sing before the altar over the whole-burnt/ perpetual offering every day, for all the days of the year, 364;/ and the offerings of the sabbaths, 52 songs." Talmon argues that the text is a reference to the "Covenanter's calendar," but the psalm is more likely to reflect the different calendars and festival calendars in wider Jewish circles. See Shemaryahu Talmon, "The Covenanters' Calendar of the Holy Seasons according to the List of King David's Compositions in the Psalms Scroll from Cave 11 (11QPsa XXVII)," in *Fifty Years of Dead Sea Scrolls Research in Memory of Jacob Licht*, ed. Gerson Brin and Bilhah Nitzan (Jerusalem: Yad Ben Zvi, 2001), 204–19; William Brownlee, 'The Significance of David's Compositions," *RevQ* 5 (1966): 569–74; James C. VanderKam, "Studies on 'David's Compositions,'" *ErIsr* 26 (1999): 212–20.

days at some points in one or more of the 364-day-year cycles to keep the calendrical date approximately in line with the seasons).[15]

Uwe Glessmer, for instance, proposes possible solutions to that effect,[16] while dismissing the prevalent theory that the 364-Day Calendar Traditions were a sectarian invention. He stated that its "roots ... go back at the very least into the third century BCE."[17] Jaubert pointed out at the earliest stage that despite there being no textual evidence to support any method of intercalation there was probably more than one method of intercalation during the long period that this calendar existed to harmonize the 364-day calendar with the solar year.[18] While some scholars argue that lack of textual support for intercalation should be taken seriously as a counter-indication that a method of calendrical correction existed, many others argue that absence of evidence is not evidence of absence.

Beckwith, who has summarized several various hypotheses concerning possible processes of intercalation, concludes that the 364-day year was not intercalated. He argues that the ideal calendar was allowed to rotate through the seasons, returning to its starting point after about 290 years. In keeping with that generation of scholars, the article expresses the view that this calendar was followed by sectarians, rather than being widely adhered

---

15. Moshe D. Herr, "The Calendar," in *The Jewish People in the First Century*, ed. Shmuel Safrai et al. (Philadelphia: Fortress, 1976), 2:834; James C. VanderKam, "The Origin, Character, and Early History of the 364-Day Calendar: A Reassessment of Jaubert's Hypothesis," *CBQ* 41 (1979): 390–411; see also Philip R. Davies, "Calendrical Change and Qumran Origins: An Assessment of VanderKam's Theory," *CBQ* 45 (1983): 80–89; Saulnier, *Calendrical Variations*, 49–50.

16. Glessmer, "Calendars in the Qumran Scrolls," 265–68, suggests two alternative systems of intercalation based on 4QOtot (4Q267). See also Uwe Glessmer, "364-Tage Kalender und die Sabbatstruktur seiner Schaltungen in ihrer Bedeutung für den Kult," in *Ernten, was man sät: Festschrift für Klaus Koch zu seinem 65. Geburtstag*, ed. Dwight R. Daniels, Uwe Glessmer, and Martin Rösel (Neukirchen-Vluyn: Neukirchener Verlag, 1991), 379–98; Glessmer, "Investigation of the Otot-text (4Q319) and Questions about Methodology," in Wise et al., *Methods of Investigation*, 429–40; Glessmer, "The Otot Texts (4Q319) and the Problem of Intercalation in the Context of the 364-Day Calendar," in *Qumranstudien: Vorträge und Beiträge der Teilnehmer des Qumranseminars auf dem internationalen Treffen der Society of Biblical Literature, Münster, 25–26 Juli 1999*, ed. Heinz-Josef Fabry, Armin Lange, and Hermann Lichtenberger (Göttingen: Vandenhoeck & Ruprecht, 1996), 125–64; VanderKam, *Calendars in the Dead Sea Scrolls*, 82–84.

17. Glessmer, "Calendars in the Qumran Scrolls," 233.

18. *Date of the Last Supper*, 38.

to.¹⁹ In a similar vein, Martin Abegg argues that the 364-day-year calendar was meant to be ideal and that it was never intended to be adjusted to the actual solar year.²⁰

The problem with the suggestion that the Jubilees-Qumran calendar is a fictional system that was possibly an ideal only, and thus never brought into line with the solar year, is that it is difficult to account for the fact that it was rooted in different genres and thematic contexts and carefully preserved, as we now know, for more than two hundred years in Hebrew manuscripts, arguably by different Jewish groups. This is really a very elaborate conceit. If this was the case, it would suggest that this ideal calendar was a phenomenon that was well-known, stable, and widespread, and, arguably, as it cannot be proved, never put into actual practice.

Some scholars' explanations, expounded by Roger Beckwith, include the idea that the later secondary text 1 En. 80.2–8 apparently warns that there will be a contraction between time and the seasons "in the days of the sinners" because of the sinners' adherence to the wrong, that is, lunisolar, calendar.²¹ However, this is an interpretation of a passage known in the Ethiopic, not in the Aramaic fragments; it is specific to the history of the reception and textual history of the Ethiopic Astronomical Book/Book of the Luminaries (1 En. 72–82), and, therefore, it cannot help to elucidate this historical-anthropological question of calendar differentiation and identity in early Judaism.

The standard position in Qumran scholarship has always been to link the Book of the Luminaries with the book of Jubilees, principally because

---

19. Roger T. Beckwith, "The Modern Attempt to Reconcile the Qumran Calendar with the True Solar Year," *RevQ* 7 (1969–1971): 379–96. See also Wacholder and Wacholder, who state that the 364-day year was "utopian" for the sect and that they thought that the true solar year "resulted from human corruption. The sect rejected this mode of calendation as a sign of human sinfulness," which echoes this view ("Patterns of Biblical Dates," 36–37).

20. Abegg, "Calendar at Qumran," 149–50. Ben-Dov states that the 364-day year could not have been regularly intercalated because it would mean admitting that the divine plan was imperfect, which was impossible, and, on the other hand, that it may have been intercalated on an ad hoc basis (*Head of All Years*, 19–20). This is not only paradoxical (it was either intercalated or not) but ahistorical, since calendars in the region had fixed cycles and methods of intercalation.

21. Beckwith, "Modern Attempt to Reconcile," 393–95. See also Wacholder and Wacholder, who compare "Enoch 80:2 ff" (*sic*) with Jub. 6.33 ("Patterns of Biblical Dates," 37 n. 73).

Jub. 6.23–38 reflects 1 En. 80.2–8 or vice versa, although neither text exists in the Qumran fragments. However, if the Hebrew fragment of Jub. 2.9 // 4Q216 IV, 7b–9 constitutes the main evidence for a polemic between the solar and luni-solar calendars in a primary source, the proposition that the 364-Day Calendar Traditions were intended to be angelic—since Jubilees is narrated by angels—is feasible. This idea may be supported by the importance of the 364-day calendar in the liturgical texts, the Songs of the Sabbath Sacrifice, and possibly 4QDaily Prayers (4Q503). Yet it seems unlikely that, if the 364-Day Calendar Traditions were actually used, a community would pray with the angels at Passover in the winter—in seventy years, the calendrical date would be a season behind—it is more probable that there was a fixed method to correct the discrepancy and still keep a mystical connection with the angels.[22]

## Aramaic Calendars and the Book of Luminaries

The luni-solar calendar with the Babylonian month names, by definition, was intercalated to harmonize the 354-day lunar year with the solar year of 365-and-one-quarter days. It was based on a cycle of nineteen solar years (known as the 19-year cycle), corresponding to 235 lunar months by the addition of seven lunar months at spaces of two- or three-year intervals.[23] In the Babylonian calendar the length of the month was determined by the observation of the first sliver of the crescent moon or, in the last three centuries BCE, precalculation of the first appearance of the moon.[24] This was in contrast to the Greek Metonic cycle, recorded from the late fifth century BCE, in which the months were alternately 29 or 30 days long.[25] Arguably, intercalation using the 19-year cycle was also used

---

22. So VanderKam, "Origin, Character," 404–6.

23. In years 1, 3, 6, 9, 11, 14, and 17 (the intercalary month was an extra twelfth month, except in year 1, when it was an additional sixth month). See Francesca Rochberg-Halton, "Calendars: Ancient Near East," *ABD* 1:810–14; John Britton, "Calendars, Intercalation and Year-Lengths," in *Calendars and Years: Astronomy and Time in the Ancient Near East*, ed. John M. Steele (Oxford: Oxbow, 2007), 115–32.

24. John M. Steele, "The Length of the Month in Mesopotamian Calendars of the First Millennium BC," in Steele, *Calendars and Years*, 133–48.

25. William Kendrick Pritchett and Otto Neugebauer, *The Calendars of Athens* (Cambridge: Harvard University Press, 1947), 1–14. First-century BCE writer Geminos describes a system of 59-day double lunar months composed of 29- and 30-day months. See James Evans and J. Lennart Berggren, *Geminos's Introduction to the Phenomena: A*

in the Mesopotamian ideal year of 360 days, composed of twelve 30-day months employed in administrative and cultic and civil calendars from circa 2600–300 BCE.[26] As with Qumran, there is no record of any intercalary procedures with the Babylonian 360-day calendar; yet, similarly, if intercalation did not take place, the Babylonian calendar dates would regress through the seasons.

## The Zodiac

The 360-day ideal calendar composed of twelve 30-day months was also used in different genres of divinatory texts, from the Neo-Assyrian period (ca. 1000–612 BCE) to the early Seleucid era.[27] From the fifth century BCE this included the zodiac signs whereby the 360-degree zodiacal circle of twelve signs equally divided into 30 degrees each could be used with the calendar for divination.[28] The final form of the uniform zodiac (that is, the

---

*Translation and Study of a Hellenistic Survey of Astronomy* (Princeton: Princeton University Press, 2006), 8.3 n. 3. The calendar of Athens from 120 BCE intercalated an extra month in years 3, 6, 9, 11, 14, 17, and 19 (see the fixed Babylonian 19-year cycle), and years 2, 5, 8, 10, 13, 16, and 18 from the late fifth century to the mid-third century BCE. See Robert Hannah, *Time in Antiquity* (London: Routledge, 2009), 30–36, 62.

26. Robert K. Englund, "Administrative Timekeeping in Mesopotamia," *JESHO* 31 (1988): 121–85; Lis Brack-Bernsen, "The 360-Day Year in Mesopotamia," in Steele, *Calendars and Years*, 83–100. There is evidence that intercalation was used to avert the date of an evil portent. See, e.g., A. Leo Oppenheim, "A Babylonian Diviner's Manual," *JNES* 33 (1974): 197–220. The diviner advises intercalating the 360-day ideal calendar to advance the date that an omen would fall and otherwise incur an unlucky prediction. David Brown argues that the text is older than the Neo-Assyrian period. See Brown, *Mesopotamian Planetary Astronomy-Astrology*, CM 18 (Groningen: Styx, 2000), 120–22; Clemency Williams, "Signs from the Sky, Signs from the Earth: The Diviner's Manual Revisited," in *Under One Sky: Astronomy and Mathematics in the Ancient Near East*, ed. John M. Steele and Annette Imhausen, AOAT 297 (Münster: Ugarit-Verlag, 2002), 473–86. For discussion and references, see Jacobus, *Zodiac Calendars*, 88–89.

27. Brown, *Mesopotamian Planetary Astronomy-Astrology*, 113–14; Francesca Rochberg, *The Heavenly Writing: Divination, Horoscopy, and Astronomy in Mesopotamian Culture* (Cambridge: Cambridge University Press, 2004), 7–8.

28. John Britton and Christopher Walker, "Astronomy and Astrology in Mesopotamia," in *Astronomy before the Telescope*, ed. Christopher Walker (New York: St Martin's, 1996), 47.

twelve zodiac signs) in circa 400 BCE directly contributed to the development of personal horoscopes.[29]

In addition, astral divination developed and took on new forms by the subdivision of the 30-day months, which corresponded schematically to the zodiac signs, into thirty schematic consecutive zodiacal units reflecting the moon's daily orbit on the zodiac circle. Referred to by modern scholars as the micro-zodiac, many late, nonhoroscopic calendrical texts used numerical schemes to represent the zodiac signs and the micro-zodiac signs in astrological hemerologies concerned with magic and medicine, celestial omen divination, and the association of plants, trees, minerals, cities, and countries.[30]

---

29. The zodiac is defined by Rochberg as "a beltway through the heavens through which the sun, moon, and planets may be seen to move. In a conception of the sky as a sphere, the zodiac is a circular belt bisected by the ecliptic and extending roughly 8° north and south of it" (*Heavenly Writing*, 126). The zodiac signs comprise equal divisions of 30° carved out of the unequal-sized zodiacal constellations, so described by Rochberg, that are centered on the middle of the path of the sun's apparent orbit on the ecliptic (it was thought that the sun moved around the earth). See John P. Britton, "Studies in Babylonian Lunar Theory: Part 3. The Introduction of the Uniform Zodiac," *AHES* 64 (2010): 619, 638–40; Barthel L. van der Waerden, "History of the Zodiac," *AfO* (1952–1953): 218–24; Ulla Koch-Westenholz, *Mesopotamian Astrology: An Introduction to Babylonian and Assyrian Celestial Divination*, CNIP 19 (Copenhagen: Museum Tusculanum, 1995), 25. For critical editions in horoscope texts, see Abraham J. Sachs, "Babylonian Horoscopes," *JCS* 6 (1952): 49–75; Francesca Rochberg, *Babylonian Horoscopes*, TAPS 88.1 (Philadelphia: American Philosophical Society, 1998).

30. The micro-zodiac used in astral divination is also referred to by some scholars as *dodekatemoria*, "twelfth part," meaning that the twelve signs of the zodiac are divided into twelve parts each month. However, in the Qumran texts discussed here the micro-zodiac consists of thirteen parts, meaning the number of zodiac signs that the moon passes through each month. (The same term is also used for an astrological system in the hemerological texts that use the thirteen-part micro-zodiac calendar to calculate alternative micro-zodiac signs to find other days when a particular form of magic could be performed, thereby doubling the choice of auspicious days in each month for performing spells or exorcism. See JoAnn Scurlock, "Sorcery in the Stars: STT 300, BRM 19–20 and the Mandaic Book of the Zodiac," *AfO* 51 [2005–2006]: 125–46.) The 360-day year of the thirteen-part micro-zodiac is based on a simple, schematic calendar that presupposes that the sun travels 1 degree on the zodiacal circle (the ecliptic) each day and that the mean motion of the moon is 13 degrees each day. Since in each month the moon returns to the same phase from which it started (known as a synodic month; in the Babylonian calendar it was the first crescent), in

The 360-day year was in use at Qumran in 4QZodiac Calendar and 4QBrontologion (4Q318) (4Q318 is registered as 4QZodiology and Brontology).[31] (Following Geza Vermes but distinguishing between the two content units in order to clearly discuss each, I use the title 4QZodiac Calendar and Brontologion in order to refer to 4QZodiac Calendar [4Q318 IV, VII, VIII, 1–6] and 4QBrontologion [4Q318 VIII, 1–6] separately where necessary.[32]) Structurally, 4Q318 is a fragmentary schematic 360-day calendar that lists the signs of the zodiac that the moon travels through on every day of a year composed of twelve 30-day synodic months in a schematic pattern.

As with some late Babylonian texts used for astral divination, 4QZodiac Calendar uses the micro-zodiac; since the months are synodic, the moon returns the same sign that it was in at the start of each month.[33] Also

---

each synodic month the moon travels 360 degrees plus the 30 degrees that the sun has traveled in that month, which totals 390°. Therefore, in one 30-day month in the 360-day calendar the moon travels 390 degrees (divided by thirty for each day equals 13 degrees per day). For critical editions of zodiacal hemerological texts that use a micro-zodiac calendar and a numerical substitution for the zodiac and micro-zodiac signs, see Arthur Ungnad, "Besprechungskunst und Astrologie in Babylonien," *AfO* 14 (1941–1944): 251–84; Markham J. Geller, *Melothesia in Mesopotamia: Medicine, Magic and Astrology in the Ancient Near East* (Boston: de Gruyter, 2014) (the latest critical editions of BRM 19–20 and related zodiacal hemerological texts); John M. Steele, "A Late Babylonian Compendium of Calendrical and Stellar Astrology," *JCS* 67 (2015): 187–215; see also Erica Reiner, *Astral Magic in Babylonia*, TAPS 85.4 (Philadelphia: American Philosophical Society, 1995), 108–18. For existing critical editions and images of some of these well-known texts, see Ernst F. Weidner, *Gestirn-Darstellungen auf Babylonischen Tontafeln*, OAWPHK 254 (Vienna: Hermann Böhlaus, 1967). For a recent overview and preliminary updating of the corpus, see M. Willis Monroe, "The Micro-Zodiac in Babylon and Uruk: Seleucid Zodiacal Astrology," in *The Circulation of Astronomical Knowledge in the Ancient World*, ed. John M. Steele, TAC 6 (Leiden: Brill, 2016), 119–38. See also John Wee, "Virtual Moons over Babylonia: The Calendar Text System, Its Micro-Zodiac of 13, and the Making of Medical Zodiology," in Steele, *Circulation of Astronomical Knowledge*, 139–229, for a revised theory that the micro-zodiac is solar.

31. Jonas C. Greenfield and Michael Sokoloff, with David Pingree and Ada Yardeni, "318. 4QZodiology and Brontology ar," in Pfann, *Qumran Cave 4.XXVI*, 259–74.

32. Jacobus, *Zodiac Calendars*, 3–4; Geza Vermes, *The Complete Dead Sea Scrolls in English* (London: Penguin, 1997), 361–62.

33. Greenfield and Sokoloff, "318. 4QZodiology and Brontology ar," 271. That is, in a synodic month "the moon travels through *thirteen* signs between its conjunctions with the Sun." For detailed case studies and explanations of the micro-zodiac

known as a selenodromion, or a lunar zodiac calendar, it is followed by a brontologion, a thunder omen text written in the archaic style of Mesopotamian omen texts based on natural phenomena or induced signs from various divination practices.[34] (Józef Milik first recognized that this combined text was well-known in medieval Byzantine astrological texts; the history of its transmission is a subject area that remains to be explored.)[35]

The selenodromion and brontologion are connected: the date according to the 360-day of the thunder clap and the corresponding fateful zodiac sign of the moon on that date can be ascertained by the schematic zodiac calendar.[36] Furthermore, both texts commence when the moon is in Taurus, rather than in Aries, the first sign of the zodiac, a subject that has given rise to various theories that link 4QZodiac Calendar with first-millennium BCE Mesopotamian astronomy-astrology known from the canonical compendium MUL.APIN or even earlier.[37] I have argued that

---

calendrical scheme that is similar to 4QZodiac Calendar, which the authors call the *dodekatemoria*, see Lis Brack-Bernsen and John M. Steele, "Babylonian Mathemagics: Two Astronomical-Astrological Texts," in *Studies in the History of Exact Sciences in Honour of David Pingree*, ed. Charles Burnett et al. (Leiden: Brill, 2004), 95–121; Jacobus, *Zodiac Calendars*, 63–83, 91–99.

34. This is a wide area. See omina, for example, in René Labat, *Un calendrier babylonien des travaux des signes et des mois: Séries iqqur îpuš* (Paris: Librairie Honoré Champion, 1965); Weidner, *Gestirn-Darstellungen*; Hermann Hunger and John Steele, *The Babylonian Astronomical Compendium MUL.APIN*, SWAMW 1 (London: Routledge, 2018); Jacobus, *Zodiac Calendars*, 208–16.

35. Józef T. Milik, *Ten Years of Discovery in the Wilderness of Judea*, trans. John Strugnell, SBT 26 (London: SCM, 1959), 42; Greenfield and Sokoloff, "318. 4QZodiology and Brontology ar," 259–74; Michael O. Wise, "Thunder in Gemini from Qumran: An Aramaic Brontologion from Qumran," in *Thunder in Gemini and Other Essays on the History, Language and Literature of Second Temple Palestine*, JSPSup 15 (Sheffield: Sheffield Academic, 1994), 23–35, 40–43; Jacobus, *Zodiac Calendars*, 184–208.

36. Matthias Albani, "Der Zodiakos in 4Q318 und die Henoch-Astronomie," *MB* 7 (1993): 3–42; Albani, "Horoscopes in the Qumran Scrolls," in Flint and VanderKam, *Dead Sea Scrolls after Fifty Years*, 2:296–301, 322–23, but see also 300 and 323; Greenfield and Sokoloff, "318. 4QZodiology and Brontology ar," 259, 262–66; Jacobus, *Zodiac Calendars*, 44–183, 208–16.

37. Albani, "Der Zodiakos in 4Q318," 27–32; Wise, "Thunder in Gemini," 39–48; Markham J. Geller, "New Documents from the Dead Sea: Babylonian Science in Aramaic," in *Boundaries of the Ancient Near Eastern World: A Tribute to Cyrus Gordon*, ed. Meir Lubetski, JSOTSup 273 (Sheffield: Sheffield Academic, 1998), 224–29; Jacobus, *Zodiac Calendars*, 53–60.

4Q318 uses contemporaneous late Babylonian–early Seleucid-period science (see below).

In 4QZodiac Calendar the months have the Aramaic translations of the Babylonian month names,[38] which is an additional link to the ideal Babylonian calendar model. When tested in actuality with the current Hebrew calendar combined with the data for the position of the moon in the zodiac given for dates in Babylonian horoscopes (which use the Babylonian calendar), the position of the moon in the zodiac on days in the month in 4Q318 is accurate for some intercalary years and close to the moon's sign on the same dates in other years, depending on the gap between the intercalations.[39] Therefore, unlike the 364-Day Calendar Traditions in the Hebrew DSS, it can be demonstrated that 4QZodiac Calendar is a calendar that probably uses the Babylonian 19-year cycle that can be adjusted to actual years. This is the purpose of a schematic calendar.

The lacunose fragment (with smaller, placed fragments) can be easily reconstructed from the text's schematic arrangement of the moon moving into the next zodiac sign every two days, two days, then three days in a recurring sequence (the reality is that the moon takes circa 2.4 days to pass through each zodiac sign). The 360-day zodiac calendar scheme is similar to late Babylonian zodiac calendar texts that use the micro-zodiac and numbers to represent the months and zodiac signs.[40] The varied situation at Qumran is summarized by James VanderKam:

---

38. The seventh month, Tishri (4Q318 IV, 9 reconstructed); the tenth month, Tevet (4Q318 VI, 8 reconstructed); and the twelfth month, Adar (4Q318 VIII, 1) (see Greenfield and Sokoloff, "318. 4QZodiology and Brontology ar," 262–64; Jacobus, *Zodiac Calendars*, 171, 172, 174, which includes full proposed reconstruction of 4QZodiac Calendar from the first month, Nisan, to Adar).

39. Jacobus, *Zodiac Calendars*, 100–115, 122–32; Helen R. Jacobus, "4QZodiac Calendar in Relation to Babylonian Horoscopes," in *Astrology in Time and Place: Cross-cultural Questions in the History of Astrology*, ed. Nicholas Campion and Dorian Gieseler Greenbaum (Newcastle: Cambridge Scholars, 2015), 217–44; Rochberg, *Babylonian Horoscopes*. On the early history of the Jewish calendar, see Judah B. Segal, "Intercalation and the Hebrew Calendar," *VT* 7 (1957): 250–307; Ben-Zion Wacholder and David B. Weisburg, "Visibility of the Moon in Cuneiform and Rabbinic Sources," *HUCA* 42 (1971): 227–42; Sacha Stern, *Calendar and Community: A History of the Jewish Calendar Second Century BCE–Tenth Century CE* (Oxford: Oxford University Press, 2001).

40. See Brack-Bernsen and Steele, "Babylonian Mathemagics."

Calendars could be put to different uses. At Qumran, dating festivals was obviously important, but some texts show that calendars were used to record important events and the names of the characters who participated in them [the historical texts, in particular 4Q322a, 4Q332, 4Q322, 4Q333]. The astrological texts also demonstrate that divination was known at Qumran. God had placed in the phenomena of the sky a code from which one could decipher what the character of a person would be [4Q186, not discussed in this essay] and what events were bound to occur [4Q318].[41]

The Aramaic calendrical texts, 4QAstronomical Enoch[a-b] (4Q208–209 1–22, 29–31, 32?, 33–39, 40? 41?),[42] and 4Q318, as well as not having the מועדים marked in the text, are not divided into weeks. 4Q208–209 and 4QZodiac Calendar explicitly focus on the position of the moon for each day in the calendar.

### Is There a Triennial Cycle in the Aramaic Fragments of 4QAstronomical Enoch[a-b]?

Milik, who produced the first critical edition some of the Aramaic fragments of 4Q208–209, identified the texts as the first year of a synchronistic calendar in which the 354-day lunar year and 364-day schematic year are harmonized into a triennial cycle by the addition of a 30-day month every three years.[43] The months consist of alternating 29- and 30-day months.

However, it has long been argued by some scholars that the Ur-text for the solar year in 1 En. 72 is 360 days.[44] If they are correct, this challenges

---

41. VanderKam, *Calendars in the Dead Sea Scrolls*, 112.

42. József T. Milik, *The Books of Enoch: Aramaic Fragments of Qumrân Cave 4* (Oxford: Clarendon, 1976), 7–22, 273–84; Eibert J. C. Tigchelaar and Florentino García Martínez, "208. 4QAstronomical Enoch[a] ar," in Pfann, *Qumran Cave 4.XXVI*, 104–31; Tigchelaar and García Martínez, "209. 4QAstronomical Enoch[b] ar," in Pfann, *Qumran Cave 4.XXVI*, 132–58, 166–71; Henryk Drawnel, *Aramaic Astronomical Book (4Q208–4Q211) from Qumran: Text, Translation and Commentary* (Oxford: Clarendon, 2011), 71–133, 134–87, 201–8.

43. Milik, *Books of Enoch*, 274–75.

44. Glessmer, "Calendars in the Qumran Scrolls," 233–34; Matthias Albani, *Astronomie und Schöpfungsglaube: Untersuchungen zum Astronomischen Henochbuch*, WMANT 68 (Neukirchen-Vluyn: Neukirchener, 1994), 155–69; Albani, "Der Zodiakos in 4Q318," 27–35; Paolo Sacchi, *Jewish Apocalyptic and Its History*, JSPSup 20 (Sheffield: Sheffield Academic, 1996), 128–39. For a summary, see James C.

Milik's hypothesis and that of the editors of 4Q208–209, Eibert Tigchelaar and Florentino García Martínez, of a solar, schematic year of 364 days in 4Q208–209.[45] Since Astronomical Enoch[a–b] is not a calendar divided into weeks, the suggestion that 4Q208–209 reflect a synchronistic solar calendar of 360 days and a lunar calendar of 354 days is more likely and demonstrable; see below.

More recently, Eshbal Ratzon has proposed that the fragments of 4Q209 contain not just the first year but all three years of the triennial cycle; however, when 4Q208–209 are mathematically reconstructed according to the text in the fragments, described below, the hypothesis is shown to be unsupported.[46]

The most valuable contribution to the field in recent years has been made by Henryk Drawnel, who reconstructed all the Aramaic astronomical fragments, which he organized into an astronomical time-related scheme and calendrical template, thereby opening up the subject to wider research possibilities.[47] Drawnel himself rejects the consensus view that 4Q208–209 represents a synchronistic, luni-solar calendar in any form at all, arguing that the references to the sun are interpolations that are grammatically incorrect and that the appearance of the "gates" in the fragments are erratic and inconsistent.[48]

---

VanderKam, "The Book of Luminaries," in *1 Enoch 2*, ed. George W. E. Nickelsburg and James C. VanderKam (Minneapolis: Fortress, 2012), 373–83; Jacobus, *Zodiac Calendars*, 272–74.

45. Milik, *Books of Enoch*, 8, 274–75; Eibert J. C. Tigchelaar and Florentino García Martínez, "208–209. Astronomical Enoch[a–b] ar: Introduction," in Pfann, *Qumran Cave 4.XXVI*, 96. The model for the 360-day solar calendar element is described in Helen R. Jacobus, "Astral Divination in the Dead Sea Scrolls," in *Hellenistic Astronomy: The Science in Its Contexts*, ed. Alan C. Bowen and Francesca Rochberg (Leiden: Brill, forthcoming).

46. Eshbal Ratzon, "The First Jewish Astronomers: Lunar Theory and the Reconstruction of a Dead Sea Scroll," *SciCon* 30 (2017): 113–39. But see Helen R. Jacobus, "Reconstructing the Calendar of 4Q208–4Q209 (and a Response to Eshbal Ratzon)," *RevQ* 31 (2019): 251–73.

47. Drawnel, *Aramaic Astronomical Book*, 71–187, 201–8.

48. Drawnel, *Aramaic Astronomical Book*, 72, 298–99.

## Discussion on 4Q208 and Streams of Transmission

Following Tigchelaar, who argued that 4Q208, possibly dating from the late third or first quarter of the second century BCE (according to the earliest dates by radiocarbon dating), probably contained the synchronistic calendar only, it may be suggested that 4Q208 was an independent document and that the ancient scribes/editors appended a later copy, 4Q209, which is Herodian,[49] to the content of 4Q209 23–28 // 1 En. 76–79, 82.

Although the higher-numbered fragments of 4Q209 are reflected in the Book of Luminaries, scholars are divided as to whether 4Q209 appeared in an abbreviated or a corrupted form, or if at all, in 1 En. 73.[50] What is not in dispute, however, is some kind of receptive relationship between 4Q208–209 and the Ethiopic MS 64 in the Bibliothèque nationale in Paris, which contains folios listing the number of days that the moon rises in each of the six gates in every month.[51] The manuscript also

---

49. Milik, *Books of Enoch*, 73; Eibert J. C. Tigchelaar, "Some Remarks on the Book of Watchers, the Priests, Enoch and Genesis, and 4Q208," *Hen* 24 (2002): 145. On the radiocarbon dating of 4Q208, see Milik, *Books of Enoch*, 273; VanderKam, "Book of Luminaries," 339–40; A. J. Timothy Jull et al., "Radiocarbon Dating of Scrolls and Linen Fragments from the Judaean Desert," *Radiocarbon* 37 (1995): 11–19. See also Israel Carmi, "Radiocarbon Dating of the Dead Sea Scrolls," in *The Dead Sea Scrolls: Fifty Years after Their Discovery*, ed. Lawrence H. Schiffman, Emanuel Tov, and James C. VanderKam (Jerusalem: Israel Exploration Society, 2000), 881–88, who date the manuscript to the first century BCE. There has been significant discussion on methods of radiocarbon dating, and there is a consensus that Milik's paleographic dating of ca. 200 BCE is close to the earliest calibrated age range according to carbon-14 testing. See Kaare L. Rasmussen et al., "Reply to Israel Carmi (2002): Are the $^{14}$C Dates of the Dead Sea Scrolls Affected by Castor Oil Contamination?," *Radiocarbon* 45 (2003): 497–499. Doudna dates 4Q208 to 172–48 BCE. See Greg Doudna, "Dating the Scrolls on the Basis of Radiocarbon Analysis," in Flint and VanderKam, *Dead Sea Scrolls after Fifty Years*, 1:467. Atwill and Braunheim date 4Q208 to 186–92 BCE. See Joseph Atwill and Steve Braunheim, "Redating the Radiocarbon Dating of the Dead Sea Scrolls," *DSD* 7 (2004): 147. See also Johannes van der Plicht, "Radiocarbon Dating and the Dead Sea Scrolls: A Comment on 'Redating,'" *DSD* 14 (2007): 82.

50. VanderKam is unconvinced that the Ethiopic derives from an original Aramaic text, contra Drawnel, who reconstructs 1 En. 73.4–8 and 1 En. 6–7 as the same preambles to the beginning of a 30-day month and a 29-day month that are subsequently described in detail in 4Q209 (VanderKam, "Book of Luminaries," 438–39; Drawnel, *Aramaic Astronomical Book*, 441, 447).

51. Sylvain Grébaut, "Table des levers de la lune pour chaque mois de l'année," *RevOrChr* 21 (1918–1019): 422–28; Otto Neugebauer, "Notes on Ethiopic Astronomy,"

lists the variations in daylight lengths for each month of the year (see 1 En. 72) and an adaptation of the introduction to the Book of Luminaries—shown to Enoch the Prophet by the angel Uriel; see 1 En. 72.1—written in the third person.[52]

The editors of 4Q208–209, Tigchelaar and García Martínez in the critical edition showed that the Ge'ez text was close to the Aramaic text,[53] and VanderKam also agrees that the data in 4QAstronomical Enoch[a–b] are close to the Ethiopic manuscript, possibly signifying separate streams of transmission in Ge'ez in the Book of Luminaries, and Ethiopic MS 64. He concluded:

1. All the fragments of 4Q208 belong to the synchronistic calendar with no surviving trace of the other topics found in *1 Enoch* 72–82.
2. Most fragments of 4Q209 present the synchronistic calendar, but offer some material present in sections of *1 Enoch* 72–82 [frgs 23–28].
3. The Ethiopic MSS do not contain the synchronistic calendar on the scale suggested in the Aramaic fragments; rather, they include only short sections that cite a few parts of it.
4. Ethiopic MS 64 from the Bibliothèque nationale, citing *1 En.* 72.1 to identify the source of its information, preserves much more detailed information about the lunar movements during the months of a full year than is now present in the Ethiopic MSS of the Book of the Luminaries.
5. This last fact suggests the possibility that at some point in its transmission history some tabular data were separated from the other sections of the Enochic astronomical work, which was left with only a condensed version of the technical lists.

Perhaps this opens up a new way of viewing the history of the text from Aramaic to Ethiopic: long, technical lists or tables were removed from the ancient text and stored in collections of such data as we find in Ethiopic MS 64. This rendered the process of copying the literary text much

---

*Orientalia* NS 33 (1964): 51–58; Milik, *Books of Enoch*, 275–78; VanderKam, "Book of Luminaries," 406–7.

52. Sylvain Grébaut, "Variations de la durée des jours et des nuits pour chaque mois de l'année," *Revue de l'Orient Chretien* 21 (1918–1919): 429–32; Grébaut, "Table les levers des la lune," 423, 426; VanderKam, "Book of Luminaries," 407 n. 290.

53. Tigchelaar and García Martínez, "208–209. Astronomical Enoch[a–b] ar," 100 and passim.

easier, while the full range of data was still accessible in other MSS should one need to consult them, as some did. We could then regard the Book of the Luminaries as a faithful but purposefully abbreviated version of the Astronomical Book. It retains essential features of the special Enochic system without the more painful lists that once made the text so very much longer.

As a result, we have reason to regard the Book of the Luminaries, not as a careless translation or copy of a longer, more understandable text, but in places as a purposefully reduced text about the Enochic astronomy, one that is more comfortably readable than the longer Aramaic work.[54]

Although VanderKam apparently accepts here that there is no evidence that 4Q208 was combined with any other material outside the synchronistic calendar, he is also contending that 4Q208 is Enochic. This may be anachronistic, since there is no evidence that it was connected to an early version of the Aramaic Astronomical Book, accepted as comprising 4Q208–211, and may give the misleading impression or lead to the misunderstanding that 4Q208 was part of an intentional Ur-text for the Book of the Luminaries when this is, in fact, not at all certain.

Although 4Q209 23–28 corresponds with a corruption of 1 En. 79–79, 82, and Ethiopic manuscript 64 is also connected with the preamble adapted from 1 En. 72.1, that does not constitute evidence that 4Q208 was originally part of a longer work. Elsewhere, VanderKam argues that the hypothesis that 4Q208 only contained the synchronistic calendar is an argument from silence and not a demonstrated point.[55] He also separates 4QZodiac Calendar from 4Q208–209, stating: "The only calendrical texts written in Aramaic found at Qumran are related to the Book of the Luminaries and thus to Enoch; the others are written in Hebrew," adding in a footnote: "4Q318 Zodiology and Brontology ar may appear to be an exception, but it is not a calendrical work in the same sense as the others from Cave 4. Also its terminology differs strongly from the Enochic texts."[56]

Yet, the different styles of 4Q318 and 4Q208 and 4Q209 do not mean that they are unrelated, since it can be shown that these Aramaic calendars

---

54. James C. VanderKam, "The Aramaic Astronomical Book and the Ethiopic Book of Luminaries," in Dobos and Köszeghy, *With Wisdom as a Robe*, 220–21.

55. VanderKam, "Aramaic Astronomical Book," 212; see also VanderKam, "Book of Luminaries," 341–42, in a similar vein.

56. VanderKam, "Aramaic Astronomical Book," 212–13 n. 12.

are similar (4QBrontologion emanates from another genre). Furthermore, it is equally possible that if 4Q208 did comprise the synchronistic calendar only, the reception of 4Q208 in 4Q209 as part of the Book of the Luminaries is a later development. In my view, based on its mathematical content, it is a related, self-contained addition.

Aramaic Calendar Reconstruction

The reconstruction for 4QZodiac Calendar is shown in table 8.1 and has been discussed in depth elsewhere.[57] The text only states the moon's zodiac sign for the days of the year, whereas 4Q208–209 uses gate numbers to represent the moon's position on the horizon at moonrise and moonset.

Reconstruction of 4QAstronomical Enoch[a–b] with the Zodiac

The ordinal month numbers or, possibly, the Babylonian month names, have not survived, if they existed. Nonetheless, by using the template of 4QZodiac Calendar, it is possible to reconstruct the year, supported by fragments in 4Q208–209 that contain the greatest amount of relevant data. The gate numbers can be substituted for the zodiac signs, as the numerical scheme in Babylonian hemerological texts that use the zodiac does (see below). It is then possible to mathematically reconstruct the month for the largest fragment of 4Q209 (7 II–III) by adapting the schematic arrangement in 4QZodiac Calendar with the numerical scheme in 1 En. 72.[58] The substitution of zodiac signs with a numerical scheme (months and their corresponding zodiac signs numbered one to twelve) is practiced in Babylonian hemerological texts that use the zodiac (see above).[59] The reconstruction is based on the largest fragment of 4Q209, containing days of the waning moon toward the end of month IX and

---

57. Jacobus, *Zodiac Calendars*, 47–51, 157–74; Helen R. Jacobus, "4Q318: A Jewish Zodiac Calendar at Qumran?," in *The Dead Scrolls: Texts and Contexts*, ed. Charlotte Hempel, STDJ 90 (Leiden: Brill, 2010), 371–74.

58. First Enoch 72 was also so interpreted by earlier scholars in the nineteenth and early twentieth centuries after the first English translation by Richard Laurence in 1821 (see summary of literature in Jacobus, *Zodiac Calendars*, 263–68).

59. Ungnad, "Besprechungskunst und Astrologie"; Scurlock, "Sorcery in the Stars"; Geller, *Melothesia in Mesopotamia*; Steele, "Late Babylonian Compendium."

## Table. 8.1. Reconstruction of 4QZodiac Calendar (4Q318 IV, VII, VIII, 1–6)

|    | Nisan | Iyyar | Sivan | Tammuz | Av | Elul | Tishri | Heshvan | Kislev | Tevet | Shevat | Adar |
|----|-------|-------|-------|--------|----|----|--------|---------|--------|-------|--------|------|
| 1  | ♉ | ♊ | ♋ | ♌ | ♍ | ♎ | ♏ | ♐ | ♑ | ♒ | ♓ | ♈ |
| 2  | ♉ | ♊ | ♋ | ♌ | ♍ | ♎ | ♏ | ♐ | ♑ | ♒ | ♓ | ♈ |
| 3  | ♊ | ♋ | ♌ | ♍ | ♎ | ♏ | ♐ | ♑ | ♒ | ♓ | ♈ | ♉ |
| 4  | ♊ | ♋ | ♌ | ♍ | ♎ | ♏ | ♐ | ♑ | ♒ | ♓ | ♈ | ♉ |
| 5  | ♋ | ♌ | ♍ | ♎ | ♏ | ♐ | ♑ | ♒ | ♓ | ♈ | ♉ | ♊ |
| 6  | ♋ | ♌ | ♍ | ♎ | ♏ | ♐ | ♑ | ♒ | ♓ | ♈ | ♉ | ♊ |
| 7  | ♋ | ♌ | ♍ | ♎ | ♏ | ♐ | ♑ | ♒ | ♓ | ♈ | ♉ | ♊ |
| 8  | ♌ | ♍ | ♎ | ♏ | ♐ | ♑ | ♒ | ♓ | ♈ | ♉ | ♊ | ♋ |
| 9  | ♌ | ♍ | ♎ | ♏ | ♐ | ♑ | ♒ | ♓ | ♈ | ♉ | ♊ | ♋ |
| 10 | ♍ | ♎ | ♏ | ♐ | ♑ | ♒ | ♓ | ♈ | ♉ | ♊ | ♋ | ♌ |
| 11 | ♍ | ♎ | ♏ | ♐ | ♑ | ♒ | ♓ | ♈ | ♉ | ♊ | ♋ | ♌ |
| 12 | ♎ | ♏ | ♐ | ♑ | ♒ | ♓ | ♈ | ♉ | ♊ | ♋ | ♌ | ♍ |
| 13 | ♎ | ♏ | ♐ | ♑ | ♒ | ♓ | ♈ | ♉ | ♊ | ♋ | ♌ | ♍ |
| 14 | ♎ | ♏ | ♐ | ♑ | ♒ | ♓ | ♈ | ♉ | ♊ | ♋ | ♌ | ♍ |
| 15 | ♏ | ♐ | ♑ | ♒ | ♓ | ♈ | ♉ | ♊ | ♋ | ♌ | ♍ | ♎ |
| 16 | ♏ | ♐ | ♑ | ♒ | ♓ | ♈ | ♉ | ♊ | ♋ | ♌ | ♍ | ♎ |
| 17 | ♐ | ♑ | ♒ | ♓ | ♈ | ♉ | ♊ | ♋ | ♌ | ♍ | ♎ | ♏ |
| 18 | ♐ | ♑ | ♒ | ♓ | ♈ | ♉ | ♊ | ♋ | ♌ | ♍ | ♎ | ♏ |
| 19 | ♑ | ♒ | ♓ | ♈ | ♉ | ♊ | ♋ | ♌ | ♍ | ♎ | ♏ | ♐ |
| 20 | ♑ | ♒ | ♓ | ♈ | ♉ | ♊ | ♋ | ♌ | ♍ | ♎ | ♏ | ♐ |
| 21 | ♑ | ♒ | ♓ | ♈ | ♉ | ♊ | ♋ | ♌ | ♍ | ♎ | ♏ | ♐ |
| 22 | ♒ | ♓ | ♈ | ♉ | ♊ | ♋ | ♌ | ♍ | ♎ | ♏ | ♐ | ♑ |
| 23 | ♒ | ♓ | ♈ | ♉ | ♊ | ♋ | ♌ | ♍ | ♎ | ♏ | ♐ | ♑ |
| 24 | ♓ | ♈ | ♉ | ♊ | ♋ | ♌ | ♍ | ♎ | ♏ | ♐ | ♑ | ♒ |
| 25 | ♓ | ♈ | ♉ | ♊ | ♋ | ♌ | ♍ | ♎ | ♏ | ♐ | ♑ | ♒ |
| 26 | ♈ | ♉ | ♊ | ♋ | ♌ | ♍ | ♎ | ♏ | ♐ | ♑ | ♒ | ♓ |
| 27 | ♈ | ♉ | ♊ | ♋ | ♌ | ♍ | ♎ | ♏ | ♐ | ♑ | ♒ | ♓ |
| 28 | ♈ | ♉ | ♊ | ♋ | ♌ | ♍ | ♎ | ♏ | ♐ | ♑ | ♒ | ♓ |
| 29 | ♉ | ♊ | ♋ | ♌ | ♍ | ♎ | ♏ | ♐ | ♑ | ♒ | ♓ | ♈ |
| 30 | ♉ | ♊ | ♋ | ♌ | ♍ | ♎ | ♏ | ♐ | ♑ | ♒ | ♓ | ♈ |

Key: Aries ♈; Taurus ♉; Gemini ♊; Cancer ♋; Leo ♌; Virgo ♍; Libra ♎; Scorpio ♏; Sagittarius ♐; Capricorn ♑; Aquarius ♒; Pisces ♓
(shaded cells = extant fragments)

Table 8.2. Reconstruction of 4Q208–209,
with zodiac signs corresponding to gate numbers

| | I | II | III | IV | V | VI | VII | VIII | IX | X | XI | XII | 29 | 30 |
|---|---|---|---|---|---|---|---|---|---|---|---|---|---|---|
| 1 | 4♈ | 5♉ | 6♊ | 6♋ | 5♌ | 4♍ | 3♎ | 2♏ | 1♐ | 1♑ | 2♒ | 3♓ | .5 | |
| 2 | 4♈ | 5♉ | 6♊ | 6♋ | 5♌ | 4♍ | 3♎ | 2♏ | 1♐ | 1♑ | 2♒ | 3♓ | 1 | .5 |
| 3 | 5♉ | 6♊ | 6♋ | 5♌ | 4♍ | 3♎ | 2♏ | 1♐ | 1♑ | 2♒ | 3♓ | 4♈ | 1.5 | 1 |
| 4 | 5♉ | ♊ | 6♋ | 5♌ | 4♍ | 3♎ | 2♏ | 1♐ | 1♑ | 2♒ | 33♓ | 4♈ | 2 | 1.5 |
| 5 | 6♊ | 4♋ | 5♌ | 4♍ | 3♎ | 2♏ | 1♐ | 1♑ | 2♒ | 3♓ | 4♈ | 5♉ | 2.5 | 2 |
| 6 | 6♊ | 6♋ | 5♌ | 4♍ | 3♎ | 2♏ | 1♐ | 1♑ | 2♒ | 3♓ | 4♈ | 5♉ | 3 | 2.5 |
| 7 | 6♋ | 5♌ | 4♍ | 3♎ | 2♏ | 1♐ | 1♑ | 2♒ | 3♓ | 4♈ | 5♉ | 6♊ | 3.5 | 3 |
| 8 | 6♋ | 5♌ | 4♍ | 3♎ | 2♏ | 1♐ | 1♑ | 2♒ | 3♓ | 4♈ | 5♉ | 6♊ | 4 | 3.5 |
| 9 | 6♋ | 5♌ | 4♍ | 3♎ | 2♏ | 1♐ | 1♑ | 2♒ | 3♓ | 4♈ | 5♉ | 6♊ | 4.5 | 4 |
| 10 | 6♌ | 4♍ | 3♎ | 2♏ | 1♐ | 1♑ | 2♒ | 3♓ | 4♈ | 5♉ | 6♊ | 6♋ | 5 | 4.5 |
| 11 | 6♌ | 4♍ | 3♎ | 2♏ | 1♐ | 1♑ | 2♒ | 3♓ | 4♈ | 5♉ | 6♊ | 6♋ | 5.5 | 5 |
| 12 | 4♍ | 3♎ | 2♏ | 1♐ | 1♑ | 2♒ | 3♓ | 4♈ | 5♉ | 6♊ | 6♋ | 5♌ | 6 | 5.5 |
| 13 | 4♍ | 3♎ | 2♏ | 1♐ | 1♑ | 2♒ | 3♓ | 4♈ | 5♉ | 6♊ | 6♋ | 5♌ | 6.5 | 6 |
| 14 | 3♎ | 2♏ | 1♐ | 1♑ | 2♒ | 3♓ | 4♈ | 5♉ | 6♊ | 6♋ | 5♌ | 4♍ | (7) | 6.5 |
| 15 | 3♎ | 2♏ | 1♐ | 1♑ | 2♒ | 3♓ | 4♈ | 5♉ | 6♊ | 6♋ | 5♌ | 4♍ | 6.5 | (7) |
| 16 | 3♎ | 2♏ | 1♐ | 1♑ | 2♒ | 3♓ | 4♈ | 5♉ | 6♊ | 6♋ | 5♌ | 4♍ | 6 | 6.5 |
| 17 | 2♏ | 1♐ | 1♑ | 2♒ | 3♓ | 4♈ | 5♉ | 6♊ | 6♋ | 5♌ | 4♍ | 3♎ | 5.5 | 6 |
| 18 | 2♏ | 1♐ | 1♑ | 2♒ | 3♓ | 4♈ | 5♉ | 6♊ | 6♋ | 5♌ | 4♍ | 3♎ | 5 | 5.5 |
| 19 | 1♐ | 1♑ | 2♒ | 3♓ | 4♈ | 5♉ | 6♊ | 6♋ | 5♌ | 4♍ | 3♎ | 2♏ | 4.5 | 5 |
| 20 | 1♐ | 1♑ | 2♒ | 3♓ | 4♈ | 5♉ | 6♊ | 6♋ | 5♌ | 4♍ | 3♎ | 2♏ | 4 | 4.5 |
| 21 | 1♑ | 2♒ | 3♓ | 4♈ | 5♉ | 6♊ | 6♋ | 5♌ | 4♍ | 3♎ | 2♏ | 1♐ | 3.5 | 4 |
| 22 | 1♑ | 2♒ | 3♓ | 4♈ | 5♉ | 6♊ | 6♋ | 5♌ | 4♍ | 3♎ | 2♏ | 1♐ | 3 | 3.5 |
| 23 | 1♑ | 2♒ | 3♓ | 4♈ | 5♉ | 6♊ | 6♋ | 5♌ | 4♍ | 3♎ | 2♏ | 1♐ | 2.5 | 3 |
| 24 | 2♒ | 3♓ | 4♈ | 5♉ | 6♊ | 6♋ | 5♌ | 4♍ | 3♎ | 2♏ | 1♐ | 1♑ | 2 | 2.5 |
| 25 | 2♒ | 3♓ | 4♈ | 5♉ | 6♊ | 6♋ | 5♌ | 4♍ | 3♎ | 2♏ | 1♐ | 1♑ | 1.5 | 2 |
| 26 | 3♓ | 4♈ | 5♉ | 6♊ | 6♋ | 5♌ | 4♍ | 3♎ | 2♏ | 1♐ | 1♑ | 2♒ | 1 | 1.5 |
| 27 | 3♓ | 4♈ | 5♉ | 6♊ | 6♋ | 5♌ | 4♍ | 3♎ | 2♏ | 1♐ | 1♑ | 2♒ | .5 | 1 |
| 28 | 4♈ | 5♉ | 6♊ | 6♋ | 5♌ | 4♍ | 3♎ | 2♏ | 1♐ | 1♑ | 2♒ | 3♓ | | .5 |
| 29 | 4♈ | 5♉ | 6♊ | 6♋ | 5♌ | 4♍ | 3♎ | 2♏ | 1♐ | 1♑ | 2♒ | 3♓ | | |
| 30 | 4♈ | | 6♊ | | 5♌ | | 3♎ | | 1♐ | | 2♒ | | | |

Gate numbers key: Aries ♈: Gate 4; Taurus ♉: Gate 5; Gemini ♊: Gate 6; Cancer ♋: Gate 6; Leo ♌: Gate 5; Virgo ♍: Gate 4; Libra ♎: Gate 3; Scorpio ♏: Gate 2; Sagittarius ♐: Gate 1; Capricorn ♑: Gate 1; Aquarius ♒: Gate 2; Pisces ♓: Gate 3 shaded areas: fragments with gate numbers; top row: months; left: days; far right, fractions of the visible moon in half-sevenths for 29- and 30-day months

days of the waxing moon after the first quarter in month X.[60] The reconstruction of the remainder of the year, shown in table 8.2, has been mathematically restored by extending the same pattern. This restoration is supported by other fragments that contain sufficient data from a few days in other months; in particular, the extant gate numbers in the fragments' data are necessary to place them in the reconstruction. The original schematic restoration for the month and then the year involved, postulating that the moon changes gates every two days, then two days, then two days, then three days in a recurring arrangement, representing a slightly different configuration from the lunar scheme in 4QZodiac Calendar, as described above.[61]

As mentioned, not one month number/month name has survived in any of the fragments. However, by adopting the editors' and Drawnel's painstaking restorations of the fractions of visibility and invisibility when the moon progressively waxes and wanes in units of half-sevenths incrementally and rises and sets throughout the day and night during the month, it is possible to propose an identification of the months from the days, fractions, and extant gate numbers in the fragments.

The restoration in table 8.2 is based on the premise that the calendrical day begins at sunset and that when a gate number is mentioned it is because the moon has risen in a new gate, that is, not the same gate as the day before, when no gate number is mentioned. The lunar months are alternately of 29 and 30 days (a 354-day lunar year), as postulated by Milik, synchronized, as here proposed, with a 360-day solar year.

The extant gate numbers in the fragments are underlined in the table. No two dates contain the same data. Only the fractions of the moon's shining, or visibility after sunset, the new calendrical day, is given in the right-hand columns for 29- and 30-day months. [62] (The text also states the fractions of the moon's invisibility for different time relations between the sun and the moon during the day and night, which can be ascertained from the right-hand columns in table 8.2 by subtracting the fractions of shining, or light, from seven sevenths). The corresponding zodiac signs to the gate numbers are shown in table 8.2, demonstrating the argu-

---

60. Month X was reconstructed on this basis from the text in Jacobus, *Zodiac Calendars*, 305–11.

61. Jacobus, *Zodiac Calendars*, 268–71, 274–83, 305–11.

62. See Pattern I (fractions for a 29-day-month) and Pattern II (fractions for a 30-day month) in Drawnel, *Aramaic Astronomical Book*, 421–25.

ment that these texts are related to 4QZodiac Calendar, rather than to the Jubilees-Qumran calendar of 364 days, which tends to be the default comparative position.

It is proposed that the fragments are to be placed in the reconstruction as follows (shaded in table 8.2 with extant gate numbers underlined):[63]

4Q209 16: Month I, nights 25–27: On night 25: the waning moon rises from gate 2 and sets in gate 3 in the morning; it is hidden for five sevenths; it shines for two sevenths and sets in gate 3. On night 26: the moon is hidden for 5.5 sevenths and rises in gate 3, shining for 1.5 sevenths and hidden for 5.5 sevenths after sunset, the new calendrical day; it sets in gate 3. The moon is in gate 3 on nights 26 (extant) and 27 (based on the fractions, it is a 30-day month).

4Q208 33: Month III, nights 27 and 28: The waning moon rises on nights 28 (extant), 29, and 30 in gate 6 after sunset, the new calendrical day, shining for 0.5 sevenths. The moon is in gate 6 on night 28 (a 30-day month).

4Q208 16: Month VII, nights 25 and 26: The waning moon would set in gate 5 after sunset on night 25, and it rises in the morning in gate 4. On night 26 the waning moon rises and shines from gate 4 after sunset, the new calendrical day, with 1.5 sevenths of light. The moon is in gate 4 on nights 26 (extant) and 27 (a 30-day month). An ancient scribal mistake states that the moon shines on night 25 for two-"and-a-half"- (ופלג) sevenths instead of for two sevenths (line 4). A scribe corrected the error with a line through the *gimel* of ופלג.

4Q209 7 II: Month IX, nights 23–27: The waning moon would set in gate 2 on night 25 in the morning. It rises and shines after sunset, the new calendrical day, on night 26 in gate 2 for 1.5 sevenths. The moon is in gate 2 on nights 26 (extant) and 27. There is a large space in the manuscript after night 27 (a 30-day month).

---

63. The fragment item numbering follows those registered in the critical editions. The numbering on the Leon Levy Dead Sea Scrolls Digital Library is currently different: 4QAstronomical Enoch[b] 4Q209 7 is numbered 4QEnastr[b] Frag. 1. (Odd-numbered months have 30 days, and even-numbered months have 29 days.) For the full set of data, see the various fragments in Tigchelaar and García Martínez, "208–209. Astronomical Enoch[a–b] ar"; Tigchelaar and García Martínez, "208. 4QAstronomical Enoch[a] ar"; Tigchelaar and García Martínez, "209. 4QAstronomical Enoch[b] ar"; Drawnel, *Aramaic Astronomical Book*.

4Q209 3 III: Month X, nights 2–4/5: The moon rises from gate 2 during daytime of day 2. It sets after sunset, the new calendrical day in gate 2 on nights 3 and 4. On night 4, the waxing moon is five-sevenths dark; it shines for two sevenths after sunset, the new calendrical day (having risen in gate 2 during the daytime). It sets in gate 3 on night 4 and rises in gate 3 during the daytime and after sunset on night 5, the new calendrical day, shining for 2.5 sevenths, in gate 3. The moon is in gate 3 on nights 5 (extant) and 6 (a 29-day month).

4Q209 7 III 3: Month X, nights 8–10: The sun rises in gate 1 (the only reference to the sun in a gate with an extant number in the texts), and the waxing moon rises in gate 5 on day 9 (in the daytime, extant). It shines in gate 5 after sunset for five sevenths, on calendrical day 10.[64] The moon is in gate 5 on nights 10 and 11 (a 29-day month, as above).

4Q208 24 I: Month XII, nights 2–4: the waxing moon sets on night 2 in an unnumbered gate (gate 3) and rises from gate 4 during the day (extant). On night 3 after sunset, the new calendrical day, the thin waxing moon is 1.5 sevenths light and dark for 5.5 sevenths in gate 4. The moon is in gate 4 on nights 3 (extant) and 4 (a 29-day month).

The efficacy of tables 8.1 and 8.2 (and their introduction of Babylonian astronomy) can be tested by using publicly available materials:

Convert a Gregorian or another calendar date to the present Hebrew calendar; note whether the year had an intercalation.[65] For a year that has

---

64. Eshbal Ratzon assigns day 8, month X to gate 5 for the first year of what she claims is a triennial cycle (in contrast to Milik's claim that 4Q208–209 represented one year of a triennial cycle; see Milik, *Books of Enoch*, 274; Ratzon, "First Jewish Astronomers," 134). According to the scheme presented in table 8.2, the moon rises in gate 5 on day 9 (daytime) and shines in gate 5 after sunset on calendrical day/night 10. Therefore, since the calendar days begin at sunset, day 10, month X should be assigned to gate 5, and day 8, month X, to gate 4, the previous gate.

65. The website Fourmilab: Calendar Converter is useful: www.fourmilab.ch/documents/calendar/. However, note that the Hebrew calendar date changes at noon on the website (and many other similar calendar converter sites), instead of at sunset, and it uses numerical historical years in the mathematical form, so, 10 BCE equates to −10. The Jewish numerical new year begins on the first day of the seventh month, Rosh Hashanah, in the autumn, Tishri. In modern Judaism, the liturgical year begins later in the seventh month, on Simchat Torah. Intercalation may take place in the spring of the same numerical year at the end of the calendrical year for the months beginning in Nisan, with the insertion of a 30-day month (ve-Adar) before the twelfth month, Adar, a 29-day month. This will have the effect of making the Hebrew calendar date

a ve-Adar (Adar II, an intercalary twelfth month, Adar) prior to Nisan, the first month, look at the date and the moon's position in the zodiac in table 8.1; for nonintercalary years, use the date and the moon's position in the zodiac in table 8.2.

To test the calendars by eye, check the day of the month in the Hebrew calendar and the phase of the moon, which should correspond, look up at the sky on a starry night, and now identify the zodiacal constellations near the moon from either of the tables, as appropriate (taking into account that the fixed stars have apparently moved some 23 degrees westward [as seen from the earth] in two thousand years,[66] which is about a hand-breadth with an outstretched arm). The zodiac signs are mathematical constructions that do not exist in the sky, but the star groups or bright stars in the constellations whose name they carry are identifiable.

One can also use an online planetarium to help identify the zodiacal constellations for the time, date, and latitude, or a planisphere. There are also many different apps for identifying the constellations and the position of the sun and moon, frequently with visual reconstructions based on various sources for the classical Greek star groups.

It is possible to test any date with astronomical computer programs that can be set for dates two thousand years ago, and further back in time, or the future.[67] For example, by computation, the dates with a gate number (gate 2) in 4Q209 7 II, 6–10 coincide with days 25–26 in Month IX according to table 8.2. Equating to Kislev to the ninth month, the date may be programmed for moonrise on 25 Kislev, 10 BCE, Jerusalem (a nonintercalary year in the retrojected Hebrew calendar), which converts to 20 December in 10 BCE.[68] According to table 8.2, the moon is in gate 3 on that

---

from Nisan, the first month, onward "late" in that year (as will be the case with Easter and Passover on 15 Nisan).

66. The rotation westward of the stars is due to the phenomenon known as the precession of the equinoxes. See Koch-Westenholz, *Mesopotamian Astrology*, 22–23; Otto Neugebauer, "The Alleged Babylonian Discovery of the Precession of the Equinoxes," *JAOS* 70 (1950): 1–8. One can use one's hand and fingers to measure the degrees between celestial objects; see Apama Kerr, "A Handy Guide to Measuring the Sky," timeanddate.com, https://tinyurl.com/SBL3554a.

67. Such as the free online program Stellarium. Note that in this program the calendar years before BCE are written in the mathematical form of a minus year, not the historical form, so, for example, 10 BCE equates to –9 in the data.

68. In the table 8.2 scheme, on 25–26 IX, the moon changes gates/signs from gate 3 (Libra) to gate 2 (Scorpio). In the Hebrew calendar the date would be ca. 25–26

date, which corresponds with the zodiac sign of Libra; thus, programmed with the images, the moon is shown to be rising when the zodiacal constellation of Libra is rising on the horizon.

Alternatively, one can also ascertain the position of the moon in the zodiac for a particular date according to table 8.1 or table 8.2 with an astrological ephemeris. These automatically ignore the westward rotation of the constellations and are fixed from the time of first-century astronomer Ptolemy. In other words, they state the position of the sun and the moon in the zodiac as they were 2,000 years ago (as well as the position of planets).[69]

The remarkable accuracy in some years, or closeness of the results in others, demonstrates the ingenuity of Babylonian astronomy in a way that can be understood today.

## Scholarly Controversy

Otto Neugebauer rejects the theory that the gates represented the zodiac signs in relation to the Book of the Luminaries, replacing it with a hypothesis based solely on horizon astronomy. He maintains that the gates in 1 En. 72 were concerned with seasonal changes in day lengths corresponding with the sun's monthly and rising and setting points on the eastern and western horizon.[70]

With reference to his study of Ethiopic MS 64, which he discusses in relation to the Ethiopic Astronomical Book, Neugebauer states that the gates of the moon represented "sixths of the arc of the horizon which

---

Kislev. Converted to the Julian calendar for 10 BCE, this equates to 20 December (in the Hebrew year 3752; Fourmilab date, Julian Calendar: December 20, –10 = Hebrew date: 25 Kislev, 3752). The image for the Julian calendar date programmed into Stellarium for about 5 a.m. when the moon would be rising (a late waning moon rises in the morning, as denoted by the day of the month, 25–26) visually depicts the waning moon between the zodiacal constellations of Libra and Scorpio. The image may be viewed on the author's website: https://manchester.academia.edu/HelenRJacobus.

69. One such link is the Swiss Ephemeris: Dieter Koch and Alois Treindl, "Astrodienst Ephemeris Tables from the Year 50 BCE for 50 Years," Astrodienst, https://tinyurl.com/SBL3554b. Note the pre–turn of the era Julian calendar date appears in the historical calendar format (BCE).

70. Neugebauer, "Notes on Ethiopic Astronomy," esp. 50–61; Albani, *Astronomie und Schöpfungsglaube*, 75–83.

contains the points of sunrise in the course of one year ... agreeing with geographical latitudes between Lower Egypt and Greece."[71] He contends:

> Nowhere in this scheme is explicit use made of the zodiacal motions of sun or moon; not even in measurement of arcs in specific units (degrees) is necessary. Thus we are dealing with an extremely primitive level of astronomy which shows no relation to the sophisticated Babylonian astronomy of the Seleucid period nor to its Hellenistic Greek sequel.[72] Of course, no chronological conclusion should be based on such negative evidence for procedures which might be of local Palestinian origin uninfluenced by contemporary scientific achievements elsewhere.[73]

Even in his later work, Neugebauer does not include the Aramaic calendrical texts in his argument. Ethiopic MS 64, if it came from an Aramaic line of transmission, as has been suggested, is a late secondary source. Furthermore, Ethiopic MS 64 describes the changing gate numbers for the moon for each day of the month, which Neugebauer does not demonstrate in the Book of Luminaries, not a numerical scheme for the sunrise throughout the year. It is unclear whether Neugebauer means that the moon rose in those same points on the horizon, corresponding to the sun's gates on the days specified in the manuscript. He does not propose an equivalent point for moonrise in the different zones on the horizon for every day of the month during the year.

More recently, scholars outside Qumran studies have been reexploring the significance of the zodiac in relation to horizon astronomy: Lis Brack-Bernsen and Hermann Hunger suggest that the zodiac "was first perceived as arcs along the horizon over which the constellations rise."[74] Their hypothesis agrees with the Uwe Glessmer's argument that 1 En. 72 is not unrelated to actual science and is based on astronomy found in MUL. APIN and that 1 En. 72 uses zodiacal system based on the horizon.[75]

---

71. Neugebauer, "Notes on Ethiopic Astronomy," 57.

72. Uwe Glessmer, "Horizontal Measuring in the Babylonian Astronomical Compendium MUL.APIN and in the Astronomical Book of 1 En," *Hen* 18 (1996): 250–82; for summaries, see VanderKam, "Book of Luminaries," 378–80.

73. Neugebauer, "Notes on Ethiopic Astronomy," 58.

74. Lis Brack-Bernsen and Hermann Hunger, "The Babylonian Zodiac: Speculations on Its Invention and Significance," *Centaurus* 41 (1999): 280–81.

75. Brack-Bernsen and Hunger, "Babylonian Zodiac," 283–85, figs. 1–2; Glessmer, "Horizontal Measuring."

Greek and Babylonian astronomical literature describe different methods of calculating the time it takes for the signs on the zodiacal circle to rise on the horizon, in the east, and set on the horizon, in the west, known as "rising time schemes."[76] (The zodiac signs between the winter solstice and summer solstice rise quickly, and the signs from the summer solstice to the winter solstice rise slowly.)[77]

There is also a revival of research into the reception and transmission of knowledge in antiquity, involving networks of scribes, astronomers, and diviners in the ancient Near East, ancient historians, traveling scholars, and scribal schools: a substratum in classics, Assyriology, and biblical studies that has been gathering speed and momentum.[78]

---

76. Otto Neugebauer, "The Rising Times in Babylonian Astronomy," *JCS* 7 (1953): 100–102. For a summary of some known sources of the textual transmission of rising time schemes of the zodiac in Babylonian astronomy to the Greek world and Roman Egypt, see, Rochberg, *Heavenly Writing*, 242. For texts on the rising times of the zodiac in cuneiform sources, see Francesca Rochberg, "A Babylonian Rising-Times Scheme in Non-tabular Astronomical Texts," in Burnett et al., *Studies in the History*, 56–94. For new editions of zodiacal rising times and the development of zodiacal calendars in Babylonian astronomy, see John M. Steele, *Rising Time Schemes in Babylonian Astronomy* (Cham, Switzerland: Springer, 2017), esp. 1–3, 9–12, 21–45, 47–104.

77. Evans and Berggren, *Geminos's Introduction to the Phenomena*, 170–74; Manilius, *Astr.* 3.275-442 (in order to calculate the ascendant or horoscope); Aratus, *Phaen.* 559–724; also see Strabo, *Geog.* 1.1.21. For ancient literature connecting the visible position in the heavens of the constellations, the zodiacal signs, including their risings in relation to the calendar, and mythology, see Ovid, *Fasti*. First-century Greek historian Diodorus Siculus discusses Babylonian astrology in relation to the rising and setting of 30 stars every 10 days (compare the Egyptian star clocks), saying that they pass messages to each other and that 12 are each assigned a month and a zodiacal sign (*Bib. hist.* 2.30.6-7). On 30 stars in Babylonian astronomical literature, see Wayne Horowitz and Joachim Oelsner, "The 30 Star-Catalogue HS 1897 and the Late Parallel BM 55502," *AfO* 44/45 (1997–1998): 176–85.

78. For example, Johannes Haubold, *Greece and Mesopotamia: Dialogues in Literature* (Cambridge: Cambridge University Press, 2013); Eleanor Robson, "The Production and Dissemination of Scholarly Knowledge," in *The Oxford Handbook of Cuneiform Culture*, ed. Karen Radner and Eleanor Robson (Oxford: Oxford University Press, 2011), 557–76; Johannes Haubold et al., eds., *The World of Berossos: Proceedings of the Fourth International Collquium on "The Ancient Near East Between Classical and Ancient Oriental Traditions," Hatfield College, Durham 7th to 9th July 2010* (Wiesbaden: Harrassowitz, 2013); Helen R. Jacobus, "Flood Calendars and Birds of the Ark in the Dead Sea Scrolls (4Q252 and 4Q254a), Septuagint, and Ancient Near East

David Pingree states that 4QZodiac Calendar "was not nonsensical,"[79] a statement that, although minimal in its evaluation of the text, may support our hypothesis that, contra Neugebauer, early Jewish astronomer-astrologers were not "uninfluenced by contemporary scientific achievements elsewhere" and that the Aramaic calendrical scrolls do show a relationship to the "sophisticated Babylonian astronomy of the Seleucid period" and "its Hellenistic Greek sequel." While direct contact may be doubted, there is strong evidence of a culture of knowledge and educational transmission within the region. The proposition that local Palestinian scholars worked in intellectual isolation may now be regarded as unlikely and outdated.

## Connections and the "Cryptic A" Calendars

There has been extensive research on the relationships between 4QAstronomical Enoch[a–b] and the Hebrew calendrical scrolls that are synchronized with the 354-day lunar year or that have lunar possible components: 4Q320 (see above), 4QCalendrical Document/Mishmarot B (4Q321; ca. 50–25 BCE), 4QCalendrical Document/Mishmarot C (4Q321a; ca. 100–50 BCE), the liturgical text 4QpapDaily Prayers (4Q503; 100–75 BCE), and the calendrical text written in the so-called Cryptic A script, 4QCryptA Lunisolar calendar (4Q317; date unknown due to the lack of comparative chronology of the script).[80]

Due to their unique terminology and text structure, Talmon suggests that the 354-day lunar year is synchronized with the *mishmarot* in the

---

Texts," in *Opening Heaven's Floodgates: The Genesis Flood Narrative, Its Context, and Reception*, ed. Jason M. Silverman, BI 12 (Piscataway, NJ: Gorgias, 2013), 85–112.

79. In Greenfield and Sokoloff, "318. 4QZodiology and Brontology ar," 271.

80. On 4Q321, see Talmon, Ben-Dov, and Glessmer, *Qumran Cave 4.XVI*, 68. On 4Q321a, see Talmon, Ben-Dov, and Glessmer, *Qumran Cave 4.XVI*, 83. On 4Q503, see Maurice Baillet, "503. Prières quotidiennes," 105–6. On 4Q317, see Milik, *Books of Enoch*, 68–69; Florentino García-Martínez and Eibert J. C. Tigchelaar, "4Q317. (4QAstrCrypt) 4QcryptA Phases of the Moon," in García Martínez and Tigchelaar, *Dead Sea Scrolls Study Edition*, 2:672–77; Martin G. Abegg, "Various Calendrical Texts: 4Q317 (4QcryptA Lunisolar Calendar)," in *Calendrical and Sapiential Texts*, vol. 4 of *The Dead Sea Scrolls Reader*, ed. Donald W. Parry and Emanuel Tov (Leiden: Brill, 2004), 58–72; Stephen J. Pfann, "Cryptic A Calendrical Documents," in Gropp, *Qumran Cave 4.XXVIII*, pls. 52–58; Ben-Dov, *Head of All Years*, 140–46; Jacobus, "Qumran Calendars and the Creation," 87–104.

six-year cycle containing the presumed unknown lunar phases of 4Q320, 4Q321, and 4Q321a.[81] Although the phases have been the subject of extensive enquiry—and a hypothesis that they emanate from Babylonian astronomical traditions[82]—they are more easily explained with reference to the 364-Day Calendar Traditions and the synchronized schematic luni-solar calendar in 4Q317. This text also contains a 364-day year synchronized with what are probably schematic lunar phases: the first day of the waxing crescent moon and first day of the waning full moon, a similar pattern to that in the *mishmarot* texts above. The alleged influence of Babylonian astronomy is not conclusive, since these phases, adduced from Babylonian observational records, have major differences with the above *mishmarot* texts and were among several actual lunar phases used for mantic purposes in Babylonian horoscopes (of unknown relevance to Qumran Hebrew texts).[83]

The text of 4Q317, however, is too fragmentary to establish the exact length of its intended calendrical cycle or the number of years represented by the fragments.[84] The largest surviving fragment, 4Q317 1+1a II, contains only the unusual scribal feature of having two interwoven texts and interlinear data; these are written by more than one hand. In 4Q317 (and the complicated system of scribal corrections in 4Q317 1+1a II), the 364-day calendar is synchronized with the moon by the superimposition of

---

81. Talmon, "320–330, 337, 394 1–2 Introduction," in Talmon, Ben-Dov, and Glessmer, *Qumran Cave 4.XVI*, 13–14, 30–31; Talmon, "4Q320. 4QCalendrical Document/Mishmarot A," in Talmon, Ben-Dov, and Glessmer, *Qumran Cave 4.XVI*, 40–41; Talmon, "4Q321. 4QCalendrical Document/Mishmarot B," in Talmon, Ben-Dov, and Glessmer, *Qumran Cave 4.XVI*, 66–68; Talmon, "4Q321a. 4QCalendrical Document/Mishmarot C," in Talmon, Ben-Dov, and Glessmer, *Qumran Cave 4.XVI*, 82–83.

82. Abegg, "Does Anyone Really Know"; Wise, "Second Thoughts on *dwq*," 98–120; Jonathan Ben-Dov and Wayne Horowitz, "The Babylonian Lunar Three in Calendrical Scrolls from Qumran," *ZA* 95 (2005): 104–20.

83. Helen R. Jacobus, "The Babylonian Lunar Three and the Qumran Calendars of the Priestly Courses: A Response," *RevQ* (2013): 21–51.

84. Jacobus, "Qumran Calendars and the Creation," 81–82 (table 4). The edition and reconstruction demonstrates that the fragment comes from a 29-day month in which Sunday falls on the 8th, 15th, 22nd, and 29th, followed by a month when Sunday falls on the 5th day of month. The conjunction falls on the 8th and the full moon on the 22nd. This would be or months XII to I in year 1 and 4 of the sexennial cycle or year 1 of the triennial cycle.

lunar fractions of fourteenths onto the days of the week and the days of the month.

The scholarly name for this script as "cryptic" contains a layer of meaning that the texts written in this form refer to encoded knowledge for purposes of concealment. In earlier scholarship Glessmer had already questioned the script's value-laden designation as cryptic because, he states, it was not certain that there was an "intention to 'conceal' something."[85] However, it is also argued by Michael Stone that the texts concerned do not differ significantly in their content from related texts that are written in noncryptic Hebrew; he has since agreed that the purpose of the script was to hide this material from unauthorized eyes.[86]

The generalized hypothesis that the Cryptic A script was created for the eyes of the Maskil only within the community is not conclusive, given the range of texts, which includes calendars that are also available to be read in Hebrew script, and also the range of individual occurrences of the letters and mixtures of script types involved.[87] (It might be preferable, therefore, if the script were renamed with a neutral nomenclature that does not make etic assumptions about the context of this written language, whether it was encoded, and which group members had access to it.)

The two texts, 4Q317 and the liturgical text 4Q503, have some striking mathematical similarities, which has been the subject of comparative research in Qumran scholarship. Although they are from different genres,

---

85. Glessmer, "Calendars in the Qumran Scrolls," 2:261.

86. Michael Stone, "Response by Michael Stone and Discussion," in *Aramaica Qumranica: Proceedings of Conference on the Aramaic Texts from Qumran, in Aix-en-Provence, 30 June–2 July 2008*, ed. Katell Berthelot and Daniel Stökl Ben Ezra, STDJ 94 (Leiden: Brill, 2010), 399–401, 428–30. For his later agreement, see Michael Stone, *Secret Groups in Ancient Judaism* (Oxford: Oxford University Press, 2017), 67–72.

87. Stephen J. Pfann, "4Qpap cryptA Midrash Sefer Moshe," in *Qumran Cave 4.XXV: Halakhic Texts*, by Joseph Baumgarten et al., DJD XXXV (Oxford: Clarendon, 1999), 1–24; Pfann, "4Q249a–i. 4Qpap cryptA Serekh ha-'Edah," in Pfann, *Qumran Cave 4.XXVI*, 547–74; Stephen J. Pfann and Menachem Kister: "298. 4QCryptA Words of the Maskil to All Sons of Dawn," in *Qumran Cave 4.XV: Sapiential Texts, Part 1*, by Torlief Elgvin et al., DJD XX (Oxford: Clarendon, 1997), 1–30; for list, see Jacobus, "Qumran Calendars and the Creation," 48–49 nn. 5, 8, 61 n. 27. For recent studies on the script, see Jonathan Ben-Dov, Daniel Stökl Ben Ezra, and Asaf Gayer, "Reconstruction of a Single Copy of the Qumran Cave 4 Cryptic-Script Serekh ha-'Edah," *RevQ* 29 (2017): 21–77; Eshbal Ratzon and Jonathan Ben-Dov, "A Newly Reconstructed Calendrical Scroll from Qumran in Cryptic Script," *JBL* 136 (2017): 905–36.

formats, and styles, both reference the moon's phases in linear progressive proportions and fractions of fourteen parts, reflecting a key component of data in 4Q208–209. Some of the poetic terminology is also similar.[88]

The Judean scholarly tradition of using sevenths and half-sevenths (fourteenths) to describe the daily incremental waxing and decremental waning of the moon dates at least from the period when 4Q208 was produced. There is no reason why these astronomical conventions were not shared among schools of scholars in the late Second Temple period. The content of 4Q317 and 4Q503 includes the tradition of using units of fourteenths, but there is nothing of the Babylonian astral sciences within them. Hence, it is doubtful that 4Q317 should be classified as Enochic, as has been the case.[89]

The long-running theory that the 364-Day Calendar Traditions arose from the ideal Babylonian 360-day year is at the heart of a consensus position that the Hebrew calendars evolved out of a pre-4Q208 calendrical paradigm.[90]

## The Alleged Mesopotamian Background to the 364-Day Calendar Traditions

Taking a separate stream of possible transmission, John Britton found that a 364-day year involving an intercalary month added every three years existed in the early history of Mesopotamian calendars in the early-first millennium BCE astrological-astronomical compendium, in MUL. APIN ii 12, and ii 16. According to the text, ten days were added every twelve months, or equivalently thirty days were added every three years. Thus, assuming a schematic month length of 29.5 days, three years would consist of 1092 days, implying that one year comprised 364 days.[91] After

---

88. For a textual comparison of 4Q503 with 4Q317 and references to other studies, see Jacobus, "Qumran Calendars and the Creation," 72–75.

89. Stephen Pfann, "A Reassessment of Qumran's Calendars," *Hen* 31 (2009): 104–10; Pfann, "The Ancient 'Library' or 'Libraries' of Qumran: The Specter of Cave 1Q," in Crawford and Wassen, *Dead Sea Scrolls at Qumran*, 183, 186–88.

90. Jonathan Ben-Dov, "The Initial Stages of Lunar Theory at Qumran," *JJS* 54 (2003): 125–38; Ben-Dov, *Head of All Years*, 34–40. See response by Jacobus, "Calendars in the Qumran Collection," 227–29. See also James C. VanderKam, "The Book of Enoch and the Qumran Scrolls," in Lim and VanderKam, *Oxford Handbook of the Dead Sea Scrolls*, 275.

91. John P. Britton, "Treatments of Annual Phenomena in Cuneiform Sources,"

the mid-eighth century BCE, it was recognized that this scheme was inaccurate.[92]

Modern scholars have discussed this calendar as possible evidence for the Judean 364-day year.[93] Horowitz argues that not only are 364-day-year lengths contained in MUL.APIN and its Hellenistic period copy, but a 364-day stellar year was implied in the second-century BCE star-list tablet AO 6478.[94] He concludes that "the Mesopotamian 364 day year" was "the ultimate source for the 364 day year found in Apocrypha and Qumran texts."[95] Horowitz's hypotheses were contested by Johannes Koch, who argued that a 360-day year is, in fact, implied in the intercalation schemes in MUL.APIN, and that AO 6478 contains a slightly shorter time, measured in degrees, for the apparent annual circuit of the stars (the latter calculation has been recently supported by John Steele).[96] Sacha Stern describes the hypothesis that a 364-day calendar existed in Mesopotamia as "implausible" and the alleged connection between MUL.APIN, AO 6478, and the 364-day calendar in the book of the Enoch as "far-fetched."[97] However, no textual, historical, or epigraphic evidence

---

in Steele and Imhausen, *Under One Sky*, 23–24; Hermann Hunger and David Pingree, *MUL.APIN: An Astronomical Compendium in Cuneiform*, AfOB 24 (Horn, Austria: Berger & Söhne, 1989); Hunger and Steele, *Babylonian Astronomical Compendium MUL.APIN*.

92. Britton, "Treatments of Annual Phenomena," 25.

93. E.g., Ben-Dov, *Head of All Years*, 35 n. 40.

94. Wayne Horowitz, "Two New Ziqpu-Star Texts and Stellar Circles," *JCS* 46 (1994): esp. 94–96; Wayne Horowitz, *Mesopotamian Cosmic Geography* (Winona Lake, IN: Eisenbrauns, 1998), 168–92.

95. Wayne Horowitz, "The 360 and 360-Day Year in Ancient Mesopotamia," *JANES* 24 (1996): 37.

96. In the subsequent debate between Horowitz and Koch. See Johannes Koch, "AO 6478, MUL APIN und das 364-Tage Jahr," *NABU* (1996): 97–99 (no. 111); Koch, "Kannte man in Mesopotamien das 364 Tage-Jahr wirklich seit dem 7. Jahrhundert v. Chr.?," *NABU* (1997): 109–12 (no. 119); Wayne Horowitz, "The 364-Day Year in Mesopotamia Again," *NABU* (1998): 49–51 (no. 49); Koch, "Ein für allemal: Das antike Mesopotamien kannte kein 364 Tage-Jahr," *NABU* (1998): 112–14 (no. 121); Steele, *Rising Time Schemes*, 15. The discussion is summarized in VanderKam, "Book of the Luminaries," 381. On the methods of intercalation that arguably imply a 364-day year in MUL.APIN ii 12, 16, and AO 6478, see Hunger and Pingree, *MUL.APIN*, 139–40, 143, 153, 194.

97. Sacha Stern, *Calendars in Antiquity: Empires, States, and Societies* (Oxford: Oxford University Press, 2012), 198–99.

has been identified to support Stern's own idea that the 364-day Judean calendar was derived originally from the Egyptian calendar and received in Judea during its rule by the Ptolemies.[98]

Arguable support for a 364-day year may exist in 4Q209 26, 2–3, which is very fragmentary and parallel to 1 En. 79.4–5: the archangel Uriel explains to Enoch that the lunar year is divided into two halves of twenty-five weeks and two days, and that it falls behind the course of the sun. In the Ethiopic text, the moon's decrease from the path of the sun (Aramaic, 4Q209 26, 3, מחסר מן דבר שמשא, from חסר, meaning "lack") is five days in each half-year—hence the solar year would be ten days more than the 354-day lunar year, a precise timescale that is not extant in the parallel, broken Aramaic fragment.[99]

Aside from whether the time length of "five days" had existed in this Aramaic text, another problem is that 4Q209 26, 3 // 1 En. 79.4–5 is a separate genre from the formulaic calendar of 4Q208–209. Therefore, if more fragments were to be found that showed that 1 En. 79.4–5 faithfully followed an Aramaic *Vorlage*, it would still remain an open question as to whether 4Q208–209 contained a 364-day solar schematic year, or, probably being derived from Babylonian astral divinatory texts, a 360-day year.

Jaubert's findings fit in well with a hypothesis that biblical writers had access to MUL.APIN and used its three-year cycle in their literature, possibly during the exilic period. The problem, however, is that it is impossible to prove a connection. Textual criticism of the layers of the Bible with the passages highlighted by Jaubert in support of her theory remains to be done. Yet, given that the 364-Day Calendar Traditions are not sectarian, and therefore need not be only written in Hebrew, if they came by way of a Mesopotamian route we should expect to find some 364-Day Calendar Traditions in Aramaic, yet none has surfaced.

---

98. Stern, *Calendars in Antiquity*, 200–203.

99. VanderKam, "Book of Luminaries," 516–20; Otto Neugebauer, *The "Astronomical" Chapters of the Ethiopic Book of Enoch (72 to 82)*, (Copenhagen: Munksgaard, 1981), 3–42, esp. 30; Drawnel, *Aramaic Astronomical Book*, 194–97, 388–89, Jacobus, *Zodiac Calendars*, 324–32. On the term meaning "lack," see Cook, *Qumran Aramaic Dictionary*, 88–89, "It is shortened from the sun's course" (מחסר, passive participle).

## The Translation Theory

To support the hypothesis that the 364-Day Calendar Traditions hark back to Mesopotamia, it is claimed by some scholars that 4Q317 was translated into the Cryptic A script (which is Hebrew with different letters) from Aramaic.[100] This idea requires some textual and sociological support. If it is likely that Hebrew was the official language of the sect, a common scholarly view, rather than Aramaic (in which they would have been fluent, or it was their primary spoken language),[101] then it is unclear why one of these surviving related texts is written in the common Hebrew script (4Q503), which is not a secret language, and one is written in the uncommon Hebrew script, Cryptic A (4Q317), which is supposedly esoteric. Neither is Aramaic a secret language, so if the alleged concealed knowledge pertaining to lunar fractions in half-sevenths/fourteenths that is common to 4Q208–209 and 4Q317 and 4Q503 were to be translated into the official sectarian tongue, Hebrew, in a coded form, then by the same token, 4Q208 should have been translated into the Cryptic A script from Aramaic at a later date. Instead, the calendar of 4Q209, a closely related text to 4Q208 was copied as part of Enoch's cosmological journey in the manuscript of 4Q209 in the colloquial language, Aramaic.

Rather than a translation from Aramaic to Cryptic A, for which there is no evidence, it is more likely that these astronomical-calendrical texts have their own independent forms and parallels with other texts, as well as noticeable marked divergencies that reflect intracultural scribal practices between schools of scholars. The original background of the Hebrew and Cryptic A 364-Day Calendar Traditions is arguably more likely to be older than "Qumranic." The inconsistent hypotheses regarding the development

---

100. Ben-Dov, "Scientific Writings in Aramaic and Hebrew at Qumran: Translation and Concealment," in Berthelot and Stökl Ben Ezra, *Aramaica Qumranica*, 393; see also Ben-Dov, "Initial Stages of Lunar Theory," 133; but compare Ben-Dov in *Head of All Years*, in which he hypothesizes that "the author of 4Q317 elected to write in Hebrew" (145).

101. Studies on Hebrew-Aramaic bilingualism in the late Second Temple period include James Barr, "Hebrew, Aramaic and Greek in the Hellenistic Age," in *The Hellenistic Age*, vol. 2 of *The Cambridge History of Judaism*, ed. William David Davies and Louis Finkelstein (Cambridge: Cambridge University Press, 1989), 82–83; Steven Fassberg, "Which Semitic Languages Did Jesus and Other Contemporary Jews Speak?," *CBQ* 74 (2012): 263–80.

of the Aramaic and the Hebrew/cryptic script calendars have blurred the intellectual identities of the different groups of scholars involved.

In conclusion, the major difference between the Hebrew and the Aramaic texts is that the Aramaic calendars are dynamic, realistic constructs that are not modeled on the Sabbath and which partly originated in Seleucid era–Babylonian magical and divinatory texts. In the case of 4Q208–209, the calendar can probably trace its roots in Greek calendrical science (which uses 29- and 30-day months alternately), late Babylonian/Seleucid calendrical science, and early Jewish astronomical concepts that use fractions in half-sevenths.

Hence, the septenary lunar fractions were absorbed into the Aramaic calendars that had their roots in Babylonian astral divination through the schools that were producing the Hebrew 364-Day Calendar Traditions. This suggested paradigm reverses the scholarly view that the Hebrew 364-Day Calendar Traditions evolved from the Aramaic 360-day calendars via a hypothetical, original Aramaic version of 4Q317. It also restores the history of the 364-Day Calendar Traditions to an earlier period, predating 4Q208, thereby reviving the theory of the importance in the early Second Temple period of the number seven (not only to the era of Qumran and possible related communities). The Hebrew 364-Day Calendar Traditions without lunar components also reflect other Judean traditions, which have been variously classified into a range of categories and subcategories by different scholars.

The revised and renewed methodology advocates that there were separate calendars for different purposes that were connected to liturgical service and praying at the same time as the angels. It challenges the unsatisfactory scholarly theory that the 364-Day Calendar Traditions were a perfect, divine system that were simply ideal and never practiced, while also apparently opposed to the working, luni-solar calendar (that, this paper argues, also involved the stars). The consensus hypothesis fails to explain the existence of two types of calendars at Qumran, Hebrew and Aramaic, except by forcing the Aramaic Astronomical Book into an unproven 364-Day Calendar Traditions triennial cycle and ditching 4Q318. This does not resolve the problem but creates further unanswered questions.

By challenging some central tenets of current Qumran calendar scholarship, we are ultimately questioning the thesis that the community that preserved these manuscripts was a homogenous group who only had one calendrical tradition in a single linear form chronologically. It is hoped that this essay has brought some of the central paradoxes, problems, and contradictions in the present consensus into a more open and discursive arena.

Bibliography

Abegg, Martin G. "The Calendar at Qumran." Pages 145–71 in *Theory of Israel*. Vol. 1 of *Judaism in Late Antiquity, Part Five: The Judaism of Qumran; A Systemic Reading of the Dead Sea Scrolls*. Edited by Alan J. Avery-Peck, Jacob Neusner, and Bruce Chilton. HOS 1/56. Leiden: Brill, 2001.

———. "Does Anyone Really Know What Time It Is? A Re-examination of 4Q503 in Light of 4Q317." Pages 396–406 in *Technological Innovations, New Texts, and Reformulated Issues: The Provo International Conference on the Dead Sea Scrolls*. Edited by Donald W. Parry and Eugene Ulrich. STDJ 30. Leiden: Brill, 1999.

———. "Various Calendrical Texts: 4Q317 (4QcryptA Lunisolar Calendar)." Pages 58–72 in *Calendrical and Sapiential Texts*. Vol. 4 of *The Dead Sea Scrolls Reader*. Edited by Donald W. Parry and Emanuel Tov. Leiden: Brill, 2004.

Albani, Matthias. *Astronomie und Schöpfungsglaube: Untersuchungen zum astronomischen Henochbuch*. WMANT 68. Neukirchen-Vluyn: Neukirchener, 1994.

———. "Der Zodiakos in 4Q318 und die Henoch-Astronomie." *MB* 7 (1993): 3–42.

———. "Horoscopes in the Qumran Scrolls." Pages 279–330 in *The Dead Sea Scrolls after Fifty Years: A Comprehensive Assessment*. Vol. 2. Edited by Peter W. Flint and James C. VanderKam. Leiden: Brill, 1999.

Alexander, Philip, and Geza Vermes. *Qumran Cave 4.XIX: Serekh Ha-Yaḥad*. DJD XXVI. Oxford: Clarendon, 1998.

Atwill, Joseph, and Steve Braunheim. "Redating the Radiocarbon Dating of the Dead Sea Scrolls." *DSD* 7 (2004): 143–57.

Baillet, Maurice. "17. Fragment de calendrier." Pages 132–33 in *Les "Petites Grottes" de Qumrân*. By Maurice Baillet, Józef T. Milik, and Roland de Vaux. DJD III. Oxford: Clarendon, 1962.

———. "503. Prières quotidiennes." Pages 105–36 in *Qumrân Grotte 4.III: 4Q482–4Q520*. Edited by Maurice Baillet. DJD VII. Oxford: Clarendon, 1982.

Barr, James. "Hebrew, Aramaic and Greek in the Hellenistic Age." Pages 79–114 in *The Hellenistic Age*. Vol. 2 of *The Cambridge History of Juda-*

*ism*. Edited by William David Davies and Louis Finkelstein. Cambridge: Cambridge University Press, 1989.

Barthélemy, Dominique. "Notes en marge de publications récentes sur les manuscrits de Qumrân." *RB* 59 (1952): 199–203.

Baumgarten, Joseph M. "4Q503 (Daily Prayers) and the Lunar Calendar." *RevQ* 12 (1986): 399–407.

Beckwith, Roger T. *Calendar, Chronology and Worship*. AGJU 61. Leiden: Brill, 2005.

———. "The Modern Attempt to Reconcile the Qumran Calendar with the True Solar Year." *RevQ* 7 (1969–1971): 379–96.

Ben-Dov, Jonathan. *Head of All Years: Astronomy and Calendars at Qumran in their Ancient Context*. STDJ 78. Leiden: Brill, 2008.

———. "The Initial Stages of Lunar Theory at Qumran." *JJS* 54 (2003): 125–38.

Ben-Dov, Jonathan, and Wayne Horowitz. "The Babylonian Lunar Three in Calendrical Scrolls from Qumran." *ZA* 95 (2005): 104–20.

Ben-Dov, Jonathan, Daniel Stökl Ben Ezra, and Asaf Gayer. "Reconstruction of a Single Copy of the Qumran Cave 4 Cryptic-Script Serekh ha-ʿEdah." *RevQ* 29 (2017): 21–77.

Bernstein, Moshe J. "4Q252: From Re-written Bible to Biblical Commentary." *JJS* 45 (1994): 1–27.

Brack-Bernsen, Lis. "The 360-Day Year in Mesopotamia." Pages 83–100 in *Calendars and Years: Astronomy and Time in the Ancient Near East*. Edited by John M. Steele. Oxford: Oxbow, 2007.

Brack-Bernsen, Lis, and Hermann Hunger. "The Babylonian Zodiac: Speculations on Its Invention and Significance." *Centaurus* 41 (1999): 280–92.

Brack-Bernsen, Lis, and John M. Steele. "Babylonian Mathemagics: Two Astronomical-Astrological Texts." Pages 95–121 in *Studies in the History of Exact Sciences in Honour of David Pingree*. Edited by Charles Burnett, Jan P. Hogendijk, Kim Plofker, and Michio Yano. Leiden: Brill, 2004.

Britton, John P. "Calendars, Intercalation and Year-Lengths." Pages 115–32 in *Calendars and Years: Astronomy and Time in the Ancient Near East*. Edited by John M. Steele. Oxford: Oxbow, 2007.

———. "Studies in Babylonian Lunar Theory: Part 3. The Introduction of the Uniform Zodiac." *AHES* 64 (2010): 617–63.

———. "Treatments of Annual Phenomena in Cuneiform Sources." Pages 21–78 in *Under One Sky: Astronomy and Mathematics in the Ancient*

*Near East*. Edited by John M. Steele and Annette Imhausen. AOAT 297. Münster: Ugarit-Verlag, 2002.

Britton, John, and Christopher Walker. "Astronomy and Astrology in Mesopotamia." Pages 42–67 in *Astronomy before the Telescope*. Edited by Christopher Walker. New York: Saint Martin's, 1996.

Brooke, George J. "252. 4QCommentary on Genesis A." Pages 185–207 in *Qumran Cave 4.XVII: Parabiblical Texts, Part 3*. By George J. Brooke et al. DJD XXII. Oxford: Clarendon, 1996.

———. "254a. 4QCommentary on Genesis D." Pages 233–36 in *Qumran Cave 4.XVII: Parabiblical Texts, Part 3*. By George J. Brooke et al. DJD XXII. Oxford: Clarendon, 1996.

———. "The Genre of 4Q252: From Poetry to Pesher." *DSD* 1 (1994): 160–79.

———. "The Thematic Content of 4Q252." *JQR* 85 (1994): 33–59.

Brown, David. *Mesopotamian Planetary Astronomy-Astrology*. CM 18. Groningen: Styx, 2000.

Brownlee, William. 'The Significance of David's Compositions." *RevQ* 5 (1966): 569–74.

Callaway, Philip. "The 364-Day Calendar Traditions at Qumran." Pages 19–29 in *Mogilani 1989: Papers on the Dead Sea Scrolls Offered in Memory of Jean Carmignac; Part I: General Research on the Dead Sea Scrolls, Qumran, and the New Testament; The Present State of Qumranology*. Edited by Zdzislaw Jan Kapera. Krakow: Enigma, 1993.

Carmi, Israel. "Radiocarbon Dating of the Dead Sea Scrolls." Pages 881–88 in *The Dead Sea Scrolls: Fifty Years after Their Discovery*. Edited by Lawrence H. Schiffman, Emanuel Tov, and James C. VanderKam. Jerusalem: Israel Exploration Society, 2000.

Daise, Michael A. "The *Temple Scroll* Calendar: Revisiting the Feast of Oil in the Calendrical Documents/*Mišmarot*." Pages 329–38 in *With Wisdom as a Robe: Qumran and Other Jewish Studies in Honour of Ida Fröhlich*. Edited by Károly Dániel Dobos and Miklos Köszeghy. Sheffield: Sheffield Academic, 2009.

Davies, Philip. R. "Calendrical Change and Qumran Origins: An Assessment of VanderKam's Theory." *CBQ* 45 (1983): 80–89.

Doudna, Greg. "Dating the Scrolls on the Basis of Radiocarbon Analysis." Pages 438–71 in *The Dead Sea Scrolls after Fifty Years*. Vol. 1. Edited by Peter W. Flint and James C. VanderKam. Leiden: Brill, 1998.

Drawnel, Henryk. *The Aramaic Astronomical Book (4Q208–4Q211) from Qumran: Text, Translation, and Commentary*. Oxford: Clarendon, 2011.

Englund, Robert K. "Administrative Timekeeping in Mesopotamia." *JESHO* 31 (1988): 121–85.

Evans, James, and J. Lennart Berggren. *Geminos's Introduction to the Phenomena: A Translation and Study of a Hellenistic Survey of Astronomy*. Princeton: Princeton University Press, 2006.

Fassberg, Steven. "Which Semitic Languages Did Jesus and Other Contemporary Jews Speak?" *CBQ* 74 (2012): 263–80.

Fitzmyer, Joseph. A. "332. 4QHistorical Text D." Pages 281–86 in *Qumran Cave 4.XXVI: Cryptic Texts*. By Stephen J. Pfann. *Miscellanea, Part 1*. By Philip S. Alexander et al. DJD XXXVI. Oxford: Clarendon, 2000.

García Martínez, Florentino, and Eibert J. C. Tigchelaar. "4Q317. (4QAstrCrypt) 4QcryptA Phases of the Moon." Pages 672–77 in *The Dead Sea Scrolls Study Edition*. Vol. 2. Leiden: Brill, 1998.

———. *The Dead Sea Scrolls Study Edition*. 2 vols. Leiden: Brill, 1997–1998.

Geller, Markham J. *Melothesia in Mesopotamia: Medicine, Magic and Astrology in the Ancient Near East*. Boston: de Gruyter, 2014.

———. "New Documents from the Dead Sea: Babylonian Science in Aramaic." Pages 224–29 in *Boundaries of the Ancient Near Eastern World: A Tribute to Cyrus Gordon*. Edited by Meir Lubetski. JSOTSup 273. Sheffield: Sheffield Academic, 1998.

Glessmer, Uwe. "364-Tage Kalender und die Sabbatstruktur seiner Schaltungen in ihrer Bedeutung für den Kult." Pages 379–98 in *Ernten, was man sät: Festschrift für Klaus Koch zu seinem 65. Geburstag*. Edited by Dwight R. Daniels, Uwe Glessmer, and Martin Rösel. Neukirchen-Vluyn: Neukirchener Verlag, 1991.

———. "Calendars in the Qumran Scrolls." Pages 213–78 in *The Dead Sea Scrolls after Fifty Years: A Comprehensive Assessment*. Vol. 2. Edited by Peter W. Flint and James C. VanderKam. Leiden: Brill, 1999.

———. "Horizontal Measuring in the Babylonian Astronomical Compendium MUL.APIN and in the Astronomical Book of 1 En." *Hen* 18 (1996): 250–82.

———. "Investigation of the Otot-text (4Q319) and Questions about Methodology." Pages 429–40 in *Methods of Investigation of the Dead Sea Scrolls and the Khirbet Qumran Site: Present Realities and Future Prospects*. ANYAS 722. Edited by Michael O. Wise, Norman Golb, John J. Collins, and Dennis G. Pardee. New York: New York Academy of Science, 1994.

———. "The Otot Texts (4Q319) and the Problem of Intercalations in the Context of the 364-Day Calendar." Pages 125–64 in *Qumranstu-*

*dien: Vorträge und Beiträge der Teilnehmer des Qumranseminars auf dem internationalen Treffen der Society of Biblical Literature, Münster, 25–26 Juli 1993*. Edited by Heinz-Josef Fabry, Armin Lange, and Hermann Lichtenberger. Göttingen: Vandenhoeck & Ruprecht, 1996.

Grébaut, Sylvain. "Table des levers de la lune pour chaque mois de l'année." *RevOrChr* 21 (1918–1919): 422–28.

———. "Variations de la durée des jours et des nuits pour chaque mois de l'année." *RevOrChr* 21 (1918–1919): 429–32.

Greenfield, Jonas, and Michael Sokoloff, with David Pingree and Ada Yardeni. "318. 4QZodiology and Brontology ar." Pages 259–74 in *Qumran Cave 4.XXVI: Cryptic Texts*. By Stephen J. Pfann. *Miscellanea, Part 1*. By Philip S. Alexander et al. DJD XXXVI. Oxford: Clarendon, 2000.

Hannah, Robert. *Time in Antiquity*. London: Routledge, 2009.

Haubold, Johannes. *Greece and Mesopotamia: Dialogues in Literature*. Cambridge: Cambridge University Press, 2013.

Haubold, Johannes, Giovanni B. Lanfranchi, Robert Rollinger, and John M. Steele, eds. *The World of Berossos: Proceedings of the Fourth International Collquium on "The Ancient Near East between Classical and Ancient Oriental Traditions," Hatfield College, Durham 7th to 9th July 2010*. Wiesbaden: Harrassowitz, 2013.

Herr, Moshe D. "The Calendar." Pages 834–64 in *The Jewish People in the First Century*. Vol. 2. Edited by Shmuel Safrai, David Flusser, Menahem Stern, and Willem Cornelis van Unnik. Philadelphia: Fortress, 1976.

Horowitz, Wayne. "The 360 and 360-Day Year in Ancient Mesopotamia." *JANES* 24 (1996): 35–44.

———. "The 364-Day Year in Mesopotamia Again." *NABU* (1998): 49–51.

———. *Mesopotamian Cosmic Geography*. Winona Lake, IN: Eisenbrauns, 1998.

———. "Two New Ziqpu-Star Texts and Stellar Circles." *JCS* 46 (1994): 89–98.

Horowitz, Wayne, and Joachim Oelsner. "The 30 Star-Catalogue HS 1897 and the Late Parallel BM 55502." *AfO* 44/45 (1997–1998): 176–85.

Hunger, Hermann, and David Pingree. *MUL.APIN: An Astronomical Compendium in Cuneiform*. AfOB 24. Horn, Austria: Berger & Söhne, 1989.

Hunger, Hermann, and John Steele. *The Babylonian Astronomical Compendium MUL.APIN*. SWAMW 1. London: Routledge, 2018.

Jacobus, Helen R. "4Q318: A Jewish Zodiac Calendar at Qumran?" Pages 365–95 in *The Dead Sea Scrolls: Texts and Contexts*. Edited by Charlotte Hempel. STDJ 90. Leiden: Brill, 2010.

———. "4QZodiac Calendar in Relation to Babylonian Horoscopes." Pages 217–44 in *Astrology in Time and Place: Cross-cultural Questions in the History of Astrology*. Edited by Nicholas Campion and Dorian Gieseler Greenbaum. Newcastle: Cambridge Scholars, 2015.

———. "Astral Divination in the Dead Sea Scrolls." Pages 539–50 in *Hellenistic Astronomy: The Science in Its Contexts*. Edited by Alan C. Bowen and Francesca Rochberg. Leiden: Brill, 2020.

———. "The Babylonian Lunar Three and the Qumran Calendars of the Priestly Courses: A Response." *RevQ* 26 (2013): 21–51.

———. "Calendars." Pages 435–48 in *The T&T Clark Companion to the Dead Sea Scrolls*. Edited by George J. Brooke and Charlotte Hempel. BC. London: Bloomsbury, 2018.

———. "Calendars in the Qumran Collection." Pages 217–43 in *The Dead Sea Scrolls at Qumran and the Concept of a Library*. Edited by Sidnie White Crawford and Cecilia Wassen. STDJ 116. Leiden: Brill, 2015.

———. "Flood Calendars and the Birds of the Ark in the Dead Sea Scrolls (4Q252 and 4Q254a), Septuagint, and Ancient Near East Texts." Pages 85–112 in *Opening Heaven's Floodgates: The Genesis Flood Narrative, Its Context, and Reception*. Edited by Jason M. Silverman. BI 12. Piscataway, NJ: Gorgias, 2013.

———. "Qumran Calendars and the Creation: A Study of 4QcrypticA Lunisolar Calendar (4Q317)." *JAJ* 4 (2013): 48–104.

———. "Reconstructing the Calendar of 4Q208–4Q209 (and a Response to Eshbal Ratzon)." *RevQ* 31 (2019): 251–73.

———. *Zodiac Calendars in the Dead Sea Scrolls and Their Reception: Ancient Astronomy and Astrology in Early Judaism*. IJS 14. Leiden: Brill, 2014.

Jaubert, Annie. *The Date of the Last Supper*. Translated by Isaac Rafferty. Staten Island, NY: Alba House, 1965.

———. "Le calendrier des Jubilés et de la secte de Qumrân. Ses origines bibliques." *VT* 3 (1953): 250–64.

———. "Le calendrier des Jubilés et les jours liturgiques de la semaine." *VT* 7 (1957): 35–61.

Jull, A. J. Timothy, Douglas J. Donahue, Magen Broshi, and Emanuel Tov. "Radiocarbon Dating of Scrolls and Linen Fragments from the Judean Desert." *Radiocarbon* 37 (1995): 11–19.

Kerr, Apama. "A Handy Guide to Measuring the Sky." timeanddate.com. https://tinyurl.com/SBL3554a.

Koch, Dieter, and Alois Treindl. "Astrodienst Ephemeris Tables from the Year 50 BCE for 50 Years." Astrodienst. https://tinyurl.com/SBL3554b.

Koch, Johannes. "AO 6478, MUL APIN und das 364-Tage Jahr." *NABU* (1996): 97–99.

———. "Ein für allemal: Das antike Mesopotamien kannte kein 364 Tage-Jah." *NABU* (1998): 112–14.

———. "Kannte man in Mesopotamien das 364 Tage-Jahr wirklich seit dem 7. Jahrhundert v. Chr.?" *NABU* (1997): 109–12.

Koch-Westenholz, Ulla. *Mesopotamian Astrology: An Introduction to Babylonian and Assyrian Celestial Divination*. CNIP 19. Copenhagen: Museum Tusculanum, 1995.

Labat, René. *Un calendrier babylonien des travaux des signes et des mois: Séries iqqur îpuš*. Paris: Librairie Honoré Champion, 1965.

Lange, Armin, and Ulrike Mittmann-Richert. "Annotated List of the Texts of the Judaean Desert Classified by Content and Genre." Pages 115–64 in *The Texts in the Judaean Desert: Indices and an Introduction to the Discoveries in the Judean Desert Series*. By Emanuel Tov. DJD XXXIX. Oxford: Clarendon, 2002.

Lim, Timothy H. "The Chronology of the Flood Story in a Qumran Text (4Q252)." *JJS* 43 (1992): 288–98.

Magness, Jodi. *The Archaeology of Qumran and the Dead Sea Scrolls*. SDSSRL. Grand Rapids: Eerdmans, 2002.

Metso, Sarianna. *The Textual Development of the Qumran Community Rule*. STDJ 21. Leiden: Brill, 1997.

Meyers, Eric. M. "Khirbet Qumran and Its Environs." Pages 21–45 in *The Oxford Handbook of The Dead Sea Scrolls*. Edited by Timothy H. Lim and John J. Collins. Oxford: Oxford University Press, 2010.

Milik, Józef T. *The Books of Enoch: Aramaic Fragments of Qumrân Cave 4*. Oxford: Clarendon, 1976.

———. *Ten Years of Discovery in the Wilderness of Judea*. Translated by John Strugnell. London: SCM, 1959.

Monroe, M. Willis. "The Micro-Zodiac in Babylon and Uruk: Seleucid Zodiacal Astrology." Pages 119–38 in *The Circulation of Astronomical Knowledge in the Ancient World*. Edited by John M. Steele. TAC 6. Leiden: Brill, 2016.

Neugebauer, Otto. "The Alleged Babylonian Discovery of the Precession of the Equinoxes." *JAOS* 70 (1950): 1–8.

———. *The "Astronomical" Chapters of the Ethiopic Book of Enoch (72 to 82)*. Copenhagen: Munksgaard, 1981.

———. "The Rising Times in Babylonian Astronomy." *JCS* 7 (1953): 100–102.

———. "Notes on Ethiopic Astronomy." *Orientalia* n.s. 33 (1964): 49–71.

Newsom, Carol. "1K. *MasShirot 'Olat ha-Shabbat*." Pages 239–52 in *Qumran Cave 4.VI: Poetical and Liturgical Texts, Part 1*. DJD XXI. By Esther Eshel et al. Oxford: Clarendon, 1998.

———. "4Q400–4Q407, Mas1K, 4Q*Shirot 'Olat ha-Shabbat*$^{a-h}$." Pages 173–401 in *Qumran Cave 4.VI: Poetical and Liturgical Texts, Part 1*. DJD XXI. By Esther Eshel et al. Oxford: Clarendon, 1998.

———. *Angelic Liturgy: Songs of the Sabbath Sacrifice*. Vol. 4B of *The Dead Sea Scrolls: Hebrew, Aramaic and Greek Texts with English Translations*. Edited by James H. Charlesworth and Carol A. Newsom. Tübingen: Mohr Siebeck, 1999.

———. "Sectually Explicit: Literature from Qumran." Pages 167–87 in *The Hebrew Bible and Its Interpreter*. Edited by William H. Propp, Baruch Halpern, and David Noel Freedman. Winona Lake, IN: Eisenbrauns, 1990.

———. *Songs of the Sabbath Sacrifice: A Critical Edition*. Atlanta: Scholars Press, 1985.

Oppenheim, A. Leo. "A Babylonian Diviner's Manual." *JNES* 33 (1974): 197–220.

Pfann, Stephen J. "4Q249a–i. 4Qpap cryptA Serekh ha-'Edah." Pages 547–74 in *Qumran Cave 4.XXVI: Cryptic Texts*. By Stephen J. Pfann et al. *Miscellanea, Part 1*. By Philip S. Alexander et al. DJD XXXVI. Oxford: Clarendon, 2000.

———. "4Qpap cryptA Midrash Sefer Moshe." Pages 1–24 in *Qumran Cave 4.XXV: Halakhic Texts*. By Joseph M. Baumgarten et al. DJD XXXV. Oxford: Clarendon, 1999.

———. "The Ancient 'Library' or 'Libraries' of Qumran: The Specter of Cave 1Q." Pages 168–216 in *The Dead Sea Scrolls at Qumran and the Concept of a Library*. Edited by Sidnie White Crawford and Cecilia Wassen. STDJ 116. Leiden: Brill, 2015.

———. "Cryptic A Calendrical Documents." Plates 52–58 in *Qumran Cave 4.XXVIII: Wadi Daliyeh II; The Samaria Papyri for Wadi Daliyeh*. By Douglas M. Gropp. *Qumran Cave 4.XXVIII: Miscellanea, Part 2*. By Eileen Schuller et al. DJD XXVIII. Oxford: Clarendon, 2001.

———. "A Reassessment of Qumran's Calendars." *Hen* 31 (2009): 104–10.
Pfann, Stephen J., and Menachem Kister. "298. 4QCryptA Words of the Maskil to All Sons of Dawn." Pages 1–30 in *Qumran Cave 4.XV: Sapiential Texts, Part 1*. By Torlief Elgvin et al. DJD XX. Oxford: Clarendon, 1997.
Plicht, Johannes van der. "Radiocarbon Dating and the Dead Sea Scrolls: A Comment on 'Redating.'" *DSD* 14 (2007): 77–89.
Pritchett, William Kendrick, and Otto Neugebauer. *The Calendars of Athens*. Cambridge: Harvard University Press, 1947.
Rasmussen, Kaare, Johannes van der Plicht, Gregory L. Doudna, Frank Moore Cross, and John Strugnell. "Reply to Israel Carmi (2002): Are the $^{14}$C Dates of the Dead Sea Scrolls Affected by Castor Oil Contamination?" *Radiocarbon* 45 (2003): 497–99.
Ratzon, Eshbal. "The First Jewish Astronomers: Lunar Theory and the Reconstruction of a Dead Sea Scroll." *SciCon* 30 (2017): 130–39.
Ratzon, Eshbal, and Jonathan Ben-Dov. "A Newly Reconstructed Calendrical Scroll from Qumran in Cryptic Script." *JBL* 136 (2017): 905–36.
Reiner, Erica. *Astral Magic in Babylonia*. TAPS 85.4. Philadelphia: American Philosophical Society, 1995.
Robson, Eleanor. "The Production and Dissemination of Scholarly Knowledge." Pages 557–76 in *The Oxford Handbook of Cuneiform Culture*. Edited by Karen Radner and Eleanor Robson. Oxford: Oxford University Press, 2011.
Rochberg-Halton, Francesca. *Babylonian Horoscopes*. TAPS 88.1. Philadelphia: American Philosophical Society, 1998.
———. "A Babylonian Rising-Times Scheme in Non-Tabular Astronomical Texts." Pages 56–94 in *Studies in the History of the Exact Sciences in Honour of David Pingree*. Edited by Charles Burnett, Jan P. Hogendijk, Kim Plofker, and Michio Yano. Leiden: Brill, 2004.
———. "Calendars: Ancient Near East." *ABD* 1:810–14.
———. *The Heavenly Writing: Divination, Horoscopy, and Astronomy in Mesopotamian Culture*. Cambridge: Cambridge University Press, 2004.
Sacchi, Paolo. *Jewish Apocalyptic and Its History*. JSPSup 20. Sheffield: Sheffield Academic, 1996.
Sachs, Abraham J. "Babylonian Horoscopes." *JCS* 6 (1952): 49–75.
Sanders, James A. *The Psalms Scroll of Qumrân Cave 11 (11QPsa)*. DJD IV. Oxford: Clarendon, 1965.

Saulnier, Stéphane. *Calendrical Variations in Second Temple Judaism: New Perspectives on the "Date of the Last Supper" Debate*. JSJSup 159. Leiden: Brill, 2012.

Schmidt, Francis. "Le Calendrier Liturgique des Prières Quotidiennes (4Q503)." Pages 55–88 in *Le Temps et les Temps: Dans les littératures juives et chrétiennes au tourant de notre ère*. Edited by Christian Grappe and Jean-Claude Ingelaere. JSJSup 112. Leiden: Brill, 2006.

Scurlock, JoAnn. "Sorcery in the Stars: STT 300, BRM 19–20 and the Mandaic Book of the Zodiac." *AfO* 51 (2005–2006): 125–46.

Segal, Judah B. "Intercalation and the Hebrew Calendar." *VT* 7 (1957): 250–307.

Steele, John M. "A Late Babylonian Compendium of Calendrical and Stellar Astrology." *JCS* 67 (2015): 187–215.

———. "The Length of the Month in Mesopotamian Calendars of the First Millennium BC." Pages 133–48 in *Calendars and Years: Astronomy and Time in the Ancient Near East*. Edited by John M. Steele. Oxford: Oxbow, 2007.

———. *Rising Time Schemes in Babylonian Astronomy*. Cham, Switzerland: Springer, 2017.

Stern, Sacha. *Calendar and Community: A History of the Jewish Calendar Second Century BCE–Tenth Century CE*. Oxford: Oxford University Press, 2001.

———. *Calendars in Antiquity: Empires, States, and Societies*. Oxford: Oxford University Press, 2012.

———. "The Sectarian Calendar of Qumran." Pages 52–74 in *Sects and Sectarianism in Jewish History*. Edited by Sacha Stern. IJS 12. Leiden: Brill, 2011.

Stone, Michael. "Response by Michael Stone and Discussion." Pages 399–401 and 428–30 in *Aramaica Qumranica: Proceedings of Conference on the Aramaic Texts from Qumran, in Aix-en-Provence, 30 June–2 July 2008*. Edited by Katell Berthelot and Daniel Stökl Ben Ezra. STDJ 94. Leiden: Brill, 2010.

———. *Secret Groups in Ancient Judaism*. Oxford: Oxford University Press, 2017.

Talmon, Shemaryahu. "320–330, 337, 394 1–2 Introduction." Pages 1–36 in *Qumran Cave 4.XVI: Calendrical Texts*. By Shemaryahu Talmon, Jonathan Ben-Dov, and Uwe Glessmer. DJD XXI. Oxford: Clarendon, 2001.

———. "4Q320. 4QCalendrical Document/Mishmarot A." Pages 37–64 in *Qumran Cave 4.XVI: Calendrical Texts*. By Shemaryahu Talmon, Jonathan Ben-Dov, and Uwe Glessmer. DJD XXI. Oxford: Clarendon, 2001.

———. "4Q321. 4QCalendrical Document/Mishmarot B." Pages 65–80 in *Qumran Cave 4.XVI: Calendrical Texts*. By Shemaryahu Talmon, Jonathan Ben-Dov, and Uwe Glessmer. DJD XXI. Oxford: Clarendon, 2001.

———. "4Q321a. 4QCalendrical Document/ Mishmarot C." Pages 81–92 in *Qumran Cave 4.XVI: Calendrical Texts*. By Shemaryahu Talmon, Jonathan Ben-Dov, and Uwe Glessmer. DJD XXI. Oxford: Clarendon, 2001.

———. "The Calendar Controversy in Ancient Judaism: The Case of the Community of the Renewed Covenant." Pages 379–95 in *Technological Innovations, New Texts, and Reformulated Issues: The Provo International Conference on the Dead Sea Scrolls*. Edited by Donald W. Parry and Eugene Ulrich. STDJ 30. Leiden: Brill, 1999.

———. "The Calendar of the Covenanters of the Judean Desert." Pages 147–99 in *The World of Qumran from Within: Collected Studies*. Jerusalem: Magnes, 1989.

———. "Calendars and Mishmarot." *EDSS* 1:108–17.

———. "The Covenanters' Calendar of the Holy Seasons according to the List of King David's Compositions in the Psalms Scroll from Cave 11 (11QPs[a] XXVII)." Pages 204–19 in *Fifty Years of Dead Sea Scrolls Research in Memory of Jacob Licht*. Edited by Gerson Brin and Bilhah Nitzan. Jerusalem: Yad Ben Zvi, 2001.

———. "Yom Hakippurim in the Habakkuk Scroll." *Bib* 32 (1951): 549–63.

Talmon, Shemaryahu, Jonathan Ben-Dov, and Uwe Glessmer. *Qumran Cave 4.XVI: Calendrical Texts*. DJD XXI. Oxford: Clarendon, 2001.

Tigchelaar, Eibert J. C. "322a. 4QHistorical Text H?" Pages 125–28 in *Qumran Cave 4.XXVIII: Wadi Daliyeh II; The Samaria Papyri for Wadi Daliyeh*. By Douglas M. Gropp. *Qumran Cave 4.XXVIII: Miscellanea, Part 2*. By Eileen Schuller et al. DJD XXVIII. Oxford: Clarendon, 2001.

———. "Some Remarks on the Book of Watchers, the Priests, Enoch and Genesis, and 4Q208." *Hen* 24 (2002): 143–45.

Tigchelaar, Eibert J. C., and Florentino García Martínez. "208–209. Astronomical Enoch[a-b] ar: Introduction." Pages 96–102 in *Qumran Cave 4.XXVI: Cryptic Texts*. By Stephen J. Pfann et al. *Miscellanea, Part 1*. By Philip S. Alexander et al. DJD XXXVI. Oxford: Clarendon, 2000.

———. "208. 4QAstronomical Enoch<sup>a</sup> ar." Pages 104–31 in *Qumran Cave 4.XXVI: Cryptic Texts*. By Stephen J. Pfann et al. *Miscellanea, Part 1*. By Philip S. Alexander et al. DJD XXXVI. Oxford: Clarendon, 2000.

———. "209. 4QAstronomical Enoch<sup>b</sup> ar." Pages 132–71 in *Qumran Cave 4.XXVI: Cryptic Texts*. By Stephen J. Pfann et al. *Miscellanea, Part 1*. By Philip S. Alexander et al. DJD XXXVI. Oxford: Clarendon, 2000.

Ungnad, Arthur. "Besprechungskunst und Astrologie in Babylonien." *AfO* 14 (1941–1944): 251–84.

VanderKam, James C. "The Aramaic Astronomical Book and the Ethiopic Book of Luminaries." Pages 207–21 in *With Wisdom as a Robe: Qumran and Other Jewish Studies in Honour of Ida Fröhlich*. Edited by Károly Dániel Dobos and Miklós Kőszeghy. Sheffield: Sheffield Academic, 2009.

———. "The Book of Enoch and the Qumran Scrolls." Pages 151–72 in *The Oxford Handbook of the Dead Sea Scrolls*. Edited by Timothy H. Lim and John J. Collins. Oxford: Oxford University Press, 2010.

———. "The Book of Luminaries." Pages 334–575 in *1 Enoch 2*. By George W. E. Nickelsburg and James C. VanderKam. Minneapolis: Fortress, 2012.

———. *Calendars in the Dead Sea Scrolls: Measuring Time*. London: Routledge, 1998.

———. "Calendrical Texts and the Origins of the Dead Sea Scrolls Community." Pages 371–88 in *Methods of Investigation of the Dead Sea Scrolls and the Khirbet Qumran Site: Present Realities and Future Prospects*. Edited by Michael O. Wise, Norman Golb, John J. Collins, and Dennis Pardee. ANYAS 722. New York: New York Academy of Sciences, 1994.

———. "The Origin, Character and Early History of the 364-Day Calendar: A Reassessment of Jaubert's Hypothesis." *CBQ* 41 (1979): 390–411.

———. "Studies on 'David's Compositions.'" *ErIsr* (1999): 212–20.

———. "The Temple Scroll and the Book of Jubilees." Pages 211–23 in *Temple Scroll Studies*. Edited by George J. Brooke. JSPSup 7. Sheffield: Sheffield Academic, 1989.

Vermes, Geza. *The Complete Dead Sea Scrolls in English*. London: Penguin, 1997.

Wacholder, Ben-Zion, and Sholom Wacholder. "Patterns of Biblical Dates and Qumran's Calendar: The Fallacy of Jaubert's Hypothesis." *HUCA* 66 (1995): 1–40.

Wacholder, Ben-Zion, and David B. Weisburg. "Visibility of the Moon in Cuneiform and Rabbinic Sources." *HUCA* 42 (1971): 227–42.

Waerden, Barthel L. van der. "History of the Zodiac." *AfO* (1952–1953): 216–30.

Wee, John. "Virtual Moons over Babylonia: The Calendar Text System, Its Micro-Zodiac of 13, and the Making of Medical Zodiology." Pages 139–229 in *The Circulation of Astronomical Knowledge in the Ancient World*. Edited by John M. Steele. TAC 6. Leiden: Brill, 2016.

Weidner, Ernst F. *Gestirn-Darstellungen auf Babylonischen Tontafeln*. OAWPHK 254. Vienna: Hermann Böhlaus, 1967.

Williams, Clemency. "Signs from the Sky, Signs from the Earth: The Diviner's Manual Revisited." Pages 473–86 in *Under One Sky: Astronomy and Mathematics in the Ancient Near East*. Edited by John M. Steele and Annette Imhausen. AOAT 297. Münster: Ugarit-Verlag, 2002.

Wise, Michael O. "Second Thoughts on *dwq* and the Synchronistic Calendar." Pages 98–120 in *Pursuing the Text: Studies in Honour of Ben Zion Wacholder on the Occasion of His Seventieth Birthday*. Edited by John C. Reeves and John Kampen. JSOTSup 184. Sheffield: Sheffield Academic. 1994.

———. "Thunder in Gemini from Qumran: An Aramaic Brontologion from Qumran." Pages 13–50 in *Thunder in Gemini and Other Essays on the History, Language and Literature of Second Temple Palestine*. JSup 15. Sheffield: Sheffield Academic, 1994.

Wise, Michael, Martin Abegg, and Edward Cook, eds. *The Dead Sea Scrolls: A New Translation*. New York: HarperCollins, 1996.

# Spirits of Controversy in My Bodily Structures: Spatiality of Body and Community in Qumran Apotropaic Prayers

Andrew R. Krause

Few issues from Second Temple Judaism are as contentious as that of spirits. During this period, we find a pervasive and increasing belief that the various aspects of evil and truth were dependent on realities and spiritual beings separate from the self and thus capable of affecting the individual in a variety of ways. In the scrolls from Qumran especially, we find that spirits could have benign or nefarious effects; they could purify or pollute. They could do so for both the individual or an entire group or movement. But how did they communicate this impurity, and how were individuals and groups to counteract such effects? Likewise, God-given spirits in these same texts often accomplish what later scholars termed atonement, as God is able to change the person and group from a life of transgression to that of divine election and torah fulfillment.

Unfortunately, we too often reduce pneumatology to a set of ideas and literary imagery, despite the fact that these spirits were spoken of as distinct agents occupying specific spaces in these texts. Thus, in the present paper, I will apply critical spatial theory to this theme in a specific set of texts that focus on this issue of spirits, holiness, and atonement. It should be noted that this might not have been viewed as entirely parallel to the atonement that other Jews of this period sought in the Jerusalem temple (or other temples), but it may very well have been the sort of prayer and moral exemplarity that took its place (4QFlor [4Q174] 1 I, 6–7; 1QS IX, 3–5). Looking primarily at the Hodayot and the various apotropaic prayers, I will use Tim Cresswell's social geography of transgression as a heuristic tool that will allow us to explicate the rhetoric and ritual expectations of these texts with regard to sin and atonement in both groups and individuals. I will argue that these Qumran texts understood sinful desires as being the effects of transgressive and polluting spirits in the personal, visceral spaces of the sectarian self, which could as a result pollute and endanger the group. Such emergent views of polluting spirits necessitated reconciliation with the idea of God's spirit as a force for good in the same spaces, bringing wisdom, torah understanding, and secret knowledge, which counteracted the effects of the evil spirits, and thus pushed sin and transgression from the individual's heart. However, the texts themselves remain vague on precisely how such spirit(s) of wisdom contend with their evil counterparts. The Yaḥad movement, which is often known for its hubristic claims of special revelation and moral perfection, evinced a considerable amount of anxiety regarding the polluting effects of evil spirits and humans in their spaces; however, God-given spirits of knowledge, law, and purity as the solution to this problem is consistent with the self-understanding of the movement as divinely elect.

## 1. Spatial Theories of Transgression and Protection

Spatial theory has revolutionized the way that we research groups and their spaces. Social valuation of spaces is a well-worn path, even within the study of the so-called Dead Sea Scrolls (DSS). Theories such as those of Henri Lefebvre, Edward Soja, and Robert Sack have been drawn on by Qumran scholars such as Alison Schofield, Angela Kim Harkins, Liv Lied, and George Brooke, who have clarified the importance of spaces such as Damascus and the ritualized space of the community for and in the ideologies of such groups as the Yaḥad movement. But what of more intimate, embodied spaces? While Harkins's work has clarified the communal body in the purported ritual narrative of the Hodayot, what can the DSS tell us about the actual body and its potential endangerment? In this short section, I will lay out the germane theories of Gaston Bachelard and Tim Cresswell and how they might help us to understand sin and transgression within the individual and the resultant effects on the larger community in those scrolls that are specifically concerned with protection of the self in Second Temple Judaism.

Bachelard's work on space begins with a warning that all treatments of such spaces are clouded in subjectivity and personal experience. For Bachelard, we must

> seek to determine the human value of the sorts of space that may be grasped, that may be defended against adverse forces, the spaces that we

love.... Attached to its protective value, which can be a positive one, are also imagined values, which soon become dominant. Spaces that have become seized upon by the imagination cannot remain indifferent space subject to the measures and estimates of the surveyor. It has been lived in, not in its positivity, but with all the partiality of the imagination.... For it concentrates being within limits that protect.[1]

Bachelard notes that our understanding of important spaces includes a need to protect that which is vulnerable to intrusion. Such spaces may hold secrets and memories that make them unobjectifiable. Bachelard specifically singles out purpose-made enclosures such as boxes, chests, and drawers as spaces that hold things of intrinsic value and thus become both protective and in need of protection.[2]

But how much more, then, do we value our bodies? They are us and they enclose us, but in an absolute sense. Our foremost unconscious impulses involve the protection of our body. Anything that we internalize, whether benign or malicious, has potentially life-changing consequences. Thus, as accounts of both nefarious and God-given spirits began to appear with greater regularity in the second and first centuries BCE, the protection and cleansing of one's body became commensurately important. Several narratives in the Hebrew Bible had already spoken of the giving of God's spirit. For example, 1 Sam 16:13–23; 18:10; 19:9 present both holy and evil spirits taking control of individuals (David and Saul respectively) in a way that controls them and renders their mental faculties inert.[3] Not surprisingly, then, both Philo (*Mos.* 1.277, 283) and Josephus (*A.J.* 4.121) present the spirit as an invading angel in their interpretations of the Balaam story, as he loses mental control.[4] Such loss of control at the filling of bodily space could lead to specific heroic acts if led by God or trespass and impurity if led by Belial or other nefarious forces.

The issue of morality and ethics of personal space is thus also important. Perhaps no spatial theorist has done as much work on transgression and space as Cresswell. Cresswell's social geography of space is based on

---

1. Gaston Bachelard, *Poetics of Space*, trans. Maria Jolas (Boston: Beacon, 1969), xxxv–xxxvi.
2. Bachelard, *Poetics of Space*, 5–7, 74–89.
3. See John R. Levison, *The Spirit in First-Century Judaism*, AGJU 29 (Leiden: Brill, 1997), 37. Levison compares this to similar treatments of possession in early Babylonian exorcism inscriptions.
4. Levison, *Spirit in First-Century Judaism*, 30–33.

the idea that all morality is spatially contingent. He argues that actions interpreted by the local culture as transgressions against the conventions of a specific space are viewed as dangerous to both the space and the society, and often represent attempts to change the natures of both. Transgressive actions are implicitly deemed out of place by the larger society.[5] The common use of spatial imagery in such ethical discourse is indicative of the role of space in such judgments; they are not merely metaphorical. For our purposes, we should also note that Cresswell argues that the language of dirt, garbage, and impurity is also commonly used in such discourse. While he uses the examples of modern pagans squatting at Stonehenge and the proliferation of graffiti in 1970s New York, Cresswell notes that "things that transgress become dirt—they are in the wrong place."[6] Those things that are deemed as inherently impure or dirty are given specific places for deposition and removal, for example, a waste bin or washroom; to put them elsewhere is viewed as a repugnant transgression and pollution of this improper place. Moral impurity is thus spoken of as being tied to a receptacle of such impurity, and the most natural place is the human body and the places that body inhabits. A clear Second Temple example of such thinking is evident in Jesus's statement of impurity regarding the Pharisees in Matt 15:10–11, 17–20:

> Then he [Jesus] called the crowd to him and said to them, "Listen and understand: it is not what goes into the mouth that defiles a person, but it is what comes out of the mouth that defiles.... Do you not see that whatever goes into the mouth enters the stomach, and goes out into the sewer? But what comes out of the mouth proceeds from the heart, and this is what defiles. For out of the heart come evil intentions, murder, adultery, fornication, theft, false witness, slander. These are what defile a person." (NRSV)

---

5. Tim Cresswell, *In Place/Out of Place: Geography, Ideology, and Transgression* (Minneapolis: University of Minnesota Press, 1996), 37–59. Christine Shepardson notes the applicability of Cresswell's theories of spatial transgressions in her work on spatial disputes between Nicene and anti-Nicene Christians in late antique Antioch. See Shepardson, *Controlling Contested Places: Late Antique Antioch and the Spatial Politics of Religious Controversy* (Berkeley: University of California Press, 2014), 154–60.

6. Cresswell, *In Place/Out of Place*, 38–39. Cresswell follows Mary Douglas's definition of impurity as "matter out of place." See Douglas, *Purity and Danger* (London: Routledge, 1966), 36.

These transgressive actions are held in the person and defile them and the community in which they are enacted. Thus, in prayer and ritual texts meant to protect the group from evil, defilement and impurity of bodily and community spaces through evil, transgression, and impurity are precisely what we should expect to be counteracted.

Philip Alexander has, in my opinion, rightly argued that demons and impurity are intimately tied in Second Temple Judaism, as both threaten and encroach on the community's space and practice. The idea of impure spirits from Zech 13:2 became common parlance by the first century CE.[7] Alexander argues that demons and other evil forces are out of place in the created order and belong to the abyss, where they will be sent in the cosmic exorcism and purification in the end of days, as we find, for example, in the curses of 4QBerakhot (4Q286–290).[8] This is entirely in keeping with Cresswell's conception of transgression and impurity as contrary to the order of a space and thus out of place. Likewise, Jodi Magness, in a study comparing Jesus's exorcisms to antidemonic texts from Qumran, has argued that both corpora share a concern for eschatological purity of groups by keeping out all defiling diseases and evil demons. Citing the War Rule, she notes that the time of eschatological blessing would lack all such evil, and God's name would be invoked over the community in order to keep it holy (4QSM [4Q285] 1, 1–11 // 11QSM [11Q14] 1 II, 5–15). Following Cecilia Wassen, Magness argues that there could be no defiling sickness, sin, or evil spirits in a community led by God-given spirits and angels; the direct intervention of God in such cases would give the afflicted a chance of entering God's eschatological kingdom.[9]

---

7. Philip S. Alexander, "The Demonology of the Dead Sea Scrolls," in *The Dead Sea Scrolls after Fifty Years: A Comprehensive Assessment*, ed. Peter W. Flint and James C. VanderKam (Leiden: Brill, 1999), 2:348–49. E.g., Matt 10:1; Mark 3:11; Acts 8:7; Rev 16:13; found also in 4QIncantations (4Q444) 1 I, 8 and 11QPs[a] XIX, 5 (Plea for Deliverance).

8. Alexander, "Demonology of the Dead Sea Scrolls," 350. On the spatiality of the curses in 4QBerakhot, see Andrew R. Krause, "Community, Alterity, and Space in the Qumran Covenant Curses," *DSD* 25 (2018): 229–36.

9. Jodi Magness, "They Shall See the Glory of the Lord (Isa 35:2): Eschatological Perfection and Purity at Qumran and in Jesus' Movement," *JSHJ* 14 (2016): 99–119; Cecilia Wassen, "What Do Angels Have against the Blind and the Deaf? Rules of Exclusion in the Dead Sea Scrolls," in *Common Judaism: Explorations in Second Temple Judaism*, ed. Wayne O. McCready and Adele Reinhartz (Minneapolis: Fortress, 2008), 115–29.

## 2. Past Research on Spirits and Bodies in Second Temple Judaism

But are these spirits understood as external realities (i.e., a cosmic dualism) or merely internal inclinations and dispositions (i.e., anthropological or psychological dualism)? When study of the Two Spirits Treatise in 1QS III, 13–IV, 26 began, it was common to speak of Zoroastrian dualism as the primary influence regarding dualism and spirits.[10] However, Preben Wernberg-Møller irrevocably changed the conversation when he argued that no such influence existed, but rather the so-called spirits were simply mythic imagery used for psychological dispositions or spiritual habits.[11] Subsequently, Shaul Shaked took a moderating view that spirits could refer to spiritual entities, opposing qualities inherent in people, or various cognitive faculties.[12] In either case, Bennie Reynolds is correct to note that various groups spoke of and utilized such spirits and demons for various purposes, as they were a productive theological and literary data set, especially in advocating apocalyptic visions and frameworks.[13]

Subsequent scholars have tended to take sides on this debate and to apply the findings to the wider corpus from Qumran. For example, Carol Newsom refers to the spirits in terms of "volitional aspects of the person," which are spoken of using the languages of wisdom character ethics and predestinarian metaphysics.[14] Conversely, Mladen Popović has argued that despite the various meanings and subtleties of usage for *spirit*, what we find is not an anthropological but rather a cosmic dualism of spirits

---

10. For a brief summary, see Herbert G. May, "Cosmological Reference in the Qumran Doctrine of the Two Spirits and in Old Testament Imagery," *JBL* 82 (1963): 1–3.

11. Preben Wernberg-Møller, "A Reconsideration of the Two Spirits in the Rule of the Community (1QS III 13–IV 26)," *RevQ* 3 (1961): 413–41. It should be noted that Werner-Møller had previously advocated for such spirits being both spiritual entities and psychological states. See Wernberg-Møller, *The Manual of Discipline* (Leiden: Brill, 1957), 67.

12. Shaul Shaked, "Qumran and Iran: Further Considerations," *IOS* 2 (1972): 436.

13. Bennie Reynolds III, "A Dwelling Place of Demons: Demonology and Apocalypticism in the Dead Sea Scrolls," in *Apocalyptic Thinking in Early Judaism: Engaging with John Collins' "Apocalyptic Imagination,"* ed. Sidnie White Crawford and Cecilia Wassen, JSJSup 182 (Leiden: Brill, 2018), 23–54.

14. Carol A. Newsom, *The Self as Symbolic Space: Constructing Identity and Community at Qumran*, STDJ 52 (Leiden: Brill, 2004), 133.

as external beings that affect the individual for good or ill.[15] John Levison has argued that we find a number of inconsistent uses of *spirit* in Second Temple literature, especially as the human spirit and disposition, an invading angel, and various qualities, all of which display a creativity and diversity of thought in this period.[16] For Levison, much of the giving of God's spirit leads to fulfilling the torah. This understanding follows the language of Ezek 36–37, in which God's spirit is placed inside the one who believes, and this occasions some form of regeneration.[17] Loren Stuckenbruck argues that these texts are an attempt to internalize their cosmic dualism "to come to terms with discrepancies between the ideology and identity they claimed for themselves on the one hand and realities of which they experienced on the other."[18] Recently, Lawrence Schiffman and Alexandra Frisch have argued that the Yaḥad movement had a unique and systematic view of the body, which has not been adequately acknowledged. They argue that the flesh and spirit of the individual comprise a single, corporate entity.[19]

### 3. Body as a Site of Protection in the Qumran Apotropaic Prayers

Thus, the relationship between spirits and flesh remains one of the oldest discussions in Judaism and Christianity, and such controversy has not spared Qumran studies. Whether such spirits are psychologized as evil inclinations or theologized as warring spirits, our understanding of the relationship between these spirits and the bodies is connected. Rather than a Platonic—or possibly Pauline—flesh/soul antithesis, the body

---

15. Mladen Popović, "Anthropology, Pneumatology, and Demonology in Early Judaism: The *Two Spirits Treatise* (1QS 3:13–4:26) and Other Texts from the Dead Sea Scrolls," in *Dust of the Ground and Breath of Life (Gen 2:7): The Problem of a Dualistic Anthropology in Early Judaism and Christianity*, ed. Jacques T. A. G. M. van Ruiten and George H. van Kooten, TBN 20 (Leiden: Brill, 2016), 58–98.

16. See Levison, *Spirit in First-Century Judaism*, 217–36.

17. John R. Levison, *Filled with the Spirit* (Grand Rapids: Eerdmans, 2009), 271.

18. Loren T. Stuckenbruck, "The Interiorization of Dualism within the Human Being in Second Temple Judaism," in *Light against Darkness: Dualism in Ancient Mediterranean Religion and the Contemporary World*, ed. Armin Lange et al., JAJSup 2 (Gottingen: Vandenhoeck & Ruprecht, 2011), 145–68.

19. Alexandra Frisch and Lawrence H. Schiffman, "The Body in Qumran Literature: Flesh and Spirit, Purity and Impurity in the Dead Sea Scrolls," *DSD* 23 (2016): 155–82.

was related to the purported actions of these spirits in such texts and the religious experience which they seek to articulate. In this section, I will discuss various apotropaic prayers as relating these spirits to the sectarian body. I will argue that the body is consistently spatial and that the spatial theories of Bachelard and Cresswell help us to clarify the uncharacteristic anxiety that these texts illustrate within the Yaḥad movement.

While many questions still exist and demand attention in this discussion, the apotropaic methods and strategies of the Yaḥad movement appear to be relatively coherent and logical, if somewhat inconsistent. Generally speaking, the key concepts here are the desire to keep evil at bay—despite evil's current (though fleeting) dominion—through methods that do not include direct invocation of the divine name as a "word of power," nor divine coercion through aggressive incantation, and the importance of personal and communal purity. Such practices pervaded the prayer and liturgical corpora from Qumran, not merely those texts generically defined as apotropaic.

David Flusser is generally regarded as the first to note a specifically Qumran apotropaic tradition. In a 1966 article titled "Qumran and Jewish 'Apotropaic' Prayers," Flusser uses the prayer of Levi in the Aramaic Levi Document (4QLevi[a] [4Q213] 1 I, 14–18) and the Plea for Deliverance (11QPs[a] XIX) to note specific traits that differed from later rabbinic boundary-marking rites.[20] For Flusser, the important points were the emphasis placed on God-given knowledge of law and wisdom, purification, protection against sin as a tangible element, and deliverance from Satan.

As more texts became available, scholars were able both to confirm to some degree and to add greater detail to Flusser's notion of a Qumran system of apotropaic practices. The most important element noted by subsequent scholars was the use of praise of God as the active element in keeping evil at bay. In the introduction to her *editio princeps* of 4QIncantation, which stands with 4QSongs of the Maskil[a–b] (4Q510–511) as the best examples of sectarian apotropaic prayer, Esther Chazon offers a list of common attributes among such sectarian boundary-marking rituals. She lists (1) the use of the phrase ואני מיראי אל, "And as for me, I spread the fear of God"; (2) the motif of contending spirits within the speaker's body; (3) the "law of God" as an element of spiritual purity and protection; (4) stress

---

20. David Flusser, "Qumran and Jewish 'Apotropaic' Prayers," *IEJ* 16 (1966): 194–205.

on divinely given gifts and attributes as prophylactic elements; (5) Enochic terminology for evil spirits; and (6) reference to the limited duration of evil's dominion.[21] In terms of divine gifts, the speaker of such communal prophylactic prayers stresses wisdom, strength, and righteousness, which are often referred to as spirits of their own.

Scholars have generally taken the Maskil's statement in 4QSongs of the Maskil[a] 1, 4–5, "And I, the *Maskil*, declare the splendor of his radiance in order to frighten and to terr[ify]all the spirits"[22] (ואני משכיל משמיע הוד תפארתו לפחד ולב[הל] כול רוחי) as a programmatic, methodological statement for the communal barring of evil spirits of all kinds.[23] For Esther Eshel, this differentiates what we find in sectarian apotropaic prayers from outside incantations, as she states, "Whereas apotropaic prayers request God's protection from threatening external evil forces, incantations address the evil forces directly, seeking to expel demons already at work."[24] However, we have good reason to problematize this definition of incantation. Incantation is better defined using James Frazer's definition of magic as the belief that "the same causes will always produce the same effects, that the performance of the proper ceremony, accompanied by the proper

---

21. Emanuel Tov, *The Texts in the Judaean Desert: Indices and an Introduction to the Discoveries in the Judean Desert Series*, DJD XXXIX (Oxford: Clarendon, 2002), 370–71.

22. Unless otherwise indicated, all translations from the DSS are mine.

23. See also 4QShir[b] 8, 4; 11, 5; Philip S. Alexander, "'Wrestling against Wickedness in High Places': Magic in the Worldview of the Qumran Community," in *The Scrolls and the Scriptures: Qumran Fifty Years After*, ed. Stanley E. Porter and Craig A. Evans, JSPSup 26 (Sheffield: Sheffield Academic, 1997), 318–37, esp. 320; Esther Eshel, "Genres of Magical Texts in the Dead Sea Scrolls," in *Die Dämonen/Demons*, ed. Armin Lange, Hermann Lichtenberger, and K. F. Diethard Römheld (Tübingen: Mohr Siebeck, 2003), 410; Eshel, "Apotropaic Prayers in the Second Temple Period," in *Liturgical Perspectives: Prayer and Poetry in Light of the Dead Sea Scrolls*, ed. Esther G. Chazon, STDJ 48 (Leiden: Brill, 2003), 69–88; Florentino García Martínez, "Magic in the Dead Sea Scrolls," in *Qumranica Minora II: Thematic Studies in the Dead Sea Scrolls*, ed. Eibert J. C. Tigchelaar, STDJ 44 (Leiden: Brill, 2007), 119; Bilhah Nitzan, *Qumran Prayer and Religious Poetry*, STDJ 12 (Leiden: Brill, 1994), 248; Andrew R. Krause, "Protected Sects: The Apotropaic Performance and Function of *4QIncantation* and *4QSongs of the Maskil* and Their Relevance for the Study of the Hodayot," *JAJ* 5 (2014): 28–29. This fits well with the common use of ואני מיראי אל in 4QIncantation 1, 1 and 4QShir[b] 35, 6.

24. Eshel, "Apotropaic Prayers," 69.

spell, will inevitably be attended by the desired result."[25] Michael Swartz is correct to note that, despite a clearly conservative and temple-focused proclivity, many of the rituals in both the Qumran and the rabbinic corpora show clear signs of formulas that expect a definitive, set result.[26] Thus, we should follow Pieter van der Horst and Judith Newman in understanding that prayer and such magical formularies are on a continuum; they are not binary oppositions.[27]

By definition, apotropaic prayers are spatial in their practice, regarding both their performance and their desired effects. That is, the evil spirits and beings are kept out of a specific space through ritual praxis in proximity to such space. As I will argue, the human, sectarian body is the primary unit of protection, which leads to the community as a secondary site of protection. This is especially the case given that these texts require the spatial presence of God-given gifts or spirits to take the place of such actions. Further, the attendant purity issues of evil forces in the body show the body to be presented as a receptacle for either divine or nefarious spirits.

While not written at Qumran, the book of Jubilees was clearly authoritative for the movement, and copies were found at Qumran (4QJub$^{a-i}$ [4Q217–223, 4Q482]). In chapter 12 (which is not extant from Qumran), Abram prays for protection against evil spirits: "Save me from the hands of evil spirits which rule over the thought of the heart of man and do not let them lead me astray from following you, O my God."[28] Interestingly, this follows shortly after Abram was warned by his father, Terah, against worshiping idols, which "are the misleading of the heart." Miryam Brand

---

25. James Frazer, *The Golden Bough* (repr., London: Chancellor, 1994), 49. For further discussion, see William J. Lyons and Andy M. Reimer, "The Demonic Virus and Qumran Studies: Some Preventative Measures," *DSD* 5 (1998): 16–32; Krause, "Protected Sects," 26–27.

26. See Michael D. Swartz, "Magical Piety in Ancient and Medieval Judaism," in *Ancient Magic and Ritual Power*, ed. Marvin Meyer and Paul Mirecki, RGRW 129 (Leiden: Brill, 1995), 167–83; Swartz, "Sacrificial Themes in Jewish Magic," in *Magic and Ritual in the Ancient World*, ed. Paul Mirecki and Marvin Meyer, RGRW 141 (Leiden: Brill, 2002), 303–15. See also discussion of similar issues in the Egyptian Greek Magical Papyri in Sarah Iles Johnston, "Sacrifice in the Greek Magical Papyri," in Mirecki and Meyer, *Magic and Ritual*, 344–58.

27. Pieter van der Horst and Judith H. Newman, *Early Jewish Prayers in Greek: A Commentary*, CEJL (Berlin: de Gruyter, 2008), 219.

28. Translation from Orval S. Wintermute, "Jubilees: A New Translation and Introduction," *OTP* 2:81.

has made the important observation that Abram's apotropaic prayer is the only place in all of Jubilees—a book replete with talk of evil spirits—in which fear of external demons is integrated with fear of them inside the body.[29]

Moving to the so-called sectarian literature from Qumran, the limited text extant from 4QIncantation evinces a prime example of this interior site of protection:

> And as for me, because of my fearing God, he opened my mouth with his true knowledge; and from his holy spirit [
> truth to a[l]l[ the]se. They became spirits of controversy in my (bodily) structure; law[s of God
> in ]blood vessels of flesh. And a spirit of knowledge and understanding, truth and righteousness, God put in [my] he[art
> ] And strengthen yourself by the laws of God, and in order to fight against the spirits of wickedness, and not [ ] (1, 1–4; Chazon, DJD XXIX)

In lines 2–3, we find two parallel references to bodily spaces: the body (מבניתי) and blood vessels/innards (תכמי),[30] both of which "spirits of controversy" (רוחי ריב) may inhabit. Lines 4–8 appear to offer further detail on the evil spirits mentioned, noting the limited dominion of these spirits and further mentioning bastards (ממזרים) and spirits of impurity (רוחי הטמא). However, we should also note the inclusion of contrary spirits of knowledge, understanding, truth, and righteousness, which may reside in the heart of the individual and counteract the effects of the nefarious spirits. These God-given spirits, along with the laws of God, will give strength and relief from the spirits of controversy and impurity. Moreover, we should not be surprised to find a spirit of truth or knowledge in the

---

29. Miryam T. Brand, *Evil Within and Without: The Source of Sin and Its Nature as Portrayed in Second Temple Literature*, JAJSup 9 (Göttingen: Vandenhoeck & Ruprecht, 2013), 206; See also Eshel, "Apotropaic Prayers," 78.

30. Chazon notes that in every case of its usage, this term relates to something evil in the person. See Esther Chazon et al., *Qumran Cave 4.XX: Poetic and Liturgical Texts, Part 2*, DJD XXIX (Oxford: Clarendon, 1999), 376. Miryam Brand challenges this translation, arguing that it gives unnecessary specificity to a term that is continually used in a metaphorical sense (Brand, *Evil Within and Without*, 204–5 n. 35). For our purposes, this challenge is helpful, though I would challenge Brand's characterization of these terms as "metaphorical" in 4QIncantation and 1QH$^a$, as they are being used in more of a locative sense, as the authors clearly view such things as being objectively and consistently inside the individual's viscera/inner parts.

heart of the proper member of the Yaḥad,[31] as the Shema (Deut 6:4–9), a particularly influential text at Qumran, counsels that proper reading of Torah will result in it occupying the heart, as the heart was generally considered the locus of understanding and moral agency. This text is common in the Qumran *tefillin*, or phylacteries. It is noteworthy that several scholars believe that the *tefillin* themselves likely took on an apotropaic usage,[32] which is all the more appropriate as they were affixed to the practitioners' bodily space. Albert Hogeterp, who uses 4QIncantation as a parallel, states that the anthropological dualism of the Two Spirits Treatise, especially 1QS IV, 15–26, presents a similarly contentious warring of dispositions or evil spirits.[33]

> By His truth God shall then purify all human deeds, and refine some of humanity so as to extinguish every perverse spirit from the inward parts of the flesh, cleansing from every wicked deed by a holy spirit. Like purifying waters, He shall sprinkle each with a spirit of truth, effectual against all the abominations of lying and sullying by an unclean spirit.
> (IV, 20–22; Wise, Abegg, Cook, *DSSR*)

In line 23 we are told that, "until now the spirits of truth and injustice have fought in the hearts of men." This leads Loren Stuckenbruck to state aptly that the theological anthropology of the Treatise on the Two Spirits "envisions the human being as the battle ground between cosmic forces, [and thus] is an interiorization of a socio-religious conflict that, given the strict ideals of the community, could no longer be circumscribed by physical boundaries."[34]

We should, however, note that such language is not limited within 1QS to this proto-Yaḥadic text, as we find similar spatiality of body and community, for example, in the so-called Hymn of the Maskil (1QS IX, 25–XI, 15). This text states

---

31. For the "spirit of truth" as a membership prerequisite, see Anja Klein, "From the 'Right Spirit' to the 'Spirit of Truth': Observations on Psalm 51 and 1QS," in *Dynamics of Language and Exegesis at Qumran*, ed. Devorah Dimant and Reinhard G. Kratz, FAT 2/35 (Tübingen: Mohr Siebeck, 2009), 180–81.

32. See Yehudah Cohn, "Were Tefillin Phylacteries?," *JJS* 59 (2008): 39–57.

33. Albert L. A. Hogeterp, "The Eschatology of the Two Spirits Treatise Revisited," *RevQ* 23 (2007): 255–56.

34. Stuckenbruck, "Interiorization of Dualism," 168.

I shall give no refuge in my heart to Belial [ובליעל לוא אשמור בלבבי]. In my mouth shall be heard neither foolishness nor sinful deceit; neither fraud nor lies shall be discovered between my lips. For thanksgiving shall I open my mouth, the righteousness of God shall my tongue recount always.... In His hand are the perfection of my walk and the virtue of my heart. (1QS X, 21–23; XI, 2; Wise, Abegg, Cook, *DSSR*)

As in the above-mentioned texts, the heart is presented as a space occupied by either evil spirits—here Belial himself is the occupying evil—or God-given virtue, both of which can control the behavior and speech of the individual. Asaf Gayer has recently argued that this hymn illustrates both the use of prayer to segregate the community from its enemies and the central role of the Maskil in this apotropaic prayer.[35] While I certainly agree with the former premise entirely and the latter in broad strokes, we should be careful not to overemphasize the place of the Maskil. While the Maskil does show considerable liturgical virtuosity in many of these prayers, several other prayers do not show such reliance on a liturgical official, at least not in their extant forms, so we should temper Gayer's claims of dependence on the Maskil as a goal in this text.

Further language of visceral indwelling and contention of spirits is also used in the Songs of the Maskil (4QShir$^{a-b}$ or 4Q510–511), the longest extant sectarian compilation of apotropaic prayers.[36] It should be noted here that this compilation is almost entirely voiced in the first-person singular. However, its ritual performance by the Maskil, a liturgical leader, and the frequent use of corporate performative markers such as "Amen, Amen" show that it was meant to have both personal and corporate ritual effects. 4Q510 1, 6 states, "[the spirits] fall upon men without warning to lead them astray from a spirit of understanding and to make their heart and their [ ] desolate" (והפוגעים פתע פתאום לתעות רוח בינה ולהשם לבבם). Likewise, 4Q511 18 II, 7–8 states, "And I detest all the deeds of impurity,

---

35. Asaf Gayer, "The Centrality of Prayer and the Stability of Trust: An Analysis of the Hymn of the Maskil in 1QS IX, 25b–XI, 15a," in *Ancient Jewish Prayers and Emotions*, ed. Stefan C. Reif and Renate Egger-Wenzel, DCLS 26 (Berlin: de Gruyter, 2016), 317–33.

36. It is important to note that Joseph L. Angel has questioned the unity of these two texts through material reconstruction using the Stegemann method. However, neither has Angel made the case definitively, nor do these arguments compromise our use of these scrolls. See Angel, "The Material Reconstruction of 4QSongs of the Maskil$^b$ (4Q511)," *RevQ* 27 (2015): 25–82.

for God made the knowledge of intelligence shine in my heart" (וכֹול מעשׂי
נדה שנתי כיא הֵאיר אלוהים דעת בינה בלבבי). Both of these passages illustrate
the work of indwelling malevolent spirits and transgression in contending directly with the divinely given, sapiential spirits, again, in the heart.
4Q511 28+29, 3–4 states in even more detail, "You have placed knowledge
in my foundation of dust (ש]מתה דעת בסוד עפרי) to [...], even though I
am a formation from spat saliva, I am moulded [from clay], and of darkness is my mixtu[re ...] /.../ and iniquity in the innards of my flesh [וְעַוְלָה
בתכמי בׂשרי]." Likewise, in 4Q511 48+49+51 II, 3–5 apotropaic elements
are said to come from within the individual, and "in the innards of my
flesh is the foundation of [ ... and in] my body wars; the laws of God are
in my heart [חוקי אל בלבבי]." Thus, as in the previous examples, both texts
present the nefarious spirits as being counteracted and fought by positive
spirits of knowledge and justice. Also, as in 4QIncantation, examples from
4Q511 present all of this taking place in bodily structures.

While the final passage above utilizes language of the foundation of
innards and heart as the spaces relating to the spirits much the same as
we have seen previously, the penultimate passage mentions the visceral
spaces as the formation of the human from dust, clay, and spittle, that is, in
the *Niedrigskeitdoxologie* tradition in which the speaker debases himself as
mere animate dirt, as in Gen 2.[37] We find similar statements in sections of
the Hodayot, for example,

> And what is flesh that it should have insight into [these things?
> And] how is [a creat]ure of dust able to direct its steps? *vacat*
> (1QH[a] VII, 34)
>
> And ] you have brought into covenant with you,
> and you have uncovered the heart of dust

---

37. Jörg Frey, "Flesh and Spirit in the Palestinian Jewish Sapiential Tradition and in the Qumran Texts," in *Wisdom Texts from Qumran and the Development of Sapiential Thought*, ed. Charlotte Hempel, Armin Lange, and Hermann Lichtenberger, BETL 159 (Leuven: Peeters, 2002), 367–404. According to Frey, the latter anthropological dualism predominates the more recently edited 1/4QInstruction (1Q26, 4Q415–418, 4Q418a) and 1/4QMysteries (1Q27, 4Q299–301). See also Stuckenbruck, "Interiorization of Dualism," 145–68. Brand notes that the spirits and demons of 4QIncantation and 4Q511 take on an "internalized" element not found in Jubilees's Watcher traditions, though it is in line with Abram's prayer in Jub. 12.19–21 (*Evil Within and Without*, 206).

> that it might guard itself [from
> [and ]from the snares of judgement corresponding to your compassion.
> And as for me, a creature [of clay and a thing mixed with water,
> a structure of d]ust and a heart of stone,
> with whom shall I be reckoned until this?
> For [ you] have set straight in the ear of dust,
> and that which will be forever
> you have engraved on the heart [of stone
> (1QH$^a$ XXI, 10–14)[38]

As we will see below, this parallel of bodily structures and the *Niedrigskeitdoxologie* is noteworthy and more diffuse than previously noted in these texts.

That the Hodayot should contain such close parallels is not surprising, as several scholars have noted generic and literary parallels between this corpus and the apotropaic prayers.[39] Perhaps the best example is in 1QH$^a$ IV,

> [Blessed are you, O God of compassi]on
> on account of the spirits that you have granted me.
> I will [f]ind a ready response,
> reciting your righteous acts and (your) patience
> [ ]k and the deeds of your strong right hand,
> and confessing the transgressions of (my) previous (deeds),
> and p[rostr]ating myself,
> and begging for mercy concerning [
> ] my deeds and the perversity of my heart,
> because I have wallowed in impurity,
> but from the council of wor[ms] I have [de]parted (IV, 29–31)

and again,

> And in order to *b* to him his humility through your disciplines,
> and through [your] tes[ts] you have [strengthened] his heart
> [ ] your servant from sinning against you

---

38. Translations follow Hartmut Stegemann, Eileen Schuller, and Carol A. Newsom, *Qumran Cave 1.III: 1QHodayot$^a$, with Incorporation of 1QHodayot$^b$ and 4QHodayot$^{a-f}$*, DJD XL (Oxford: Clarendon, 2009).

39. Alexander, "Wrestling against Wickedness," 320; Eshel, "Genres of Magical Texts," 410; Eshel, "Apotropaic Prayers," 69–88; Krause, "Protected Sects," 28–29.

> and from stumbling in all the matters of your will.
> Strengthen [his] loi[ns
> that he may sta]nd against spirits [
> and that he may w]alk in everything that you love
> and despise everything that [you] hate,
> [and do] what is good in your eyes.
> [ ] their [domi]nion in his members;
> for your servant (is) a spirit of flesh.
> *vacat*
> [Blessed are you, God Most High,
> that you have spread your holy spirit upon your servant
> [and you] have purified *m* [ ]*t* his heart
> (1QH<sup>a</sup> IV, 34–38)

Again, the apotropaic means of God are placed in the heart in order to defeat the contentious spirits that defile and control the flesh; here, spirits of strength, knowledge, and purity are all given to the individual in order to purify the heart, just as all of the afflictions are brought "by means of a spirit" (IV, 13–20).[40] As in the previously quoted text of 1QS IV, the glory and covenant of Adam are spoken of as related to the cleansing of the clay structures. As in 4Q510 1, 6, 1QH<sup>a</sup> X states, "You have made straight in] my [hea]rt all the deeds of iniquity, and you have purifi[ed me] [ and] you placed faithful gu[ardians in the face of (my) distress], righteous [re] provers for all the violen[ce done to me]" (5–6), and later, "You placed it in his heart to open up the source of knowledge to all who understand" (18), once again making the heart both the site of protection and purification. This may also help us to make sense of the common, though problematic, statement about "the spirit of flesh," which is clearly spoken of as a malevolent spirit; thus, we might think of this designation as being spatial, as such evil spirits are usually spoken of as actually inhabiting the viscera. According to Angela Kim Harkins,

> In the case of the *hodayot*, religious experience is described through language of the body and understood as an extraordinary phenomenal and transformative encounter with the divine. The transformative expe-

---

40. See also "You expel a perverted spirit from within me" (1QH<sup>a</sup> XVI, 1–2); "cleanse me with Your righteousness" (XIX, 33–34); "And You opened a foun[tain] to correct the way of the creature of clay, and the guilt of one born of a woman according to his deeds" (XXIII, 13–14).

rience appears as a number of different kinds: from danger to safety (rescue); from weakness to strength (empowering); from impurity to purity (cleansing); from ordinary knowing to revealed knowing (illumination); from a lowly state to an exalted one (elevation); and from human to angelic company (union with angels). These categories of transformation are not mutually exclusive ones, and reports of rescue and empowerment can be conflated.[41]

For Harkins, this is part of the general movement in 1QH[a] from debasement and impurity to heavenly glory, which the entire community seeks in the purported narrative progression of this Cave 1 scroll. The transformative effects of the knowledge are thus both increased wisdom and purity, and the casting out of iniquitous spirits.[42] Torah, as the very law of God to which the movement aspires, would be a natural remedy to internal transgression and impurity. Even though this is often stated in the first-person singular, as in 4Q510–511, the ritual setting of these texts and recital by the Maskil point to a corporate understanding; thus, as each individual seeks internal personal purity, it is done as a collective group, with a liturgical leader reciting the prayers.

Such ritual performance and theological concerns are not limited to groups led by such functionaries in seclusion, though. In 4QBarkhi Nafshi[a–e] (4Q434, 435–438), a text whose relation to the sectarian nature is far from certain, we find a deep concern for such bodily purity and the need to protect visceral space, but in a specifically urban, multicultural context[43] and using different terminology:

---

41. Angela Kim Harkins, *Reading with an "I" to the Heavens: Looking at the Qumran Hodayot through the Lens of Visionary Traditions*, Ekstasis 3 (Berlin: de Gruyter, 2011), 29–31.

42. See Joseph Angel's contention that the primary experiential function of apotropaic prayers is the transmission of group and institutional knowledge. See Angel, "Maskil, Community, and Religions Experience in the Songs of the Sage (4Q510–511)," *DSD* 19 (2012): 1–27. Angel follows Roy Rappaport's dictum that "ritual is not only informative, but self-informative." See Roy Rappaport, *Ritual and Religion in the Making of Humanity*, CSCA 110 (Cambridge: Cambridge University Press, 1999), 104.

43. These hymns continually call on God to protect the individual and community as being in the midst of the nations (גוים) in a way that speaks of ongoing personal interactions (e.g., 4QBarkhi Nafshi[a] 1 I, 8; 4QBarkhi Nafshi[d] 2, 5). Discussion of the unity and origins of this collection goes beyond the scope of this paper, but for a recent, detailed discussion, see Mika J. Pajunen, *The Land of the Elect and Justice for*

And you have prevailed over the heart [of the contrite], so that he should walk in your ways. You have commanded my heart, and my kidneys/inmost parts [כליותי] you have taught well, lest your statutes be forgotten. [On my heart ] you [have enjoined] your law, on my kidneys/inmost parts [כליותי] you have engraved it; and you have prevailed upon me, so that I pursue after you[r] ways.... [The heart of stone] you have [dri]ven with rebukes far from me, and have set a pure heart in its place. The evil inclination [you] have driven with rebukes [from my inmost parts] [and the spirit of ho]liness you have set in my heart. Adulterousness of the eyes you have removed from me (4QBarkhi Nafshi[c] 1 Ia,b, 4–6; 1 Ia,b, 10–II, 1; Weinfeld and Seely, DJD XXIX [partially emended])

The bodily imagery that pervades this text should not merely be taken as metaphorical, either to speak of giving new attributes or personal transformation.[44] Conversely, George Brooke argues that the authors of these hymns took scriptural metaphors and gave them concrete meanings, as proof of membership meant that a real transformation had taken place through the giving of spirits and virtues in the elect, while the transgressor is physically unsatisfactory.[45] Brooke specifically cites 4QZodiacal Physi-

---

*All: Reading Psalms in the Dead Sea Scrolls in Light of 4Q381*, JAJSup 14 (Göttingen: Vandenhoeck & Ruprecht, 2013), 66–70.

44. The latter is a more convincing argument, especially given the use of evil inclination (יצר רע) as the previous state before the pure heart is given, as it presents the penitent as expecting real bodily change (4QBarkhi Nafshi[c] 1 I, 10). See Mika S. Pajunen, "Exodus and Exile as Prototypes of Justice: Prophecies in the *Psalms of Solomon* and the *Barkhi Nafshi* Hymns," in *Functions of Psalms and Prayers in the Late Second Temple Period*, ed. Mika S. Pajunen and Jeremy Penner, BZAW 486 (Berlin: de Gruyter, 2017), 269–71; Eibert J. C. Tigchelaar, "The Evil Inclination in the Dead Sea Scrolls, with a Re-edition of 4Q468i (4QSectarian Text?)," in *Empsychoi Logoi: Religious Innovations in Antiquity*, ed. Alberdina Houtman, Albert de Jong, and Magda Misset-van de Weg, AGJU 73 (Leiden: Brill, 2008), 347–57. The former argument does contend in greater detail the language of bodily space, though it reduces it to a metaphorical imagery for the giving of specific virtues to the individual. See David Rolph Seely, "Implanting Pious Qualities in the *Barki Nafshi* Hymns," in *The Dead Sea Scrolls: Fifty Years after Their Discovery*, ed. Lawrence H. Schiffman, Emanuel Tov, and James C. VanderKam (Jerusalem: Israel Exploration Society, 2000), 322–31.

45. George J. Brooke, "Body Parts in *Barkhi Nafshi* and the Qualifications of Membership in the Worshipping Community," in *Sapiential, Liturgical, and Poetical Texts from Qumran*, ed. Daniel Falk, Florentino García Martínez, and Eileen M. Schuller, STDJ 35 (Leiden: Brill, 2000), 79–94. Brooke specifically cites 4QPhysionomic Text (4Q186), in which the physical attributes of an individual can illustrate

ognomy (4Q186), in which the physical attributes of an individual can illustrate the types of spirit within them, as a text with similar teachings regarding bodies and their parts as spaces of spiritual contention.[46] Brooke also ties the rejection of those with physical deformities to this belief in the physical transformation of the truly elect by God. This provided a God-given distinction that the performative community believed differentiated it from other Jews and their neighbors. According to Brooke, "Since most often it seems as if such texts might be used at times of private prayer or public worship, it can be concluded that prayer and worship acted as significant means of control within the community."[47] Thus, while different organs are cited, for example, the kidneys (כליות), as the places of contention, we find a similar presentation of the community and bodily spaces in these hymns.

## Conclusions and Implications

It has too often been assumed that the Yaḥad movement and their various neighbors tended to treat the individual as a whole, possibly with a body or flesh and a specific spirit of their own. Likewise, it is often simply assumed that the language relating to the body is merely poetic. However, as I have argued, the apotropaic prayers of Qumran use markedly consistent language when speaking of the relationship between spirits and the human body. These spirits are spoken of in a locative sense relating to various anatomical parts. God-given spirits and knowledge are spoken of as relating to the heart, whereas malevolent spirits are spoken of as occupying the viscera, though also potentially forcing the spirits of knowledge from the heart. This would lead to "hypocrites, [who] concoct devilish plans, and seek you with a divided heart [וידרשוכה בלב ולב]" (1QH[a] XII, 14–15). Thus, in order to understand the effects of the various spirits, I have argued

---

the types of spirit within them, as a text with similar teachings regarding bodies and their parts as spaces of spiritual contention.

46. Brooke, "Body Parts in *Barkhi Nafshi*," 87–91. For further discussion of this text, see Philip S. Alexander, "Physiognomy, Initiation, and Rank in the Qumran Community," in *Geschichte-Tradition-Reflexion*, ed. Hubert Cancik, Hermann Lichtenberger, and Peter Schäfer (Tübingen: Mohr Siebeck, 1996), 1:385–94; Mladen Popović, *Reading the Human Body: Physiognomics and Astrology in the Dead Sea Scrolls and Hellenistic-Early Roman Period Judaism*, STDJ 67 (Leiden: Brill, 2007), 17–66.

47. Brooke, "Body Parts in *Barkhi Nafshi*," 91.

that we must better understand the relationship between these indwelling spirits and the bodily spaces they inhabit, and thus the community spaces made up of the various bodies, and the relationship between spaces, transgression, and protection.

Following Bachelard and Cresswell, enclosed spaces may be sites of protection or transgression. In this exposition of Qumran prayer and psalmody, I have argued that this is precisely what we find: the heart and viscera as containing spirits of either transgression and impurity or God-given wisdom. Like Cresswell, I have argued that framing this discussion as fundamentally spatial in terms of the human body and community of bodies clarifies both the impetuses and dangers of sin and the possibility of divine atonement in these texts. Though this would not have been considered akin to the atonement found in the contemporary temple, it was viewed as the direct action of God in the historical circumstances of the movement to cleanse them from their transgressions and transgressive natures in a way similar to how Jesus's actions would be understood by the early Christ believers. Such atonement came in the form of knowledge and law as spirits that possessed their own agency and ability to fight against the spirits of deception, transgression, and impurity. However, God alone gives sufficiently strong spirits to overcome the nefarious spirits, thus safeguarding the Yaḥad's sense of divine election, and in a way that is consistent with the movement's claims to special revelation. Conversely, giving deception and evil agency allowed the Yaḥad to justify their own experience of moral and spiritual failure. In other communities such as the Lot of Belial, where these spirits had control, their individual and corporate spaces were defiled through transgression. Such individuals and communities must therefore be avoided and even ritually cast out if they had entered the Yaḥadic communities, as we find in both the Rule of the Community and Damascus Document (1QS VI, 24–VII, 26; CD XIV, 18–23 // 4QD^a [4Q266] 10 I, 10–II, 15).

Internal spaces could hold impurity in ways that few others could, as noted by Jesus in Matt 15. Perhaps a most accurate analogy would be the body of the transgressor becomes like a defiled earthenware vessel, which communicates the impurity of what it has held. This would fit especially well with the frequent use of the *Niedrigskeitdoxologie*, which stresses the clay structure of the postulant. This would also aptly describe the spatial understanding of the body as a potentially impure vessel in need of cleansing. Such an analogy fits with the need for not only divine forgiveness and empowerment but for ablutions as a cleansing ritual for the individual as well. As an enclosed space, like a pot, the body (both individual and corporate) would need to be protected.

## Bibliography

Alexander, Philip S. "The Demonology of the Dead Sea Scrolls." Pages 331–53 in *The Dead Sea Scrolls after Fifty Years: A Comprehensive Assessment*. Vol. 2. Edited by Peter W. Flint and James C. VanderKam. Leiden: Brill, 1999.

———. "Physiognomy, Initiation, and Rank in the Qumran Community." Pages 385–94 in *Geschichte-Tradition-Reflexion*. Vol. 1. Edited by Hubert Cancik, Hermann Lichtenberger, and Peter Schäfer. Tübingen: Mohr Siebeck, 1996.

———. "'Wrestling against Wickedness in High Places': Magic in the Worldview of the Qumran Community." Pages 318–37 in *The Scrolls and the Scriptures: Qumran Fifty Years After*. Edited by Stanley E. Porter and Craig A. Evans. JSPSup 26. Sheffield: Sheffield Academic, 1997.

Angel, Joseph L. "Maskil, Community, and Religions Experience in the Songs of the Sage (4Q510–511)." *DSD* 19 (2012): 1–27.

———. "The Material Reconstruction of 4QSongs of the Maskil[b] (4Q511)." *RevQ* 27 (2015): 25–82.

Bachelard, Gaston. *Poetics of Space*. Translated by Maria Jolas. Boston: Beacon, 1969.

Brand, Miryam T. *Evil Within and Without: The Source of Sin and Its Nature as Portrayed in Second Temple Literature*. JAJSup 9. Göttingen: Vandenhoeck & Ruprecht, 2013.

Brooke, George J. "Body Parts in *Barkhi Nafshi* and the Qualifications of Membership in the Worshipping Community." Pages 79–94 in *Sapiential, Liturgical, and Poetical Texts from Qumran*. Edited by Daniel K. Falk, Florentino García Martínez, and Eileen M. Schuller. STDJ 35. Leiden: Brill, 2000.

Chazon, Esther, et al. *Qumran Cave 4.XX: Poetic and Liturgical Texts, Part 2*. DJD XXIX. Oxford: Clarendon, 1999.

Cohn, Yehudah. "Were Tefillin Phylacteries?" *JJS* 59 (2008): 39–57.

Cresswell, Tim. *In Place/Out of Place: Geography, Ideology, and Transgression*. Minneapolis: University of Minnesota Press, 1996.

Douglas, Mary. *Purity and Danger*. London: Routledge, 1966.

Eshel, Esther. "Apotropaic Prayers in the Second Temple Period." Pages 69–88 in *Liturgical Perspectives: Prayer and Poetry in Light of the Dead Sea Scrolls*. Edited by Esther G. Chazon. STDJ 48. Leiden: Brill, 2003.

———. "Genres of Magical Texts in the Dead Sea Scrolls." Pages 395–414 in *Die Dämonen/Demons*. Edited by Armin Lange, Hermann Lichtenberger, and K. F. Diethard Römheld. Tübingen: Mohr Siebeck, 2003.

Flusser, David. "Qumran and Jewish 'Apotropaic' Prayers." *IEJ* 16 (1966): 194–205.

Frazer, James. *The Golden Bough*. Repr., London: Chancellor, 1994.

Frey, Jörg. "Flesh and Spirit in the Palestinian Jewish Sapiential Tradition and in the Qumran Texts." Pages 367–404 in *Wisdom Texts from Qumran and the Development of Sapiential Thought*. Edited by Charlotte Hempel, Armin Lange, and Hermann Lichtenberger. BETL 159. Leuven: Peeters, 2002.

Frisch, Alexandra, and Lawrence H. Schiffman. "The Body in Qumran Literature: Flesh and Spirit, Purity and Impurity in the Dead Sea Scrolls." *DSD* 23 (2016): 155–82.

García Martínez, Florentino. "Magic in the Dead Sea Scrolls." Pages 109–30 in *Qumranica Minora II: Thematic Studies in the Dead Sea Scrolls*. Edited by Eibert J. C. Tigchelaar. STDJ 44. Leiden: Brill, 2007.

Gayer, Asaf. "The Centrality of Prayer and the Stability of Trust: An Analysis of the Hymn of the Maskil in 1QS IX, 25b–XI, 15a." Pages 317–33 in *Ancient Jewish Prayers and Emotions*. Edited by Stefan C. Reif and Renate Egger-Wenzel. DCLS 26. Berlin: de Gruyter, 2016.

Harkins, Angela Kim. *Reading with an "I" to the Heavens: Looking at the Qumran Hodayot through the Lens of Visionary Traditions*. Ekstasis 3. Berlin: de Gruyter, 2011.

Hogeterp, Albert L. A. "The Eschatology of the Two Spirits Treatise Revisited." *RevQ* 23 (2007): 247–58.

Horst, Pieter van der, and Judith H. Newman. *Early Jewish Prayers in Greek: A Commentary*. CEJL. Berlin: de Gruyter, 2008.

Johnston, Sarah Iles. "Sacrifice in the Greek Magical Papyri." Pages 344–58 in *Magic and Ritual in the Ancient World*. Edited by Paul Mirecki and Marvin Meyer. RGRW 141. Leiden: Brill, 2002.

Klein, Anja. "From the 'Right Spirit' to the 'Spirit of Truth': Observations on Psalm 51 and 1QS." Pages 171–91 in *Dynamics of Language and Exegesis at Qumran*. Edited by Devorah Dimant and Reinhard G. Kratz. FAT 2/35. Tübingen: Mohr Siebeck, 2009.

Krause, Andrew R. "Community, Alterity, and Space in the Qumran Covenant Curses." *DSD* 25 (2018): 217–37.

———. "Protected Sects: The Apotropaic Performance and Function of 4QIncantation and 4QSongs of the Maskil and Their Relevance for the Study of the Hodayot." *JAJ* 5 (2014): 25–39.

Levison, John R. *Filled with the Spirit*. Grand Rapids: Eerdmans, 2009.

———. *The Spirit in First-Century Judaism*. AGJU 29. Leiden: Brill, 1997.

Lyons, William J., and Andy M. Reimer. "The Demonic Virus and Qumran Studies: Some Preventative Measures." *DSD* 5 (1998): 16–32.

Magness, Jodi. "They Shall See the Glory of the Lord (Isa 35:2): Eschatological Perfection and Purity at Qumran and in Jesus' Movement." *JSHJ* 14 (2016): 99–119.

May, Herbert G. "Cosmological Reference in the Qumran Doctrine of the Two Spirits and in Old Testament Imagery." *JBL* 82 (1963): 1–14.

Newsom, Carol A. *The Self as Symbolic Space: Constructing Identity and Community at Qumran*. STDJ 52. Leiden: Brill, 2004.

Nitzan, Bilhah. *Qumran Prayer and Religious Poetry*. STDJ 12. Leiden: Brill, 1994.

Pajunen, Mika S. "Exodus and Exile as Prototypes of Justice: Prophecies in the *Psalms of Solomon* and the *Barkhi Nafshi* Hymns." Pages 252–77 in *Functions of Psalms and Prayers in the Late Second Temple Period*. Edited by Mika S. Pajunen and Jeremy Penner. BZAW 486. Berlin: de Gruyter, 2017.

———. *The Land of the Elect and Justice for All: Reading Psalms in the Dead Sea Scrolls in Light of 4Q381*. JAJSup 14. Göttingen: Vandenhoeck & Ruprecht, 2013.

Popović, Mladen. "Anthropology, Pneumatology, and Demonology in Early Judaism: The *Two Spirits Treatise* (1QS 3:13–4:26) and Other Texts from the Dead Sea Scrolls." Pages 58–98 in *Dust of the Ground and Breath of Life (Gen 2:7): The Problem of a Dualistic Anthropology in Early Judaism and Christianity*. Edited by Jacques T. A. G. M. van Ruiten and George H. van Kooten. TBN 20. Leiden: Brill, 2016.

———. *Reading the Human Body: Physiognomics and Astrology in the Dead Sea Scrolls and Hellenistic-Early Roman Period Judaism*. STDJ 67. Leiden: Brill, 2007.

Rappaport, Roy. *Ritual and Religion in the Making of Humanity*. CSCA 110. Cambridge: Cambridge University Press, 1999.

Reynolds, Bennie, III. "A Dwelling Place of Demons: Demonology and Apocalypticism in the Dead Sea Scrolls." Pages 23–54 in *Apocalyp-*

*tic Thinking in Early Judaism: Engaging with John Collins' "Apocalyptic Imagination."* Edited by Sidnie White Crawford and Cecilia Wassen. JSJSup 182. Leiden: Brill, 2018.

Seely, David Rolph. "Implanting Pious Qualities in the *Barki Nafshi* Hymns." Pages 322–31 in *The Dead Sea Scrolls: Fifty Years after Their Discovery.* Edited by Lawrence H. Schiffman, Emanuel Tov, and James C. VanderKam. Jerusalem: Israel Exploration Society, 2000.

Shaked, Shaul. "Qumran and Iran: Further Considerations." *IOS* 2 (1972): 433–46.

Shepardson, Christine. *Controlling Contested Places: Late Antique Antioch and the Spatial Politics of Religious Controversy.* Berkeley: University of California Press, 2014.

Stegemann, Hartmut, Eileen Schuller, and Carol A. Newsom. *Qumran Cave 1.III: 1QHodayot$^a$, with Incorporation of 1QHodayot$^b$ and 4QHodayot$^{a-f}$.* DJD XL. Oxford: Clarendon, 2009.

Stuckenbruck, Loren T. "The Interiorization of Dualism within the Human Being in Second Temple Judaism." Pages 145–68 in *Light against Darkness: Dualism in Ancient Mediterranean Religion and the Contemporary World.* Edited by Armin Lange, Eric M. Meyers, Bennie H. Reynolds, and Randall Styers. JAJSup 2. Gottingen: Vandenhoeck & Ruprecht, 2011.

Swartz, Michael D. "Magical Piety in Ancient and Medieval Judaism." Pages 167–83 in *Ancient Magic and Ritual Power.* Edited by Marvin Meyer and Paul Mirecki. RGRW 129. Leiden: Brill, 1995.

———. "Sacrificial Themes in Jewish Magic." Pages 303–15 in *Magic and Ritual in the Ancient World.* Edited by Paul Mirecki and Marvin Meyer. RGRW 141. Leiden: Brill, 2002.

Tigchelaar, Eibert J. C. "The Evil Inclination in the Dead Sea Scrolls, with a Re-edition of 4Q468i (4QSectarian Text?)." Pages 347–57 in *Empsychoi Logoi: Religious Innovations in Antiquity.* Edited by Alberdina Houtman, Albert de Jong, and Magda Misset-van de Weg. AGJU 73. Leiden: Brill, 2008.

Tov, Emanuel. *The Texts in the Judaean Desert: Indices and an Introduction to the Discoveries in the Judean Desert Series.* DJD XXXIX. Oxford: Clarendon, 2002.

Wassen, Cecilia. "What Do Angels Have against the Blind and the Deaf? Rules of Exclusion in the Dead Sea Scrolls." Pages 115–29 in *Common Judaism: Explorations in Second Temple Judaism.* Edited by Wayne O. McCready and Adele Reinhartz. Minneapolis: Fortress, 2008.

Wernberg-Møller, Preben. *The Manual of Discipline: Translated and Annotated with an Introduction.* STDJ 1. Leiden: Brill, 1957.

———. "A Reconsideration of the Two Spirits in the Rule of the Community (1QS III 13–IV 26)." *RevQ* 3 (1961): 413–41.

Wintermute, Orval S. "Jubilees: A New Translation and Introduction." *OTP* 2:35–142.

Part 3
The Body

# Sexuality and Self-Deprecation in the Thanksgiving Psalms: Questions of Celibacy and the Presence of Women in the Yaḥad

Nicholas Meyer

Within a year of the initial discoveries, Eleazar Sukenik had made a link between the archeological finds at Qumran and the Essenes, the ancient Judean group known to scholars by the secondhand descriptions of, primarily, Philo, Josephus, and Pliny the Elder.[1] This Essene hypothesis seemed to find striking confirmation in the apparent sexual exclusiveness of the group described in the Rule of the Community (1QS), a text that captured the imagination of scholars like few others, for despite Josephus's late admission that a group of Essenes did in fact marry and procreate, the classical descriptions tended to make the group's celibacy—and maleness—defining features of its identity.[2] Importantly, they attributed these

---

1. In fact, it is likely that Josephus had some firsthand knowledge of the Essenes, even if we permit ourselves some skepticism of the self-portrait in *Vita* 9–12, and Pliny seems not to identify them as Jews. For a recent review of these sources in relation to the Scrolls, see Joan E. Taylor, "The Classical Sources on the Essenes and the Scrolls Communities," in *The Oxford Handbook of the Dead Sea Scrolls*, ed. Timothy H. Lim and John J. Collins (Oxford: Oxford University Press, 2010), 173–99; Taylor, *The Essenes, The Scrolls, and the Dead Sea* (Oxford: Oxford University Press, 2012). An account of the development of the Essene hypothesis is provided by Hartmut Stegemann, "The Qumran Essenes—Local Members of the Main Jewish Union in Late Second Temple Times," in *The Madrid Qumran Congress: Proceedings of the International Congress on the Dead Sea Scrolls, Madrid, 18–21 March, 1991*, ed. Luis Vegas Montaner and Julio Trebeolle Barrera, STDJ 11 (Leiden: Brill, 1992), 1:83–166.

2. According to Pliny, they are "without women and renouncing love entirely, without money, and having for company only the palm trees"; "for thousands of centuries a race has existed which is eternal yet into which no one is born" (*Nat.* 5.73). Philo says, "no Essaean takes a woman" (*Hypoth.* 11.14) and that "they are men of

qualities to a negative view of pleasure and to misogyny, and in the case of those who did marry, Josephus imputed the dutiful motive to prolong the human race.[3] Thus celibacy was interpreted as the norm, male, and entangled in a negative view of sexuality. The Rule of the Community offered little resistance to these assumptions.[4]

Today, however, the understanding of sectarian praxis around marriage, sexuality, and family has changed dramatically. The widespread presence of women and children and the strict regulation, rather than the complete rejection, of sexual relations among the sectarians are widely accepted as following from the evidence. So what changed? With the full publication of the Scrolls, scholars have been able to reopen the conversation around sex and marriage by highlighting not just the new but also the

---

ripe years already inclining to old age" (*Hypoth.* 11.3). And Josephus maintains, "they disdain marriage for themselves" (*B.J.* 2.120) and "take no wives" (*A.J.* 18.21), and yet, "there exists another order of Essenes who, although in agreement with the others on the way of life, usages, and customs, are separated from them on the subject of marriage" (*B.J.* 2.160–161). Translations follow Geza Vermes and Martin Goodman, eds., *The Essenes: According to the Classical Sources* (Sheffield: JSOT Press, 1989).

3. Philo: "No Essaean takes a woman because women are selfish, excessively jealous, skillful in ensnaring the morals of a spouse and in seducing him by endless charms. Women set out to flatter, and wear all sorts of masks, like actors on the stage; then, when they have bewitched the eye and captured the ear, when, that is to say, they have deceived the lower senses, they next lead the sovereign mind astray" (*Hypoth.* 11.14–15). Josephus: "The Essenes renounce pleasure as an evil, and regard continence and resistance to the passions as a virtue. They disdain marriage for themselves.... It is not that they abolish marriage, or the propagation of the species resulting from it, but they are on their guard against the licentiousness of women and are convinced that none of them is faithful to one man" (*B.J.* 2.120–121). As Eileen Schuller notes, these explanations are transparently interpretive glosses reflecting in the first place the views of Philo and Josephus. See Schuller, "Evidence for Women in the Community of the Dead Sea Scrolls," in *Voluntary Associations in the Graeco-Roman World*, ed. John S. Kloppenborg and Stephen G. Wilson (London: Routledge, 1996), 255.

4. On celibacy in general, see Pieter Willem van der Horst, "Celibacy in Early Judaism," *RB* 109 (2002): 390–402; Gary M. Anderson, "Celibacy or Consummation in the Garden: Reflections on Early Jewish and Christian Interpretations of the Garden of Eden," *HTR* 82 (1989): 121–48; Joseph M. Baumgarten, "Celibacy," *EDSS* 1:122–25. On celibacy in the Greco-Roman world, see Calvin J. Roetzel, "Sex and the Single God: Celibacy as Social Deviancy in the Roman Period," in *Text and Artifact in the Religions of Mediterranean Antiquity: Essays in Honour of Peter Richardson*, ed. Stephen G. Wilson and Michel Desjardins (Waterloo, ON: Wilfried Laurier University Press, 2000), 231–48.

familiar evidence that had been overshadowed by the exaggerated impact of the Rule of the Community.[5] Familiar texts, such as the Damascus Document (CD) and the Rule of the Congregation, which take marriage as the norm, are no longer left on the periphery of these questions, bolstered as they now are by abundant corroborating testimony.[6] Even the most androcentric texts, such as the Rule of the Community, have proven amenable to feminist readings pressing home the difference between rhetorical representation and reality, and suggesting indications of the presence of women and children among the sectarians.[7] Meanwhile, the relatively few excavated gravesites found in the cemetery (or cemeteries) adjacent to the ancient buildings, which were once thought to provide clear confirmation

---

5. Important studies that contributed to broadening scholarly perspective on the presence of women include Joseph M. Baumgarten, "The Qumran-Essene Restraints on Marriage," in *Archaeology and History in the Dead Sea Scrolls: The New York University Conference in Memory of Yigael Yadin* (Sheffield: JSOT Press, 1990), 13–24; Lawrence H. Schiffman, *Reclaiming the Dead Sea Scrolls: The History of Judaism, the Background of Christianity, the Lost Library of Qumran* (New York: Doubleday, 1994), 127–43; Eileen M. Schuller, "Women in the Dead Sea Scrolls," in *Methods of Investigation of the Dead Sea Scrolls and the Khirbet Qumran Site: Present Realities and Future Prospects*, ed. Michael O. Wise et al., ANYAS 722 (New York: New York Academy of Science, 1994), 115–31; Schuller, "Women in the Dead Sea Scrolls," in *The Dead Sea Scrolls after Fifty Years: A Comprehensive Assessment*, ed. Peter W. Flint and James C. VanderKam (Leiden: Brill, 1999), 2:117–44; Sidnie White Crawford, "Not according to Rule: Women, the Dead Sea Scrolls and Qumran," in *Emanuel: Studies in Hebrew Bible, Septuagint, and Dead Sea Scrolls in Honor of Emanuel Tov*, ed. Shalom M. Paul et al., VTSup 94 (Leiden: Brill, 2003), 127–50; Cecilia Wassen, *Women in the Damascus Document*, AcBib 21 (Atlanta: Society of Biblical Literature, 2005).

6. For recent summaries, see Eileen M. Schuller, "Women in the Dead Sea Scrolls: Research in the Past Decade and Future Directions," in *Dead Sea Scrolls and Contemporary Culture: Proceedings of the International Conference Held at the Israel Museum, Jerusalem (July 6–8, 2008)*, ed. Adolfo D. Roitman, Lawrence H. Schiffman, and Shani Tzoref, STDJ 93 (Leiden: Brill, 2011), 571–88; Tal Ilan, "Women in Qumran and the Dead Sea Scrolls," in Lim and Collins, *Oxford Handbook of the Dead Sea Scrolls*, 123–47.

7. See Maxine L. Grossman, "Gendered Sectarians: Envisioning Women (and Men) at Qumran," in *Celebrate Her for the Fruit of Her Hands: Essays in Honor of Carol L. Meyers*, ed. Susan Ackerman, Charles E. Carter, and Beth Alpert Nakhai (Winona Lake, IN: Eisenbrauns, 2015), 265–88; Grossman, "Rethinking Gender in the Community Rule: An Experiment in Sociology," in Roitman, Schiffman, and Tzoref, *Dead Sea Scrolls and Contemporary Culture*, 497–512; Joan E. Taylor, "Women, Children, and Celibate Men in Serekh Texts," *HTR* 104 (2011): 171–90.

of the classical descriptions, have proven to be complex, indecisive, and of diminished relevance when we acknowledge that the sectarians lived not just in one location but in "camps" (CD VII, 6, etc.) and "dwellings" (1QS VI, 2) throughout the land.[8] Thus, celibacy, once regarded as the norm, has become the exception—and for some has fallen out of the picture entirely.[9]

In this context, it is natural for scholars to seek a fresh evaluation of the sectarian attitude toward sexuality starting from the primary rather than the secondary evidence. Here, some of the most recent work, while admitting the patriarchal and condescending posture of much of the material, nevertheless registers an affirming and positive view of women and sexual life on the part of the sectarians.[10] For instance, the testi-

---

8. Recent summaries include Schuller, "Women in the Dead Sea Scrolls: Research," 578–81; Eric M. Meyers, "Khirbet Qumran and Its Environs," in Lim and Collins, *Oxford Handbook of the Dead Sea Scrolls*, 36–37; Rachel Hachlili, "The Qumran Cemetery Reassessed," in Lim and Collins, *Oxford Handbook of the Dead Sea Scrolls*, 65–67.

9. Such is the case for Paul Heger, "Celibacy in Qumran: Hellenistic Fiction or Reality? Qumran's Attitude toward Sex," *RevQ* 26 (2013): 53–90. Hartmut Stegemann also attempts to explain how the Essenes may have merely *appeared* celibate. See Stegemann, *The Library of Qumran: On the Essenes, Qumran, John the Baptist, and Jesus* (Leiden: Brill, 1998), 193–98. For some, the rejection of celibacy entails the rejection of the Essene hypothesis as well. See Albert I. Baumgarten, "Who Cares and Why Does It Matter? Qumran and the Essenes, Once Again!," *DSD* 11 (2004): 174–90; Eyal Regev, "Cherchez les femmes: Were the Yaḥad Celibates?," *DSD* 15 (2008): 253–84. Scholars are also less inclined to think only in terms of the absolute rejection of marriage but also of foregoing sex after childbearing years, of prolonged abstention from sex during pregnancy, or perhaps of regular, extended periods of sexual abstinence when away from the household. For cautions against the binary of marriage/celibacy, see Taylor, "Women, Children, and Celibate Men," 189; Maxine Grossman, "Queerly Sectarian: Jewish Difference, the Dead Sea Scrolls, and Marital Disciplines," *JJI* 11 (2018): 87–105; Grossman, "The World of Qumran and the Sectarian Dead Sea Scrolls in Gendered Perspective," in *Early Jewish Writings: Apocrypha*, ed. Eileen M. Schuller and Marie-Theres Wacker, BW 3.1 (Atlanta: SBL Press, 2017), 245; Crawford, "Not according to Rule," 146–47.

10. See Cecilia Wassen, "Women, Worship, Wilderness, and War: Celibacy and the Constructions of Identity in the Dead Sea Scrolls," in *Sibyls, Scriptures, and Scrolls: John Collins at Seventy*, ed. Joel Baden, Hindy Najman, and Eibert J. C. Tigchelaar, JSJSup 175 (Leiden: Brill, 2017), 1361–85; Wassen, "The Importance of Marriage in the Construction of Sectarian Identity in the Dead Sea Scrolls," in *Social Memory and Social Identity in the Study of Early Judaism and Early Christianity*, ed. Samuel Byrskog, Raimo Hakola, and Jutta Jokiranta, NTOA/SUNT (Göttingen: Vandenhoeck & Ruprecht, 2016), 127–50; Heger, "Celibacy in Qumran"; William R. G. Loader, *The*

mony and intelligence of women could be prized (1QSa I, 11; 4Q502 1–3, 6–7), promises of fruitful seed may not be simply metaphorical (1QS IV, 7; 1QH^a IV, 26–27), and the bond between male and female is affirmed by reference to Gen 1:27 (CD IV, 21; see 4Q502 1–3, 3–7), a text whose reception in rabbinic Judaism is often read back into these texts to affirm the rightful place of sex among the sectarians. On this view, if celibacy was practiced, its basis must not have been in a negative view of sex, of women, or even perhaps of ritual impurity, but in a desire to maximize one's time for devotion and study and/or as a by-product of the stricter regulation of sexual life in sectarian halakah, including stipulations against remarriage (possibly, CD IV, 20–21; see 11Q19 LVII, 17–19) and nonprocreative sex (4Q270 2 II, 15–17; 7 I, 12–13).[11] The old rationales for celibacy have dissolved: the Scrolls are supposed to display neither the patent misogyny that Philo and Josephus associate with the Essenes, nor, in the words of William Loader, any "implication that human sexuality is something negative."[12]

It is here I want to suggest that the texts known as the Thanksgiving Psalms, or Hodayot (1QH^a), become relevant. These texts have not featured prominently in the discussion around celibacy, primarily meriting reference for a positive appreciation of the processes of giving birth and nursing (1QH^a XI, 6–19 and XVII, 36). However, not only do they supply a strong counterperspective to the positive picture that is now frequently reconstructed by scholars, but they can also be placed within the textual lineage (CD VII; 1QS VIII, IX, and XI) that reflects the best indications that celibacy was practiced by some sectarians. In these latter texts, a composite profile emerges of an elite wing within the sectarians who strove for perfect holiness with the goal of facilitating their performance of a spiritual priesthood in the company of angels. In my conclusion, I will reflect on how the depreciative view of sexuality in the Thanksgiving Psalms might reflect on the practice of celibacy, the inclusion of women, and the view of the female sex more generally.

---

*Dead Sea Scrolls on Sexuality: Attitudes towards Sexuality in Sectarian and Related Literature at Qumran* (Grand Rapids: Eerdmans, 2009).

11. These restraints are discussed by Baumgarten, "Qumran-Essene Restraints"; Crawford, "Not according to Rule."

12. Loader, *Dead Sea Scrolls*, 387. Arguing that the scrolls do "not display any disdain for women or for sexual life," Paul Heger concludes that the celibacy of the Essenes was a pure fiction ("Celibacy in Qumran," 54).

## Celibacy, Perfection of Way, and Priestly Communion with Angels

I begin by tracing the textual lineage, which helps us to contextualize the negative view of sexuality in the Thanksgiving Psalms within a practice of celibacy and a vision of priestly communion with angels. Women's presence and the practice of marriage are well attested even in plainly sectarian documents, so we must ask: Does there remain good reason to think that some practice of celibacy was also to be found among the sectarians? I approach the question with two aims in mind: to ascertain whether there is strong internal evidence of a division within the covenanters along these lines and, if so, to recover the symbolic framework within which celibacy operated.

The strongest evidence for a celibate group within the covenanters is in fact found in a work that plainly presumes its members marry and have children. Column VII of CD sets up a contrast between those who "walk ... in perfect holiness [בתמים קדש]" (VII, 4–5), for whom "God's covenant is an assurance to them to bring them life for a thousand generation(s)" (VII, 5–6),[13] on the one hand, and "all those who despise" God's covenant and can look forward to his wrath (VII, 9), on the other. Sitting intrusively between these contrasts, however, is the introduction of a division within the covenanters, which Joseph Baumgarten and Elisha Qimron have interpreted as indicative of the difference between marrying and nonmarrying sectarians.[14] Cecilia Wassen has effectively criticized aspects of their reading but still allows that the text constitutes evidence for the practice of celibacy.[15] In what follows, the text is presented with additional material from the parallel in CD B XIX, 2–5:

---

13. For text and translation, see the edition prepared by Joseph Baumgarten and Daniel R. Schwartz in *Damascus Document, War Scroll, and Related Documents*, vol. 2 of *The Dead Sea Scrolls: Hebrew, Aramaic, and Greek Texts with English Translations*, ed. James H. Charlesworth, PTSDSSP (Louisville: Westminster John Knox, 1995).

14. Baumgarten, "Qumran-Essene Restraints on Marriage"; Elisha Qimron, "Celibacy in the Dead Sea Scrolls and the Two Kinds of Sectarians," in *The Madrid Qumran Congress: Proceedings of the International Congress on the Dead Sea Scrolls, Madrid, 18-21 March, 1991*, ed. Luis Vegas Montaner and Julio Trebeolle Barrera, STDJ 11 (Leiden: Brill, 1992), 1:287–294; see also John J. Collins, *Beyond the Qumran Community: The Sectarian Movement of the Dead Sea Scrolls* (Grand Rapids: Eerdmans, 2010), 31–33.

15. Wassen, *Women in the Damascus Document*, 122–30; Wassen, "Women, Worship, Wilderness, and War," 1362.

But if they live (in) camps, according to the rule of the Land [manuscript B: which is as it was previously], and take wives [manuscript B: according to the custom of the Torah] and beget sons, then they shall walk according to the Torah and the precept established according to the rule of the Torah, as he said, "Between a man and his wife and between a father and his son." (CD VII, 6–9)

Wassen has made the point that, on the basis of the whole of CD, the initial introduction of those who "walk in perfect holiness" (VII, 4–5) should be read as a reference to the entire community, which clearly consists of families.[16] However, the intrusive "but if" (ואם) makes family life the implied exception to what precedes, for the provision of normalizing qualifications ("according to the rule of the land," "as it was previously," "according to the custom of the Torah") is a strange way to refer to what is supposed to be taken for granted.[17] For these reasons, the text may be best regarded as an interpolation, a redactional element, reflecting the reception of CD among celibates. If this is the case, it becomes apparent that not only were there celibate sectarians, but that they (or, rather, the ones in evidence here) lived apart from those who married and dwelt in camps and that they regarded their own way of life as that which constituted the way of perfection, par excellence.[18]

The motivation for this practice of celibacy can be detected in the contrast created between walking "in perfect holiness" (בתמים קדש) and marrying and having children. Celibacy emerged from a desire to achieve a more consistent experience and perhaps degree of holiness, probably interpreted in part as consisting of ritual purity. They lived apart from

---

16. See Wassen, *Women in the Damascus Document*, 122–30, citing CD II, 15–16; XX, 2, 5, 7. At the very least, it includes men who have families (CD XX, 13).

17. It is these "normalizing qualifications" that justify the translation of ואם as "but if." For the sense of "whenever," see Gen 38:9; Ps 78:34; 1QSa I, 25 and II, 11.

18. One might push back that the text need not be read this way; it is also true, however, that there would have been no need to include "in camps" if this were not also relevant to the distinction being made. Furthermore, it is possible that the alternative, more perfect path, is contained in the immediately preceding statement that "they shall live a thousand generations," which could have been construed as envisioning a radically different (celibate) future from what is introduced by ואם. This, however, breaks down the contrast between those who walk in perfect holiness and await God's blessing and the wicked, who await his cursing. Moreover, there would be a surplus of rhetoric in the description of marriage and childbearing if there were no preference for (or awareness of) an alternative lifestyle that already calls for a state of celibacy.

the camps, presumably, to more readily manage and minimize impurity. Qimron has suggested that the implicit counterpart to "camps" is the holy camp of the temple city, Jerusalem.[19] It may be, then, that these ascetics dwelled in Jerusalem, where, according to sectarian law, sexual activity was forbidden (11Q19 XLV, 7-12; XLVI, 16-18; CD XII, 1-2), perhaps at Qumran, and/or various places throughout the land, as a metaphorical temple. Wherever they dwelt, they seem to have distinguished themselves on the level of holiness maintained in their daily lives (by refraining from marriage/sex) and in their social spheres (by dwelling apart from the camps).

The profile of an elite priestly group that employs temple symbolism in its self-definition is to be found, above all, in the Rule of the Community.[20] Beginning in column V, the "council of the *yaḥad*" takes center stage (1QS V, 7; VI, 3, 10, 12-13, 14; VII, 2, 22, 24; VIII, 1, 5, 11, 22; but also III, 2 and 6). It is possible that this is a unique group within the broader *yaḥad* (as 1QSa might imply), or it may be a synonym for the *yaḥad*.[21] In any case, columns VIII and IX do seem to envision the emergence of an elite group within the *yaḥad*, which is especially characterized by holiness and sanctuary symbolism, so that wherever one sees the internal distinction, there is a striking agreement with the situation implied by CD VII.[22]

---

19. See Qimron, "Celibacy in the Dead Sea Scrolls," 289, citing 4QMMT B 29-30, 59-62.

20. The relationship of Serekh ha-Yaḥad (S) to the Damascus Document (D) is commonly regarded to be more complex than previously allowed, but some important distinctions remain: the text is androcentric in a way that D is not, in part due to the near total omission of matters related to the maintenance of ritual/sexual purity in its regulations; it describes a more totalizing pattern of community structure, involving communal property, pure meals, and constant study; and it prefers to describe the group as the יחד instead of D's עדה. For a relatively recent accounting of the relationship between these texts, see Collins, *Beyond the Qumran Community*, 54-60.

21. Taylor, who detects the presence of "hidden women" in cols. I-IV, suggests that the "council of the *yaḥad*" addresses an elite celibate wing within the *yaḥad* ("Women, Children, and Celibate Men," 181-82). Collins, however, takes the "council of the *yaḥad*" in 1QS simply as a synonym for the (in his view, probably celibate) *yaḥad*, although in 1QSa, which he argues legislates for the future, he sees it as addressing an elite group within the congregation of all Israel (*Beyond the Qumran Community*, 69-78, 150-51).

22. On cols. VIII-IX, see Shane Berg, "An Elite Group within the *Yaḥad*: Revisiting 1QS 8-9," in *Qumran Studies: New Approaches, New Questions*, ed. Michael Thomas Davis and Brent A. Strawn (Grand Rapids: Eerdmans, 2007), 161-77.

Temple function is briefly described in 1QS V, 5-6, but the symbolism is only developed in column VIII with the description of "an eternal plant, the House of Holiness for Israel, a most holy assembly for Aaron ... offering up a sweet odor ... a house of perfection and truth in Israel ... to atone for the land" (1QS VIII, 5-10), making atonement not with offerings of flesh but of the lips and perfection of behavior.[23] Column IX elaborates:

> When ... these become in Israel a foundation of the Holy Spirit in eternal truth, they shall atone for iniquitous guilt and for sinful unfaithfulness, so that (God's) favor for the land (is obtained) without the flesh of burnt-offerings and without the fat of sacrifices. The proper offerings of the lips for judgment (is as) a righteous sweetness, and the perfect of the way (are as) a pleasing freewill offering. At that time the men of the Community shall separate themselves (as) a House of Holiness for Aaron, for the Community of the most Holy Ones, and a house of the Community for Israel; (these are) the ones who walk perfectly [ההולכים בתמים]. (1QS IX, 3-6)

There is admittedly much that is uncertain about the precise identity of the group described herein, but that something like it did in fact emerge seems confirmed by column XI. The priestly attributes described in the previous columns are now expressed in terms of the present mystical communion with the heavenly world. The author professes to have beheld eternal, hidden truths and a hidden spring of glory (1QS XI, 3-7), and then speaks of the elect:

> Those whom God has chosen he has set as an eternal possession. He has allowed them to inherit the lot of the holy ones. With the sons of heaven he has joined together their assembly for [or "to form"] the Council of the Community [לעצת היחד]. (Their) assembly (is) a House of Holiness for [or "to form"] the eternal plant during every time to come. (1QS XI, 7-9)

As a member of the Council of the Community, the author has seen heavenly realities and is joined to the sons of heaven. In some sense, he celebrates an angelic life, and this, as we know, was to be a life without

---

23. For text and translation (at times lightly modified here), see James H. Charlesworth, ed., *Rule of the Community and Related Documents*, vol. 1 of *The Dead Sea Scrolls: Hebrew, Aramaic, and Greek Texts with English Translations*, PTSDSSP (Louisville: Westminster John Knox, 1994).

sex (see 1 En. 15; Mark 12:25).[24] The totalizing form of communal life described in 1QS V–IX is focused on the performance of this liturgical mysticism, and such a raison d'être would be well served by normalizing sexual abstinence.[25] It is a strong inference, therefore, that CD's celibates, those who regarded themselves first and foremost as ones who walked in perfect holiness, were in fact to be found in the elite community described in 1QS V–IX.[26]

In general, the outline above is not unique to me, nor does it address a myriad of complications of textual and social development and diversity that are still being worked out in the literature.[27] I have attempted only to outline the best evidence for a practice of celibacy and the symbolic system within which it appears to have operated. Given that there is thus good evidence for the practice and that it was set over against marriage by its provision of greater holiness, it does seem incongruous or at least unexpected that when scholars attempt to survey sectarian attitudes toward sexuality, many of them are reporting only positive findings. Was no expression given to the sense that sexuality posed an obstacle to ritual purity, let alone to the heavenly life?[28]

---

24. See Crispin H. T. Fletcher-Louis, *All the Glory of Adam: Liturgical Anthropology in the Dead Sea Scrolls*, STDJ 42 (Leiden: Brill, 2002), 131–34; John J. Collins, "The Angelic Life," in *Metamorphoses: Resurrection, Body and Transformative Practices in Early Christianity*, ed. Turid Karlsen Seim and Jorunn Økland, Ekstasis 1 (Berlin: de Gruyter, 2009), 301–2; Devorah Dimant, "Men as Angels: The Self-Image of the Qumran Community," in *Religion and Politics in the Ancient Near East*, ed. Adele Berlin (Bethesda: University Press of Maryland, 1996), 102.

25. I agree with Cecilia Wassen that the vision would not require celibacy; my argument is that it would be advanced by celibacy, and given the evidence of the presence of elite celibates and of their dwelling in distinct communities, it seems a valid inference to correlate the two (see Wassen, "Women, Worship, Wilderness, and War," 1372–73).

26. However, one need not think only in terms of the absolute rejection of sex and marriage; the group may consist of elders, who are now celibate, for instance. This would be one possibility to explain how in 1QSb priests, apparently members of the Council of the Community, appear also to be heads of families (see II, 28; III, 2, 4).

27. See the discussion of many such issues in Collins, *Beyond the Qumran Community*.

28. Fletcher-Louis has suggested that we find such in claims to have transcended the flesh בשר, stating that they are "certainly not *limited to*, but probably *include*[*s*], a fully sexual life." As he notes, בשר can function euphemistically for the genitals in the Hebrew Bible, but in none of the Scrolls he cites (Sir 45:4; Jub. 31.14; 1QH$^a$ VII, 20 [=

## Sexuality as Self-Deprecation in the Thanksgiving Psalms

Enter the sectarian psalms. These psalms, especially the Thanksgiving Psalms, or Hodayot, are well known for celebrating the kind of access to the heavenly world described in 1QS in the Psalm of the Maskil, as they speak of becoming princes in the eternal lot and growing into an eternal planting (1QH<sup>a</sup> XIV, 17–18; XVI, 5–23), of being granted access to angelic knowledge (1QH<sup>a</sup> VIII, 12–16; XI, 20–24), or of being raised to the eternal height to be with the divine beings (1QH<sup>a</sup> XI, 20–24; XXVI, 27–28).[29] The Psalm of the Maskil, 1QS IX, 26–XI, 22, serves for us as a textual link between CD VII and its association of celibacy with perfection of holiness and the sexual self-deprecation we are to study in the Thanksgiving Psalms.[30] In the latter half of this psalm, such proximity to heavenly realities immediately evokes a passage of anthropological abasement: "But, I belong to wicked *adam*," says the speaker, as he goes on to lament human sinfulness, at times using the language of impurity ("he cleanses me of the *niddah* of the human being," 1QS XI, 9, 14–15) and reciting the fact of his being "born of woman" (ילוד אשה, 1QS XI, 21).[31] In this and four closely related texts, in which the human condition is debased within the context of the praise of God, the language of sexuality features prominently.[32] However, the language of such texts has been frequently overlooked in discussions of celibacy, generally referred to as primarily expressive of moral impurity, or regarded as expressing mere human lowliness without any

---

l. 30 in DJD XL]; 4Q491c 1, 7) does it clearly have this meaning (Fletcher-Louis, *All the Glory*, 134). His intuition, however, will receive support in the texts considered here.

29. Texts could be multiplied many times. See Nicholas A. Meyer, *Adam's Dust and Adam's Glory in the Hodayot and the Letters of Paul: Rethinking Anthropogony and Theology*, NovTSup 168 (Leiden: Brill, 2016), 32–37, 64–94.

30. עצת היחד does not occur in the Hodayot, but עצת קודש (1QH<sup>a</sup> XV, 13; see 1QS II, 25; VIII, 21; 1QSa II, 9), עדת יחד (1QH<sup>a</sup> XXVI, 28), and יחד on its own, with a particularly close association with angelic communion in XIX, 17 (see ll. 13–17), do so appear. Moreover, many psalms, or groups of psalms, in 1QH<sup>a</sup> are also attributed to the Maskil (V, 12; VII, 21; XX, 7; XXV, 34).

31. A similar passage is found in the Psalms of the Sabbath Sacrifice, 4Q400 2, 7: the earthly priests ask, "[What] is the offering of our tongue of dust (compared) with the knowledge of the div[ine beings?"

32. These have the form of the much discussed *Niedrigkeitsdoxologien*, on which see Meyer, *Adam's Dust and Adam's Glory*, 32–37.

implicit notion of negativity, such as sinfulness or disgust.[33] But as we shall see, the rhetoric of self-abasement in these texts is sexually charged, and its expression bears the imprint of a subjectivity chastened by the experience of heavenly election.

For the sake of space, here I cite only three of the texts that will be drawn on in the discussion below, those from the Thanksgiving Psalms.[34] They provide the clearest expressions of sexual self-deprecation, which, once understood, will allow us to see these resonances elsewhere in more terse expressions as well.

> 1QH[a] V, 31-33: What is one born of woman [ילוד אשה] amid all your [gre]at fearful acts? He is a thing constructed of dust and kneaded with water [מבנה עפר ומגבל מים]. Sin[ful gui]lt is his foundation [א[שמה וחט] אה סודו], obscene shame [ערות קלון], and a sp[ring of (sexual) im]purity [ומ[קור הנ]דה]. And a perverted spirit [ורוח נעוה] rules him.

---

33. Jonathan Klawans references these texts in the discussion of the application of terms for ritual impurity to the matter of moral impurity. See Klawans, *Impurity and Sin in Ancient Judaism* (Oxford: Oxford University Press, 2000), 75, 78. Jason Maston likewise refers to the language of these texts as referring in the first place to a person's "sinful deeds." See Maston, *Divine and Human Agency in Second Temple Judaism: A Comparative Study*, WUNT 297 (Tübingen: Mohr Siebeck, 2010), 88 (see also 84). William Loader, admitting that the language of these texts may retain sexual references, nevertheless insists that "nothing suggests that the author sees either the substances or the processes of creation or of procreation as something evil or dirty" and "nothing links nakedness/shame to sin, such as in the Eden story which sees awareness of nakedness as its consequence; nor are the impurities of being human signs of sinfulness" (*Dead Sea Scrolls*, 247, 248). The overlooking of the language of such texts is true of those arguing for and against the practice. While such passages are briefly referenced by Lawrence Schiffman (who sees them as exceptional), they do not feature in discussions considering celibacy by, among others, Cecilia Wassen, Paul Heger, and John J. Collins (Schiffman, *Reclaiming the Dead Sea Scrolls*, 141, 151; Wassen, "Women, Worship, Wilderness, and War"; Wassen, "Importance of Marriage"; Heger, "Celibacy in Qumran"; Collins, *Beyond the Qumran Community*; Collins, "Angelic Life"). This may be due to the fact that these texts are understood to refer to moral impurity, a reading I presently challenge.

34. The others include 1QS XI, especially, XI, 21-22, and from the Songs of the Sage, 4Q511 28+29. With some modifications, texts from the Thanksgiving Psalms are cited from the composite edition of Hartmut Stegemann, Eileen M. Schuller, and Carol A. Newsom, *Qumran Cave 1.III: 1QHodayot[a], with Incorporation of 1QHodayot[b] and 4QHodayot[a-f]*, DJD XL (Oxford: Clarendon, 2009).

1QHªIX, 23–25: Yet I am a creature of clay [יצר החמר] and a thing kneaded with water [ומגבל המים], a foundation of obscenity [סוד הערוה] and a spring of (sexual) impurity [ומקור הנדה], a furnace of iniquity [כור העוון], and a structure of sin [ומבנה החטאה], a spirit of error [רוח התועה], and a perverted being [ונעוה], without understanding, and terrified by righteous judgements.

1QHª XX, 27–30, 35: As for me, from dust [you] took [me [מעפר לקח]תני] and from clay] I was [n]ipped [ומחמר ק[ורצתי] as a spring of (sexual) impurity [למקור נדה] and obscene shame [וערות קלון], a heap of dust [מקוי עפר] and a thing kneaded [with water [מגבל] במים], a council of magg]ots [ה[סוד רמ], a dwelling of darkness [ומדור חושך]. And there is a return to dust for the vessel of clay at the time of [your] anger [...] dust returns to that from which it was taken.... According to my knowledge I have spoken, a creature mixed from clay [מצורוק יצר חמר].

Four features of these texts gain particular significance in the context of this priestly communion with heaven: the first is their unified focus on humanity's earthly origins; the second is the prevalence of terms that reflect sexuality; the third feature is the appearance of several such terms elsewhere in contexts concerned with ritual purity; and, finally, there is the negative estimation that is made of the sexed body. I take each feature in turn.

Focus on earthiness: Each of these texts is concerned with the human creature per se, and its outstanding feature turns out to be earthiness. They interrogate what it means to be earth-born. Multiple expressions point to the condition: "a thing constructed of dust" (1QHª V, 32), "a creature of clay" (1QHª IX, 23), "from dust you took me" (1QHª XX, 27), "from clay I was nipped" (1QHª XX, 27), "a heap of dust" (1QHª XX, 28), "a kneading from dust" (1QS XI, 21), and "moulded from clay" (4Q511 28+29, 4), and so on. Another term, "a thing kneaded with water" (מגבל [ב/ה[מים], 1QHª V, 32; IX, 23; XX, 28 [reconstructed], et al.), likely reflects a reading of Gen 2:7 in light of verse 6 so that God is understood to create the *adam* from dust moistened with the water that had just come up from the ground (see Gen. Rab. 14.1; Exod. Rab. 30.13). Hence we also get the phrases "whose kneading is from dust" (מעפר מגבלו, 1QS XI, 21), "from darkness is my mixture" (מחושך מגבל[י), 4Q511 28+29, 4), and, possibly, elsewhere, "kneaded with nought and nothingess" (מגב[ל און ואפס, 1QHª XXI, 30). This language also at times reflects the decree of Gen 3:19 ("you are dust, and to dust you shall return")[35] when the earthiness of humanity becomes a token of mortality: "dust returns to that from which it was taken" (1QH[a] XX, 29–30), "whose corpse [or "dwelling"] is food for maggots" (1QS XI, 21), "for dust is his longing" (1QS XI, 22), and the total reduction, he is "a council of maggots" (1QH[a] XX, 28). This focus on earthiness likely reflects the observation recorded in the biblical psalms that "the heavens are the LORD's heavens, but the earth he has given to human beings" (Ps 115:16). The worshiper feels a deep disconnect between his or her earthly origin and heavenly lot.

*Terms reflecting sexuality:* These texts move easily between earthiness and sexuality. We find the phrase "born of woman" (ילוד אשה) in 1QH[a] V, 31 as well as in 1QS XI, 21 and elsewhere. The status or nature of one "born of a woman" is interrogated both times and immediately answered by reference to the earthly origins of the human being. As far as can be told, the term is consistently paired with earthiness, just as it is in the book of Job (14:1; 15:14; 25:4), to which the anthropology of these psalms owes so much.[36] There is strong reason to think that in these contexts the term means not just "human being" but "one who is womb-born," thus evoking a deliberate play on the relatedness of earth and womb. This sexual connotation is picked up by Job 14:4 ("Who can bring a clean thing out of an unclean?") and by the attendant terms of a ritual/sexual nature that follow in our present texts, such as "spring of *niddah*" and "obscene shame" (or the related "foundation of obscenity"), discussed below. The term "furnace of iniquity" (כור העוון, 1QH[a] IX, 24) employs a word, כור, that two columns later becomes a transparent metaphor for "womb" (1QH[a] XI, 9, 11, 13).[37] This latter psalm also associates terms such as "womb opening of death"

---

35. Unless otherwise indicated, Scripture quotations follow the NRSV.

36. See Meyer, *Adam's Dust and Adam's Glory*, 58–64; Carol A. Newsom, "Deriving Negative Anthropology through Exegetical Activity: The Hodayot as a Case Study," in *Is There a Text in This Cave? Studies in the Textuality of the Dead Sea Scrolls in Honour of George J. Brooke*, ed. Ariel Feldman, Maria Cioată, and Charlotte Hempel, STDJ 119 (Leiden: Brill, 2017), 258–74. On "born of woman" being paired with earthiness, see 1QH[a] XXIII, 13–14, "vessel of clay ... born of woman"; XXI, 2 and 9–10 are partially preserved and fragmentary, but for references to creation from the earth, see XXI, 9–12; the term is also restored in the very fragmentary 4Q482 1, 4.

37. See also 1QapGen VI, 1. For discussion of this sense of the word in 4Q416 2 III, 17, see John Strugnell, Daniel J. Harrington, and Torleif Elgvin, *Qumran Cave 4.XXIV: Sapiential Texts, Part 2*, DJD XXXIV (Oxford: Clarendon, 1999), 121. Jastrow cites b. Shabb. 140b as a possible use of this word for female pudenda. See Marcus

(משברי מות, XI, 9), "chords of sheol" (חבלי שאול, XI, 10), and "womb opening of the pit" (משברי שחת, XI, 13), clearly reflecting the metaphorical blending of earth and womb.[38] Though often overlooked, the gendering of the earth as feminine and the feminine as earthly is common affair, as when Job affirms, "Naked I came from my mother's womb, and naked I shall return there" (Job 1:21), or when it is asserted that that the angels of heaven are exclusively male (1 En. 15).

There are other terms here that likely riff on earth and womb, specifically by employing double entendres of divine creation and procreation, reflecting the thought of the biblical psalmist, who says, "You knit me together in my mother's womb.... I was ... intricately woven in the depths of the earth" (Ps 139:13, 15), or of Job, who asks of the one whose "hands fashioned" him from clay: "Did you not pour me out like milk and curdle me like cheese?" (Job 10:8–10). Hence, even if they (primarily) reflect creation from the earth, it is likely that many of the following terms evoke procreation. The terms "a dwelling of darkness" (מדור חושך, 1QH$^a$ XX, 28–29) and "from darkness is my mixture" (מחושך מגב[לי, 4Q511 28+29, 4) are readily seen as evoking the darkness of the womb (see Ps 139:11–13; 4Q184 1, 4–10). It has already been suggested that "a thing kneaded with water" takes Gen 2:6 into verse 7 and evokes the mixing/kneading of earth with water as an image of divine creation. It is not unlikely that the earth that secrets water in Gen 2:6 evoked the womb (as it did for Philo in *Opif.* 131–134), which is elsewhere implicitly compared to a spring (Lev 12:7; Prov 5:15; Song 4:12–15), so that "kneaded with water" reflects too the female element of procreation and perhaps the theory that the human being is formed in part from uterine fluid (see Wis 7:1–2).[39] Conversely,

---

Jastrow, *A Dictionary of the Targumim, the Talmud Babli and Yerushalmi, and the Midrashic Literature* (New York: Judaica, 1971), 625.

38. The term משבר when used in the plural suggests the meaning of "(ocean) breakers," and yet the reference is clearly to the womb or cervix. This is part of a complex metaphorical play between womb and underworld torrents in the psalm. See Carol A. Newsom, *The Self as Symbolic Space: Constructing Identity and Community at Qumran*, STDJ 52 (Leiden: Brill, 2004), 246–48.

39. Confirmation of this occurs in each of the texts cited above, from cols. V, IX, and XX, for the term is consistently followed immediately by references to the polluted foundations of the human being with terms discussed below. Wernberg-Møller suggested that מים in this phrase stands for semen (citing Mek. Shir. 8 et al.), but this interpretation was quickly challenged by Jonas Greenfield, who cites rabbinic parallels employing the same verbal root in reference to the creation of Adam from water and

the male element in procreation may be in play via double entendres in the difficult term מצורוק, translated above as though it meant simply "a mixture" (1QH ͣ XX, 35; see 1QS XI, 21; 4Q511 28+29, 3) but that may include a reference to saliva/semen, as well as in the phrase "shaped by hand" (יוצר יד, 1QS XI, 22).⁴⁰ Again, these terms are likely first to reflect creation from the earth, but in contexts discussing what it means to be "born of woman" (or otherwise evoking the sexed body) they are likely to carry sexual resonances as well.

Contexts of ritual purity: Several of the above terms are prominent in contexts concerned with ritual/sexual impurity.⁴¹ In tantalizing fashion, 1QH ͣ XX, 27–29 begins with a reflection on the creation of humankind from the earth and immediately interprets that via a *lamed* of purpose with the quality of being "a spring of *niddah*" and "obscene shame," terms that reappear in column V. These terms are highly redolent of the inextricably sexed nature of the human creature, as the variant phrase סוד הערוה in column IX highlights: "foundation of obscenity."

"Spring of *niddah*" and "obscene shame" (or "foundation of obscenity") always come as a set pair. The latter is the construction ערות קלון. The term קלון, "shame," can be used euphemistically for the genitals (as is Jer 13:26; Nah 3:5), while ערוה, "nakedness," refers immediately either to male or female genitalia (Ezek 16:8, 36; 22:10). ערוה is prominent in the Levitical legislation, where it refers often to female genitalia (e.g., Lev 18:19, alongside נדה), and it occurs in halakic and regulatory contexts in CD V, 10 and 1QS VII, 14 of male nakedness. It has the latter sense also in the War Scroll, where a concern with male ritual purity in the presence of angels is connected to a stipulation against wicked or immodest nakedness (1QM VII, 3–7; X, 1; see Deut 23:15 MT), and finally it occurs in

---

dust in Gen 2:6–7. Greenfield is right to point to Gen 2:6–7 but wrong in supposing that this excluded a reference to procreation. However, it is not the male element that is likely in view but the female, since the water comes from the earth. See Preben Wernberg-Møller, *The Manual of Discipline: Translated and Annotated with an Introduction*, STDJ 1 (Leiden: Brill, 1957), 155; Jonas C. Greenfield, "Root GBL in Mishnaic Hebrew and in the Hymnic Literature from Qumran," *RevQ* 2 (1959): 155–62.

40. For these terms, see Wernberg-Møller, *Manual of Discipline*, 155, and Charlesworth, *Rule of the Community*, 51.

41. I use the phrase "ritual/sexual impurity" to designate a subset within the category of ritual impurity, namely, those impurities associated with the normal sexual functions of human biology. For the distinction between ritual and moral impurity, see Klawans, *Impurity and Sin*, 3–42.

the purity codes of 4Q251 1, 7 in the phrase "naked flesh" ערוה בשר and 4Q512 29–32, 9 in the phrase "purify me from impure obscenity [ערות נדה]," where, arguably, "nakedness" defines a kind of ritual/sexual impurity (also 4Q512 36–38, 6).

The second term, "spring of *niddah*," is מקור הנדה. "Let your spring [מקור] be blessed," says Prov 5:18, where מקור serves as a sexual metaphor and parallels an exhortation to "rejoice in the wife of your youth" (also 5:16). מקור also refers to the flow of blood after childbirth in Lev 12:7 and to menstruation in Lev 20:18, where it is parallel to ערוה. Again, in the War Scroll VII, which speaks of immodest ערוה, מקור is applied to the male sex, as one is forbidden to go to war with the camps who has not cleansed himself of his "spring." The reason: "the holy angels are with the armies" (1QM VII, 6). The same apparent reference to seminal emission is found in 4Q514 1 I, 4. "Spring" is determined by נדה, "impurity," which of course is used primarily of menstrual blood, but also of generalized moral impurity (already in late biblical texts).[42] Little remarked on is the application of נדה to male ritual/sexual impurity. It may have this meaning in 4Q251 1, 6; it seems to include this sense in 4Q512, in the phrase just cited, "purify me from ערות נדה" (36–38, 6); and it certainly has this sense in 11Q19 XLV, 10, referring to a nocturnal emission (see, too, CD XII, 2, of intercourse). When *niddah* is combined with "spring" and stands alongside "nakedness" as a description of the "foundation" of the one "taken from dust" and/or "born of a woman," its ritual/sexual connotations are strongly to the fore.[43] The mutually interpretive significance of the earth and the womb provide the occasion to belittle the status of the one taken from the ground as both ritually defiled and defiling. In this way can we comprehend the statement "from clay I was nipped as a spring of (sexual) impurity" (1QH[a] XX, 27–28).[44]

---

42. Lichtenberger's judgment that נדה is less well attested in the sexual sense than in the Hebrew Bible and that it more often refers to "waters of purification" and moral impurity in the DSS is negated now by the full publication of the DSS. Yet, he rightly remarks that "wobei in unseren Texten eine strenge Scheidung zwischen kultisch und sittlich nicht immer möglich ist." See Hermann Lichtenberger, *Studien zum Menschenbild in Texten der Qumrangemeinde*, SUNT 15 (Göttingen: Vandenhoeck & Ruprecht, 1980), 85. For the distribution of senses in DSS, see Hannah K. Harrington, "נדה," TWQ 2:885–90.

43. Here I differ from Harrington, who, along with those cited earlier, places these occurrences under the category of *moralische Verschmutzung* (Harrington, "נדה").

44. For the expression of this thought in Jub. 3.8–14 and 4Q265 7, 11–13, see Meyer, *Adam's Dust and Adam's Glory*, 48–50.

Finally, the negative estimation of ritual/sexual impurity: What is additionally noteworthy about these terms is that ritual/sexual impurity and mortality are embedded in semantic networks evoking sinfulness and spiritual perversion, even creatively blending these categories, as in "sinful guilt is his foundation" (1QH$^a$ V, 32), or "a foundation of obscenity, a spring of impurity, a furnace of iniquity, a structure of sin, a spirit of error" (1QH$^a$ IX, 24). There is no concern here to treat the ritual and the moral separately,[45] but that does not mean the ritual has collapsed into the moral. The language of ritual impurity here, as well as other terms evoking human sexuality, name and disparage the sexed body, which has become a source of shame and disgust.[46] This attitude is not as foreign to the biblical mind-set as often thought. The most striking example may be Ezek 36:17, which states that the deplorable deeds of Israel are in God's sight "like the uncleanness of a woman in her menstrual period" (כטמאת הנדה). This statement hardly reflects positively on human (female) sexuality, but at least it appears to be only occasionally problematic. In the Thanksgiving Psalms, the human being per se is reduced to the polluting sexual organs.[47] As an innately sexed being, our author becomes to himself an object of disgust.

How does this happen? Contextual cues point toward heavenly communion. Just as in 1QS the mystical communion of heaven leads to self-abasement and the interrogation of one "born of woman," so in 1QH$^a$ XI a statement celebrating heavenly exaltation (XI, 20–24) is immediately followed up by "But I, a vessel of clay, what am I? A thing kneaded with water" (XI, 24–25), and in XXVI, in a similar context celebrating heavenly knowledge and access, the author asks, "What is flesh in relation to these things?" (XXVI, 35–36). The experience of otherworldly communion exposes the humanity of the worshiper, causes him to reflect on his

---

45. See Klawans, *Impurity and Sin*, 75–88.

46. See Johanna Stiebert, "Shame and the Body in Psalms and Lamentations of the Hebrew Bible and in Thanksgiving Hymns from Qumran," *OTE* 20 (2007): 798–829. For the lived reality of impurities, involving shame, withdrawal from ritual performance, and isolation, see the two chapters "Thinking beyond the Abstract" and "Everyday Living," in Jessica M. Keady, *Vulnerability and Valour: A Gendered Analysis of Everyday Life in the Dead Sea Scrolls Communities*, LSTS 91 (London: Bloomsbury, 2017).

47. It is no argument against the sexual reference of the terms "spring of *niddah*" and "obscene shame" that the whole human being is so named, as suggested by Loader (*Dead Sea Scrolls*, 248 n. 51; citing Lichtenberger, *Studien zum Menschenbild*, 85). This figure of speech occurs in the poetic books, e.g., Prov 5:15; Song 4:12–15, and enables one to highlight rather than obscure the sexed body.

inadequacy, much as an intense light reveals what is otherwise obscured. In our texts, it is especially the earthen/sexed body that seems out of place in the divine presence and among the *elim*. The worshiper now, more than ever, experiences the body as an obstacle to holiness. The emotional content that is generated by human sexuality will thus vary in part depending on the context in which it is experienced or evaluated against. While, on the one hand, sexuality can be appreciated as a good for its obvious utility in extending human, mortal life on earth, on the other hand, when set within the context of one's participation in a priestly and asexual vision of the heavenly world, innate sexuality may become a mark of alienation, unworthiness, and a source of shame and disgust.

## Conclusion

I have suggested that the self-deprecation of the Thanksgiving Psalms, in which the earthly body is negatively characterized as sexually impure, should be understood as a response to the experience of otherworldly communion. The importance of context in estimations of the value of human sexuality thus becomes apparent. Of course, one need not be a celibate to utter the words of these texts, although they plainly reveal a negative attitude toward sexuality such as is sometimes judged to be absent from the Scrolls and which might motivate the practice of extraordinary sexual abstinence. Moreover, the textual links that have been traced to connect these texts, through 1QS and the Psalm of the Maskil to CD VII, suggest that they might indeed give expression to the experience of those celibates who sought to walk in perfect holiness. If so, these texts seemingly reveal the lived reality of those who pursued such a goal as one of at least partial frustration. The speaker's total reduction of the self to the sexual organ ("a spring of *niddah*," "a foundation of obscenity") reveals the illusory goal of total purity. Even abstinence from all sexual acts does not prevent the body from emitting its impurity on occasion, and it would be easy to interpret any lapse in this regard, particularly for males, as indicative of sin. Thus, there is good reason to suspect that the inclusion of the sexed body in the trope of self-abasement reflects not only the chastened subjectivity of one exposed to the heavenly world but also the frustrations experienced by those who, for the goal of communion with this world, sought to eliminate exposure to the bodily conditions associated with ritual/sexual impurity.

What, however, can be learned about the presence of women and the representation of their sexuality? Too often, it is simply assumed that a celibate community would exclude women, whether for the sake of reducing temptation or exposure to impurity. Recently, however, Jessica Keady has pushed back against the tendency to assume that female impurity is more problematic and less easily controlled than male impurity, noting rather the unpredictability of nocturnal emission.[48] (The contrast to males is even stronger when postmenopausal women are included.) The present study has uncovered evidence that supports the suggestion that impurity due to seminal emission was indeed a frustration for some of the sectarians. On the other hand, it is noteworthy that by drawing the womb and the earth into metaphorical association, these texts position the feminine on the lower half of the heavenly/earthly duality. And yet this metaphorical logic has a long prehistory and is not used to develop a specifically female construction of impurity. Rather, these psalms speak of human beings per se as fundamentally impure, and specific terms reflecting sexuality can be redolent of either female or male qualities, or of both at the same time.[49] A man or a woman might lament of being "a spring of *niddah*," and in these texts no one doubts that men, at least, do just that. Moreover, Wassen has remarked on the importance of the plantation metaphor for the sectarians, noting that, in lacking an altar, the plantation may be particularly well-suited for thinking about the community as a sanctuary.[50] We ought to recall, therefore, that both Adam *and* Eve are permitted to enter the garden sanctuary, the original plantation, after periods of ritual purification are endured, according to Jubilees and 4Q265. The sexually differentiated times of their purification may point to the ongoing male construction of the female as more prone to impurity, but Keady's reminder that female

---

48. Keady, *Vulnerability and Valour*, 134–38, 168–70.

49. Jonathan Klawans has suggested that the use of *niddah* to refer to moral impurity in sectarian texts is at least potentially misogynistic. See Klawans, "Purity in the Dead Sea Scrolls," in Lim and Collins, *Oxford Handbook of the Dead Sea Scrolls*, 390. This potential, however, is reduced when we recognize that *niddah* has become a term not just for moral impurity but for generalized ritual/sexual impurity, whether male or female, and in some cases, specifically male. In this sense, the use of *niddah* in the texts considered here achieves an equality of impurity. Jessica Keady makes a similar point with reference to 4Q274 1 I (*Vulnerability and Valour*, 133–34).

50. Cecilia Wassen, "Do You Have to Be Pure in a Metaphorical Temple? Sanctuary Metaphors and Construction of Sacred Space in the Dead Sea Scrolls and Paul's Letters," in *Purity, Holiness, and Identity in Judaism and Christianity: Essays in Memory of Susan Haber*, ed. Carl S. Erhlich, Anders Runesson, and Eileen M. Schuller, WUNT 305 (Tübingen: Mohr Siebeck, 2013), 63.

impurity may in practice be more readily managed than male should be borne in mind when asking about the lived realities of forming a community around maximal purity. What can be said is that the reduction of the human being to a sexual impurity in these texts *includes* the male. Therefore, since a male who is fundamentally impure can partake in this heavenly priesthood, we may be permitted to wonder whether so too could a female.[51] In contrast to Philo and Josephus, then, who interpret celibacy as a symptom of misogyny, the kind of negative estimation of sex that is made here equally qualifies male and female and appears rather to be a symptom of priestly concerns for ritual purity and heavenly worship.

In conclusion, the four features of self-abasement I have traced in the Thanksgiving Psalms—namely, the stress on earthiness, the equation between the earthly vessel and the sexed body, the priestly inflection of that body as ritually polluted and polluting, and the negative estimation of the sexed body—readily cohere against the backdrop of a human being's experience of an otherworldly calling. The heavenly communion exposes the worshiper's earthly constitution, especially his or her sexuality, as a matter of being out of place, a source of shame, and a cause of frustration. Therefore, it cannot be said that the Scrolls give no indication of a denigration of sex or sexuality such as might be related to the practice of celibacy. Rather, the morose view of the sexed body traced here can be textually correlated to the distinction within the covenanters reflected in the interpolated text of the Damascus Document, and plausibly also in 1QS V–IX, a distinction that would roughly correspond to that which Josephus makes between Essenes who marry and those who do not.

## Bibliography

Anderson, Gary M. "Celibacy or Consummation in the Garden: Reflections on Early Jewish and Christian Interpretations of the Garden of Eden." *HTR* 82 (1989): 121–48.

---

51. See the exploration of this possibility in Jennifer Zilm, "Multi-coloured like Woven Works: Gender, Ritual Clothing and Praying with the Angels in the Dead Sea Scrolls and the Testament of Job," in *Prayer and Poetry in the Dead Sea Scrolls and Related Literature: Essays in Honor of Eileen Schuller on the Occasion of Her Sixty-Fifth Birthday*, ed. Jeremy Penner, Ken M. Penner, and Cecilia Wassen, STDJ 98 (Leiden: Brill, 2012), 437–51.

Baumgarten, Albert I. "Who Cares and Why Does It Matter? Qumran and the Essenes, Once Again!" *DSD* 11 (2004): 174–90.

Baumgarten, Joseph M. "Celibacy." *EDSS* 1:122–25.

———. "The Qumran-Essene Restraints on Marriage." Pages 13–24 in *Archaeology and History in the Dead Sea Scrolls: The New York University Conference in Memory of Yigael Yadin*. Sheffield: JSOT Press, 1990.

Berg, Shane. "An Elite Group within the Yaḥad: Revisiting 1QS 8–9." Pages 161–77 in *Qumran Studies: New Approaches, New Questions*. Edited by Michael Thomas Davis and Brent A. Strawn. Grand Rapids: Eerdmans, 2007.

Charlesworth, James H., ed. *Damascus Document, War Scroll, and Related Documents*. Vol. 2 of *The Dead Sea Scrolls: Hebrew, Aramaic, and Greek Texts with English Translations*. PTSDSSP. Louisville: Westminster John Knox, 1995.

———, ed. *Rule of the Community and Related Documents*. Vol. 1 of *The Dead Sea Scrolls: Hebrew, Aramaic, and Greek Texts with English Translations*. PTSDSSP. Louisville: Westminster John Knox, 1994.

Collins, John J. "The Angelic Life." Pages 291–310 in *Metamorphoses: Resurrection, Body and Transformative Practices in Early Christianity*. Edited by Turid Karlsen Seim and Jorunn Økland. Ekstasis 1. Berlin: de Gruyter, 2009.

———. *Beyond the Qumran Community: The Sectarian Movement of the Dead Sea Scrolls*. Grand Rapids: Eerdmans, 2010.

Crawford, Sidnie White. "Not according to Rule: Women, the Dead Sea Scrolls and Qumran." Pages 127–50 in *Emanuel: Studies in Hebrew Bible, Septuagint, and Dead Sea Scrolls in Honor of Emanuel Tov*. Edited by Shalom M. Paul, Robert A. Kraft, Lawrence H. Schiffman, and Weston W. Fields. VTSup 94. Leiden: Brill, 2003.

Dimant, Devorah. "Men as Angels: The Self-Image of the Qumran Community." Pages 93–103 in *Religion and Politics in the Ancient Near East*. Edited by Adele Berlin. Bethesda: University Press of Maryland, 1996.

Fletcher-Louis, Crispin H. T. *All the Glory of Adam: Liturgical Anthropology in the Dead Sea Scrolls*. STDJ 42. Leiden: Brill, 2001.

Greenfield, Jonas C. "Root GBL in Mishnaic Hebrew and in the Hymnic Literature from Qumran." *RevQ* 2 (1959): 155–62.

Grossman, Maxine L. "Gendered Sectarians: Envisioning Women (and Men) at Qumran." Pages 265–88 in *Celebrate Her for the Fruit of Her Hands: Essays in Honor of Carol L. Meyers*. Edited by Susan Ackerman, Charles E. Carter, and Beth Alpert Nakhai. Winona Lake, IN: Eisenbrauns, 2015.

———. "Queerly Sectarian: Jewish Difference, the Dead Sea Scrolls, and Marital Disciplines." *JJI* 11 (2018): 87–105.

———. "Rethinking Gender in the Community Rule: An Experiment in Sociology." Pages 497–512 in *Dead Sea Scrolls and Contemporary Culture: Proceedings of the International Conference Held at the Israel Museum, Jerusalem (July 6–8, 2008)*. Edited by Adolfo D. Roitman, Lawrence H. Schiffman, and Shani Tzoref. STDJ 93. Leiden: Brill, 2011.

———. "The World of Qumran and the Sectarian Dead Sea Scrolls in Gendered Perspective." Pages 225–46 in *Early Jewish Writings: Apocrypha*. Edited by Eileen M. Schuller and Marie-Theres Wacker. BW 3.1. Atlanta: SBL Press, 2017.

Hachlili, Rachel. "The Qumran Cemetery Reassessed." Pages 46–78 in *The Oxford Handbook of the Dead Sea Scrolls*. Edited by Timothy H. Lim and John J. Collins. Oxford: Oxford University Press, 2010.

Heger, Paul. "Celibacy in Qumran: Hellenistic Fiction or Reality? Qumran's Attitude toward Sex." *RevQ* 26 (2013): 53–90.

Horst, Pieter Willem van der. "Celibacy in Early Judaism." *RB* 109 (2002): 390–402.

Ilan, Tal. "Women in Qumran and the Dead Sea Scrolls." Pages 123–47 in *The Oxford Handbook of the Dead Sea Scrolls*. Edited by Timothy H. Lim and John J. Collins. Oxford: Oxford University Press, 2010.

Jastrow, Marcus. *A Dictionary of the Targumim, the Talmud Babli and Yerushalmi, and the Midrashic Literature*. New York: Judaica, 1971.

Keady, Jessica M. *Vulnerability and Valour: A Gendered Analysis of Everyday Life in the Dead Sea Scrolls Communities*. LSTS 91. London: Bloomsbury, 2017.

Klawans, Jonathan. *Impurity and Sin in Ancient Judaism*. Oxford: Oxford University Press, 2000.

———. "Purity in the Dead Sea Scrolls." Pages 377–402 in *The Oxford Handbook of the Dead Sea Scrolls*. Edited by John J. Collins and Timothy H. Lim. Oxford: Oxford University Press, 2010.

Lichtenberger, Hermann. *Studien zum Menschenbild in Texten der Qumrangemeinde*. SUNT 15. Göttingen: Vandenhoeck & Ruprecht, 1980.

Loader, William R. G. *The Dead Sea Scrolls on Sexuality: Attitudes towards Sexuality in Sectarian and Related Literature at Qumran*. Grand Rapids: Eerdmans, 2009.

Maston, Jason. *Divine and Human Agency in Second Temple Judaism: A Comparative Study.* WUNT 297. Tübingen: Mohr Siebeck, 2010.

Meyer, Nicholas A. *Adam's Dust and Adam's Glory in the Hodayot and the Letters of Paul: Rethinking Anthropogony and Theology.* NovTSup 168. Leiden: Brill, 2016.

Meyers, Eric M. "Khirbet Qumran and Its Environs." Pages 21–45 in *The Oxford Handbook of the Dead Sea Scrolls.* Edited by Timothy H. Lim and John J. Collins. Oxford: Oxford University Press, 2010.

Newsom, Carol A. "Deriving Negative Anthropology through Exegetical Activity: The Hodayot as a Case Study." Pages 258–74 in *Is There a Text in This Cave? Studies in the Textuality of the Dead Sea Scrolls in Honour of George J. Brooke.* Edited by Ariel Feldman, Maria Cioată, and Charlotte Hempel. STDJ 119. Leiden: Brill, 2017.

———. *The Self as Symbolic Space: Constructing Identity and Community at Qumran.* STDJ 52. Leiden: Brill, 2004.

Qimron, Elisha. "Celibacy in the Dead Sea Scrolls and the Two Kinds of Sectarians." Pages 287–94 in *The Madrid Qumran Congress: Proceedings of the International Congress on the Dead Sea Scrolls, Madrid, 18–21 March, 1991.* Vol. 1. Edited by Luis Vegas Montaner and Julio Trebeolle Barrera. STDJ 11. Leiden: Brill, 1992.

Regev, Eyal. "Cherchez les femmes: Were the Yaḥad Celibates?" *DSD* 15 (2008): 253–84.

Roetzel, Calvin J. "Sex and the Single God: Celibacy as Social Deviancy in the Roman Period." Pages 231–48 in *Text and Artifact in the Religions of Mediterranean Antiquity: Essays in Honour of Peter Richardson.* Edited by Stephen G. Wilson and Michel Desjardins. Waterloo, ON: Wilfried Laurier University Press, 2000.

Schiffman, Lawrence H. *Reclaiming the Dead Sea Scrolls: The History of Judaism, the Background of Christianity, the Lost Library of Qumran.* New York: Doubleday, 1994.

Schuller, Eileen M. "Evidence for Women in the Community of the Dead Sea Scrolls." Pages 252–65 in *Voluntary Associations in the Graeco-Roman World.* Edited by John S. Kloppenborg and Stephen G. Wilson. London: Routledge, 1996.

———. "Women in the Dead Sea Scrolls." Pages 115–31 in *Methods of Investigation of the Dead Sea Scrolls and the Khirbet Qumran Site: Present Realities and Future Prospects.* Edited by Michael O. Wise, Norman Golb, John J. Collins, and Dennis Pardee. ANYAS 722. New York: New York Academy of Science, 1994.

———. "Women in the Dead Sea Scrolls." Pages 117–44 in *The Dead Sea Scrolls after Fifty Years: A Comprehensive Assessment*. Vol. 2. Edited by Peter W. Flint and James C. VanderKam. Leiden: Brill, 1999.

———. "Women in the Dead Sea Scrolls: Research in the Past Decade and Future Directions." Pages 571–88 in *Dead Sea Scrolls and Contemporary Culture: Proceedings of the International Conference Held at the Israel Museum, Jerusalem (July 6–8, 2008)*. Edited by Adolfo D. Roitman, Lawrence H. Schiffman, and Shani Tzoref. STDJ 93. Leiden: Brill, 2011.

Stegemann, Hartmut. *The Library of Qumran: On the Essenes, Qumran, John the Baptist, and Jesus*. Leiden: Brill, 1998.

———. "The Qumran Essenes—Local Members of the Main Jewish Union in Late Second Temple Times." Pages 83–166 in *The Madrid Qumran Congress: Proceedings of the International Congress on the Dead Sea Scrolls, Madrid 18–21 March, 1991*. Vol. 1. Edited by Luis Vegas Montaner and Julio Trebeolle Barrera. STDJ 11. Leiden: Brill, 1992.

Stegemann, Hartmut, Eileen M. Schuller, and Carol A. Newsom, eds. *Qumran Cave 1.III: 1QHodayot$^a$, with Incorporation of 1QHodayot$^b$ and 4QHodayot$^{a-f}$*. DJD XL. Oxford: Clarendon, 2009.

Stiebert, Johanna. "Shame and the Body in Psalms and Lamentations of the Hebrew Bible and in Thanksgiving Hymns from Qumran." *OTE* 20 (2007): 798–829.

Strugnell, John, Daniel J. Harrington, and Torleif Elgvin. *Qumran Cave 4.XXIV: Sapiential Texts Part 2*. DJD XXXIV. Oxford: Clarendon, 1999.

Taylor, Joan E. "The Classical Sources on the Essenes and the Scrolls Communities." Pages 173–99 in *The Oxford Handbook of the Dead Sea Scrolls*. Edited by Timothy H. Lim and John J. Collins. Oxford: Oxford University Press, 2010.

———. *The Essenes, the Scrolls, and the Dead Sea*. Oxford: Oxford University Press, 2012.

———. "Women, Children, and Celibate Men in Serekh Texts." *HTR* 104 (2011): 171–90.

Vermes, Geza, and Martin Goodman, eds. *The Essenes: According to the Classical Sources*. Sheffield: JSOT Press, 1989.

Wassen, Cecilia. "Do You Have to Be Pure in a Metaphorical Temple? Sanctuary Metaphors and Construction of Sacred Space in the Dead Sea Scrolls and Paul's Letters." Pages 55–86 in *Purity, Holiness, and Identity in Judaism and Christianity: Essays in Memory of Susan Haber.*

Edited by Carl S. Ehrlich, Anders Runesson, and Eileen M. Schuller. WUNT 305. Tübingen: Mohr Siebeck, 2013.

———. "The Importance of Marriage in the Construction of Sectarian Identity in the Dead Sea Scrolls." Pages 127–50 in *Social Memory and Social Identity in the Study of Early Judaism and Early Christianity*. Edited by Samuel Byrskog, Raimo Hakola, and Jutta Jokiranta. NTOA/SUNT. Göttingen: Vandenhoeck & Ruprecht, 2016.

———. *Women in the Damascus Document*. AcBib 21. Atlanta: Society of Biblical Literature, 2005.

———. "Women, Worship, Wilderness, and War: Celibacy and the Constructions of Identity in the Dead Sea Scrolls." Pages 1361–85 in *Sibyls, Scriptures, and Scrolls: John Collins at Seventy*. Edited by Joel Baden, Hindy Najman, and Eibert J. C. Tigchelaar. JSJSup 175. Leiden: Brill, 2017.

Wernberg-Møller, Preben. *The Manual of Discipline: Translated and Annotated with an Introduction*. STDJ 1. Leiden: Brill, 1957.

Zilm, Jennifer. "Multi-coloured like Woven Works: Gender, Ritual Clothing and Praying with the Angels in the Dead Sea Scrolls and the Testament of Job." Pages 437–51 in *Prayer and Poetry in the Dead Sea Scrolls and Related Literature: Essays in Honor of Eileen Schuller on the Occasion of Her Sixty-Fifth Birthday*. Edited by Jeremy Penner, Ken M. Penner, and Cecilia Wassen. STDJ 98. Leiden: Brill, 2012.

# Masculinities and the Men of the Qumran Communities: Reevaluating the Ideals of Purification, Power, and Performance in the Dead Sea Scrolls

Jessica M. Keady

## Introduction

In most cases where ancient texts are related to ancient social groups, the scholarly focus has been on elites. As such, the ancient literary portrayals are not necessarily understood as representative of the lived reality of most everyday people. I argue, however, that the Dead Sea Scrolls (DSS) actually provide verifiable depictions of mixed communities of elites and ordinary people and, consequently, can offer insights into the lives of the Essenes during the Second Temple period.[1] Scholars who have discussed issues of

---

The initial research for this chapter can be seen in my monograph, Jessica M. Keady, *Vulnerability and Valour: A Gendered Analysis of Everyday Life in the Dead Sea Scrolls Communities*, LSTS 91 (London: Bloomsbury, 2017). I was given the opportunity to present a form of the current chapter to the participants of the Centenary Summer Meeting of the Society for Old Testament Study (London, 17–20 July 2017), for which I am very grateful.

1. DSS scholars who follow the Essene identification behind the DSS communities include John J. Collins, "Sectarian Communities in the Dead Sea Scrolls," in *The Oxford Handbook of the Dead Sea Scrolls*, ed. Timothy H. Lim and John J. Collins (Oxford: Oxford University Press, 2010), 151; Cecilia Wassen, *Women in the Damascus Document*, AcBib 21 (Atlanta: Society of Biblical Literature, 2005), 5; Alison Schofield, *From Qumran to the Yaḥad: A New Paradigm of Textual Development for the Community Rule*, STDJ 77 (Leiden: Brill, 2009). As well as the Essene hypothesis, there is also the Groningen hypothesis, which argues that the origins of the Essene movement and the origins of the Qumran community are distinct from each other: the Essene movement developed out of the Palestinian apocalyptic tradition, and the Qumran community emerged later from the same movement after a split from the founding

purity and impurity in the DSS (e.g., Hannah Harrington and Jonathan Klawans)[2] have constructed their understanding of Jewish purity systems with the focus on priestly traditions and the relationships between purity and sin within the relevant texts. Although such discussions are important to understanding the use and influence of purity and impurity in Second Temple Judaism, these scholarly discussions usually have to be qualified because real life among the DSS communities would almost certainly not have been so systematic and rigid. Using masculinity studies as a larger framework, this chapter will argue that aspects of the DSS provide verifiable depictions of mixed communities, of elites and ordinary people, and, consequently, they can offer insights into the lives of the Essenes during the Second Temple period and the potential links between being impure and being socially perceived as less masculine.

A new wave of scholarship is beginning to emerge in which scholars are starting to question the abstract and systemic views and portrayals of purity and impurity in ancient Judaism. For example, the dynamic nature of purity has once again been emphasized by Christian Frevel and Christophe Nihan, who have argued that purity in the ancient world is not to be treated—or understood—as an isolated phenomenon, but rather set within a diachronic and synchronic modality, which constructs purity in a "dynamic framework" rather than an abstract one.[3] Furthermore, Tracy Lemos has begun to question the current systemic approach in scholarly literature on purity and impurity, and she sees it as misguided, since a systemic, singular understanding of purity does not encapsulate how purity and impurity were truly constructed in the ancient world. Accord-

---

group, which resulted in the physical withdrawal to Qumran. See Florentino García Martínez and Adam S. van der Woude, "A 'Groningen' Hypothesis of Qumran Origins and Early History," *RevQ* 14 (1990): 521–41. Among other views, the Sadducean hypothesis was revived by Lawrence Schiffman based on views expressed in MMT that are "identical" to those attributed to the Sadducees in rabbinic sources. See Lawrence H. Schiffman, *The Halakhah at Qumran*, SJLA 16 (Leiden: Brill, 1975). See also Charlotte Hempel, "Qumran Community," in *EDSS* 2:746–51, for a more detailed explanation of these theories related to the identity of the DSS communities.

2. See, e.g. Hannah K. Harrington, *The Purity Texts*, CQS 5 (London: T&T Clark, 2004); Jonathan Klawans, *Impurity and Sin in Ancient Judaism* (Oxford: Oxford University Press, 2000).

3. Christian Frevel and Christophe Nihan, "Introduction," in *Purity and the Forming of Religious Traditions in the Ancient Mediterranean World and Ancient Judaism*, ed. Christian Frevel and Christophe Nihan, DHR 3 (Leiden: Brill, 2013), 10.

ingly, there is still a need to understand the diversity of purity issues and examine the "relationship between impurity constructions and the lived experiences of Israelites."[4] While I agree with these critiques, I would argue further that a fresher methodology needs to be used to enhance the understanding of ordinary male and female experiences of purity and impurity in the ancient world. My own research has attempted to enter this interdisciplinary market, and I have found gender studies to be a useful framework for reading the constructions of purity and impurity in the DSS.

Historically, menstrual cycles have been read as a sign of women's lack of control over their bodies; women leaked, while men remained contained. The reduction of men's bodily fluids to the productive and pleasurable elements has allowed men to spatially distance themselves from the leaky, uncontrollable, and disruptive aspects of the corporeal female body.[5] Such essentialist arguments relating to the rationality of men and the boundless nature of women have been challenged and redefined, not only by feminist scholars but also by social constructionists who have argued that there is no natural body. Rather, the body is always "culturally mapped; it never exists in a pure or un-coded state."[6] While it is usual for the female to be negatively positioned in such leaky and uncontrollable ways, the methods I have found most useful are ones that challenge that position, and I have found masculinity studies a useful tool to bring the uncontrollable aspects of the impure and vulnerable male into the fold of discussion.

Ilona Zsolnay has recently put forward the following questions as being fundamentally important when looking at the constructions of masculinities in antiquity:

What does it mean to be a man?
What does society believe the ideal construct of masculinities to be?
How do I demonstrate my masculinity?

---

4. Tracy Lemos, "Where There Is Dirt, Is There System? Revisiting Biblical Purity Constructions," *JSOT* 37 (2013): 265–94. The contemporary focus on the lived experiences and embodiment in the social sciences is an important shift away from the Cartesian dichotomies and should be incorporated in the understanding of purity and impurity in the ancient Jewish world (see Lemos, "Where There Is Dirt," 265).

5. Elizabeth Grosz, *Volatile Bodies: Toward a Corporeal Feminism* (Bloomington: Indiana University Press, 1994), 200.

6. Diana Fuss, *Essentially Speaking: Feminism, Nature and Difference* (London: Routledge, 1990), 6.

How do I negotiate my performance of it?[7]

I fully accept that there are risks in imposing modern methodologies onto ancient texts and traditions, but I am also in agreement with Maria Wyke, who, in her understanding of gender and antiquity, argues that ancient bodies continue to be sites on which discussions of modern sexualities and genders can be discussed, confronted, and assessed.[8] With that in mind, this chapter will cover four areas: first, I will outline the masculinities framework of Raewyn Connell, which I have found most useful when discussing constructs of the male; second, I will introduce the War Texts, focusing particularly on the War Scroll (1QM), and how the text might have functioned among the Qumran communities; third, I will take some examples relating to the constructions of the male in the War Scroll in relation to the wider gendered framework; and I will conclude with some general reflections on purification, power, and performance in relation to masculinities.

## Raewyn Connell and Hegemonic Masculinity

In the 1990s, Connell started to rethink the relationship between the male and the female body by acknowledging that, in culture, the physical sense of maleness and femaleness is central to the cultural interpretation of gender, rather than being biologically determined.[9] Connell reinserted the plurality and diversity of bodies and argued that all too often the body is described in monolithic terms and that it is crucial to remember that masculinities vary and change across time and space, within societies, and through wider life courses.[10] For Connell, a historical account of masculinity cannot be understood as linear. Accordingly, she proposes to move beyond the ideological and biological rationale of masculinity and gender to search for their practical bases in everyday life. Relationships constructing masculinities are dialectical, and the recognition of different types and

---

7. Ilona Zsolnay, ed., *Being a Man: Negotiating Ancient Constructs of Masculinity* (New York: Routledge, 2016).

8. Maria Wyke, "Introduction," in *Parchments of Gender: Deciphering the Bodies of Antiquity*, ed. Maria Wyke (Oxford: Clarendon, 1998), 1–11.

9. Raewyn W. Connell, *Masculinities* (Cambridge: Polity, 1995), 52.

10. Connell, *Masculinities*, 52; Jeff Hearn, "Masculinities," in *International Encyclopedia of Men and Masculinities*, ed. Michael Flood et al. (London: Routledge, 2007), 391.

transgressions of masculinities must be made to adjust the existing fixed categories of gender.

For Connell, there are four types of masculinities, which are each positioned hierarchically in relation to one another: hegemony, subordination, complicity, and marginalization.[11] I am particularly focused on the hegemonic position and turn now to describe its meaning in more detail.

Applying Hegemonic Masculinities to the Dead Sea Scrolls

Hegemonic Position

Hegemonic masculinity has a threefold purpose in Connell's work: it is a position in the system of gender relations; it is the system itself; and it is also the current ideology that serves to reproduce masculine domination.[12] The hegemonic position is the accepted male ideal, and this image changes over time and place.[13] Drawing on Antonio Gramsci's hegemonic analysis of class relations, Connell defines hegemonic masculinity as "the configuration of gender practice which embodies the currently accepted answer to the problem of legitimacy of patriarchy, which guarantees (or is taken to guarantee) the dominant position of men and the subordination of women."[14] Consequently, the characteristics associated with hegemonic masculinity have allowed society to understand how men and women are positioned and have performed differently in communities, and the extent to which this has affected social structure in everyday life.

The most visible bearers of hegemonic masculinity are not always the most powerful, and as such the models of hegemonic masculinity express ideals, fantasies, and desires that men construct, which in itself is revealing.[15] The masculine ideals and constructs that are often portrayed

---

11. Connell, *Masculinities*, 77–78.
12. Donald P. Levy, "Hegemonic Masculinity," in Flood et al., *International Encyclopedia of Men*, 253.
13. Connell, *Masculinities*, 77.
14. Connell, *Masculinities*, 77. See Antonio Gramsci, *Selection from the Prison Notebooks* (London: Biddles, 1971).
15. Connell, *Masculinities*, 77. See also Raewyn W. Connell and James W. Messerschmidt, "Hegemonic Masculinity: Rethinking the Concept," *GS* 19 (2005): 840. In this review of the use and function of hegemonic masculinity over the past few decades, Connell and Messerschmidt assess the use and application of hegemonic masculinity in a variety of disciplines. For example, the concept of hegemonic masculinity has

are quite unrealistic for ordinary men to aspire to. Hegemonic masculinity embodies an accepted strategy, and when conditions for the defense of patriarchy change, the bases for the dominance of a particular masculinity are eroded.[16] That seems to suggest that masculine frameworks, constructs, and performances can indeed change.

In a recent review of the place of hegemonic masculinity as a methodological concept, Connell and James Messerschmidt remind scholars that the concept of hegemonic masculinity was originally formulated alongside hegemonic femininity (renamed as "emphasized femininity"), which reinstated the "asymmetrical position of masculinities and femininities in a patriarchal gender order." In subsequent research on men and hegemonic masculinities over the last few decades, the relationship between masculinities and femininities in the hegemonic model has not been adequately addressed and, as a result, has become neglected. Connell and Messerschmidt defend, very convincingly, why this lack of scholarly engagement with the female standpoint alongside the male is regrettable, since "gender is always relational and patterns of masculinity are socially defined in contradiction." Women are central in many of the social and physical processes that construct masculinities. Consequently, Connell and Messerschmidt have now called for research on hegemonic masculinity to give much closer and more detailed attention to the practices of women and the "historical interplay of femininities and masculinities."[17]

Subsequently, in biblical scholarship, there is a methodological move to understand the more dynamic place of ancient women, and, as such, the traditional portrayals of a hierarchical position of gender and patriarchy are beginning to be challenged. For example, Carol Meyers argues that there is a need to move beyond the term *patriarchy* and instead proposes

---

been used in education studies as a way of understanding how the dynamics of a classroom have affected bullying, achievement, and friendship groups. See Wayne Martino, "Boys and Literacy: Exploring the Construction of Hegemonic Masculinities and the Formation of Literate Capacities in the English Classroom," *EA* 112 (1995): 11–24. The use of hegemonic masculinity has also proven insightful in the field of criminology, where the concept has helped to theorize the relationship among masculinities and crime, including rape and murder. See James W. Messerschmidt, *Masculinity and Crime: Critique and Reconceptualization of Theory* (Lanaham, MD: Rowman & Littlefield, 1993).

16. Connell, *Masculinities*, 77.
17. Connell and Messerschmidt, "Hegemonic Masculinity: Rethinking," 184.

the use of the term *heterarchy*.[18] That term reflects the complexity of gender dynamics and acknowledges that ancient women were not dominated in all aspects of society but were "autonomous actors in multiple aspects of households and community life."[19] Masculinities and femininities are not fixed categories, and it is therefore essential to recognize the dynamism of the relationship in which gender is constituted.[20]

One of the main arguments I want to make with regards to masculinity and certain DSS is that the fluidity and dynamic nature of masculinity also reflects the fluidity and dynamic nature of purity and impurity; such dialectical views of purity are important when trying to move beyond the current systemic approaches in scholarship. The interplay between different forms of masculinities is a key aspect of how a patriarchal social order works.[21] Connell wants to demonstrate three wider ideas in her reconstruction of what masculinities mean in society: first, how some men have succeeded in making it appear normal, natural, and necessary for them to enjoy power over other men and most women; second, why it is that so many men and women have participated willingly in their own oppression; and third, how resistance to hegemonic masculinity can promote gender justice.[22] It is the third idea, resistance to hegemonic masculinity, that I find particularly relevant, since impurity among the DSS communities (in relation to men) may have brought about aspects of resistance, and reversal, to the traditional social/patriarchal order among the communities. It is in everyday relations and daily activities that Connell sees the practice of gender, and with the wider masculine framework in mind, I turn now to the War Texts.

---

18. Ross Kraemer has discussed the interchangeability of masculinity in relation to its constructions within societies and variations according to social class, and reinforces the notion that "gender is always hierarchical." See Ross S. Kraemer, "Women and Gender," in *The Oxford Handbook of Early Christian Studies*, ed. Susan Ashbrook Harvey and David Hunter (Oxford: Oxford University Press, 2010), 466.

19. See Carol L. Meyers, "Hierarchy or Heterarchy? Archaeology and the Theorizing of Israelite Society," in *Confronting the Past: Archaeological and Historical Essays on Ancient Israel in Honor of William G. Dever*, ed. Seymour Gitin, J. Edward Wright, and J. P. Dessel (Winona Lake, IN: Eisenbrauns, 2006), 249–51. See also Meyers, "Was Ancient Israel a Patriarchal Society," *JBL* 133 (2014): 8–27.

20. Connell, *Masculinities*, 38.

21. Raewyn W. Connell, *Gender and Power: Society, the Person and Sexual Politics* (London: Polity, 1987), 183.

22. Connell and Messerschmidt, "Hegemonic Masculinity: Rethinking," 184.

## What Are the War Texts?

The War Texts is the name given to a small group of DSS that depict the preparation for the eschatological battle between the "Sons of Light," led by God, and the "Sons of Darkness," led by Belial.[23] The longest of the War Texts is known primarily from a manuscript found in Cave 1 and labeled 1QM (Milḥamah), and it is this manuscript that will be the main focus of my discussion. The eschatological war presented in 1QM culminates with God's own intervention, which results in the total extermination of the army of Belial and leaves the Sons of Light to enjoy everlasting redemption and blessing.[24] Outside the DSS there are no other literary parallels known of this kind in Second Temple literature, which highlights the importance and unique nature of the sectarian War Scroll material.[25]

As Jean Duhaime has argued, 1QM represents the most complete copy of the War Scroll and can be seen to show the final form of its literary development.[26] For Duhaime, the early Herodian script of 1QM points to a date in the last part of the first century BCE.[27] As such, looking at 1QM will give a view of the male one hundred years later than Serekh ha-Yaḥad (S) in 1QS form. Although the bottom part of 1QM is missing, it is still possible to infer that there were a minimum of twenty-one to twenty-two lines in an average column. In the discoveries from Cave 4, six fragmentary manuscripts of the War Scroll, as well as a War Scroll–like fragment (4Q497), have been identified (4Q491–496 = 4QM 1–6).[28] The language of 1QM and the related fragmentary manuscripts that have been discovered

---

23. Jean Duhaime, *The War Texts: 1QM and Related Manuscripts*, CQS 6 (London: T&T Clark, 2004), 4.
24. Jean Duhaime, "War Scroll," in *Damascus Document, War Scroll, and Related Documents*, vol. 2 of *The Dead Sea Scrolls: Hebrew, Aramaic, and Greek Texts with English Translations*, ed. James H. Charlesworth, PTSDSSP 2 (Tübingen: Mohr Siebeck, 1995), 81.
25. Brian Schultz, *Conquering the World: The War Scroll (1QM) Reconsidered*, STDJ 76 (Leiden: Brill, 2009), 10.
26. Duhaime, "War Scroll," 80–82.
27. Jean Duhaime, "War Scroll," 80. Not all scholars are in agreement over this dating; Salomo A. Birnbaum has argued for a date in the third quarter of the first century BCE. See Birnbaum, *Text*, vol. 1 of *The Hebrew Scripts* (Leiden: Brill, 1971).
28. Duhaime, "War Scroll," 80.

is Hebrew. It is significant that the language of the War Scroll shares features of the Hebrew in other DSS.[29]

Duhaime has put forward the argument that the War Scroll appears to be in the form of a "tactical treatise," which provides military rules and regulations on the organization of the army and the varying equipment needed for certain military procedures that was applicable to varying military situations. For example, in the work of Asclepiodotus, there is an older example of a "tactical treatise" that has similar characteristics to 1QM II–IX. Drawing on the theoretical aspect of the treatise and the fragments from Cave 4, it is likely that the War Scroll is a compilation of at least three different documents (cols. II–IX, X–XIV, XV–XIX), and each unit may have been transmitted and modified over many recensions.[30] George Brooke has also described the War Scroll as a "ritual campaign manual for those who have to fight an external enemy other."[31] Brian Schultz, in light of the manuscripts found in Cave 4, concludes that the manuscript was originally composed to describe warfare as it was expected to be carried out during the eschatological age but that it was modified over time to include a description of the very battle that would bring about the expected messianic age.[32]

The War Scroll was one of the texts analyzed by Alexander Samely for the collaborative research project "Typology of Anonymous and Pseudepigraphic Jewish Literature in Antiquity, c. 200 BCE to 700 CE,"[33] and he

---

29. Duhaime, "War Scroll," 83. The structure and date of the original composition of the War Scroll are unknown, but Duhaime has argued that there is textual evidence to demonstrate that at least two different recensions of this work were in circulation during the second part of the first century BCE.

30. Duhaime, "War Scroll," 84.

31. George J. Brooke, "Text, Timing, and Terror: Thematic Thoughts on the War Scroll in Conversation with the Writings of the Martin G. Abegg Jr.," in *The War Scroll, Violence, War and Peace in the Dead Sea Scrolls and Related Literature: Essays in Honour of Martin G. Abegg on the Occasion of His Sixty-Fifth Birthday*, ed. Kipp Davis et al., STDJ 115 (Leiden: Brill, 2015), 48.

32. Schultz, *Conquering the World*, 7. The "M material" for Schultz relates to the work reflecting 1QM and all its possible recensions, including 4Q491–496, 4Q471.

33. The results of the wider project were published in Alexander Samely, ed., *Profiling Jewish Literature in Antiquity: An Inventory from Second Temple Texts to the Talmuds* (Oxford; Oxford University Press, 2013). For the website results of the project, see "Typology of Anonymous and Pseudepigraphic Jewish Literature in Antiquity, c. 200 BCE to c. 700 CE," Modern Languages and Cultures, https://tinyurl.com/SBL3554c.

argues that the text presents itself as speaking to certain persons, groups, or entities, and is explicitly projecting a certain image of its addressee. Consequently, the laws, commandments, or norms of behavior that are described in the text lie entirely in a future that is anticipated as coming unconditionally. The norms are not projected as being for some eventuality, which may or may not arise; they will be required to be applied at some future date. With that in mind, the manuscript could have been used on the battlefield as a guide for legitimation and religious motivation.[34] Although the War Scroll is set within an eschatological setting, the numerous copies of the text have led scholars, such as Philip Alexander, to argue that "members of the sect presumably took it literally and studied it as a manual to train themselves."[35] If viewed from this perspective, even in an eschatological setting, everyday lives are being affected and taken as a preparation guide for battle, in which case the text may have been performed and acted in preparation of the pending battles. There does appear to be a growing interest throughout the War Texts in laymen and people other than priests, which may have to do with making the war traditions accessible to a wider audience.[36]

Although there is no way of knowing what the precise use of the War Scroll was among the Qumran communities, references to the training aspects of the rules in the M material are significant to my own interpretation. The patterns, behaviors, and practices that were described in the manuscripts may have been performed and/or taken literally.[37] I am taking the War Scroll as a manuscript that is outlining masculine, particularly hegemonic, ideologies. It is very possible that the Qumran communities expected the war imminently, and I am interested in the possible significance that this may have had on the constructions of patterns, behaviors, practices, and performances of male behaviors.

### The Construction/s of the Male in the War Scroll

The construction of the men outlined in the War Scroll represent the ideal—the ideal ages (1QM VI, 14–VII, 1): "The men of the rule shall be

---

34. Duhaime, "War Scroll," 85.
35. Philip S. Alexander, "Rules," *EDSS* 2:803.
36. This viewpoint has been argued by Hanna Vanonen, "Stable and Fluid War Traditions: Re-thinking the War Material from Qumran" (PhD diss., University of Helsinki, 2017).
37. Alexander, "Rules," 803.

from forty years to fifty. Those who order the camps shall be from fifty years to sixty. The officers shall also be from forty years to fifty. All those who strip the slain, seize plunder, purify the land, keep watch over the weapons and the one who prepares the provisions, all of them shall be from twenty-five years to thirty"—the ideal fight (1QM VI, 12), the ideal qualities (1QM VI, 16–17), and the ideal purity: "They shall all be volunteers for war, perfect ones of spirit and flesh, and ready for the Day of Vengeance" (1QM VII, 5).[38] It appears that even in the ideal, reality is at play. It is not just the men who should be masculinized: even the horses are described in masculine terms, as they are to be "male horses [סוסים], swift of foot, soft of mouth, long of breath" (1QM VI, 12), and those riding them shall be "men of worth" (1QM VI, 13). Violence in the War Scroll is used in a way that expands able-bodied men's masculinity, since "All of them shall be ready ... to shed the blood of the slain of their guiltiness" (1QM VI, 15) and not to "become defiled in their unclean blood" (1QM VIII, 8). In these examples, the idealized males are represented as pure and ready to provoke violence among others. They are also to avoid tarring their purity and becoming defiled, since they would not be able to fight; here, their impurity affects masculine behaviors.

The definitions of warfare, masculinity, and purity can be used as concepts that relate to whether a man among the DSS communities was able to go to war and therefore prove his masculinity. For example, in 1QM VII, 1–7 there is a detailed description of who is and who is not permitted to enter the battlefield, which are concerns largely based on purity, as well as age, gender, and modesty. It is stated that "No young boy or woman [ובול נער זעטוט ואשה] shall enter their camps when they leave Jerusalem to go to battle until their return" (1QM VII, 3). Such prohibitions may demonstrate that there were age and gender restrictions placed on the people of the DSS communities, but it may also have been that women were restricted from entering the camps for purity reasons—with their possible menstrual uncleanness and also the temptation for the men to have sexual intercourse with the women.

In relation to enforcing the laws of purity and conducting rituals, the priests and the Levites play a fundamentally important role during war (1QM VII, 7–IX, 9; XIII, 1–2; XV, 4–7). Deuteronomy is one of the major sources of inspiration for the War Scroll, especially with the laws

---

38. The War Scroll translation is according to Duhaime, "War Scroll," 80–141.

of purity, since purification laws are to be strictly enforced because God stands among the camps (1QM X, 1-2; Deut 7:21-22). The laws about exclusion and purity in the camps (1QM VII, 3-7 and 4Q491 1-3, 6-10) are applications derived from Deut 23:10-15 in which the concept of holiness does not mean a particular enhancement of human moral qualities. In observing the ritual customs prescribed in Deut 23:10-15, Israel was segregated from the unclean things, and bodily impurities were particularly important in terms of separation (see Lev 15; Num 5:1-4).[39] It is also instructed in 1QM VII, 7 that there should be a place away from the camp "two thousand cubits or so" for the toilet (see Deut 23:13; 11QT$^a$ XLVI, 13), and there is to be no "indecent nakedness" around the camps. Such exclusivist language portrayed in the War Scroll not only defines who *does* what, but, ultimately, who *is* what within a community.[40]

In Deuteronomy, the soldier becomes the symbol for the holiness of the camp, and if a soldier becomes unclean because of a nocturnal emission (מקרה לילה), as seen in Deut 23:10-11, then he is to wait until evening and wash himself with water, and only when the sun has set is he to return back into the camp. In masculine terms, when the soldier is in danger of losing his purity he is instructed to leave the camp since he is not able to participate in a pure manner.[41] For David Biale, God was involved in the "power of the procreative fluids," such as menstrual blood and semen, and Biale tries to understand the reason sexual intercourse was deemed impure in Leviticus as a result of semen being attributed to demonic forces. Biale argues that the priests seemed to have understood ejaculation as a temporary loss of a man's "vital power," which, from a masculinist perspective, may equate

---

39. Gerhard von Rad, *Deuteronomy*, trans. Dorothea Barton (London: SCM, 1966), 58.

40. David H. J. Morgan, "Theater of War: Combat, the Military and Masculinities," in *Theorizing Masculinities*, ed. Harry Brod and Michael Kaufman (London: Sage, 1994), 180. For Thomas Hentrich, the impact biblical purity laws had on disabled or otherwise afflicted people forced them to become "the Other" within society. See Thomas Hentrich, "Masculinity and Disability in the Bible," in *"This" Abled Body: Rethinking Disabilities in Biblical Studies*, ed. Hector Avalos, Sarah J. Melcher, and Jeremy Schipper (Atlanta: Society of Biblical Literature, 2007), 73-80. Such relations between disability and masculinity could also be used to enhance debates on purity and the DSS and take further Harrington's comparative work between 4QMMT, Durkheim, and Douglas.

41. Udo Rüterswörden, "Purity Conceptions in Deuteronomy," in Frevel and Nihan, *Purity and the Forming of Religious Traditions*, 414.

with a loss of masculinity.[42] The man who is not ritually clean "in respect to his genitals on the day of battle shall not go down with them into battle" (1QM VII, 6) for the holy angels are present among their army. For me, such images relating to impurity can be equated with a loss of masculinity; he has now lost a part of him that once made him inclusive, dominant, and masculine within the communal setting, but since he is now impure he has lost a part of his identity that made him part of the community.

The historical association of war and hegemonic masculinity affected those who were unable to take part in the war, and if members of particular communities were unable to go to war due to purity issues, then the ways that they would have been perceived by the pure members of the same DSS communities, whether male or female, would have been affected. Bryan Turner, in his discussion of disability and the body, argues that a sociological understanding of the body is needed that combines both an appreciation of the lived body in the everyday world and a clear understanding that the body is constructed.[43] Such an understanding of masculinity and disability studies has recently occurred in biblical scholarship with Thomas Hentrich, in his discussion of masculinity and disability in the Bible, revealing how the gender of a person is only second to their disability.[44] Drawing on the secondary nature of gender in the Hebrew Bible, the impurity of those described in the War Scroll is based on bodily blemishes. The men are described as "lame," "blind," "crippled," "blemished," and "unclean": their male body has become impure in the eyes of God and in the wider communities (1QM VII, 6). In masculine terms, impure men trouble the hegemonic ideal type.

## Constructing Hegemonic Ideals in the War Scroll

Joane Nagel has demonstrated the intimate connection between war and manhood as long-standing.[45] For Nagel, the attributes associated with

---

42. David Biale, *Eros and the Jew: From Biblical Israel to Contemporary America* (London: HarperCollins, 1992), 29.

43. Bryan S. Turner, "Disability and the Sociology of the Body," in *Handbook of Disability Studies*, ed. Gary L. Abrecht, Katherine D. Seelman, and Michael Bury (London: Sage, 2001), 253.

44. Hentrich, "Masculinity and Disability," 73.

45. Joane Nagel, "War," in Flood et al., *International Encyclopedia of Men and Masculinities*, 626.

hegemonic masculinity "across time and space mirror the cultural components of warrior traditions: bravery, toughness, daring, honour, strength and courage."[46] The intimate connection between war and masculinity is long-standing, and one way to reach this is by looking at the constructions of the masculine body in specific texts that discuss war, ideology, and behavior.[47] For example, drawing on images of soldiers from republican and imperial Rome, Richard Alston has argued that violence has been constructed as a particularly male attribute and that the violence associated with soldiers has come to represent the ideals of manhood.[48] Given that Warren Rosenberg has argued that the "ideal Jewish male became a biblical scholar, a congregant and a loving husband and father, who rejected violence,"[49] the construction of violence in the War Scroll is worthy of further attention. Is it possible that the War Scroll's construction of masculinity is purposefully different from the construction of the male in other biblical texts? In the violent examples from the War Scroll, the idealized males are represented as pure and ready to provoke violence among others. They are also to avoid tarring their purity and becoming defiled, since they will not be able to fight; consequently, potential impurity may affect their masculine performance.

In the War Scroll, an exclusive group of males is created who are portrayed and constructed as the physical and inclusive members of the Qumran communities.[50] The men are to be "perfect ones of spirit and flesh" (1QM VII, 5) and nothing less. In 1QM VII, 1–7 there is a detailed description of who is and who is not permitted to enter the battlefield, which are concerns largely based on purity, as well as age, gender, and modesty. It is stated that "No young boy or woman [וכול נער זעטוט ואשה] shall enter their camps when they leave Jerusalem to go to battle until their return. Neither lame, nor blind, nor crippled, nor a man in whose flesh

---

46. Nagel, "War," 626.

47. Nagel, "War," 626.

48. Richard Alston, "Arms and the Man: Soldiers, Masculinity and Power in Republican and Imperial Rome," in *When Men Were Men: Masculinity, Power and Identity in Classical Antiquity*, ed. Lin Foxhall and John Salmon (London: Routledge, 1998), 205.

49. Warren Rosenberg, "Jewish Masculinities," in Flood et al., *International Encyclopedia of Men and Masculinities*, 350.

50. Joseph Roisman, *The Rhetoric of Manhood: Masculinity in the Attic Orators* (Berkeley: University of California Press, 2005), 105.

there is a permanent blemish, nor a man stricken by some uncleanliness in his flesh, none of them shall go to battle with them" (1QM VII, 3–5).

The War Scroll outlines how a man should react in the appointed time of vengeance; he is to be "strong and brave" (1QM XV, 7), and he is not to be "terrified, alarmed or trembling" (1QM XVII, 7–8). Just as the men permitted to be in the military had to meet masculine expectations that were set up alongside the permitted masculine ideology, so the eschatological battle outlines to all those who are listening to and reading this scroll how to be a man, a Son of Light, and what is needed to be "pure of spirit and flesh" (1QM VII, 5). The brave, disciplined, pure, strong man brought honor to himself, his family, and the wider communities, but without the purity element, no man could prove his bravery, strength, or worth (1QM XV, 7). Drawing on the ideas of masculine preservation, purity, and warfare, masculinity and purity can be understood as related concepts when discussing the men behind the War Scroll. The real question here is one of the possible spilling of blood and all the resonance that this has on purity status; it is a question of keeping a physically whole, blood-free, and scar-free body. The male would consequently have to stay pure and retain his masculinized physical flesh while fighting; they were to shed the blood of the guilty (1QM VI, 17) but not their own. It is assumed in 1QM XIV that all the Sons of Light, when they have slayed the enemy, shall "clean their garments and wash themselves of the blood of the guilty corpses" (1QM XIV, 2–3). Accordingly, it is not presumed that the Jewish men are themselves impure but are simply to "return to the place where they had taken position" (1QM XIV, 3). This hope is almost beyond reality and again points to the vulnerable position in which men found themselves.

The people whom God chooses to redeem are described in terms that relate to the improvement and enhancement of their male body, since God has "taught war to the weak. [...] He gives to the staggering knees, strength to stand and steadiness of loins to the smitten back" (1QM XIV, 6–7; 4Q491 8 I, 4–5). The effects of masculine ideologies allow the body to become an object of society where power is produced in order to be controlled, identified, and reproduced.[51] The male bodies are pure, masculinized, and ready to do God's work (1QM XIV, 12).

---

51. Bryan S. Turner, *The Body and Society: Explorations in Social Theory* (London: Sage, 1996), 48.

These ideals provide rules and routines that would have been followed in certain respects in daily life, and how to act and behave when the war did come. Since the War Scroll is an eschatological text, the actuality of whether men did go to war can never be known, but the ideological images that are portrayed provide an idealized setting and vision for the men to aspire to, which, in turn, affected the wider DSS communities. It seems that both reality and the ideal were aspired to as they each affected involvement in daily life.

Purity, Power, and Performance:
The Constructions of Masculinist Ideologies in the War Texts

It was the goal of men to not be characterized as belonging to other imperfectly masculinized groups of men, especially the Sons of Darkness. During the times the War Scroll texts were being produced, rewritten, and reused, masculinity took on different aspects and redefinitions based on the historical circumstances. Potentially, in more stable societies, the ideas and ideals of masculinity would also have remained stable, and any change or redefinition of masculine behaviors would have reflected the chaos of the time; the stable portrayal of masculinity is not to be found in the construction of the masculine in the War Scroll.[52] The texts portray an ideal male in various ways, but the everyday, ordinary man cannot adhere to this, as people's daily lives aspire to such ideals and can never obtain them.

The constructions of the ideal traits that are presented in the DSS provide a hypothetical, ideal masculinity that men living among the communities were encouraged to take as their model. This is where the distinction between the idealized daily life and the reality of daily life would have come into consistent interaction, since in waiting for the reign of Belial to end and in living daily life in the present age, there would always have been a reason to strive to be a better person, a perfected version of oneself that was not yet attainable. Men were not "just men all the time";[53] they strove to be better people, to be pure and different from the impure and lustful norms that they saw before them in the reign of Belial. As such, they strove to perfect their purity and their masculinity in ways that would

---

52. Alston, "Arms and the Man," 220.
53. See Kirsten Hastrup, "The Semantics of Biology: Virginity," in *Defining Females: The Nature of Women in Society*, ed. Shirley Ardener (Oxford: BERG, 1993), 42.

differentiate them, not only before God and other communities but also among themselves. It is impurity that troubled the hegemonic ideal and left men in vulnerable positions among their wider communities.

This chapter has revealed the vulnerable position in which impure men found themselves and subsequently has demonstrated the following key points. First, masculinity can be enhanced through being pure and defiant in either men's membership or attitude to war. Second, the correlation between loss of masculinity and loss of purity was highlighted, which reveals an inherent vulnerability of men's purity; it was not static but evolving. Studying ancient texts should not distract us from attempting to reconstruct the people, communities, and social situations behind the manuscripts. By using gendered and everyday methodologies that discuss the male in an eschatological setting, it is possible to engender ancient Judaism through a modern lens that makes the people behind the War Texts more visible and embodied, rather than systemic and passive. In order to enhance understanding of the purity rules in those texts, the present chapter has highlighted both the vulnerability of the prevailing scholarly abstractions about purity, and the interpretative potential of putting the problematic impure male at the center of quests for the ideologies of gender and masculinity in the ancient communities of the DSS.

It seems to me, at least, that many of the masculine characteristics, qualities, and attributes, as constructed in the War Scroll, depended on the male being and remaining pure; anything less left them vulnerable. When read within a masculine framework, there is a relationship to be found between purity, power, and performance that in itself reveals an inherent vulnerability of male impurity; neither masculinity nor purity are static, they are, therefore, both constantly evolving. It appears that in the War Scroll, it was the goal of men to avoid being characterized as belonging to the Other—the impure other, the marginalized other, the imperfect other. Gender is not constructed in this text on a male-versus-female scale; rather, the constructions of men in the War Scroll are paired against other men. Using masculinity as a lens to read the War Scroll, the construction of the eschatological hegemonic ideal is formed as a social construct, which, I would argue, could not have been realized on a daily basis. However, it is possible that the formation of the ideal may have been imagined and/or performed at certain times; consequently, the position and performance of being a man was in itself vulnerable, fluctuating, and dependent on external factors.

## Bibliography

Alexander, Philip S. "Rules." *EDSS* 2:799–803.

Alston, Richard. "Arms and the Man: Soldiers, Masculinity and Power in Republican and Imperial Rome." Pages 205–23 in *When Men Were Men: Masculinity, Power and Identity in Classical Antiquity*. Edited by Lin Foxhall and John Salmon. London: Routledge, 1998.

Biale, David. *Eros and the Jew: From Biblical Israel to Contemporary America*. London: HarperCollins, 1992.

Birnbaum, Salomo A. *Text*. Vol. 1 of *The Hebrew Scripts*. Leiden: Brill, 1971.

Brooke, George J. "Text, Timing, and Terror: Thematic Thoughts on the War Scroll in Conversation with the Writings of the Martin G. Abegg Jr." Pages 46–66 in *The War Scroll, Violence, War and Peace in the Dead Sea Scrolls and Related Literature: Essays in Honour of Martin G. Abegg on the Occasion of His Sixty-Fifth Birthday*. Edited by Kipp Davis, Kyung S. Baek, Dorothy Peters, and Peter W. Flint. STDJ 115. Leiden: Brill, 2015.

Collins, John J. "Sectarian Communities in the Dead Sea Scrolls." Pages 151–72 in *The Oxford Handbook of the Dead Sea Scrolls*. Edited by Timothy H. Lim and John J. Collins. Oxford: Oxford University Press, 2010.

Connell, Raewyn W. *Gender and Power: Society, the Person and Sexual Politics*. London: Polity, 1987.

———. *Masculinities*. Cambridge: Polity, 1995.

Connell, Raewyn W., and James W. Messerschmidt. "Hegemonic Masculinity: Rethinking the Concept." *GS* 19 (2005): 829–59.

Duhaime, Jean. "War Scroll." Pages 80–141 in *Damascus Document, War Scroll, and Related Documents*. Vol. 2 of *The Dead Sea Scrolls: Hebrew, Aramaic, and Greek Texts with English Translations*. Edited by James H. Charlesworth. PTSDSSP 2. Tübingen: Mohr Siebeck, 1995.

———. *The War Texts: 1QM and Related Manuscripts*. London: T&T Clark, 2004.

Frevel, Christian, and Christophe Nihan. "Introduction." Pages 1–47 in *Purity and the Forming of Religious Traditions in the Ancient Mediterranean World and Ancient Judaism*. Edited by Christian Frevel and Christophe Nihan. DHR 3. Leiden: Brill, 2013.

Fuss, Diana. *Essentially Speaking: Feminism, Nature and Difference*. London: Routledge, 1990.

García Martínez, Florentino, and Adam S. van der Woude. "A 'Groningen' Hypothesis of Qumran Origins and Early History." *RevQ* 14 (1990): 521–41.

Gramsci, Antonio. *Selection from the Prison Notebooks*. London: Biddles, 1971.

Grosz, Elizabeth. *Volatile Bodies: Toward a Corporeal Feminism*. Bloomington: Indiana University Press, 1994.

Harrington, Hannah K. *The Purity Texts*. CQS 5. London: T&T Clark, 2004.

Hastrup, Kirsten. "The Semantics of Biology: Virginity." Pages 34–49 in *Defining Females: The Nature of Women in Society*. Edited by Shirley Ardener. Oxford: BERG, 1993.

Hearn, Jeff. "Masculinities." Pages 390–94 in *International Encyclopedia of Men and Masculinities*. Edited by Michael Flood, Judith Kegan Gardiner, Bob Pease, and Keith Pringle. London: Routledge, 2007.

Hempel, Charlotte. "Qumran Community." *EDSS* 2:746–51.

Hentrich, Thomas. "Masculinity and Disability in the Bible." Pages 73–91 in *"This" Abled Body: Rethinking Disabilities in Biblical Studies*. Edited by Hector Avalos, Sarah J. Melcher, and Jeremy Schipper. Atlanta: Society of Biblical Literature, 2007.

Keady, Jessica M. *Vulnerability and Valour: A Gendered Analysis of Everyday Life in the Dead Sea Scrolls Communities*. LSTS 91. London: Bloomsbury, 2017.

Klawans, Jonathan. *Impurity and Sin in Ancient Judaism*. Oxford: Oxford University Press, 2000.

Kraemer, Ross S. "Women and Gender." Pages 465–93 in *The Oxford Handbook of Early Christian Studies*. Edited by Susan Ashbrook Harvey and David Hunter. Oxford: Oxford University Press, 2010.

Lemos, Tracy. "Where There Is Dirt, Is There System? Revisiting Biblical Purity Constructions." *JSOT* 37 (2013): 265–94.

Levy, Donald P. "Hegemonic Masculinity." Pages 253–55 in *International Encyclopedia of Men and Masculinities*. Edited by Michael Flood, Judith Kegan Gardiner, Bob Pease, and Keith Pringle. London: Routledge, 2007.

Martino, Wayne. "Boys and Literacy: Exploring the Construction of Hegemonic Masculinities and the Formation of Literate Capacities in the English Classroom." *EA* 112 (1995): 11–24.

Messerschmidt, James W. *Masculinity and Crime: Critique and Reconceptualization of Theory*. Lanaham, MD: Rowman & Littlefield, 1993.

Meyers, Carol L. "Hierarchy or Heterarchy? Archaeology and the Theorizing of Israelite Society." Pages 249–51 in *Confronting the Past: Archaeological and Historical Essays on Ancient Israel in Honor of William G. Dever*. Edited by Seymour Gitin, J. Edward Wright, and J. P. Dessel. Winona Lake, IN: Eisenbrauns, 2006.

———. "Was Ancient Israel a Patriarchal Society." *JBL* 133 (2014): 8–27.

Morgan, David H. J. "Theater of War: Combat, the Military and Masculinities." Pages 165–83 in *Theorizing Masculinities*. Edited by Harry Brod and Michael Kaufman. London: Sage, 1994.

Nagel, Joane. "War." Pages 626–29 in *International Encyclopedia of Men and Masculinities*. Edited by Michael Flood, Judith Kegan Gardiner, Bob Pease, and Keith Pringle. London: Routledge, 2007.

Rad, Gerhard von. *Deuteronomy*. Translated by Dorethea Barton. London: SCM, 1966.

Roisman, Joseph. *The Rhetoric of Manhood: Masculinity in the Attic Orators*. Berkeley: University of California Press, 2005.

Rosenberg, Warren. "Jewish Masculinities." Pages 349–51 in *International Encyclopedia of Men and Masculinities*. Edited by Michael Flood, Judith Kegan Gardiner, Bob Pease, and Keith Pringle. London: Routledge, 2007.

Rütersworden, Udo. "Purity Conceptions in Deuteronomy." Pages 423–39 in *Purity and the Forming of Religious Traditions in the Ancient Mediterranean World and Ancient Judaism*. Edited by Christian Frevel and Christophe Nihan. DHR 3. Leiden: Brill, 2013.

Samely, Alexander, ed. *Profiling Jewish Literature in Antiquity: An Inventory from Second Temple Texts to the Talmuds*. Oxford: Oxford University Press, 2013.

Schiffman, Lawrence H. *The Halakhah at Qumran*. SJLA 16. Leiden: Brill, 1975.

Schofield, Alison. *From Qumran to the Yaḥad: A New Paradigm of Textual Development for the Community Rule*. STDJ 77. Leiden: Brill, 2009.

Schultz, Brian. *Conquering the World: The War Scroll (1QM) Reconsidered*. STDJ 76. Leiden: Brill, 2009.

Turner, Bryan S. *The Body and Society: Explorations in Social Theory*. London: Sage, 1996.

———. "Disability and the Sociology of the Body." Pages 252–66 in *Handbook of Disability Studies*. Edited by Gary L. Abrecht, Katherine D. Seelman, and Michael Bury. London: Sage, 2001.

"Typology of Anonymous and Pseudepigraphic Jewish Literature in Antiquity, c. 200 BCE to c. 700 CE." Modern Languages and Cultures. https://tinyurl.com/SBL3554c.

Vanonen, Hanna. "Stable and Fluid War Traditions: Re-thinking the War Material from Qumran." PhD diss., University of Helsinki, 2017.

Wassen, Cecilia. *Women in the Damascus Document*. AcBib 21. Atlanta: Society of Biblical Literature, 2005.

Wyke, Maria. "Introduction." Pages 1–11 in *Parchments of Gender: Deciphering the Bodies of Antiquity*. Edited by Maria Wyke. Oxford: Clarendon, 1998.

Zsolnay, Ilona, ed. *Being a Man: Negotiating Ancient Constructs of Masculinity*. New York: Routledge, 2016.

# Circumcision of the Heart in the Dead Sea Scrolls and in the Second Temple Period: Spiritual, Moral, and Ethnic

Carmen Palmer

Daniel Schwartz argues that the sectarian movement affiliated with the Dead Sea Scrolls (DSS) was prone to spiritualization and that matters of descent had lost value.[1] He suggests that for members of that movement, "differential descent, while a fact of life, was not a very significant way to categorize people. Other ways, such as viewing them as good or bad ... are more meaningful."[2] Something that made a person good or bad in the sectarian movement was the extent to which one followed the correct covenant. For example, 1QS II, 25–26; V, 7–8; and X, 10 all describe entering the "covenant of God" (ברית אל). 1QS III, 6–9 articulates that in order to do so, a combination of correct repentance and ritual action of sprinkling waters is required.[3] This overlap of ritual and moral purity, observed through a mingling of correct thought and actions, could be regarded as a type of "spiritualizing" or "religious practice."[4] Where Schwartz is concerned, it

---

This chapter is an expansion from arguments discussed in Carmen Palmer, *Converts in the Dead Sea Scrolls: The* Gēr *and Mutable Ethnicity*, STDJ 126 (Leiden: Brill, 2018).

1. On the tendency to spiritualize specifically, see Daniel R. Schwartz, "Ends Meet: Qumran and Paul on Circumcision," in *The Dead Sea Scrolls and Pauline Literature*, ed. Jean Sébastien Rey, STDJ 102 (Leiden: Brill, 2014), 307.

2. Schwartz, "Ends Meet," 303. Schwartz bases his overall thesis on the notion that the farther removed from the temple, the less descent would matter.

3. Harrington uses this example when describing the unique overlap of ritual and moral purity present within "Qumran literature." See Hannah K. Harrington, *The Purity Texts*, CQS 5 (London: T&T Clark, 2004), 27.

4. The term *religious practice* is offered in response to scholarly discussion concerning the time frame for the beginnings of religion as a separate entity. See, for example, David M. Miller, "Ethnicity, Religion and the Meaning of *Ioudaios* in Ancient

is this type of spiritualizing, or focusing on matters of religious practice, that leads to a diminished focus on kinship. Among the DSS, one finds a number of texts that clearly describe a circumcision of the foreskin of the heart. Obviously, the sectarian movement was not performing heart surgery, and so we can call these heart circumcisions metaphorical. We can also call them spiritual, because, as we shall see, they stem from scriptural predecessors that touch upon the notion of spiritual, or spiritual-moral, obedience to covenantal regulations. If one follows Schwartz's theory, this heart circumcision would pertain only to matters of the spiritual, or, said differently, religious practice, and would have dismissed anything to do with kinship and descent.

However, I argue that kinship matters for this metaphorical heart circumcision, just as it does for physical circumcision. Physical circumcision has traditionally been recognized as a marker of identity in scriptural tradition, connected to kinship and descent by means of marking the children of Abraham eight days after birth, as in Gen 17:12.[5] According to the instrumentalist pole of ethnicity studies, ethnicity comprises all features of a group's identity. Broadly speaking, these are features of kinship and culture, with other elements such as religious practice, language, and customs included within that.[6] Scholarship has recognized that components of identity within the ancient Mediterranean fit within such descriptive parameters. For example, Jonathan Hall, in studying ancient Greece, argues that primary ethnic identity markers include "descent and kinship," a connection to a "specific territory," and a "sense of shared history," although other features, such as language and religion, are also present.[7]

---

'Judaism,'" *CurBR* 12 (2014): 216–65, esp. his conclusion on 255; Steve Mason, "Jews, Judaeans, Judaizing, Judaism: Problems of Categorization in Ancient History," *JSJ* 38 (2007): 482; Philip F. Esler, *Conflict and Identity in Romans: The Social Setting of Paul's Letter* (Minneapolis: Fortress, 2003), 70. See also the discussion that follows on religious practice as one component of ethnic identity.

5. Each subsequent section will discuss the relationship between physical circumcision and kinship and descent according to the text under consideration.

6. See, for example, Fredrik Barth, "Introduction," in *Ethnic Groups and Boundaries: The Social Organization of Cultural Difference*, ed. Fredrik Barth (Boston: Little, Brown, 1969), 9–38; John Hutchinson and Anthony D. Smith, "Introduction," in *Ethnicity*, ed. John Hutchinson and Anthony D. Smith (Oxford: Oxford University Press, 1996), 3–14.

7. Jonathan M. Hall, *Hellenicity: Between Ethnicity and Culture* (Chicago: University of Chicago Press, 2002), 9.

Something spiritual would fit within this category of religion or religious practice, or more broadly culture. This description means that a full change between groups would also entail a change between all features of ethnicity. Where there is the spiritual, there is kinship, and vice versa. Thus, if circumcision of the heart contains a notion of the spiritual, there must also be kinship, allowing for a full ethnic identity. In other words, emphasis on the spiritual does not imply a dismissal of kinship, when considering matters of identity.

In the present essay, I will argue that descent has not lost value, despite a multiplicity of expanding views toward a required circumcision of the heart within the period of late Second Temple Judaism. This finding will stand both with regard to the sectarian movement affiliated with the DSS and with regard to writings pertaining to other groups in late Second Temple Judaism. Furthermore, circumcision of the heart relates to matters of both kinship and culture, and is therefore an integral component of ethnic identity. As Robert Kugler articulates, the sectarian affiliations of the movement need not imply that we define the group through only a religious (or spiritual) taxonomy.[8] The present essay continues Kugler's discussion by first observing the qualities of ethnic identity relating to kinship and the spiritual (or "religious") in circumcision, both physical and of the heart, in the DSS. Following that, this investigation casts comparative nets to three other texts from within late Second Temple Judaism that also draw on the imagery of circumcision of the heart, namely, Jubilees, selected texts from among the works of Philo, and Paul's Letter to the Romans. The goal is to see how heart circumcision may compare or contrast as an ethnic marker among these various texts. We will discover that these texts offer varying models of ethnic identity expressed in heart circumcision, and the comparisons among them will highlight a usage within the Yaḥad tradition that is very exclusive.

---

8. Robert Kugler, "The War Rule Texts and a New Theory of the People of the Dead Sea Scrolls: A Brief Thought Experiment," in *The War Scroll, Violence, War and Peace in the Dead Sea Scrolls and Related Literature: Essays in Honour of Martin G. Abegg on the Occasion of His Sixty-Fifth Birthday*, ed. Kipp Davis et al., STDJ 115 (Leiden: Brill, 2016), 164. Kugler concludes that, in the case of the War Scroll, in a later stage of the community, traits we might call "religion" did emerge, from the "over-narrowing of ethnic identities around ethnicity traits that contribute to what we have come to call religion" ("War Rule Texts," 171).

## Circumcision in the Dead Sea Scrolls

A number of passages relating to circumcision of the heart exist within the DSS. These texts include 1Q Pesher Habakkuk XI, 12–13; 4Q177 Catena A 9, 8; 4Q434 Barkhi Nafshi[a] 1 I, 4; 4Q504 Words of the Luminaries[a] 4, 11; and 4Q509 Festival Prayers frag. 287.[9] Some of these passages might predate the sectarian movement affiliated with the DSS, such as the fairly complete example of a passage identifying circumcision of the heart in Barkhi Nafshi: "And he has circumcised the foreskins of their heart [וימול עורלות לבם], and he has delivered them on account of his lovingkindness, and he set their feet to the way."[10] Nevertheless, the motif of circumcision of the heart is clearly subsequently appropriated by the movement. The Rule of the Community (1QS), one of the major rule traditions found at Qumran, describes a spiritual and metaphorical circumcision, using the term *form* or *inclination* (יצר) in 1QS V, 4–5: "No man shall wander in the stubbornness of his heart, to err following his heart, 5 his eyes, and the plan of his inclination. He shall rather circumcise in the Community the foreskin of the inclination [יאאם למול ביחד עורלת יצר] (and) a stiff neck."[11] David Rolph Seely notes that one may deem the "inclination" coterminous with the heart, in particular when the inclination is affiliated with a good or bad spirit or inclination.[12] Indeed, as noted by Roger Le Déaut, this יצר is not something independent from the heart, when considering passages

---

9. These passages can be found among the various partial lists: Martin G. Abegg, "The Covenant of the Qumran Sectarians," in *The Concept of the Covenant in the Second Temple Period*, ed. Stanley E. Porter and Jacqueline C. R. de Roo, JSJSup 71 (Leiden: Brill, 2003), 82; David Rolph Seely, "The 'Circumcised Heart' in 4Q434 Barki Nafshi," *RevQ* 17 (1996): 532.

10. Text and translation from Moshe Weinfeld and David Seely, "Barkhi Nafshi," in *Qumran Cave 4.XX: Poetic and Liturgical Texts, Part 2*, by Esther Chazon et al., DJD XXIX (Oxford: Clarendon, 1999), 270–71. See George J. Brooke, "Body Parts in *Barkhi Nafshi* and the Qualifications for Membership of the Worshipping Community," in *Sapiential, Liturgical and Poetical Texts from Qumran*, ed. Daniel Falk, Florentino García Martínez, and Eileen M. Schuller, STDJ 35 (Leiden: Brill, 2000), 79; Eileen M. Schuller, "Prayers and Psalms from the Pre-Maccabean Period," *DSD* 13 (2006): 314 and n. 28.

11. Text and translation for all passages from 1QS follow Elisha Qimron, "Rule of the Community (1QS)," in *Rule of the Community and Related Documents*, vol. 1 of *The Dead Sea Scrolls: Hebrew, Aramaic, and Greek Texts with English Translations*, ed. James H. Charlesworth, PTSDSSP 1 (Tübingen: Mohr Siebeck, 1994), 5–51.

12. Seely, "Circumcised Heart," 532–33.

describing an evil spirit that influences the heart (e.g., CD II, 15–16).[13] This rule is specifically for those men of the community, identified as the Yaḥad: וזה הסרכ לאנשי היחד, (1QS V, 1).[14] Consequently, the motif of circumcision of the heart is uniquely affiliated with what one might call a Yaḥad tradition of the sectarian movement.

What did this circumcision of the heart mean for those following the rules of the Yaḥad tradition? All scriptural passages that could serve as antecedents, including Deut 10:16; 30:6; and Jer 4:4, suggest the need for spiritual obedience.[15] For example, Deut 10:16 is recounted in the context of reminding Israel "of its basic obligations before God," in other words, the covenantal obligations to keep the commandments.[16] Werner Lemke has argued that, taken together as a whole, Jer 4:4; 6:10; and 9:24–25 articulate the requirement of spiritual obedience to God, often in light of needing to repent from disobedience.[17] In the context of the Yaḥad community, to what, exactly, is obedience required? The Yaḥad community borrowed this motif to exhort spiritual obedience for that community's special and eternal covenant (1QS III, 11–12). As articulated by Le Déaut, the obedience requires uprightness of heart, humility of spirit, and "meticulous observation of the Law," all moral conditions that distinguished the

---

13. Roger Le Déaut, "Le thème de la circoncision du coeur (Dt. XXX 6; Jér. IV 4) dans les versions anciennes (LXX et Targum) et à Qumrân," in *Congress Volume: Vienna 1980*, ed. John A. Emerton, VTSup 32 (Leiden: Brill, 1981), 191–92. Seely refers to Le Déaut, although Seely puts more emphasis on rabbinic comparisons between the inclination and the heart, whereas Le Déaut suggests that the inclination is within the heart (see Seely, "Circumcised Heart," 532–33; Le Déaut, "Le thème de la circoncision du coeur," 192 and n. 55).

14. It is clear that the other occasions of heart circumcision are found within texts that might best affiliate with those individuals linked to this rule. For example, 1QpHab, which refers to a heart circumcision (XI, 12–13), also draws on this special *yaḥad* terminology (in this case, the council of the community, עצת היחד), in XII, 4.

15. On scriptural antecedents for 1QS V, 5 specifically, see Brooke, "Body Parts in Barkhi Nafshi," 82; Seely, "Circumcised Heart"; Le Déaut, "Le thème de la circoncision du coeur," esp. 192. It should be noted that Le Déaut considers only Deut 10:16 as a scriptural reference and not Deut 30:6.

16. Werner E. Lemke, "Circumcision of the Heart: The Journey of a Biblical Metaphor," in *A God So Near: Essays on Old Testament Theology in Honor of Patrick D. Miller*, ed. Brent A. Strawn and Nancy R. Bowen (Winona Lake, IN: Eisenbrauns, 2003), 300.

17. Lemke, "Circumcision of the Heart," 303–7.

Yaḥad community from other Israelites.[18] This new covenant, to be followed through correct moral obedience, was exclusive to this community.

Clearly one can see a spiritual dimension in this heart/form circumcision, through the moral dimension required in following the new covenant. With this spiritual dimension, there is a possibility that physical circumcision, and consequently descent and kinship, would diminish. After all, Schwartz has argued that for the sectarian movement, "descent does not matter much."[19] In a similar vein, Sandra Jacobs argues that the high regard expressed in 1QS V, 4 for "circumspectly walking in all their ways," affiliated with the spiritual circumcision in 1QS V, 4–6, "highlights the lack of interest of the covenant of [physical] circumcision in the rewritten biblical traditions found at Qumran."[20] However, while not plentiful, references to physical circumcision are nevertheless present within the DSS. CD XVI, 4–6 rewrites Abraham's initial circumcision as described in Gen 17:9–14 and articulates that "Abraham was circumcised on the day of his knowing [על כן נימול {ב} אברהם ביום דעתו]."[21] Added to this first example, one can reconstruct a regulation from Lev 12 concerning eighth-day circumcision, within 4Q266 6 II, 6: "And on the eighth day the flesh of his] foreskin [shall be circumcised" ([ו]ביום השמיני ימול בשר עׇרְלָתֹ]).[22] Finally, a third passage, CD XII, 10–11, might refer to the act of physical circumcision, in prohibiting the sale of servants who have entered the "covenant of Abraham" (ברית אברהם). Schwartz suggests that physical circumcision may not pertain to this instance due to the inclusion of female slaves in the statement.[23] On

---

18. Le Déaut, "Le thème de la circoncision du coeur," 193–94. English translation of the French is mine.

19. Schwartz, "Ends Meet," 305.

20. Sandra Jacobs, "Expendable Signs: The Covenant of the Rainbow and Circumcision at Qumran," in *The Dead Sea Scrolls in Context: Integrating the Dead Sea Scrolls in the Study of Ancient Texts, Languages, and Cultures*, ed. Armin Lange, Emanuel Tov, and Matthias Weigold, VTSup 140 (Leiden: Brill, 2011), 571.

21. All texts and translation from CD follow Joseph M. Baumgarten and Daniel R. Schwartz, "Damascus Document (CD)," in *Damascus Document, War Scroll, and Related Documents*, in *The Dead Sea Scrolls: Hebrew, Aramaic, and Greek Texts with English Translations*, ed. James H. Charlesworth, PTSDSSP 2 (Tübingen: Mohr Siebeck, 1995), 4–79.

22. Text and translation for this 4QD manuscript follow Joseph M. Baumgarten, *Qumran Cave 4.XIII: The Damascus Document (4Q266–273)*, DJD XVIII (Oxford: Clarendon, 1996), 55–56.

23. On this matter, see Schwartz, "Ends Meet," 301.

the other hand, one may assume physical circumcision for the male, in light of the reference to Abraham's circumcision in CD XVI. In such a case, we find three passages that indicate the ongoing importance of physical circumcision for the sectarian movement overall, or at least, for the tradition relating to the Damascus Document.

One notes that no passages within 1QS or other documents that refer to the Yaḥad tradition (such as 1QpHab, mentioned above, and here in XII, 4) refer to physical circumcision specifically. Nevertheless, the overall dominant view within late Second Temple Judaism that physical circumcision was an important feature of Jewish identity would lay the burden of proof to argue otherwise for the sectarian movement on any extant texts that deny the importance of physical circumcision. On this topic, there are none among the DSS.[24] Instead, it appears that both forms of circumcision were understood as requirements for these Yaḥad followers, with heart circumcision being a secondary circumcision that followed an assumed physical circumcision. In fact, 1QS V, 6 describes those who join the movement as הנלוים, a term that assumed the meaning "converts" during this time period, literally, "the ones who attached themselves."[25] It appears that followers of the Yaḥad had undergone a sort of secondary conversion to an exclusive group.

In summary, where circumcision in the DSS is concerned, matters of kinship are definitely involved. References to physical circumcision

---

24. The importance of circumcision is evident when considering that Godfearers were still considered thus, even when performing temple sacrifices, if they did not undergo circumcision. In other words, circumcision seemed a definitive step of conversion. See, for example, Paula Fredriksen, "Judaism, the Circumcision of Gentiles, and Apocalyptic Hope: Another Look at Galatians 1 and 2," in *The Galatians Debate: Contemporary Issues in Rhetorical and Historical Interpretation*, ed. Mark D. Nanos (Peabody, MA: Hendrickson, 2002), 238; Terence Donaldson, *Judaism and the Gentiles: Jewish Patterns of Universalism (to 135 CE)* (Waco, TX: Baylor University Press, 2007), 10; Lawrence H. Schiffman, *Who Was a Jew? Rabbinic and Halakhic Perspectives on the Jewish-Christian Schism* (Hoboken, NJ: Ktav, 1985), esp. 23–25, 37.

25. The Second Temple verb לוה is usually found in the *niphal*, "to attach oneself" or "to join oneself," such as in Esth 9:27. See José Ramírez Kidd, *Alterity and Identity in Israel*, BZAW 283 (Berlin: de Gruyter, 1999), 72. The verb has been understood to indicate an act of conversion when found in later Second Temple Judaism. Included are those later texts that use a Greek rendering of the verb (whether from Hebrew or Aramaic), such as those who "attach themselves [προσκειμένοις]" to the sons of Israel in Tob 1:8. See also Jdt 14:10 (see Donaldson, *Judaism and the Gentiles*, 42, 207).

appear within the Damascus Document and related 4QD material, and suggest a connection to the covenant of Abraham. References to a circumcision of the heart that refers to spiritual and moral behaviors exist in other scrolls, and the Rule of the Community alludes to this type of circumcision with a coterminous reference to a circumcision of form. While the Rule of the Community does not also refer to a physical circumcision, it seems more likely that the circumcision of the heart is a type of secondary circumcision, rather than an alternative to physical circumcision. Through circumcision of the heart, members of the Yaḥad community become a new kind of convert. Matters of kinship and culture (through correct religious practices) are combined through both forms of circumcision, resulting in a full ethnic identity within the DSS. Let us now move on to the comparisons to Jubilees, selected passages from the works of Philo, and Romans.

## Jubilees

While physical circumcision has an important ideological role to play in Jubilees (which shall be discussed further below), Jub. 1.23 is the sole verse in the work containing a reference to circumcision of the heart. The reference occurs within the context of the Lord's response to an intercessory prayer by Moses, on behalf of the Israelites, to avoid exile due to disobedience:

> And the LORD said to Moses: "I know their contrariness and their thoughts and their stubbornness. And they will not obey until they acknowledge their sin and the sins of their fathers. But after this they will return to me in all uprighteousness and with all of (their) heart and soul. And I shall cut off the foreskin of their heart and the foreskin of the heart of their descendants. And I shall create for them a holy spirit, and I shall purify them so that they will not turn away from following me from that day and forever." (Jub. 1.22–23)[26]

This one metaphorical occasion of circumcision of the heart reworks Deut 30:6: "Moreover, the LORD your God will circumcise your heart and the heart of your descendants, so that you will love the LORD your God with all your heart and with all your soul, in order that you may live."[27] The

---

26. Translations for Jubilees follow Orval S. Wintermute, "Jubilees: A New Translation and Introduction," *OTP* 2:35–142.

27. Regarding Deut 30:6 as the scriptural antecedent in question, see Matthew

Deuteronomy passage occurs within the context of the curses and blessings described that will follow from either disobedience or obedience to the covenant established between the people of Israel and the Lord. The passage iterates that whenever the people return to the Lord after a time of disobedience, they will be brought back from whatever location to which they may be exiled to the land of their ancestors, and, as cited above, God will circumcise their hearts and the hearts of their descendants. In this passage, it is God's agency that performs the heart circumcision for the sake of loving God.[28]

Where the Jubilees passage is concerned, however, Kyle Wells observes that prior to receiving the circumcision of the heart, some *initial* effort is required on the part of the people that comes with the recognition of past sins and sinful behavior. Jubilees 1.22 introduces the reference to heart circumcision, with the stipulation that "they will not obey until they acknowledge their sin and the sins of their fathers [ancestors]." Whereas Deut 30:1–10 advocates a "divinely initiated restoration," in Jubilees, restoration is reliant first on "Israel's turning" prior to divine transformation of "human nature."[29] Wells concludes that divine gifts are bestowed "on those who comply with that order [found within God's law] to some degree."[30] These divine gifts are circumcision of the heart followed by the creation of a holy spirit and the Lord's purification of the people for the

---

Thiessen, *Contesting Conversion: Genealogy, Circumcision, and Identity in Ancient Judaism and Christianity* (Oxford: Oxford University Press, 2011), 71. Translation followed is that of the NRSV. Scholarship has established that Jubilees originally would have been composed in Hebrew, as fifteen fragments or portions thereof of Jubilees in Hebrew have been discovered at Qumran. See James C. VanderKam, *The Book of Jubilees*, CSCO 511 (Leuven: Peeters, 1989), vi–xi; Michael Segal, *The Book of* Jubilees: *Rewritten Bible, Redaction, Ideology, and Theology*, JSJSup 117 (Leiden: Brill, 2007), 1.

28. Le Déaut, "Le thème de la circoncision du coeur," 181.

29. Kyle B. Wells, *Grace and Agency in Paul and Second Temple Judaism: Interpreting the Transformation of the Heart*, NovTSup (Leiden: Brill, 2015), 150, 161–62.

30. Wells, *Grace and Agency*, 163. Wells overall is arguing against the conclusion drawn by David Lambert, namely, that Jubilees works within an understanding that humanity's transformation (in the circumcision of the heart) is divinely initiated. Lambert argues that Jubilees is resolving the exegetical problem caused by human agency suggested in Deut 4:29–31, contrasted against divine agency apparent in Deut 30:1–10. See David Lambert, "Did Israel Believe That Redemption Awaited Its Repentance? The Case of *Jubilees* 1," *CBQ* 68 (2006): esp. 634, 640.

sake of perpetual future obedience.[31] The reliance of Jub. 1.23 on Deut 30:6, a scriptural antecedent in which the heart circumcision occurs in order to love God fully and live, combined with the observation in Jub. 1.23 that initial obedience is required to acquire heart circumcision and a holy spirit, forges a particular sentiment: circumcision of the heart is representative of God's restorative activity that will create the holy spirit and purification required for the people to obey, *predicated* on some initial human obedience. Within the context of Jubilees, circumcision of the heart is therefore spiritual, as it is a divine activity arising from human obedience to a divinely commanded law.

The question arises, then, as to what would constitute initial human obedience and acknowledgment of sins in Jubilees. As is well known, within Jubilees, eighth-day circumcision is imperative.[32] The topic arises first in Jub. 15.11–14, with the specifications that all males in the household will be circumcised on the eighth day and that any "soul [individual]" not circumcised on the eighth day will be "uprooted from its family" (Jub. 15.14). Whether the result of a later addition or not,[33] Jub. 15.25–34 then proceeds to add further specification that there is "no circumcising of days and there is no passing a single day beyond eight days because it is an eternal ordinance ordained and written in the heavenly tablets" (Jub. 15.25). The phrase "no circumcising of days" has been interpreted to mean that there should be no reduction of days.[34] Furthermore, anyone not circum-

---

31. Wells suggests that references to the "heart," the verb to "create," and a "spirit" can be seen in both Jub. 1.23 and also Ps 51:12 [Heb.]. (Wells, *Grace and Agency*, 149).

32. Thiessen suggests that Jubilees drew from a version of Gen 17:14 that included the reference to eighth-day circumcision (Thiessen, *Contesting Conversion*, 72). (The MT of Gen 17:14 makes no reference to the specificity of circumcision on the eighth day.) Segal makes a similar comment, noting that the addition regarding the eighth day in Jubilees versus MT Gen 17:14 is not an addition on the part of the individual he identifies as the "reviser," but rather, the reference is found in other textual witnesses such as the Samaritan Pentateuch and the LXX (Segal, *Book of* Jubilees, 230, n. 2).

33. Kugel argues that Jub. 15.24–34 is an addition on the part of an "Interpolator." See James L. Kugel, *A Walk through* Jubilees: *Studies in the* Book of Jubilees *and the World of Its Creation*, JSJSup 156 (Leiden: Brill, 2012), 257.

34. See Jacques T. A. G. M. van Ruiten, "The *Book of Jubilees* as Paratextual Literature," in *In the Second Degree: Paratextual Literature in Ancient Near Eastern and Ancient Mediterranean Culture and Its Reflections in Medieval Literature*, ed. Philip S. Alexander, Armin Lange, and Renate J. Pillinger (Leiden: Brill, 2010), 87–88, for a summary of scholarly views that generally suggest the phrase "no circumcising of

cised by the eighth day after birth is, in fact, destined for destruction and "uprooted from the earth" and does not belong to the people of Abraham (Jub. 15.26). As noted by Jacques van Ruiten, following the commandment to circumcise at the appropriate time "requires human action."[35] This eighth-day circumcision could be the initial human obedience necessary to receive God's circumcision of the heart.

What impetus would there be to include such specificity regarding circumcision occurring exactly on the eighth day after birth? The severe reprimand might likely be in response to historically committed perceived sins. One option is that a view existed in the second- or first-century BCE time frame of Jubilees that was similar to the halakic position found in m. Shabb. 19:5. This rabbinic passage articulates that under certain circumstances, circumcision could be delayed up until the twelfth day: "An infant is circumcised on the eighth, ninth, tenth, eleventh, or twelfth days [קטן נמול לשמונה לתשעה ולעשרה ולאחד עשר ולשנים עשר]."[36]

Another option also exists that relates specifically to the ethnic feature of kinship, namely, that in order to be circumcised on the eighth day after birth, an individual must be born into a Jewish household. This restriction means that adult (male) gentiles desiring to convert are ineligible to do so. Since entering Jewish peoplehood generally entailed circumcision, such as what is reported by Josephus concerning the Idumeans undergoing circumcision in *A.J.* 13.257–258, eighth-day circumcision regulations would

---

days" to mean no reduction in days. See also Kugel, *Walk through* Jubilees, 257, who holds the same opinion.

35. Van Ruiten, "Book of Jubilees," 89.

36. English translation according to Jacob Neusner, *The Mishnah: A New Translation* (New Haven: Yale University Press, 1988), 203. Reasons that would permit the delay include matters regarding timing, such as whether the baby was born at twilight or on the Sabbath. Segal suggests that the argument concerns delaying circumcision and is not a matter of whether it was performed at all (*Book of* Jubilees, 236–37 n. 22). In the same note, Segal furthermore draws on the argument of Menahem Kister that such a debate pertains to halakic argumentation and not to a Hellenistic setting. However, as noted by Kugel, the concern raised in Jub. 15.33 that some children of Israel are not circumcising fully, in order to conceal the circumcision, appears to relate to the historical setting of hellenizing Jews (e.g., Josephus, *A.J.* 12.241; 1 Macc 1:11). It is possible that disputes regarding delaying circumcision could have a historical setting as well. See Menahem Kister, "Concerning the History of the Essenes: A Study of the *Animal Apocalypse*, the *Book of Jubilees*, and the *Damascus Covenant* (Heb.)," *Tarbiz* 56 (1986): 6–7 n. 26; Kugel, *Walk through* Jubilees, 258 and n. 40. See also van Ruiten, "Book of Jubilees," 89, who provides an overview of the discussion.

have prohibited gentile conversions to Judaism.[37] In this vein, Matthew Thiessen looks to the connection in Jubilees between law and identity to argue the following: "Jubilees links law observance inextricably with birth and therefore with genealogy, insisting that eighth-day circumcision is the principal indicator of Jewish identity."[38]

Based on Jub. 15, physical circumcision that must happen on the eighth day after birth consequently incorporates multiple features of ethnicity beyond simply that of religious practice or the spiritual. Features of religious practice are indeed present through proper obedience of the divinely sanctioned law, but so too are a connection to the land and a notion of shared kinship. These features of ethnicity prevalent in the command regarding eighth-day physical circumcision relate back to the initial action required and acknowledgment of sin discussed in Jub. 1. Jubilees 15 discusses disobedience of the commandment resulting in uprooting from the land and exclusion from the covenant made for Abraham. Chapter 1 discusses the fear that the people will be put into exile for not being obedient to the law, which relates to the very uprooting identified in chapter 15. Finally, eighth-day circumcision is available to and required of the children of Abraham.

To bring these findings together, where Jubilees is concerned, an integrated notion of ethnicity beyond solely a component of the spiritual or proper religious practice is still of importance, despite the spiritualization present in the circumcision of the heart named in Jub. 1.23. The reason for this integration is that eighth-day physical circumcision constituted the initial compliance with God's laws, which was imperative in order to receive the heart circumcision from God that would, in turn, permit future restorative obedience. These findings mean that without eighth-day circumcision, which was fully ethnic, there could be no heart circumcision. Therefore, heart circumcision was also completely ethnic, as it was fully reliant on eighth-day circumcision, which, for Jubilees, was heavily reliant on both kinship (or genealogy, or descent, to use the terminologies of Thiessen and Schwartz) and culture (including the practice of following God's law).

---

37. Cohen suggests that the circumcision of the Idumeans is the earliest example of conferring Judean citizenship on outsiders and becoming Judean in a political sense. See Shaye J. D. Cohen, *The Beginnings of Jewishness: Boundaries, Varieties, Uncertainties* (Berkeley: University of California Press, 1999), esp. 110, 118.

38. Thiessen, *Contesting Conversion*, 85 (notwithstanding his view of one author contra that of multiple redactors).

In this fashion, circumcision of the heart is similar in Jubilees to that in the Yaḥad tradition of the DSS; both are secondary, and both are fairly exclusive. There is no heart circumcision for gentiles, even those who may have undergone circumcision and consider themselves to have become Jewish.

## Philo

There are two forms of circumcision, one physical, of the flesh, and one of the mind or heart where Philo is concerned. Maren Niehoff argues that Philo develops a notion of twofold circumcision based on Philo's reading of Gen 17:10–11, where there is reference to "every male" being circumcised as well as reference to physical circumcision.[39] According to Niehoff, Philo interprets these references as two types of circumcision (evidenced in QG 3.46), one physical and fleshly, and one metaphorical of the mind. Philo's interpretation is made possible by the fact that he views the mind as male: "That which is, properly speaking, masculine in us is the intellect" (QG 3.46).[40] Subsequently, Philo draws on the only pentateuchal reference to circumcision that is metaphorical, Deut 10:16, which draws on the metaphor of the circumcision of the heart. It is in this fashion that Philo can draw a connection between circumcision of the mind as a circumcision of the heart.[41]

What more can be said about Philo's understanding of circumcision of the heart, specifically? Philo describes it as spiritual, when arguing it is this type of circumcision required of converts in QE 2.2 (although he also argues for the need for physical circumcision as well, which will be discussed below): "He shows most evidently that he is a proselyte, inasmuch as he is not circumcised in the flesh of his foreskin, but in the pleasures and appetites, and all the other passions of the soul; for the Hebrew race was not circumcised in Egypt."[42] This spiritual element emerges from the moral

---

39. On the two circumcisions and the connection between the mind and maleness, see Maren R. Niehoff, "Circumcision as a Marker of Identity: Philo, Origen and the Rabbis on Gen 17:1–14," *JSQ* 10 (2003): 95.

40. English translations for Philo follow Charles D. Yonge, trans., *The Works of Philo: Complete and Unabridged*, new updated ed. (Peabody, MA: Hendrickson, 1993).

41. Niehoff, "Circumcision as a Marker," 96. See also Wells, *Grace and Agency*, 201, who comments that "Philo sees the heart as the seat of the mind."

42. Niehoff, "Circumcision as a Marker," 101.

perfection of Abraham that redefines his covenantal relationship with God.[43] Heart circumcision generates the intellect: Philo argues that "the generative principle of the soul is the intellect ... which is rather the generative principle of the heart. And in truth there is nothing to which it is found more like than the circumcision of the heart" (*QG* 3.48). Furthermore, there is a resemblance between this heart circumcision and physical circumcision.[44] Philo describes this union in *Spec.* 1.6: "There is the resemblance of the part that is circumcised to the heart; for both parts are prepared for the sake of generation; for the breath contained within the heart is generative of thoughts, and the generative organ itself is productive of living beings." In this manner, physical and heart circumcision go hand in hand as two generative principles. Where the heart circumcision generates thoughts, the physical circumcision generates kinship through offspring.[45]

In fact, this intertwined rapport between heart and physical circumcision is also strong for another reason. According to Philo, in addition to a connection to kinship and descent through generation of living beings, physical circumcision is also "a symbol of the excision of the pleasures which delude the mind" (*Spec.* 1.9).[46] Eradicating mind-deluding pleasures facilitates seeking out clearness of truth and the one living God. In fact, it seems that Philo leans on Deut 10:16 to suggest that circumcising one's heart for the sake of relinquishing stubbornness refers to physical circumcision (*Spec.* 1.304–306). Such a statement implies that physical circumcision will at once also elucidate heart circumcision. It seems that where Philo is concerned, to a point heart circumcision is reliant on physical circumcision.

---

43. Niehoff, "Circumcision as a Marker," 93–95.

44. Mireille Hadas-Lebel, *Philo of Alexandria: A Thinker in the Jewish Diaspora*, trans. Robyn Fréchet, ed. Francesca Calabi and Robert Berchman, SPhA 7 (Leiden: Brill, 2012), 96.

45. Wells, *Grace and Agency*, 201. See also Richard D. Hecht, "The Exegetical Contexts of Philo's Interpretation of Circumcision," in *Nourished with Peace: Studies in Hellenistic Judaism in Memory of Samuel Sandmel*, ed. Frederick E. Greenspahn, Earle Hilgert, and Burton L. Mack, HS (Chico, CA: Scholars Press, 1984), 62.

46. See also *QG* 3.48; Everett Ferguson, "Spiritual Circumcision in Early Christianity," *SJT* 41 (November 1988): 486. Additional passages to consult include *Migr.* 92; *Spec.* 1.305; Peter Borgen, "The Early Church and the Hellenistic Synagogue," *ST* 37 (1983): 64. See also Hadas-Lebel, *Philo of Alexandria*, 96; Niehoff, "Circumcision as a Marker," 100. Finally, according to Hecht, the reason for this arrogance is found in *Migration* 92, that man believes he is behind generation ("Exegetical Contexts," 74).

To this end, despite Philo's acknowledgment and perhaps even sympathy toward a spiritual circumcision of the heart, noted above in *QE* 2.2, scholarship suggests that Philo regards both types of circumcision to be required. For example, in Niehoff's terms, Philo believes that spiritual circumcision should not have preference over physical, as physical circumcision offers "educational value."[47] Peder Borgen argues that even though Philo's focus on spiritual heart circumcision (which Borgen calls "ethical circumcision") for converts in *QE* 2.2 may appear to emphasize this type of circumcision over that of physical, nevertheless, Philo is merely commenting on those Jews who uphold such a view. Philo's own view supports the need for physical circumcision in general.[48] Similarly, John Collins has argued that Philo focuses on physical circumcision not as a "prerequisite for membership" but as "a duty consequent on admission" into Judaism.[49] A common passage to support these views is *Migr.* 92: "Nor because the rite of circumcision is an emblem of the excision of pleasures and of all the passions, and of the destruction of that impious opinion, according to which the mind has imagined itself to be by itself competent to produce offspring, does it follow that we are to annul the law which has been enacted about circumcision."

In light of the dual requirement of both physical and heart circumcision, and physical circumcision's role in producing offspring, one can see that descent has not diminished where Philo is concerned. One can observe a further connection to descent when looking specifically at Philo's views toward circumcision and convert conversion. Having discerned that circumcision, both physical and spiritual of the heart, is a critical component of conversion, a closer look at the nature of the conversion itself will also reveal that descent maintains an important role in identity. For Philo, the process of conversion involves a convert having forsaken all of the following:

---

47. Hadas-Lebel, *Philo of Alexandria*, 97; Niehoff, "Circumcision as a Marker," 101. Here also, Niehoff draws a connection between Mosaic law and circumcision, per *Migr.* 91–93.

48. Borgen, "Early Church," 67–68.

49. John J. Collins, "A Symbol of Otherness: Circumcision and Salvation in the First Century," in *"To See Ourselves as Others See Us": Christians, Jews, "Others" in Late Antiquity*, ed. Jacob Neusner and Ernest S. Frerichs (Chico, CA: Scholars Press, 1985), 173–74; also see Nolland, who believes Philo does expect converts to undergo physical circumcision. See John Nolland, "Uncircumcised Proselytes?," *JSJ* 12 (1981): 173–79, esp. 179.

their natural relations by blood, and their native land and their national customs, and the sacred temples of their gods, and the worship and honour which they had been wont to pay to them, and have migrated with a holy migration, changing their abode of fabulous inventions for that of the certainty and clearness of truth, and of the worship of the one true and living God. (*Virt.* 102)

Thus, we find converts having given up elements related to both kinship and culture, including religious practice as well as citizenship via a connection to land. In the act of their holy migration, these converts have relinquished their prior identity, including blood relations and cultural affiliations (including worship of foreign gods). Borgen interprets Philo to mean that converts have made a break with "pagan society" and have instead migrated to "another ethnic group, the Jewish nation."[50] Physical and spiritual circumcision, as an integral part of this migration, also include notions of descent and kinship, land, and religious practice.

Overall, matters of descent and kinship are important to Philo's combined concepts of physical and heart circumcision. Jonathan Smith has suggested that for Philo, circumcision "seems to have little to do with either ethnic [meaning descent] or religious identity."[51] Smith notes that Philo defends physical circumcision for reasons that include emphasis on matters of hygiene (*Spec.* 1.5) and also relates the physical organ symbolically to the heart (*Spec.* 1.6), noted above to evoke the mind. But, in fact, we have found that heart circumcision, despite its relationship to the mind and the perfecting of thoughts, is intertwined with physical circumcision, which reflects descent in its connection to the physical organ and the generation of human beings. This interconnection is present because both forms of circumcision are required. One may possibly go even further to suggest that the excision of pleasures and conceit performed by physical circumcision may assist in the perfecting of the mind. Furthermore, descent features prominently as part of the holy migration undertaken by converts.

---

50. Borgen also observes that this passage highlights a main theme regarding converts to Judaism, which is that of the transition to the God within Jewish law ("Early Church," 60, 61).

51. Jonathan Z. Smith, *Imagining Religion: From Babylon to Jonestown*, ed. Jacob Neusner, CSHJ (Chicago: University of Chicago Press, 1982), 14.

Intriguingly, because heart circumcision was required of converts as well, Philo's concept of identity is more permeable and contrasts against that of the Yaḥad tradition, where there, heart circumcision was exclusive.

## Romans

Of all the passages concerning heart circumcision discussed in this essay, the one concerning which the most ink has been spilled is Paul's passage from Rom 2:28–29: "For the Jew is not one evidently so, nor is circumcision evident and in the flesh [ἐν σαρκὶ]. The Jew is the hidden Jew and circumcision is of the heart [καρδίας], in the Spirit [ἐν πνεύματι] not in the letter; his praise comes not from humankind but from God."[52] The passage in question interprets a number of possible scriptural antecedents, such as Jer 9:23–26; Ezek 36:26; and Deut 30:6, as well as Gen 17, a chapter that discusses the Israelites' covenantal obedience to God.[53] Physical circumcision, in its rapport to "the flesh," is related to both Jewish ritual and religious practice as well as kinship.[54]

Where circumcision of the heart is concerned, many scholars share the understanding that Paul intends to redefine Jewish identity, by arguing that a spiritual obedience based on faith in Christ will lead to salvation.[55] In this view, circumcision of the heart represents a biblical metaphor, which is this obedience. While its essence is construed differently by various schol-

---

52. As per John M. G. Barclay, "Paul and Philo on Circumcision: Romans 2.25–9 in Social and Cultural Context," *NTS* 44 (1998): 545. As noted by Barclay and others, it is preferable to use a translation with as few additions as possible for this elliptical passage. See also Matthew Thiessen, "Paul's Argument against Gentile Circumcision in Romans 2:17–29," *NovT* 56 (2014): 376–77.

53. In particular, for a study of innerscriptural references that can be observed in Rom 2:28–29, see Timothy W. Berkley, *From a Broken Covenant to Circumcision of the Heart: Pauline Intertextual Exegesis in Romans 2:17–29*, SBLDS 175 (Atlanta: Society of Biblical Literature, 2000).

54. Boyarin makes this argument in reference to "morally neutral" occasions of "according to the flesh [κατὰ σάρκα]," such as in Rom 4:1; 9:3. See Daniel Boyarin, *A Radical Jew: Paul and the Politics of Identity* (Berkeley: University of California Press, 1994), 72.

55. For a general overview on the outlook concerning salvation from faith in Christ, see, e.g., Berkley, *From a Broken Covenant*, 11, 216–17; Boyarin, *Radical Jew*, 9; Stanislaus Lyonnet, "La circoncision du coeur, celle qui relève de l'Esprit et non de la lettre," in *L'évangile hier et aujourd'hui: mélanges offerts au Professeur Franz-J. Leenhardt* (Genève: Editions Labor et Fides, 1968), 96.

ars, overwhelmingly heart circumcision is understood to focus on faithful behaviors (whether from humans or from God) that are removed from descent and kinship. For example, Jörg Frey argues that physical circumcision is soteriologically invalid and that the required circumcision of the heart is equivalent to justification without works.[56] Joseph Modrzejewski concludes that circumcision of the heart is "nothing else but being Christian" and becomes synonymous with baptism.[57] Ellen Christiansen argues that Paul reinterprets circumcision of the heart "to be an image of the gift of the divine Spirit."[58] Christiansen concludes thus because, in her argument, circumcision maintains "national, racial, gender, moral and social" features that now no longer apply in Christ.[59] The theme of a replacement of or distancing from descent with circumcision of the heart can also be found in Daniel Boyarin's work. Boyarin has argued that Paul works within a dualist ideology whereby "circumcision in the flesh," as a kind of cultural practice representative of kinship, and "physical kinship," both have "spiritual referents."[60] According to Boyarin, although Paul's "flesh/spirit dualism" would not result in actual "liberation from the body," the spiritual counterpart would enable an "escape" from desire and ethnicity (meaning physical kinship).[61] Indeed, all of the above examples display a decreased focus on descent or kinship and support Schwartz's thesis that "bodies lose their significance."[62]

---

56. Jörg Frey, "Paul's Jewish Identity," in *Jewish Identity in the Greco-Roman World*, ed. Jörg Frey, Daniel R. Schwartz, and Stephanie Gripentrog, AGJU 71 (Leiden: Brill, 2007), 313.

57. Joseph Mélèze Modrzejewski, "'Filios Suos Tantum': Roman Law and Jewish Identity," in *Jews and Gentiles in the Holy Land in the Days of the Second Temple, the Mishnah and the Talmud: A Collection of Articles*, ed. Menachem Mor et al. (Jerusalem: Yad Ben-Zvi, 2003), 115–16. Spiritual circumcision may be practiced possibly through baptism (see Gal 3:27). On the other hand, Ferguson argues that the "association of baptism with circumcision is actually secondary, and ... derived from the identification of the seal with the Holy Spirit. The earliest texts associate the seal of the new covenant with the gift of the Holy Spirit and do not identify baptism with circumcision." He points to Rom 4:11 and 2 Cor 1:22 (Ferguson, "Spiritual Circumcision," 491–92).

58. Ellen Juhl Christiansen, *The Covenant in Judaism and Paul: A Study of Ritual Boundaries as Identity Markers*, AGJU 27 (Leiden: Brill, 1995), 289.

59. Christiansen, *Covenant in Judaism*, 291.

60. Boyarin, *Radical Jew*, 72.

61. Boyarin, *Radical Jew*, 60, 68.

62. Schwartz, "Ends Meet," 305.

Not all, however, are of the opinion that kinship has lost significance in the relationship between circumcision both physical and of the heart. Arguing against the notion that Paul redefines Judaism, Matthew Thiessen concludes that Paul upholds eighth-day circumcision requirements, per Gen 17:14 LXX, and therefore circumcised Jews as well as uncircumcised gentiles are pleasing to God through circumcision of the heart.[63] In this outlook, descent and kinship are still very much an important factor in Paul's outlook. Physical circumcision, in its eighth-day requirement, is very much connected to descent. But above and beyond physical circumcision, arguably kinship is present within Paul's notion of heart circumcision as well. Ethnicity theory has found Paul to think through an ethnic lens. Denise Kimber Buell has suggested that a statement such as Gal 3:28 ("There is no longer Jew or Greek, there is no longer slave or free, there is no longer male and female; for all of you are one in Christ Jesus" [NRSV]) does not imply an "escape" (to borrow from Boyarin) from kinship, but rather a transformation of ethnic identity.[64] If one combined Boyarin's notion of a spiritual referent to kinship and Kimber Buell's notion of the creation of a new ethnicity, then one might understand Paul to be fashioning a kind of spiritual ethnicity, a kind of spiritual ethnogenesis. Those who practice spiritual circumcision can gain a dual ethnicity,[65] as either Jew and Christ follower, or gentile and Christ follower, with the spiritual Christ-follower essence being the link. Seen this way, circumcision of the heart's ability to draw together Jew and gentile need not be removing ethnicity, but rather adding to it, forming dual ethnicities. This ethnicity would be part flesh (Jew or gentile) and part spiritual in faith in Christ. This new *ethnos* in Christ brings together both kinship as well as culture in religious practice.

In this case, heart circumcision is still very much related to kinship, and not only culture, here implying the religious practice of faith in Christ. Heart circumcision seems to be what enables the ethnogenesis, or formation of a new ethnicity, for what were different groups to fit within one new, multifaceted elasticity. Therefore, a major difference between heart

---

63. Thiessen, "Paul's Argument." See also the discussion above in the section on Jubilees for Thiessen's argument regarding eighth-day circumcision, and corresponding notes.

64. Denise Kimber Buell, *Why This New Race: Ethnic Reasoning in Early Christianity* (New York: Columbia University Press, 2005), 138.

65. Esler describes dual or multi ethnicities (*Conflict and Identity*, 73).

circumcision within the Yaḥad tradition and this passage in Romans is its mutable nature and accessibility to both Jews and gentiles.

## Conclusions

The present essay set out to demonstrate that descent has not lost value, despite a burgeoning literary tradition concerning circumcision of the heart, within both the DSS and other literature from the late Second Temple period. According to ethnicity theory, identity comprises features of both kinship and culture, meaning that identity within the sectarian movement should not become a matter of religious practice alone. The ethnic dimensions of kinship and descent, especially prevalent in physical circumcision, should still hold importance even when notions of circumcision of the heart emerge. The study tested this theory and found that notions of kinship and descent are indeed integral to circumcision of the heart, and not only in the sectarian movement but also within other texts from within late Second Temple Judaism. Sometimes heart circumcision is incorporated with descent in physical circumcision, and other times it is reliant on descent in physical circumcision, but always circumcision of the heart is part of a full ethnic identity in each case. Nevertheless, it represents something slightly different in each text and exhibits differing levels of permeability, too.

Within the DSS linked to the Yaḥad tradition, circumcision of the heart represents a spiritual obedience to follow a special covenant. This heart circumcision is a secondary circumcision to physical circumcision, which is still assumed to be practiced and relating to kinship, in light of other passages that describe both Abraham's circumcision and an infant's circumcision at eight days after birth. Overall, due to heart circumcision's secondary nature to and reliance on physical circumcision, identity for the Yaḥad community is fully comprising ethnic features of kinship and culture. Furthermore, for the Yaḥad, circumcision of the heart is exclusive to those members who are followers of the special covenant. Within Jubilees, circumcision of the heart represents God's restorative activity for an initial obedience, most likely represented in eighth-day circumcision, which provokes future obedience to the laws and salvation. Once again, circumcision of the heart is reliant on physical circumcision, and again it is exclusive in its insistence on the eighth-day requirement of the physical circumcision. Within Philo, physical circumcision eradicates the pleasures that delude the mind, to permit the perfection of the mind provided by circumcision of the heart. Furthermore, the intertwined nature of these two forms of circumcision relates to kinship as well as to a spiritual essence, evidenced in the change of kinship that takes place at the time of a convert's conversion. In this regard, while both forms of circumcision are required, they are accessible to all Jews and converts to Judaism. Finally, in Paul, circumcision of the heart, linked to faith in Christ, enables the ethnogenesis of a spiritual ethnicity; this ethnicity is also dual, in that it is the means to bring together both a Jew and a Christ follower, and a gentile and a Christ follower. Physical circumcision is again related in that Jews who circumcise on the eighth day are pleasing to God, just as are gentiles for whom physical circumcision is prohibited.

In this essay, ethnicity theory served as a template to assess whether descent lost value for various groups within late Second Temple Judaism. In conclusion, the argument holds that heart circumcision is not a dismissal of the ethnic feature of kinship: physical and heart circumcision are generally viewed either as one being imperative for the other, or both blending together so fully, that the overall impression is one of kinship and culture combined. Furthermore, this assessment of circumcision of the heart through the lens of ethnicity theory provided a window through which to observe the identity of the Yaḥad tradition of the sectarian movement. On the one hand, the Yaḥad tradition follows a similar trend as other groups within late Second Temple Judaism, by using the motif of circumcision of the heart. On the other hand, we can see that this tradition uses the motif in the most exclusive manner among all the texts under consideration, showcasing a particular stream within the sectarian movement with a high level of impermeability.

## Bibliography

Abegg, Martin G. "The Covenant of the Qumran Sectarians." Pages 81–97 in *The Concept of the Covenant in the Second Temple Period*. Edited by Stanley E. Porter and Jacqueline C. R. de Roo. JSJSup 71. Leiden: Brill, 2003.

Barclay, John M. G. "Paul and Philo on Circumcision: Romans 2.25–9 in Social and Cultural Context." *NTS* 44 (1998): 536–56.

Barth, Fredrik. "Introduction." Pages 9–38 in *Ethnic Groups and Boundaries: The Social Organization of Cultural Difference*. Edited by Fredrik Barth. Boston: Little, Brown, 1969.

Baumgarten, Joseph M. *Qumran Cave 4.XIII: The Damascus Document (4Q266–273)*. DJD XVIII. Oxford: Clarendon, 1996.

Baumgarten, Joseph M., and Daniel R. Schwartz. "Damascus Document (CD)." Pages 4–79 in *Damascus Document, War Scroll, and Related Documents*. Vol. 2 of *The Dead Sea Scrolls: Hebrew, Aramaic, and Greek Texts with English Translations*. Edited by James H. Charlesworth. PTSDSSP 2. Tübingen: Mohr Siebeck, 1995.

Berkley, Timothy W. *From a Broken Covenant to Circumcision of the Heart: Pauline Intertextual Exegesis in Romans 2:17–29*. SBLDS 175. Atlanta: Society of Biblical Literature, 2000.

Borgen, Peter. "The Early Church and the Hellenistic Synagogue." *ST* 37 (1983): 64.

Boyarin, Daniel. *A Radical Jew: Paul and the Politics of Identity*. Berkeley: University of California Press, 1994.

Brooke, George J. "Body Parts in *Barkhi Nafshi* and the Qualifications for Membership of the Worshipping Community." Pages 79–94 in *Sapiential, Liturgical and Poetical Texts from Qumran*. Edited by Daniel K. Falk, Florentino García Martínez, and Eileen M. Schuller. STDJ 35. Leiden: Brill, 2000.

Christiansen, Ellen Juhl. *The Covenant in Judaism and Paul: A Study of Ritual Boundaries as Identity Markers*. AGJU 27. Leiden: Brill, 1995.

Cohen, Shaye J. D. *The Beginnings of Jewishness: Boundaries, Varieties, Uncertainties*. Berkeley: University of California Press, 1999.

Collins, John J. "A Symbol of Otherness: Circumcision and Salvation in the First Century." Pages 163–86 in *"To See Ourselves as Others See Us": Christians, Jews, "Others" in Late Antiquity*. Edited by Jacob Neusner and Ernest S. Frerichs. Chico, CA: Scholars Press, 1985.

Donaldson, Terence. *Judaism and the Gentiles: Jewish Patterns of Universalism (to 135 CE)*. Waco, TX: Baylor University Press, 2007.

Esler, Philip F. *Conflict and Identity in Romans: The Social Setting of Paul's Letter*. Minneapolis: Fortress, 2003.

Ferguson, Everett. "Spiritual Circumcision in Early Christianity." *SJT* 41 (1988): 485–97.

Fredriksen, Paula. "Judaism, the Circumcision of Gentiles, and Apocalyptic Hope: Another Look at Galatians 1 and 2." Pages 235–60 in *The Galatians Debate: Contemporary Issues in Rhetorical and Historical Interpretation*. Edited by Mark D. Nanos. Peabody, MA: Hendrickson, 2002.

Frey, Jörg. "Paul's Jewish Identity." Pages 285–321 in *Jewish Identity in the Greco-Roman World*. Edited by Jörg Frey, Daniel R. Schwartz, and Stephanie Gripentrog. AGJU 71. Leiden: Brill, 2007.

Hadas-Lebel, Mireille. *Philo of Alexandria: A Thinker in the Jewish Diaspora*. Translated by Robyn Fréchet. Edited by Francesca Calabi and Robert Berchman. SPhA 7. Leiden: Brill, 2012.

Hall, Jonathan M. *Hellenicity: Between Ethnicity and Culture*. Chicago: University of Chicago Press, 2002.

Harrington, Hannah K. *The Purity Texts*. CQS 5. London: T&T Clark, 2004.

Hecht, Richard D. "The Exegetical Contexts of Philo's Interpretation of Circumcision." Pages 51–79 in *Nourished with Peace: Studies in Hellenistic Judaism in Memory of Samuel Sandmel*. Edited by Frederick E. Greenspahn, Earle Hilgert, and Burton L. Mack. HS. Chico, CA: Scholars Press, 1984.

Hutchinson, John, and Anthony D. Smith. "Introduction." Pages 3–14 in *Ethnicity*. Edited by John Hutchinson and Anthony D. Smith. Oxford: Oxford University Press, 1996.

Jacobs, Sandra. "Expendable Signs: The Covenant of the Rainbow and Circumcision at Qumran." Pages 563–75 in *The Dead Sea Scrolls in Context: Integrating the Dead Sea Scrolls in the Study of Ancient Texts, Languages, and Cultures*. Edited by Armin Lange, Emanuel Tov, and Matthias Weigold. VTSup 140. Leiden: Brill, 2011.

Kidd, José Ramírez. *Alterity and Identity in Israel*. BZAW 283. Berlin: de Gruyter, 1999.

Kimber Buell, Denise. *Why This New Race: Ethnic Reasoning in Early Christianity*. New York: Columbia University Press, 2005.

Kister, Menahem. "Concerning the History of the Essenes: A Study of the *Animal Apocalypse*, the *Book of Jubilees*, and the *Damascus Covenant* (Heb.)." *Tarbiz* 56 (1986): 1–18.

Kugel, James L. *A Walk through* Jubilees: *Studies in the* Book of Jubilees *and the World of Its Creation*. JSJSup 156. Leiden: Brill, 2012.

Kugler, Robert. "The War Rule Texts and a New Theory of the People of the Dead Sea Scrolls: A Brief Thought Experiment." Pages 163–72 in *The War Scroll, Violence, War and Peace in the Dead Sea Scrolls and Related Literature: Essays in Honour of Martin G. Abegg on the Occasion of His Sixty-Fifth Birthday*. Edited by Kipp Davis, Dorothy M. Peters, Kyung S. Baek, and Peter W. Flint. STDJ 115. Leiden: Brill, 2015.

Lambert, David. "Did Israel Believe That Redemption Awaited Its Repentance? The Case of *Jubilees* 1." *CBQ* 68 (2006): 631–50.

Le Déaut, Roger. "Le thème de la circoncision du coeur (Dt. XXX 6; Jér. IV 4) dans les versions anciennes (LXX et Targum) et à Qumrân." Pages

178–205 in *Congress Volume: Vienna 1980*. Edited by John A. Emerton. VTSup 32. Leiden: Brill, 1981.

Lemke, Werner E. "Circumcision of the Heart: The Journey of a Biblical Metaphor." Pages 299–319 in *A God So Near: Essays on Old Testament Theology in Honor of Patrick D. Miller*. Edited by Brent A. Strawn and Nancy R. Bowen. Winona Lake, IN: Eisenbrauns, 2003.

Lyonnet, Stanislaus. "La circoncision du coeur, celle qui relève de l'Esprit et non de la letter." Pages 87–97 in *L'évangile hier et aujourd'hui: mélanges offerts au Professeur Franz-J. Leenhardt*. Genève: Editions Labor et Fides, 1968.

Mason, Steve. "Jews, Judaeans, Judaizing, Judaism: Problems of Categorization in Ancient History." *JSJ* 38 (2007): 457–512.

Miller, David M. "Ethnicity, Religion and the Meaning of *Ioudaios* in Ancient 'Judaism.'" *CurBR* 12 (2014): 216–65.

Modrzejewski, Joseph Mélèze. "'Filios Suos Tantum': Roman Law and Jewish Identity." Pages 108–36 in *Jews and Gentiles in the Holy Land in the Days of the Second Temple, the Mishnah and the Talmud: A Collection of Articles*. Edited by Menachem Mor, Aharon Oppenheimer, Jack Pastor, and Daniel R. Schwartz. Jerusalem: Yad Ben-Zvi, 2003.

Neusner, Jacob. *The Mishnah: A New Translation*. New Haven: Yale University Press, 1988.

Niehoff, Maren R. "Circumcision as a Marker of Identity: Philo, Origen and the Rabbis on Gen 17:1–14." *JSQ* 10 (2003): 89–123.

Nolland, John. "Uncircumcised Proselytes?" *JSJ* 12 (1981): 173–79.

Palmer, Carmen. *Converts in the Dead Sea Scrolls: The* Gēr *and Mutable Ethnicity*. STDJ 126. Leiden: Brill, 2018.

Qimron, Elisha. "Rule of the Community (1QS)." Pages 5–51 in *Rule of the Community and Related Documents*. Vol. 1 of *The Dead Sea Scrolls: Hebrew, Aramaic, and Greek Texts with English Translations*. Edited by James H. Charlesworth. PTSDSSP 1. Tübingen: Mohr Siebeck, 1994.

Ruiten, Jacques T. A. G. M. van. "The *Book of Jubilees* as Paratextual Literature." Pages 65–95 in *In the Second Degree: Paratextual Literature in Ancient Near Eastern and Ancient Mediterranean Culture and Its Reflections in Medieval Literature*. Edited by Philip S. Alexander, Armin Lange, and Renate J. Pillinger. Leiden: Brill, 2010.

Schiffman, Lawrence H. *Who Was a Jew? Rabbinic and Halakhic Perspectives on the Jewish-Christian Schism*. Hoboken, NJ: Ktav, 1985.

Schuller, Eileen M. "Prayers and Psalms from the Pre-Maccabean Period." *DSD* 13 (2006): 306–18.

Schwartz, Daniel R. "Ends Meet: Qumran and Paul on Circumcision." Pages 295–307 in *The Dead Sea Scrolls and Pauline Literature*. Edited by Jean Sébastien Rey. STDJ 102. Leiden: Brill, 2014.

Seely, David Rolph. "The 'Circumcised Heart' in 4Q434 *Barki Nafshi*." *RevQ* 17 (1996): 527–35.

Segal, Michael. *The Book of Jubilees: Rewritten Bible, Redaction, Ideology, and Theology*. JSJSup 117. Leiden: Brill, 2007.

Smith, Jonathan Z. *Imagining Religion: From Babylon to Jonestown*. Edited by Jacob Neusner. CSHJ. Chicago: University of Chicago Press, 1982.

Thiessen, Matthew. *Contesting Conversion: Genealogy, Circumcision, and Identity in Ancient Judaism and Christianity*. Oxford: Oxford University Press, 2011.

———. "Paul's Argument against Gentile Circumcision in Romans 2:17–29." *NovT* 56 (2014): 373–91.

VanderKam, James C. *The Book of Jubilees*. CSCO 511. Leuven: Peeters, 1989.

Weinfeld, Moshe, and David Seely. "Barkhi Nafshi." Pages 255–334 in *Qumran Cave 4.XX: Poetic and Liturgical Texts, Part 2*. By Esther Chazon et al. DJD XXIX. Oxford: Clarendon, 1999.

Wells, Kyle B. *Grace and Agency in Paul and Second Temple Judaism: Interpreting the Transformation of the Heart*. NovTSup. Leiden: Brill, 2015.

Wintermute, Orval S. "Jubilees: A New Translation and Introduction." *OTP* 2:35–142.

Yonge, Charles D., trans. *The Works of Philo: Complete and Unabridged*. New updated ed. Peabody, MA: Hendrickson, 1993.

# Experiencing the Solidity of Spaces in the Qumran Hodayot

Angela Kim Harkins

This essay proposes that Second Temple narrative prayers in first-person voice seek to make otherworldly spaces accessible with firsthand vividness, what we might call an experience of presence. *Presence* is a cognitive state in which a reader gains awareness of being in a particular narrative world or otherworldly space.[1] The first-person voice is the mechanism by which a reader could gain access to an immersive experience of the narrative world of the prayer, thus experiencing in part the things that the speaker describes with the vividness of presence. This study uses relevant aspects of cognitive literary theory to consider how spaces are described in the Qumran Hodayot (1QH$^a$) in such a way as to allow for the phenomenon of immersive reading.[2] How might a reader become lost in a

---

An earlier version of this paper was presented at the International Meeting of the Society of Biblical Literature in Rome, Italy, July 2019.

1. Anežka Kuzmičová, "Presence in the Reading of Literary Narrative: A Case for Motor Enactment," *Sem* 189 (2012): 24.

2. The English translation of the Hodayot used in this essay is my own, based on the reconstructed Hebrew text edited by Eileen M. Schuller and based on the work of Hartmut Stegemann, which was used in Hartmut Stegemann, Eileen M. Schuller, and Carol A. Newsom, *Qumran Cave 1.III: 1QHodayot$^a$ with Incorporation of 1QHodayot$^b$ and 4QHodayot$^{a-f}$*, DJD XL (Oxford: Clarendon, 2009), available now as Schuller and Newsom, *The Hodayot (Thanksgiving Psalms): A Study Edition of 1QH$^a$*, EJL 36 (Atlanta: Society of Biblical Literature, 2012). See also Hartmut Stegemann, "Rekonstruktion der Hodajot: Ursprüngliche Gestalt und kritisch bearbeiteter Text der Hymnenrolle aus Höhle 1 von Qumran" (PhD diss., University of Heidelberg, 1963). It is the view of the present author that the first group of Community Hymns known as 1QH cols. I–VIII was likely not a part of the Cave 1 Hodayot based on material and literary arguments discussed in Angela Kim Harkins, "Another Look at

narrative landscape? These questions about how otherworldly spaces achieve the quality of solidity will rely on observations and strategies that literary theorists have made for the writing of fiction and fantasy literature, both of which seek to create compelling narrative worlds for readers. Our discussion will begin by examining elements that encourage the readerly response of ruminating on the text itself, seeking to understand it. The first of these includes the effect that bizarre and counterintuitive features of the landscape might have on a reader, leading to a slower reading pace that allows for more cognitive and emotional engagement with the text. Then we will consider how the first-person voice allows a reader to enact the experiences of the hymnist, who describes being in a particular narrative place, thereby enscripting the prayer's embodied experiences for a reader to enact. These embodied experiences will be discussed as either interoceptive experiences (bodily experiences associated with the viscera, including pain, hunger, temperature, and also emotions) or proprioceptive experiences, which presume an extended body moving through space (movement, balance, and any kind of kinesthetic action). The first-person narration that is characteristic of prayers provides many details about the interoceptive and proprioceptive experiences of the hymnist, thus giving access to what it might be like to experience the narrative world of the Hodayot. The possible effects of reading 1QH$^a$ XVI, 5–XVII, 36 on the people who read and transmitted them seek to take into account the embodied (biological) and cultural contexts of the people of the DSS, who were living in an ancient Mediterranean culture.[3]

---

the Cave 1 Hodayot: Was CH I Materially Part of the Scroll 1QHodayot$^a$?," *DSD* 25 (2018): 185–216. This essay continues and improves the general argument presented in Harkins, "A New Proposal for Thinking about 1QH$^a$ Sixty Years after Its Discovery," in *Texts from Cave 1 Sixty Years after Their Discovery*, ed. Daniel K. Falk et al., STDJ 91 (Leiden: Brill, 2010), 101–34.

3. See Armin W. Geertz, "Religious Bodies, Minds and Places: A Cognitive Science of Religion Perspective," in *Spazi e Luoghi Sacri: Espressioni ed Esperienze di Vissuto Religioso*, ed. Laura Carnevale (Santo Spirito [Bari]: Edipuglia, 2017), 35–52, for an updated discussion of integrative approaches to the study of religion, such as cognitive science of religion. The basic point that is being made here in this study— that texts can express a vividness and an experiential quality of presence—is known in the classical world as the various literary strategies that achieve vividness or *enargeia*. See Ruth Webb, "Imagination and the Arousal of Emotions in Greco-Roman Rhetoric," in *The Passions in Roman Thought and Literature*, ed. Susanna M. Braund and Christopher Gill (Cambridge: Cambridge University Press, 1997), 112–27; Graham

## 1. Counterintuitive Aspects of Otherworldly Spaces

The Hodayot are narrative prayers that describe various scenes of otherworldly spaces that include strange and counterintuitive details. For example, the *hodayah* in 1QH<sup>a</sup> XI, 6–37 makes explicit reference to an otherworldly netherworld space that has "eternal bars" for imprisoning (XI, 18–19) and also "cords of death that bind with no (hope of) escape" (XI, 29). The text goes on to describe the "fiery rivers of Belial that will bubble over the riverbanks" (XI, 30), devouring everything as far as Abaddon (XI, 33). The mental image of the landscape engulfed in flames during the conflagration (XI, 32) is one that stays with the reader; it is also reminiscent of apocalyptic visionary texts of otherworldly scenes.[4]

Recognizable references to the landscape in 1QH<sup>a</sup> XI present the reader with familiar geographic components. The swollen rivers in line 30 as well as the mountain and expanse of land referenced in line 32 are presented to the reader in such a way as to appeal to our lived experience of such landscapes; yet the conflagration and details that suggest that this is a place of imprisonment remind readers and hearers that this religious geography is not the world as we know it. These spaces not only effect a strong emotional response in the reader—fear or terror—they stimulate the naturally occurring associative processes of memory reinvigoration. The process of remembering is surprisingly imperfect, "not a literal reproduction of the past, but rather ... a constructive process in which bits and pieces of information from various sources are pulled together."[5] The first-person narration of experiences can also simulate

---

Zanker, *Modes of Viewing in Hellenistic Poetry and Art* (Madison: University of Wisconsin Press, 2004). See too the application of classical *enargeia* to Paul's writings by Jane Heath, "Absent Presences of Paul and Christ: *Enargeia* in 1 Thessalonians 1–3," *JSNT* 32 (2009): 3–38. Dionysius of Halicarnassus speaks of *enargeia* as a literary style that has the effect of making the reader "suppose that he is seeing the things being presented actually happening" (*De Lys.* 7.14.17–15.1, discussed by Heath, "Absent Presences," 9–12).

4. For a discussion of how the landscape in this *hodayah* in 1QH<sup>a</sup> XI resonates with the otherworldly scenes described in the Enochic Book of the Watchers, see Angela Kim Harkins, *Reading with an "I" to the Heavens: Looking at the Qumran Hodayot through the Lens of Visionary Traditions*, Ekstasis 3 (Berlin: de Gruyter, 2011), 141–47.

5. Daniel L. Schacter and Donna Rose Addis, "The Cognitive Neuroscience of Constructive Memory: Remembering the Past and Imagining the Future," *PTRS* 362 (2007): 773.

episodic memory construction and reconstruction, which is a highly adaptive cognitive process that simulates the imagining of personalized possible experiences set in the future.[6] Such striking images of a burning landscape or of eternal bars for imprisonment remind the reader that this is not the world as he or she experiences it. According to Laura Feldt, one strategic effect of counterfactual or surprising details, such as those that appear in 1QH[a] XI, is to generate confusion and destabilize the reader.[7] Narratives that include disorienting and counterintuitive elements slow down the process of reading and function to allow readers to engage the text more deeply at an emotional level, perhaps moving readers to go back to reread or to ruminate over the unsettling passage. Counterintuitive elements and the role of suspense slow down the pace of reading, allow for rumination, and invite deeper thinking about a passage. Disorientation can lead to further experiences of meaningful contemplation. The generation of interpretation from such a process remains an undetermined process, since emotion's naturally associative function in memory reinvigoration would engage the remembering of texts and experiences at the level of the individual.[8]

Turning now to the well-irrigated garden in 1QH[a] XVI, 5–XVII, 36, the landscape here can be said to optimize environmental features that befit the culture and historical period of the DSS. Even so, cross-cultural studies of otherworldly spaces such as paradise note the similarity between the general features of the narrative landscape and its notable differences in specific counterintuitive ways that remind the reader that this is not the world as we know it.[9] Cross-cultural narratives about paradise

---

6. Schacter and Addis, "Cognitive Neuroscience," 778.

7. Laura Feldt, "Religious Narrative and the Literary Fantastic: Ambiguity and Uncertainty in Ex. 1–18," *Rel* 41 (2011): 255. Feldt's work successfully applies the theoretical framework of fantasy literature found in the work of Renate Lachmann to the supernatural elements in the plague narratives of the book of Exodus. See Lachmann, *Erzählte Phantastik: Zu Phantasiegeschichte und Semantik phantastischer Texte* (Frankfurt am Main: Suhrkamp, 2002). Fantasy literature in particular is well suited to the study of apocalypses, which also use bizarre and counterintuitive elements. Such writings have a greater chance of generating cognitive processes that seek understanding.

8. Feldt, "Religious Narrative," 275; on emotion's naturally associative function in memory construction and reconstruction, see Harkins, *Reading with an "I,"* 69–113, esp. 94–96.

9. Jani Närhi, "Beautiful Reflections: The Cognitive and Evolutionary Foundations of Paradise Representations," *MTSR* 20 (2008): 339–65.

include counterintuitive elements such as divine inhabitants, exotic cultivars, and the absence of conflict, disease, or perishability, all serving to remind readers that this is an otherworldly realm.[10] The *hodayah* in 1QH$^a$ XVI, 5–XVII, 36 makes mention of a number of features of the landscape:

> I thank [you, O Lo]rd, that you have placed me at the source of brooks in a dry land, (by) a spring of water in a parched land, and (by) a watered garden, and a wetland ○○○○ the field, (you) plant cypress and elm together with boxwood for the sake of your glory; trees of life at a spring of mystery, hidden in the midst of all the wetland-trees. And they were there so that a shoot might be made to sprout into an eternal planting. Before taking root, they sprouted out and stretched out their roots to the strea[m]. And its stem was exposed to the living waters, and it became an eternal source. All the an[ima]ls of the forest grazed on its leafy shoot. Its rootstock was a grazing place for all who passed on the way, and its branch is for every winged-bird. And all the wetland-tr[ees] towered over it; even though in their planting they grow tall, they do not stretch out (their) root to the stream. The h[o]ly shoot is made to sprout into a plant of truth; it is concealed. It is without regard and not perceived, it seals up its mystery. And you, [O G]od, have fenced in its fruit with the mystery of strong warriors, spirits of holiness, and flaming fire moving every which way [מתהפכת], so that no [stran]ger might [come] to the fountain of life, nor with the eternal trees drink the waters of holiness, nor bear its fruit with the plantation of heaven. For he sees without recognizing, and he considers without believing in the source of life, and so he gives away the pro[d]uce of the eternal sprout. But I became like the things [wa]shed up by rivers swollen-by-floodwaters, because they cast their mud on me. *vacat.* (XVI, 5–16)

In this detailed description of a wetland garden, the hymnist describes the various types of vegetation within it, including the exotic cultivar known from the garden of Eden, the trees of life (XVI, 6–7). In addition to the wide range of vegetation, both this-worldly (e.g., "cypress," "elm,"

---

10. On the counterintuitiveness of religious concepts, see Pascal Boyer, *The Naturalness of Religious Ideas: A Cognitive Theory of Religion* (Berkeley: University of California Press, 1994); Boyer, *Religion Explained: The Evolutionary Origins of Religious Thought* (New York: Basic Books, 2001); Boyer and Charles Ramble, "Cognitive Templates for Religious Concepts: Cross-cultural Evidence for Recall of Counter-intuitive Representations," *CS* 25 (2001): 535–64; Ilkka Pyysiäinen, Marjaana Lindeman, and Timo Honkela, "Counterintuitiveness as the Hallmark of Religiosity," *Rel* 33 (2003): 341–55.

"boxwood," mentioned in XVI, 6) and otherworldly cultivars ("trees of life," עֲצֵי חִיִּ֫ים, XVI, 6–7) are specified in this passage. Also, a clear reference is made to angelic beings: "strong warriors, spirits of holiness, and flaming fire moving every which way" (XVI, 13) in a manner that recalls the image of the cherubim with their flaming sword "moving every which way" (הַמִּתְהַפֶּכֶת) to guard the entrance to the garden of Eden.[11] The *hodayah* then moves from a detailed description of the lush garden to the hymnist himself. The speaker makes a self-referential remark about his God-given teaching being like the soft rain showers that keep the wetland garden moist and which supply the waterways of the landscape: "But You, O my God, have put (your teachings) in my mouth, like early rains for all [...], and a spring of living waters. He will not fail to open the heavens, they will not languish, they will become a torrent overflowing ov[er all the ]wetland [trees] and (pouring) into seas, without end" (XVI, 17–18). The name Eden appears in XVI, 21 and is also referenced in a previous *hodayah*, which identifies the garden that produces the "eternal planting" as Eden (1QH<sup>a</sup> XIV, 18–19; see XVI, 7).

Perhaps in a manner not unlike the thematic turn found in the Genesis story of Eden, which culminates in a series of curses, the *hodayah* also shifts to an extended lament of the hymnist, language that will be investigated in the second half of this study. The focus of the text abruptly turns to the speaker's affliction and misery, poignantly depicted in 1QH<sup>a</sup> XVI, 26–XVII, 7. The core imagery of the *hodayah* has now become the hymnist's anguish. One of the effects on the reader of this unexpected change in tone is confusion and disorientation about why this has happened. The tension generates a deeper desire to understand the speaker's experiences and slows down the pace of reading, perhaps even inviting readers to reread or to ruminate over why this has taken place. This can be said to resemble the readerly experience of fantasy narratives, which also routinely make use of destabilizing strategies. Such strategies, according to Feldt, seek to pull the reader in more deeply into the narrative world.[12] As a reader, the heavily emotional and personal first-person narrative invites a searching for an explanation for the speaker's agony, and it also leads us to contemplate more deeply the speaker's experiences.

---

11. Gen 3:24: וַיְשַׁכֵּן מִקֶּדֶם לְגַן־עֵדֶן אֶת־הַכְּרֻבִים וְאֵת לַהַט הַחֶרֶב הַמִּתְהַפֶּכֶת לִשְׁמֹר אֶת־דֶּרֶךְ עֵץ הַחַיִּים׃

12. Feldt, "Religious Narrative," 272.

## 2. Enactive Reading That Immerses the Reader in a Narrative World

Literary theorists argue that heavily detailed descriptions of spaces alone are insufficient in generating an immersive experience of reading; it is the enactive process of reading first-person narration that is crucial. The landscape described in 1QH$^a$ XVI, 5–XVII, 36 is more than just a literary backdrop for the events that take place in the foreground. The wetland garden that is described in 1QH$^a$ XVI, 5–XVII, 36 not only gives us a detailed account of an otherworldly space, but it also includes a significant description of the speaker's physical and emotional experiences within those spaces as well.[13] The narrative world, the landscape, the environment and geography, and also any nonhuman beings that are encountered within that space, can take on a quality of solidity as readers gain information about the experiences of the *hodayot* hymnist who interacts and emotionally responds to the space.

These narrative worlds, sometimes referred to as "possible and fictional worlds" by critical literary theorists, are described as experientially fluid spaces that are generated in part by the text and in part by the reader's imaginative experiencing of the text through what are called enactive processes.[14] Texts provide only a glimpse of a narrative world that readers must then extend and complete in their imaginations. Marco Caracciolo illustrates this phenomenon in the following way: "Just as you don't need to download, say, the entire *New York Times* to be able to read it on your desktop, so you don't need to construct a representation of all the detail of the scene in front of you to have a sense of its detailed presence."[15] A reader

---

13. Nancy Easterlin gives the example of a preschool in her explanation of what is meant by environment. When she speaks of a bad or a good environment for a small child, she is not referring to just the condition of the furniture or toys in a classroom, or where they may be located. She is thinking comprehensively about an overall experience of the child in that environment, one that includes the relationships had with the people in those environments and the events that took place there. Easterlin gives the example of being bitten by another child and the child's own emotional responses to those events. See Nancy Easterlin, "Loving Ourselves Best of All: Ecocriticism and the Adapted Mind," *Mosaic* 37 (2004): 8–9.

14. Helpful is the discussion by Marco Caracciolo, "Ungrounding Fictional Worlds: An Enactivist Perspective on the 'Worldlikeness' of Fiction," in *Possible Worlds Theory and Contemporary Narratology*, ed. Alice Bell and Marie-Laure Ryan (Lincoln: University of Nebraska Press, 2019), 113–31.

15. Caracciolo, "Ungrounding Fictional Worlds," 127. He borrows this example from Alva Noë, *Action in Perception* (Cambridge: MIT Press, 2004), 50.

knows intuitively that there is much more to the *Times* than what can be seen, without having been shown its entirety in excruciating detail. So too the narrative world is extended and completed when it is enacted by the reader's imagination. In other words, detailed descriptions of spaces alone do not create immersive experiences; it is the description of those spaces as they are experienced and enacted by the figures in the text.

Critical literary theory as it is applied to narrative spaces is an integrative approach that emerged in the late twentieth century.[16] It considers how the embodied experience of reading could engage immersive cognitive processes of mental imaging through practices, such as enactive reading and enactive perception, and through the first-person voice. Enactivism is a way of speaking phenomenologically about the mental imagery that is generated in varying degrees during the activity of reading.[17] The cognitive processing areas of the mind are engaged by language about the sensory experiences of the body, which can be described as proprioceptive experiences, which include kinesthetic and movement-related experiences, and interoceptive experiences.[18] This cognitive process of enactive reading can heighten a reader's ability of having an immersive experience of the text.

Language about these sensory experiences of the hymnist can be enacted in the imagination by a reader, thus making the two-dimensional literary environment of the garden into a three-dimensional space. The first-person voice can also intensify a reader's experience by providing

---

16. Stephen Kaplan, "Environmental Preference in a Knowledge-Seeking, Knowledge-Using Organism," in *The Adapted Mind: Evolutionary Psychology and the Generation of Culture*, ed. Jerome Barkow, Leda Cosmides, and John Tooby (New York: Oxford University Press, 1992), 581–98; Glen A. Love, "Ecocriticism and Science: Toward Consilience?," *NLH* 30 (1999): 661–76; Easterlin, "Loving Ourselves Best of All"; Nancy Easterlin, *A Biocultural Approach to Literary Theory and Interpretation* (Baltimore: Johns Hopkins University Press, 2012); also the essays in Lisa Zunshine, ed., *Introduction to Cognitive Cultural Studies* (Baltimore: Johns Hopkins University Press, 2010); Karin Kukkonen and Marco Caracciolo, "Introduction: What Is the 'Second Generation'?," *Style* 48 (2014): 261–74; Marco Caracciolo, *The Experientiality of Narrative: An Enactivist Approach* (Berlin: de Gruyter, 2014); Caracciolo, "Cognitive Literary Studies and the Status of Interpretation: An Attempt at Conceptual Mapping," *NLH* 47 (2016): 187–207.

17. Anežka Kuzmičová, "Mental Imagery: A View from Embodied Cognition," *Style* 48 (2014): 275–76; also Kuzmičová, "Presence in the Reading," 23–48; Nicole K. Speer et al., "Reading Stories Activates Neural Representations of Visual and Motor Experiences," *PS* 20 (2009): 289–99.

18. Kuzmičová, "Mental Imagery," 275–76.

access to the elements that we associate with consciousness, the interior emotional experiences (interoception) and the presumption of a fully extended sensing body (proprioception). The more a reader is able to imagine the *hodayot* hymnist with a fully extended physical body and with the complexities of an interior consciousness, the more likely it is that a reader will be able to deeply empathize with the *hodayot* hymnist. We do well to remind readers that the ancient readers of the 1QH$^a$ XVI, 5–XVII, 36, of course, were never predetermined to have any particular kind of reading experience. Awareness of the literary details that best encourage enactive reading processes can draw our attention to the question of how a flesh-and-blood reader might have experienced the *hodayot*.[19]

Cognitive literary theorists such as Anežka Kuzmičová and Marco Caracciolo argue that the phenomenon of immersive reading, that is, achieving an experience of presence in a narrative world, relies on first-person narration of interoceptive and proprioceptive experiences. Cognitive literary approaches remind modern Western DSS scholars of our interpretive bias that privileges a sensorium that limits discussion of sensory perception to just the five senses that are highlighted by Aristotle: seeing, hearing, smelling, tasting, and touching. Using cross-cultural anthropology and literary studies of the Hebrew Bible, Israeli scholar Yael Avrahami similarly challenges the classic model of five sense in her study *The Senses of Scripture*.[20] Avrahami argues persuasively that the Hebrew Bible repeatedly conceptualizes how the human body is able to know and understand experientially and to perceive through a sensorium of *seven* senses: "sight, hearing, *kinaesthesia*, speech, taste, touch, and smell."[21] Cognitive literary

---

19. Jenefer Robinson, *Deeper than Reason: Emotion and Its Role in Literature, Music, and Art* (Oxford: Clarendon, 2007); David S. Miall, "Emotions and the Structuring of Narrative Responses," *PT* 32 (2011): 323v48; Marco Caracciolo, "Fictional Consciousnesses: A Reader's Manual," *Style* 46 (2012): 42–65. According to Caracciolo, vivid language about a character's bodily and emotional experiences allows us to construct an idea of that character's consciousness: "Readers experience the fictional world through the consciousness of a character.... Readers can enact a fictional consciousness, they can perform it on the basis of textual cues" (43). So too, the thesis of Harkins, that the first-person voice allows readers to emotionally reenact the experiences of the text (*Reading with an "I"*).

20. Yael Avrahami, *The Senses of Scripture: Sensory Perception in the Hebrew Bible* (London: T&T Clark, 2012).

21. Avrahami, *Senses of Scripture*, 2, emphasis added. These seven are discussed in ch. 2 of *Senses of Scripture*, 65–112.

studies emphasize the strategic role that descriptions of interoception and proprioception provide in constructing immersive narrative experiences.

## 2.1. Interoception

Interoception complicates the ways we might imagine the interior consciousness of literary characters in ways that are helpful in thinking about the *hodayot* hymnist and his emotional experiences because it integrates the physiological basis for emotional processes. Interoception refers to an individual's "sense of the internal physiological condition of the body," but could also be extended to include sensory experiences that we would perceive through our bodies, such as "temperature, pain, itch, tickle, sensual touch, muscular and visceral sensations, vasomotor flush, hunger, thirst."[22] It is the case that these physiological states are evaluated by the self and inflected with some kind of motivational or emotional quality. For example, both extreme hot or cold temperatures are disliked or avoided. The arousal of certain emotions such as fear or anguish can have a visceral and physiological basis and so can be considered to be part of an interoceptive experience.[23] Herein lies the Hebrew idioms for emotions that locate these experiences in various internal organs (heart, liver, belly, womb).[24] Mark Smith's anthropology-based discussion of emotion language in the Hebrew Bible begins with the classic example of Lam 2:11, a passage that makes multiple references to the viscera in its poignant description of anguish over the people's political destruction, "My eyes are spent with weeping; my belly is in turmoil [חמרמרו מעי]; my liver is poured out on the ground [נשפך לארץ כבדי] because of the destruction of my people, because infants and babes faint in the streets of the city."

The *hodayot* hymnist gives readers access to his interior emotional state through his references to the body and its physiological experiences. Vasomotor experiences may be described as blushing or the blanching of the face, which are uncontrollable yet visible manifestations of a range of interior states (e.g., shame, shyness, embarrassment, and even fear) that

---

22. Arthur D. Craig, "How Do You Feel? Interoception: The Sense of the Physiological Condition of the Body," *NRN* 3 (2002): 655.

23. Anil K. Seth, "Interoceptive Inference, Emotion, and the Embodied Self," *TCS* 17 (2013): 565–73.

24. Mark S. Smith, "The Heart and Innards in Israelite Emotional Expressions: Notes from Anthropology and Psychobiology," *JBL* 117 (1998): 427–36.

point to complex human experiences of self-consciousness. So too, emotional states associated with the viscera are counted among interoceptive experiences and speak to the ways in which our experience of emotions are profoundly located within our physiological experiences. Experiences of having "knots in your stomach" or "feeling sick to your stomach" can express the depths of dismay or regret. Such access to the interoceptive experiences of the speaker of the *hodayot* assists greatly, in how the hymnist can be imagined with all of the complexities of human interior consciousness that we might associate with our own lived experiences and emotional states.

In the following passage (1QH<sup>a</sup> XVI, 26–XVII, 16), the speaker moves from a poignant description of his own personal anguish and torment (esp. XVI, 26–XVII, 7) to an emotional state of hope and confidence in God (XVII, 8–16):[25]

> In the heat, its leaves wither and are not restored by the spri[ng of water.... My] dwelling is with the sick, and [my] heart k[no]ws agonies. I have become like a man who is forsaken by [...] there is no refuge for me. For my agony breaks out to bitterness, and an incurable pain without stopping, [... ro]ars over me, like those who descend into Sheol. Among the dead my spirit searches, for [my] li[fe] goes down to the pit [...] my soul is faint day and night without rest. And my agony breaks out as a burning fire shut up within [my] b[ones] whose flame consumes for days on end, putting an end to my strength without ceasing and destroying my flesh without end. The billows break over me and my soul is completely worn down. For my strength is departed from my body, my heart is poured out as water, and my flesh is melted as wax. My courage [literally, "the strength of my loins"] has become terror, my arm is shattered at the shoulder, and (I am) [un]able to stretch forth my hand; my [foo]t is enfettered, my knees buckle like water and are unable to take a step—there is no sound to my footfall ... are pulled loose by stumbling chains, and my tongue that You had strengthened in my mouth, is no longer, it is unable to make a sound and (unable) to give forth its voice for instru[ction] to revive the spirits of those who stumble, and (unable) to encourage the weary with a word. The sound of my lips is silence [...] with chains of judgment [...] or in the bitterness [...] heart ... dominion [...] the earth [...] [...] they have been silenced as not [...] humankind, not ... (*vacat*?) [...] [...] by night and [...] [...] without compassion. In wrath He awakes mistrust and completely [...] the breakers of death and

---

25. See the notes on the translation in Harkins, *Reading with an "I,"* 231–32.

Sheol are over my couch. My bed lifts up a lamentation, [and my pallet] a sound of groanings. My eyes (burn) like a fire in a furnace, and my weeping flows like rivers of water. My eyes fail to rest, my [strength] stands far from me, and my life has been put to the side. But as for me, from ruin to desolation, from pain to agony, and from travails to torments, my soul meditates on Your wonders.

This is perhaps one of the most moving passages in the Hodayot. Emotional responses are a significant part of how a literary environment is experienced, and they can be far more compelling than a physical description of a building or landscape and the things found within it. The hymnist gives a palpable account of his anguished emotional state, making several references to his visceral sensations of anguished emotion. He writes, "my agony breaks out like a burning fire shut up within [my] b[ones] whose flame consumes for days on end" in XVI, 31. Shortly thereafter, we find the literal expression "the strength of my loins has become a terror," which expresses some kind of visceral fear in XVI, 34 and has been translated here as "my courage has become terror." Through the first-person voice, the hymnist discloses a great deal about his emotional experiences of distress, fear, and worry.

2.2. Proprioception

Proprioception includes the embodied sensations of moving through space that are often reported in apocalypses that detail otherworldly journeying. Proprioception can refer to both conscious or unconscious and active or passive experiences. In general, it refers to the embodied self in a spatial realm, as it moves and experiences the environment around it. The speaker's extended body is described from head to toe in some of the most poignant descriptions of personal distress: "my arm is broken at the shoulder, [and I can]not raise my hand; my [foo]t is enfettered, my knees buckle like water, and unable to take a step—there is no sound to my footfall" (XVI, 34–35). Such experiences correspond to the five senses of the body—seeing, tasting, touching, hearing, smelling—and also include the extended body in motion, which is further specified as kinesthetic perception.[26]

---

26. See Avrahami, *Senses of Scripture*.

The *hodayah* in 1QHᵃ XVI, 5–XVII, 36 emphasizes the visual details of the wetland garden, but they are also accompanied by other wide-ranging details about the hymnist's proprioceptive experiences of physical embeddedness within that otherworldly environs. In addition to reporting his interior emotional responses to the things that are seen and experienced, the speaker describes how his extended body interacts with the wetland garden. The hymnist reports, "when I stretch out a hand to hoe its furrows, its roots strike into the flinty rock.... When I withdraw (my) hand, it becomes like a juniper [in the wilderness,] and its rootstock like nettles in salty ground" (1QHᵃ XVI, 23–25). Because the well-irrigated garden is described only in piecemeal in 1QHᵃ XVI, 5–XVII, 36, the reader must extend the fragmentary references to imagine the speaker's fully extended body in a larger otherworldly landscape. These spaces and the events that take place in them elicit an emotional response from the hymnist, although the otherworldly spaces are only partially described in the *hodayah*.

Both interoceptive and proprioceptive experiences are described by the Hodayot hymnist in great detail. For the person who imaginatively reads this text, the repeated use of the first-person pronoun serves as a reminder that these are eyewitness reports of an otherworldly scene. Reports of these interoceptive reports in first-person voice can greatly facilitate how the vision might be experienced in the body of a subsequent reader with an intensity that conveys a quality of presence.[27]

---

27. Aldo Tagliabue, "An Embodied Reading of Epiphanies in Aelius Aristides' *Sacred Tales*," *Ramus* 45 (2016): 214. The visual perception is enhanced by the convergence of other bodily senses in the narrated experience, an important one being that of motion. See also G. Gabrielle Starr, "Multisensory Imagery," in *Introduction to Cognitive Cultural Studies*, ed. Lisa Zunshine (Baltimore: Johns Hopkins University Press, 2010), 275–91; Starr, *Feeling Beauty: The Neuroscience of Aesthetic Experience* (Cambridge: MIT Press, 2015). For a description of the enactive mental imaging of a scene, see the detailed description of breakfast in Hemmingway's novel *The Garden of Eden*, in which a wide range of sensory imagery achieves the state of experiencing the breakfast (taste, smell, touch, movement), in Anežka Kuzmičová, "Does It Matter Where You Read? Situating Narrative in Physical Environment," *CT* 26 (2015): 223. This kind of phenomenal experience is related to imitative and mirroring processing in the brain. See Elhanan Borenstein and Eytan Ruppin, "The Evolution of Imitation and Mirror Neurons in Adaptive Agents," *CSR* 6 (2005): 229–42. Marie-Laure Ryan uses the term *mental simulation* to refer to this phenomenon in immersive reading in which the reader mirrors the emotional experiences or consciousness had by the characters in the text. See Ryan, "The Text as World: Theories of Immersion," in *Narrative*

This process of enactive reading is one in which interoceptive and proprioceptive experiences are processed by sensorimotor areas of the mind in such a way that the embodied mind experiences in part the action that is being described.[28] Cognitive literary theorists who study the experiential effects of reading emotionally arousing fantasy literature note that language about the emotional experiences of the protagonists assists in deepening a reader's immersive experiences. In such studies, "immersion ratings were significantly higher for fear-inducing than for neutral passages."[29] Both enactive reading and enactive perception speak to the ways that first-person referential descriptions of embodied experiences contribute qualities of vividness and also solidity to the spaces in 1QH[a] XVI, 5–XVII, 36.

## Conclusion

Scholars of the DSS do well to consider how emerging cognitive approaches might contribute to our study of the past in a way that textures and complicates the experience of reading. Such approaches profitably expand the way we conceptualize the emotional and sensory experiences that are described in the Hodayot, and work to overcome a problematic Cartesian dualism that severs the mind from the body. Michael Swartz does well to remind us that the process of reading is itself far more complex than most text-based scholars may be willing to keep in mind: "Indeed, the force of recitation needs to be taken quite seriously as a potent form of ritual behavior and as an example of the actualization of sacred space in time. Memorization, recitation and performance, we must remember, are physical acts, requiring intensive preparation, stamina, and physical prowess."[30]

---

as *Virtual Reality 2: Revisiting Immersion and Interactivity in Literature and Electronic Media* (Baltimore: Johns Hopkins University Press, 2015), 61–84, esp. 78–84.

28. Speer et al., "Reading Stories Activates Neural Representations of Visual and Motor Experiences"; Vittorio Gallese, "Embodied Simulation and Its Role in Cognition," *RSL* 13 (2018): 31–46.

29. See Chun-Ting Hsu, Markus Conrad, and Arthur M. Jacobs, "Fiction Feelings in Harry Potter: Haemodynamic Response in the Mid-cingulate Cortex Correlates with Immersive Reading Experience," *Neuroreport* 25 (2014): 1356.

30. Michael D. Swartz, "Ritual about Myth about Ritual: Towards an Understanding of the Avodah in the Rabbinic Period," *JJTP* 6 (1997): 153. See too Ophir Münz-Manor, "Narrating Salvation: Verbal Sacrifices in Late Antique Liturgical Poetry," in *Jews, Christians, and the Roman Empire: The Poetics of Power in Late*

Swartz's comments highlight the various performative and embodied aspects of reading prayers that I think are helpful for thinking about how we might imagine how 1QH$^a$ XVI, 5–XVII, 36 was read. The activity of reading and pondering destabilizing images or counterintuitive details in the Hodayot can generate a state of rumination and deeper contemplation of what is described, allowing ancient readers access to experiences of presence of otherworldly phenomena and beings.

Literary theorists who study the phenomenon of immersive reading look to neurological studies of the brain and its cognitive processes of spatial reasoning, and remind DSS scholars that texts are experienced in complex ways by flesh-and-blood readers. The descriptions of imagined spaces and places can generate various effects on a reader's imagination; the landscape is more than just a literary backdrop for staging the main action of the narrative. How the Hodayot hymnist interacts with the spaces that are described can significantly enrich how readers might imagine the *hodayah* with an immersive quality and invite deeper emotional engagement on the part of the reader. The spaces in 1QH$^a$ XVI, 5–XVII, 36 gain solidity in conjunction with the dramatic and poignant descriptions of the hymnist's interoceptive and proprioceptive experiences of the garden in first-person voice. This integrative approach to understanding reading offers a potentially rich way to conceptualize how flesh-and-blood readers might have read a text like the Hodayot immersively, with an experience of presence. Even so, as with most ritual practices, the necessary predispositions must be cultivated over time through formative behaviors and within communities; immersive experiences of presence are not instantaneous effects produced at will by merely imagining intently.[31] Even so, such experiences of presence could be said to contribute ultimately to the cultivation of emotional predispositions needed for courage and perseverance in the face of adversity or uncertainty.[32] In closing, the compelling quality of the

---

*Antiquity*, ed. Annette Y. Reed and Natalie B. Dohrmann (Philadelphia: University of Pennsylvania Press, 2013), 154–66.

31. Tanya Luhrmann, *When God Talks Back: Understanding the American Evangelical Relationship with God* (New York: Knopf, 2012). Luhrmann's study discusses a multitude of practices that individuals engage in within communities that regularly experience moments of presence during prayer. Again, as Swartz's comments indicate about religious reading, these formative prayer practices are both mentally and physically intense.

32. This emotional effect of reading narratives with strong emotional overtones is described well by Ari Mermelstein, who uses a social-constructivist understanding

Hodayot may have very little to do with its presumed historical author,[33] and more to do with the text's ability to create compelling experiences of presence for the reader.

## Bibliography

Avrahami, Yael. *The Senses of Scripture: Sensory Perception in the Hebrew Bible.* London: T&T Clark, 2012.

Borenstein, Elhanan, and Eytan Ruppin. "The Evolution of Imitation and Mirror Neurons in Adaptive Agents." *CSR* 6 (2005): 229–42.

Boyer, Pascal. *The Naturalness of Religious Ideas: A Cognitive Theory of Religion.* Berkeley: University of California Press, 1994.

———. *Religion Explained: The Evolutionary Origins of Religious Thought.* New York: Basic Books, 2001.

Boyer, Pascal, and Charles Ramble. "Cognitive Templates for Religious Concepts: Cross-cultural Evidence for Recall of Counter-intuitive Representations." *CS* 25 (2001): 535–64.

Caracciolo, Marco. "Cognitive Literary Studies and the Status of Interpretation: An Attempt at Conceptual Mapping." *NLH* 47 (2016): 187–207.

———. *The Experientiality of Narrative: An Enactivist Approach.* Berlin: de Gruyter, 2014.

———. "Fictional Consciousnesses: A Reader's Manual." *Style* 46 (2012): 42–65.

———. "Ungrounding Fictional Worlds: An Enactivist Perspective on the 'Worldlikeness' of Fiction." Pages 113–31 in *Possible Worlds Theory and Contemporary Narratology.* Edited by Alice Bell and Marie-Laure Ryan. Lincoln: University of Nebraska Press, 2019.

---

of emotion to consider how emotions are used in the formation of common values and beliefs. See Mermelstein, "Constructing Fear and Pride in the Book of Daniel: The Profile of a Second Temple Emotional Community," *JSJ* 46 (2015): 450.

33. The ability to immerse oneself in reading does not depend upon the text being historically true. According to Cain Todd, humans have the natural capacity to suspend disbelief, even when the content is known to be fictional. See Todd, "Fictional Immersion: Attending Emotionally to Fiction," *JVI* (2012): 449–65. Also see Angela Kim Harkins, "The Pro-social Role of Grief in Ezra's Penitential Prayer," *BibInt* 24 (2016): 466–91, esp. 490–91; Sarah Iles Johnston, "How Myths and Other Stories Help to Create and Sustain Beliefs," in *Narrating Religion*, ed. Sarah Iles Johnston (London: MacMmllan, 2016), 141–56; Johnston, *The Story of Myth* (Cambridge: Harvard University Press, 2018).

Craig, Arthur D. "How Do You Feel? Interoception: The Sense of the Physiological Condition of the Body." *NRN* 3 (2002): 655–66.
Easterlin, Nancy. *A Biocultural Approach to Literary Theory and Interpretation*. Baltimore: Johns Hopkins University Press, 2012.
———. "Loving Ourselves Best of All: Ecocriticism and the Adapted Mind." *Mosaic* 37 (2004): 1–18.
Feldt, Laura. "Religious Narrative and the Literary Fantastic: Ambiguity and Uncertainty in Ex. 1–18." *Rel* 41 (2011): 251–83.
Gallese, Vittorio. "Embodied Simulation and Its Role in Cognition." *RSL* 13 (2018): 31–46.
Geertz, Armin W. "Religious Bodies, Minds and Places: A Cognitive Science of Religion Perspective." Pages 35–52 in *Spazi e Luoghi Sacri: Espressioni ed Esperienze di Vissuto Religioso*. Edited by Laura Carnevale. Santo Spirito (Bari): Edipuglia, 2017.
Harkins, Angela Kim. "Another Look at the Cave 1 Hodayot: Was CH I Materially Part of the Scroll 1QHodayot[a]?" *DSD* 25 (2018): 185–216.
———. "A New Proposal for Thinking about 1QH[a] Sixty Years after Its Discovery." Pages 101–34 in *Texts from Cave 1 Sixty Years after Their Discovery*. Edited by Daniel K. Falk, Sarianna Metso, Donald W. Parry, and Eibert J. C. Tigchelaar. STDJ 91. Leiden: Brill, 2010.
———. "The Pro-social Role of Grief in Ezra's Penitential Prayer." *BibInt* 24 (2016): 466–91.
———. *Reading with an "I" to the Heavens: Looking at the Qumran Hodayot through the Lens of Visionary Traditions*. Ekstasis 3. Berlin: de Gruyter, 2011.
Heath, Jane. "Absent Presences of Paul and Christ: *Enargeia* in 1 Thessalonians 1–3." *JSNT* 32 (2009): 3–38.
Hsu, Chun-Ting, Markus Conrad, and Arthur M. Jacobs. "Fiction Feelings in Harry Potter: Haemodynamic Response in the Mid-cingulate Cortex Correlates with Immersive Reading Experience." *Neuroreport* 25 (2014): 1356–61.
Johnston, Sarah Iles. "How Myths and Other Stories Help to Create and Sustain Beliefs." Pages 141–56 in *Narrating Religion*. Edited by Sarah Iles Johnston. London: Macmillan, 2016.
———. *The Story of Myth*. Cambridge: Harvard University Press, 2018.
Kaplan, Stephen. "Environmental Preference in a Knowledge-Seeking, Knowledge-Using Organism." Pages 581–98 in *The Adapted Mind: Evolutionary Psychology and the Generation of Culture*. Edited by

Jerome Barkow, Leda Cosmides, and John Tooby. New York: Oxford University Press, 1992.

Kukkonen, Karin, and Marco Caracciolo. "Introduction: What Is the 'Second Generation'?" *Style* 48 (2014): 261–74.

Kuzmičová, Anežka. "Does It Matter Where You Read? Situating Narrative in Physical Environment." *CT* 26 (2015): 290–308.

———. "Mental Imagery: A View from Embodied Cognition." *Style* 48 (2014): 275–93.

———. "Presence in the Reading of Literary Narrative: A Case for Motor Enactment." *Sem* 189 (2012): 23–48.

Lachmann, Renate. *Erzählte Phantastik: Zu Phantasiegeschichte und Semantik phantastischer Texte*. Frankfurt am Main: Suhrkamp, 2002.

Love, Glen A. "Ecocriticism and Science: Toward Consilience?" *NLH* 30 (1999): 661–76.

Luhrmann, Tanya. *When God Talks Back: Understanding the American Evangelical Relationship with God*. New York: Knopf, 2012.

Mermelstein, Ari. "Constructing Fear and Pride in the Book of Daniel: The Profile of a Second Temple Emotional Community." *JSJ* 46 (2015): 449–83.

Miall, David S. "Emotions and the Structuring of Narrative Responses." *PT* 32 (2011): 323–48.

Münz-Manor, Ophir. "Narrating Salvation: Verbal Sacrifices in Late Antique Liturgical Poetry." Pages 154–66 in *Jews, Christians, and the Roman Empire: The Poetics of Power in Late Antiquity*. Edited by Annette Y. Reed and Natalie B. Dohrmann. Philadelphia: University of Pennsylvania Press, 2013.

Närhi, Jani. "Beautiful Reflections: The Cognitive and Evolutionary Foundations of Paradise Representations." *Method & Theory in the Study of Religion* 20 (2008): 339–65.

Noë, Alva. *Action in Perception*. Cambridge: MIT Press, 2004.

Pyysiäinen, Ilkka, Marjaana Lindeman, and Timo Honkela. "Counter-Intuitiveness as the Hallmark of Religiosity." *Rel* 33 (2003): 341–55.

Robinson, Jenefer. *Deeper than Reason: Emotion and Its Role in Literature, Music, and Art*. Oxford: Clarendon, 2007.

Ryan, Marie-Laure. *Narrative as Virtual Reality 2: Revisiting Immersion and Interactivity in Literature and Electronic Media*. Baltimore: Johns Hopkins University Press, 2015.

Schacter, Daniel L., and Donna Rose Addis. "The Cognitive Neuroscience of Constructive Memory: Remembering the Past and Imagining the

Future." *Philosophical Transactions of the Royal Society B* 362 (2007): 773–86.

Schuller, Eileen M., and Carol A. Newsom. *The Hodayot (Thanksgiving Psalms): A Study Edition of 1QH$^a$*. EJL 36. Atlanta: Society of Biblical Literature, 2012.

Seth, Anil K. "Interoceptive Inference, Emotion, and the Embodied Self." *TCS* 17 (2013): 565–73.

Smith, Mark S. "The Heart and Innards in Israelite Emotional Expressions: Notes from Anthropology and Psychobiology." *JBL* 117 (1998): 427–36.

Speer, Nicole K., Jeremy R. Reynolds, Khena M. Swallow, and Jeffrey M. Zacks. "Reading Stories Activates Neural Representations of Visual and Motor Experiences." *PS* 20 (2009): 289–99.

Starr, G. Gabrielle. *Feeling Beauty: The Neuroscience of Aesthetic Experience*. Cambridge: MIT Press, 2015.

———. "Multisensory Imagery." Pages 275–91 in *Introduction to Cognitive Cultural Studies*. Edited by Lisa Zunshine. Baltimore: Johns Hopkins University Press, 2010.

Stegemann, Hartmut. "Rekonstruktion der Hodajot: Ursprüngliche Gestalt und kritisch bearbeiteter Text der Hymnenrolle aus Höhle 1 von Qumran." PhD diss., University of Heidelberg, 1963.

Stegemann, Hartmut, Eileen M. Schuller, and Carol A. Newsom, eds. *Qumran Cave 1.III: 1QHodayot$^a$ with Incorporation of 1QHodayot$^b$ and 4QHodayot$^{a-f}$*. DJD XL. Oxford: Clarendon, 2009.

Swartz, Michael D. "Ritual about Myth about Ritual: Towards an Understanding of the Avodah in the Rabbinic Period." *JJTP* 6 (1997): 135–55.

Tagliabue, Aldo. "An Embodied Reading of Epiphanies in Aelius Aristides' *Sacred Tales*." *Ramus* 45 (2016): 213–30.

Todd, Cain. "Fictional Immersion: Attending Emotionally to Fiction." *JVI* (2012): 449–65.

Webb, Ruth. "Imagination and the Arousal of Emotions in Greco-Roman Rhetoric." Pages 112–27 in *The Passions in Roman Thought and Literature*. Edited by Susanna M. Braund and Christopher Gill. Cambridge: Cambridge University Press, 1997.

Zanker, Graham. *Modes of Viewing in Hellenistic Poetry and Art*. Madison: University of Wisconsin Press, 2004.

Zunshine, Lisa, ed. *Introduction to Cognitive Cultural Studies*. Baltimore: Johns Hopkins University Press, 2010.

# Contributors

**Kyung S. Baek** teaches in the area of biblical studies at Trinity Western University and other theological institutions. In addition, he is a Research Associate in the Dead Sea Scrolls Institute at TWU and Director of Biblical and Theological Studies at Pacific Life Bible College. He is coauthor of *Leviticus at Qumran: Text and Interpretation* (Brill, 2017), as well as coeditor of *Reading the Bible in Ancient Traditions and Modern Editions: Studies in Memory of Peter W. Flint* (Society of Biblical Literature, 2017); *The War Scroll, War and Peace in the Dead Sea Scrolls and Related Literature* (Brill, 2016); and *Celebrating the Dead Sea Scrolls: A Canadian Collection* (Society of Biblical Literature, 2011). His main research interests focus on the Dead Sea Scrolls, gospels, use of the Hebrew Bible in the New Testament, and biblical interpretation.

**Brandon Diggens** is a graduate student and assistant at Trinity Western University, researching unidentified Aramaic fragments.

**Angela Kim Harkins** is an Associate Professor of New Testament at Boston College School of Theology and Ministry. Prior to taking up this position, she was the Marie Curie International Incoming Fellow at the University of Birmingham, England. She is the author of *Reading with an "I" to the Heavens: Looking at the Qumran Hodayot through the Lens of Visionary Traditions* (de Gruyter, 2012). Harkins has coedited four volumes of collected essays on the Watchers, religious experience and the Dead Sea Scrolls, and studies of the Second Temple period. She is the author of over thirty-five essays, with journal articles appearing in *Dead Sea Discoveries, Journal for the Study of the Pseudepigrapha, The Journal Henoch, Biblical Interpretation, The Journal for the Study of the New Testament, Theological Studies,* and *the Journal of Cognitive Historiography*. Currently, she is working on a long-term project on the Shepherd of Hermas.

**Helen R. Jacobus** is an Honorary Research Fellow at the University of Manchester in the Department of Religions and Theology. Her research is in the Hebrew Bible, Second Temple Judaism, and early Jewish calendars and astronomy. She is the author of *Zodiac Calendars in the Dead Sea Scrolls and Their Reception: Ancient Astronomy and Astrology in Early Judaism* (Brill, 2014), a revision of her doctoral thesis at the University of Manchester under the supervision of George J. Brooke. She received the Sean W. Dever Memorial Award when she was a PhD candidate. Jacobus is coeditor of *Studies on Magic and Divination in the Biblical World* (Gorgias, 2013) and has published many articles and chapters in multicontributor volumes, encyclopedias, and reference books.

**Jessica M. Keady** is Lecturer in Biblical Studies and Gender at the University of Wales Trinity Saint David, United Kingdom. She is the author of *Vulnerability and Valour: A Gendered Analysis of Everyday Life in the Dead Sea Scrolls Communities* (T&T Clark Bloomsbury, 2017); coeditor of *Scripture as Social Discourse: Social-Scientific Perspectives on Early Jewish and Christian Writings* (T&T Clark Bloomsbury, 2018 with Todd Klutz and Casey A. Strine); and coeditor of the *Dead Sea Discoveries* themed issue on "Gender Studies and the Dead Sea Scrolls" (Brill, 2019 with Jutta Jokiranta). Keady's research interests are related to Second Temple Jewish writings, especially the Dead Sea Scrolls, and uncovering their ancient and social context from a gendered perspective. Her teaching areas include the Dead Sea Scrolls, the Hebrew Bible, gender and Judaism, contemporary approaches to biblical texts, and the book of Genesis.

**Andrew R. Krause** (PhD, McMaster University) is Assistant Academic Director and biblical studies faculty at ACTS Seminaries of Trinity Western University in Langley, BC, Canada. Previously, he was Postdoctoral Research Fellow in the Exzellenzcluster "Religion und Politik" and Institutum Judaicum Delitzschianum at Westfälische Wilhelms-Universität in Münster, Germany. He is the author of *Synagogues in the Works of Flavius Josephus: Rhetoric, Spatiality, and First-Century Jewish Institutions* (Brill, 2017) and coeditor of *Synagogues in the Hellenistic Roman Period: New Finds—New Theories—New Methods* (Vandenhoeck & Ruprecht, forthcoming). His research focuses upon prayer, institutional formation, and scripturalization in the Dead Sea Scrolls, Septuagint, and Hebrew Bible.

**Heather Macumber** is Associate Professor of Biblical Studies at Providence University College and Seminary in Manitoba, Canada. Her primary interests revolve around the intersection of the divine and human realms in prophetic, apocalyptic, and pseudepigraphic works. The use of Monster Theory as a critical lens, focusing on the books of Daniel and John's Apocalypse, is the subject of her recent publications in the *Journal of Hebrew Scriptures* and *Biblical Interpretation*. Her forthcoming book entitled *Monstrous Visions: Hybridity and Liminality in John's Apocalypse* will be published with Lexington Books/Fortress Academic.

**Sarianna Metso** is Associate Professor in the Department of Historical Studies and the Department of Near and Middle Eastern Civilizations at the University of Toronto and an Associate Member of the University of Toronto Centre for Jewish Studies. She is the author of *The Textual Development of the Qumran Community Rule* (Brill, 1997); *The Serekh Texts* (T&T Clark, 2007); and *The Community Rule: A Critical Edition with Translation* (SBL Press, 2019). As a member of the official publication team of the Dead Sea Scrolls, she has coedited two fragmentary manuscripts of the book of Job for the Discoveries in the Judaean Desert series (DJD XVI; Oxford, 2000). Her other publications include *The Community of the Dead Sea Scrolls*, a coedited thematic issue for the journal *Dead Sea Discoveries* (Brill, 2009), and two coedited conference volumes, *Qumran Cave 1 Revisited: Texts from Cave 1 Sixty Years after Their Discovery* (Brill, 2010) and *The Dead Sea Scrolls: Transmission of Traditions and Production of Texts* (Brill, 2010). She has written numerous articles on various aspects of the Dead Sea Scrolls and the Bible, particularly on issues of ancient Jewish legislation, community identity development, and methodology of historical reconstruction.

**Nicholas Meyer** is a Sessional Lecturer at Huron University and McMaster University. His research interests are in theological anthropology, theodicy, and traditions of creation in Second Temple Judaism. He holds a PhD in Religious Studies from McMaster University and is the author of *Adam's Dust and Adam's Glory in the Hodayot and the Letters of Paul: Rethinking Anthropogony and Theology* (Brill, 2016). Meyer's present research aims to uncover recollections and to trace the trajectories of the motif of the childlike innocence of Adam and Eve in Second Temple literature.

**Carmen Palmer** (PhD, University of St. Michael's College) is Adjunct Faculty at Martin Luther University College in biblical studies and global citizenship. Prior to that she taught in the areas of Biblical Hebrew and Hebrew Bible at Emmanuel College at the Toronto School of Theology. Palmer's research focuses on notions of identity and/or conversion within the Hebrew Bible, the Dead Sea Scrolls, ancient Judaism, and the ancient Mediterranean more broadly. Related to these topics, she has written foreigner and gentile entries in the *Encyclopedia of the Bible and Its Reception* and a journal article on the female slave as a gentile convert in the Dead Sea Scrolls in *Jewish Law Association Studies* (forthcoming). She is the author of *Converts in the Dead Sea Scrolls: The Gēr and Mutable Ethnicity* (Brill, 2018).

**Andrew B. Perrin** (PhD, McMaster University) is Canada Research Chair in Religious Identities of Ancient Judaism and Director of the Dead Sea Scrolls Institute at Trinity Western University. His publications include the monograph *The Dynamics of Dream-Vision Revelation in the Aramaic Dead Sea Scrolls* (Vandenhoeck & Ruprecht, 2015), winner of the Manfred Lautenschlaeger Award for Theological Promise, and a forthcoming article in *Journal of Theological Studies* on the formation of Daniel traditions at Qumran, winner of the David Noel Freedman Award for Excellence and Creativity in Hebrew Bible Scholarship. Perrin's research explores the conceptual and cultural worlds of Second Temple Judaism through the lens of the Qumran Aramaic texts.

**Eileen Schuller** is Professor Emerita of Religious Studies at McMaster University, Hamilton, Canada, where she taught since 1990 and held the Senator William McMaster Chair in the Study of Religion. She has been involved with the publication of the Dead Sea Scrolls since 1980, especially manuscripts of prayers and hymns. She edited the Cave 4 Hodayot manuscripts for the Discoveries in the Judaean Desert series (DJD XXIX; Oxford, 1999) and, with Hartmut Stegemann, the reedition of 1QH$^a$ (DJD XL; Oxford, 2009). She has written extensively on women in the Dead Sea Scrolls. Schuller has been a Lady Davis Visiting Professor at Hebrew University, Jerusalem (2013), recipient of the Alexander von Humboldt Research Prize at Georg-August University, Göttingen (2005–2006), and was elected to the Royal Society of Canada (2015). In 2018, she was president of the Catholic Biblical Association.

**John Screnock** (PhD, Toronto) is Research Fellow in Hebrew Bible in the Faculty of Oriental Studies at the University of Oxford. From 2015–2018, he was Kennicott Junior Research Fellow at Oxford. His publications include *Traductor Scriptor: The Old Greek Translation of Exodus 1–14 as Scribal Activity* (Brill, 2017); *Esther: A Handbook on the Hebrew Text* (Baylor, 2015); and articles in the *Journal of Biblical Literature, Vetus Testamentum, Biblica, Dead Sea Discoveries, Journal of Semitic Studies, Hebrew Studies*, and *Textus*. At Oxford, John teaches Esther, Psalms, Hebrew, and Ugaritic. His current project examines scribal activity in the textual witnesses to Psalms for insights into the language, poetics, and interpretation of the Psalms.

**Jonathan Vroom** is an Assistant Professor (Teaching Stream) and Writing Specialist at the University of Toronto Mississauga. He received his PhD in Hebrew and Judaic Studies at the University of Toronto and is the author of *The Authority of Law in the Hebrew Bible and Early Judaism: Tracing the Origins of Legal Obligation from Ezra to Qumran* (Brill, 2018), in addition to a number of essays and articles on related topics. Prior to his present focus on the fields of university pedagogy and writing studies, he taught numerous courses in the areas of Hebrew Bible and Judaism at the University of Toronto.

**Matthew L. Walsh** is Assistant Professor of Biblical Studies and Dean of Students at Acadia Divinity College in Wolfville, Nova Scotia. He is the author of *Angels Associated with Israel in the Dead Sea Scrolls: Angelology and Sectarian Identity at Qumran* (Mohr Siebeck, 2019), and he coauthored the "Angels" entry for Oxford Bibliographies Online (Oxford, 2019). His research and teaching areas include Hebrew, Greek, Hebrew Bible, Judaism in the Second Temple period, and hermeneutics.

# Ancient Sources Index

## Hebrew Bible/Old Testament

### Genesis
| | |
|---|---|
| 1:14–19 | 200 |
| 1:20–21 | 154 |
| 1:27 | 283 |
| 2 | 264 |
| 2:6–7 | 293–94 |
| 3:19 | 291 |
| 3:24 | 16, 358 |
| 7:4 | 77 |
| 16:7–14 | 150 |
| 17 | 343 |
| 17:9–14 | 332 |
| 17:10–11 | 339 |
| 17:12 | 328 |
| 17:14 | 336 |
| 17:14 (LXX) | 345 |
| 21:15–19 | 150 |
| 38:9 | 285 |
| 49:28 | 76 |

### Exodus
| | |
|---|---|
| 3 | 150 |
| 21:1–22:16 | 43 |

### Leviticus
| | |
|---|---|
| 10:10 | 10 |
| 11–15 | 28 |
| 12 | 332 |
| 12:7 | 293, 295 |
| 15 | 316 |
| 18:19 | 294 |
| 20:18 | 295 |
| 22:16 | 29 |

### Numbers
| | |
|---|---|
| 5:1–4 | 316 |
| 7:84 | 74 |
| 18:16 | 84 |
| 21:6 | 147 |

### Deuteronomy
| | |
|---|---|
| 6:4–9 | 262 |
| 7:9 | 70 |
| 7:21–22 | 316 |
| 8:15 | 147 |
| 10:16 | 331, 339–40 |
| 23:10–15 | 316 |
| 23:15 | 294 |
| 30:1–10 | 335 |
| 30:6 | 331, 334, 343 |

### Joshua
| | |
|---|---|
| 5:13–14 | 178 |
| 15:41 | 74 |

### Judges
| | |
|---|---|
| 13:5 | 126, 129 |

### 1 Samuel
| | |
|---|---|
| 16:13–23 | 253 |
| 18:10 | 253 |
| 19:9 | 253 |

### 1 Kings
| | |
|---|---|
| 6:27 | 147 |
| 7:3 | 75 |
| 9:28 | 84 |
| 19 | 150 |

## 2 Chronicles
| | |
|---|---|
| 3:3 | 83 |
| 32:9 | 192 |

## Ezra
| | |
|---|---|
| 2:5 | 78 |
| 2:6 | 78 |
| 2:58 | 78 |

## Esther
| | |
|---|---|
| 9:27 | 333 |

## Job
| | |
|---|---|
| 1:21 | 293 |
| 10:8–10 | 293 |
| 14:1 | 292 |
| 14:4 | 292 |
| 15:14 | 292 |
| 24:5 | 149 |
| 25:4 | 292 |
| 38:7 | 175 |

## Psalms
| | |
|---|---|
| 29:3–4 | 154 |
| 51:12 | 336 |
| 65:7 | 154 |
| 74:13–14 | 155 |
| 74:14 | 149 |
| 78:2 | 126 |
| 78:34 | 285 |
| 89:9–10 | 155 |
| 93:3–4 | 154 |
| 104:19 | 200 |
| 104:25–26 | 154 |
| 139:13 | 293 |
| 139:15 | 293 |
| 146:7–8 | 132 |

## Proverbs
| | |
|---|---|
| 5:15 | 293, 296 |
| 5:16 | 295 |
| 5:18 | 295 |
| 26:4–5 | 41 |

## Song of Songs
| | |
|---|---|
| 4:12–15 | 293, 296 |

## Isaiah
| | |
|---|---|
| 1:15 | 134 |
| 1:17 | 134 |
| 1:21 | 123 |
| 1:23–26 | 123 |
| 2:2 | 134 |
| 2:15 | 123 |
| 2:17 | 123 |
| 2:19–21 | 122 |
| 2:22 | 123 |
| 5:1–7 | 133–34 |
| 5:6 | 149 |
| 5:8–20 | 134 |
| 5:10–14 | 123 |
| 5:11–14 | 122 |
| 6:2 | 147 |
| 6:9–10 (LXX) | 130–31 |
| 6:10 (Tg.) | 133 |
| 7:9–12 | 123, 134 |
| 7:14–15 | 123 |
| 7:14 | 126, 129 |
| 7:14 (LXX) | 136 |
| 7:17 | 122 |
| 8:7 | 123 |
| 8:11 | 122 |
| 8:14 | 134 |
| 8:23–9:1 (LXX) | 137 |
| 9:5–6 | 191 |
| 10:13–14 | 123 |
| 11:1 | 126, 129 |
| 11:2 | 134 |
| 13:10 | 131–33 |
| 14:11 | 131 |
| 14:11–15 | 134 |
| 14:13–15 | 131, 133 |
| 14:27 | 123 |
| 14:29 | 123 |
| 19:2 | 130, 134 |
| 22:4 | 134 |
| 22:22 | 134 |
| 22:22 (LXX) | 133 |
| 22:22 (Tg.) | 133 |

| | | | |
|---|---|---|---|
| 24:17 | 122 | 52:1 | 134 |
| 24:19 | 133 | 52:7 | 122 |
| 24:21–23 | 175 | 52:15 | 134 |
| 24:23 | 131–32 | 53:3 | 134 |
| 26:19 | 132 | 53:4 | 126 |
| 26:20 | 134 | 53:4 (LXX) | 137–38 |
| 27:1 | 155 | 53:10–12 | 134 |
| 27:13 | 133–34 | 53:11–12 | 133–34 |
| 28:12 | 134 | 54:1–2 | 122 |
| 28:16 | 134 | 54:9 | 134 |
| 29:13 | 131, 133 | 56:7 (LXX) | 130–31 |
| 29:13 (LXX) | 130 | 57:15 | 134 |
| 29:14 | 134 | 58:3 | 134 |
| 29:18 | 132 | 58:5–14 | 134 |
| 29:23 | 134 | 58:7 | 134 |
| 30:6 | 147 | 59:19 | 132 |
| 30:15–18 | 122 | 60:6 | 134 |
| 31:8 | 122 | 61:1 | 131–32, 134 |
| 34:4 | 132–33 | 61:1–2 | 133 |
| 34:12–15 | 149 | 61:2 | 134 |
| 34:13–14 | 150 | 62:11 | 126 |
| 34:14 | 134 | 63:16 | 134 |
| 34:8 | 134 | 64:7–8 | 134 |
| 35:4–6 | 131–33 | 65:4 | 134 |
| 36:7 | 134 | 66:1 | 133–34 |
| 36:20 | 134 | | |
| 40:1–5 | 122 | Jeremiah | |
| 40:3 | 122, 126, 136 | 4:4 | 331 |
| 40:8 | 134 | 6:10 | 331 |
| 42:1 | 134 | 7:11 | 130 |
| 42:1–4 | 126 | 9:23–26 | 343 |
| 42:1–4 (LXX) | 138 | 9:24–25 | 331 |
| 42:18 | 132–33 | 13:26 | 294 |
| 43:5 | 130, 132 | 18:1–2 | 126–27, 129 |
| 43:16 | 134 | 19:1–13 | 129 |
| 45:10–14 | 123 | 19:11 | 131 |
| 48:1–2 | 134 | 31:15 | 126 |
| 49:12 | 130, 132 | 32:6–9 | 126–27, 129 |
| 49:24–25 | 134 | | |
| 50:6 | 134 | Lamentations | |
| 50:11 (Tg.) | 133 | 2:11 | 362 |
| 51:7 | 134 | | |
| 51:8 | 134 | Ezekiel | |
| 51:9–10 | 155 | 10:2–20 | 147 |
| 51:17–22 | 134 | 12:2 | 130 |

*Ezekiel (cont.)*

| | |
|---|---:|
| 32:7 | 131 |
| 33:31 | 130 |
| 36–37 | 257 |
| 36:17 | 296 |
| 36:26 | 343 |

Daniel

| | |
|---|---:|
| 2:28 | 109 |
| 4:2 | 109 |
| 4:7 | 109 |
| 4:10 | 109 |
| 6:14 | 39 |
| 7–12 | 12, 171–81 |
| 7:1 | 109 |
| 7:9–10 | 173 |
| 7:11–12 | 173 |
| 7:13–14 | 172 |
| 7:17–18 | 174 |
| 7:18 | 173 |
| 7:21 | 173 |
| 7:22 | 192 |
| 7:26–27 | 173 |
| 7:27 | 184–85, 192 |
| 8:5–9 | 176 |
| 8:10–12 | 175–76 |
| 8:11 | 178 |
| 8:25 | 176 |
| 9:20 | 180 |
| 10:1–11:1 | 177 |
| 10:13 | 177–78 |
| 10:20–21 | 177–78, 192 |
| 10:23 | 192 |
| 11:2–12:4 | 177 |
| 11:40 | 177 |
| 12:1 | 177, 179, 192 |
| 12:3 | 179 |
| 12:5–13 | 177 |
| 11:33 | 180 |
| 11:36 | 176 |
| 12:2–3 | 170 |

Hosea

| | |
|---|---:|
| 11:1 | 126, 129 |

Joel

| | |
|---|---:|
| 2:10 | 131 |
| 2:31 | 131 |
| 3:15 | 131 |

Micah

| | |
|---|---:|
| 5:2 | 129 |
| 5:4 | 129 |

Nahum

| | |
|---|---:|
| 3:5 | 294 |

Habakkuk

| | |
|---|---:|
| 2:5–6 | 128 |

Zephaniah

| | |
|---|---:|
| 2:9 | 149 |

Zechariah

| | |
|---|---:|
| 9:9 | 126 |
| 11:12–13 | 126–29 |

### Ancient Near Eastern Texts

| | |
|---|---:|
| AO 6478 | 233 |

MUL.APIN

| | |
|---|---:|
| ii 12 | 232 |
| ii 16 | 232 |

### Deuterocanonical Books

Tobit

| | |
|---|---:|
| 1:8 | 333 |
| 3:8 | 158 |
| 6:7 | 105 |
| 6:8 | 158 |
| 6:14–15 | 158 |
| 6:15 | 105 |
| 7:1 | 105 |
| 7:2 | 105 |
| 8:2 | 158 |
| 14:3 | 105 |

## Ancient Sources Index

| | | | |
|---|---|---|---|
| Judith | | 77.3 | 104 |
| 14:10 | 333 | 79 | 218 |
| | | 79.4–5 | 234 |
| Ben Sira | | 80.2–8 | 207 |
| 43:6–8 | 200 | 82 | 216, 218 |
| 45:4 | 288 | 83–90 | 99 |
| 50:6 | 200 | 89.12 | 101 |
| | | 89.29 | 101 |
| Wisdom of Solomon | | 89.30 | 101 |
| 5:5 | 170 | 104.2–6 | 170, 179 |
| 7:1–2 | 293 | | |
| | | 2 Enoch | |
| 1 Maccabees | | 20.1 | 147 |
| 1:11 | 337 | | |
| | | Jubilees | |
| Pseudepigrapha | | 1.22–23 | 334–36 |
| | | 1.23 | 338 |
| 2 Baruch | | 1.27–29 | 186 |
| 10.6–8 | 150 | 2.1 | 186 |
| | | 2.5 | 200 |
| 1 Enoch | | 2.9 | 200, 208 |
| 1–36 | 99 | 3.8–14 | 295 |
| 2.2 | 101 | 6.23–38 | 200, 208 |
| 3.1 | 101 | 6.33 | 207–8 |
| 5.1 | 101 | 10.7–14 | 158 |
| 6–7 | 216 | 12.19–21 | 260, 265 |
| 6.4 | 101 | 15.11–14 | 336 |
| 6.7 | 101 | 15.25–34 | 336–37 |
| 6.8 | 101 | 31.14 | 288 |
| 7.1 | 101 | | |
| 10.9 | 148 | Dead Sea Scrolls | |
| 15 | 288, 293 | | |
| 15.11–16.1 | 148 | Aramaic Levi Document (ALD) | |
| 16.1–2 | 155 | 8 | 102 |
| 31.3 | 101 | 96 | 102 |
| 32.1 | 101 | 97 | 102 |
| 61.10 | 147 | | |
| 71.7 | 147 | Cairo Damascus Document (CD) | |
| 72 | 217, 219, 227 | I, 4–5 | 72 |
| 72–82 | 99, 217 | I, 5–6 | 72, 82 |
| 72.1 | 218 | I, 10 | 72 |
| 73 | 216 | II, 15–16 | 331 |
| 76–79 | 216 | IV, 14 | 72 |
| 77.1 | 104 | IV, 16–17 | 72 |
| 77.2 | 104 | IV, 20–21 | 72, 283 |

## Ancient Sources Index

*Cairo Damascus Document (cont.)*

| | |
|---|---|
| V, 10 | 294 |
| VI, 14–21 | 10, 28 |
| VI, 20–VII, 3 | 50 |
| VII | 283, 286 |
| VII, 4–6 | 284 |
| VII, 6 | 282 |
| VII, 6–9 | 285 |
| VII, 9 | 284 |
| IX, 2–8 | 50 |
| IX, 22–23 | 72 |
| X, 4 | 60, 72 |
| X, 6–7 | 72 |
| X, 8 | 72 |
| X, 14–XI, 18 | 42, 54 |
| XI, 22–23 | 72 |
| XII, 1–2 | 286, 295 |
| XII, 5 | 72 |
| XII, 10–11 | 332 |
| XIII, 1 | 72 |
| XIV, 4 | 72 |
| XIV, 6 | 72 |
| XIV, 7 | 72 |
| XIV, 9 | 72 |
| XIV, 13 | 72 |
| XIV, 18–20 | 42 |
| XIV, 18–23 | 270 |
| XIV, 21 | 72, 82 |
| XVI, 4–6 | 332–33 |
| XIX, 1 | 72 |
| XIX, 2 | 70, 72, 285 |
| XIX, 2–5 | 284 |
| XX, 5 | 285 |
| XX, 7 | 285 |
| XX, 13 | 285 |
| XX, 15 | 72, 77 |
| XX, 22 | 72 |

| | |
|---|---|
| 1QIsa<sup>a</sup> | 123 |

1QpHab
| | |
|---|---|
| VII, 4–5 | 29 |
| VIII, 8–11 | 128 |
| XI, 12–13 | 330–31 |

1Q20
| | |
|---|---|
| 0, 8 | 111 |
| 0, 13 | 111 |
| II, 22 | 111 |
| II, 23 | 111 |
| VI, 3 | 111 |
| VII, 19 | 111 |
| XX, 9 | 109 |
| XX, 16–29 | 158 |
| XX, 26 | 111 |
| XX, 29 | 111 |
| XX, 34 | 109 |
| XXI, 32–33 | 111 |

1Q21
| | |
|---|---|
| 4, 1 | 102 |
| 45, 1 | 102 |

| | |
|---|---|
| 1Q23 | 100 |

| | |
|---|---|
| 1Q24 | 100 |

1QS
| | |
|---|---|
| I, 13–III, 12 | 181 |
| II, 25–26 | 327 |
| II, 25 | 289 |
| III, 2 | 286 |
| III, 6 | 286 |
| III, 6–9 | 327 |
| III, 11–12 | 331 |
| III, 13–IV, 26 | 13, 181–83, 256–57 |
| III, 18 | 72 |
| III, 20–21 | 145 |
| III, 20–26 | 191–92 |
| III, 21–22 | 182 |
| III, 24 | 157, 191 |
| IV, 5–6 | 191 |
| IV, 7 | 283 |
| IV, 15–26 | 14, 262 |
| V, 1 | 331 |
| V, 4–5 | 330, 332 |
| V, 5–6 | 287 |
| V, 6 | 333 |
| V, 7–8 | 327 |
| V, 7 | 286 |

# Ancient Sources Index 385

| | | | |
|---|---|---|---|
| V, 13–20 | 29 | 1QSa | |
| V, 24–VI, 1 | 50 | I, 8 | 72 |
| VI, 2 | 282 | I, 10 | 72 |
| VI, 3 | 286 | I, 11 | 283 |
| VI, 10 | 286 | I, 12 | 72 |
| VI, 12–13 | 286 | I, 13 | 72 |
| VI, 14 | 286 | I, 26 | 72 |
| VI, 24–XII, 25 | 42, 270 | II, 9 | 289 |
| VII, 2 | 286 | II, 28 | 288 |
| VII, 3 | 72 | III, 2 | 288 |
| VII, 5 | 72 | III, 4 | 288 |
| VII, 6 | 72 | | |
| VII, 7–8 | 48 | 1QM | |
| VII, 8 | 72 | I, 5–14 | 191 |
| VII, 9 | 72 | I, 13 | 72 |
| VII, 10–11 | 45, 72 | I, 25 | 285 |
| VII, 12 | 72 | II–IX | 313 |
| VII, 13–14 | 48, 72 | II, 1 | 60, 72–73 |
| VII, 14–15 | 72 | II, 1–3 | 80, 81 |
| VII, 17–18 | 43–44, 72 | II, 1–6 | 201 |
| VII, 18–21 | 46–47 | II, 2 | 72–73, 77 |
| VII, 19 | 72 | II, 4 | 72 |
| VII, 20 | 286 | II, 6 | 72 |
| VII, 22 | 286 | II, 9 | 72 |
| VIII | 283 | II, 10 | 86 |
| VIII, 1 | 72, 81, 286 | II, 11 | 285 |
| VIII, 5 | 286 | II, 13 | 72 |
| VIII, 5–10 | 151, 287 | II, 14 | 72 |
| VIII, 11 | 286 | III, 14 | 72 |
| VIII, 21 | 289 | IV, 5 | 72 |
| VIII, 22 | 286 | IV, 15 | 72, 83 |
| IX | 283 | IV, 16 | 72 |
| IX, 3–6 | 251, 287 | IV, 17 | 72 |
| IX, 25–XI, 15 | 14, 262–63, 289 | V, 1 | 72 |
| IX, 26 | 203 | V, 2 | 72 |
| X, 3–6 | 287 | V, 3 | 72 |
| X, 10 | 327 | V, 7 | 72 |
| XI | 283 | V, 12 | 72 |
| XI, 3–9 | 287 | V, 13 | 72 |
| XI, 21–22 | 290 | V, 14 | 72 |
| XII, 4 | 331, 333 | V, 16 | 72 |
| XXI, 21 | 294 | VI, 1 | 72 |
| XXI, 22 | 294 | VI, 2 | 72 |
| | | VI, 4 | 72 |
| | | VI, 6 | 186, 193 |

*1QM (cont.)*

| | |
|---|---|
| VI, 8–9 | 72 |
| VI, 10 | 72 |
| VI, 12 | 315 |
| VI, 13 | 315 |
| VI, 14 | 72 |
| VI, 14–VII, 1 | 314 |
| VI, 15 | 315 |
| VI, 16–17 | 315 |
| VI, 17 | 319 |
| VII, 1–7 | 318 |
| VII, 1 | 72 |
| VII, 2 | 72 |
| VII, 3 | 72, 315 |
| VII, 3–5 | 319 |
| VII, 3–7 | 294, 316, 319 |
| VII, 5 | 315, 318 |
| VII, 6 | 188, 295, 317 |
| VII, 7–IX, 9 | 315 |
| VII, 8–9 | 188–89 |
| VII, 9–10 | 72 |
| VII, 14 | 72 |
| VII, 15 | 72 |
| VII, 16 | 72 |
| VII, 18 | 72 |
| VIII, 1–2 | 72, 315 |
| VIII, 4 | 72 |
| VIII, 6 | 72 |
| VIII, 8 | 315 |
| VIII, 8–9 | 72 |
| VIII, 13 | 72 |
| VIII, 14 | 72 |
| IX, 4–5 | 72 |
| IX, 11 | 72 |
| IX, 12 | 72 |
| IX, 13 | 72 |
| X, 1–2 | 316 |
| X, 9–10 | 185–87, 193 |
| XI, 8–9 | 72 |
| XII, 8 | 186, 193 |
| XII, 8–9 | 186 |
| XIV, 2–3 | 319 |
| XIV, 6–7 | 319 |
| XIV, 12 | 319 |
| XV, 4–7 | 315 |
| XV, 7 | 319 |
| XVI, 1 | 186–87, 193 |
| XVI, 7 | 72 |
| XVII, 5–8 | 189–93 |
| XVII, 7–8 | 319 |

*1QH$^a$*

| | |
|---|---|
| IV, 13–20 | 266 |
| IV, 26–27 | 283 |
| IV, 29–31 | 265 |
| IV, 34–38 | 265–66 |
| V, 12 | 289 |
| V, 31–33 | 290–92 |
| V, 32 | 296 |
| VII, 20 | 288 |
| VII, 21 | 289 |
| VII, 34 | 264 |
| VIII, 12–16 | 289 |
| IX, 23–25 | 291–92 |
| IX, 24 | 296 |
| X, 5–6 | 266 |
| X, 18 | 266 |
| XI, 6–19 | 283 |
| XI, 6–37 | 355–56 |
| XI, 9 | 292–93 |
| XI, 10 | 293 |
| XI, 11 | 292 |
| XI, 13 | 292–93 |
| XI, 17–19 | 155 |
| XI, 20–24 | 289, 296 |
| XI, 21 | 291–92 |
| XI, 22–23 | 187 |
| XI, 22–24 | 151 |
| XI, 24–26 | 159, 296 |
| XII, 14–15 | 269 |
| XII, 25–26 | 151 |
| XIV, 17–18 | 289 |
| XV, 13 | 289 |
| XVI, 1–2 | 266 |
| XVI, 5–16 | 357–58 |
| XVI, 5–23 | 289 |
| XVI, 5–XVII, 36 | 16, 354, 356, 359, 361, 365 |
| XVI, 6–7 | 16, 357 |
| XVI, 7 | 358 |

Ancient Sources Index 387

| | | | |
|---|---|---|---|
| XVI, 18–19 | 358 | 4Q7 | |
| XVI, 23–25 | 365 | 2, 2–8 | 200 |
| XVI, 26–XVII, 7 | 358–59, 363 | | |
| XVI, 26–XVII, 16 | 16, 363 | 4Q10 | |
| XVI, 31 | 16, 364 | 1–4 | 200 |
| XVI, 34–35 | 364 | | |
| XVII, 8–16 | 363–64 | 4Q159 | 70 |
| XVII, 36 | 283 | | |
| XVIII | 176 | 4Q161 | 122 |
| XIX, 13–17 | 151, 289 | | |
| XIX, 14–15 | 187 | 4Q162 | 122 |
| XIX, 16 | 145 | | |
| XIX, 33–34 | 266 | 4Q163 | 122 |
| XX, 7 | 289 | | |
| XX, 27–30 | 291–95 | 4Q164 | 122 |
| XX, 35 | 294 | | |
| XXI, 10–14 | 264–65 | 4Q165 | 122 |
| XXI, 30 | 291 | | |
| XXIII, 13–14 | 266 | 4Q169 | 24 |
| XXV, 34 | 289 | | |
| XXVI, 27–28 | 289 | 4Q174 | |
| XXVI, 35–36 | 296 | 1 I, 6–7 | 251 |
| | | | |
| 2Q24 | | 4Q177 | |
| 1, 2 | 107–8 | A 9, 8 | 330 |
| 1, 3 | 107–8 | | |
| 4, 14 | 108 | 4Q184 | |
| | | 1, 4–10 | 293 |
| 2Q26 | 100 | | |
| | | 4Q186 | 214, 268 |
| 3Q4 | 122 | | |
| | | 4Q196 | |
| 3Q15 | | 13, 2–3 | 105 |
| I, 4 | 74 | 14 I, 6 | 105 |
| II, 6 | 78 | 14 I, 9 | 105 |
| II, 8 | 74 | 14 II, 6 | 105 |
| IV, 18 | 72 | 14 II, 8 | 105 |
| VII, 5 | 72 | 18, 16 | 105 |
| VIII, 5–6 | 74 | | |
| IX, 2 | 74 | 4Q197 | |
| XI, 10 | 74 | 4 I, 12 | 105 |
| | | 4 I, 19 | 109 |
| 4Q2 | | 4 II, 3 | 109 |
| 1 I, 16–22 | 200 | 4 II, 10 | 105 |
| | | 4 III, 3 | 105 |

## Ancient Sources Index

4Q197 (cont.)
- 4 III, 4 — 105
- 4 III, 11 — 111

4Q198
- 1, 2 — 105

4Q201
- 1 I, 21 — 99
- 1 II, 1 — 100–101, 111
- 1 II, 2 — 99, 101
- 1 II, 5–6 — 100–101
- 1 II, 9 — 101
- 1 II, 11 — 101
- 1 II, 13 — 111
- 1 II, 19 — 111
- 1 II, 20 — 111
- 1 III, 2 — 101
- 1 III, 4 — 111
- 1 III, 5 — 101
- 1 III, 9 — 100–101
- 1 III, 10 — 101
- 1 III, 11 — 101
- 1 III, 12 — 101
- 1 III, 13 — 101
- 1 III, 14 — 101
- 1 III, 15 — 101
- 1 IV, 1 — 111
- 1 XII, 29 — 101
- 1 XII, 30 — 101

4Q202
- 1 II, 7 — 101
- 1 II, 15 — 101
- 1 II, 17 — 101
- 1 II, 18 — 101
- 1 II, 27 — 111

4Q203 — 100

4Q204
- 1 I, 20 — 100–101
- 1 I, 21 — 101
- 1 I, 24–25 — 100–101
- 1 I, 28 — 101
- 1 I, 30 — 101
- 1 II, 24 — 101
- 1 II, 26 — 100–101
- 1 II, 28 — 101
- 1 VI, 13 — 111
- 1 VI, 14 — 111
- 1 XII, 29 — 100
- 4, 1 — 101

4Q205
- 2 I, 26 — 100–101
- 2 II, 27 — 101
- 2 II, 29 — 101
- 2 II, 30 — 101
- 5 II, 17 — 112

4Q206
- 1 XXVI, 16 — 100–101
- 1 XXVI, 17 — 101
- 2–3 — 100
- 4 I, 21 — 112
- 4 II, 13 — 100–101
- 4 II, 20 — 112
- 4 III, 19 — 101
- 4 III, 21 — 101

4Q208
- 23 — 103
- 24, 1 — 224
- 33 — 223

4Q209
- 1–22 — 214
- 3 III — 224
- 7 II — 223
- 7 II–III — 219
- 7 II, 6–10 — 225
- 7 III, 3 — 224
- 16 — 223
- 23–28 — 215, 218
- 23, 3 — 104
- 23, 5 — 103–4
- 23, 6 — 103
- 23, 7–8 — 103–4
- 23, 8 — 104

| | | | |
|---|---|---|---|
| 26, 2–3 | 234 | 4Q246 | |
| 29–31 | 214 | 1 I, 5 | 112 |
| 32 | 214 | | |
| 33–39 | 214 | 4Q251 | |
| 40 | 214 | 1, 6 | 295 |
| 41 | 214 | 1, 7 | 295 |
| 4Q210 | | 4Q252 | 69–70 |
| 1 II, 15 | 104 | II, 2–3 | 205 |
| 1 II, 16 | 103–4 | | |
| 1 II, 17 | 104 | 4Q256 | 29 |
| 1 II, 18–19 | 103–4 | | |
| | | 4Q258 | 29 |
| 4Q211 | | | |
| 1 I, 3 | 112 | 4Q259 | |
| | | I, 4 | 49 |
| 4Q213 | | I, 4–15 | 42 |
| 1 I, 14–18 | 258 | I, 11–13 | 48 |
| 1 II, 4 | 102 | II, 3–9 | 42 |
| 1 II, 6 | 102 | IV, 8 | 203 |
| | | VI, 9–VII, 8 | 203 |
| 4Q213a | | | |
| 3–4, 2 | 112 | 4Q261 | |
| 3–4, 6 | 112 | 3, 2–4 | 42 |
| | | 4a–b, 1–7 | 42 |
| 4Q213b | | 5a–c, 1–9 | 42 |
| 1, 4 | 102 | 6a–e, 1–5 | 42 |
| 4Q214 | | 4Q265 | |
| 2, 3 | 101–2 | 4 I, 2–II, 2 | 42 |
| | | 4 I, 4 | 72 |
| 4Q214a | 101 | 4 I, 6 | 72 |
| | | 4 I, 9 | 72 |
| 4Q214b | | 4 I, 11 | 72 |
| 2–3, 8 | 102 | 4 I, 12 | 72 |
| 2–6 I, 4 | 112 | 4 II, 2 | 72 |
| 2–6 I, 9 | 102 | 7, 5–6 | 72 |
| 8, 1 | 102 | 7, 11–13 | 295 |
| 8, 2 | 102 | 10 II, 6–8 | 45 |
| 4Q216 | | 4Q266 | |
| VI, 5 | 200 | 2 I, 10 | 72 |
| VI, 7b–9 | 200, 208 | 2 I, 13 | 72 |
| | | 6 II, 3 | 72 |
| | | 6 II, 6 | 332 |

| | | | |
|---|---|---|---|
| 4Q266 (cont.) | | IV, 8 | 213 |
| 8 III, 6 | 72 | VII | 211, 220 |
| 10 I–II | 42 | VIII, 1 | 213 |
| 10 I, 10–II, 15 | 270 | VIII, 1–6 | 211, 220 |
| 10 II, 1 | 72, 82 | | |
| 10 II, 2 | 72 | 4Q319 | 201–2 |
| 10 II, 3–4 | 72 | | |
| 10 II, 6 | 72, 82 | 4Q320 | 13, 200, 230 |
| 10 II, 7 | 72 | | |
| 10 II, 8 | 72, 82 | 4Q321 | 229–30 |
| 10 II, 13 | 72 | I, 4 | 70 |
| | | | |
| 4Q267 | 42 | 4Q321a | 229–30 |
| 9 V, 11 | 72 | | |
| | | 4Q322 | 214 |
| 4Q268 | | | |
| 1, 13 | 72 | 4Q322a | |
| | | 2 | 203, 214 |
| 4Q269 | 42 | | |
| | | 4Q324d | 70, 204 |
| 4Q270 | | | |
| 2 II, 15–17 | 283 | 4Q325 | 70, 204 |
| 6 IV, 12 | 72 | | |
| 6 IV, 16 | 72 | 4Q326 | 204 |
| 6 IV, 17 | 72 | | |
| 6 IV, 18 | 72 | 4Q327 | 204 |
| 7 I | 42 | | |
| 7 I, 8–10 | 46–47 | 4Q332 | |
| 7 I, 9 | 82 | 2 | 203, 214 |
| 7 I, 12–13 | 283 | | |
| 7 I, 13–14 | 43–44 | 4Q333 | 214 |
| 7 I, 14 | 82 | | |
| | | 4Q334 | |
| 4Q274 | | 2–4 | 70 |
| 1 I | 298 | | |
| | | 4Q364 | 30, 70 |
| 4Q285 | | | |
| 1, 1–11 | 255 | 4Q364a | 204 |
| | | | |
| 4Q317 | | 4Q365 | 30 |
| 1+1a II | 230 | 2 II, 2 | 69 |
| 1+1a II, 12 | 69 | | |
| | | 4Q365a | 69–70 |
| 4Q318 | | | |
| IV | 211, 220 | 4Q366 | 30 |

|  |  |  |  |
|---|---|---|---|
| 4Q367 | 30 | 3 II, 16 | 72 |
|  |  | 8–9, 5 | 72 |
| 4Q385 | 70 | 13, 3 | 72 |
|  |  | 13, 4 | 72 |
| 4Q394 | 69–70 | 13, 5 | 72 |
|  |  | 15 II–16, 5 | 72 |
| 4QMMT |  | 20 II–21, 6 | 72 |
| B 29–30 | 286 | 64–67, 2 | 72 |
| B 59–62 | 286 | 64–67, 3 | 72 |
|  |  |  |  |
| 4Q400 |  | 4Q416 |  |
| 2, 5–7 | 145, 151 | 2 III, 17 | 292 |
| 2, 7 | 289 |  |  |
|  |  | 4Q417 |  |
| 4Q403 |  | 2 I, 5 | 176 |
| 1 I, 1 | 72 |  |  |
| 1 I, 2 | 72 | 4Q418 |  |
| 1 I, 3 | 72 | 140, 4 | 176 |
| 1 I, 4 | 72 |  |  |
| 1 I, 5 | 72 | 4Q434 |  |
| 1 I, 11 | 72 | 1 I, 4 | 330 |
| 1 I, 12 | 72 | 1 I, 8 | 267 |
| 1 I, 13 | 72 |  |  |
| 1 I, 16 | 72 | 4Q436 |  |
| 1 I, 19 | 72 | 1 Ia–b, 4–6 | 268 |
| 1 I, 20 | 72 | 1 Ia–b, 10–II,1 | 268 |
| 1 I, 21–22 | 72 |  |  |
| 1 I, 23 | 72 | 4Q437 |  |
| 1 I, 24 | 72 | 2, 5 | 267 |
| 1 I, 25 | 72 |  |  |
| 1 I, 26 | 72 | 4Q444 |  |
| 1 II, 11 | 72 | 1 I, 1 | 259 |
| 1 II, 15–16 | 147 | 1 I, 1–4 | 261 |
| 1 II, 21 | 72 | 1 I, 8 | 255 |
| 1 II, 22 | 72 |  |  |
| 1 II, 27 | 72 | 4Q461 |  |
|  |  | 1 I, 2 | 112 |
| 4Q404 | 70 |  |  |
|  |  | 4Q491 | 70 |
| 4Q405 |  | 1–3, 6–10 | 316 |
| 3 II, 2 | 72 | 8 I, 4–5 | 319 |
| 3 II, 4 | 72 |  |  |
| 3 II, 5 | 72 | 4Q491c |  |
| 3 II, 8 | 72 | 1, 7 | 289 |
| 3 II, 13 | 72 |  |  |

| | | | |
|---|---|---|---|
| 4Q496 | 70 | 4Q530 | |
| | | 1 I, 7 | 112 |
| 4Q502 | | 2 II+6–12, 16 | 112 |
| 1–3, 3–7 | 283 | 2 II+6–12, 24 | 112 |
| 4Q503 | 70, 208, 229, 231, 235 | 4Q531 | |
| | | 15, 3 | 112 |
| 4Q504 | | 22, 8 | 112 |
| 4, 11 | 330 | | |
| | | 4Q532 | |
| 4Q509 | | 1 II, 2 | 106 |
| 287 | 330 | 1 II, 3 | 106 |
| | | 1 II, 6–8 | 106 |
| 4Q510 | | 1 II, 8 | 106 |
| 1, 4 | 153, 158 | | |
| 1, 4–6 | 157, 259, 266 | 4Q534 | |
| 1, 7–8 | 155 | 1 I, 4 | 112 |
| | | 7 I, 1 | 112 |
| 4Q511 | | | |
| 1, 3–8 | 153 | 4Q543 | |
| 2 I, 7–10 | 161 | 2a–b, 1 | 109 |
| 8, 4 | 153, 259 | 4, 2 | 109 |
| 8, 7–8 | 160 | 5–9, 7 | 109 |
| 10, 8–9 | 157 | | |
| 11, 5 | 259 | 4Q541 | |
| 18 | 159 | 9 I, 6 | 112 |
| 18 II, 7–8 | 263 | | |
| 28+29, 2–4 | 159, 264 | 4Q542 | |
| 28+29, 3 | 294 | 1 II, 7 | 113 |
| 28+29, 4 | 291, 293 | | |
| 30, 1–4 | 155 | 4Q544 | |
| 35, 2–4 | 160 | 1, 1 | 109 |
| 35, 3–4 | 152 | 1, 2 | 109 |
| 35, 6–8 | 157 | 1, 3 | 110 |
| 35, 6 | 259 | 1, 4 | 110 |
| 48, 49+51 II, 1–4 | 158 | 1, 8 | 110 |
| 48+49+51 II, 3–5 | 264 | 1, 10 | 109–10 |
| | | 1, 13 | 113 |
| 4Q512 | | 1, 14 | 109 |
| 29–32, 9 | 295 | 2, 16 | 113 |
| 36–38, 6 | 295 | | |
| | | 4Q545 | |
| 4Q514 | | 1a I, 14 | 109 |
| 1 I, 4 | 295 | 1a–b II, 13 | 109 |
| | | 1a–b II, 15 | 109–10 |

| | | | |
|---|---|---|---|
| 1a–b II, 17 | 110 | 4Q556a | |
| 1a–b II, 19 | 110 | 5 I, 7 | 113 |
| 4Q547 | | 4Q558 | |
| 1–2 III, 6 | 109 | 29, 4 | 113 |
| 1–2 III, 7 | 110 | 33 I, 8 | 113 |
| 1–2 III, 9 | 109–10 | 33 II, 5 | 113 |
| | | 51 II, 4 | 113 |
| 4Q548 | | 57, 4 | 113 |
| 1 II+2, 7 | 113 | | |
| | | 4Q560 | 152 |
| 4Q553 | | 1 I, 5 | 113 |
| 3+2 II+4, 2 | 106 | | |
| 3+2 II+4, 3 | 106 | 4Q561 | |
| 3+2 II+4, 5 | 106 | 1 I, 5 | 113 |
| 3+2 II+4, 5–6 | 106 | | |
| | | 4Q564 | |
| 4Q554 | | 1 II, 2 | 113 |
| 1 II, 12 | 107 | | |
| 1 II, 13 | 107–8 | 4Q565 | |
| 1 II, 14 | 107–8 | 1, 3 | 114 |
| 1 II, 15 | 107 | | |
| 1 II, 16 | 108 | 4Q586 | |
| 1 II, 17 | 107 | b, 2 | 114 |
| 1 II, 18 | 107–8 | | |
| 1 II, 19 | 107 | 5Q15 | |
| 1 II, 20 | 107–8 | 1 I, 1 | 107–8 |
| 1 II, 21 | 107 | 1 I, 1–2 | 107–8 |
| 1 III, 13 | 107 | 1 I, 3 | 107–8 |
| 1 III, 14 | 107–8 | 1 I, 4 | 107–8 |
| 1 III, 15 | 107–8 | 1 I, 5 | 107–8 |
| 1 III, 16 | 107–8 | 1 I, 6 | 107 |
| 1 III, 18 | 107 | 1 I, 16 | 107 |
| 1 III, 19 | 108 | 1 I, 17 | 107–8 |
| 1 III, 20 | 108 | 1 I, 18 | 107–8 |
| 1 III, 21 | 107–8 | 1 I, 19 | 107–8 |
| | | 1 II, 1 | 107 |
| 4Q554a | | 1 II, 2 | 108 |
| 1, 4 | 108 | 1 II, 3 | 108 |
| 1, 7 | 107 | 1 II, 4 | 107–8 |
| 1, 10 | 108 | 1 II, 7 | 108 |
| | | 1 II, 8 | 107 |
| 4Q556 | 100 | 1 II, 11 | 107 |
| 1, 6 | 113 | 1 II, 13 | 108 |

| | | | |
|---|---|---|---|
| 6Q8 | 100 | **Ancient Jewish Writers** | |
| 6Q17 | 201 | Josephus, *Antiquitates judaicae* | |
| 11Q5 | | 4.121 | 253 |
| XIX, 5 | 255 | 12.241 | 337 |
| XIX, 13–16 | 158 | 13.257–258 | 337–38 |
| XXVII | 70, 73–74 | 15.136 | 186 |
| XXVII, 4–5 | 72 | 18.21 | 280 |
| XXVII, 4–10 | 79, 81 | Josephus, *Bellum judaicum* | |
| XXVII, 5–7 | 72–73, 78–79 | 2.120–121 | 280 |
| XXVII, 5–9 | 205 | 2.160–161 | 280 |
| XXVII, 7 | 72 | | |
| XXVII, 8 | 72 | Philo of Alexandria, *De migratione Abrahami* | |
| XXVII, 9–10 | 72–73, 78–79 | 92 | 341 |
| 11Q10 | | | |
| 11, 8 | 114 | Philo of Alexandria, *De opificio mundi* | |
| 28, 5–6 | 114 | 131–134 | 293 |
| 32, 9 | 114 | | |
| | | Philo of Alexandria, *De specialibus legibus* | |
| 11Q11 | | 1.6 | 340 |
| V, 4–11 | 156 | 1.9 | 340 |
| V, 6 | 149 | 1.304–306 | 340 |
| 11Q13 | | Philo of Alexandria, *De virtutibus* | |
| II, 8–9 | 184–85, 191, 193 | 102 | 341–42 |
| 11Q14 | | Philo of Alexandria, *De vita Mosis* | |
| 1 II, 5–15 | 255 | 1.277 | 253 |
| | | 1.283 | 253 |
| 11Q17 | 204 | | |
| | | Philo of Alexandria, *Hypothetica* | |
| 11Q18 | | 11.3 | 280 |
| 20, 5 | 108 | 11.14 | 279, 280 |
| 11Q19 | 23, 69 | Philo of Alexandria, *Quaestiones et solutiones in Exodum* | |
| XLV, 10 | 295 | | |
| XLVI, 13 | 316 | 2,2 | 339, 341 |
| LVI, 18 | 109 | | |
| LVII, 17–19 | 283 | Philo of Alexandria, *Quaestiones et solutiones in Genesin* | |
| 11Q29 | 42 | 3.46 | 339 |
| | | 3.48 | 340 |
| Mas1K | 202, 204 | | |

# Ancient Sources Index

## New Testament

### Matthew
| | |
|---|---:|
| 1:1 | 120 |
| 1:20 | 128–29 |
| 1:22–23 | 126, 129 |
| 1:23 | 125, 136 |
| 2:1–2 | 128 |
| 2:6 | 129 |
| 2:11 | 134 |
| 2:12 | 129 |
| 2:13 | 129 |
| 2:13–15 | 128 |
| 2:15 | 126, 129 |
| 2:17–18 | 126 |
| 2:18 | 129 |
| 2:19 | 129 |
| 2:22 | 129 |
| 2:23 | 126, 129 |
| 3:3 | 126–27, 136–37 |
| 3:16–17 | 134 |
| 4:5 | 134 |
| 4:7 | 134 |
| 4:14 | 125 |
| 4:15–16 | 126, 137 |
| 5:1–12 | 128 |
| 5:4 | 134 |
| 5:14 | 134 |
| 5:17 | 130–31 |
| 5:34–35 | 133–34 |
| 5:39 | 134 |
| 6:6 | 134 |
| 6:7 | 134 |
| 6:9 | 134 |
| 6:16 | 134 |
| 6:19 | 134 |
| 8:11 | 130, 132, 134 |
| 8:17 | 126, 137–38 |
| 8:28 | 134 |
| 9:14 | 134 |
| 10:1 | 255 |
| 11:4–5 | 133 |
| 11:5 | 131–32, 134 |
| 11:21 | 134 |
| 11:23 | 131, 133–34 |
| 11:25 | 134 |
| 12:17–21 | 126, 138 |
| 12:43 | 134 |
| 13:13 | 133 |
| 13:13–15 | 130–31 |
| 13:16 | 134 |
| 13:35 | 126 |
| 13:52 | 131 |
| 15:8–9 | 130–31, 133 |
| 15:10–20 | 254, 270 |
| 16:19 | 133–34 |
| 16:23 | 134 |
| 17:9 | 128–29 |
| 20:28 | 134 |
| 21:4–5 | 126 |
| 21:13 | 130–31, 133 |
| 21:33 | 133–34 |
| 21:42 | 134 |
| 23:13–36 | 128 |
| 23:13 | 134 |
| 23:23 | 134 |
| 24:7 | 131, 134 |
| 24:15 | 125 |
| 24:29 | 131–34 |
| 24:31 | 133 |
| 24:35 | 134 |
| 24:37 | 134 |
| 25:35 | 134 |
| 26:15 | 126 |
| 26:28 | 134 |
| 26:39 | 134 |
| 26:52 | 133 |
| 26:67 | 134 |
| 26:75 | 134 |
| 27:9–10 | 126–27, 129 |
| 27:12 | 134 |
| 27:19 | 129 |
| 27:30 | 134 |
| 27:38 | 134 |
| 27:43 | 134 |

### Mark
| | |
|---|---:|
| 1:3 | 125–27 |
| 3:11 | 255 |
| 4:12 | 133 |

*Mark (cont.)*
- 7:6–7     130–31, 133
- 9:9       129
- 4:12      130–31
- 11:17     130, 133
- 12:1      133
- 12:25     288
- 13:14     125
- 13:24–25  133

Luke
- 3:4       125–26
- 4:18–19   132
- 8:10      130–31, 133
- 9:36      129
- 10:15     133
- 13:29     130
- 17:18–23  133
- 19:46     130, 133
- 20:9      133
- 21:25     133

John
- 1:23      125–26

Acts
- 2:17      129
- 7:53      186
- 8:7       255
- 28:26–27  130

Romans
- 2:28–29   343
- 4:11      344
- 11:8      130

2 Corinthians
- 1:22      344

Galatians
- 3:19      186
- 3:27      344
- 3:28      345

Philippians
- 4:18      130

Colossians
- 2:22      130

Hebrews
- 2:2       186

Revelation
- 16:13     255

### Rabbinic Works

Genesis Rabbah
- 14.1      291

Exodus Rabbah
- 30.13     291

m. Shabbat
- 19:5      337

### Greco-Roman Literature

Aratus, *Phaenomena*
- 559–724   228

Manilius, *Astronomica*
- 3.275–442 228

Pliny the Elder, *Naturalis historia*
- 5.73      279

Strabo, *Geographica*
- 1.1.21    228

# Author Index

Abegg, Martin G.   61, 64, 79, 88, 95, 111, 114, 121, 201–2, 204, 207, 229–30, 237, 249, 262–63, 330, 347
Addis, Donna Rose   355–56, 370–71
Albani, Matthias   212, 214, 226, 237
Alexander, Philip S.   49, 55, 148, 152–53, 157–58, 163, 177, 181, 194, 203, 237, 255, 259, 265, 269, 271, 314, 322
Alston, Richard   318, 320, 322
Anderson, Gary M.   280, 299
Anderson, Robert T.   27, 32
Angel, Joseph L.   155, 157, 160, 163, 170, 194, 263, 267, 271
Arnold, Russell C. D.   6, 17
Asma, Stephen T.   147, 163
Atwill, Joseph   216, 237
Avigad, Nahman   93–94, 114
Avrahami, Yael   361, 364, 368
Bachelard, Gaston   252–53, 258, 270–71
Baek, Kyung S.   96, 120, 129, 139, 141
Bailey, Charles   68, 88
Baillet, Maurice   104, 107, 114, 153, 163, 201, 204, 229, 237
Ballentine, Debra Scoggins   154, 163
Bampfylde, Gillian   172–73, 176, 178, 184, 194
Barclay, John M. G.   343, 347
Barr, James   235, 237–38
Barth, Fredrik   328, 347
Barthélemy, Dominique   93, 116, 201, 238
Baumgarten, Albert I.   282, 300
Baumgarten, Joseph M.   43, 55, 204, 238, 280–81, 283–84, 300, 332, 347–48
Bautch, Richard J.   182, 194

Beal, Timothy K.   146–47, 163
Beaton, Richard   125, 139
Beckwith, Roger T.   202, 206–7, 238
Bell, Catherine   6
Ben Zvi, Ehud   29, 32
Ben-Dov, Jonathan   70, 90, 200–203, 207, 229–33, 235, 238, 245
Benveniste, Émile   146, 163
Berg, Shane   286, 300
Bergey, Ronald   70, 88
Berggren, J. Lennart   208–9, 228, 240
Bergsma, John S.   182, 194
Berkley, Timothy W.   343, 348
Bernstein, Moshe J.   5, 17, 27, 30, 32, 205, 238
Beyer, Klaus   103, 111–14
Biale, David   316–17, 322
Birnbaum, Salomo A.   312, 322
Boccaccini, Gabriele   4, 17
Boda, Mark J.   6, 17
Borenstein, Elhanan   365, 368
Borg, Alexandra   60, 88
Borgen, Peter   340–42, 348
Boyarin, Daniel   343–45, 348
Boyer, Pascal   357, 368
Brack-Bernsen, Lis   211–13, 227, 238
Brand, Miryam T.   260–61, 264, 271
Braunheim, Steve   216, 237
Breed, Brennan W.   175, 196
Briggs, Richard S.   135, 139
Britton, John P.   208–10, 232–33, 238–39
Brooke, George J.   4, 8, 17, 122, 124, 129, 139, 149, 164, 205, 239, 252, 268–69, 271, 313, 322, 330–31, 348, 374

Broshi, Magen 242
Brown, David 209, 239
Brownlee, William 205, 239
Buth, Randall 84, 88
Callaway, Philip 202, 239
Campbell, Jonathan G. 7, 17
Caracciolo, Marco 359–61, 368, 370
Caragounis, Chrys C. 174, 194
Carmi, Israel 216, 239
Carmignac, Jean 112, 186–89, 191, 194
Carroll, Noel 147, 149, 164
Charlesworth, James H. 43, 48, 55, 284, 300
Chazon, Esther G. 5, 17, 151, 164, 258–59, 261, 271
Christiansen, Ellen Juhl 344, 348
Cohen, Jeffrey J. 146–48, 156, 161–62, 164
Cohen, Shaye J. D. 338, 348
Cohn, Yehudah 262, 271
Collins, John J. 1, 8, 17, 49, 55, 150–52, 161, 164, 171–75, 177, 179–80, 182, 184–88, 192–94, 284, 286, 288, 290, 300, 305, 322, 341, 348
Connell, Raewyn W. 308–11, 322
Conrad, Markus 366, 369
Cook, Edward M. 11, 79, 105, 110–14, 201, 234, 249, 262–63
Cook, John A. 66, 88
Craig, Arthur D. 362, 369
Crawford, Sidnie White 26, 30–32, 44, 55, 281–83, 300
Cresswell, Tim 251–55, 258, 270–71
Cross, Frank Moore 245
Crystal, David 66–67, 88
Daise, Michael A. 204, 239
Darwall, Stephen L. 39, 55
Davidson, Maxwell J. 191–94
Davies, Philip R. 36, 55, 191–92, 195, 206, 239
Davis, Michael Thomas 7, 17
Day, John 155, 164
Dequeker, Luc 173, 184, 186–88, 195
Dhali, Maruf A. 7, 17
DiLella, Alexander A. 176, 178–79, 195

Dimant, Devorah 4–5, 8, 18, 288, 300
DiTommaso, Lorenzo 107, 115
Doering, Lutz 24, 32
Donahue, Douglas J. 242
Donaldson, Terence 333, 348
Doudna, Gregory L. 216, 239, 245
Douglas, Mary 6, 254, 271, 316
Drawnel, Henryk 96, 102–3, 112, 115, 214–16, 222–23, 234, 239
Dresher, B. Elan 66, 68, 89
Duhaime, Jean 185–86, 189–90, 192–93, 195, 312–15, 322
Duke, Robert R. 97, 109, 115
Dupont-Sommer, André 111
Easterlin, Nancy 359–60, 369
Edelman, Diana V. 29, 32
Elgvin, Torleif 292, 303
Englund, Robert K. 209, 240
Eshel, Esther 27, 32, 96, 102, 115, 152, 157, 164, 259, 261, 265, 272
Eshel, Hanan 27, 32
Esler, Philip F. 328, 345, 348
Evans, Craig A. 5, 19, 119, 133, 139
Evans, James 208–9, 228, 240
Falk, Daniel K. 5–8, 17–18, 120, 141
Fassberg, Steven E. 63–65, 75, 84, 89, 235, 240
Feldt, Laura 151–52, 164–65, 356, 358, 369
Ferch, Arthur J. 172, 195
Ferguson, Everett 340, 344, 348
Fields, Weston W. 123, 139
Fitzmyer, Joseph A. 96, 104–5, 111–12, 115, 126, 131–32, 139–40, 203, 240
Fletcher-Louis, Crispin H. T. 170, 195, 288–89, 300
Flint, Peter W. 5, 11–12, 18, 95, 114, 119–23, 128, 136, 140
Flusser, David 258, 272
Forbes, Dean 68, 89
Fraade, Steven D. 53, 55
Frazer, James 259–60, 272
Fredriksen, Paula 333, 348
Frevel, Christian 306, 316, 322
Frey, Jörg 264, 272, 344, 348

Frisch, Alexandria   159, 165, 257, 272
Frölich, Ida   149, 153, 165
Fuss, Diana   307, 322
Gallese, Vittorio   366, 369
Gamble, Harry   130, 140
García Martínez, Florentino   4–5, 7, 17–18, 96, 103–4, 107, 114–16, 145, 165, 183–84, 195, 203, 214–15, 217, 223, 229, 240, 247–48, 259, 272, 306, 323
Gayer, Asaf   231, 238, 263, 272
Geertz, Armin W.   354, 369
Geller, Markham J.   211–12, 219, 240
Giles, Terry   27, 32
Gillihan, Yonder Moynihan   36, 49, 55
Gilmore, David   146–47, 165
Glessmer, Uwe   70, 90, 200, 202–3, 206, 214, 227, 229–31, 240–41
Goldingay, John E.   175–76, 179–80, 195
Goldstone, Matthew   50, 55
Goodblatt, David   5, 18
Goodman, Martin   280, 303
Gramsci, Antonio   309, 323
Grébaut, Sylvain   216–17, 241
Green, Dennis   24, 32
Greenfield, Jonas C.   96, 102, 111–12, 115, 117, 211–13, 229, 241, 293–94, 300
Grossman, Maxine L.   8, 18, 281–82, 300–301
Grosz, Elizabeth   307, 323
Gruber, Mayer I.   24, 32
Gundry, Robert H.   127, 140
Hachlili, Rachel   282, 301
Hadas-Lebel, Mireille   340–41, 349
Hale, Mark   68, 89
Hall, Jonathan M.   328, 349
Hallermayer, Michaela   96, 115
Hannah, Darrell D.   170, 183, 189, 192, 195
Hannah, Robert   209, 241
Hanneken, Todd R.   178, 195
Harkins, Angela Kim   6, 18, 252, 266–67, 272, 353–56, 361, 363, 368–69
Harrington, Daniel J.   292, 303
Harrington, Hannah K.   6, 18, 295, 305–6, 316, 323, 327, 349
Harris, William   130, 140
Hartman, Louis F.   176, 178–79, 195
Hastrup, Kirsten   320, 323
Haubold, Johannes   228, 241
Hays, Richard B.   124–25, 130, 133, 140
He, Sheng   17
Hearn, Jeff   308, 323
Heath, Jane   355, 369
Hecht, Richard D.   340, 349
Heger, Paul   282–83, 290, 301
Heiser, Michael   172–73, 184, 190, 195
Hempel, Charlotte   8, 18, 35–36, 42–43, 45, 55–56, 95, 115, 181, 195, 306, 323
Hentrich, Thomas   316–17, 323
Herr, Moshe D.   206, 241
Hershovitz, Scott   39, 56
Hogeterp, Albert L. A.   262, 272
Holmstedt, Robert D.   7, 18–19, 66–70, 89–90, 186–87, 195–96
Honkela, Timo   357, 370
Hornkohl, Aaron   67, 89
Horowitz, Wayne   228, 230, 233, 238, 241
Horst, Pieter Willem van der   260, 272, 280, 301
Hsu, Chun-Ting   366, 369
Huet, Marie Hélène   147, 165
Hughes, Julie A.   132–33, 141
Hunger, Hermann   212, 227, 233, 238, 241
Hurtado, Larry W.   169, 196
Hutchinson, John   328, 349
Hutter, Manfred   148, 165
Ilan, Tal   281, 301
Jacobs, Arthur M.   366, 369
Jacobs, Jared   61, 89
Jacobs, Sandra   332, 349
Jacobus, Helen R.   201, 203–4, 209, 211–13, 215, 219, 228–32, 234, 242
Jassen, Alex P.   6–7, 19, 47, 56, 128, 141
Jastrow, Marcus   292–93, 301
Jaubert, Annie   201–2, 206, 234, 242
Johnston, Sarah Iles   260, 272, 368–69
Jokiranta, Jutta   6–7, 19, 29, 32, 53–54, 56, 374
Jull, A. J. Timothy   216, 242

Kampen, John 5, 17
Kaplan, Stephen 360, 369–70
Kartveit, Magnar 27–28, 30–32
Keady, Jessica M. 6, 19, 296, 298–99, 301, 305, 323
Kerr, Apama 225, 243
Kidd, José Ramírez 333, 349
Kimber Buell, Denise 345, 349
Kister, Menachem 231, 245, 337, 349
Klawans, Jonathan 290, 294, 296, 298, 301, 306, 323
Klein, Anja 262, 272
Kloppenborg, John S. 95, 115
Klutz, Todd 374
Knowles, Dudley 38, 56
Knowles, Michael 133, 141
Koch-Westenholz, Ulla 210, 225, 243
Koch, Dieter 226, 243
Koch, Johannes 233, 342
Kraemer, Ross S. 311, 323
Kratz, Reinhard G. 45, 56
Krause, Andrew R. 255, 259–60, 265, 273
Kugel, James L. 336–37, 349
Kugler, Robert A. 5, 19, 329, 349
Kukkonen, Karin 360, 370
Kuzmičová, Anežka 353, 360–61, 365, 370
Labat, René 212, 243
Lachmann, Renate 356, 370
Lacocque, Andre 176–78, 196
Lambert, David 335, 349
Lane-Mercier, Gillian 132, 141
Lanfranchi, Giovanni B. 241
Lange, Armin 204, 243
Langlois, Michael 111
Le Déaut, Roger 330–32, 335, 349–50
Lefebvre, Henri 252
Lefebvre, Michael 52, 56
Lemke, Werner E. 331, 350
Lemos, Tracy 306–7, 323
Levison, John R. 253, 257, 273
Levy, Donald P. 309, 323
Lichtenberger, Hermann 153, 165, 295–96, 301

Lied, Liv Ingeborg 150–51, 162, 165, 252
Lim, Timothy H. 205, 243
Lindeman, Marjaana 357, 370
Loader, William R. G. 282–83, 290, 296, 301
Love, Glen A. 360, 370
Luhrmann, Tanya 367, 370
Luz, Ulrich 127–28, 141
Lyonnet, Stanislaus 343, 350
Lyons, William John 7, 17, 260, 273
Mach, Michael 169, 196
Machiela, Daniel A. 111–12, 128, 141
Magness, Jodi 202, 243, 255, 273
Martino, Wayne 310, 323
Mason, Eric F. 183–84, 196
Mason, Steve 328, 350
Maston, Jason 290, 302
May, Herbert G. 256, 273
Meier, John P. 24, 32
Menken, Maarten J. J. 126–27, 141
Mermelstein, Ari 367–68, 370
Messerschmidt, James W. 309–311, 322–23
Metso, Sarianna 8, 18–19, 24–26, 28–29, 33, 35–36, 43, 46, 53, 56, 181–82, 196, 203, 243
Meyer, Nicholas A. 289, 292, 295, 302
Meyers, Carol L. 310–11, 324
Meyers, Eric. M. 202, 243, 282, 302
Miall, David S. 361, 370
Michalak, Aleksander R. 169–70, 178, 189, 196
Milgrom, Jacob 6
Milik, Józef T. 93–94, 99–100, 102–4, 106–7, 111–12, 115–16, 212, 214–17, 222, 224, 229, 243
Miller, David M. 327–28, 350
Mittmann-Richert, Ulrike 204, 243
Modrzejewski, Joseph Mélèze 344, 350
Monroe, M. Willis 211, 243
Morgan, David H. J. 316, 324
Morrow, Francis J., Jr. 122, 141
Moshavi, Adina 62, 70, 84, 89
Moussy, Claude 146, 165

# Author Index

Moyise, Steve   130–31, 135, 141
Mroczek, Eva   97, 116
Mullen, E. Theodore, Jr.   175, 196
Münz-Manor, Ophir   366–67, 370
Muraoka, Takamitsu   59, 89, 100, 103, 105, 110, 116
Nagel, Joane   317–18, 324
Najman, Hindy   8, 19, 97, 116, 150–51, 165
Närhi, Jani   356, 370
Nati, James   35, 49, 57
Naudé, Jacobus A.   7, 19, 66, 68, 89–90
Neugebauer, Otto   208, 216–17, 225–29, 234, 243–45
Neusner, Jacob   337, 350
Newman, Judith H.   6–7, 19, 95, 115, 152, 159, 165–66, 260, 272
Newsom, Carol A.   6–7, 19, 53–54, 57, 145, 151, 156–61, 166–67, 175–76, 180, 188, 196, 202–4, 244, 256, 265, 273–74, 290, 292–93, 302–3, 353, 371
Ngunga, Abi T.   123, 141
Nickelsburg, George W. E.   99, 116, 162, 166, 180, 182, 196
Niehoff, Maren R.   339–41, 350
Nihan, Christophe   306, 316, 322
Nissinen, Martti   128, 141
Nitzan, Bilhah   153, 155–57, 166, 259, 273
Noë, Alva   359, 370
Noegel, Scott B.   128–29, 141
Nolan, Brian M.   135, 141
Nolland, John   341, 350
Norin, Stig   96, 116
Novakovic, Lidija   55
Oelsner, Joachim   228, 241
Oppenheim, A. Leo   211, 244
Pajunen, Mika S.   97, 116, 267–68, 273
Palmer, Carmen   327, 350
Parry, Donald W.   18
Penner, Ken M.   7, 19
Penny, Douglas L.   152, 166
Perrin, Andrew B.   96, 112–13, 116, 120, 141
Pfann, Stephen J.   229, 231–32, 244–45

Pietersen, Lloyd K.   7, 17
Pingree, David   211, 229, 233, 241
Pinnick, Avital   5, 18
Plicht, Johannes van der   216, 245
Ploeg, Jan van der   186, 196
Polzin, Robert   62, 90
Popović, Mladen   7, 17–18, 112, 256–57, 269, 273
Porter, Stanley E.   5, 19
Poythress, Vern S.   173, 197
Pritchett, William Kendrick   208, 245
Przybylski, Benno   134, 141
Puech, Émile   94, 96–97, 100, 106–9, 112–14, 116–17
Pyysiäinen, Ilkka   357, 370
Qimron, Elisha   4, 7, 10, 19, 43–44, 46, 48, 57, 59, 61–65, 69, 71–76, 83–84, 86–87, 90, 182–83, 197, 284, 286, 302, 330, 350
Rad, Gerhard von   316, 324
Ramble, Charles   357, 368
Rappaport, Roy   267, 273
Rappaport, Uriel   4–5, 18
Rasmussen, Kaare L.   216, 245
Ratzon, Eshbal   215, 224, 231, 245
Raz, Joseph   38–39, 57,
Regev, Eyal   35, 57, 282, 302
Reimer, Andy M.   260, 273
Reiner, Erica   211, 245
Rendsburg, Gary   74, 90
Reymond, Eric   7, 19, 59, 61, 63, 90
Reynolds, Bennie, III   256, 273–74
Reynolds, Jeremy R.   371
Rezetko, Robert   68, 90
Rietz, Henry W. M.   55
Robinson, Jenefer   361, 370
Robson, Eleanor   228, 245
Rochberg-Halton, Francesca   208–10, 213, 228, 245
Roetzel, Calvin J.   280, 302
Roisman, Joseph   318, 324
Rollinger, Robert   241
Rosen, Arie   40, 48–49, 57
Rosenberg, Warren   318, 324
Rothstein, Susan   62, 70, 84, 89

Ruiten, Jacques T. A. G. M. van  336–37, 350
Ruppin, Eytan  365, 368
Rüterswörden, Udo  316, 324
Ryan, Marie-Laure  359, 365–66, 370
Sacchi, Paolo  214, 245
Sachs, Abraham J.  210, 245
Sack, Robert  252
Samely, Alexander  313, 324
Sanders, E. P.  36, 57, 185, 197
Sanders, James A.  205, 245
Saulnier, Stéphane  201, 206, 246
Schacter, Daniel L.  355–56, 370–71
Schäfer, Peter  189, 197
Schaper, Joachim  123, 141
Schattner-Rieser, Ursula  100, 103, 110, 117
Schauer, Frederick  39, 47–48, 51, 57
Schiffman, Lawrence H.  4–5, 8, 19–20, 29, 33, 50, 53, 57, 159, 165, 182, 197, 257, 272, 281, 290, 302, 306, 324, 333, 350
Schilling-Estes, Natalie  68, 91
Schmidt, Francis  204, 246
Schniedewind, William  59, 87–88, 90
Schofield, Alison  6–8, 20, 48–49, 57, 149–51, 166, 252, 305, 324
Schomaker, Lambert  17
Schuller, Eileen M.  5–6, 8, 18–20, 145, 167, 170, 197, 265, 274, 280–82, 290, 302–3, 330, 350, 353, 371
Schultz, Brian  185, 197, 312–13, 324
Schwartz, Daniel R.  5, 18, 284, 327–28, 332–33, 338, 344, 348, 351
Scott, Niall  147, 166
Screnock, John  7, 18–19, 60, 62, 64, 66–70, 75, 85–86, 90, 186–87, 195–96
Scurlock, JoAnn  210, 219, 246
Seely, David Rolph  268, 274, 330–31, 351
Segal, Judah B.  213, 246
Segal, Michael  27, 33, 171–72, 177, 197, 335–37, 351
Segal, Moses H.  75, 90
Seth, Anil K.  362, 371

Shaked, Shaul  256, 274
Shemesh, Aharon  24, 33
Shepardson, Christine  254, 274
Smith, Anthony D.  328, 349
Smith, Jonathan Z.  342, 351
Smith, Mark S.  149, 167, 362, 371
Soja, Edward W.  151, 167, 252
Sokoloff, Michael  111, 114, 211–13, 229, 241
Speer, Nicole K.  360, 366, 371
Stadel, Christian  111
Stanley, Christopher D.  130, 135, 142
Starky, J. L.  112
Starr, G. Gabrielle  365, 371
Steele, John M.  208, 211–13, 219, 228, 233, 238, 241, 246
Stegemann, Hartmut  4, 20, 30, 33, 145, 167, 263–64, 274, 279, 282, 290, 303, 353, 371, 376
Stendahl, Krister  127, 142
Stern, Sacha  200, 213, 233–34, 246
Steudel, Annette  42, 57, 184, 197
Stökl Ben Ezra, Daniel  113, 231, 235, 238
Stone, Michael E.  96, 102, 112, 115, 117, 231, 246
Strawn, Brent A.  7, 17
Strine, Casey A.  374
Strugnell, John  245, 292, 303
Stuckenbruck, Loren T.  97, 99–101, 112, 117, 148, 152–53, 158, 167, 257, 262, 264, 274
Sukenik, Eleazar  86, 90, 279
Sullivan, Kevin P.  189, 197
Swallow, Khena M.  371
Swanson, Dwight D.  30, 33, 69, 90
Swartz, Michael D.  260, 274, 366–67, 371
Tagliabue, Aldo  365, 371
Talmon, Shemaryahu  70, 90, 149, 167, 181–82, 197, 199–200, 202–3, 205, 229–30, 246–47
Taylor, Joan E.  8, 20, 279, 281–82, 286, 303
Tervanotko, Hanna  6, 20

# Author Index

Thiessen, Matthew 334–36, 338, 343, 345, 351
Tigchelaar, Eibert J. C.   17, 96, 103–4, 107, 115, 117, 145, 165, 183–84, 195, 203, 214–17, 223, 229, 240, 247–48, 268, 274
Todd, Cain   368, 371
Tov, Emanuel   4–5, 19–20, 27, 242, 259
Trebolle Barrera, Julio   4, 18, 20
Treindl, Alois   226, 243
Trever, John C.   123, 142
Tso, Marcus K. M.   43, 58
Turner, Bryan S.   319, 324
Turner, Victor   6
Tuschling, Ruth M. M.   183, 189, 193, 197
Tzoref, Shani   8, 20
Ulrich, Eugene   25–26, 33, 95, 114, 117–19, 122–24, 128, 140, 142
Ungnad, Arthur   211, 219, 248
van der Woude, Adam S.   183–84, 195, 306, 323
VanderKam, James C.   5, 18–20, 199, 204–6, 208, 213–18, 227, 232–34, 248, 335, 351
Vanonen, Hanna   314, 325
Vaughn, Michael S.   51, 58
Vegas Montaner, Luis   4, 20
Vermes, Geza   49, 55, 203, 211, 237, 248, 280, 303
Vroom, Jonathan   36, 42, 52, 58, 87, 90
Wacholder, Ben-Zion   30, 34, 202, 207, 213, 248
Wacholder, Sholom   202, 207, 248
Waerden, Barthel L. van der   210, 249
Walker, Christopher   209, 239
Walsh, Matthew L.   169, 197
Wassen, Cecilia   6, 20, 183, 197, 255, 274, 281–82, 284–85, 288, 290, 298, 303–305, 325
Webb, Ruth   354, 371
Wee, John   211, 249
Weidner, Ernst F.   211–12, 249
Weinfeld, Moshe   268, 330, 351
Weisburg, David B.   213, 248

Weissenberg, Hanne von   35, 58
Weitzman, Steven   65, 74, 90
Wells, Kyle B.   335–36, 339–40, 351
Werline, Rodney A.   6, 17
Wernberg-Møller, Preben   181, 198, 256, 275, 293–94, 304
Williams, Clemency   209, 249
Wintermute, Orval S.   260, 275, 334, 351
Wise, Michael O.   79, 111, 152, 166, 201, 204, 212, 230, 249, 262–63
Wolfram, Walt   68, 91
Wright, Archie T.   152, 156, 161, 167
Wyke, Maria   308, 325
Yadin, Yigael   93–94, 114, 187, 190, 198
Yardeni, Ada   211, 241
Yonge, Charles D.   339, 351
Young, Ian   68, 90
Zacks, Jeffrey M.   371
Zahn, Molly   27, 30, 34
Zanker, Graham   354–55, 371
Zevit, Ziony   172, 198
Zhang, Lening   51, 58
Zhang, Yan   51, 58
Zilm, Jennifer   299, 304
Zsolnay, Ilona   307–8, 325
Zunshine, Lisa   360, 371

www.ingramcontent.com/pod-product-compliance
Lightning Source LLC
Chambersburg PA
CBHW021928290426
44108CB00012B/765